Modern Spain

Modern Spain
Politics and Society since 1874

Francisco J. Romero Salvadó

BLOOMSBURY ACADEMIC
LONDON • NEW YORK • OXFORD • NEW DELHI • SYDNEY

BLOOMSBURY ACADEMIC
Bloomsbury Publishing Plc
50 Bedford Square, London, WC1B 3DP, UK
1385 Broadway, New York, NY 10018, USA
29 Earlsfort Terrace, Dublin 2, Ireland

BLOOMSBURY, BLOOMSBURY ACADEMIC and the Diana logo are trademarks of Bloomsbury Publishing Plc

First published in Great Britain 2024

Copyright © Francisco J. Romero Salvadó, 2024

Francisco J. Romero Salvadó has asserted his right under the Copyright, Designs and Patents Act, 1988, to be identified as Author of this work.

For legal purposes the Acknowledgements on p. xi constitute an extension of this copyright page.

Cover image: Anarchist attack on King Alfonso XIII of Spain, rue de Rivoli, Paris. Engraving, 'Le petit journal', June 11, 1905. © Stefano Bianchetti / Bridgeman Images

All rights reserved. No part of this publication may be reproduced or transmitted in any form or by any means, electronic or mechanical, including photocopying, recording, or any information storage or retrieval system, without prior permission in writing from the publishers.

Bloomsbury Publishing Plc does not have any control over, or responsibility for, any third-party websites referred to or in this book. All internet addresses given in this book were correct at the time of going to press. The author and publisher regret any inconvenience caused if addresses have changed or sites have ceased to exist, but can accept no responsibility for any such changes.

A catalogue record for this book is available from the British Library.

A catalog record for this book is available from the Library of Congress.

ISBN: HB: 978-1-3504-5518-4
PB: 978-1-3504-5517-7
ePDF: 978-1-3504-5519-1
eBook: 978-1-3504-5520-7

Typeset by RefineCatch Limited, Bungay, Suffolk
Printed and bound in Great Britain

To find out more about our authors and books visit www.bloomsbury.com and sign up for our newsletters.

For my wife Alison and my daughter Rachel, with much love
And in memory of my mother

CONTENTS

List of Maps x
Preface and Acknowledgements xi
List of Abbreviations xv

1 The Restoration Monarchy, 1874–1914: The Fading Charm of a Political Comedy 1
   Spain in the Age of Liberal Revolution 1
   The Political Comedy 5
   A Modernizing Nation 9
   The Protest of the Disenfranchised 11
   A Vicious Circle of Terror 16
   El Desastre: Reality, Myth, and Aftermath 19
   The Regeneration Chimera 28
   Notes 35

2 The Restoration Monarchy, 1914–1931: The Twilight of an Era 49
   Fatal Neutralities 49
   1917: Spain was not Russia 53
   The European Civil War 58
   The CNT's Finest Hour 60
   Red Mirage, Black Storm 64
   The Death of the Liberal Order: Euthanasia or Infanticide? 67
   Regeneration from Above 69
   The Disintegration of the Dictatorship 74
   The Twilight of an Era: Alfonso XIII's Departure 79
   Notes 85

3 Shattered Hopes: The Second Republic, 1931–1936 95
   La Niña Bonita 95
   A Short-Lived Honeymoon 99
   The Republic Besieged 104

An Illusion: A Republican's Republic 109
The CEDA's Hour 112
The Slippery Path to the Abyss 116
Notes 121

4 The Spanish Tragedy, 1936–1939 129

The Death of Reason 129
The Outbreak of Apocalypse 130
Foreign Intervention 136
The Grand Charade 144
In the City of God 147
In the City of the Devil 152
The Republic's Dogged Resistance 155
Franco's Victory 158
Notes 165

5 The Long Dictatorship of General Francisco Franco, 1939–1975 177

The Myth of Neutrality 177
Francoism by the Grace of God 184
Años de Hambre, Años de Silencio 186
From International Ostracism to Respectability 191
The Economic Miracle 198
The Twilight of the Regime 201
Notes 209

6 A Success Story: The Recovery of Democracy 219

Hope, Uncertainty, Fear 219
Walking a Tightrope: The Democratic Transition 222
A Golden but Brief Honeymoon 226
Francoism's Last Stand 230
The End of the Transition: The PSOE in Power 235
Towards a New *Turno*: The Return of the Right 245
Notes 248

7 *Quo Vadis* Spain? The Challenges of a New Century 253

From Euphoria to Disillusion 253
The Fragile Foundations of the Economic Miracle 255
The Three Fateful Cs: *Caínismo, Crispación*, Corruption 258
The Democratic Transition Under Attack 268

    The Catalan Challenge: *El Procés* 269
    Challenge in Madrid: The Emergence of New Parties 279
Quo Vadis, Spain? 282
Notes 288

Bibliography 297
Index 323

MAPS

1	Regions and provinces of Spain	xxi
2	The Spanish Empire in 1898	xxii
3	The Spanish African Empire in 1912	xxiii
4	Spain, 22 July 1936	xxiv
5	August 1936–January 1937	xxv
6	February 1937–February 1938	xxvi
7	March 1938–November 1938	xxvii
8	December 1938–April 1939	xxviii
9	Autonomous Regions of Spain	xxix

PREFACE AND ACKNOWLEDGEMENTS

I have always compared the process of planning, researching, and completing a book with a long journey. It is indeed a voyage in which moments of uncertainty coexist with those of discovery until reaching, finally, one's destination successfully. This particular journey was especially nostalgic since it coincided to a certain extent with my first ever venture, a book titled *Twentieth Century Spain: Politics and Society in Spain, 1898–1998* (Macmillan, 1999).

This voyage constitutes the culmination of 35 years of teaching, researching, and writing about modern Spanish history and politics, including the publication of eight monographs. Something that never changes is the large number of debts incurred along the way. This ambitious enterprise could not have been accomplished without learning from or discussions with many colleagues during my long academic career. First, I need to mention three outstanding scholars whose magisterial influence has largely shaped the course of my endeavours: Paul Preston, Helen Graham, and Enrique Moradiellos. I am also indebted to Gabriel Alonso for his suggestions to improve the script for this book. It is impossible to remember – and therefore I apologize to anyone I may have overlooked – the many people whose different contributions throughout my career have been crucial for successfully completing this voyage: Manel Aisa, Miguel Ángel del Arco Blanco, Sebastian Balfour, Soledad Bengoechea, Teresa Carnero, Ángela Cenarro, Francisco Cobo Romero, Ricardo Costa, Chris Ealham, Eduardo González Calleja, María Jesús González Hernández, Pablo La Porte, Javier Moreno Luzón, Carlos Navajas, Fernando Padilla, Javier Ponce, Alejandro Quiroga, Donald Sassoon, Adrian Shubert, Jonathan Smele, and Franz Snowden. I am also extremely grateful to Josué Sánchez for designing the maps and to April Snider from Rowman & Littlefield for granting permission to use those that were first published in my *Historical Dictionary of the Spanish Civil War* (2013). I should also thank the four anonymous referees of the original proposal. Their suggestions were crucial in determining its final content. Finally, I must thank my wife Alison and my daughter Rachel, to whom I dedicate this book. Their patience, good humour, and tolerance towards someone who spends much of his time on long trips living in the past are admirable, but they are also a constant reminder that one should never forget the real priorities of life.

This is, in qualitative as well as quantitative terms, a new product compared with the book I published in 1999. It covers a wider and more logical framework and offers a fresher perspective. No longer restricted by the proverbial centenary of the year 1898, it commences with the restoration of the Bourbon dynasty to the throne in December 1874. This ushered in a long period of seemingly political stability based on the consolidation of a constitutional and parliamentarian regime. The Restoration Monarchy is here analysed in two chapters. The first ends on the eve of the outbreak of the Great War. The second includes the overthrow of the liberal order in September 1923, the establishment and gradual collapse of an authoritarian regime under General Miguel Primo de Rivera in January 1930, and the final implosion of the monarchy in April 1931. Following on chronologically, there are three revamped and updated central chapters dealing with key historical periods: the Second Republic (1931–1936), the Civil War (1936–1939), and the dictatorship of General Francisco Franco (1939–1975). The book ends with two chapters that bring us up to the present day. The first covers the successful democratic transition and the establishment of a new peaceful alternation in office between the Socialists (PSOE) and Conservatives (PP). The second focuses on the challenges brought about by the twenty-first century that have gradually undermined the confidence and optimism of the previous decades and exacerbated structural problems that had, seemingly, been overcome.

This book's main objective is, above all, the enhancement of the study and debate of the history and politics of modern Spain, as well as an innovative and genuine attempt to be an essential point of reference and influence for scholarship in the field. It reveals new theoretical frameworks to engage with existing academic discussion. A key goal is to demonstrate how the Spanish case can serve to enlighten a long period of impressive modernization and transformation in all areas (technological, cultural, socio-economic, political, etc.) within a broader European framework. Such dramatic changes in Spain, as elsewhere, produced unprecedented levels of social violence, political polarization, and ideological radicalism. Within these parameters, it is important to emphasize that I share with the French scholar, Emmanuel de Waresquiel, the idea that historians should be meteorologists. The events chosen for analysis should help us discover what the weather was like during that period. Of course, this does not mean whether it rained or not, but rather coming to terms with the *Zeitgeist* (spirit of the age). By doing so, existing myths, assumptions, and all sorts of historical distortions, simplifications, and manipulations can be unearthed and challenged.

Indeed, a long-established myth has been the idea of the exceptional nature of Spain within a European context. From an Anglo-Saxon perspective, Spain's often turbulent history was tellingly regarded as a labyrinth in the words of the English writer Gerald Brennan, who fell in love and chose to settle in Spain in 1919 where he spent most of the rest of his life. This concept of 'exceptionalism' was reinforced by such leading scholars as Raymond Carr, Eric Hobsbawm, and James Joll. They viewed Spain's often bloodied and chaotic political evolution as a colourful but dystopian and disconcerting history that could largely be explained by idiosyncratic, exotic, and romantic arguments supposedly congenital to the character of the Spanish people: their hot-headedness, fierce pride, and profoundly passionate and individualist character. Ironically, for different reasons, the various Spanish regimes and many Spaniards themselves have come to accept that idea.

This book rejects such bizarre conclusions based on stereotypical prejudices. Certainly, Spain has its distinctive idiosyncrasies – but all countries have them. The success of Bolshevism is a peculiar phenomenon associated with Russia, as is the Nazi regime with Germany and Brexit with the United Kingdom. Many – though not only – Anglo-Saxon authors appear to have drawn their conclusions on Spain by taking a comparative approach with the UK, the apparent embodiment of economic modernization and political stability, and a very peculiar case, rather than the rule, vis-à-vis most of continental Europe. Notwithstanding its vital particularities (the persistence of a militarized public order, the overriding socio-economic and ideological power of the Catholic Church, the existence of a powerful anarcho-syndicalist tendency within the organized labour movement, etc.), the political, socio-economic, and cultural history of Spain did not follow an independent path but was part of an overall European process. It underwent, as did all its neighbours, a similar – albeit faster or slower depending on the comparative analysis – degree of modernization since the nineteenth century. In fact, the Spanish model, far from embodying an exceptional case, constitutes a truly valid example to illustrate the same troubled path to modernity, or the long and often violent transition from elites to mass politics, which marked European societies from most of the long nineteenth century up to the end of the Second World War.

For blatant political purposes, the apologists for and hagiographers of General Franco continued to foster this idea of Spain being essentially different to the rest of a continent dominated by liberalism, socialism, Protestantism, and other pernicious principles. Ironically, they were not altogether wrong. The Spanish Dictatorship, together with that in neighbouring Portugal, remained untouched by the new world order that followed the defeat of the Axis in 1945: western Europe embraced liberal democracy while eastern Europe became part of Soviet-dominated territory.

After 40 years of Francoism, Spain surprised domestic as well as foreign observers by undergoing a successful and relatively peaceful and quick transition to genuine democracy. The degree of startling socio-economic and political modernization was such that it became a beacon to emulate by the states then emerging from decades of dictatorships in eastern Europe and Latin America. It joined the club of modern European democracies in 1986, the European Union (EU), and is today considered one of the most progressive, tolerant, and envied societies for its climate, health system, and transport network.

The far-reaching impact of the economic crisis, which began in earnest in 2008, served to prick considerably that euphoric image. Spain, as elsewhere in Europe, to a greater or lesser extent, experienced an upsurge of anti-system, populist, and extremist socio-political movements. In the Spanish case, they illustrated the existence of structural tensions that had always existed but were lying dormant: an economy that depends largely on high levels of private consumption, tourism, and the construction industry; a persistently high unemployment rate; the unsettled territorial question; deeply rooted corrupt practices; the politics of polarization, and so on.

The construction of modern democracy in Spain is still a work in progress. However, the country has now clearly embraced the rule of law and the principles of tolerance, defence of human rights, and civil liberties that characterize the European Union. These are the essential foundations to face the future challenges of a rapidly evolving world with optimism.

ABBREVIATIONS

ACNP   *Asociación Católica Nacional de Propagandistas* (National and Catholic Association of Propagandists). Influential Catholic lay association created in 1909.

ANC   *L'Assemblea Nacional Catalana* (Catalan National Assembly). Social movement established in 2011 with the objective of achieving the independence of Catalonia.

AP   *Alianza Popular* (Popular Alliance). Party created by ex-Francoist ministers in 1976 and led by Manuel Fraga Iribarne.

AVE   *Alta Velocidad Española*. Cutting-edge, high-speed new trains.

CCOO   *Comisiones Obreras* (Workers' Commissions). Communist-controlled trade union which first emerged in the late 1950s.

CDC   *Convergència Democràtica de Catalunya* (Democratic Convergence of Catalonia). Right-wing party founded by Jordi Pujol in 1974 that constituted the senior partner of CiU in 1978.

CDS   *Centro Democrático y Social* (Democratic and Social Centre). A centre-left party headed by Adolfo Suárez that broke away from the UCD in 1982.

CEDA   *Confederación Española de Derechas Autónomas* (Spanish Confederation of Autonomous Rightist Parties). Right-wing and Catholic coalition founded in 1933 and led by Jose María Gil Robles.

CEOE   *Confederación Española de Organizaciones Empresariales* (Spanish Confederation of Employers' Organizations). Main industrialist body founded in 1977.

CiU   *Convergència i Unió Democràtica de Catalunya* (Convergence and Democratic Union of Catalonia). Right-wing nationalist coalition formed in 1978 which, under Jordi Pujol, became the dominant political force in Catalonia.

CNCA	*Confederación Nacional Católica Agraria* (National Catholic Confederation of Agrarians). Founded in 1917 and closely connected to the ACNP. It provided the populist base for CEDA.
CNT	*Confederación Nacional del Trabajo* (National Labour Confederation). An anarcho-syndicalist trade union created in 1910.
CTV	*Corpo di Truppe Volontarie* (Volunteer Troop Corps). Italian forces sent to Spain to fight for the Nationalists during the civil war.
CUP	*Candidatura d'Unitat Popular* (Popular Unity Candidacy). Far-left Catalan assembly-based organization founded in 1991. Its programme combines a socialist type of revolution with the independence of the so-called Catalan countries (Catalonia, Valencia, and the Balearic Islands).
EE	*Euzkadiko Ezquerra* (Basque Left). Party formed in 1977 closely linked to the political-military branch of ETA. It merged with a section of the Basque communists in 1981 and was absorbed by the PSOE in 1993.
EEC	European Economic Community.
ERC	*Esquerra Republicana de Catalunya* (Catalan Republic Left). Political coalition formed by diverse parties in Catalonia in 1931. Its programme since 1989 includes secession from Spain.
ETA	*Euzkadi Ta Askatasuna* (Basque Nation and Liberty). Basque radical movement founded in 1959. It began the armed struggle in 1968. In October 1974, it split in two: a political-military branch (ETA-PM) that was willing to collaborate with other Spanish left-wing parties and contemplated its gradual abandonment of violence in exchange for genuine political concessions, and a military branch (ETA-M) for whom the terror campaign to achieve independence had primacy.
EU	European Union. It succeeded the EEC after the Maastricht Treaty, signed in February 1992, which called for further European social and political integration.
FAI	*Federación Anarquista Ibérica* (Iberian Anarchist Federation). Created by anarchists in 1927. It came to control the CNT in the 1930s.
FET	*Falange Española Tradicionalista* (Spanish Traditionalist Falange). Francoist single party also known as the 'National

	Movement' created by the merging of all the forces supporting the nationalist camp in April 1937.
FNTT	*Federación Nacional de Trabajadores de la Tierra* (National Federation of Land Workers). Agrarian section of the UGT established in 1930.
FRAP	*Frente Revolucionario Anti-Fascista y Patriótico* (Anti-Fascist and Patriotic Revolutionary Front). Extreme-left terrorist group which appeared in 1973.
FRE	*Federación Regional Española de la Primera Internacional* (Spanish Regional Federation of the First International). It lasted from 1870 to 1881.
FRTE	*Federación Regional de Trabajadores Españoles* (Regional Federation of Spanish Workers). The successor of the FRE that existed from 1881 to 1888.
GAL	*Grupos Antiterroristas de Liberación* (Anti-Terrorist Liberation Group). State-sponsored anti-terrorist group active in the 1980s.
GDP	Gross domestic product.
GRAPO	*Grupos de Resistencia Antifascista Primero de Octubre* (Groups of Anti-Fascist Resistance First of October). Ultra-left terrorist group which began its activities in the mid-1970s and was thought to be infiltrated by the police.
HB	*Herri Batasuna* (People's Unity). Formed in 1978 as a coalition of left-wing and radical Basque nationalist groups. It acted as ETA's political front. It has been re-founded several times, its most recent incarnation being *Bildu* (Unity), established in 2012.
HOAC	*Hermandades Obreras de Acción Católica* (Workers' Brotherhood of Catholic Action). Catholic workers' associations which began to function in the 1940s.
INI	*Instituto Nacional de Industria* (National Industrial Institute). A national corporation created in 1941 to supervise and regulate industrial production.
IRS	*Instituto de Reformas Sociales* (Institute for Social Reforms). Body created in 1903 composed of state experts and employers' and labour representatives whose goal was to suggest measures to improve workers' living conditions.
IU	*Izquierda Unida* (United Left). Coalition of left-wing groups created after the NATO referendum in 1986. Its main component was the PCE.

JAP	*Juventudes de Acción Popular* (Popular Action Youth). Youth section of the CEDA.
JOC	*Juventud Obrera Católica* (Catholic Workers' Youth Movement). Catholic workers' association which began its activities in the 1940s.
JONS	*Juntas de Ofensiva Nacional Sindicalista* (Committees of National Syndicalist Offensive). The result of a merger of two small fascist groups: *La Conquista del Estado* (The Conquest of the State) and the *Juntas Castellanas de Actuación Hispánica* (Castilian Groups of Hispanic Action) in October 1931. It merged with the Falange in February 1934.
JSU	*Juventudes Socialistas Unificadas* (United Socialist Youth). The result of the merger, in March 1936, of the Socialist and the Communist Youth. It effectively fell under communist control during the civil war.
NATO	North Atlantic Treaty Organization. Western defensive alliance created in 1949.
NIA	Non-Intervention Agreement. French initiative intended to avoid foreign military intervention in Spain. It had been signed by all 27 European countries by September 1936.
NIC	Non-Intervention Committee. Based in London, it was created to supervise the Non-Intervention Agreement. Ambassadors in Britain represented their respective nations.
PCE	*Partido Comunista de España* (Spanish Communist Party). Founded in 1921.
PDeCAT	*Partit Demòcrata Europeu Català* (Catalan European Democratic Party). Party created out of the re-foundation of CDC in 2016.
PNV	*Partido Nacionalista Vasco* (Basque Nationalist Party). Leading nationalist force in the Basque Country founded in 1895.
POUM	*Partido Obrero Unificado Marxista* (Workers' Party of Marxist Unification). Small revolutionary Marxist group fiercely opposed to the PCE and created in 1935 by the merger of the Left Communist Party, led by the former Trotskyist Andreu Nin, and Joaquín Maurín's Bloc of Workers and Peasants.
PP	*Partido Popular* (Popular Party). Successor to AP in 1989 led by a new generation that sought to rally the centre-right forces in Spain.

PRSS	*Partido Republicano Radical-Socialista* (Radical-Socialist Republican Party). Founded in 1929 after the split from the more left-wing and fiercely anti-clerical section of the Radical Party. In 1933, its largest faction joined Azaña to form *Izquierda Republicana*, while the other faction formed *Unión Republicana* with Martínez Barrio.
PSC	*Partit dels Socialistes de Catalunya* (Catalan Socialist Party). Socialist party in Catalonia associated with the PSOE.
PSOE	*Partido Socialista Obrero Español* (Spanish Socialist Workers Party). Spanish socialist party founded in 1879.
PSP	*Partido Socialista Popular* (Popular Socialist Party). Independent socialist party founded by Professor Tierno Galván in 1968. It joined the PSOE in 1978.
PSUC	*Partido Socialista Unificado de Cataluña* (United Socialist Party of Catalonia). Formed in July 1936 by the fusion of four small socialist and communist groups, including the Catalan sections of the PCE and the PSOE.
RENFE	*Red Nacional de los Ferrocarriles Españoles*. Spain's national railway.
RTVE	*Radio y Televisión Española*. Spain's state radio and television.
UCD	*Unión de Centro Democrático* (Union of the Democratic Centre). Centrist coalition formed by Adolfo Suárez in 1977.
UDC	*Unió Democràtica de Catalunya* (The Democratic Union of Catalonia). Christian-democratic party founded in 1931. It became the minor partner in the CiU coalition created in 1978.
UGT	*Unión General de Trabajadores* (General Union of Labourers). Socialist-controlled trade union created in 1888.
UMD	*Unión Militar Democrática* (Democratic Military Union). Clandestine organization of democratic military officers which came to the surface in the summer of 1975.
UN	United Nations. International organization established in June 1945.
UP	*Unión Patriótica* (Patriotic Union). Political movement created in April 1924 to support the dictatorship of General Primo de Rivera.
UPOD	*Unidas Podemos* (United We Can). Coalition formed by *Podemos* and IU in 2016.

UR	*Unión Republicana* (Republican Union). Created by the merger of a splinter section of the Radical Party and a faction of the PRRS in 1933.
VAT	Value added tax.

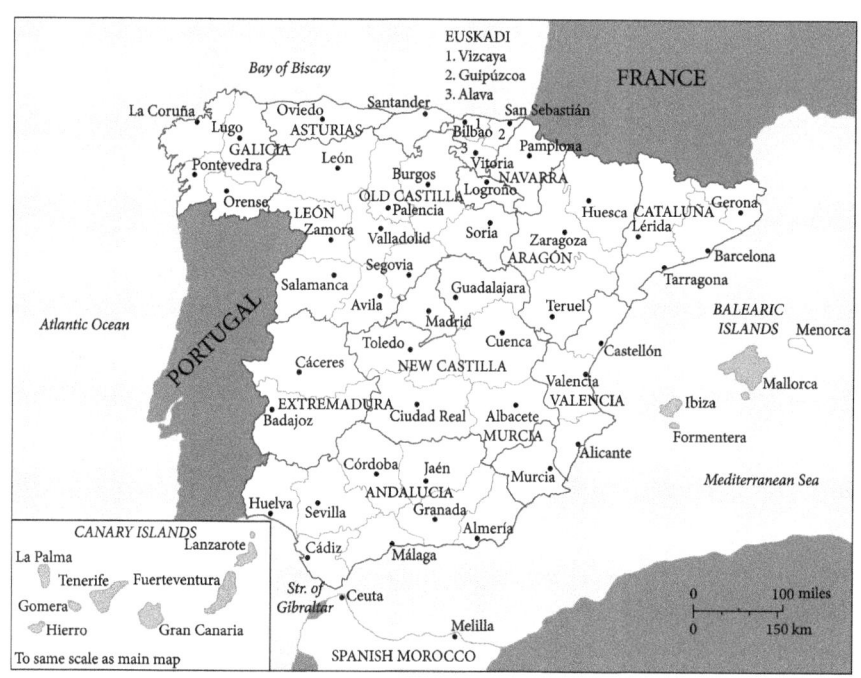

MAP 1 *Regions and provinces of Spain.*

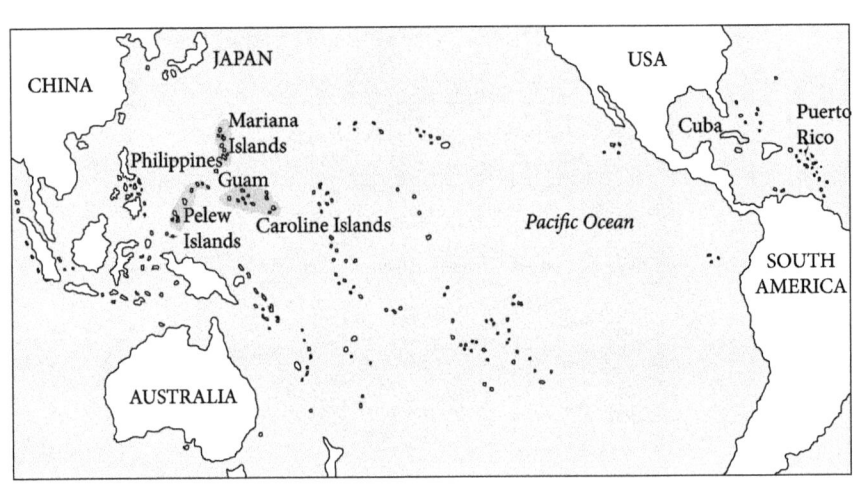

MAP 2 *The Spanish Empire in 1898.*

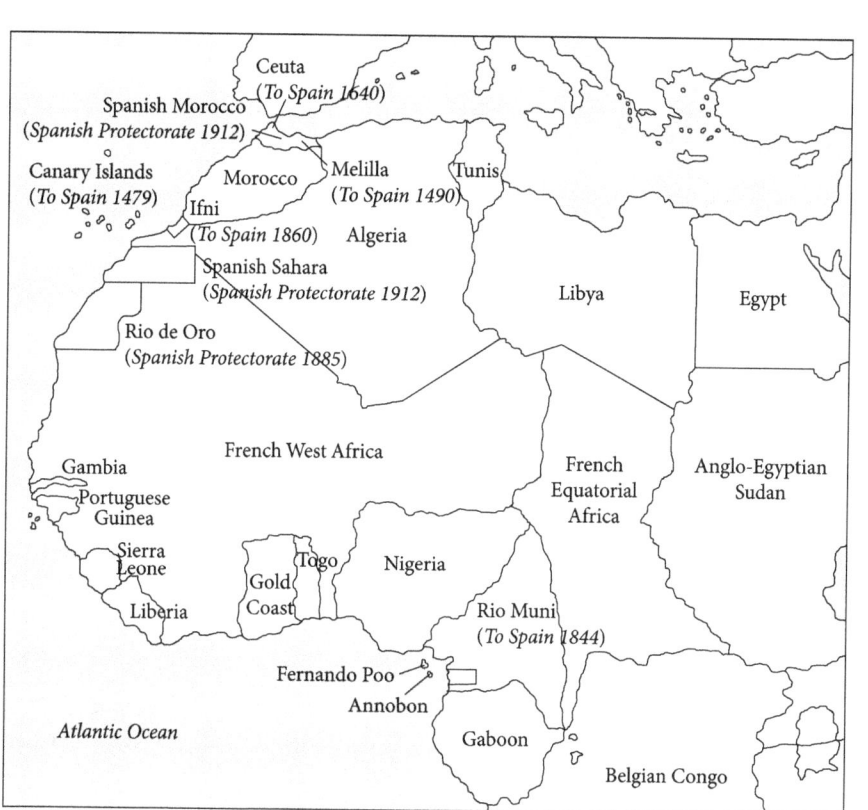

MAP 3 *The Spanish African Empire in 1912.*

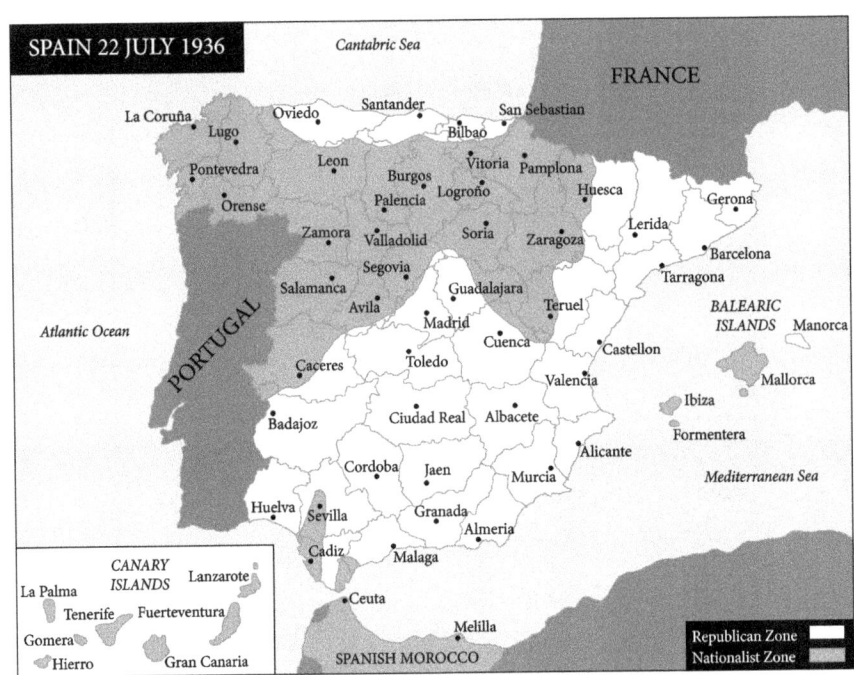

MAP 4 *Spain, 22 July 1936*.

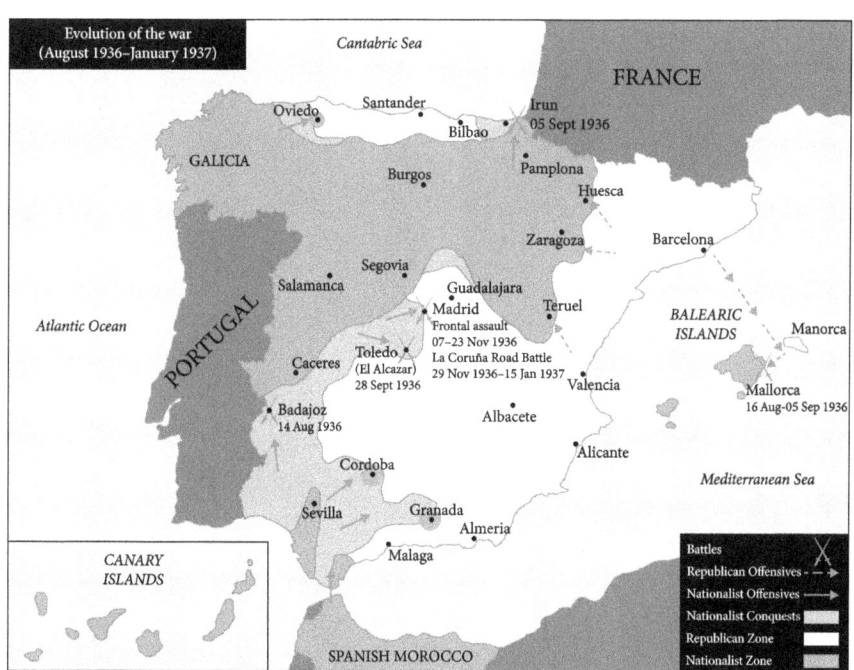

MAP 5 *August 1936–January 1937.*

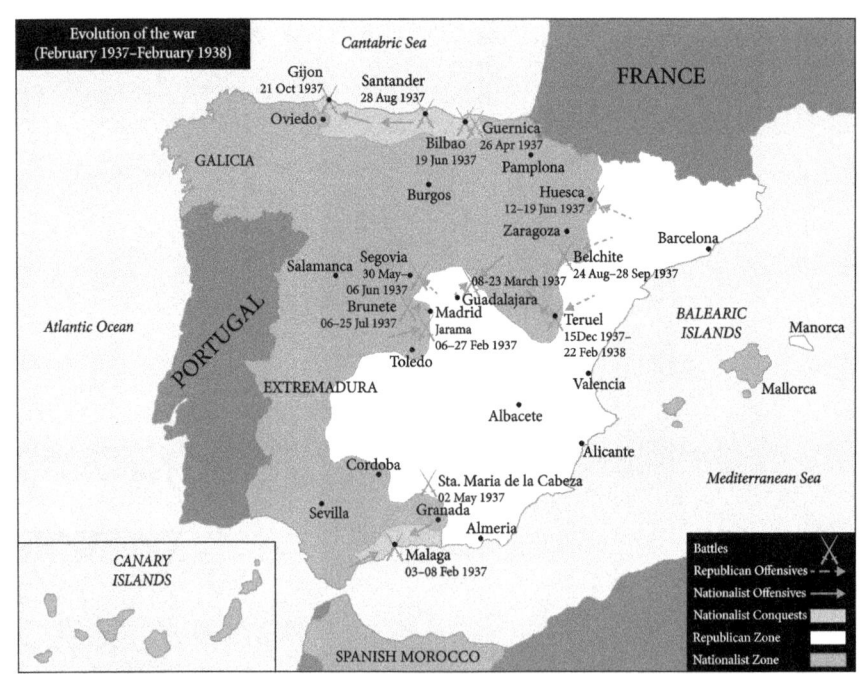

MAP 6 *February 1937–February 1938.*

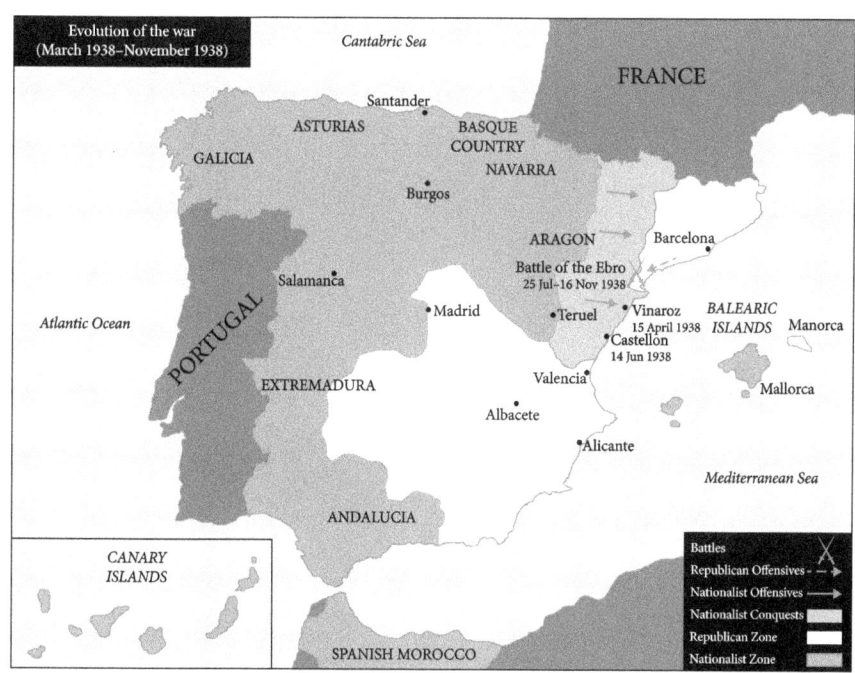

MAP 7 *March 1938–November 1938.*

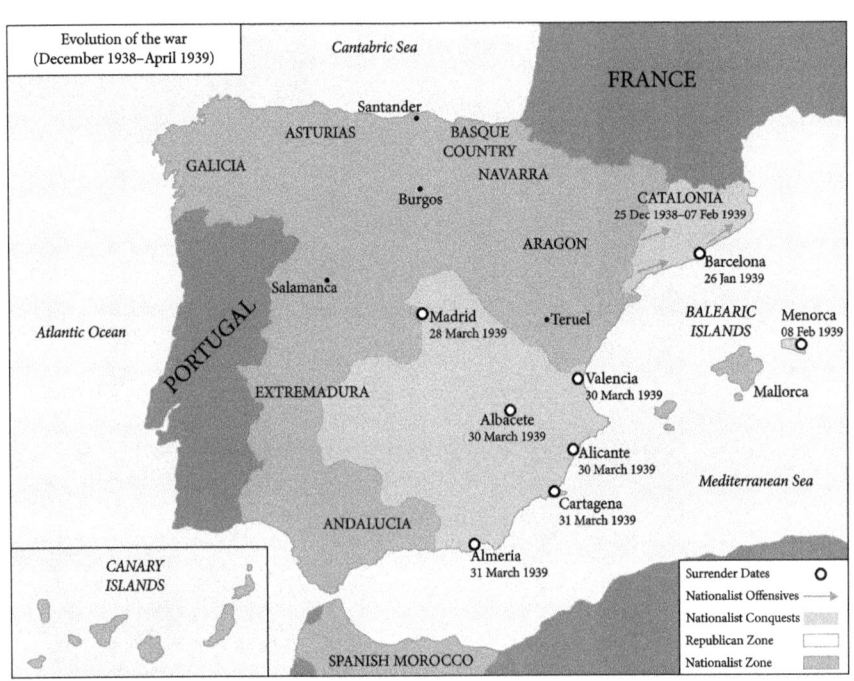

MAP 8 *December 1938–April 1939.*

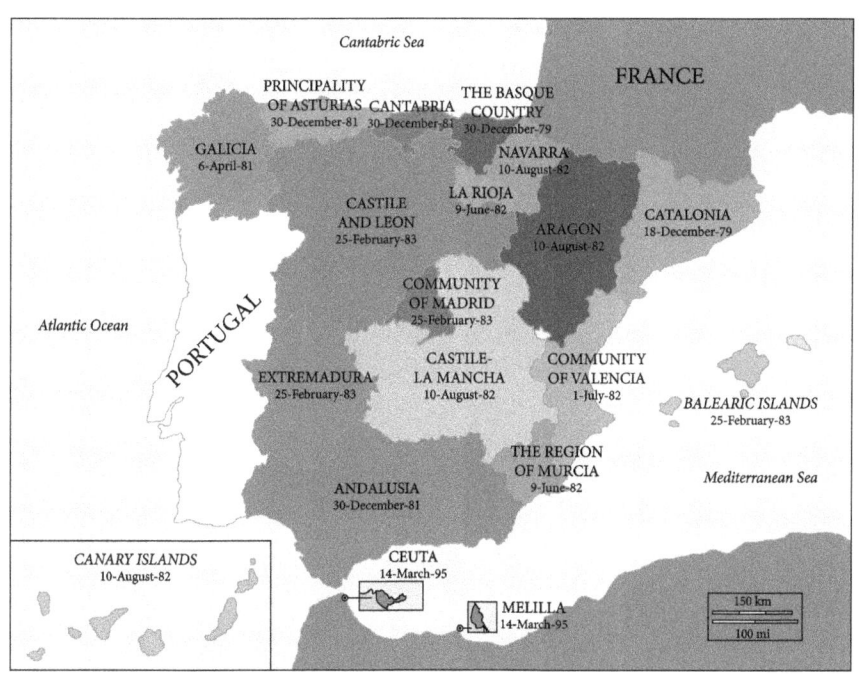

MAP 9 *Autonomous Regions of Spain.*

1

The Restoration Monarchy, 1874–1914: The Fading Charm of a Political Comedy

Spain in the Age of Liberal Revolution

On 29 December 1874, a *pronunciamiento* (military uprising) led by General Arsenio Martínez Campos in Sagunto (Valencia) ended the short-lived First Republic (established in February 1873). The new regime (the Restoration or Liberal Monarchy) restored to the throne from exile the Bourbon dynasty in the shape of Alfonso XII and ushered in a relatively long period of stability. Socio-political upheaval and praetorian intervention had marked the previous decades. They formed part of the age which characterized the transition from the *Ancien Régime* to liberalism in Europe.[1]

At the start of the nineteenth century, the possession of a subsoil rich in mineral resources (coal, lead, mercury, copper, etc.) and the largest colonial empire on earth seemed to suggest that Spain would remain one of the great powers. Just 100 years later, however, she had been relegated to the European periphery.

The country was torn apart between 1808 and 1814 during the badly mislabelled war of independence.[2] Initially allied to France, Spain lost its navy in the joint defeat at Trafalgar (1805). Three years later, the quarrel between the feeble King Charles IV and his son Ferdinand was solved by Napoleon:[3] both were summoned to Bayonne in May 1808, forced to abdicate (in exchange for generous pensions), and the emperor's brother Joseph assumed the throne. Napoleon believed that this manoeuvre would not attract major opposition. If anything, he was doing Spain a favour in supplanting the incompetent French incumbents (the Bourbons) with a new enlightened dynasty to modernize a country still largely under the yoke of aristocracy and inquisition. However, it triggered a large-scale insurrection. The term 'liberal' was coined in Spain to describe the delegates from the diverse provincial juntas fighting against who they considered the foreign usurper. Gathering in Cádiz, the centre of resistance, they drafted the country's first modern constitution, which accommodated progressive and reactionary tendencies: it confirmed that national sovereignty resided in the people represented by the *Cortes* (parliament) elected by universal suffrage, and that all Spaniards enjoyed equality before the law and civil liberties. It abolished the inquisition and the old feudal order, thus putting an end to the privileges of the clergy and aristocracy and the absolute power of the Crown. However, it confirmed that the monarchy was sacrosanct, recognized the property rights of the feudal lords, and the confessional character of the state with Catholicism as the only tolerated religion.[4]

Known during his exile in France as 'the desired', Ferdinand VII turned out to be one of the most infamous monarchs in Spanish history. On his return to Spain, he repudiated the constitution, restored absolutism and the inquisition, and imprisoned and executed the very same people who had been fighting on his behalf. His rule was a period of obscurantism. Royal troops, except for a brief liberal stage between 1820 and 1823, succeeded in suppressing insurrections but lost all the colonies on mainland America.[5]

After three childless marriages, an ailing king fathered two daughters with his fourth wife, Maria Christina of the Two Sicilies: Isabel (1830) and Luisa Fernanda (1832). He then passed the Pragmatic Sanction that set aside the Salic Law, which had banned female descendants from ascending the throne. On his death in September 1833, his daughter Isabel, then just three years old, was proclaimed sovereign (Isabel II) with her mother acting as Queen Regent. The king's brother, Don Carlos, who had been for years the presumptive heir, refused to recognize his niece. His rebellion ushered in four decades of socio-economic strife amidst three civil wars: the first from 1833 to 1840; a second between 1846 and 1849 that was confined to Catalonia; and the third from 1872 to 1876.

The Carlist Wars, known by the name adopted by Don Carlos' followers, were not just dynastic disputes between two rival pretenders to the throne. They were the embodiment of a local version of the much broader conflict, then taking place throughout Europe, between liberalism and absolutism. Carlism, also known as traditionalism, was, above all, a protest movement against the potentially disruptive impact of change and its threat to the fabric of traditional life. It represented an idyllic view of a past ruled by a paternal king, defender of the poor and keeper of justice, in which the Catholic faith remained the cornerstone of the nation and was threatened by the evils of liberalism. Spurred by local priests, resistance to secularism and hostility to modernity drove thousands of Catholic farmers and artisans, especially from rural areas of Navarre, the Basque Country, Catalonia, and Valencia, to join the *requetés* (the troops of the pretender). These were the parts of Spain that were better integrated socio-economically. Being on the periphery, they were deeply distrustful of the centre and opposed the abolition of medieval legislation that protected regional peculiarities. Their rallying cry was '*Dios, Patria y Rey*' (God, Fatherland, and King), to which the term *Fueros* (old laws) was later added. They never managed to control any major city or threaten the state apart from a daring short-lived sortie towards Madrid in 1837. Nevertheless, unlike the poorly motivated Liberal army, made up of conscript soldiers, they fought stubbornly for what they almost regarded as a holy cause. They proved extremely successful in holding out in their strongholds where the mountainous terrain suited their guerrilla style of warfare. Due to the drastic material and human differences, the war inexorably tilted in favour of the Liberals, who were recognized diplomatically and even helped militarily by France and Britain. In August 1839, widespread war-weariness led the Carlist generals on the northern front to abandon the cause of the Pretender. In return, they obtained guarantees of no future reprisals and were absorbed with full pay into the ranks of the Liberal army. A year later, the last of the Carlist eastern bulwarks had been defeated.[6]

Spain's liberal revolution unleashed market forces that saw a transition from feudalism to capitalism. This process began in the 1830s with finance minister Juan Álvarez Mendizábal's *desamortización* (freeing property from entail), and concluded with Pascual Madoz's – another finance minister – Law of Disentailment (1855).[7] Liberalism did not necessarily herald the advent of democracy. Constitutions, parties, and parliaments certainly curtailed the authority of the Crown and the seigneurial privileges of the feudal lords. However, liberalism meant, above all, a shift in terms of power from social birth to wealth. It consolidated in Spain (as in many other countries) a new ruling class formed by the vested landed interests and the new rising, albeit still weak, industrial and financial bourgeoisie.[8]

The nature of the liberal revolution in Spain explained both Carlism's obstinate strength and the permanent state of upheaval that reigned over the country. The Liberals who embraced the cause of Isabel II were an alliance between the urban middle classes, financiers, and merchants with the landed oligarchy. The latter's sudden conversion to liberal principles was not miraculous. The dismantling of the feudal state secured the socio-economic power of the oligarchs, as in most of Europe, since in return for accepting the loss of their ancestral seigneurial privileges, their hereditary rights were transformed into property titles. Furthermore, they were reimbursed by the state for relinquishing several feudal dues and managed, in many cases, to retain their domains and even expand their holdings.[9] The *desamortización* occurred amidst a savage civil war, with a Treasury heavily indebted and starved of capital, following the loss of the immense revenues from the Americas. Land, the largest source of wealth, became a commodity that could be freely traded. But the urgent need for funds to underpin the throne of Isabel II resulted in the land being sold rapidly in large chunks at public auction to the highest bidder: the old feudal lords, speculators, financiers, and wealthy farmers who could afford the high purchase prices. The southern half of the country (Castile, Extremadura, and Andalusia), where the nobility had owned large estates since the *Reconquista* (711–1492) – the epic struggle to expel the Muslims from the Iberian Peninsula – underwent a process of land concentration (*latifundismo*).[10]

The liberal revolution saw the clergy and the peasantry suffer the greatest losses. After the expropriation of land held in mortmain, the Church relinquished a great deal of its former power. Simultaneously, the *desamortización* inflicted a lethal blow on the peasantry. Priced out of available plots of land, the peasantry lost its traditional access to the now sold commons. Furthermore, its long-term leases and inherited rights enshrined in the old order between lord and vassal gave way to new market laws where the property owner could impose whatever conditions it wanted. The often-absentee big landowners left overseers in charge who sought to maximize profits through labour-intensive exploitation rather than investing in new technology. The landless peasants became *jornaleros*, working for a fixed salary (*jornal*), or *braceros*, working with their arms (*brazos*), toiling in the *latifundios* from sunrise to sunset for what was a measly wage. Their employability depended on the whim of the overseers and seasonal need.[11]

The end of the civil war in 1840 failed to provide stability. Brigands and Carlist gangs operated with impunity in some areas. Banditry and revolts became so endemic, particularly in the countryside in the south, that in 1844 a new force was created – the civil guard, commanded by military officers – to bring law and order to rural Spain. Its members were dispatched far from their homes so as they would not identify with the locals. Detested in particular by the southern peasantry, they were regarded as the landowners' private army.[12] The military became the final guarantor of the state. As only a tiny minority of wealthy property owners were entitled to vote, parties had a limited popular following. They rallied around generals, who acted as *espadones* (big swords). Rather than military dictators, they were political *caudillos* who, once in power, sought to exclude others from office, leading them to resort to *pronunciamientos*.[13]

Short-lived administrations and recurring praetorian intervention hindered economic progress. Aware of their precarious hold on power, politicians sought to line their pockets while still in office. Moreover, governments, dependent on military benevolence, devoted over half of the budget to maintaining an inflated standing army. A growing state deficit and indebtedness led to short-term solutions. Thus, spurred by its monetary difficulties, the state became the main recipient of capital that otherwise could have been diverted into productive efforts.[14] Furthermore, the pressure of a flailing Treasury, as well as administrative short-sightedness, led to the bartering of mineral concessions for short-term pecuniary relief. In 1868, a new mining law amounted practically to a speculators' charter in which Spain transferred its most important resources to foreign capitalists. By 1913, 29 percent of Spanish mining companies and about half of the mining capital was in overseas control.[15] From its former imperial greatness, Spain had become a financial colony.

For over three decades, *pronunciamientos* became the regular means of political change. Not only were cabinets toppled but also regimes. In 1840, the Regent Maria Christina had to flee the country. In 1868, Isabel II was dethroned. By then, the queen had become an object of widely held scorn. With his signature sarcastic approach, the writer Ramón del Valle Inclán described her reign as a 'court of miracles and debauchery' marked by intrigue and scandals alongside a grotesque combination of religious fanaticism and sexual promiscuity (married for state reasons to her homosexual cousin, Francisco de Asís, both kept a legion of lovers).[16]

The 'Glorious Revolution' of 1868 represented the Spanish version of the European revolutions of 1848. However, the well-intentioned efforts during the *Sexenio Democrático* (democratic six years) between 1868 and 1874 all failed.[17] The cause that had cemented the revolutionary alliance, hatred for the queen, disappeared upon her departure. An initial compromise was to summon Constituent *Cortes*, elected by universal suffrage, which decided to establish a progressive monarchy. Ironically, the search for a foreign prince led to a continental conflagration when, in 1870, Emperor Napoleon III's veto of the candidacy of a member of the Hohenzollern family led to war between France and Prussia. Eventually, the crown was offered to Amadeo of Savoy, the second son of Vittorio Emmanuel II who had just completed the process of unifying Italy. The hapless new monarch acted as the first sincere constitutional sovereign in Spanish history. Yet his rule was marred by an anti-colonial insurrection in Cuba, constant plotting by republicans and Bourbon monarchists, and in 1872 a new Carlist rising. In February 1873, a tired Amadeo abdicated and quietly left the country. Amidst the ensuing power vacuum, the First Republic was proclaimed by default. Rather than bringing about stability, the establishment of a federal system of government led to regional anarchy: an upsurge of independent small city-states (*cantones*) across south-eastern Spain. After four successive executives in less than a year and with the country threatened by Carlism in the north and anarchy in the south and east, the army took matters into its own hands. On 3 January 1874, General Manuel Pavía stormed parliament and installed General Francisco Serrano as acting president until his ousting by Martínez Campos the following December.

The Political Comedy

The Restoration Monarchy initiated a period of political consistency facilitated by two military successes: the Carlist challenge was crushed (1876) and the war in Cuba ended with the Pact of Zanjón (1878). The architect of the new regime was Antonio Cánovas del Castillo. A leading politician during the reign of Isabel II, he later became the main adviser to the queen's heir, Prince Alfonso, and the mastermind behind restoring the Bourbons to the throne. Above all a pragmatist, once in office Cánovas understood that the new regime could not mean a *status quo ante* or a mere return to the situation before 1868. Aware that the exclusive monopoly of power held by one faction left *pronunciamientos* as the instrument to change governments, he pursued a tangible break with the past: he forced the queen to remain in exile in France and to abdicate in favour of her son Alfonso (XII). On 1 December 1874, soon before acceding to the throne, the young monarch endorsed the so-called Manifesto of Sandhurst, where he was studying at the Royal Military College, which blended respect for tradition and identification with modern liberal principles.[18] Furthermore, Cánovas sought a rapprochement with the politicians of 1868. While he led the merger of different factions into the *Partido Liberal Conservador* (Conservative Party), he also helped a former rival, Práxedes Mateo Sagasta, to establish the *Partido Liberal Fusionista* (Liberal Party), made up of several groups on the left of those identifying as conservative.[19]

Liberal principles marked the spirit of the constitution approved in 1876. A significant modicum of civil liberties (freedom of the press, speech, assembly, etc.) was enshrined and even though Catholicism was declared the state religion, the private practice of other faiths was allowed. The Restoration's longest administration headed by Sagasta (November 1885 to July 1890) expanded the constitutional framework to include progressive measures such as the abolition of slavery, a Law of Associations (which permitted the legal existence of parties and unions), trial by popular jury for both ordinary and political crimes, and universal suffrage for males aged above 25.[20]

Yet, like practically everywhere else in Europe, the constitution preserved gender inequalities. Women were not allowed to take part in public life, and were thus denied the vote. Whilst remaining single they retained some independence in terms of being able to conduct business and manage their affairs, once married they were virtual legal appendages of their husbands, to whom they owed strict obedience. Article 57 of the Civil Code of 1889 noted: 'the husband must protect his wife, and she must obey her husband'.[21] In a patriarchal society, women remained subject to the decisions of fathers and husbands, and were expected, once married, to attend to household chores. The hegemonic role of the Church on public mores stressed that their cultural identity was to be shaped through marriage and motherhood.[22] Catholic schools that normally filled the void caused by insufficient state provision for girls emphasized the importance of Christian values and strongly rejected co-education as an offence to morality. Spain was one of the last western nations to admit women to universities: they could attend courses and graduate in some instances, but it was only in 1910 that they were allowed to access higher education without restrictions.[23] The percentage of women in the workforce was relatively low, and certainly lower than in neighbouring western societies until the 1980s. For middle- and upper-class women, charitable volunteerism, largely organized by the Church, was the most acceptable type of work until well into the twentieth century. The first professions to open their doors to women were primary school teaching, nursing, and midwifery. The total number employed in the liberal professions (lawyers, doctors, etc.) was negligible. It was only after the Great War that female shop clerks became a familiar feature and women could attain civil service positions. The number of working women was much higher amongst poor families, most of whom were employed in agriculture or domestic service. Regarding the industrial workforce, women were to be found working in textiles, food processing, and some all-female trades such as cigarette manufacture.[24]

In 1885, at the deathbed of King Alfonso XII, the Conservative and Liberal parties formally sealed the 'Pact of *El Pardo*', an agreement to alternate in office, the so-called *turno pacífico* (peaceful rotation). This consolidated a political formula through which the ruling elites could enjoy power without the need to resort to praetorian intervention. If Restoration Spain was a liberal order, it was certainly not democratic. Despite all its constitutional trappings, a governing oligarchy formed by two dynastic parties monopolized power. They were committees of notables connected by nepotism and clientele networks, which extended from the capital to the provinces.[25] They rotated in office with the consistency of a pendulum; the by-product of an institutionalized comedy, which allowed their mutual sharing of governmental spoils and administrative graft. Apart from the slightly anti-clerical rhetoric of the Liberals, there was hardly any difference between them and the Conservatives.

In Restoration Spain, elections did not produce governments but were a farce whose outcome had been rigged in advance. Dynastic candidates did not even bother to canvass their constituencies. The *Ministro de la Gobernación* (minister of the interior) manufactured the so-called *encasillado* before ballotting day. This was a byzantine process of negotiations with the dynastic notables (the monarchist opposition was allotted a sizeable minority of seats) to fill the different *casillas* (pigeon-holes), which represented each constituency in the electoral register to ensure that the government had an overall majority. There were some independent constituencies, normally large urban districts, where the popular will was respected and members of the non-monarchist opposition could be elected.[26]

The *caciques* were tantamount to the kingpins of the entire political structure.[27] They were the local bigwigs who delivered the governmental majorities. In the process, they made universal male suffrage redundant and thwarted a potentially democratic system. Sometimes, they used fraudulent practices and coercion to ensure the election of the official candidate. However, it was a misconception that *caciques* prevented people from expressing their will in the ballot box using sheer force. A liberal regime, which allowed freedom of association and expression, could not resort systematically to constant repression against the voters and get away with it. The ruling order depended on mass political apathy and, only exceptionally, physical repression. Normally, the *caciques* delivered the 'right' results without any organized resistance. The significant levels of cultural and economic underdevelopment, combined with poor national integration, favoured the development of the patron-client network. The *caciques* were perceived by their fellow citizens as the local representatives of the central administration, and thus the official link between their communities and the distant state. No government dared to move against them, as remaining in power depended on them. Hence the *caciques* could run their territories as their fiefdoms, having extraordinary powers to settle local affairs, appoint officials, undertake public works, and even levy taxes.[28]

Restoration Spain was not a bizarre anomaly but the local version of the oligarchic orders that reigned over most of Europe. Notwithstanding its inherent peculiarities, it constituted an enlightening example to analyse the troubled transition from elite to mass politics and a laboratory *par excellence* of the social conflict associated with that process.[29] Everywhere, this transition took place in stages: from absolute monarchies to oligarchies and expanded suffrage that incorporated the middle and later the working classes.[30] Elements of the *Ancien Régime* remained ingrained in Europe's civil and political societies. Before the Great War, a variety of mechanisms (limited suffrage, excessive weight of the rural vote, the responsibility of cabinets to the Crown only, etc.) helped manufacture docile majorities in parliament.[31] Electoral fraud and clientelism were the usual devices in southern Europe.[32]

In Spain, like elsewhere, the Crown (emperors, tsars, kings, etc.) was the state's centrepiece.[33] The monarch was the commander-in-chief of the armed forces, could veto legislation, appoint and dismiss cabinets, grant titles, and select 50 percent of the Senate (parliament's upper house) from amongst political, ecclesiastical, and military dignitaries, and members of the aristocracy. The constitution of 1876 proclaimed that national sovereignty was shared by the monarch and parliament. This amounted to a difficult compromise between the feudal divine right and popular sovereignty.[34] The king, and not a genuine ballot of the electorate, was the real arbiter of public life, ensuring the smooth functioning of the *turno*. When he felt that the party in power was 'exhausted', the opposition was appointed in its place. Still, he had to abide by a series of rules: governments were only ousted during a crisis or following a glaring loss of support in parliament, often due to schisms, a common occurrence due to the nature of the dynastic parties.[35] Any political notable who received a decree of dissolution of parliament from the king, knew that the new elections would grant him an overall majority to rule comfortably.

Notwithstanding the prolonged secularization and decline in piety throughout Europe in the nineteenth century, the different established churches conserved their might in rural areas and amongst the upper classes. They also gave legitimacy to the ruling dynasties through their powerful symbolism.[36] In Spain, the *Reconquista*, followed by America's evangelization, conferred upon the Catholic Church an unparalleled status. Temporarily caught off-kilter due to its staunch opposition to liberalism, it suffered the expropriation of vast swathes of land. However, given its fundamental role as a bulwark of social order, Cánovas sought to solve the religious question with a compromise. Article 11 of the constitution allowed freedom of worship but confirmed Catholicism as the state's official religion and cemented its fiscal privileges.[37] After the arrival of a more tolerant Pope, Leo XIII (1878–1903), the ecclesiastical hierarchy, apart from some recalcitrant prelates, aligned themselves with the regime.[38] This honeymoon period facilitated the expansion of religious orders and their paramount role in children's education and social services (charities, orphanages, hospitals, etc.). By 1912, the Church had recovered its previous economic might. Invested in speculation and trade, it represented almost one-third of Spain's wealth.[39]

The armed forces of Europe were no longer an entrenched monopoly of the aristocracy but an institution that allowed for upward social mobility, something that had been enabled in Spain by civil and colonial conflicts. Still, their values were deeply anchored in the past. Indoctrinated in military academies with the principles of hierarchy, duty, and discipline, officers' primary loyalty was to their sovereign and their essential mission was the defence of the ruling order.[40] It is misleading to state that the Liberal Monarchy resulted in the eradication of praetorian practices. On the contrary, it facilitated the establishment of autonomous military power and sowed the seeds of its interference in public affairs in the twentieth century. Both dynastic parties often responded to episodes of social agitation by suspending constitutional guarantees and declaring martial law, which amounted to granting the military control of public order. Civil liberties were limited in all or parts of the country for a period of about 25 years, half the lifetime of the regime.[41] Politics ostensibly remained in the hands of civilians but in exchange, they were not to interfere in military matters. Officers were rewarded with lucrative posts, aristocratic titles, seats in cabinets and the Senate, and so on. Governments abstained from tackling military inefficiency, exemplified by a generous budget to pay the salaries of an inflated officer corps that left very little for new equipment.[42] In contrast with the scrupulous respect for military expenditure, the limited resources destined for the police meant an underpaid (and often corrupted), small, and overburdened constabulary in the cities (unlike the effective paramilitary force, the civil guard, in the countryside).[43]

A Modernizing Nation

As recent scholarship demonstrates, the Restoration was a more complex period than traditionally assumed. It cannot be simplified to an era solely determined by political fraud.[44] Spain saw a decisive transformation of both its economy and society. Scientific and technological discoveries were applied to the fields of transport, industry, and medicine. Although gradual, public education began the eradication of illiteracy. Spain was behind the most prosperous western nations (Britain, France, Germany, etc.) but was ahead of many eastern and southern states in terms of economic growth, living standards, and average incomes. Still, Spain's structural modernization was much greater in the north and the east and the cities.[45]

By the end of the nineteenth century, Spain's backbone began to take shape with the consolidation of a national market facilitated by the railway system and the first major roads. A sort of 'dual economy' emerged that widened the socio-economic disparity between the regions. A modern capitalist economy developed around the Catalan cotton textile industry, the Basque iron and steel factories, and the Asturian mining concerns. Nonetheless, their goods could not compete with British or German products for foreign outlets and they were left at the mercy of the low purchasing power of the domestic market, thus stifling industrial growth.[46] The transport revolution and the significant reduction of freight charges produced by steam navigation meant the arrival of cheap grain from Russia and the American continent, which devastated the agrarian sector in Europe. In Spain, it provoked mass migration: from the 1880s to the First World War, more than 3 million Spaniards departed for foreign lands, the majority of whom chose to settle in Latin America.[47] Many others migrated internally to Spain's main cities. The constant influx of rural labour resulted in old medieval walls being torn down and extensions (*ensanches*) built to accommodate the growing population. By the turn of the century, Madrid and Barcelona had over half a million inhabitants each, followed by Valencia with over 200,000 and ten other cities with over 100,000 (including Bilbao, Sevilla, Zaragoza, and Málaga).[48] Electricity put an end to the darkness. Streets began to be populated by motor vehicles, tramways, cafeterias, and department stores. Rising employment in new domains such as an enlarged bureaucracy, the service and financial sectors, and white-collar professions resulted in the enlargement of the middle class. There was also a notable increase in the urban proletariat employed in transport, construction, clothing, food processing, metallurgy, and so on. In the process, urban space was socially divided. With their well-lit, broad streets and modern buildings with gas, sewers, and proximity to schools and gardens, the *ensanches* became the residences of the middle and wealthy classes. The proletariat was pushed into the suburbs or the dingy inner-city slums, where they had to endure overcrowded tenements, delinquency, prostitution, and filth. Their deplorable situation was worsened by the shocking state of their workplaces. Without any social benefits or insurance, workers spent 10–15 hours a day in unsanitary conditions lacking the most elementary safety measures.[49]

The economic crisis brought about an alliance of Basque and Catalan industrialists with Castilian wheat-growers in a common demand for state protection. Their efforts were rewarded with the introduction of high tariff barriers in 1891, which were increased again in 1907, transforming Spain into the most heavily protected economy on the continent. Securing the domestic market was seen by the socio-economic elites as a preferred alternative to investment and improvement to allow them to compete in the international marketplace. In 1914, the agrarian sector still employed 66 percent of the active population.[50]

In political terms, Restoration Spain represented a progressive advance. Its enemies were not systematically censored or persecuted. On the contrary, the system was willing to integrate those prepared to accept the constitutional framework. There were examples of former opponents who rose to prominent positions in government.[51] Indeed, the regime avoided confrontation and instead sought compromise. At election time, the party in power respected the strongholds of the opposition and even the seats of leading Republicans or Carlists. Ironically, the fraudulent practices of the time were well known and regularly exposed in literature and the press – after all, this was a liberal system whose constitutional foundations prevented the permanent repression of its detractors. Political fraud often collapsed when confronted in constituencies by a genuinely democratic vote.[52] Like other European nations, Spain was faced with the challenge of modernity. The pressing issue was to overcome the hindrances of the past in order to efficiently conduct a transition from an elitist society to a democratic state where large sectors of the population would feel represented.[53]

The Protest of the Disenfranchised

The regime's 'charm' had its limits. It enshrined basic civil liberties but sacrificed administrative efficiency and political democracy. A governing oligarchy in Madrid dependent on the omnipotent local *caciques* in the countryside perpetuated a state of permanent fraudulence, with detrimental effects on a population whose real needs were systematically ignored. The Liberal Monarchy consolidated a national market, unified administration, and currency. Yet, despite a chronic deficit, governments failed to alter a financial system based on regressive taxation. Wealth was not taxed, whereas consumption was. Spain suffered from both a low total tax collection as well as a high dependence on indirect taxes, tariffs, and monopolies. Furthermore, a significant proportion of income was spent on interest payments and the military.[54] Attempts at budgetary reform were predisposed to fail given structural constraints: no central administration dared to tackle the startling corruption on which, ultimately, the regime rested or act against its main perpetrator, the *caciques*. This meant costly and inefficient public services, an inept national civil service, as well as the lack of a modern health system and school facilities.[55]

The regime's pursuit of demobilization resulted in widespread apathy towards public affairs. Traditionally, scholars argued that during the Restoration, the regime was unable to ingrain nationalist sentiments in a large part of the population.[56] Modern literature tends to be more nuanced. It recognizes that during this period, national institutions – such as banks, the press, and symbols – emerged that marked the establishment of modern nation-states.[57] However, the liberal regime could hardly expect to integrate the population in a political sense since it was obliged to delegate its day-to-day tasks to the *caciques*, which controlled the local networks.[58] The inability to create a mechanism to provide the populace with a shared sense of belonging to a national community was compounded by the strength of historical linguistic and peculiar traditions, cultural and socio-economic regional differences, and a deficient transport system in the face of massive geographic obstacles (long rivers, high mountain ranges, etc.). Consequently, while Restoration Spain was theoretically a highly centralized state, it was in real terms a politically disjointed country with strong expressions of localism.[59] As late as 1921, the philosopher José Ortega y Gasset stressed the persistence of a largely invertebrate society.[60]

A grave error was to overlook education as a tool for national integration. Regimes such as the French Third Republic (1871–1940) invested heavily in compulsory state education. French teachers were trained to instil secular and republican values via national curriculums whose content was carefully regulated. By the early twentieth century, religious orders were even denied the right to teach or to run schools. The outcome was a gradual eradication of regional linguistic differences and the emergence of a sense of national community. In contrast, Restoration Spain denied resources to public education so that the great majority of children remained illiterate, mostly but not only in the countryside. In contrast, religious education thrived – an education that was based on theocratic principles of conformity, hierarchy, and discipline.[61] Military service also failed to produce national integration. In countries like Germany and France, universal conscription played a crucial role in bringing youth together so that they viewed one another as compatriots. It also subjected recruits to rhetoric on the need to place the good of the *Patria* above local interests. In contrast, the army in Spain was never a unifying agency in the sense of a 'nation in arms'. Crucially, recruitment was not universal but was limited to those poorer households which most needed their young ones to contribute financially. Those who were well-off could afford to avoid three years of conscription.[62]

The persistence of the political comedy fed an ongoing social tragedy. Although Spaniards – the audience of the farce – enjoyed, in theory, a voice and even the vote, it was meaningless in practice. The *turno* did not respond to a genuine popular mandate, and thus did not make any meaningful change to the lives of citizens. Parliament remained a talking shop in which dynastic politicians spent their time bartering for graft while making verbose and empty speeches. Consequently, the regime systematically ignored the will of most of the population, perpetuated an unjust socio-economic structure, and presided over an explosive situation. Those effectively disenfranchised from the political process were left with stark alternatives: apathy, emigration, or protest and conflict that often resulted in a vicious circle of popular upheaval and police/military repression.

Traditional forms of protest remained, mostly in the shape of spontaneous outbursts of collective mobilization, or *echarse a la calle* (taking to the streets), to vent anger against what were perceived to be blatant injustices, such as *motines de subsistencias* (food riots) due to shortages or spiralling prices, *consumos* (taxes on basic food items), and *quintas* (military recruitment).[63] These protests were normally led by women, who, in charge of the household budget, were painfully aware of their precarious economic situation. The trigger often related to the distribution of and access to acceptably priced basic consumer goods (bread, meat, coal, etc.). Premeditation was rare and protests mostly erupted in so-called 'hotspots' (markets, docks, bakeries, etc.). Women often paraded with their hungry children in initially peaceful demonstrations that could quickly deteriorate into violent scenes involving destruction or robbery of goods, assaults on shops, and even physical attacks. The outcome of many consumer protests was favourable to women since the police could not be easily ordered to charge or shoot at female demonstrators.[64] Furthermore, the southern countryside simultaneously endured widespread banditry and insurrectional *jacqueries*. With a quasi-religious fervour, peasants rose time and again in the belief that one day the oppressed would seize the land and an ideal society be born. A disorganized and local phenomenon, they were easily quashed by the civil guard. Although sometimes the authorities heeded these outbursts of popular discontent, they normally regarded economic grievances and protests as threats to public order. The constitution was then suspended, martial law often ensued, and the army called out to regain control.[65] By responding *manu militari* to socio-economic vindications, the governing oligarchy undermined the foundations of a state that could have been strengthened if a broad consensus had been sought.[66]

Carlists and Republicans were initially the main beneficiaries of popular discontent. Yet, by the turn of the century, they had lost the support of large chunks of their working-class constituencies. After the short-lived experiment of the First Republic (1873–1874), Republicans retained considerable sympathies amongst sectors of the labour movement, yet they were small factions, dominated by old notables bickering constantly and lacking a national organization and a programme to tackle social issues. With the establishment of the International Working Men's Association (the First International) in 1864, the labouring classes finally had a working-class movement they could join.

A striking feature of Spain's labour movement was its ideological and geographical division between two antagonistic factions: a Marxist tendency in the centre and north, and a libertarian or anarchist tendency in the south and east. Their profound mutual hostility made the possibility of workers' unity extremely elusive. A noteworthy feature was the libertarian movement's ability to remain a highly appealing vehicle of popular protest. A good deal of literature has mythicized Spanish anarchism, explaining its success using idiosyncratic arguments supposedly congenital to the character of Spaniards:

their hot temperament, fierce pride, etc. – a population accustomed to centuries of religious fanaticism thus readily embraced anarchism.[67] However, such arguments rest on very misleading stereotypes. They overlook the strength of libertarian principles in other states (Italy, France, Russia, Switzerland). By concentrating on a mythical and seemingly homogeneous Andalusia of large estates and masses of landless peasants, they also fail to explain how the same doctrine was also popular in cities such as Barcelona.[68] The scholarly interpretation, certainly embraced by Catalan nationalists, that anarchism was an alien phenomenon introduced by constant migratory currents of radicalized southern peasants does not match the facts. Until the Great War, most migrants came from the Catalan hinterland and neighbouring Valencia and Aragón.

Initially, Libertarian success in Spain was simply because the International's first messenger was the Italian Giuseppe Fanelli, a collaborator of the Russian anarchist leader Mikhail Bakunin. He landed in Barcelona in October 1868 and later travelled to Valencia and Madrid. With his passionate speeches, he electrified his audiences and won over a legion of converts.[69] Anarchist principles (an apolitical stance and emphasis on economic struggle) dominated the two first workers' national organizations: the *Federación Regional Española de la Primera Internacional* (FRE, Spanish Regional Federation of the First International, 1870–1881) and the *Federación Regional de Trabajadores Españoles* (FRTE, Regional Federation of Spanish Workers, 1881–1888). Membership was relatively modest: the FRE at its peak had nearly 30,000 affiliates and its successor, the FRTE, nearly 58,000.[70]

Anarchist success cannot be explained merely in terms of chronology. In December 1871, Paul Lafargue, Karl Marx's son-in-law, visited Spain. Although he mastered Spanish, having been born in Cuba, his influence was very limited: the conversion of a small group, mostly typographers who belonged to the *Asociación General del Arte de Imprimir* (General Association of the Printing Art). Expelled from the FRE, they formed the nucleus of the *Partido Socialista Obrero Español* (PSOE, Spanish Workers' Socialist Party), which was founded in 1879.[71]

In August 1888, the Socialists established the *Unión General de Trabajadores* (UGT, General Workers' Union) with its headquarters in Barcelona and 5,000 members mostly from that city.[72] The moment seemed auspicious: it coincided with the vacuum left by the demise of the FTRE. Nevertheless, Spanish socialism failed to attain labour hegemony due to its theoretical and functional deficiencies. It was termed *Pablismo* given the dominant role played by its founder, Pablo Iglesias Posse, who, with a reduced number of militants, controlled both the UGT and the PSOE.[73] The absence of intellectuals amongst the leadership produced a lack of ideological debate and the consolidation of an orthodox interpretation of Marxism, which bore little relation to the country's socio-economic or political situation. Spanish socialism constituted one of the most flagrant examples of the economic determinism that dominated the Second International, the new workers' organization founded in 1889. Its leaders' blind belief in the historical inevitability of the victory of the proletariat had led to a certain paralysis: it did not make any sense to take excessive risks on revolutionary adventures when, after all, capitalism was doomed. It was, therefore, usual to see in the Socialists' mouthpiece, *El Socialista*, the fiercest radical editorials followed by enthusiastic greetings of small economic gains achieved by negotiation. The result was a paradox: whilst revolution was constantly advocated, in practice the instinct for day-to-day survival prevailed.[74]

Despite electoral falsification being intrinsic, the Socialists threw themselves with admirable courage into the electoral contest. Yet they isolated their organization from contact with other progressive forces that might 'contaminate' it with bourgeois ideas. To make matters worse, unlike the active canvassing in rural areas of their counterparts in France, Germany, and Italy, the Spanish Socialists' dogmatic reading of Marxism gave marginal attention to the crucial agrarian question in a country where two-thirds of the population were part of that sector.[75] They waited until the national congress of 1918 to draft their first agrarian programme. Astonishingly, the UGT's agrarian section, the *Federación Nacional de Trabajadores de la Tierra* (FNTT, National Federation of Land Workers) was not established until 1930.[76] Consequently, electoral success was slow in coming and that was only in local elections. Socialist councillors began to get elected in small numbers in the 1890s in the Basque Country and finally, in 1905, in Madrid, where Iglesias and two others obtained seats in the municipal administration. Ironically, they resorted to fraudulent methods (the forging of ballot papers) to secure electoral success.[77]

Socialism failed to achieve a breakthrough in Barcelona. Spain's main industrial metropolis seemed fertile ground given the long tradition of organized labour. Furthermore, it was the UGT's headquarters and initial stronghold, having gained a foothold amongst the stevedores, typographers, and textile workers. Nevertheless, support soon waned dramatically: from 75 percent of the UGT's early membership to 7 percent in 1900 and token figures later. This was the result of their isolationist stance vis-à-vis progressive bourgeois parties that clashed with the traditionally pragmatic approach of Catalan trade unionism of collaboration with local republicans. Furthermore, from the 1890s, Socialists' ambiguity – if not outright opposition – regarding industrial action saw them alienated from an increasingly radicalized Catalan proletariat. This feeling of estrangement was greatly enhanced when the UGT transferred its headquarters from Barcelona to Madrid in 1899. The price of betting on a centralized organization whose primacy was state politics rather than the economic struggle was to become a spent force in Barcelona.[78]

Spanish socialism was noted for its relatively slow but steady progress based on perseverance and organizational skills. It gained a solid foothold in Madrid and the provincial cities of Castile, whose economy was dominated by light industry, skilled craftsmanship, and service sectors. In January 1913, the UGT claimed nearly 150,000 members. The crucial breakthrough was its organizing of the Asturian miners, the Basque shipbuilding and metallurgy workers, and the railway workers.[79] However, socialist centralization, administrative obsession, and internal discipline failed to arouse widespread mass enthusiasm. In contrast, anarchism appeared to be a more suitable vessel to express social grievances. Spain's libertarian movement has been compared with a river that vanishes in some stretches and reappears later in strength.[80] Its ideological simplicity and belief in the autonomy of the local sections appealed to many workers. Furthermore, its emphasis on a spontaneous revolutionary response to exploitation fed into a tradition of social upheaval. Crucially, unlike socialist indifference towards the rural south, anarchist 'apostles' carried the new gospel from village to village, converting the downtrodden labourers by heralding the arrival of a new age of justice and land redistribution. Anarchism seemed to provide ideological coherence to a reality in which the masses, distrusting the state and politics, were told that their emancipation should be the result of their efforts through so-called direct action (the economic struggle against employers without political interference).[81]

A Vicious Circle of Terror

Returning to the analogy of the river, despite periods of repression and persecution, the libertarian movement managed to re-emerge with force time and time again. This was largely the result of it being firmly rooted in the social fabric of the community due to its emphasis on bottom-up solutions rather than the more distant top-down strategy embraced by the Socialists. Unlike the latter's focus on high politics and administrative issues, the anarchists established close links within their *barrios* (quarters) by identifying clear local needs such as disputes revolving around consumption of goods and services.[82] They championed the struggle for neighbourhood self-reliance and freedom from external authority. As Chris Ealham notes, firm believers in the spontaneous self-expression of the masses, and in opposition to the Socialists who maintained a sharp distinction between the revolutionary and the criminal, the Libertarians emphasized the inalienable right of the poor and the needy to secure their existence, by whatever means necessary, legal or illegal. Widespread alienation inspired by years of political corruption provided the ideal context for anarchist anti-politicism and made the idea of direct action by the workers themselves appealing.[83] The anarchists were also ahead of the Socialists in terms of creating alternative grassroots social infrastructure comprising newspapers, cultural associations, and social clubs. A key institution was the *ateneo*, a popular centre that provided a range of services to its working-class members, including reading rooms, libraries, a space to hold conferences and debates, and, crucially, tuition in grammar and general education for adults and their children.[84]

Anarchist activities were crucial to provide the Spanish working classes with a language of class identity.[85] However, the anarchists' emphasis on the spontaneity of the masses together with their decentralized and loosely structured body often resulted in the harnessing of popular energies to badly planned revolutionary outbursts that frequently ended in defeat.

Another handicap was the existence of a subculture, whereby the labour organization existed side by side with small action groups that implemented so-called 'propaganda by the deed' or violence against the class enemy. Unlike Marxist doctrinal rigidity, the libertarian movement welcomed diverse groups: trade unionists, bohemians, and naturists, as well as all sorts of marginal forces. Yet, that vast heterogeneity exacerbated structural tensions between two tendencies that co-existed in a complex relationship: apolitical labour activists who favoured the creation of an effective mass movement to extract significant social concessions, and those who favoured the secret activities of the action groups which, regarding themselves as the 'guardians of ideological purity', often perceived union activities as an obstacle to the revolutionary dream.[86] Indeed, a hardened minority believed that avenging terrorism was the tool with which to begin the demolition of the ruling order and awaken the lethargic downtrodden masses.[87] The mixture of exaltation and impotence led to the search for a shortcut to revolution, which provided the authorities with the excuse to crush workers' organizations. Terrorist activities carried out by action groups (and often *agents provocateurs*) were met by indiscriminate repression, which, in turn, triggered new acts of terror.[88] It was a struggle that workers, faced with the mighty machinery of the state, could never win and only helped enshrine the libertarian movement's romantic but also tragic story.

This dynamic was well-illustrated in Jerez in 1882. In December of that year, the civil guard claimed to have discovered certain documents hidden under a stone in the countryside. They revealed the existence of a secret society, the *Mano Negra* (Black Hand), whose objective was the liquidation of its class enemies. This fantastic plot produced a wave of hysteria, which led to mass arrests on charges built on informers' testimonies and confessions extracted through torture. It resulted in eight executions and many stiff prison sentences, including 15 life sentences.[89] An immediate consequence was the FTRE's dissolution in 1888. Its successor was a weak two-headed movement: the *Federación de la Sociedades de Resistencia al Capital* (known as *Pacto de Unión y Solidaridad*), whose focus was on economic struggle through union activity, and the *Organización Anarquista de la Región Española*, an umbrella organization for the action groups. Both soon disappeared.

On 8 January 1892, Jerez again became the epicentre of social violence. Some 600 badly armed peasants invaded the city intending to storm the local jail to free some recently arrested comrades. When troops appeared, the crowds dispersed but some of them fell upon and killed two passers-by, their crime being the wearing of bourgeois clothes. Once again, workers' societies were closed, hundreds of militants were arrested, and many were tortured to produce confessions. A trial without any legal guarantees led to dozens of prison sentences and four executions. Despite the apocalyptic rhetoric, the events were, above all, a mass riot without any impetus beyond the release of prisoners. It was *agents provocateurs* who spurred on the crowds who had gathered outside Jerez. By then, troops had received reinforcements and waited strategically across the city.[90]

Mass repression in Andalusia fuelled calls for revenge. Coinciding with the executions in Jerez, a bomb exploded in the *Plaza Real* of Barcelona, leaving one person dead and several wounded.[91] Over the following years, the Catalan capital became the epicentre of a lethal spiral of bloody terrorism and draconian reaction. Two *atentados* (terror attacks) were particularly horrific. On 7 November 1893, a bomb was thrown from one of the top floors of the *Liceu* Theatre, a venue usually packed with the cream of the city's bourgeoisie. The initial figure of 15 dead began to mount over the following days given the large number of wounded. Then, on 7 June 1896, a bomb exploded during a religious procession in the Barcelona's old quarter. Six people died instantly and 40 were wounded (six others died later from their injuries); many were children.[92]

The callousness of such massacres created an atmosphere favourable to large-scale repression under military control as the havoc was followed by the suspension of constitutional guarantees and the declaration of martial law. Its indiscriminate nature, together with the mounting feeling of social injustice, transformed the alleged killers into martyrs and contributed to the creation of anarchist mythology. A contemporary commented that the authorities' cruelty had done more for anarchism than all the activities of its militants.[93] Indeed, one month after the *atentado* at the *Liceu*, the authorities boasted that several anarchists had confessed. The arrest of the real perpetrator, a certain Santiago Salvador, revealed how those confessions had been extracted through torture, including mock executions by firing squad. Still, they were not freed. Their depositions were used to court-martial them for a previous terrorist attack. In May 1894, four were sentenced to life imprisonment and six were executed.[94]

In June 1896, Barcelona experienced a new staggering judicial perversion. The full truth might never be known. The *atentado* was especially baffling: the bomb was not thrown at the head of the procession, where the city's high dignitaries marched, but at the tail occupied by the humblest citizens. Today, the most accepted thesis is that the culprit was a certain François Girault, a French anarchist who was not familiar with local habits as indicated by the location of the explosion.[95]

Once again, reaction was draconian and the priority did not seem to be the genuine discovery of the truth. Altogether, some 700 people were rounded up and jailed. Some were chained and taken to the colossal Castle of Montjuïc, which looks out over the city. Their confessions were obtained after weeks of brutal coercion. During the court martial, held behind closed doors, the accused were not allowed to produce defence witnesses. The only proof of their guilt was their confessions. The verdict, revised by the Supreme Council of War and the Navy in April 1897, was 62 absolutions, 20 different terms of prison, and five death sentences. On 6 May, facing the firing squad, the five continued to proclaim their innocence. To add insult to injury, those absolved, together with the many prisoners still languishing in jail, were expelled from Spain. Abroad, they revealed the scandalous perversion of justice they had suffered.

In August 1897, Cánovas was shot dead while on holiday in the Spa of Santa Águeda in Mondragón (Guipúzcoa). The gunman was an Italian anarchist, Michelle Angiolillo, who had lived in Barcelona and befriended some of those arrested and executed, having worked with them in the printing plant of the anarchist journal, *Ciencia Social*. Tellingly, the last event at which Angiolillo was seen was at a gathering in England where a former prisoner in Montjuïch and deportee, Francisco Gana, narrated his horrific experiences and showed the dreadful marks that had been left on his body.[96] Cánovas, the prime minister who had condoned the infamous repression, was an obvious target. Still, his murder was not exceptional in the last decade of the nineteenth century, as many dignitaries fell victim to 'propaganda by the deed'. His death was sandwiched between that of the French president, Marie François Sadi Carnot (1894), and King Umberto I of Italy (1900). Their assassinations were carried out by two Italian anarchists, Sante Geronimo Caserio and Gaetano Bresci respectively, as a response to the repression in those countries.[97]

Angiolillo's execution added another name to the already long list of anarchist 'martyrs'. Still, with the shameful events surrounding the Montjuïc trial still fresh in the mind, there was no mass repression. His confession that he had acted alone was accepted.[98] In the summer of 1897, while discredited by the shameful spectacle of judicial perversion in Barcelona, Spain also faced a bloody and expensive colonial war.

El Desastre: Reality, Myth, and Aftermath

Since the loss of its vast possessions on the American continent in the 1820s, the Spanish empire had been reduced to the islands of Cuba and Puerto Rico in the Caribbean, some archipelagos in the Pacific (the most important of which was the Philippine islands), and a few enclaves in Africa. The crown's pearl was Cuba, the world's largest producer of sugar, a magnet for financial investment, and the main destiny for colonial administrators and peninsular migration. This island was, above all, an essentially captive market for Spanish products and finance, and its lucrative raw materials (sugar, tobacco, coffee, cotton) helped to compensate for Spain's chronic trade deficit.[99] The first warning of rising discontent was in 1868. The insurrection lasted 10 years, until the Peace Treaty of Zanjón, which promised the introduction of a generous regime of home rule. However, that promise was never fulfilled. A powerful colonial lobby (which included Castilian wheat growers, Catalan industrialists, officers of the overseas army, and civil servants) ensured that any demands for autonomy and free trade were systematically rejected.

In February 1895, there was a new colonial revolt in Cuba. The authorities in Madrid responded by closing ranks and declaring in bold speeches that, if necessary, 'Spain was willing to spend its last peseta and give its children's last drop of blood in defence of its rights and territory'.[100] Cuba was considered an intrinsic part of Spain. One of the first territories discovered by Christopher Columbus, it had belonged to the Spanish Crown for over 400 years. Furthermore, thousands of Spaniards had settled there and maintained close links with the mainland.

On paper, the revolt should have been crushed in a relatively short time due to Spain's overwhelming superiority, both in manpower and weaponry. Some 200,000 troops were dispatched. They were aided by Cuban volunteers, whose number stood at around 90,000 in February 1897, three times the number of rebels.[101] Nonetheless, grandiloquent rhetoric and far superior firepower did not result in decisive victories on the battlefield.

Several issues hindered Spain's efforts. First, the rebels avoided large frontal battles on open ground. Instead, they adopted a guerrilla style of warfare, using hit-and-run tactics, employing very mobile and small cavalry columns against which material superiority could not prove decisive. After an attack, they swiftly dispersed and blended into the countryside.[102] Spain was also forced to divert resources to the Philippines where a revolt broke out in 1896. Furthermore, her attempts to maintain the fiction of a past golden age relied on outdated warships and poorly trained soldiers.[103] The recruits sent to the colonies came from humble households that could not afford the 2,000 pesetas to release them from conscription. They were thrown into an unsanitary and inhospitable setting. Overall, only 4 percent of casualties were as a result of fighting. The other 96 percent were down to a combination of tropical diseases (malaria, yellow fever, etc.) and the dismal state of the health services.[104] The initial *union sacrée* began gradually to give way to war weariness and even opposition. In 1896, *El Socialista* launched a campaign demanding a fair draft system under the slogan: 'Conscription for all!'[105]

However, it was an external agent that determined the outcome of the Cuban revolt: the United States. With the country unified after the badly termed 'conquest of the west', the obvious geopolitical target of US dollar diplomacy (the Caribbean and the Pacific) coincided with Spain's waning power. Notwithstanding the existing high tariff barriers, Cuba, just a few miles off the coast of Florida, was moving into the orbit of the northern industrial colossus that, unlike Spain, could invest massively in the island's economy and absorb its produce (sugar, tobacco, coffee, etc.). The rebels obtained military supplies and were endorsed by viscerally anti-Spanish propaganda. Press barons such as William Randolph Hearst and Joseph Pulitzer inflamed public opinion with sensationalist reports of the alleged atrocities committed by the Spaniards.[106] In March 1897, diplomatic relations deteriorated further with the assumption of office of a Republican administration headed by William McKinley, which included outspoken advocates of intervention such as the Assistant Secretary of the Navy, Theodore Roosevelt. In January 1898, the US government sent a warship (the USS *Maine*) to Cuba with the alleged purpose of protecting American property and lives. When on 15 February an explosion destroyed it in Havana harbour, killing 266 members of the crew, the US imperialist lobby and sensationalist press at last had the pretext to intervene. In April, the United States was at war with Spain.[107]

Given the contrast between military and economic resources, combined with the geographical location, it seemed a temerity to wage war against the United States. Furthermore, decades of diplomatic isolation, avoiding any entanglements with either of the two camps emerging in Europe, had left Spain without any solid allies. Although perfectly aware of the impossibility of sustaining a long drawn-out campaign, the government headed by Sagasta was even more fearful that capitulation could result in such a backlash amongst the army and the colonial lobby that it would endanger the survival of the regime.[108] The solution to that dilemma was to embark upon a suicidal struggle to end the dispute honourably. During the 113 days of the conflict, the dynastic elites forged a quixotic farce built upon patriotic speeches. While the Church described the war as a crusade against a mercantilist and protestant nation, a jingoistic press fantasized about how eternal Spain, represented by an old lion, was about to thrash the American scum, depicted as pigs, vultures, or avaricious Jews.[109]

The navy, concentrated in Cavite (Philippines) and Santiago (Cuba), was sacrificed: two American fleets, on 1 May and 3 July respectively, which were overwhelmingly superior in numbers and firepower, destroyed the obsolete Spanish warships. This quixotic episode, hailed a glorious defeat, was illustrated later by the following: ¡*Más vale honra sin barcos que barcos sin honra!* ('Better honour without ships than ships without honour!'). Without a significant naval force, it was impossible to continue the war. Thus, nobody objected when Sagasta sued for peace in early August.[110] Spain had not lost her last peseta or drop of blood, but the price was extremely high: some 2,000 million pesetas and close to half of the contingent of 200,000 soldiers who had died or fallen ill. Furthermore, the treaty signed in Paris in December confirmed the loss of the last significant remnants of its empire. Cuba, Puerto Rico, and Guam were ceded to the United States, which also obtained, after a payment of US$20 million, the Philippines. Germany paid 25 million marks for the last territories in the Pacific (the Mariana, the Caroline, and the Palau Islands).[111]

Henceforth, the year 1898 became synonymous with '*desastre*'. Today, the saying *más se perdió en Cuba* ('more was lost in Cuba') is used to mean that nothing can get worse. Coinciding with a golden period for Spanish culture, leading members of the country's intellectual elite (Miguel de Unamuno, José Ortega y Gasset, Joaquín Costa, Pío Baroja), known as the 'Generation of 98', invented a nostalgic past based on Spain's previous imperial greatness and denounced the present as the epitome of decadence: *caciquismo*, backwardness, clericalism, and so on. They insisted on the urgency of national regeneration, or the profound rekindling of the country's moral and ideological foundations. However, they prescribed different formulas: some believed in democratic modernization and others in regeneration from above implemented by an intellectual elite (Ortega) or an 'iron surgeon' (Costa).[112] The magnitude of this feeling of discontent must be understood in the context of an era in which overseas possessions were seen as the hallmark of a vigorous nation. In an age of colonial expansion and Social Darwinism, Spain was reduced overnight from the status of Great Power to that of a second-rate nation.[113] This feeling was illustrated in a cartoon depicting the brutal contrast between the beginning of Spain's imperial mission (the caravels in 1492 on a voyage of discovery) and its bitter end 400 years later (the return of thousands of emaciated soldiers crammed on the decks of ships).[114]

Subsequent Spanish regimes perpetuated the concept of national disaster to denigrate the Liberal Monarchy. However, modern scholarship suggests that Spain's *fin de siècle* must be seen in the context of an age of international redistribution of power and the parallel emergence of new great powers (Japan, the United States, Germany) and setbacks (particular versions of the '98') for others, such as the Ottoman Empire (in open retrenchment), Portugal (humiliated by Germany and Britain in southern Africa), Italy (defeated by the Ethiopians in 1896 in Adowa), and Russia (beaten by Japan in 1905).[115] It cannot be said that 1898 constituted a symbolic dividing line between two different periods. Spain neither enjoyed a golden era in previous years nor faced a calamitous situation afterwards. In fact, unlike other national debacles such as the French defeat in the Franco-Prussian War that brought down the Third Empire in 1870 or the revolutionary upsurge which shook the foundations of the all-powerful Tsarist regime in 1905, there were no major institutional crises in Spain. Sagasta was back in office two years later, the *turno* continued unabated, and the Bourbon dynasty remained on the throne.[116] Therefore, this view of doom in 1898 was an exaggeration. In general, society continued to function practically the same as before. It was the socio-political and cultural elites whose overblown perception of the events led them to spread the image of a collective disgrace of apocalyptic dimensions.[117] Francisco Silvela, Cánovas' successor as leader of the Conservative Party, stated that 'Spain had lost its heartbeat'.[118]

The status quo remained intact because the governing classes could embrace, in words rather than deeds, and with different degrees of conviction, the idea of regeneration. The deeply rooted phenomenon of local *caciquismo* meant that in a society with poor communications and a high level of illiteracy, the traditional networks of social control continued to function.[119] Reformist challenges, such as that led by the essayist Joaquín Costa, who attempted to use the Chambers of Commerce and Agriculture to create a party of producers, the National Union, with which to challenge dynastic hegemony were thwarted. Costa's objective was to modernize the country through the development of irrigation canals and reservoirs, public works, and so on. Yet farmers and tradesmen were powerless to break the domination of the local *caciques*. In 1901, a frustrated Costa published *Oligarquía y caciquismo como la forma actual de gobierno en España* ('Oligarchy and *caciquismo* as the sources of governance in Spain'). He concluded that a national *caudillo* or an 'iron surgeon' might be needed to implement surgical methods (remove the tumour of *caciquismo*) to regenerate Spain.[120]

The regime's most outspoken enemies were too weak to take advantage of a potentially favourable conjuncture. Carlism was a declining force, the Republicans were divided after the fiasco of the First Republic, and the army lacked a charismatic *espadón*. Only General Camilo Polavieja, a hero of the Philippines, was briefly tempted to lead a government whose aim was a programme of national regeneration and administrative decentralization, which relied on the enthusiastic support of the main Catalan economic corporations. However, he encountered the opposition of the Queen Regent, Maria Christina of Austria, who believed that such an endeavour might endanger the dynasty. In March 1899, Polavieja accepted the War portfolio in a government formed by Silvela, whose declared objective was to bring dignity back to politics.[121] During the two brief governments presided over by Silvela (March 1899 to October 1900 and December 1902 to July 1903), the first significant social legislation was introduced by interior minister Eduardo Dato: for workplace accidents, the regulation of women and children's labour, the celebration of 1 May as a holiday (labour day), and the creation of the *Instituto de Reformas Sociales* (IRS), a body composed of state experts and representatives of employers and labour with the aim of implementing measures to improve workers' living conditions.[122]

The absence of a major economic upheaval helped political stability. A deflationary programme based on modest fiscal reform, new taxation on utilities, and public spending cuts, devised by the minister of finance, Raimundo Fernández Villaverde, led to years of budgetary surpluses. His scheme of public debt conversion was covered 25 times over. Also, the repatriation of capital (over 1,600 million pesetas) proved crucial, and the currency's devaluation helped increase exports.[123]

Still, defeat had put an end to a false consciousness, anchored in a glorious imperial past, of still being a leading power when, in fact, Spain was a marginal state within Europe. Furthermore, the unreformed persistence of the political comedy continued to fuel social tragedy, given the major issues that the country was to face after the turn of the century: the emergence of peripheral nationalisms, the bitter class struggle, and the existence of a bloated and now bruised army searching for a new *raison d'être*.[124]

The colonial disaster gave motivation to centrifugal tendencies. They crystallized in the two regions marked by the greatest economic modernization and previous mass adherence to Carlism in their rural hinterland: the Basque Country and Catalonia.

Basque Nationalism inherited Carlism's ultra-Catholic and reactionary aspects, embodied in the motto 'God and Ancient Laws', to which now was added a xenophobic and separatist position. The *Partido Nacionalista Vasco* (PNV, Basque Nationalist Party), founded by Sabino Arana in 1895, warned that the 'purity' of the Basque race was threatened by the growing number of immigrants attracted by that region's industrial development. However, before his death in 1903, he rejected independence and backed home rule within Spain. This dichotomy between an autonomic and a separatist tendency within the PNV has persisted until the present day. Still, it had to wait until 1918 to get its first significant electoral breakthrough and remained mostly confined to the province of Vizcaya.[125]

In contrast, the first political expression of Catalan nationalism,[126] the *Lliga Regionalista de Catalunya* (*Lliga*), enjoyed astounding electoral success in April 1901 in Barcelona, one month after its foundation. The emergence of Catalan nationalism was the product of a collaboration between a group of well-educated conservative youth (including Francesc Cambó, Enric Prat de la Riba, and Joan Ventosa) with economic concerns about a regime unable to protect their interests overseas and which later presided over a deflationary budget, rising taxation, and legislation favourable to the workers.[127] In opposition to Villaverde's economic plan, shopkeepers, industrialists, and businessmen across Spain, particularly in Barcelona, backed a 'strike of tax-payers' by stopping their activities: *tancament de caixes* (closure of tills). In October 1899, the government declared martial law. A few shopkeepers were jailed. The movement collapsed but brought about the divorce of these sectors from the *turno*.[128]

Above all, the *Lliga* represented the so-called *gent de bé* (the good citizens) and identified with an ideal Catalonia of social order and economic progress. Labour conflicts were often dismissed as being inspired by outside agitators or caused by migrant rabble.[129] It was a social-conservative force with strong Catholic roots that pursued home rule but not separatism. It formed part of the nationwide movement of regeneration which sprang up after 1898. This new generation of Catalan politicians saw the Spanish state as archaically structured, ineffective, and plagued by corruption.[130] Within this context and given the authorities' perceived disregard for industrial interests, instead pandering to the southern landed estates, it prescribed the idea of an '*Espanya Catalana*': Spain could only regain its past greatness as a nation-state of 'nations' led by an economically advanced Catalonia.[131] Thus, it was imperative to destroy the dynastic monopoly of power. However, its instinctive conservatism continued to prevail. Its acceptance of the monarchist legal framework caused breakaway factions from its republican and federal wings.[132]

The colonial disaster injected new life into Republicanism. In 1903, most republican factions established an electoral alliance, led by a former president of the First Republic, Nicolás Salmerón. The introduction of universal suffrage helped them increase their parliamentary representation in the cities where results were harder to manipulate. They were often led by (or counted amongst their ranks) well-known intellectuals such as the writer Vicente Blasco Ibáñez in his native city of Valencia, one of the first places where *caciquismo* was vanquished.[133] The new century saw the emergence of new republican leaders. Melquiades Álvarez, a distinguished law professor, was to champion a moderate position and in 1912 founded the Reformist Party, which initially included many intellectuals (including Manuel Azaña, Américo Castro, and José Ortega y Gasset). It was prepared to accept the monarchy if the regime was genuinely committed to undertake a real process of democratization.[134] The journalist Alejandro Lerroux represented the Jacobin tendency. Modern scholarship has rescued him from the traditional accusation of being an unprincipled opportunist sent by Madrid to counter the recently born Catalan nationalism and divide the proletariat in Barcelona.[135] He certainly had no qualms in sealing a variety of underhand deals with some notables of the Liberal Party.[136] However, his murky transactions only took place after his electoral success. Moreover, far from being a monarchist puppet, he never renounced conspiring against the regime. It was his reputation that persuaded local republicans to recruit his services to rekindle their ailing movement.[137]

In his youth, Lerroux joined the *Partido Republicano Progresista*, the most radical republican faction, headed by Manuel Ruiz Zorrilla, the mastermind of numerous conspiracies against the monarchy from his exile in Paris.[138] Lerroux was thrust into the limelight and gained widespread support among the Catalan proletariat when his newspaper *El Progreso* became a leading voice in the campaign against the injustices of Montjuïc.[139] Succeeding where the PSOE had failed, he profited from the collapse of the organized labour movement after the repression of the 1890s and presided over the meteoric upsurge of the republican cause in Barcelona. A consummate orator, he transformed demagogy into an art and built a formidable political machine. He lured the previously passive masses by mobilizing them with rousing speeches, incendiary pamphlets, and popular leisure activities such as picnics and dances. His discourses consisted of vague promises of a forthcoming revolution, fierce anti-clericalism, and hostility towards Catalan nationalism since the *Lliga* was the party of the employers. He resonated with a radicalized constituency who had seen their organization destroyed by years of indiscriminate repression. The hold that Lerroux acquired over the proletariat was such that he was known as 'the *Paralelo*'s Emperor', the *Paralelo* being the working-class area where he used to make his speeches.¹⁴⁰ That influence gradually diminished as the workers began to reorganize themselves. A new labour federation, *Solidaridad Obrera*, was created in August 1907. It sponsored revolutionary syndicalist principles that urged workers to unite regardless of ideological leanings, abandon politics, and adopt methods of direct action.¹⁴¹

In 1902, Alfonso XIII ascended to the throne. King before birth, months after the death of his father, he was educated by military and religious preceptors and spent his childhood shielded from the real world.¹⁴² Aged 16, he was confronted with the task of reigning. From the start, unlike his parents, who had avoided meddling with the executive, the young monarch abused the principle of shared national sovereignty and never concealed his contempt for his politicians who he treated as mere lackeys.¹⁴³ The internecine feuds of the dynastic parties resulting from their artificial nature facilitated royal intervention in dismissing or appointing cabinets: there were ten governments alone between 1902 and 1906. Most crises were known as *orientales*, since they were manufactured at the *Palacio de Oriente*, the royal residence.¹⁴⁴

Alfonso's reign commenced under the shadow of two dark realities: terrorism and colonial debacle. Like other European monarchs, Alfonso XIII was a constant target. The two most serious attempts on his life occurred on the 31st of May of two consecutive years, 1905 and 1906. In the first instance, a bomb was thrown at the carriage in which he was travelling with the French President Émile François Loubet in Paris. Several passers-by were injured and one of the escort officers was killed. The perpetrator was never apprehended. One year later it was his wedding to Princess Victoria Eugenie of Battenberg, King Edward VII's niece. Amidst the cheers of the crowds cramming the narrow old streets in the centre of Madrid, a procession of carriages bearing Spain's aristocracy and the heirs to all the crowns of Europe began its slow journey to the royal palace. Widespread happiness turned into a macabre spectacle when a powerful explosive, concealed in a bunch of flowers, was thrown at the royal carriage from the balcony of the fourth floor of a guesthouse. The horses suffered the brunt of the blast, although 23 people were killed and 108 wounded; miraculously the royal couple escaped unscathed.¹⁴⁵

The following morning, the terrorist committed suicide, ensuring that secrecy persisted. His name was Mateo Morral, the son of a well-off textile manufacturer from Sabadell (Barcelona), whose last known job was as a librarian in the *Escuela Moderna*. Its owner, Francisco Ferrer Guardia, had inherited a fortune from one of his students in France allowing him to realize his pedagogical dream, to open a school in Barcelona, as well as financing a wide range of projects, including terrorism. Given that Alfonso XIII had no descendants and the regime rested on an institutionalized fraud, regicide as a means for major political change was neither naive nor absurd.¹⁴⁶

Ferrer and Lerroux were two of the conspirators behind the *atentados* in 1905 and 1906. In their youth, both of them had belonged to Zorrilla's radical republican faction, later collaborated in the campaign against Montjuïc, and landed in Barcelona in 1901. Tellingly, on the day of the royal wedding, they were together in *Café de la Alhambra* in *Plaza de Cataluña* anxiously awaiting news from Madrid.[147] However, the outcome was not as expected. Based on his display of courage in the face of death, Alfonso XIII's popularity was enhanced. Ferrer was arrested and tried a year later. However, unlike the perversion of justice displayed by the 1890s court martials, the civil court behaved impeccably.[148] Despite his collaboration and ideological affinity with Morral, the absence of material proof or any direct witnesses introduced enough doubt to guarantee his absolution.[149]

Having inherited the trauma of 1898, Alfonso XIII considered it his duty to pursue national regeneration through the restoration of Spain's imperial prestige. This was facilitated by one of the last episodes of Africa's colonial redistribution: the partition of Morocco between France and Spain that gave the latter control of a strip of land of some 22,000 square kilometres on the northern coast (Rif) around its historical enclaves of Ceuta and Melilla. Such was the royal enthusiasm for this venture that he was nicknamed 'Alfonso the African'.[150] His imperial quest brought the monarch closer to the military.

The army was the institution most affected by the defeat of 1898. Ortega noted that 'it was like a loaded shotgun without a target to shoot'.[151] Rising social unrest and peripheral nationalism offered them one – the safeguarding of the fatherland's sacred values (national unity and social order). In the process, the military found the constitutional framework inadequate to fight separatism and labour unrest.[152] The army also became highly sensitive to any criticism regarding its competence. The catalyst for intervention, not surprisingly, emerged in Barcelona. The Catalan capital encapsulated the structural tensions produced by the process of modernity: an industrial bourgeoisie averse to social compromise, a proletariat with a long tradition of militancy, two mass parties – one republican and Jacobin and the other social-conservative and regionalist – and a garrison prone to intervention in civil affairs, was a lethal combination. Its ignition had a decisive impact on Spain's fate.[153]

On 23 November 1905, a cartoon published by the satirical Catalanist *¡Cu-Cut!* incensed the local garrison. It depicted a cavalry officer and a passer-by standing together while a crowd was entering a reception hall. Informed by his companion that they were attending a victory banquet, the military concluded that it ought to be then a civilian affair. That night, some 300 officers ransacked the journal's offices and later those of the *Lliga*'s mouthpiece, *La Veu de Catalunya*.[154] The government was caught between widespread Catalan calls for the officers to be punished and military solidarity. There were also rumours that officers were planning to storm the *Cortes*. Finally, the monarch dismissed his cabinet headed by Eugenio Montero Ríos and replaced him with another notable also from the Liberal Party, Segismundo Moret, who was more amenable to placating the army. In

March 1906, the Law of Jurisdictions was passed whereby any offence against the army, the monarchy, or the fatherland fell under military jurisdiction. This concession to praetorian violence was a devastating blow to civilian supremacy.[155]

The *Lliga*'s leaders profited from the general indignation. Parties, from Carlists to Republicans, followed their rallying call and joined an electoral coalition, *Solidaridad Catalana*, founded on the idea of civic responsibility vis-à-vis military brutality. Only Lerroux remained aloof due to his belief that the bulk of the working classes were not prepared to align themselves with a campaign led by their class enemies.[156] The elections of April 1907 were marked by violent incidents, including an armed attack on the car in which Salmerón and Cambó travelled. The latter was gravely wounded.[157] Overall, although Lerroux's republicans obtained more votes than in previous polls, they were crushed by their rivals' broad coalition. *Solidaridad Catalana* won 41 out of the 44 seats.[158] Having lost his own seat, and thus lacking parliamentary immunity, Lerroux went into exile after founding his own *Partido Republicano Radical* (Radical Party).

The Regeneration Chimera

Many dynastic notables embraced the idea of regeneration. This often meant a somewhat rhetorical stance. However, between 1907 and 1912, Spain was ruled by the two monarchist leaders most associated with a genuine overhaul of the ruling order and whose charisma shone through amidst dynastic mediocrity: Antonio Maura and José Canalejas. Yet even their attempts ended in abject failure.

Lerroux recognized Maura's stature and charisma as a statesman: 'he is the axis of national politics. Either you are with him or against him'.[159] Having started his political career in the Liberal Party, Maura's Catholic faith and beliefs in economic protectionism led to his gradual marginalization by a party for whom anti-clericalism (at least, in rhetorical terms) and free trade were then important tenets. In his first cabinet post, as minister for overseas (December 1892 to March 1894), Maura's comprehensive programme of decentralization for Cuba met total opposition, even from his own party, and forced his resignation.[160] In 1901, he joined the Conservatives who, then headed by Silvela, appeared more in tune with his calls for regeneration. When a demoralized Silvela chose to retire from politics in October 1903, he nominated Maura as his official successor to fulfil the task.[161]

No other dynastic notable was as polemic as Maura. Indeed, he differed radically from most of his colleagues who happily abided by the motto *ir tirando* ('live from day to day'). In July 1901, he declared in parliament that there was a growing fissure between the government and the people. Therefore, 'unless a revolution was carried out from above, a more formidable challenge would come from below'.[162] The opportunity to carry out his reformist programme appeared to have arrived when he headed one of the longest dynastic administrations (January 1907 to October 1909).[163] For over two years, the *Cortes* experienced an unknown period of debate of a large number of proposals whose declared objective was to 'purify' politics, awaken the so-called *masas neutras* (the apathetic middle classes), and eradicate *caciquismo*. It constituted the only comprehensive programme endorsed by a dynastic politician in the pursuit of citizens' participation in public life. It included reforming the electoral system and the judiciary. His pet project was the Law of Local Administration, which in pursuing administrative decentralization, would grant towns more independence and thus wrest control of their fiefdoms from their *caciques*.[164]

Although he obtained a legion of fervent supporters, his messianic arrogance, sense of infallibility, and mordant rhetoric ensured hostility from the entire political spectrum. Even Alfonso XIII, who described him sarcastically as 'Superman', never felt at ease with someone who relegated him to a secondary role and was so markedly different from the typical court minion he could manipulate.[165] His plans to clean up politics infuriated the Liberals and even many Conservatives, who feared losing their privileged position in a genuine democracy. He awakened levels of hostility in the Liberal Party that were unprecedented in the Restoration's framework of dynastic harmony. They were incensed when they were trounced in the elections of April 1907. Going against much of his previous rhetoric, Maura presided over one of the most sordid electoral contests.[166] To help ensure a huge parliamentary majority, he put Juan de la Cierva in the Home Office, a stereotype of the politics Maura claimed he wanted to eradicate. Still, any prime minister who pursued a reformist agenda had to confront the paradoxical premise that change depended on a parliament being docile enough to allow it to happen.[167] The Liberals were aware that while the Conservatives could aspire to become the party of the Catholic middle classes, without the *caciquista* apparatus, they had to compete with Republicans and Socialists for the vote of the progressive urban middle and working classes. In their eagerness to oust Maura and his 'revolution from above', they would be prepared to break the dynastic consensus and side with a revolution from below, which they believed could be manipulated. The conflictive agenda in Barcelona permitted them to advance their objective to defenestrate Maura.

Although Barcelona was not the only city to be rocked by social upheaval, it remained the epicentre of violence. From 1903, an epidemic of explosions earned it the sobriquet of 'the city of bombs'. The explosions ended in 1910 in the same abrupt way they had first begun. The campaign had no clear objectives. The aim of the bombings appeared to be to spread public insecurity and keep tensions raised.[168] The blame fell on the anarchists. The first bombs went off after the ill-fated general strike of 1902 and several labour conflicts in 1903 (carters, carpenters, tram drivers, etc.). However, as they were arrested after each explosion and jailed for long periods of preventive custody, the anarchists could not have kept up the campaign. Furthermore, the terrorist attacks were condemned in the strongest terms by the same libertarian media that had justified them in the previous decade.[169] The highly volatile situation in Barcelona produced the perfect environment in which different elements coalesced to maintain the climate of terror (the bitter class conflict, the violent confrontation between Lerroux's followers and those of *Solidaridad Catalana*, criminal opportunism, etc.).[170] The few ever apprehended turned out to be individuals without means or trade (vagabonds, indigents, etc.). It is absurd to believe that anarchists paid others to plant their bombs for them.[171] The perpetrators consisted also of police informers who made a lucrative business out of terrorism. The most notorious, Joan Rull, was a member of an anarchist group, who ended up selling his services to three civil governors. He was finally arrested when it became blatantly clear that the period of intensive bombing coincided with the authorities' unwillingness to yield to his economic demands. Rull was sentenced to death and executed in August 1908.[172]

Maura appointed Ángel Ossorio as Barcelona's civil governor. A young lawyer with moderate leanings, he behaved with impeccable objectivity during the 1907 general elections. He worked frenetically, passing decrees, increasing the number of police on the streets, investing heavily in informers, and so on. His hyperactivity gave way to demoralization when the bombing campaign continued unabated. Overwhelmed, Ossorio offered his resignation several times but it was not accepted. When he demanded harsh measures, the government introduced, in January 1908, a controversial bill for the repression of terrorism: it would threaten freedom of the press, shut down workers' centres and expel from Spain anyone who, by word or deed, supported or justified illegal activities.[173] The surprise was not the uproar that ensued but that the Liberal Party took the unprecedented step of joining Republicans in a 'leftist bloc'.[174] Their sudden staunch defence of civil liberties seemed hollow: the bloc's outspoken leader was Moret, who two years earlier had introduced the Law of Jurisdictions. In early 1909, the bill was dropped, but Maura's days in office were numbered. An unexpected affair brought about his fall: Morocco.

Unlike other dynastic notables and the monarch, Maura never showed any imperialist ambitions. Nevertheless, international agreements compelled the government to act when, in the spring of 1909, a rebellion threatened the construction of a railway near Melilla. Both the king and Moret readily supported military intervention. However, with the debacle of 1898 still fresh in their minds, the lower classes were not prepared to become once more the cannon fodder of a colonial war. Moreover, there were no historical links as in the Cuban case. The Moroccan venture was regarded as the king's enterprise backed by some narrow interests that were behind the construction of the railway network. To add insult to injury, on 12 July reservists from 1903 to 1907 were drafted. Accompanied by friends and families, the troops' farewells became scenes of grief and anger, which often led to violent clashes with the police.[175]

Labour leaders, including Iglesias, were rounded up to forestall a general strike. Still, on 26 July, a 24-hour stoppage went ahead in Barcelona. It lasted seven days, the so-called 'Tragic Week'.[176] Sympathy for the protest was such that the picket lines' efforts to bring the city to a standstill counted on the complicity of most employers.[177] The strike also benefited from the authorities' deadlock: Cierva wanted to send in the army, but the governor believed it was a mistake to use troops to put down an anti-war demonstration. Finally, the minister imposed his view and martial law was declared.[178]

During the first three days, outnumbered by the protesters, the soldiers were mostly used to protect key buildings. Consequently, the leaderless masses became the virtual owners of the city. Overwhelmed by events, the strike committee (formed by a Socialist, an anarchist, and an activist from *Solidaridad Obrera*) had no plans beyond a 24-hour stoppage. Republicans, both Lerroux's followers and those in *Solidaridad Catalana*, refused to head the movement. Without any clear political objectives, the crowds stormed armouries and built barricades. Spurred by years of Lerroux's fierce anti-clerical discourse, popular anger turned towards ecclesiastical property. Clouds of smoke covered the skies of Barcelona as religious buildings were burnt down. Macabre scenes included the looting of convents, desecration of graves, and processions carrying the corpses of mummified nuns. The army, bolstered by reinforcements from other regions, finally crushed the revolt. Official sources registered 80 ecclesiastical buildings attacked (at least 50 destroyed), some 120 people killed, and 399 injured.[179] Court martials tried 1,725 people between August 1909 and May 1910. Over 200 workers were deported, 49 condemned to life imprisonment, 17 to death, and the rest to jail sentences of varying lengths.[180] There were only five executions, the last of which was considered another blatant judicial outrage: that of Ferrer.

After two years abroad, Ferrer's return to *Mas Germinal* (the family home on the outskirts of Barcelona) in June 1909 was not to stage a revolution but because of the poor health of his sister-in-law and her niece, a girl aged nine, who tragically died of meningitis after his arrival.[181] Caught at the outbreak of the revolt in Barcelona where he had gone to discuss editorial matters, his participation in the unfolding events was minimal: discussing the situation with some Radical leaders that day and visiting the Radical mayors of the two villages near his home the following morning. He never formed part of the strike committee, participated in the destruction of religious property, or fought on any barricade. Nevertheless, being a marked man since 1906, his presence, although accidental, led the authorities to order his arrest. Ferrer went into hiding but was caught while trying to escape to France. He was jailed under the absurd charge of being the leader of a leaderless revolution. As in previous cases (the Black Hand, the Montjuïc trial, etc.), he was made a convenient scapegoat to explain the complexities of the social unrest. In October, he was court-martialled, sentenced to death, and shot.[182]

Hardly anyone came out in defence of Ferrer in Spain. Consulted by the government about granting a pardon, Moret affirmed that justice should be implemented; otherwise, the cabinet would fail to live up to its 'virile duties'.[183] In contrast, there were massive protests abroad to save Ferrer and later to denounce inquisitorial Spain. In France, these demonstrations often turned into violent clashes. The movement spread throughout European and American cities (Brussels, Rome, Montevideo, New York, Buenos Aires). Brussels' city hall even approved the establishment of a monument to the 'martyr of freedom of conscience'.[184]

The Tragic Week had crucial consequences. First, having seen its leaders jailed, its press censored, and its centres closed, the PSOE abandoned its political isolation and sealed a *conjunción* (electoral alliance) with the Republicans in November 1909. The alliance's breakthrough came in May 1910, when Iglesias became the first Socialist to be returned to parliament.[185] Secondly, the Radical Party's ambiguous stance during the revolt led to the gradual loss of its grip over Barcelona's proletariat. After his return from exile, Lerroux's strategy was to embrace a more moderate stance and transform his party into a major national force.[186] A new labour federation filled the vacuum left by the Radicals: the *Confederación Nacional del Trabajo* (CNT, National Confederation of Labour), a nationwide expansion of *Solidaridad Obrera*. Founded at a congress held in Barcelona (30 October to 1 November 1910), it counted some 25,000 members, mostly from that city. Based on revolutionary syndicalist principles, it rejected any state mediation and subordination to a political party. Its emphasis was on direct action through sabotage, boycotts, strikes, and so on.[187]

In the aftermath of the Tragic Week, dynastic intrigues and the crown's active participation further weakened the stability of the regime. Once the *Cortes* reopened, traditional dynastic harmony turned into violent rhetoric. On 21 October, Maura visited the royal palace and was astounded when the monarch accepted a resignation that he had never tendered. According to his eldest son Gabriel, he saw his father in tears for the first time.[188] In a democracy, his position would have been secure given his overwhelming parliamentarian majority. However, these were not normal times and Spain was not a democracy. Maura never blamed the king but declared his implacable hostility to the Liberals.

The crisis consolidated royal pre-eminence. Moret remained in power for just four months. He was already rigging the elections when the monarch denied him a decree of dissolution of Parliament and instead entrusted power to another liberal baron, José Canalejas. This can be deemed a smart move. Canalejas constituted the Liberal response to Maura's revolution from above. A republican in his youth, Canalejas (who claimed to be a radical on the left of his party) was expected to diffuse revolutionary tension while dismantling Moret's leftist bloc. His tragic death two years later helped build an idealized vision of his premiership as the last lost opportunity for meaningful regeneration.[189] Well before that time, however, his reformist reputation lay in ruins.

Canalejas advocated replacing the traditional economic laissez-faire with state interventionism to improve working conditions and so find a modus vivendi with sections of the labour movement.[190] His programme included an array of issues but was significantly diluted before its introduction: for instance, religious concerns (*Ley del Candado* – Law of Padlock – to halt the expansion of religious orders only lasted two years), the territorial question (establishment of the *Mancomunidad*, an institution which absorbed the administrative powers enjoyed by the four Catalan county councils, was only introduced by royal decree by a Conservative administration in 1914), and military conscription (included the *cuota* or payment which permitted the rich a huge reduction in their term in the army and to eat and sleep in their own homes).[191]

Unlike Maura, Canalejas believed the king should be closely involved in political decision-making, something that pleased Alfonso XIII.[192] Both also shared the same enthusiasm for an active role in Morocco. From the spring of 1911, disregarding Maura's advice,[193] Spain competed with France in an interventionist campaign in that territory that concluded with the establishment of a formal protectorate in November 1912.[194] Consequently, Spain was rocked in 1911 by anti-war protests and industrial strikes. In early August, a mutiny broke out on the frigate *Numancia*, anchored in Tangier. Although the affair lasted only a few minutes and there were no casualties, its leader, Antonio Sánchez Moya, was executed. The movement reached its peak in September when a nationwide general strike was called. The worst incidents occurred in the province of Valencia where railway lines were uprooted, several town halls were stormed, and in Cullera a magistrate, a local court officer, and a bailiff were stabbed to death. Canalejas' response matched that of previous governments: constitutional guarantees were suspended, workers' centres closed, the CNT declared illegal, and labour leaders arrested.[195] Iglesias sarcastically described the government as 'the black cabinet' and even wrote that Canalejas was worse than Maura.[196] In October 1912, he again incensed the labour movement when, to crush a railway strike, he passed a bill that declared stoppages in vital public services illegal and militarized the sector, thus equating absence from work to desertion. Ironically, Maura stood in parliament to defend the right to strike.[197] One month later the prime minister was killed.

Canalejas' death was a tragic twist of fate. On 12 November, he was walking absentmindedly ahead of his police escort. When he stopped to look in the window of a bookshop in Madrid's central square, *Puerta del Sol*, a man approached him from behind and shot him three times at point-blank range. The killer, finding himself cornered, turned the gun on himself. He was Manuel Pardiñas and had returned recently from his exile in Tampa (Florida), a well-known centre of Spanish and Italian anarchists. Canalejas should have been in his office. However, his regular meeting early in the day with the monarch had been altered due to an unexpected change in the royal agenda. Awaiting his chance to murder the king, who was expected to travel through the *Puerta del Sol*, Pardiñas must have been surprised to run into a distracted Canalejas. Taking advantage of the opportunity, he settled for killing the prime minister.[198]

After three years of political ostracism, Maura believed that Canalejas' death meant his automatic return to power. He was upset, therefore, when he learnt that the king had decided to back a new Liberal cabinet headed by the maverick Count Romanones, the ultimate *cacique* archetype and professional politician with a unique record for intrigues.[199] On 1 January 1913, an embittered Maura declared that he could no longer share responsibilities or rotate in office with the existing administration or others to be formed with similar elements.[200] Maura's note revealed his messianic arrogance and extraordinary ingenuity. Neither the Liberal notables nor the monarch were prepared to recognize that they had erred in 1909. Furthermore, Maura naively believed he was backed by his party, when in fact he was almost alone.[201] In October 1913, when the government fell due to the Liberals' internecine squabbling, he discovered that the Conservative barons were eager to enjoy the spoils of office after four years in the wilderness. They rallied around the leadership of a former minister and wealthy company lawyer, Eduardo Dato, who was well known for his consensual stance and servile attitude towards the crown. A contemporary author put it bluntly: 'Walking on his tiptoes, Dato learnt to go far. Maura, treading firmly, was banished. The king naturally preferred humble servants'.[202]

Maura's defenestration split his party. Dato controlled the apparatus, the *caciquista* networks, and the support of most notables. While Cierva formed his faction, a significant number of young monarchists responded to Ossorio's call and formed a new movement that even adopted the name of their admired leader, *Maurismo*. Staunch critics of the ruling order's atrophy, unlike the traditional dynastic parties, took an active role in terms of propaganda and street mobilization. They represented the first attempt to create a modern right-wing party and regenerate the 'country from above'. However, they never formed a coherent party, instead remaining a broad church, united by their devotion to Maura (who ironically never felt comfortable with the populist agitation of his young followers), their monarchism, and bitter dislike of the *turno*. There was a reformist Christian Democratic faction led by Ossorio, and an anti-liberal tendency headed by Antonio Goicoechea.[203]

In 1913, the hopes of regeneration awakened by Maura and Canalejas had turned out to be a chimera. The political comedy could go on as both dynastic parties were in the 'safe hands' of Romanones and Dato. However, slowly but steadily, the social, urban, and economic modernization of the country began eroding the pillars of apathy and ignorance on which the system rested. Furthermore, the liberal regime was about to face a catastrophe, the Great War.

Notes

1 Eric J. Hobsbawm, *The Age of Revolution, 1789–1848* (London: Weidenfeld & Nicolson, 1962).

2 The 'War of Independence' against the French invader was, above all, a civil war among Spaniards. It constituted a massively chaotic period of popular implosion against the symbols of authority mostly identified now with the new ruler, Joseph Bonaparte, combined with clerical reaction. Simultaneously, the Iberian Peninsula became a theatre of the wider imperial dispute between France and Britain. The victors manipulated the narrative of the events and constructed a highly emotive vision based on one-sided patriotism and anti-foreign xenophobia that has survived until the present day. Those who fought on the side of Joseph Bonaparte – not an insignificant figure given the thousands of Spaniards who sought exile in France – were referred contemptuously as *afrancesados*. José Cepeda Gómez, 'La invención de dos mitos: norteamericanos y españoles ante sus guerras de Independencia', in Antonio Rodríguez and Rosario Ruiz (eds.), *1808. Controversias historiográficas* (Madrid: Actas, 2010), pp. 194–208.

3 Ferdinand (VII) had staged a palace coup against his father in March 1808.

4 Juan Ignacio Marcuello, 'Las Cortes de Cádiz, Monarquía y gobierno de Asamblea. Valoraciones historiográficas sobre la formación de gobierno en el sistema constitucional de 1812', in Rodríguez and Ruiz (eds.), *1808*, pp. 146–72.

5 The troops that had gathered in Cádiz to embark to quell the colonial rebellions mutinied in January 1820 and forced the king to restore the constitution of 1812. As the conservative reaction gathered momentum in the continent, Ferdinand VII sought help from his Bourbon relatives in France. Louis XVIII, supported by the Holly Alliance (Austria, Prussia, and Russia), complied, and sent an army of 100,000 men in April 1823 that restored absolutism and ushered in a tyrannical period known as the 'ominous decade'.

6 Jordi Canal, *El Carlismo* (Madrid: Alianza, 2000), pp. 18–24.

7 Adrian Shubert, *A Social History of Modern Spain* (London: Unwin Hyman, 1990), pp. 58–9.

8 David Blackbourn and Geoff Eley, *The Peculiarities of German History: Bourgeois Society and Politics in Nineteenth-Century Germany* (Oxford: Oxford University Press, 1991), p. 174.

9 Shubert, *A Social History*, pp. 60–4.

10 Edward Malefakis, *Reforma agraria y revolución campesina en la España del Siglo XX* (Barcelona: Ariel, 1971), pp. 82–4.

11 Ibid., pp. 125–7.

12 Manuel Ballbé, *Orden público y militarismo en la España constitucional, 1812–1983* (Madrid: Alianza, 1985), pp. 142–6.

13 Carlos Seco Serrano, *Militarismo y civilismo en la España contemporánea* (Madrid: IEC, 1984), 78–81.

14 Jordi Nadal, 'The Failure of the Industrial Revolution in Spain, 1830–1914', in Carlo M. Cipolla (ed.), *The Fontana Economic History of Europe, vol. VI, Part Two: The Emergence of Industrial Nations* (Hassocks: Harvester Press, 1976), p. 541.

15 Clive Trebilcock, *The Industrialization of the Continental Powers, 1780–1914* (London: Longman, 1981), p. 307.

16 Ramón del Valle Inclán, *La corte de los Milagros* (Madrid: Espasa Calpe, 1968 [1927]), p. 35.

17 Gregorio de la Fuente Monge, *Los revolucionarios de 1868, elites y poder en la España liberal* (Madrid: Marcial Pons, 2000).

18 Fidel Gómez Ochoa, 'El conservadurismo canovista y los orígenes de la Restauración: la formación de un conservadurismo moderno', in Manuel Suárez Cortina (ed.), *La Restauración, entre el liberalismo y la democracia* (Madrid: Alianza, 1997), pp. 127–30, 143–4.

19 Sagasta had been minister of the Interior in the provisional government following the fall of Isabel II. He later served as prime minister both with King Amadeo and General Serrano. Carlos Dardé, 'Sagasta o cómo sobrevivir en política', in Javier Moreno Luzón (ed.), *Progresistas* (Madrid: Taurus, 2006), 103–25.

20 José Ramón Milán García, 'La revolución entra en Palacio. El liberalismo dinástico de Sagasta, 1875–1903', *Berceo*, 139 (2000), p. 95.

21 Victoria Lorée Enders and Pamela Beth Radcliff, 'Introduction', in Victoria Lorée Enders and Pamela Beth Radcliff (eds.), *Constructing Spanish Womanhood* (New York: State University of New York Press, 1999), p. 21.

22 Mary Nash, 'Un/Contested Identities: Motherhood, Sex Reform and the Modernization of Gender Identity in Early Twentieth Century Spain', in Enders and Radcliff (eds.), *Constructing Spanish Womanhood*, p. 27.

23 Katharina Rowold, *The Educated Woman: Minds, Bodies, and Women's Higher Education in Britain, Germany, and Spain, 1865–1914* (London: Routledge, 2010), pp. 160, 185.

24 Enders and Radcliff, 'Work Identities', in Enders and Radcliff (eds.), *Constructing Spanish Womanhood*, pp. 125–8. In 1910, the percentage of working women was 36 percent in France, 32 percent in England, 27 percent in Germany, and 13.5 percent in Spain.

25 Ramón Villares, 'Alfonso XII y Regencia, 1875–1902', in Ramón Villares and Javier Moreno, *Historia de España, vol. 7: Restauración y Dictadura* (Madrid: Marcial Pons, 2009), p. 54.

26 Javier Tusell, 'El sufragio universal en España (1891–1936): un balance historiográfico', *Ayer*, 3 (1991), pp. 25–32.

27 The name came from the local chieftains of the native tribes in America whose co-option enabled the Spanish *conquistadores* to control vast areas of that continent.

28 Antonio Robles (ed.), *Política en penumbra* (Madrid: Siglo XXI, 1996); José Varela Ortega, *Los amigos Políticos. Partidos, elecciones y caciquismo en la Restauración, 1875–1900* (Madrid: Alianza, 1977) and (ed.), *El poder de la influencia. Geografía del caciquismo en España, 1875–1923* (Madrid: Marcial Pons, 2001).

29 Francisco J. Romero Salvadó, *Political Comedy and Social Tragedy: Spain, a Laboratory of Social Conflict, 1892–1921* (Brighton: Sussex University Press, 2020), p. 10.

30 James Simpson and Juan Carmona, *Why Democracy Failed: The Agrarian Origins of the Spanish Civil War* (Cambridge: Cambridge University Press, 2020), p. 19.

31 Arno Mayer, *The Persistence of the Old Regime: Europe to the Great War* (London: Croom Helm, 1981), pp. 152–3.

32 *Trasformismo* in Italy or Portugal's *rotativismo* represented the local variety of oligarchic liberalism. Villares, 'Alfonso XII', p. 101.

33 Mayer, *The Persistence of the Old Regime*, pp. 15–20, 32–3.

34 Pedro Carlos González Cuevas, 'El pensamiento político de Antonio Cánovas', in Javier Tusell and Florentino Portero (eds.), *Antonio Cánovas y el sistema político de la Restauración* (Madrid: Biblioteca Nueva, 1998), pp. 47, 68–9.

35 Javier Moreno Luzón, 'The Government, Parties and King, 1913–1923', in Francisco J. Romero Salvadó and Angel Smith (eds.), *The Agony of Spanish Liberalism: From Revolution to Dictatorship, 1913–1923* (Basingstoke: Palgrave Macmillan, 2010), p. 36.

36 Mayer, *The Persistence of the Old Regime*, pp. 244–5. There were important exceptions. The clash with the French Third Republic reached a peak during the Émile Combes administration (1902–1905) that decreed the separation of Church and state and banned teaching by religious orders. The Italian *Risorgimento* – which effectively unified the country – concluded with the occupation of Rome in 1870, which ended the Papacy's rule. Pius IX declared himself to be a prisoner and pronounced a *non expedit* policy, admonishing Catholics not to collaborate with the new state.

37 Frances Lannon, *Privilege, Persecution and Prophecy: The Catholic Church in Spain, 1875–1975* (Oxford: Oxford University Press, 1987), pp. 119–20.

38 William J. Callahan, *The Catholic Church in Spain, 1875–1998* (Washington, DC: Catholic University of America Press, 2000), p. 27.

39 Joan Connelly Ullman, *The Tragic Week: A Study of Anticlericalism in Spain, 1875–1912* (Cambridge, MA: Harvard University Press, 1968), p. 35.

40 Samuel E. Finer, *The Man on Horseback: The Role of the Military in Politics* (London: Pall Mall Press, 1967), pp. 8–10.

41 Eduardo González Calleja, *La razón de la fuerza. Orden público, subversión y violencia política en la España de la Restauración, 1875–1917* (Madrid: CSIC, 1998), pp. 55–72.

42 In 1900, the army consisted of 499 generals, 578 colonels, and over 23,000 officers for some 80,000 men (six times more officers than France, which relied on an army of 180,000 soldiers). Seco Serrano, *Militarismo*, p. 233.

43 At the start of the twentieth century, Spain's security forces amounted to some 4,000 men, half of them in Madrid. There were 9,000 police agents in Paris and 14,000 police officers in London. González Calleja, *La razón de la fuerza*, p. 43.

44 Manuel Suárez Cortina, 'Introducción', in Suárez Cortina (ed.), *La Restauración*, pp. 12–13; Mercedes Cabrera and Fernando del Rey, 'De la oligarquía y el caciquismo a la política de intereses. Por una relectura de la Restauración', in Manuel Suárez Cortina (ed.), *Las máscaras de la libertad. El liberalismo español, 1808–1950* (Madrid: Marcial Pons, 2003), pp. 289–325; Javier Moreno Luzón, *Modernizing the Nation: Spain During the Reign of Alfonso XIII, 1902–1931* (Brighton: Sussex Academic Press, 2012), pp. 1–4.

45 León Prados, *De imperio a nación, 1780–1930* (Madrid: Alianza, 1988), pp. 241–4.

46 Jordi Nadal, 'A Century of Industrialization in Spain, 1833–1930', in Nicolás Sánchez-Albornoz (ed.), *The Economic Modernization of Spain, 1830–1930* (New York: New York University Press, 1987), p. 64.

47 Blanca Sánchez Alonso, 'Those Who Left and Those Who Stayed Behind: Explaining Emigration from the Regions of Spain, 1880–1914', *Journal of Economic History*, 60 (2000), p. 730.

48 The Cerdá Plan for Barcelona (1859) and the Castro Plan for Madrid (1860) sparked a process of urban expansion in other cities: San Sebastián, Pamplona, Valencia, and Bilbao (1865), Gijón (1867), Alicante (1874), Málaga (1878), and so on. José Luis García Delgado (ed.), *Las ciudades en la modernización de España. Los decenios interseculares* (Madrid: Siglo XXI, 1992).

49 Chris Ealham, *Class, Culture and Conflict in Barcelona, 1898–1937* (London: Routledge, 2005), pp. 4–6, 23–4; Benjamin Martin, *The Agony of Modernization: Labor and Industrialization in Spain* (New York: Cornell University Press, 1990), pp. 49–52.

50 Prados, *De Imperio*, pp. 172–5.

51 Segismundo Moret, José Canalejas, Santiago Alba, for example.

52 José Varela Ortega, 'De los orígenes de la democracia en España, 1845–1923', in Salvador Forner (ed.), *Democracia, elecciones y modernización en Europa, Siglos XIX–XX* (Madrid: Cátedra, 1997), p. 162.

53 Ramón Villares and Javier Moreno, 'Prólogo', in Villares and Moreno, *Historia*, p. xvii.

54 No government considered to impose direct taxation. Levies provided the main source of income, such as that on real estate (large property owners easily falsified their accounts and hid their properties), state monopolies, and indirect duties. Over 27 percent of public spending went to pay interest on debt. Paul Preston, *A People Betrayed: A History of Corruption, Political Incompetence and Social Division in Modern Spain, 1874–2018* (London: HarperCollins, 2020), p. 7; Miguel Martorell Linares, *El santo temor al déficit* (Madrid: Alianza, 2000), pp. 45–63.

55 Javier Moreno Luzón, 'El poder público hecho cisco. Clientelismo e instituciones políticas', in Robles (ed.), *Política*, pp. 184–90.

56 Borja de Riquer i Permanyer, 'El surgimiento de las nuevas identidades contemporáneas: propuestas para una discusión', *Ayer*, 35 (1999), pp. 44–7.

57 See, for instance, the publication 'La nacionalización en España', *Ayer*, 90 (2013). Particularly interesting is the article by Alejandro Quiroga, 'La nacionalización en España. Una propuesta teórica', pp. 17–38.

58 José Álvarez Junco, *Spanish Identity in the Age of Nations* (Manchester: Manchester University Press, 2011), pp. 328–9.

59 Borja de Riquer i Permanyer, 'La débil nacionalización española del Siglo XIX', *Historia Social*, 20 (1994), p. 106.

60 José Ortega y Gasset, *La España invertebrada* (Madrid: Espasa Calpe, 1999 [1921]), p. 91.

61 Carolyn P. Boyd, *Historia Patria. Política, historia e identidad nacional en España: 1875–1975* (Barcelona: Pomares, 2000), pp. 18–19, 66–7.

62 In 1882, the cost of redemption from military service was 1,500 pesetas for a normal recruit and 2,000 pesetas for those in the overseas army. In 1904, it was 1,500 pesetas across the board. Valentina Fernández Vargas, *Sangre o dinero. El mito del ejército nacional* (Madrid: Alianza, 2004), p. 24.

63 Carlos Gil Andrés, *Echarse a la calle. Amotinados, huelguistas y revolucionarios, La Rioja, 1890–1936* (Zaragoza: Prensas Universitarias de Zaragoza, 2000), pp. 9–10; Daniel Castro Alfín, 'Agitación y orden en la Restauración', *Historia Social*, 5 (1989), pp. 37–49.

64 See works by Pamela B. Radcliff, *From Mobilization to Civil War* (Cambridge: Cambridge University Press, 1996), pp. 51–3 and 'Women's Politics: Consumer Riots in Twentieth Century Spain', in Enders and Radcliff (eds.), *Constructing Spanish Womanhood*, pp. 302–12.

65 Juan Díaz del Moral, *Historia de las agitaciones campesinas andaluzas* (Madrid: Alianza, 1995 [1929]), pp. 201–2.

66 Eduardo González Calleja, 'Una perspectiva de la violencia política en la España de la Restauración', *Ayer*, 13 (1994), p. 89.

67 Gerald Brennan, *The Spanish Labyrinth: An Account of the Social and Political Background of the Civil War* (Cambridge: Cambridge University Press, 1943), p. 157; Eric J. Hobsbawm, *Primitive Rebels* (Manchester: Manchester University Press, 1959), pp. 74–92; James Joll, *The Anarchists* (London: Eyre & Spottiswoode, 1964), p. 224.

68 Manuel González de Molina, 'Los mitos de la modernidad y la protesta campesina. A propósito de rebeldes primitivos de Eric J. Hobsbawm', *Historia Social*, 25 (1996), pp. 113–57.

69 Anselmo Lorenzo, *El proletariado militante. Memorias de un internacional* (Madrid: Solidaridad Obrera, 2013 [1901–1923]), pp. 47–52.

70 Josep Termes, *Anarquismo y sindicalismo en España, 1864–1881* (Barcelona: Crítica, 2000 [1961]), pp. 183, 304–5.

71 Juan José Morato, *Pablo Iglesias* (Barcelona: Ariel, 2000 [1931]), p. 86.

72 Santiago Castillo (ed.), *Historia de la UGT, vol. 1: Un sindicalismo consciente, 1873–1914* (Madrid: Siglo XXI, 2008), pp. 92–6.

73 Manuel Pérez Ledesma, *El obrero consciente* (Madrid: Alianza, 1987), pp. 144–51.
74 Dick Geary, *European Labour Protest, 1848–1939* (London: Methuen, 1984), pp. 112–13; Paul Heywood, *Marxism and the Failure of Organized Socialism in Spain, 1879–1936* (Cambridge: Cambridge University Press, 1990), pp. 1–3; Pérez Ledesma, *El obrero,* pp. 168–93; Santos Juliá, *Los socialistas en la política española, 1879–1982* (Madrid: Taurus, 1997), pp. 21–49.
75 Salvador Cruz Artacho, Francisco Acosta Ramírez, Francisco Cobo Romero et al., 'El socialismo español y la cuestión agraria, 1879–1923. Luces y sombras en el debate teórico y en la práctica sindical y política', *Ayer,* 54 (2002), pp. 141–3.
76 Díaz del Moral, *Historia,* p. 140.
77 Morato, *Pablo Iglesias,* p. 162.
78 Xavier Cuadrat, *Socialismo y Anarquismo en Cataluña, 1890–1911* (Madrid: Revista de Trabajo, 1976), pp. 33–9; Josep Maria Huertas, *Obrers a Catalunya* (Barcelona: Avenç, 1982), pp. 94–7; 129–30; Pere Gabriel, 'El ugetismo socialista catalán, 1888–1923', *Ayer,* 54 (2004), pp. 166–7, 176.
79 Juan Pablo Fusi, *Política obrera en el País Vasco, 1880–1923* (Madrid: Turner, 1975), pp. 82–103; Adrian Shubert, *The Road to Revolution in Asturias* (Chicago, IL: University of Illinois Press, 1987), pp. 111–12.
80 José Luis Gutiérrez Molina, *El estado frente a la anarquía. Los grandes procesos contra el anarquismo español, 1883–1982* (Madrid: Síntesis, 2008), p. 11.
81 Murray Bookchin, *The Spanish Anarchists: The Heroic Years, 1868–1939* (New York: Free Life, 1977), pp. 30–1.
82 Radcliff, *From Mobilization to Civil War,* pp. 259–60.
83 Ealham, *Class, Culture and Conflict,* pp. 36, 39.
84 Ibid., pp. 45–6.
85 George R. Esenwein, *Anarchist Ideology and the Working-Class Movement in Spain, 1868–1898* (Berkeley, CA: University of California Press, 1989), p. 6.
86 Julián Casanova, 'La cara oscura del anarquismo', in Santos Juliá (ed.), *Violencia política en la España del Siglo XX* (Madrid: Taurus, 2000), p. 68; Susanna Tavera, 'La historia del anarquismo español: una encrucijada interpretativa nueva', *Ayer,* 45 (2002), p. 31.
87 Rafael Núñez Florencio, 'El terrorismo', in Julián Casanova (ed.), *Tierra y Libertad. Cien años de anarquismo en España* (Barcelona: Crítica, 2010), p. 64.
88 Esenwein, *Anarchist Ideology,* p. 9.
89 José Luis Pantoja Antúnez and Manuel Ramírez López, *La Mano Negra. Memoria de una represión* (Cádiz: Quorum, 2010); Clara Lida, 'Para repensar la mano negra. El anarquismo español durante la clandestinidad', *Historia Social,* 74 (2012), pp. 3–22.
90 Juan Avilés Farré, *La daga y la dinamita. Los anarquistas y el nacimiento del terrorismo* (Barcelona: Tusquets, 2013), pp. 213–34.

91 Grupo de Afinidad Quico Rivas, *La Barcelona de la dinamita, el plomo y el petróleo, 1884–1909* (Barcelona: El ojo portátil, 2009), p. 21.

92 Antoni Dalmau i Ribalta, *El procés de Montjuïc. Barcelona al final del Segle XIX* (Barcelona: Base, 2010); Avilés Farré, *La daga*, pp. 273–340; Ángel Herrerín López, *Anarquía, dinamita y revolución social. Violencia y repression en la España de entre siglos, 1868–1900* (Madrid: Catarata, 2011), pp. 98–191; Juan Avilés and Ángel Herrerín, 'Propaganda por el hecho y propaganda por la represión: anarquismo y violencia en la España de fines del Siglo XIX', *Ayer*, 84 (2010), pp. 177–210.

93 Guillermo Núñez de Prado, *Los dramas del anarquismo* (Barcelona: Maucci, 1904), p. 13.

94 Dalmau i Ribalta, *El procés*, pp. 201–10.

95 He fled to Paris where he confessed his crime to some of his colleagues. Rudolf Rocker, *En la borrasca, Años de destierro* (Puebla: Cajica, 1967), p. 117; Rafael Núñez Florencio, *El terrorismo anarquista, 1888–1909* (Madrid: Siglo XXI, 1983), pp. 162–4.

96 Francesco Tamburini, 'Michelle Angiolillo e l'assassinio di Cánovas del Castillo', *Spagna Contemporanea*, 9 (1996), pp. 102–5.

97 Romero Salvadó, *Political Comedy and Social Tragedy*, p. 37.

98 Tamburini, 'Michelle Angiolillo', pp. 120–4.

99 Carlos Serrano, *Final del Imperio. España, 1895–1898* (Madrid: Siglo XXI, 1984), pp. 47–64.

100 Cánovas used these words, for the first time, in the *Cortes* in July 1891. Sagasta repeated them in March 1895.

101 It is an often overlooked fact that more Cubans fought on the Spanish side than on the rebellion. Fernando Padilla, *Volunteers of the Spanish Empire, 1855–1898* (PhD thesis: University of Bristol, 2018), pp. 165, 168.

102 Michael Golay, *The Spanish-American War* (New York: Facts on File, 1995), p. 4.

103 Serrano, *Final del Imperio*, pp. 38–40.

104 Antonio Elorza and Elena Hernández Sandoica, *La Guerra de Cuba, 1895–98* (Madrid: Alianza, 1998), pp. 213–14.

105 Carlos Serrano, *Le Tour Du Peuple. Crise nationale, mouvements populaires et populisme en Espagne, 1890–1910* (Madrid: Bibliotheque de la Casa de Velázquez, 1987), pp. 64–97.

106 Joseph Smith, *The Spanish-American War: Conflict in the Caribbean and the Pacific, 1895–1902* (London: Longman, 1994), pp. 18–20, 28–33.

107 Recent scientific research proves that a coal bunker fire that ignited its ammunition stock caused the explosion. It seems preposterous to argue that the Spanish authorities would be so inept and Machiavellian to have planned to blow up the *Maine* while entertaining its officers at a dance party. Golay, *The Spanish-American War*, pp. 11–18, 32–3.

108 Conde de Romanones, *Las responsabilidades del antiguo Régimen, 1875–1923* (Madrid: Renacimiento, 1923), p. 33.

109 Sebastian Balfour, *The End of the Spanish Empire, 1898–1923* (Oxford: Oxford University Press, 1997), pp. 25–7, and 'The Lion and the Pig: Nationalism and National Identity in *Fin-de-Siècle* Spain', in Clare Mar-Molinero and Angel Smith (eds.), *Nationalism and the Nation in the Iberian Peninsula: Competing and Conflicting Identities* (Oxford: Berg, 1996), pp. 107–17. José Varela Ortega, 'Aftermath of the Splendid Disaster: Spanish Politics Before and After the Spanish American War of 1898', *Journal of Contemporary History*, 15 (1980), pp. 319–22; Manuel Pérez Ledesma, 'La sociedad española, la guerra y la derrota', in Juan Pan-Montojo (ed.), *Más se perdió en Cuba. España, 1898 y la crisis de fin de siglo* (Madrid: Alianza, 1998), pp. 104–5.

110 Varela, 'Aftermath of the Splendid Disaster', pp. 322–5.

111 Balfour, *The End of the Spanish Empire*, pp. 45–7.

112 The philosopher Ortega coined the term 'Generation of 98' in February 1913. However, their diverse leanings make it difficult to apply the concept of a generation. Yet, their common call for self-examination and regeneration had a vital influence on subsequent thinking. Vicente Cacho Viu, *Repensar el noventa y ocho* (Madrid: Biblioteca Nueva, 1997), pp. 117–71.

113 Balfour, *The End of the Spanish Empire*, p. 49.

114 *La Campana de Gracia* (10 September 1898).

115 José María Jover Zamora, *España en la política internacional. Siglos XVIII–XX* (Madrid: Marcial Pons, 1999), pp. 154–5.

116 Juan Pan-Montojo, 'Introducción. ¿98 o fin de siglo?', p. 10 and Juan Pro Ruiz, 'La política en tiempos del Desastre', p. 125, both in Pan-Montojo (ed.), *Más se perdió*.

117 José Álvarez Junco, 'La nación en duda', in Pan-Montojo (ed.), *Más se perdió*, p. 411.

118 His article appeared in *El Tiempo* (16 August 1898).

119 Balfour, *The End of the Spanish Empire*, p. 82.

120 Joaquín Costa, *Oligarquía y caciquismo como la forma actual de gobierno en España: urgencia y modo de cambiarla* (Madrid: Biblioteca Nueva, 2001 [1898]), pp. 115–16. Still, he maintained that it did not necessarily mean a dictatorship. This strong leader should collaborate with an independent judiciary and parliament (pp. 170–1).

121 Joaquín Romero Maura, *La Rosa de Fuego. El obrerismo barcelonés de 1899 a 1909* (Madrid: Alianza, 1989 [1975]), pp. 14–28.

122 Despite its good intentions, the IRS remained grossly underfunded. Furthermore, its legislative recommendations were normally met with hostility by the employers and rarely implemented. María José Espuny Tomás, 'Eduardo Dato y la legislación obrera', *Historia Social*, 43 (2002), p. 4.

123 Joseph Harrison, *The Spanish Economy in the Twentieth Century* (London: Croom Helm, 1985), p. 28.

124 Romero Salvadó, *Political Comedy and Social Tragedy*, p. 46.

125 José Luis de la Granja Sainz, *El Nacionalismo Vasco: Un siglo de historia* (Madrid: Tecnos, 2002), pp. 33–8.

126 Catalanism defended the promotion of the distinctive national identity of Catalonia (and Catalan-speaking territories such as Valencia and the Balearic Islands) – its language, traditions, and culture – vis-à-vis the threat presented by Spanish uniformity. It had focused on cultural aspects throughout the nineteenth century during the so-called *Reinaxenca* (Rebirth). *L'Oda a la Pàtria* (Ode to the Fatherland) by Bonaventura Carles Aribau in 1833 is considered its starting point.

127 Tellingly, the Lliga's first four candidates in the elections of April 1901 in Barcelona were the presidents of the most important Catalan industrial, cultural, and landowning organizations. Borja de Riquer i Permanyer, *Regionalistes i Nacionalistes, 1898–1931* (Barcelona: Dopesa, 1979), pp. 42–8, 191–206; Joseph Harrison, 'The Catalan Industrial Elite, 1898–1923', in Paul Preston and Frances Lannon (eds.), *Elites and Power in Twentieth Century Spain: Essays in Honour of Sir Raymond Carr* (Oxford: Oxford University Press, 1990), pp. 53–8.

128 Joan Garriga, *Memòries d'un liberal catalanista, 1871–1939* (Barcelona: Edicions 62, 1987), pp. 123–4.

129 José Antonio González Casanova, *Federalismo y autonomía. Cataluña y el estado español, 1868–1938* (Barcelona: Crítica, 1979), p. 179.

130 Borja de Riquer i Permanyer, *Francesc Cambó, L'últim retrat* (Barcelona: Edicions 62, 2022), p. 14.

131 Angel Smith, 'The Lliga Regionalista, the Catalan Right and the Making of the Primo de Rivera Dictatorship', in Romero Salvadó and Smith (eds.), *The Agony of Spanish Liberalism*, p. 147; Borja de Riquer i Permanyer, *Alfonso XIII y Cambó. La monarquía y el catalanismo político* (Barcelona: RBA, 2013), p. 21.

132 Francisco J. Romero Salvadó, 'Between the Catalan Quagmire and the Red Spectre, Spain 1918–19', *Historical Journal*, 60/3 (2017), pp. 4–5.

133 John R. Mosher, *The Birth of Mass Politics in Spain: Lerrouxismo in Barcelona, 1901–1909* (New York: Garland, 1991), p. 401.

134 Manuel Suárez Cortina, *El Reformismo en España* (Madrid: Siglo XXI, 1986), pp. 66–72.

135 Joan B. Culla i Clara, *El republicanisme Lerrouxista a Catalunya, 1901–1923* (Barcelona: Curial, 1986), pp. 80–3; José Álvarez Junco, *El Emperador del Paralelo. Lerroux y la demagogia populista* (Madrid: Alianza, 1990), p. 358; Mosher, *The Birth of Mass Politics*, pp. 165–8; Romero Maura, *La Rosa de Fuego*, pp. 115–16.

136 Examples of Lerroux's underhand deals can be found in the documents of dynastic notables in the Biblioteca de la Real Academia de la Historia. For instance, see *Natalio Rivas's Papers*, 11/8895 (December 1909); 11/8898 (January/February 1910).

137 Romero Maura, *La Rosa de Fuego*, p. 80.

138 Ruiz Zorrilla held several posts during the period 1868–74, including speaker of the lower house and prime minister for King Amadeo. After years of endorsing numerous ill-fated initiatives against the monarchy, he was allowed to return to Spain in 1895 a few months before his death.

139 Álvarez Junco, *El Emperador del Paralelo*, pp. 159–70.
140 Huertas, *Obrers a Catalunya*, p. 125.
141 Antonio Bar, *La CNT en los años rojos: Del sindicalismo revolucionario al anarcosindicalismo, 1910–1926* (Madrid: Akal, 1981), pp. 54–9.
142 Javier Moreno Luzón, 'El rey de papel', in Javier Moreno Luzón (ed.), *Alfonso XIII* (Madrid: Marcial Pons, 2003), pp. 28–9; Morgan C. Hall, *Alfonso XIII y el ocaso de la monarquía liberal, 1902–1923* (Madrid: Alianza, 2005), pp. 47–8; Gabriel Cardona, *Alfonso XIII, el rey de espadas* (Barcelona: Planeta, 2010), pp. 14, 33–9; Javier Tusell and Genoveva Queipo de Llano, *Alfonso XIII* (Madrid: Taurus, 2001), pp. 101–8.
143 Cardona, *Alfonso XIII*, p. 52.
144 Melchor Fernández Almagro, *Historia del reinado de Alfonso XIII* (Barcelona: Montaner y Simón, 1977 [1933]), p. 38.
145 Juan Avilés Farré, 'Contra Alfonso XIII: Atentados frustrados y conspiración revolucionaria', in Juan Avilés and Ángel Herrerín (eds.), *El nacimiento del terrorismo en Occidente. Anarquía, nihilismo y violencia revolucionaria* (Madrid: Siglo XXI, 2008), pp. 141–58; Fundació Ferrer i Guàrdia, *Causa por Regicidio frustrado (31 mayo 1906)*, 5 vols. (Madrid: Sucesores de J.A. García, 1911), vol. 4, pp. 54–63.
146 Álvarez Junco, *El Emperador del Paralelo*, p. 310.
147 González Calleja, *La razón de la fuerza*, pp. 372–81; Joaquín Romero Maura, *La Romana del diablo* (Madrid: Marcial Pons, 2000), pp. 25–34; Francisco Bergasa, *¿Quién mató a Ferrer i Guardia?* (Madrid: Aguilar, 2009), p. 94.
148 The Supreme Court decided in favour of civil jurisdiction since the latter's remit included regicide, the most important of the crimes committed.
149 Fundació Ferrer i Guàrdia, *Causa*, vol. 4, p. 401.
150 Andrée Bachoud, *Los españoles ante las campañas de Marruecos* (Madrid: Espasa, 1988), p. 79.
151 Ortega y Gasset, *La España invertebrada*, pp. 61, 64.
152 Francisco J. Romero Salvadó, 'The Failure of the Liberal Project of the Spanish Nation-State, 1909–1923', in Molinero and Smith (eds.), *Nationalism*, p. 121.
153 Romero Salvadó, *Political Comedy and Social Tragedy*, p. 59.
154 Romero Maura, *La Romana del diablo*, pp. 130–3.
155 Ballbé, *Orden público y militarismo*, pp. 277–9.
156 Romero Maura, *La Rosa de Fuego*, pp. 376–8.
157 Mosher, *The Birth of Mass Politics*, pp. 239–43.
158 Albert Balcells, *Catalan Nationalism* (London: Macmillan, 1996), pp. 55–8.
159 Gabriel Maura and Melchor Fernández Almagro, *Por qué cayó Alfonso XIII: Evolución y disolución de los partidos históricos durante su reinado* (Madrid: Ambos Mundos, 1948), p. 268.
160 Javier Tusell, *Antonio Maura. Una biografía política* (Madrid: Alianza, 1994), pp. 23–35.

161 María Jesús González Hernández, *El universo conservador de Antonio Maura* (Madrid: Biblioteca Nueva, 1997), p. 59.
162 Maura and Fernández Almagro, *Por qué cayó Alfonso XIII*, p. 40.
163 His first premiership hardly lasted a year, from December 1903 to December 1904.
164 González Hernández, *El universo*, pp. 133–5.
165 Ibid., p. 124.
166 Maura and Fernández Almagro, *Por qué cayó Alfonso XIII*, p. 112.
167 Miguel Martorell Linares, *José Sánchez Guerra. Un hombre de honor, 1859–1956* (Madrid: Marcial Pons, 2011), p. 154.
168 Antoni Dalmau i Ribalta, 'La oleada de violencia en la Barcelona de 1904–1908', *Ayer*, 85 (2012), pp. 161–2.
169 Romero Maura, *La Rosa de Fuego*, pp. 470–1.
170 Romero Salvadó, *Political Comedy and Social Tragedy*, p. 80.
171 Herrerín López, *Anarquía*, pp. 252–3.
172 Antoni Dalmau i Ribalta, *El Cas Rull. Viure del terror a la ciutat de las bombas, 1901–1908* (Barcelona: Columna, 2008); Herrerín López, *Anarquía*, pp. 266–72.
173 Romero Maura, *La Romana del diablo*, pp. 74–6.
174 Maura and Fernández Almagro, *Por qué cayó Alfonso XIII*, pp. 125–6.
175 Eloy Martín Corrales, 'Movilizaciones en España contra la guerra de Marruecos, julio-agosto de 1909', in Eloy Martín Corrales (ed.), *Semana Trágica. Entre las barricadas de Barcelona y el Barranco del Lobo* (Barcelona: Bellaterra, 2011), p. 130.
176 The classic study is Connelly Ullman, *The Tragic Week*. A plethora of works were published to mark its centenary. See, for instance, Antoni Dalmau i Ribalta, *Set dies de fúria. Barcelona i la Setmana Trágica* (Barcelona: Columna, 2009); David Martínez Fiol, *La Setmana Trágica* (Barcelona: Pòrtic, 2009); Josep Pich Mitjana, *La Setmana Tràgica (1909): Sagnant, Roja, Negra o Gloriosa* (Barcelona: UPF, 2009); Eloy Martín Corrales (ed.), *Semana Trágica*; Gemma Rubí, 'Protesta, desobediencia y violencia subversiva; La Semana Trágica de julio de 1909 en Cataluña', *Revista de Historia Contemporánea*, 10 (2011), pp. 244–68.
177 Amadeu Hurtado, *Quaranta anys de avocat. Història del meu temps, 1894–1936* (Barcelona: Edicions 62, 2011 [1956]), p. 146.
178 Ángel Ossorio, *Barcelona. Julio de 1909* (Madrid: Imprenta de Ricardo Rojas, 1910), pp. 58–68; Juan de la Cierva, *Notas de mi vida* (Madrid: Reus, 1955), pp. 135–42.
179 Dalmau i Ribalta, *Set dies de fúria*, pp. 107–11.
180 Connelly Ullman, *The Tragic Week*, pp. 287–8.
181 Sol Ferrer, *Vida y obra de Francisco Ferrer* (Barcelona: Luis de Caralt, 1980), pp. 147–8.
182 Fundació Ferrer i Guàrdia, *Ferrer, páginas para la historia. Consejo de Guerra: acusación, defensa y sentencia* (Barcelona, 1912). Juan Avilés Farré,

Francisco Ferrer Guardia. Pedagogo, anarquista y mártir (Madrid: Marcial Pons, 2006), pp. 233–6.

183 Romero Salvadó, *Political Comedy and Social Tragedy*, p. 96.
184 Vincent Robert, 'La protesta universal contra la ejecución de Ferrer: las manifestaciones de octubre de 1909', *Historia Social*, 14 (1992), pp. 61–82.
185 Morato, *Pablo Iglesias*, p. 187.
186 Culla i Clara, *El republicanisme*, p. 231.
187 See the works by Antonio Bar, *La CNT*, pp. 176–207 and 'The CNT: the Glory and Tragedy of Spanish Anarchosyndicalism', in Marcel Van der Linden and Wayne Thorpe (eds.), *Revolutionary Syndicalism: An International Perspective* (Brookfield, VT: Scholar Press, 1990), pp. 123–4.
188 Maura and Fernández Almagro, *Por qué cayó Alfonso XIII*, p. 155.
189 Salvador Forner, *Canalejas y el partido liberal democrático* (Madrid: Cátedra, 1993), p. 39; Javier Moreno Luzón, 'José Canalejas. La democracia, el estado y la nación', in Moreno Luzón (ed.), *Progresistas*, p. 167.
190 Forner, *Canalejas*, pp. 55–62.
191 Ibid., pp. 74–90.
192 Javier Moreno Luzón, 'Alfonso XIII, 1902–1931', in Villares and Moreno, *Historia*, p. 384.
193 Maura and Fernández Almagro, *Por qué cayó Alfonso XIII*, pp. 187–95.
194 Bachoud, *Los españoles*, pp. 51–4.
195 Santiago Pérez Blasco, *Cullera, 1911. La protesta d'un poble* (Valencia: 7 i Mig, 1999), pp. 28–30; Bachoud, *Los españoles*, pp. 177–8.
196 Romero Salvadó, *Political Comedy and Social Tragedy*, p. 105.
197 Maura and Fernández Almagro, *Por qué cayó Alfonso XIII*, p. 227.
198 Susana Sueiro, 'El asesinato de Canalejas y los anarquistas españoles en Estados Unidos', in Avilés and Herrerín (eds.), *El Nacimiento*, pp. 159–88; Joaquín J. Palacios, *Las cartas de Clonard* (Madrid: Visión, 2013), pp. 37–8.
199 Javier Moreno Luzón, *Romanones: caciquismo y política liberal* (Madrid: Alianza, 1998), pp. 19–20, 271; Thomas G. Trice, *Spanish Liberalism in Crisis: A Study of the Liberal Party during Spain's Parliamentary Collapse, 1913–1923* (New York: Garland, 1991), pp. 45–7; Javier Tusell, *La política y los políticos en los tiempos de Alfonso XIII* (Barcelona: Planeta, 1976), p. 61.
200 Maura and Fernández Almagro, *Por qué cayó Alfonso XIII*, pp. 231–4.
201 Manuel Burgos y Mazo, *El verano de 1919 en Gobernación* (Cuenca: Tipos, 1921), pp. 17–18.
202 Maura and Fernández Almagro, *Por qué cayó Alfonso XIII*, pp. 262–4; María Jesús González Hernández, *Ciudadanía y acción. El conservadurismo maurista, 1907–1923* (Madrid: Siglo XXI, 1990), pp. 39–40.

203 Javier Tusell and Juan Avilés, *La derecha española contemporánea: sus orígenes, el Maurismo* (Madrid: Espasa Calpe, 1986); Alejandro Quiroga, 'Nation and Reaction: Spanish Conservative Nationalism and the Restoration Crisis', in Romero Salvadó and Smith (eds.), *The Agony of Spanish Liberalism,* p. 205.

2

The Restoration Monarchy, 1914–1931: The Twilight of an Era

Fatal Neutralities

Darkness descended over Europe in the summer of 1914. The Great War was a cataclysm that resulted in the spine-chilling slaughter of some 9 million soldiers and 10 million civilians due to malnutrition, epidemics, shortages, and so on.[1] It reshaped the map of the continent and initiated a period of unprecedented socio-political radicalism that has been dubbed 'the age of catastrophe'.[2] It constituted the twilight of an era. The clock of history could not be turned back to the pre-war universe, as it heralded the arrival of mass politics. Hierarchical, clientelist, and elitist politics broke down when confronted with the unwelcome prospect of genuine democracy and, from 1917, with the fast-advancing threat of revolution.[3]

When the war broke out, the Dato government rapidly decreed Spain's strict neutrality. A distant conflict in the Balkans was no reason to break with Spain's traditional international isolation. Above all, neutrality was a logical decision imposed by reality.[4] It reflected economic weakness, military impotence, and Spain's marginal status. Dato even confided to Maura that only an ultimatum or flagrant aggression could lead to abandoning neutrality.[5] Ironically, the country's poor military prowess eliminated the danger of facing pressure to enter the war.

Neutrality avoided a human bloodbath and material destruction but could not isolate the country. Maybe Spain did not enter the war but the war entered Spain, and its political and socio-economic effects undermined the foundations of the regime. There was an unprecedented polarization in public opinion. Simultaneously, socio-economic dislocation fuelled the demands of Catalan regionalism, the labour movement, and the army.

Initially, save for some extreme exceptions, the country readily accepted neutrality. However, that consensus gradually began to break down. The war came to be perceived as an ideological clash in which each of the warring factions symbolized certain transcendent principles. The quarrel between the partisans of the two camps generated such a violent debate that it almost acquired the moral quality of 'a civil war of words' between two opposing views on Spain's future.[6] The passion was such that it produced family divisions, destroyed long-lasting friendships, and caused rows in the workplace.[7] Public opinion split between *Germanophiles* and *Francophiles*. The former predominated among conservative social sectors (the clergy, aristocracy, army, landowning oligarchy). Its most vociferous political voices were Carlists and *Mauristas*. They considered a German victory the best guarantee of protecting fundamental values such as monarchism, tradition, and social hierarchy. In contrast, the *Francophiles* were mostly those hostile to the status quo: Republicans, Socialists, and intellectuals. They identified themselves with the Allies, in particular France, the model of a secular nation that they wished to emulate.[8]

By 1916, the term neutrality changed its initial meaning. The entry of Italy and Portugal (May 1915 and March 1916, respectively) into the struggle left Spain surrounded by Allied nations. Consequently, the *Francophiles* began to demand a departure from strict neutrality, more of a compromise with the Allies, or even the rupture of relations with the Central Powers. The *Germanophiles*, aware of the military suicide that joining the war on Germany's side would entail, became ardent defenders of strict neutrality, which they described as national independence.[9]

Society's traditional fabric was drastically altered by the cruel combination of opulence and misery. Basking in its neutral status, Spain enjoyed a financial boom based on the growing industrial and food requirements of the belligerents. A radical drop in imports together with the rise in the volume and prices of exports meant that the country, almost overnight, saw its balance of trade changing from a vast deficit to registering fabulous profits. Commercial enterprises, joint-stock companies, and financial ventures enjoyed spectacular profits.[10] However, this sudden prosperity exacerbated the country's structural differences. Rural areas entered a period of crisis due to the falling demand for certain products (bananas, oranges, tomatoes, etc.) and a lack of raw materials and fertilizers. In contrast, industrial centres experienced feverish activity. Industrial barons, financial tycoons, shipowners, and speculators amassed fortunes that were often squandered on gambling, jewellery, property, and so on.[11] In contrast, for ordinary people, the war meant worsening living standards due to galloping inflation, shortages of staple products, and depressed earning power. Additionally, the demographic blast produced by the avalanche of cheap labour from the southern rural areas searching for work in the booming industrial centres resulted in squalor, overcrowding, and misery.[12]

After Romanones' return to office in December 1915, Spain witnessed the mobilization of key sectors – the armed forces, labour movement, and industrialists. Simultaneously, the polarization around the issue of neutrality reached a new high.[13]

In June 1916, the Liberal Party's flamboyant rising star, Santiago Alba, at the Treasury, introduced a far-reaching plan of national reconstruction through an extraordinary budget intended for public works, military and naval reforms, education, and more. Its cost (some 2,134 million pesetas) would be paid for in 10 years largely by levying a tax on excess war profits made by industry and trade but not, significantly, by agriculture.[14] The plan represented a decisive break from the state's traditional laissez-faire approach to the economy but drew fierce opposition.

As industry benefited the most from the financial boom, the *Lliga* believed the moment had finally arrived to put an end to a *turno* that was perceived to favour the interests of the landowning classes. Its offensive was also politically motivated. A few months earlier, Alba, then at the Home Office, had become its *bête noire* after supervising the establishment of a broad Catalan coalition, including Republicans, for the elections of April 1916.[15] Fighting under the slogan '*Per Catalunya i l'Espanya Gran*' ('For Catalonia and a Greater Spain'), in allusion to its *leitmotif* of Spain as a nation of nations where Catalonia offered an overwhelmingly agrarian country its model for a modern society, the *Lliga* increased its overall vote.[16] Emboldened by the results, its parliamentarian minority introduced the question of home rule in the *Cortes*. It was rapidly rejected in the chamber but introduced the 'Catalan question'.[17]

Alba's ambitious project enabled the *Lliga* to become the champions of industrial interests and, in the process, to stop the ministers' approaching apotheosis. During the following months, its deputies pursued a strategy of obstructionism in parliament where each clause of the project was dissected. Simultaneously, industrial groups mounted an unrelenting campaign.[18] Their efforts were aided by dynastic rivalries. Many notables, including Romanones, were delighted to see Alba's meteoric rise come to an end.[19] By late 1916, not only had Alba's grandiose plans collapsed but he had even failed to pass the ordinary budget. This ultimately revealed the contradiction between reformist projects and political reality.[20]

The government also faced the challenge of a galvanized labour movement. Hoarding, profiteering, and massive exports of basic goods resulted in shortages and sky-rocketing prices that devastated the already stretched budgets of lower-class households. From 1916, assaults on shops, clashes in markets, and demonstrations demanding cheaper food were ubiquitous. Mounting popular anger was accompanied by a significant escalation in strike activity. In July 1916, given the dramatic social crisis and under pressure from their rank-and-file, the UGT and the CNT temporarily put their historic antagonisms aside and signed a historic labour alliance.[21] Although reluctant to collaborate with the CNT's 'trouble-makers', the Socialists finally did so because their superior strength put them in the driving seat: the UGT had then over 80,000 members throughout Spain while the CNT, which had begun its reconstruction after an international congress held in El Ferrol in October 1915, had only 30,000, mostly in Catalonia.[22]

Inherent differences were apparent from the start. The Socialists did not plan an insurrection but a long campaign to raise workers' class consciousness and force the hand of the government. Therefore, they had to constantly restrain their more impetuous partners who had greeted the alliance as a sign that revolution was imminent.[23] Nonetheless, there existed huge revolutionary potential. The labour movement was more aligned than ever before and crucially, for the first time, the popular protest was being channelled into a movement not just against local injustices but the state that presided over them.

The labour movement demonstrated its might in July 1916 when the railway workers went on strike. Besides the customary pay rises, they demanded the official recognition of their union's right to represent them. When the miners threatened to endorse a strike in solidarity with the railway workers, Romanones, reluctant to use force *per se*, pressed both camps to accept the mediation of the *Instituto de Reformas Sociales* (IRS), whose final verdict was favourable to the strikers. On 9 August, a royal decree recognized the trade unions as workers' representatives in companies running public services.[24]

The crisis also hurt civil servants' hitherto relatively stable living standards, including those of army officers. They resorted to corporatist solutions. In 1917, *juntas* (committees) were established throughout the administration (Post Office, Treasury, etc.).[25] The military, while experiencing a significant fall in their purchasing power, grew increasingly anxious at being dragged into a war for which they knew themselves to be unprepared. In 1916, the government passed a Bill of Military Reform, which tackled the sensitive question of reducing the vastly overmanned officers' corps by introducing tests of physical and intellectual ability and with those savings to acquire new equipment and increase the number of frontline troops. This constituted, for the first time, a dynastic breach of the tradition of non-intervention in army matters and struck at the job security of middle-ranking officers.[26] Thus, frustrated officers up to the rank of colonel began to join the so-called *Juntas Militares de Defensa*, a type of military trade union whose headquarters were in Barcelona. In early 1917, its chairman, Colonel Benito Márquez, boasted that these *Juntas* had spread throughout Spain except for Madrid and Morocco. They denounced the corruption of the ruling politicians and attacked the favouritism enjoyed by privileged officers either based in the king's military household or serving in Africa, where, from their viewpoint, royal nepotism facilitated the awarding of promotions.[27] Above all, their primary objective was to defend the corps' collective interests: pay conditions and the *escala cerrada* (promotion according to seniority).[28]

Simultaneously, polarization around the neutrality issue reached its zenith. Unlike most dynastic politicians' determination to remain aloof from the conflict, Romanones took an active interest. Already by August 1914, his mouthpiece, *El Diario Universal*, published an article entitled *Neutralidades que matan* ('Fatal Neutralities'), which argued that, for economic and geopolitical reasons, Spain should stand with the Allies, her natural partners; otherwise, it risked being marginalized.[29] This initiative was probably a response to economic interests rather than to ideological principles: Romanones was a major shareholder in several mining corporations whose production was exported to France. Nevertheless, it constituted an audacious attempt to restore a significant measure of international prestige and enlarge the colonial empire.[30] Observing the negative backlash his article unleashed, the calculating count denied its authorship, blaming one of his collaborators, and declared his total identification with the government's strict neutrality. Nevertheless, he had revealed his sympathies. Once in office, foreign policy overshadowed pressing domestic issues.

An epic struggle between Romanones and *Germanophile* Spain marked his premiership. The belligerents' growing intervention transformed the country into a theatre of operations. Thus, Spain suffered significant erosion of sovereignty, freedom of trade, and control over its coastline and territorial waters.[31] Germany's aggressive stance made a mockery of her host's neutrality: it established a sophisticated spy network, which infiltrated anarchist groups and enrolled the services of all sorts of characters (prostitutes, waiters, dancers, etc.) to sabotage the production destined for the Allies.[32] Information on the sea routes and departures of merchant vessels bound to Allied ports was then passed to submarines.[33] Additionally, German agents in Spanish Morocco supplied money, weapons, and advisers to rebel tribes in the French zone. Levels of complicity with Spanish colonial officers reached scandalous levels. In Guinea, they openly fraternized with the interned German troops from Cameroon.[34] Moreover, the rising cost of paper facilitated the purchase of newspapers by the belligerents to influence public opinion. Through its control of some 500 publications, from different ideological leanings, Germany was able to justify her illegal activities (including submarine operations).[35] Any challenge to neutrality was labelled as treason or as an attempt to drag the proletariat into an imperialist war by its right- or left-wing newspapers, respectively.

1917: Spain was not Russia

The year 1917 constituted a watershed. Three years of military cataclysm combined with increasing material dislocation, and war-weariness exacerbated the movements of socio-political dissent that had existed before the outbreak of hostilities and fostered the threat of revolution. The troops' discipline began to disintegrate as industrial unrest increased across Europe. Russia became the revolutionary epicentre. There, a spontaneous insurrection in Petrograd led to the abdication of Tsar Nicholas II in March. In November, the Bolsheviks, headed by Vladimir Ilich Ulianov (Lenin), had gained enough popular support for their opposition to the war, calls for power to the

Soviets (councils of soldiers, workers, and peasants), and land redistribution to topple the provisional government that had failed to fill the power vacuum left by the fall of the monarchy with hardly any resistance. Russia's March and November Revolutions were mesmerising examples.

Spain's progressive circles enthusiastically greeted Nicholas II's fall. Left-wing editorials stressed the need to follow Russia's lead, liquidate the decadent monarchy, and join the Allies. On 27 March, Julián Besteiro, a Madrid University Professor of Logic and Iglesias's deputy in the PSOE, drew up a manifesto jointly subscribed by the UGT and the CNT. Aimed at the country rather than solely the proletariat, it accused the regime of allowing widespread social distress and threatened to overthrow it, at the right time, via an indefinite general strike.[36] This document was the most radical yet endorsed by the Socialists and constituted a real challenge to the state.

By 1917, the duel between Romanones and Germany (and her Spanish supporters) left only two possible outcomes: the rupture of diplomatic relations or the prime minister's fall. In April, Romanones believed the sinking of the steamer *San Fulgencio* was the right moment to break relations with Germany. By then, 30 Spanish vessels had been sunk. Still, this new attack was particularly outrageous. The *San Fulgencio* was torpedoed while heading towards Spanish waters with a vital cargo of coal after having travelled to Newcastle under a German safe conduct. The count wanted to mirror the reaction of several hitherto neutral countries, including the United States and some Latin American republics, after the German announcement of the intensification of her submarine campaign from 1 February 1917.[37] In reality, Spain's neutral status was never at risk. Russia's revolutionary events sent waves of panic among the Spanish ruling elites. Amidst the existing turbulent domestic situation, they perceived entry into the war as madness. After all, Spain was neither militarily nor economically prepared and the main supporters of intervention were enemies of the regime. Romanones lacked significant support amongst the general staff and most of the governing class, including his own party. Tellingly, the government that replaced him was headed by a rival baron, the rather colourless Marquis of Alhucemas, and contained many previous ministers. Still, his fall was ultimately the king's choice. For the monarch, the key factor in his final decision was Russia. Alfonso XIII was shocked by the fall of Nicholas II and moved firmly into the *Germanophile* camp when the Entente seemed to ignore the Tsar's fate and recognize the new provisional government.

Royal intervention triggered the chain of Spain's revolutionary events of 1917. The monarch's decision to oust Romanones' government incensed the *Francophiles*. On 27 May, they organized a gathering at Madrid's bull-ring attended by 20,000 people. They claimed that neutrality was a shameful surrender of national dignity and threatened Alfonso XIII, described as the chief of *Germanophile* Spain, with the fate of Nicholas II.[38] Rattled by this head-on challenge and terrified by the events in Russia, Alfonso was increasingly worried by the existence of officers' trade unions whose leaders openly criticized royal favouritism. Wrongly perceiving them to be in the same mutinous state as the tsarist officer corps, a frantic king ordered their dissolution.[39] He could not have anticipated the consequences: the leading *Junteros* refused to disband the organization and were arrested. On 1 June, a provisional central *Junta* gave the government a 12-hour deadline to free their leaders, give guarantees of no future reprisals, and recognize their organization's statutes. Plans for a coup accompanied the ultimatum. The Alhucemas government resigned after less than two months in office.[40]

The *Juntas'* victory constituted a devastating blow to civilian sovereignty. Praetorian defiance spread amongst other sectors in the civil service as well as non-commissioned officers.[41] Amidst a deafening clamour for a thorough political overhaul, Alfonso XIII acted as if nothing had changed. Scrupulously following the *turno* fiction, he entrusted Dato with power, who duly resorted to the usual practices: closing parliament, suspending the constitution, and introducing tight censorship. Even the monarchist press reacted with despair – one claimed that revolution was not only desirable but had become inescapable.[42]

The *Juntas'* rebellion was, above all, an act of indiscipline.[43] Yet, the language used by their mouthpiece, *La Correspondencia Militar*, lambasting the regime as 'the repulsive rule of *caciques* and oligarchs', galvanized all the forces critical of the status quo (Republicans, Socialists, Catalan Regionalists, and *Mauristas*). They believed that the army was leading the way to national regeneration.[44] Still, if they had managed to coordinate their activities with the military protest, the ruling system would have been doomed.

The *Lliga*'s leaders seized the initiative. They were not necessarily anti-monarchist and certainly not revolutionary. Far from seeking to storm the Bastille, they sought to channel praetorian defiance and popular discontent towards structural reform of the state. Otherwise, they believed, a discredited and unreformed regime would result in a more widespread social revolt.[45] The *Lliga* summoned an alternative parliament in Barcelona where deputies were to discuss how to implement national renovation, in which Republicans and Socialists were delighted to participate. On 19 July, in open defiance of the government, the so-called Assembly of Parliamentarians took place. It was the most serious attempt in Restoration Spain to carry out political reform by peaceful means. Sixty-eight members of parliament attended. Before being forcefully stopped by the police, they denounced a regime based on fraud and demanded the establishment of a Constituent *Cortes* after general elections supervised by a government representing the national will. They set up three sub-committees to consider, respectively, constitutional reform and home rule for those regions that wanted it; defence, education, and justice; and the economy.[46]

However, the Assembly failed to attract *Maurismo*. Gabriel Maura noted that if his father had taken a stance against the regime, a good deal of Spain's political right would have abandoned the monarchy, or at least, Alfonso

XIII.[47] After eight years of ostracism, he was courted by both the *Juntas* and Assembly. The political comedy could hardly have survived if Maura had accepted becoming the crucial link between them. Without him, it was extremely unlikely that the army would back a manoeuvre led by Catalan Regionalists, Republicans, and Socialists. At this crucial moment, many *Mauristas* were enthusiastic to join the Assembly. Yet, despite the encouragement of Ossorio and his son Miguel, Maura declined to play that vital role. Notwithstanding all his fierce attacks on the *turno*, he was ultimately an old-fashioned liberal unwilling to sanction any manoeuvre that could endanger the throne or the supremacy of civil power.[48]

Maura's stance aided the government in regaining the initiative, helped avoid fissures developing within the governing class, and eliminated the nightmare of a possible alliance between reformist-minded parties, the labour movement, and the *Juntas*. Dato, often perceived as an anodyne court lackey, proved to be more cunning than many expected and took a reckless gamble that involved dividing the opposition by luring the proletariat into carrying out its threat of a general strike. The plan was based on the belief that once confronted with the spectre of revolution, the moderate sectors of the Assembly would abandon their reformist schemes, the army would quell the disturbances, and the government could boast of having saved the social order and preserved neutrality.[49]

The *Juntas*' indiscipline was condoned, their statutes were recognized, and the defence budget was increased. Governor Leopoldo Matos acted in Barcelona as the go-between for Madrid and the central *Junta*. Simultaneously, the government implemented a strategy of deception and manipulation of public opinion whereby its enemies were accused of being financed by foreign gold to launch a revolution, proclaim a republic, and enter the war on the side of the Allies.[50] The recent case of Greece, whereby Allied pressure had fomented the fall of the pro-German King Constantine I, married to a sister of the Kaiser, seemed to reinforce that thesis.[51] Furthermore, Republican and Socialist pro-Allied rhetoric seemed to give authenticity to the slanders and, consequently, their acceptance by the Crown and military circles.[52] Ironically, while the Entente, reliant on the regular supply of Spain's mineral resources for its war effort, wished for political stability and averted any close identification with its Spanish left-wing supporters, Germany, the beacon of monarchist Spain, promoted industrial unrest.

The government's plan proved successful. In mid-July, a railway dispute broke out in Valencia. Following a declaration of martial law in that city, the UGT threatened a nationwide stoppage in solidarity throughout the sector to begin on 10 August. Nevertheless, until the very last moment it sought a compromise, but its attempts to do so were met with intransigence on the part of the company encouraged by the government. In short, the UGT was given a stark choice: surrender unconditionally or fulfil its threat. By a majority vote of just one, the railway workers opted to proceed with the strike. Otherwise, they felt their union would be destroyed. The Socialist leadership decided then to implement, on 13 August, the indefinite general strike announced in March.[53]

For the Socialists, endorsing a revolutionary endeavour of such scope would have been unthinkable before the war. However, after recent events, they believed they had the sympathy of both the Assembly – after all the strike was about implementing its programme – and the army officers, or at the very least their neutrality. The optimism was such that, for once, they even refused to listen to Iglesias, who, from his sickbed argued for limiting the strike to a show of solidarity with the railway workers.[54] They were sure that, as had happened in Petrograd, the regime would collapse like a pack of cards. But Spain was not Russia. Despite its obvious shortcomings, Spain was a constitutional monarchy unlike autocratic Russia and, crucially, was not at war. Also, unlike the fall of Tsarism in March and the Bolshevik takeover in November, the Spanish revolutionary movement lacked the former's spontaneity and the latter's clinical efficiency. Also, the historic conditions that had facilitated the tsar's downfall did not exist in Spain. In Petrograd, three years of war-weariness helped transform a popular protest into a revolution against the detested autocracy. Unlike Russia, the Spanish regime did not experience crucial fractures in its governing class, its army was not demoralized by the war, and there was no Bolshevik Party. The Socialists fell prey to the trap hatched by the government. Blinded by excessive optimism and under pressure from their CNT partners, they agreed to lead an ill-prepared insurrectionary movement.[55]

From the start, the strike was an utter fiasco. The stoppage only materialized in the main urban centres (Madrid, Barcelona, Valencia, Bilbao) and some mining areas, in particular Asturias. Any hopes of collusion between the labour movement, Assembly, and army were soon dashed. Catalan Regionalists and most of their parliamentarian partners sat on the fence waiting to see how events would unfold. Had the revolution succeeded, they would have been catapulted to power, but they hastened to distance themselves from it as it was blatantly failing. Ultimately, the regime's fate was in the hands of the military. Unlike the fraternization between soldiers and strikers in Petrograd, the streets resembled a pitched battle in which workers threw stones and were met by volleys of bullets. In some instances, the troops used machine guns and artillery to quell the pockets of resistance. The soldiers, not traumatized by the war-weariness of their Russian counterparts, obeyed the orders of their officers, who, in turn, followed the instructions of their generals. Rumours spread by the government that foreign gold was behind the disturbances removed any further hesitation: it was better to shoot workers in Spain than to dig trenches in France. Within a week, the bloody revolution was over apart from Asturias, where the miners continued to resist for another couple of weeks. The official figures – 71 dead, 200 injured, and 2,000 arrests – did not reflect reality.[56]

Dato's reckless gamble resulted in a short-lived victory. When the constitutional guarantees were restored, there was universal condemnation of the government's chicanery. On 4 October, the trial against the strike committee concluded with a verdict of life imprisonment for its four members (Julián Besteiro, Francisco Largo Caballero, Daniel Anguiano, and Andrés Saborit). However, that trial enabled its spokesman, Besteiro, to transform the defence into a denunciation of the cabinet's immorality for having turned a railway conflict into a general strike.[57] Also, the officer corps discovered that their recent popularity had evaporated after their brutal repression of the strike. Their indignation grew in parallel with their suspicion of having been manipulated to crush a revolt that the government itself had provoked. Finally, on 26 October, the army delivered a message to the king demanding the removal of the Dato government. In return, they guaranteed the dissolution (by force, if necessary) of any new parliament that represented a threat to the dynasty.[58]

The European Civil War

The defenestration of three governments in just a few months revealed the regime's structural crisis. The *turno pacífico*, the cornerstone of the seamless functioning of the liberal order, was shattered. Both dynastic parties were badly mauled and divided into a myriad of rival factions.[59] Some scholars have noted that, although formally surviving the revolutionary experience of 1917, the system was practically finished.[60] However, if that was the case, an explanation is needed as to how such an ailing system could last for another six years.

In fact, nothing was predetermined in 1917. If dynastic political hegemony lay in tatters, it was still able to prevent the triumph of the forces that advocated change. If the monarchist parties were faction-ridden and, except for *Maurismo*, devoid of any popular base, the opposition offered no alternative. The Republicans were small committees of notables with a scant following outside their urban fiefdoms. The Socialists possessed nationwide grassroots and organization, but traumatized by the events of August 1917, were not willing to embark on a new confrontation with the state. Moreover, the regime showed its ability to adapt to changing circumstances. The discarded *turno* gave way to a variety of new formulas, ranging from all sorts of coalitions to faction-based administrations. It also broadened its base by integrating forces such as the *Lliga* and the Reformist Party.

In November 1917, constitutional practices remained in place but the alliance of the Crown with an unchecked officer corps struck an ominous note for the future. The crisis was solved, after a record eight days of power vacuum, by the establishment of a monarchist coalition presided over by Alhucemas. It comprised members of most dynastic factions and, for the first time, two Catalan nationalists, and a civilian at the War Department, Cierva, who lacking Maura's liberal scruples, agreed to be the *Juntas'* representative to ensure that their demands were met.[61] The *Lliga*'s entry into the cabinet showed its opportunism, but also growing importance in national politics. It discarded the Assembly as soon as some of its main objectives were achieved: liquidation of the *turno* and two ministerial portfolios, including the coveted control of the economy (Joan Ventosa at the Treasury).[62]

The coalition hardly lasted five months. In March 1918, it imploded when Cierva introduced by royal decree a military reform bill, whose aim was solely to satisfy the *Juntas*. That month and demonstrating a startling difference in his treatment of civil subversion, Cierva ordered the militarization of the postal and telegraph services to solve an ongoing strike in that sector.[63] The clash between Cierva's heavy-handed manners vis-à-vis his cabinet colleagues' more moderate stance led to the collapse of the government. Rumours, confirmed by British intelligence, indicated that Cierva planned to form a cabinet made up of army officers since the *Juntas* were not willing to let their champion leave the War Department.[64]

Amidst the ensuing panic, the governing classes temporarily managed to bury their feuds and collaborate in a government of national unity headed by Maura, the only leader with enough authority to avert the praetorian threat. On 22 March, the Restoration's most impressive administration to date was announced. It contained three former premiers: Dato (Foreign Office), Romanones (Justice), Alhucemas (Home Office), and leading politicians such as Alba (Education) and Cambó (Public Works).[65] Maura's return to power meant that the former 'Messiah' had found a new role: 'fireman' or the last resort of the political comedy in peril.[66] Widespread enthusiasm greeted the so-called *Ministerio de Primates* (Cabinet of Titans). The country's social life was normalized with the rapid introduction of an amnesty for the members of the strike committee, who had been returned to parliament during the elections of February 1918. Allowed to take their seats, the *Cortes* became the scene of lively debates over the events of the previous August. However, the flamboyant national government never lived up to expectations. Its legislative record was rather modest. Furthermore, once the panic that had sealed monarchist unity faded, traditional petty squabbling resurfaced. When parliament reopened in October, a frustrated Maura witnessed the sad spectacle of ministers attacking one another.[67] The government collapsed in early November. It was followed by a short-lived coalition of liberal factions presided over by Alhucemas (9 November to 5 December 1918), which was replaced by a faction-based Romanones administration.

The national government's end coincided with the culmination of the Great War. The armistice did not usher in an era of stability but a period of unprecedented socio-political radicalism that could be described as a European Civil War, which linked umbilically the two world wars.[68] A return to the political universe of 1914 was impossible. Years of human bloodshed and socio-economic upheaval seemed to have created the necessary conditions for the revolutionary triumph augured by the Bolsheviks. They had always believed that their revolution was not a uniquely Russian event but the start of a worldwide phenomenon. It seemed plausible that if Russia's downtrodden masses had overthrown the most repressive regime of all, the experience could surely be emulated elsewhere. Furthermore, tired of being cannon fodder in an imperialist conflict, the proletariat was ready to revolt against rulers whose delusions of grandeur had produced unprecedented suffering.[69]

In the former Central Powers, councils of soldiers and workers filled the vacuum left by the flight of their rulers, as had happened in Russia after Nicholas II's dethronement. The red tide seemed to lap at every corner of the continent. Economic dislocation and food and fuel shortages prompted soldiers, workers, and peasants to engage in riots, mutinies, and uprisings. Then in March 1919, the Bolsheviks founded the Third International (Comintern) to coordinate the diverse revolutionary efforts.[70]

The CNT's Finest Hour

Spain was caught in a spiral of social conflict and political radicalism sweeping across Europe after the armistice. In the aftermath of the Great War, inflation reached a peak, widening the gap between the prices of staple goods and real wages.[71] The country found itself sliding into a revolutionary situation that, unlike 1917, now possessed an urban and a rural dimension.

After years of relative apathy, depressing living standards brought about by galloping inflation revived the endemic bitter class struggle in the rural south. The dazzling spell cast by Russian events provided the necessary myth to generate a climate of popular exaltation. Hundreds of enthusiastic apostles travelled to villages to spread the new faith to the avid masses: the despotic tsarist regime had been overthrown and the people were about to create a new Arcadia. Spain's southern countryside experienced three years of revolutionary euphoria (*Trienio Bolchevique*, 1918–1920). Its great innovation was its coordination and solidarity: just about everyone (artisans, peasants, teachers, domestic service) participated in the movement. Consequently, stoppages acquired the character of general strikes. Initial successes contributed to the growth of class consciousness and encouraged new demands: wage increases, suppression of piecework, restriction of employment to outsiders, and so on. Caught by surprise, the ruling classes were terrified. Many even fled to the relative safety of the provincial capitals while pressuring the authorities to implement drastic measures. The agrarian unions filled the subsequent power vacuum.[72]

Strike activity, extending from the southern countryside to the mining basins, reached its peak in the years 1918–1920.[73] Simultaneously, food riots and assaults on shops and bakeries, where women played a leading role, became more frequent.[74] In January 1918, they set an example to follow in Barcelona, where for days women staged massive rallies from which men were banned. They denounced hoarders, stormed bakeries and coal stores, engaged in violent confrontations with the police, and forced, on more than one occasion, meetings with the civil governor. Martial law was declared and troops were stationed to guard markets and businesses. The rioting women achieved a certain degree of success: Madrid replaced the discredited civil governor, approved the regulation of prices of basic products, and forbade their exportation or hoarding. However, governmental guidelines were not always followed by merchants and shopkeepers.[75]

Women also began to take the initiative in industrial action. For instance, they staged strikes at the *La Fortuna* biscuit factory and in the cigarette-making factory, both in Madrid, in April and July 1920 respectively. On both occasions, there were violent clashes when the employers tried to replace their striking force affiliated with the UGT with members of Catholic unions.[76]

Spain seemed to present the ideal conditions for communist success: widespread socio-economic distress, popular alienation from a governing class installed in its comfortable political comedy and disconnected from the concerns of the masses, and enthusiasm for the Russian Revolution. Yet, communism proved an utter failure. The Communist Party (*Partido Comunista de España*, PCE), created in April 1920, resulted from a split in the Socialist Youth, a tiny force that sought to hide its irrelevance behind verbal violence. Still, Spain was not a priority like Germany for Moscow. The first Comintern delegates arrived at the relatively late date of December 1919, and only after receiving instructions to stop on their way from Mexico to Moscow. They were the Russian Mikhail Borodin, Charles Shipman (aka Jesús Ramírez), a young American who had fled to Mexico to avoid military conscription and ended up playing a central role due to his knowledge of Spanish, and the Indian Manabendra Nath (alias Roy). This picturesque trio was penniless, inexperienced, and completely oblivious to Spanish politics. After landing in La Coruña (Galicia), they went to Madrid. Any knowledge of the situation would have led them to Barcelona, the proletarian centre of the country and bastion of the CNT, which had just voted in a national congress to join the Comintern.[77] Blinded by impatience and dogmatism, they chose to transform what they perceived as the PSOE's only section with an authentic revolutionary pedigree, the Socialist Youth, into the Communist Party. Unfortunately for the trio, only 2,000 of its 7,000 members took that step. Their PSOE elders disdainfully called the PCE the party of the 100 children. A second Communist Party was created in April 1921 after a split in the PSOE. After months of vicious infighting between the two communist parties, in November 1921 the Comintern imposed their merger. It remained a small force with less than 5,000 militants.[78]

Believing that Bolshevism was identical to its revolutionary vision, the CNT initially adhered provisionally to the Comintern.[79] With the organization decapitated by mass arrests, in 1921 the CNT fell under the spell of a faction of pro-Bolshevik syndicalists headed by Andreu Nin and Joaquín Maurín.[80]

However, in June 1922, now better acquainted with the situation after the publication of a report by Ángel Pestaña, who had attended the Comintern congress held in Moscow in the summer of 1920, the CNT abandoned the Communist International.[81] Consequently, communism failed to establish a solid foothold in Spain. Its appeal fell into an ideological ether, neither able to displace the socialist view of a historically inevitable but rather distant revolution, nor the anarcho-syndicalist belief in revolutionary spontaneity.[82] The PCE became a marginal force marked by constant internal squabbling and purges and targeted by police repression.

With the UGT-PSOE still traumatized by the events of August 1917, the CNT capitalized upon the growing popular turmoil. Unlike the Socialists, who distinguished between the revolutionary and the criminal, the CNT defended the inalienable right of the victims of capitalist exploitation to fight for their survival by any means.[83] Furthermore, rather than the impossible quest of conquering state power through the ballot box, its active identification with popular causes such as the struggle against the high prices of commodities and rents consolidated its neighbourhood strength and facilitated its staggering expansion: from some 15,000 members in October 1915 to 699,369 militants and 56,738 unaffiliated workers (over three times that of the UGT) at its second national congress in December 1919.[84] The CNT's spread across the country was astounding, particularly in its historical bastion of Barcelona.

During the war, the Catalan capital became the most graphic example of the obscene contrast between factory owners' extraordinary profits and workers' penury. The CNT's reconstruction resulted from the collaboration of different groups that joined in their rejection of socialist bloated bureaucracy, centralism, and participation in bourgeois politics. They all believed in direct action and operating from the bottom-up alongside a federal structure. Three groups proved instrumental: the diehards from the action groups, the arrival during the war years of a significant number of propagandists and theorists, who were to fill the key posts at the national committee and libertarian press, and a new generation of labour activists whose most charismatic exponent was Salvador Seguí.[85]

In the summer of 1918, a congress held in Sants (Barcelona), with delegates representing 75,150 workers, established the Catalan Regional Confederation and approved its reorganization based on the so-called *sindicato único* (single union) or the grouping of all the workers' associations of the same industrial sector in each locality. They rejected all kinds of political tutelage, welcomed workers regardless of their ideological leaning, and maintained the libertarian tradition of federalism and local autonomy.[86] The *sindicatos únicos* put an end to the fragmentation of scattered trades and craft societies, which had hitherto weakened proletarian solidarity. With the working force now divided into 13 branches, labour disputes would decrease, but their impact would be amplified as the unions could pool all their forces within each industrial sector in every major conflict.

Delegates travelled to other parts of the country to rebuild the organization nationwide.

The *sindicatos únicos* soon demonstrated their might. In February 1919, a dispute at the Catalan capital's main energy supplier, the Barcelona Traction Light and Power Company (known as *La Canadiense* as most of its capital was Anglo-Canadian), constituted a watershed. The conflict was initially over wages. Yet, when eight employees were sacked for attempting to create a union, it developed into a titanic struggle that lasted 44 days. As the entire workforce went on strike, they requested help from the CNT's *sindicato único* of gas, water, and electricity. The usual panoply of repressive measures was introduced, including the declaration in mid-March of martial law by the city's captain general Joaquín Miláns del Bosch. However, nobody anticipated the solidarity of the local proletariat. Barcelona was left in darkness. With food riots rocking Madrid and other cities, the countryside in revolt, and the UGT threatening a nationwide solidarity strike, the Romanones government blinked. A more liberal civil governor, Carlos Montañés, and chief of police, Geraldo Doval, were sent to Barcelona. The CNT had won a spectacular victory: it was officially recognized as the collective representative of the proletariat, and the company agreed to rehire its discharged employees (without penalties of any kind), raise salaries, and reimburse a fortnight's pay in February and a full month's wages for the days lost in March during the dispute. In turn, the government promised an amnesty for all those imprisoned and introduced an eight-hour working day in the construction sector (with a promise that it would be extended to all industries by 1 October).[87]

The prestige acquired after the *Canadiense* conflict and the revolutionary optimism unleashed by the Bolshevik Revolution assured the CNT of a receptive audience. Its national congress of December 1919 represented the apogee of its power. Its Catalan section comprised a staggering 427,086 members, practically the whole of the proletariat of the region.[88] Nonetheless, the revolutionary rhetoric of the delegates contrasted dramatically with reality. The *Canadiense* strike was an extraordinary example of workers' solidarity, efficiently organized by the union leaders. However, that great triumph was soon upstaged by a terrorist maelstrom. Barcelona became the microcosm of a violent social war, which destroyed the remaining essence of the liberal state.

By 1914, anarchist terrorism had fallen into disrepute – years of propaganda by the deed had only achieved repression of the workers. However, the war saw its resurgence, but also its transformation into a phenomenon with a new dimension. Its protagonists were no longer small cells or solitary individuals who carried out spectacular attacks against political dignitaries, but professionals of the pistol whose target was the class enemy (employers, foremen, scabs, etc.).[89] The so-called *pistolerismo* (gun law) resulted from the convergence of exogenous causes (German espionage) with domestic factors (the recrudescence of the class struggle). It found an ideal milieu in the undeclared war fought in Spain by the belligerent powers. Germany ran a vast spy network whose tendrils stretched far and wide, infiltrating anarchist groups and hiring the services of adventurers, criminals, and police officers such as the chief of Barcelona's political brigade, Manuel Brabo Portillo. The objective was to hinder trade with the Allies by any means, including sabotage and assassinations. The most notorious killing was that of Josep Albert Barret, whose company was a leading supplier of artillery ammunition to France. The assassination was carried out by an anarchist group on the orders of the union leader, Eduardo Ferrer, who was an *agent provocateur* working for Portillo.[90]

The war fostered the resurgence of anarchist action groups. They consisted of a few militants, mostly young people linked by ties of friendship and with strong roots in their neighbourhoods and local unions. They were joined by displaced immigrants, already radicalized by their own experiences, who suddenly found themselves in the powder keg that was wartime Barcelona. Passionate and idealistic, they were initially at the vanguard of the struggle: shock-troops in the skirmishes against the police and scabs, protecting union activities, and coordinating the pickets.[91] They played a vital role in the CNT's rapid expansion. The incorporation of workers' societies into the *sindicatos únicos* was not always the result of their own free will but of the aggression of the anarchists.[92] They also offered a decisive formula to win in industrial disputes: the shooting of stubborn employers. The latter's compliance, after a few *atentados*, bolstered their reputation and provided a clear incentive for the consolidation of terrorist practices.

Rising social violence reopened the internal antagonisms that had haunted the libertarian universe for decades. Labour leaders, including Seguí and Pestaña, condemned terrorism. They believed it would undermine trade union legitimacy and, consequently, the future of the entire organization.[93] Moreover, they were aware that anarcho-syndicalism could not withstand the arsenal of its enemies. However, they were unable to prevent the groups from gradually becoming an integral part of the CNT. As their prestige grew, their members acquired full-time jobs as professional *pistoleros* who received special dues from some unions for services rendered. The original altruistic urban fighters were joined by elements of the criminal underworld, for whom killing was a lucrative business. As the union struggle gave way to open warfare, they were the best equipped to operate underground and, in the process, their most charismatic members became icons of the noble fight against social injustice.

Red Mirage, Black Storm

A bizarre consequence of the Bolshevik Revolution was that the inter-war years were an era of virtually uninterrupted working-class defeats.[94] By

1921, the revolutionary *élan* had petered out just about everywhere. A black wave of nationalist and militaristic reaction was about to occupy the void left by the fleeting red tide. The fear caused by the growing strength of the organized labour movement persuaded the ruling socio-economic classes of many states to support authoritarian formulas of governance.

Like almost everywhere in Europe, there was no genuine threat of social revolution in Spain. Its would-be protagonist, the CNT, though a formidable mass protest movement, never offered a genuine challenge to the regime. Its actions were channelled into the economic sphere and its emphasis on the primacy of the revolutionary spontaneity of the masses was a world apart from Bolshevism. The national congress of December 1919 exposed its structural contradictions. It praised Bolshevism and even voted to join the Comintern provisionally, while the principles of libertarian communism were officially subscribed to for the first time. The model of *sindicato único* was adopted. However, national industry federations were rejected due to the belief of many anarchists that this would increase bureaucracy and limit local autonomy.[95] Thus, the CNT remained a conglomerate of regional confederations without any effective collective discipline or leadership.

The combination of disturbing reports on revolutionary activities throughout Europe and social unrest in Spain triggered a wave of panic. From 1919, Andalusian landowners and Catalan industrialists, like their counterparts across the country, were gripped by fear. The augmentation of *atentados*, growing union power, and the dreadful news from Russia, led them to perceive that their world was being inverted.[96] They did not see subtle distinctions between communism, socialism, and anarcho-syndicalism. For them, they were all variations of the same red menace.

Although opposed to a structural reform that endangered their hegemony, dynastic politicians were not insensitive to the social question and were prepared to embrace reformist measures that could defuse tensions.[97] Nonetheless, any attempt at social conciliation through progressive concessions clashed with employers' intransigence. From the spring of 1919, Spain became a laboratory of social warfare whose epicentre was Barcelona.[98] The *Canadiense* was a turning point. It was neither the violence of the strike (relatively timid compared with previous disputes) nor the objectives (better wages and conditions) but rather union discipline that shocked. Industrialists felt indignant at what they considered the capitulation of the authorities to the demands of troublemakers.[99] Faced with Madrid's inability or unwillingness to crush the revolutionary challenge, they decided to take matters into their own hands, closed ranks in defence of their corporate interests, and prepared for war.[100] They hired gangs of thugs as their private police force, whose actions ranged from being bodyguards to acting as *agents provocateurs*, as well as beating and even killing labour activists.[101] One of the existing employers' associations, the *Confederación Patronal Española* (*Patronal*), was reorganized as an instrument of combat.[102] They also sealed an alliance with the local garrison.

Under the pretext of defending the social order, Catalan industrialists and the military began to operate as a true anti-state – a parallel power acting in the shadows that forced governments in Madrid to choose between complicity in the violent reaction or being the victim of their subversion. In less than a year, three coups, not yet against the state, but against different cabinets, delivered a lethal blow to the regime. In late March 1919, General Miláns, incensed by Madrid's conciliatory policy, sought to reignite the conflict by disobeying the government's instructions to free those prisoners in military custody. When the CNT declared a general strike, the streets were occupied by troops aided by a paramilitary force, the *Somatén*, a rural militia to fight local banditry dating from medieval times. It was the Spanish version of the patriotic militias that emerged across Europe to combat the perceived red threat. After its success in Barcelona, its model was exported to other cities.[103] In April, the army 'invited' the civil governor and the police chief to take the train back to Madrid, which led to the fall of the Romanones administration. Their crime had been to seek a negotiated solution to the strike.[104] In December, a Conservative administration was ousted by an all-out lockout staged by the *Patronal* (3 November 1919 to 26 January 1920). The lock-out had two objectives: to sabotage the initiative devised by interior minister Manuel Burgos y Mazo to restore social harmony through a state-sponsored Joint Employer and Labour Arbitration Commission, and to starve the workers into abandoning the CNT. Instead, it fanned the flames of social hatred and played into the hands of the anarchist *exaltés*.[105] In November 1920, Catalan employers forced the removal of the city's civil governor, the liberal-minded Carlos Bas, who was replaced by General Severiano Martínez Anido, the hard-line military governor.[106]

Spain underwent a small-scale civil war. The vicious cycle of violence spread from Barcelona to other cities, especially those where the CNT had a strong presence such as Valencia and Zaragoza. Hundreds of workers were arrested and often deported to their places of birth, making long trips chained and on foot. Labour activists were victims of attacks perpetrated by employers' gunmen or the infamous *Ley de Fugas* (the shooting of prisoners while allegedly trying to escape).[107] As union leaders were rounded up or became victims of *atentados*, the CNT began to fall into the hands of the extremists. Three general secretaries were shot down, one of them being Seguí in March 1923. In turn, the action groups carried out 'revolutionary expropriations' (armed robberies) and maintained their campaign of assassinations, including those of prime minister Dato and the Archbishop of Zaragoza, shot dead in March 1921 and June 1923, respectively.

The Death of the Liberal Order: Euthanasia or Infanticide?

In September 1923, Miguel Primo de Rivera, captain general of Barcelona, staged a coup d'état. The influential Hispanist, Raymond Carr, offered a thought-provoking explanation: while Primo claimed he was finishing off a diseased body he was strangling a newborn, since the regime was evolving towards a more democratic system.[108] That thesis triggered a wide-ranging debate that continues to this day, not least because it is inseparable from the key question of Spain's troubled transition from elite to mass politics.[109] A compromise can be found somewhere in the middle, although closer to the idea of euthanasia than infanticide.[110] A regime that ruled Spain for almost 50 years cannot be considered newborn when, furthermore, it had just thwarted in 1917 an attempt to bring democratic change from above (Assembly) or from below (revolutionary strike). Tellingly, at the time, a British intelligence report noted that a leopard could not change its spots; in other words, Spain's governing classes were not going to collaborate in the destruction of a political system that was so beneficial to them.[111] Their fear of democracy had not changed significantly since Cánovas' days. A dynastic notable, Natalio Rivas, confided in his diary that a clean ballot meant for them a straight road to political oblivion, especially in the cities.[112] In fact, despite promises of far-reaching reforms, nothing substantial was delivered by the last Restoration government, a Liberal coalition led by Alhucemas. The usual ballot-rigging practices in the elections of December 1922 led to an overall majority in parliament, including a record number of deputies (146) returned by Article 29 (associated with the *caciques* since it meant the automatic election of those candidates without opposition in their constituencies) and a shockingly large number (144) linked by family ties – Alhucemas and Romanones counted nine each.[113]

Carr's dictum suffers from a certain determinism, ignores the crucial weight of agency and contingency during events, and overlooks the extent that Spain's structural tensions were the domestic version of the general crisis that engulfed most European states in the post-war years. Returning to the symbolic biological comparison, Primo used the codename 'the patient has been operated upon' to announce the beginning of the insurrection to his co-conspirators in other provinces.[114] Of course, the patient was not saved but finished off in an exercise that was certainly not a mercy killing. The military's previous subversive actions had placed the state they were supposed to protect in a 'coma'. They had in the past refrained from switching off the patient's life support before but this time it was different.

Although mauled, the patient showed time and again a remarkable ability to recover. The last two cabinets – a Conservative one headed by José Sánchez Guerra (March–December 1922) and a Liberal one led by Alhucemas (December 1922 to September 1923) – never embraced genuine democratic reform but attempted to bring back constitutional normality. This encompassed an end to emergency legislation, restoration of full civil liberties including normal trade union activity, and the adoption of a more neutral stance in social affairs. Constitutional guarantees, suspended for three years, were restored in March 1922 and decisive steps were taken to dismantle the existing system of terror such as the removal of General Martínez Anido from his post in Barcelona in October 1922.

Following the legalization of the CNT, social violence resumed in earnest. The emptiness of the union's coffers galvanized the action groups to engage in daring armed robberies. To the horror of the employers, the reconstruction of union power translated into an escalation of industrial conflict. In May 1923, a major transport strike began in Barcelona.[115] Memories of the dreaded *Canadiense* were uppermost as the city was brought to a halt. Consequently, the seditious alliance between industrialists and the garrison was rekindled. The key difference was that Primo, appointed captain general of Barcelona in 1922, was willing, unlike his predecessors, to go beyond ousting a cabinet. Having previously served as captain general in Valencia, another centre of social conflict, he concluded that the constitutional framework was inadequate to combat labour unrest.[116] After over three months of a transport strike, he became the hero of the local ruling classes when, by-passing the local authorities, he stepped in and forced the unions to concede defeat.[117]

Faced with a *pronunciamiento*, the government, lacking genuine electoral mandate and grass roots support, was unable to appeal to popular mobilization. The working class had no reason to defend the ruling order. Thus, apart from the PCE's short-lived attempt to organize a one-day general strike in Bilbao, the labour movement received the coup with apathy. After years of brutal repression, the CNT was exhausted and unwilling to take on the army while the Socialists adopted a strategy of 'wait and see'.[118] The regime's hope, the loyalty of the armed forces and royal intervention, was quickly dashed. Most senior commanders endorsed what could be termed a 'negative *pronunciamiento*': they neither came out openly in support of the rebellion nor were prepared to terminate it by fighting fellow officers. That stance left the monarch as the sole decision-maker. Thus, even if a 'smoking gun' directly linking Alfonso XIII with the coup wasn't found, he could not plead innocence. He did nothing to oppose the coup. On the contrary, he quickly showed his readiness to welcome a dictatorship.[119]

From his ascent to the throne, Alfonso XIII never concealed his contempt for parliamentary politics. In July 1921, a new harrowing colonial debacle further rallied the Crown and army against the regime. A military offensive in the central Rif petered out in the Battle of Annual. The subsequent retreat turned into a rout: some 9,000 troops were massacred and control over the eastern part of the protectorate collapsed. It provoked a national uproar demanding that those responsible be brought to account. Several officers were charged and tried, but the main target of the popular outcry was Alfonso XIII. His interest in the campaign was well known, including how he had encouraged his close friend, Manuel Fernández Silvestre, to launch the reckless advance that turned into a slaughter.[120] King and army were incensed with the politicians, who, while covering up their role in the affair, let the press and parliament freely debate the disaster. They even allowed the establishment of a cross-party select committee to investigate the question of responsibilities.

The coup took place just a few days before the opening of parliament, which after the summer recess was to discuss the recommendations of the committee.[121] In August, Gabriel Maura informed his father that Alfonso XIII, obsessed with Bolshevism and worried by his implication in the colonial debacle, had confided to him that he was toying with the idea of taking on the role of national saviour and establishing a personal dictatorship. That was enough to prompt Maura to run to the palace to dissuade the sovereign from his avowed intentions, arguing that it was too risky an enterprise. He advised the monarch to let 'those who do not let others govern assume the responsibility of the government themselves'.[122] And that is what the monarch did. Surprised by the coup while spending his summer holidays in San Sebastián, he asked the head of his military household, the hard-line former captain general of Barcelona Miláns, to sound out the opinion of the country's military authorities. Once satisfied with their steadfast support of the throne, he returned to Madrid the following morning. There, he quickly dismissed his government and invited Primo to form a military cabinet. Captured on camera, the king seemed unconcerned by the most serious crisis of his reign. He was pictured in military uniform, displaying a broad smile.[123] Continuing the biological allegory, Primo took the mantle of 'iron surgeon' and switched off the life support of the patient. Having thought to do so himself, the hospital's chief consultant, Alfonso XIII, was untroubled at signing the death certificate.[124]

Regeneration from Above

Primo seized power through a traditional *pronunciamiento*. However, his coup represented a breach with the past. He was no longer the *espadón* of a particular faction but Costa's iron surgeon, the interpreter of the aspirations of a country tired of the reigning political corruption. The manifesto that accompanied the coup was peppered with populist rhetoric, regeneration ideals, and *machista* clichés. Primo claimed to lead a 'movement of men' in response to the widespread popular demand to be freed from the professional politicians whose mismanagement had led to the disaster of 1898 and national decline. He implied that his rule would be a short parenthesis in the life of the nation during which, supported by all good citizens, thorough solutions would be found to deal with Spain's maladies (terrorism, communism, separatism, economic dislocation, the colonial quagmire, etc.).[125]

The coup formed part of the reactionary backlash that swept across Europe in the inter-war years.[126] The destruction of the Hungarian Soviet Republic in August 1919 followed by the establishment of the dictatorship of Admiral Miklós Horthy initiated that black wave. In October 1922, the seizure of power in Italy by the Fascists, with the complicity of traditional institutions (army, crown, and socio-economic elites), was a model to emulate, at least in some of its features. It was a new political phenomenon: a youthful and dynamic interclass mass movement marked by street violence, military choreography, and rejection of liberal practices. By 1923, the clamour for a similar example in Spain became deafening. Many right-wing newspapers (the monarchist *El ABC*, the Carlist *El Correo Catalán*, the Maurista *La Acción*, etc.) stressed how Italian fascism showed the way to crush red subversion.[127] Tellingly, Alfonso XIII's first trip abroad after the coup was to Italy in November 1923. There, he exultantly introduced Primo to King Vittorio Emanuele III as 'my Mussolini'.[128]

Indeed, the Dictatorship formed part of the historical context of inter-war Europe. Spanish nationalism embodied by Primo de Rivera sought to be an element of social integration destined to overcome the class struggle. The attack on liberal elitism, the repression of the labour movement, the rejection of democratic postulates along with the adoption of populist speeches were common elements in the counter-revolutionary dictatorships that emerged in the 1920s (Poland, Bulgaria, Portugal, Yugoslavia, etc.).[129]

The *pronunciamiento* had a clear social component. Believing that the constitutional order was no longer an efficient formula for social control, the dominant classes welcomed the coup. Cambó wrote that the turmoil that reigned over Barcelona paved the way for military dictatorship.[130] Indeed, it was hatched and carried out in that region's capital with the enthusiastic support of significant sectors of its economic elites. After years of growing separation from the ruling order, they concluded that the preservation of their social hegemony was worth the establishment of an authoritarian system. Some of the city's personalities accompanied the captain general during the night of the coup. Catching the train bound for Madrid to form a new administration, Primo was seen off by some 4,000 leading citizens, including the president of the *Mancomunidad*, the mayor, and presidents of the main corporations.[131]

The Catholic Church, the chambers of commerce, and most industrial and agrarian organizations greeted the coup with jubilation.[132] Overall, the benevolence with which it was received revealed the widening gap between society and dynastic politics.[133] The government's reaction revealed its impotence. After being ousted from his post of prime minister, Alhucemas greeted the rebellion with a mixture of cynicism and relief. He told the assembled press that he could now add Primo to his list of Saints for having removed him from the nightmare of governing.[134]

Primo established a *directorio militar* (military directorate) with a general from each of the eight military regions and one admiral, declared martial law (which lasted until May 1925), suspended the constitution, banned political opposition, ended trial by jury, and dissolved the *Cortes*. Repressive practices and arbitrary decisions became an ingrained feature, particularly the widespread use of censorship to silence all criticism, the restriction of basic civil liberties, the imprisonment of hundreds of political suspects, the purge of the civil service, and interference in the judiciary.[135]

Primo, an Andalusian landowner, a devout Catholic, a good monarchist, and as captain general of Barcelona the spokesman for the Catalan industrial bourgeoisie, seemed to possess the right qualifications to find a new equilibrium of forces by accommodating agrarian and industrial interests.[136] He soon renounced his claim of only needing 90 days to save Spain. However, from the start, it was obvious that he lacked a clear political philosophy. Still, his first few years in power proved quite successful. In this period, Primo mostly confined his role to that of an 'iron surgeon' performing radical surgery to release Spain from the grip of its old politics and solve the more pressing problems. Most Spaniards, tired of dynastic elitism, welcomed his *bonhomie*. The dictator possessed charm, spoke the language of the street, and did not conceal the vulgarity of his manners. He was a gargantuan eater, an inveterate gambler, loved binges, and frequently went on inebriated rampages.[137]

Given the strong emphasis on regeneration, Primo made his priority the *descuaje del caciquismo*, or the extirpation of old politics by destroying the *cacique* networks.[138] As early as 18 September and 1 October 1923, two royal decrees sought to reorganize public administration based on concepts of bureaucratic efficiency and simplification, as well as economic austerity.[139] The official press denigrated the dynastic notables as corrupt politicians misgoverning the country. Generals were appointed civil governors, town councils were dissolved, and army officers sent to every province as *delegados gubernativos*. They were to be 'apostles of the fatherland' or 'pocket iron surgeons' in an anti-*caciquista* crusade to bring about the moralization of public life throughout the country. They were to supervise the election of new councillors and administrative staff, enlist the collaboration of good citizens, foster patriotic values, and seek out the enemies of the fatherland (anarchists, communists, separatists, etc.). Initially, the *delegados gubernativos*' zeal in uprooting old practices, aided by an avalanche of anonymous public denunciations, translated into such a high number of arrests of former municipal councillors and *caciques* that Madrid had to stop it. Gradually, the purification began to lose momentum. Given the power they held, these 'apostles of the fatherland' either turned into a new sort of *caciques* themselves or were lured by vested interests.[140]

One success of the Dictatorship was the restoration of law and order. The appointment of Martinez Anido as interior minister, who had engineered the dirty war against the CNT in Barcelona, revealed the new regime's determination to adopt a hard line.¹⁴¹ The PCE and CNT were banned and hundreds of their militants were imprisoned. The action groups were hunted down or went into exile. Terrorism saw a dramatic fall, from 819 *atentados* in 1923 to 18 the following year.¹⁴² Still, state repression was relatively moderate compared with previous years. A genuine attempt to improve labour affairs facilitated this seemingly new era of social peace. A significant innovation was the regime's experiment with social policies. The Socialists were singled out as a responsible organization that could be drawn into a modus vivendi. After initial hesitation, the reluctance to collaborate with the regime by the movement's political wing led by the ex-deputy for Bilbao, Indalecio Prieto, was ended. Besteiro, who replaced Iglesias after his death in 1925, and the trade union wing, led by Largo Caballero, welcomed the opportunity. They believed that Socialists could best defend workers' interests by attaining positions of influence within the state, regardless of its political nature. Moreover, they could not only avoid proscription but also expand without competition.¹⁴³ Indeed, the UGT became a sort of partner of the Dictatorship and its leaders obtained posts in economic institutions. Largo, the UGT secretary, joined the prestigious Council of State and served in the Council of Labour, which had replaced the IRS.¹⁴⁴ However, the UGT only saw a modest expansion, growing from 210,000 affiliates in 1923 to 225,000 in 1929.¹⁴⁵

The Dictatorship created the National Corporative Organization, whose main task was to establish *comités paritarios* (joint arbitration committees) formed by representatives of workers and employers. Their objective was to solve conflicts and discuss pertinent legislation.¹⁴⁶ Significantly, these committees, consolidated by law in November 1926, never adopted the all-embracing style of fascism but were characterized by altruistic paternalism. Syndicalist freedom was respected and workers were not represented by a single fascist union. The UGT acquired the lion's share of labour representation, more so than the Catholic trade unions, which infuriated the Church. Moreover, while employers bore the burden of financing the committees and had to abide by the decisions adopted, the proletariat still had the right to resort to strike action.¹⁴⁷ Even the CNT's old guard led by Pestaña contemplated participating in the regime's corporatism. Yet this was furiously opposed by hard-liners who, in turn, founded, in a secret meeting in Valencia in July 1927, the *Federación Anarquista Ibérica* (FAI) to capture the leadership of the organization once it could resume its activities legally.¹⁴⁸

The Dictatorship presided over a significant drop in the mortality rate and a considerable increase in life expectancy.¹⁴⁹ Urban workers enjoyed years of gradual improvement in living standards, safe employment, and their rights were defended in the *comités paritarios*. The prices of basic commodities fell, public spending on education, social benefits, and health increased, and ambitious public works projects were undertaken. Nevertheless, the countryside remained untouched by these paternalist experiments so as not to infuriate the powerful landed interests. Agrarian stagnation contrasted dramatically with industrial expansion, which registered annual growth of 5.5 percent.[150]

Up until 1929, there was a period of economic development. Heavy protectionism and state intervention replaced traditional laissez-faire. The Dictatorship bet on economic nationalism based on state control, a commitment to high tariffs, support for national industry, and enlargement of the public sector.[151] It was a programme of economic modernization through the development of national resources and heavy investment in public works such as road construction and renewal of the railway system. In 1924, the National Council of the Economy was created to defend national agrarian and industrial interests. Alongside Italy and the Soviet Union, Spain became one of Europe's most heavily protected economies with a large public sector. The copious amounts of public spending resulted in a huge deficit that was mostly paid for by an extraordinary budget that was expected to raise capital from the surpluses in the ordinary budget and public debt.[152] The state's encouragement of industrial takeovers and monopolies benefited big companies. The consequence was widespread corruption and vast fortunes being made by the dictator's cronies.[153]

The Dictatorship succeeded in ending the colonial quagmire in Morocco. Primo was an *abandonista*: he often spoke against the continuity of that enterprise, a constant financial and human haemorrhage that the country could not afford. His stance, including the suggestion of exchanging Gibraltar for Ceuta, cost him the post of military governor of Cádiz in 1917 and captain general of Madrid in 1921.[154] He again maintained that position in his initial manifesto: 'we are not imperialists, nor do we hold that the honour of the army depends upon a stubborn insistence in Morocco'. Nevertheless, the so-called *africanistas* (colonial officers), upset by the accusation of responsibility for the Annual disaster and the permanent underfunding of their campaign, supported the coup. They soon became outraged, however, when the Dictatorship filled the administration with *Junteros* and ordered a general retreat to new defensive lines and the repatriation of large numbers of conscripts in Morocco. There were even talks of kidnapping the dictator during his tour of the Protectorate in 1924. In almost every garrison he visited, snubs marked his reception. Allegedly, during a dinner offered in his honour at the Foreign Legion's headquarters, the commander of the garrison, Lieutenant Colonel Francisco Franco, ordered a meal to be served consisting mainly of *huevos* (eggs). Being the Spanish slang for testicles, the message was clear: the dictator lacked them. In other words, he was a coward.[155]

Fortune seemed to smile on the dictator. The rebel chieftain, Muhammad ibn Abd-el-Krim, perceived the Spanish retreat as proof of weakness. Hence, he not only continued harassing the Spanish troops, but emboldened by his successes began the invasion of French Morocco. The outcome was a Franco-Spanish Conference held in Madrid (17 June to 25 July 1925) that led to a joint military operation. The Spanish offensive was led by General José Sanjurjo. On 8 September, Franco headed the landing of a contingent of over 13,000 troops on Alhucemas Bay, in the heart of rebel territory. Simultaneously, the French army advanced from the south. In May 1926, caught in this vice-like squeeze, outnumbered and outgunned, Krim's forces were forced into an unconditional surrender.[156]

The Disintegration of the Dictatorship

If Primo had retired in 1925 or 1926, he might have gone down in history as one of Spain's most popular statesmen.[157] Yet, ignoring his early pledge of a temporary stay in power to solve Spain's most pressing maladies, he sought to perpetuate his rule, liquidate the liberal state, and found a new regime.

In 1923, the army became the lynchpin of a broader counter-revolutionary coalition. At the helm, Primo failed as the architect of a new order. His ultimate failure was the combination of excessive amateurism and improvisation with unsolved ideological contradictions (paternalist tendencies vis-à-vis authoritarian objectives).

On 17 September 1923, the paramilitary *Somatén* was transformed into a national corps. Headed by the captain general of every military region, it was intended to become the new order's praetorian guard and a school of citizenship and indoctrination. Its mission was also to display mass support for the regime through choreographed parades, patriotic ceremonies, and colourful rituals. Boasting 175,000 members by the autumn of 1924, it reached a peak of 217,584 in August 1928.[158]

In April 1924, civilians replaced generals as provincial governors and a pro-regime party, *Unión Patriótica* (UP), was established. This was a decisive step towards the institutionalization of a new order.[159] The party was meant to embody the living proof of popular support for the regime. It was also an attempt to mobilize and integrate the middle classes into an organization orchestrated from above that could then boast legitimacy.[160] The *delegados gubernativos* were instructed to enlist the services of all good citizens to join the UP. Rather than a party, it was meant to be a mass movement with ambiguous ideological tenets. Apart from embracing the idea of 'regeneration from above' and traditional conservative principles (monarchy, property, family, etc.), the emphasis lay on National Catholicism. The regime's ideologues proclaimed Catholicism to be intrinsic to the Spanish soul. The internal enemies (Liberals, Communists, anarchists, etc.) were labelled 'the anti-Spain'.[161]

Primo took two further far-reaching steps to perpetuate his rule. First, the military directorate gave way to a civilian administration in December 1925. The cabinet incorporated technocrats and prominent members of the UP. The new star was the former *Maurista* José Calvo Sotelo at the Treasury.[162] Secondly, in September 1926, the establishment of an *Asamblea Nacional*

Consultativa (National Consultative Assembly) was announced and approved that month by a plebiscite in which only 50 percent of the electorate participated. The Assembly had 400 members drawn from representatives of the state, the provinces, and the municipalities; trades and professions; and the UP. Its objective was to advise the government on legislative matters and to draft a new constitution that would be the structural foundation of the regime. That project sought to replace the former liberal regime with a new authoritarian order based on a corporative model with fascist undertones.[163]

Like the Italian fascists, the Spanish dictatorship constituted the local solution to the crisis of oligarchic liberalism in the age of mass politics. Primo admired Mussolini, banned any press attacks on his fascist regime, and established strong relations with Italy.[164] Indeed, the regime borrowed ideas from fascism: corporatism, economic nationalism, well-choreographed parades, and so on. Lavish propaganda contributed to the personality cult of the leader. Thus, Primo was portrayed as the embodiment of Spain; a gifted leader with values such as humanism, justice, and patriotism. His portrait was paraded during official ceremonies. Towns and villages named squares and streets after Primo.[165] Nonetheless, the Dictatorship lacked fascism's revolutionary rhetoric, dynamism, and mass mobilization. There was never the intention of embracing totalitarian objectives and wiping out all political opposition. For all his posturing, Primo remained an improviser in politics. He always preferred to be liked rather than feared. Furthermore, the party and militia remained flimsy copies of the Italian original.

The UP's social constituency, made up mostly of the upper and middle classes, was a world apart from the plebeian and street-rousing nature of its Italian counterpart. It failed to attract 'new men' except for some Castilian Catholics and *Mauristas*. Yet, until his death in 1925, Maura criticized the Dictatorship and even forewarned the king his support for Primo might lead to the fall of the monarchy.[166] Lacking any organic vitality, the UP remained a governmental creation nurtured from above. It became the perfect protective umbrella for thousands of careerists thirsty for jobs and official protection. Rather than being the backbone of a new order, it merely became an instrument to offer credibility to the Dictatorship through the facade of public involvement and mass parades of homage to the leader. When the regime began to show signs of exhaustion, its membership fell dramatically, from 2 million in August 1924 to 600,000 in December 1929.[167] Equally, the *Somatén* was not the fascist Black Shirts. In Italy, they were crucial to seize first control of the streets and then the state. In contrast, the *Somatén* was created from above and under military control.[168]

The regime's policy towards women was both emancipatory and protective. The dictator's macho proclivities were the antithesis of any feminist-inclined features. In fact, the regime's propagandists promoted an idea of national masculinity whereby the dictator was presented as a providential leader, a good family man, and a virile soldier.[169] However,

Spain shared with her western neighbours a general liberalization. It became acceptable for women to smoke in public, use cosmetics, visit nightclubs, and so on. Although not regarded as men's equals, there was some advance regarding participation in public life, voting in municipal and plebiscitary elections, and running for local office. A significant innovation was the invitation of 14 women to participate in the National Assembly. Their representation among the university population rose from 4.7 to 8.3 percent. Also, protective legislation was passed such as safeguards for women and child labour, modest financial aid to large families, and maternity subsidies.[170]

From 1926, the Dictatorship faced mounting opposition. Despite Primo's initial alliance with Catalan nationalists, including promises of some degree of home rule, his regime soon turned against any expression of regional diversity. As early as 18 September 1923, it passed a decree against separatism. Henceforth, crimes against the unity of the fatherland fell under military jurisdiction. For the first time, Castilian became the compulsory language of public education, regional languages were forbidden in official functions, the state took greater control of the school curriculum, the teaching staff was purged, and regional symbols were banned in public buildings. The *Mancomunidad* lost most of its jurisdiction and its president, the Regionalist Josep Puig i Cadafalch, was replaced by the monarchist Alfonso Sala. That institution was finally abolished in April 1925.[171] Consequently, the hegemony within Catalan nationalism shifted towards a more radical and separatist formation, *Estat Catalá*, led by the eccentric Francesc Maciá, a former army colonel. From his exile in France, Maciá's adventures hardly went beyond symbolic gestures and often ended in a ridiculous fiasco. For instance, his well-published invasion across the Pyrenees via Prats de Molló, in November 1926, was infiltrated by informants and aborted by the prompt intervention of the French authorities. Yet, the subsequent trial served to give notoriety to his movement and rekindle the spirit of resistance against the regime.[172]

The intellectuals composed another bulwark of opposition. They denounced Primo's arbitrary rule and advocated the return of basic freedoms. In 1924, Miguel de Unamuno was deported to the small Canary Island of Fuerteventura. Others such as Vicente Blasco Ibáñez went into exile, from where he launched devastating attacks against both the dictator and the monarch.[173] Outraged by a decree of May 1926 enabling the government to bypass the law in times of emergency, intellectuals flooded into the republican movement. The decree of March 1928, making religious studies compulsory in the first two years of higher education and allowing Catholic colleges to give university degrees, mobilized the academic world. Universities closed their doors as professors symbolically vacated their chairs. Campuses became battlegrounds as police charged against the demonstrating students. Primo backed down, but the damage was done. Class disruptions and youth protests lasted until his last days in power.[174]

The army also began to mount a greater challenge. Up until 1925, this had come mostly from the *africanistas*. However, after the successful conclusion of the Moroccan campaign, Primo not only reconciled with them but also began to promote them to key positions. Franco himself was appointed director of the Military Academy at Zaragoza in 1928. Criticism and even attempts to overthrow the regime then shifted. Many senior generals had been prepared to accept Primo's *pronunciamiento* as a necessary temporary intervention to undertake the task of national regeneration. But they were furious at the idea of transforming an interim regime into one of permanent rule. Additionally, attempts to cut the military budget, reduce the inflated officer corps, and deal with the promotion system, infuriated his former allies in the *Juntas*. Their staunch defence of the *escala cerrada* suffered a lethal blow with the introduction of two decrees, on 9 June and 26 July 1926, entrusting promotions to a junta appointed by the dictator and in which senior generals were bypassed. This measure was regarded as a despotic and nepotistic decision. It was opposed in particular by the aristocratically dominated artillery corps, where promotion had always been by seniority.[175]

On 24 June 1926, veteran generals Weyler and Aguilera, in close touch with old politicians like Romanones and even some Republicans and anarcho-syndicalists, intended to stage a coup to restore the 1876 constitution. Such a farcical combination was easily dismantled by the authorities. The wealthy Romanones was fined half a million pesetas and poorer anarcho-syndicalists like Pestaña 1,000 pesetas.[176]

The next significant conspiracy was headed by Sánchez Guerra, head of the Conservative Party since Dato's assassination in March 1921. In 1926, the establishment of the National Assembly revealed to many monarchists that the door to a return to constitutional times had been slammed shut. After warning the king that he was undermining monarchist loyalty, Sánchez Guerra went into exile and became the champion of the violated legitimacy.[177] In January 1929, he landed in Valencia to lead a revolt. Once again it relied on an incohesive combination of members of the old governing classes, anarcho-syndicalists, and army officers. Most officers involved in the plot hesitated, giving the government time to nip the coup in the bud. The rebellion was only successful among artillery officers, but these only gained the upper hand in the small town of Ciudad Real. Their uprising was easily put down. Primo dissolved the artillery corps by decree, but in testament to his weakening grip, a military court found Sánchez Guerra not guilty. The implication was clear: the rebellion against a regime founded on illegality could not be condemned.[178]

These revolts, although unsuccessful, revealed the dwindling support within the army for the regime and coincided with the Dictatorship's glaring incapacity to build a new authoritarian order. Indeed, it was political deadlock and ideological confusion that sealed its fate. Primo could never balance, or suppress, the competing interests within the system. The final draft of a new constitution by the National Assembly was published in July 1929. Its intermediate position between an authoritarian and a liberal formula did not placate anyone: it guaranteed basic civil liberties, including the right to strike, and defended the establishment of a corporative chamber consisting of representatives of the state, the provinces, the municipalities, and members of the UP. Half of them were to be appointed and the other half elected by universal male suffrage. Yet the new parliament would basically rubber-stamp the dictator's decisions as the executive was only responsible to the king. The project was criticized by the press, attacked across the political spectrum, and even undermined by Primo who found it 'too authoritarian'. The project was abandoned leaving the regime without a clear vision for the future.[179]

The final blow came with the onset of worldwide economic depression. The trade slump of 1929 brought about a sharp drop in exports and rising prices. Regarding the maintenance of the peseta as an indicator of economic prosperity, the regime intervened to defend the exchange rate. Speculators helped themselves to juicy pickings of the country's gold and currency reserves. Finally, the peseta had to be devalued. Years of lavish public spending meant a huge budget deficit and a lack of funds.[180]

The withdrawal of support by the socio-economically well off sank the regime.[181] Ironically, the same groups who had hailed the coup now became outspoken detractors. Landowners and industrialists rejected a fiscal policy that paved the way for more progressive taxation and, in a clear vote of no confidence, refused to contribute the credit that Primo was desperate to raise. The dictator was vilified and his paternalism, mainly institutionalized in the arbitration committees, was portrayed as a tragic error, a sell-out to the Socialists, causing irrevocable damage to the economy.[182]

Even the Socialists undertook a drastic U-turn. In 1927, a UGT national congress rejected participation in the National Assembly. In the summer of 1929, Prieto's pro-republican wing gained the upper hand. By then, even Largo, ever sensitive to grassroots sentiment, had come to accept the imminent fall of the regime and the need to distance himself from it.[183]

The king also sought to disassociate himself from the Dictatorship. Determined to escape the consequences of the growing unpopularity of the regime, he thought that by dismissing the dictator, he might save the throne. The monarch had welcomed the Dictatorship, but it was not long before he began to regret the demise of the old order. Unlike King Vittorio Emanuele III, Alfonso XIII was reluctant to play second fiddle to the dictator. He could no longer form and dismiss cabinets and was upset by Primo's mordant outbursts that he would not be 'Bourbonized'.[184] The monarch had to agree to the dictator's arbitrary decisions. There was nothing he could do while the regime basked in its economic and military successes. However, as soon as the dictator's fortune began to fade in 1929, Alfonso was eager to be rid of him and began to approach members of the old governing elites to find an alternative. He was aware of a new intrigue headed by General Manuel

Goded, military governor at Cádiz, which counted on the support of many garrisons in the south and the sympathy of the captain general of the region, the king's brother-in-law, Carlos of Bourbon.[185]

In January 1930, the king used the existing economic downturn and the army's growing discontent to exert pressure on Primo to retire quietly. By then, the dictator was a sick man suffering from diabetes and alcoholism. His last resort was to write personally to the captain general of each military region to determine whether he still could count on their backing. This was a last-ditch attempt to cling to power and an open display of disrespect towards the head of the state. When all of them were evasive in their response, Primo realized that he no longer enjoyed the support of the military and resigned on 28 January 1930.[186] Thus ended the rule of such a remarkable man that even one of his greatest detractors, Miguel Maura, wrote: 'Amidst the dictators that countries had to endure, he was the most easy-going, harmless, and picturesque'.[187] He died in exile two months later in a small hotel in Paris.

From an academic point of view, Alejandro Quiroga's recent biographical study has delved comprehensively into the complexity and contradictions of the dictator. He concluded that beyond the crude myth of being a mere paternalist leader, Primo de Rivera's nationalism was an original approach. He pursued the salvation, regeneration, and indoctrination of Spaniards not as abstract concepts but as objectives of national redemption. He was also an innovator in the use of a populist rhetoric, which hardly served to conceal that, above all, his demagogy, double standards, and lack of scruples were part of his modus operandi. Primo was an affable man and a leader willing to take risks, but he was also corrupt and capricious, and, if necessary, willing to order the bombing of civilians with chemical weapons in Morocco.[188]

The Twilight of an Era: Alfonso XIII's Departure

Having cast his lot in with the praetorian takeover in 1923, the monarch thought he was securing his throne. In fact, he was destroying his constitutional underpinnings and aligning his fate with that regime. Romanones succinctly noted: 'these long seven years had a profound impact. It destroyed the foundations of the monarchist state as well as the prestige of the king. Simultaneously, the dynastic parties were in disarray after receiving constant criticism and scorn'.[189]

Showing a clear divorce from the national will, the king entrusted power to another general, Dámaso Berenguer, then head of the Royal Military Household, with instructions to dismantle gradually Primo's political apparatus and organize a return to the constitutional normality of the pre-

1923 years. This interregnum was known as the *Dictablanda* ('Soft Dictatorship'). The royal choice of a 'bayonet with a civilian touch' was a colossal error.[190] The king appeared to confirm his reluctance to undertake a thorough break with the past. Furthermore, Berenguer was one of the most disliked officers. Having been the High Commissioner of Morocco at the time of the Annual disaster, his name was forever associated with that catastrophe.[191]

Primo's sudden departure had left a dangerous power vacuum. Alfonso XIII might have believed that there could be a return to business as usual in the good old liberal times, but the stamp of authoritarian rule could not be erased overnight. The monarch appeared to have forgotten that if the dictatorship had been established because the oligarchic liberal order could no longer work, it was ludicrous to expect it to function smoothly seven years later. The political spectrum in 1930 vis-à-vis that of 1923 had changed dramatically in two crucial respects. First, the dictatorship constituted a completely new experiment; a laboratory of ideas that openly challenged the traditional liberal cannon.[192] And, secondly, the army was badly fragmented and far from ready to prop up the throne at any price.[193]

The old liberal regime was an anachronism in the much more modern country of 1930. It was a fallacy to attempt to turn back the clock of history. The dictatorship's expansionist economic policies unleashed a process of transformation that altered Spain's social fabric, and over a million people had migrated from the countryside to the large cities such as Barcelona, Madrid, and Valencia. Agriculture, although still the largest sector of the economy, fell from 57.3 to 45.51 percent of the workforce, while the industrial and service sectors grew from 21.9 and 20.81 to 25.61 and 27.98 percent, respectively. Increasing urbanization was accompanied by a similar dramatic rise in literacy, spectacular development in the railway and road systems, and the production of telephones, radios, and other signs of modernity.[194]

The reconstruction of the dynastic parties was never a viable solution. Fragmented and in crisis before 1923, they were in total turmoil in 1930. Banned from public office, their clientelist networks destroyed, and constantly vilified in the press as corrupt professional politicians, the former governing elites appeared not only as obsolete figures from a past era but also little better than thieves. Moreover, when Alfonso XIII recalled their services to save the throne, many could neither forgive nor forget that the monarch had identified himself for years with a regime that denigrated them. Alba refused to return from exile. Others joined the republican camp. Some like Sánchez Guerra, and prominent dynastic notables, declared themselves monarchists without a king. Known as Constitutionalists, they supported elections to a constituent assembly which would draw up a new constitution, discuss Alfonso XIII's recognition of the dictatorship, and debate the kind of regime to follow.[195] As old habits die hard, those dynastic notables still prepared to rally around the Crown soon engaged in their traditional petty squabbles as they attempted to revive their old clientelist practices. The two leading Liberal leaders, Romanones and Alhucemas, could not conceal their anger when Berenguer filled his administration with members of the Conservative Party. Believing it was their *turno* to manipulate the next elections, they sought to bring down the government. For them, nothing had changed and the sooner they returned to power the sooner they could resume business as usual.[196]

By contrast, the republican cause had never seen better days. According to Ángel Ossorio, even his cat was now a Republican.[197] Censorship and other arbitrary measures lured thousands of small entrepreneurs and members of liberal professions to the republican camp. They hoped to find a remedy for their grievances by opting for thorough political change. Instead of regarding the unknown with apprehension, they considered a change of regime as the best means to leave behind the clerical obscurantism and social backwardness of the old regime.[198]

In February 1926, *Alianza Republicana* was created. It comprised old political formations such as Lerroux's Radical Party and new forces led by younger leaders whose programmes included social and economic measures that would appeal to the lower classes. Manuel Azaña, President of the *Ateneo*, Madrid's cultural centre, stood out among this new generation. The alliance sought to minimize differences and collaborate on common goals: engage in a campaign that could lead to the summoning of a Constituent *Cortes* and the establishment of a modern and progressive Republic.[199]

With the gradual return of civil liberties of expression and association in 1930, the Republicans went on the offensive. Unlike the monarchists clinging to the old clientelist system, they excelled at the new reality of mass politics, attracting thousands of people to rallies in which Alfonso XIII was accused of perjury by violating his own constitution and supporting the Dictatorship. That campaign benefited enormously from the constant defections of former monarchists who joined the republican bandwagon, such as Niceto Alcalá Zamora, leader of one of the factions of the Liberal Party, and Antonio Maura's son, Miguel.

On 17 August 1930, representatives of different republican groups, Catalan nationalists, and the Socialists Indalecio Prieto and Fernando de los Ríos, met in San Sebastian where they agreed to collaborate in an electoral campaign to bring about a Constituent *Cortes* that would lead to the proclamation of a republic and grant autonomy to Catalonia. In October, a provisional government was established. The Socialists acquired three portfolios while diverse republican parties shared the rest. To dissipate the fear among the middle classes that a republican takeover would mean a complete social revolution, the crucial posts of prime minister and interior minister were taken by Alcalá Zamora and Miguel Maura, respectively. According to the latter, they offered a 'mattress' upon which the new regime would land softly; a system of order avoiding demagogy and anarchy while filling the dangerous power vacuum created by the disintegration of the monarchy.[200]

Nevertheless, feeling the national mood for radical change, the Provisional Government also engaged in revolutionary activity to accelerate the demise of the old order. They believed that the Berenguer administration, rocked by growing industrial action and students' protests, would collapse with a mere show of force. Also, they did not want to be overtaken by the subversive activities of discontented officers in collusion with the rapidly expanding CNT after its legalization the previous April. After many hesitations and postponements, an insurrection was organized for 15 December 1930. Chastened by the bitter memories of 1917, the Socialists proceeded cautiously waiting for the military to show their hand before committing themselves. However, three days before the agreed date, the impulsive Captain Fermín Galán jumped the gun and rebelled in the isolated northern garrison of Jaca (Huesca), near the French border. Upset by so many vacillations, he believed that his daring action would be the spark to ignite an all-embracing movement. Being aware of Galán's intentions, the Provisional Government sent one of its members, the Galician republican Santiago Casares Quiroga, to stop him but he arrived too late. The following day, troops sent from Zaragoza defeated Galán's small detachment. He and his second in command were tried and summarily executed. Most compromised officers remained passive, except for a minority who, after seizing the airbase of Cuatro Vientos outside Madrid, confined their actions to flying over the capital and dropping leaflets before escaping abroad. The members of the Provisional Government were arrested or went into hiding.[201]

The insurrection of 15 December was an utter disaster. However, despite its failure, it contributed to undermining the regime. The Republic now had its martyrs and Alfonso XIII could be presented as a cruel monarch willing to consolidate his reign by any means. Additionally, the revolt revealed that elements in the military were no longer plotting against the Dictatorship but the dynasty itself.

Berenguer's hopes to restore normality were dashed in February 1931. Ironically, having survived the December revolution, it was political abstention that brought down the government. The Liberal notables delivered the final blow when they refused to participate in the elections since the Conservatives would be the group to benefit from it. Berenguer had no alternative but to resign.[202] Realizing that the power vacuum was endangering the throne, the king entrusted Sánchez Guerra, hitherto one of his most bitter critics, with the creation of a new cabinet. This move, which might have been appropriate one year earlier, now smacked of despair. Indeed, Sánchez Guerra hurried to prison to offer the bewildered members of the Provisional Government portfolios in his cabinet. It was either an extremely cunning move to incorporate – or at least split – the opposition, or the final proof of monarchist desperation. Once they got over their initial surprise, the prisoners declined. By asking for their collaboration, Sánchez Guerra indicated the precariousness of the monarchy.[203]

On 18 February, a new national government was announced. However, it was considered a feeble alternative compared with the initially acclaimed administration of Maura in 1918. It included old notables (Romanones, Alhucemas, Cierva), representatives of the financial and landowning elites, and two declining forces: the *Lliga*, gravely affected by its initial support of the Dictatorship, and those fragments of *Maurismo* led by Gabriel Maura who had not deserted the monarchy.[204] Thus, the survival of the existing order rested on the shoulders of a mix of discredited dynastic politicians and representatives of the more economically privileged. It proved fatal: the old governing elites were gripped from the start by a paralysing mood of defeatism and gloom. Gabriel Maura, one of the ministers, described it as feeling like escorting the Crown to its funeral.[205] They quickly returned to their old habits of mutual distrust and spoil-sharing. They agreed that the hapless Berenguer should remain in the cabinet at the War Office. The key posts of prime minister and interior minister were given to two non-political persons, the octogenarian Admiral Juan Bautista Aznar and the Marquis of Hoyos, respectively. As the competing factional interests had to be accommodated, nobody could be seen to have an edge over the others. Finally, in order to have time to reorganize their old clientelist networks, they decided first to hold municipal elections the following April.[206]

While the monarchist administration offered a precarious view, the imprisoned members of the Provisional Government resembled a shadow cabinet ready to take control, receiving thousands of letters and visitors, and being treated with extreme respect by their jailors. Their trial in March was a farce. The government, eager to be seen to be tolerant and merciful, advocated leniency for the distinguished prisoners. However, the military court went beyond that. Its President, General Burguete, one of the fiercest repressors of the revolutionary movement of August 1917, revealed how times had changed. He allowed the accused to travel from prison in private cars and agreed to hold the trial in the biggest room available so that a large favourable audience could attend. Lawyers were permitted to turn the defence of their clients into a diatribe against the regime. The core of the defence was that there could not have been a rebellion against the constitutional order since the king himself had violated it in 1923. The verdict was a virtual acquittal: the minimum sentence of six months and one day. They were emancipated and greeted as heroes by enthusiastic crowds. Burguete even commented that he voted for their total absolution.[207]

For the municipal elections, the Republican-Socialist coalition engaged in a frenzied exercise in popular mobilization, arguing in their programme that the outcome would be a plebiscite on the monarchy.[208] Their activities contrasted with the passivity of the government, whose members, not familiar with the reality of mass politics, devoted themselves to reconstructing their old clientelist networks. The task of gaining the popular vote was left to 'patriotic' ladies, members of the nobility, some former partisans of the Dictatorship, and, above all, the Church.[209]

The results of the elections stunned the population. The monarchists obtained overwhelming majorities in the countryside but 47 of the 52 provincial capitals voted for the Republican-Socialist coalition. Old-timers such as Romanones and Cierva were dumbfounded when they heard of the scale of the defeat in their fiefdoms of Guadalajara and Murcia, respectively. The count recalled in his memoirs how he knew that everything was lost when even the aristocratic quarters in the centre of Madrid voted Republican.[210] As Gabriel Maura recognized, where public opinion could be expressed freely it had voted massively against the regime.[211] The rural vote was meaningless, just traditional sheep-like obedience orchestrated by the local *caciques*.

It was, above all, monarchist disarray that proved decisive. During the crucial 24 hours following the results, the regime simply crumbled. There was never even a tentative attempt to present the manufactured overall majority delivered in the countryside as proof of victory. The Crown was destined to oblivion by a group of confused politicians overtaken by a mixture of weariness and defeatism. The mood of the members of the Provisional Government changed from utter joy, as the results were being announced, to fear at the possible imposition of martial law, and euphoria at the spectacle of the monarchist edifice collapsing before their eyes.[212]

Governmental defeatism commenced when Berenguer dispatched a circular, on the night of 12 April, to the regional military authorities urging them to avoid clashing with the people and accepting the expression of the national will. The following day, the prime minister, Juan Bautista Aznar, conceded defeat. Asked by journalists, he retorted naively that there could be no bigger crisis than that of a country that went to bed monarchist and woke up republican. Except for the hard-liner Cierva, most ministers attending the extraordinary council of 13 April agreed with Romanones to inform the king that negotiations with the opposition should begin as soon as possible.[213] Alfonso XIII soon became aware not just of the demoralization of his politicians, but also crucially of the desertion of his army. Having acted in the past as the dynasty's praetorian guard, after the experience during the Dictatorship, the harmony of the military corps was shattered.[214] The neutrality of the army meant that popular will was to prevail over royal sovereignty for the very first time in Spain.

Romanones' visit to Alcalá Zamora on the afternoon of 14 April to negotiate a truce confirmed to the Republicans that victory was theirs. An emboldened Zamora gave the king an ultimatum: he had until sunset to leave the country – otherwise, he could not guarantee the safety of the royal family. Earlier in the morning, General Sanjurjo, head of the civil guard, had gone to the house of Miguel Maura to assert the loyalty of the force to the Republic.[215] Slowly but steadily, unchallenged enthusiastic crowds began to pack the streets of the main cities. One town after another proclaimed the

Republic. Nobody stood to defend the regime. On 14 April, the monarchy was no more. Miguel Maura noted: 'power lay in the gutter, we only had to pick it up'.[216]

The Second Republic represented the culmination of a process of political modernization. The Dictatorship in 1923 offered an alternative of regeneration from above, but its failure cleared the way for the initiative from below. While the members of the Provisional Government were taking possession of the official buildings, Alfonso XIII, the symbol of a past era, was on his way to exile swept away by the tide of history.

Notes

1 David Stevenson, *Cataclysm: The First World War as Political Tragedy* (New York: Basic Books, 2005), pp. 442–3.

2 Eric J. Hobsbawm, *Age of Extremes: The Short Twentieth Century, 1914–91* (London: Penguin, 1994), pp. 6–7.

3 Martin Blinkhorn, 'Introduction: Allies, Rivals or Antagonists? Fascists and Conservatives in Modern Europe', in Martin Blinkhorn (ed.), *Fascists and Conservatives* (London: Unwin Hyman, 1990), p. 3.

4 Francisco J. Romero Salvadó, 'Spain and the First World War: The Logic of Neutrality', *War in History,* 26/1 (2019), p. 46.

5 Maura and Fernández Almagro, *Por qué cayó Alfonso XIII*, pp. 472–3.

6 Gerald Meaker, 'A Civil War of Words', in Hans A. Schmitt (ed.), *Neutral Europe between War and Revolution, 1917–1923* (Charlottesville, VA: University of Virginia Press, 1988), pp. 1–2.

7 Pedro Gual Villalbi, *Memorias de un industrial de nuestro tiempo* (Barcelona: Sociedad General de Publicaciones, 1923), pp. 102–3.

8 Meaker, 'A Civil War of Words', pp. 1–31; Maximiliano Fuentes Codera, *España en la Primera Guerra Mundial: una movilización cultural* (Madrid: Akal, 2014), pp. 61–111.

9 Francisco J. Romero Salvadó, *Spain, 1914–1918: Between War and Revolution* (London: Routledge, 1999), pp. 10–11.

10 José Luis García Delgado (ed.), *La modernización económica en la España de Alfonso XIII* (Madrid: Espasa, 2002), pp. 108–22.

11 Gual Villalbi, *Memorias*, pp. 104–21.

12 Instituto de Reformas Sociales, *Movimiento de los precios al por menor durante la guerra y la posguerra, 1914–1922* (Madrid: Sobrinos de la Sociedad de M. Minuesa, 1923), pp. 10–21.

13 Francisco J. Romero Salvadó, 'The Great War and the Crisis of Liberalism in Spain, 1916–17', *Historical Journal*, 46/4 (2003), p. 895.

14 Mercedes Cabrera, Francisco Comín, and José Luis García Delgado, *Santiago Alba. Un programa de reforma económica en la España del primer tercio del siglo XX* (Madrid: Instituto de Estudios Fiscales, 1989).

15　Francesc Cambó, *Memorias* (Madrid: Alianza, 1987), pp. 223–6.
16　Jesús Pabón, *Cambó, 1876–1947* (Barcelona: Alpha, 1999 [1952–1968]), pp. 359–63; Charles E. Ehrlich, '*Per Catalunya i l'Espanya Gran*: Catalan Regionalism on the Offensive, 1911–1919', *European History Quarterly*, 28/2 (1998), pp. 190–1.
17　Romero Salvadó, *Spain, 1914–1918*, pp. 46–7.
18　Cabrera, Comín, and García Delgado, *Santiago Alba*, pp. 375–422.
19　Cambó, *Memorias*, pp. 234–40.
20　Cabrera, Comín, and García Delgado, *Santiago Alba*, p. 223.
21　Gerald Meaker, *The Revolutionary Left in Spain 1914–23* (Stanford, CA: Stanford University Press, 1974), pp. 39–42.
22　Andrés Saborit, *Julián Besteiro* (México: Pablo Iglesias, 1961), pp. 90–1.
23　Ángel Pestaña, *Lo que aprendí en la vida* (Murcia: Zero, 1971 [1933]), vol. 1, p. 59.
24　Andrés Saborit, *Asturias y sus hombres* (Toulouse: UGT, 1963), pp. 162–4.
25　Francisco Villacorta Baños, *Profesionales y burócratas. Estado y poder corporativo en la España del Siglo XX, 1890–1923* (Madrid: Siglo XXI, 1989), pp. 372–3.
26　Carolyn P. Boyd, *Praetorian Politics in Liberal Spain* (Chapel Hill, NC: University of North Carolina Press, 1979), pp. 51–5.
27　Benito Márquez and José María Capó, *Las Juntas Militares de Defensa* (La Habana: Porvenir, 1923), pp. 23–5.
28　Alberto Bru Sánchez-Fortún, 'Para repensar la Juntas Militares de 1917', *Hispania*, LXXVI/252 (2016), pp. 190–1.
29　Conde de Romanones, *Notas de una vida, 1912–1931* (Madrid: Marcial Pons, 1999 [1934]), p. 379.
30　Francisco J. Romero Salvadó, 'Fatal Neutrality: Pragmatism or Capitulation? Spain's Foreign Policy during the Great War', *European History Quarterly*, 33 (2003), p. 295.
31　Fernando García Sanz, *España en la Gran Guerra. Espías, diplomáticos y traficantes* (Madrid: Galaxia Gutenberg, 2014), p. 70.
32　Anne Rosenbusch, 'Total War in Neutral Territory: German Activity in Spain during the First World War', *Hispania Nova*, 15 (2017), pp. 364–70.
33　On 17 August 1915, *El Isidoro* was the first Spanish ship to be sunk. Jesús Perea Ruiz, 'Guerra submarina en España', *Espacio, Tiempo y Forma*, 16 (2004), pp. 193–229.
34　García Sanz, *España en la Gran Guerra*, pp. 209–14.
35　Ron M. Carden, *German Policy Toward Neutral Spain, 1914–18* (New York: Garland, 1987), pp. 64–86; Eduardo González Calleja and Paul Aubert, *Nidos de espías. España, Francia y la Primera Guerra Mundial* (Madrid: Alianza, 2014), pp. 239–65; Javier Ponce, 'Propaganda and Politics: Germany and Spanish Public Opinion', in Troy R.E. Paddock (ed.), *World War I and Propaganda* (Leiden: Brill, 2014), pp. 293–321.

36 *El Socialista*, 'The Proletariat Speaks to the Nation' (28 March 1917).
37 The United States broke relations with Germany on 3 February and entered the war on 6 April. Some Latin American countries (Peru, Bolivia, Brazil, etc.) followed suit.
38 Moreno Luzón, *Romanones*, p. 339.
39 Conde de Romanones, *Notas de una vida*, pp. 412–15.
40 José Buxadé, *España en crisis. La bullanga misteriosa de 1917* (Barcelona: Bauzá, 1917), pp. 43–59.
41 Villacorta Baños, *Profesionales y burócratas*, pp. 374–8; Ana I. Alonso Ibáñez, 'Las Juntas de Defensa de las clases de tropa, 1917–18', *Cuadernos de Historia Contemporánea*, 21 (1999), pp. 259–78.
42 *El Heraldo de Madrid*, 'The Revolution Has Begun' (6 June 1917).
43 Gabriel Cardona, *El poder militar en la España contemporánea hasta la guerra civil* (Madrid: Siglo XXI, 1983), p. 60.
44 Meaker, *The Revolutionary Left*, p. 69.
45 Juan Antonio Lacomba, *La crisis española de 1917* (Málaga: Ciencia Nueva, 1970), p. 201.
46 Luis Simarro, *Los sucesos de agosto en el parlamento* (Madrid: LIF, 1918), pp. 365–79.
47 Maura and Fernández Almagro, *Por qué cayó Alfonso XIII*, p. 302.
48 Francisco J. Romero Salvadó, 'Antonio Maura: From Messiah to Fireman', in Alejandro Quiroga and Miguel Ángel del Arco Blanco (eds.), *Right-Wing Spain in the Civil War Era: Soldiers of God and Apostles of the Fatherland* (London: Continuum, 2012), pp. 10–12.
49 Francisco J. Romero Salvadó, 'Spain's Revolutionary Crisis of 1917: A Reckless Gamble', in Francisco J. Romero Salvadó and Angel Smith (eds.), *The Agony of Spanish Liberalism: From Revolution to Dictatorship, 1913–1923* (Basingstoke: Palgrave, 2010), p. 76.
50 Romero Salvadó, 'Spain and the First World War', pp. 59–60.
51 A former prime minister, Eleftherios Venizelos, seized power. Greece entered the war in July 1917.
52 González Calleja and Aubert, *Nidos de espías*, pp. 294–7.
53 Andrés Saborit, *La huelga de agosto de 1917* (México: Pablo Iglesias, 1967), pp. 67–8.
54 Morato, *Pablo Iglesias*, pp. 202–3.
55 Francisco J. Romero Salvadó, '¡España no era Rusia! La revolución española de 1917: anatomía de un fracaso', *Hispania Nova*, 15 (2017), pp. 437–41.
56 Lacomba, *La crisis*, pp. 260–72; Francisco Sánchez Pérez, 'La crisis social: Las tres huelgas de agosto', in Eduardo González Calleja (ed.), *Anatomía de una crisis. 1917 y los españoles* (Madrid: Alianza, 2017), pp. 244–77.
57 Saborit, *Julián Besteiro*, pp. 103–4.
58 Márquez and Capó, *Las Juntas*, pp. 68–71.

59 The Conservatives were split into three factions led by Dato, Maura, and Cierva respectively. The Liberals were divided into three main factions led by Alhucemas, Romanones, and Alba respectively, together with two smaller ones headed by Rafael Gasset and Niceto Alcalá.

60 Lacomba, *La crisis*, p. 287; Meaker, *The Revolutionary Left*, p. 63.

61 Lacomba, *La crisis*, pp. 315–18.

62 Francisco J. Romero Salvadó, *The Foundations of Civil War: Revolution, Social Conflict and Reaction in Liberal Spain, 1916–1923* (London: Routledge, 2008), pp. 102–3.

63 It imposed the closed scale, increased the war budget by over 90 million for officers' salaries to the detriment of modernization and efficiency, and worsened the chronic top-heavy organizational structure by increasing the number of divisions from 14 to 16. Boyd, *Praetorian Politics*, pp. 102–4.

64 National Archives, *Foreign Office Papers* (FO), Intelligence Department (3 April 1918).

65 Romanones, *Notas de una vida*, pp. 421–2, claimed that it was his idea. He convinced Alfonso XIII to summon all the dynastic leaders, on the night of 21 March, and threaten them with his abdication if they were not prepared to collaborate.

66 The *Maurista* Cesar Silió coined the term 'fireman' to describe how Maura was only recalled to power in those grave situations in which 'a fire needed to be put out'. Cited in González Hernández, *Ciudadanía*, p. 117.

67 Fernández Almagro, *Historia*, p. 267.

68 Robert Gerwarth, *The Vanquished: Why the First World War Failed to End, 1917–1923* (London: Penguin, 2016), p. 7; Mayer, *The Persistence of the Old Regime*, p. 14.

69 Robert Service, *Comrades – Communism: A World History* (Basingstoke: Macmillan, 2007), p. 85.

70 Kevin McDermott and Jeremy Agnew, *The Comintern: A History of International Communism from Lenin to Stalin* (London: Macmillan, 1996), pp. 13–14.

71 Instituto de Reformas Sociales, *Movimiento*, pp. 10–11. Overall prices between 1914 and 1918 shot up by 72.8 percent in the cities and 61.8 percent in the countryside, while salaries increased by only 25.6 and 35.1 percent for the average male and female worker, respectively.

72 Francisco Cobo Romero, 'The Red Dawn of the Andalusian Countryside: Peasant Protest during the Bolshevik Triennium, 1918–1920', in Romero Salvadó and Smith (eds.), *The Agony of Spanish Liberalism*, pp. 121–37; Jacques Maurice, 'A propósito del Trienio Bolchevique', in José Luis García Delgado (ed.), *La crisis de la Restauración: España entre la Primera Guerra Mundial y la II República* (Madrid: Siglo XXI, 1986), pp. 337–47.

73 José Luis Martín Ramos, *Historia de la UGT, vol. 2: Entre la revolución y el reformismo, 1914–1931* (Madrid: Siglo XXI, 2008), p. 229: there were a record 1,060 strikes in 1920.

74 Radcliff, 'Women's Politics', p. 303.

75 Lester Golden, 'The Women in Command: The Barcelona Women's Consumer War of 1918', *UCLA Historical Journal,* 6 (1985), pp. 5–32.

76 Rosa María Capel, 'Life and Work in the Tobacco Factories: Female Industrial Workers in the Early Twentieth Century', in Enders and Radcliff (eds.), *Constructing Spanish Woman hood,* p. 146.

77 Confederación Nacional del Trabajo, *Memoria del Congreso celebrado en el Teatro de la Comedia de Madrid, los días 10 al 18 de diciembre de 1919* (Barcelona: Cosmos, 1932), pp. 372–4.

78 Manabendra Nath Roy, *Memoirs* (London: George Allen & Unwin, 1964), pp. 223–36; Charles Shipman, *It Had to be Revolution: Memoirs of an American Radical* (Ithaca, NY: Cornell University Press, 1993), pp. 86–97; Francisco J. Romero Salvadó, 'The Comintern Fiasco in Spain: The Borodin Mission and the Birth of the Spanish Communist Party', *Revolutionary Russia,* 21/2 (2008), pp. 159–63; Juan Avilés Farré, *La fe que vino de Rusia: la revolución bolchevique y los españoles, 1917–1931* (Madrid: Biblioteca Nueva, 1999), pp. 116–24.

79 Ibid., pp. 56–8.

80 Chris Ealham, 'An Impossible Unity: Revolution, Reform and Counter-Revolution and the Spanish Left, 1917–23', in Romero and Smith (eds.), *The Agony of Spanish Liberalism,* pp. 101–5.

81 Francisco J. Romero Salvadó, 'The Views of an Anarcho-Syndicalist on the Soviet Union: The Defeat of the Third International in Spain', *Revolutionary Russia,* 8/1 (1995), pp. 26–103. A lucid analysis of the divorce between the CNT and the Comintern can be found in Arturo Zoffmann's article, 'An Uncanny Honeymoon: Spanish Anarchism and the Bolshevik Dictatorship of the Proletariat, 1917–22', *International Labour and Working Class History,* 94 (2018), pp. 1–26.

82 Meaker, *The Revolutionary Left,* p. 483.

83 Ealham, *Class, Culture and Conflict in Barcelona,* p. 36.

84 This figure is the product of my own calculations based on the data in Confederación Nacional del Trabajo, *Memoria,* pp. 9–34. In its 14th national congress (June 1920), the UGT had 211,312 militants.

85 Pere Gabriel, 'Red Barcelona in the Europe of War and Revolution, 1914–30', in Angel Smith (ed.), *Red Barcelona: Social Protest and Labour Mobilization in the Twentieth Century* (London: Routledge, 2002), pp. 40–52.

86 Confederación Regional del Trabajo, *Memoria del Congreso celebrado en Barcelona, los días 28, 29, 30 de junio y el 1 de julio de 1918* (Barcelona: CRT, 1918), pp. 26–78; Angel Smith, *Anarchism, Revolution and Reaction: Catalan Labour and the Crisis of the Spanish State, 1898–1923* (Oxford: Berghahn, 2007), pp. 240–1.

87 Smith, *Anarchism, Revolution and Reaction,* pp. 292–5.

88 Confederación Nacional del Trabajo, *Memoria,* pp. 16–23.

89 León Ignacio, *Los años del pistolerismo. Ensayo de una guerra civil* (Madrid: Planeta, 1981); Eduardo González Calleja, *El Máuser y el sufragio. Orden público, subversión y violencia política en la crisis de la Restauración, 1917–1931* (Madrid: CISC, 1999); Albert Balcells, *El pistolerisme. Barcelona, 1917–1923* (Barcelona: Pòrtic, 2009); Paco Ignacio Taibo II, *Que sean fuego las estrellas. Barcelona, 1917–1923* (Barcelona: Crítica, 2016).

90 Barret's murder was immortalized in a novel by Eduardo Mendoza, translated into English as *The Truth About the Savolta Case* (London: HarperCollins, 1993). González Calleja and Aubert, *Nidos de espías*, pp. 335–8.

91 Farquhar McHarg, ¡*Pistoleros! 1: 1918* (Hastings: Christie Books, 2009), pp. 158–9.

92 Smith, *Anarchism, Revolution and Reaction,* p. 246.

93 Pestaña, *Lo que aprendí en la vida*, vol. 1, pp. 79–90.

94 Helen Graham and Paul Preston (eds.), *The Popular Front in Europe* (London: Macmillan, 1987), p. 1.

95 Confederación Nacional del Trabajo, *Memoria*, pp. 261–307.

96 Fernando del Rey Reguillo, 'El empresario, el sindicalista y el miedo', in Rafael Cruz and Manuel Pérez Ledesma (eds.), *Cultura y movilización en la España contemporánea* (Madrid: Alianza, 1997), pp. 239–41.

97 Ángeles Barrio Alonso, *La modernización de España, 1917–1939. Política y sociedad* (Madrid: Síntesis, 2004), p. 36.

98 Romero Salvadó, *Political Comedy and Social Tragedy*, p. 178.

99 Fomento del Trabajo Nacional, *Memoria de la Junta Directiva del Fomento del Trabajo Nacional correspondiente a 1919–1920* (Barcelona: Hijos de Domingo Casanova, 1920), pp. 18–22.

100 Francisco J. Romero Salvadó, '*Si Vis Pacem Para Bellum*: The Catalan Employers' Dirty War, 1919–1923', in Romero Salvadó and Smith (eds.), *The Agony of Spanish Liberalism*, pp. 175–201.

101 The most notorious was led by the former police chief, Manuel Brabo Portillo. After his assassination in September 1919, his gang was led by the German adventurer Fritz Stallmann, known as Baron Koenig. González Calleja and Aubert, *Nidos de espías*, pp. 355–64.

102 Soledad Bengoechea, *Organització Patronal i conflictivitat social a Catalunya* (Barcelona: l'Abadia de Montserrat, 1994), pp. 192–5.

103 Eduardo González Calleja and Fernando del Rey Reguillo, *La defensa armada contra la revolución* (Madrid: CSIC, 1995), pp. 71–9.

104 Romanones, *Notas de una vida*, pp. 436–40.

105 Soledad Bengoechea, *El Locaut de Barcelona* (Barcelona: Curial, 1998).

106 Meaker, *The Revolutionary Left*, pp. 328–30.

107 The *Ley de Fugas* was used for the first time in June 1920 in Valencia when three prisoners were 'executed' by the civil guards escorting them.

108 Raymond Carr, *Spain, 1808–1975* (Oxford: Oxford University Press, 1982), p. 523.

109 Francisco J. Romero Salvadó and Angel Smith, 'The Agony of Spanish Liberalism and the Origins of Dictatorship', in Romero Salvadó and Smith (eds.), *The Agony of Spanish Liberalism*, p. 10.

110 Francisco J. Romero Salvadó, 'Building Alliances against the New? Monarchy and the Military in Industrializing Spain', in Helen Graham (ed.), *Interrogating Francoism* (London: Bloomsbury, 2016), pp. 50–1.

111 The National Archives, *Foreign Office*, 371/3034-186,698 (26 September 1917).
112 Rivas was Moret's closest lieutenant and later Alba's. Biblioteca de la Real Academia de la Historia, *Natalio Rivas' Papers*, 11-8904 (26 October 1917).
113 María Teresa González Calbet, *La dictadura de Primo de Rivera. El Directorio Militar* (Madrid: El Arquero, 1987), pp. 96–100; Javier Tusell, *Radiografía de un golpe de estado: El ascenso al poder del General Primo de Rivera* (Madrid: Alianza, 1987), pp. 21–3; Eduardo González Calleja, *La España de Primo de Rivera. La modernización autoritaria 1923–1930* (Madrid: Alianza, 2005), p. 30.
114 Romero Salvadó, *The Foundations of Civil War*, p. 294.
115 Bengoechea, *Organitzatió Patronal*, p. 270.
116 Romero Salvadó, *The Foundations of Civil War*, p. 231.
117 Tusell, *Radiografía*, pp. 62–83.
118 Shlomo Ben-Ami, *Fascism from Above: The Dictatorship of Primo de Rivera in Spain, 1923–1930* (Oxford: Oxford University Press, 1983), pp. 80–1.
119 José Luis Gómez-Navarro, *El régimen de Primo de Rivera* (Madrid: Cátedra, 1991), pp. 126–9.
120 Pablo Laporte, 'The Moroccan Quagmire and the Crisis of Spain's Liberal System', in Romero Salvadó and Smith, *The Agony of Spanish Liberalism*, pp. 230–54.
121 Carolyn P. Boyd, 'El Rey-Soldado', in Moreno Luzón (ed.), *Alfonso XIII*, pp. 232–3.
122 Gabriel Maura, *Bosquejo histórico de la dictadura* (Madrid: Tipografía de archivos, 1930), pp. 20–1.
123 The picture can be seen in Moreno Luzón (ed.), *Alfonso XIII*, p. 338.
124 Romero Salvadó, *The Foundations of Civil War*, p. 294.
125 An English version of the manifesto can be found in Joe Cowans, *Modern Spain: A Documentary History* (Philadelphia, PA: University of Pennsylvania Press, 2003), pp. 126–8. A superb new biography of the Dictatorship is Alejandro Quiroga, *Miguel Primo de Rivera. Dictadura, Populismo y Nación* (Barcelona: Crítica, 2022).
126 Several countries saw the establishment of authoritarian orders in the decade 1919–1929: Hungary, Bulgaria, Poland, Portugal, Lithuania, etc.
127 Romero Salvadó, *The Foundations of Civil War*, p. 282.
128 Gómez-Navarro, *El régimen de Primo de Rivera*, pp. 129–30.
129 Quiroga, *Miguel Primo de Rivera*, p. 299.
130 Pabón, *Cambó*, p. 921.
131 Fomento del Trabajo Nacional, *Memoria de la Junta Directiva del Fomento del Trabajo Nacional correspondiente a 1923–1924* (Barcelona: Hijos de Domingo Casanova, 1924), pp. 63–7; Fernando del Rey Reguillo, 'El Capitalismo Catalán y Primo de Rivera: En torno a un golpe de estado',

Hispania, XLVIII/168 (1988), pp. 294–307; Angel Smith, 'The Catalan Counter-revolutionary Coalition and the Primo de Rivera Coup, 1917–1923', *European History Quarterly*, 37/1 (2007), pp. 28–9; Romero Salvadó, *The Foundations of Civil War*, p. 192.

132 Manuel Tuñón de Lara, *Poder y sociedad en España, 1900–1931* (Madrid: Espasa-Calpe, 1992), pp. 121–6.
133 Gómez-Navarro, *El régimen de Primo de Rivera*, p. 66.
134 Tusell, *Radiografía*, pp. 230–1.
135 González Calleja, *La España*, pp. 54–62.
136 Tuñón, *Poder y sociedad en España*, p. 290.
137 Preston, *A People Betrayed*, p. 183.
138 González Calleja, *La España*, p. 63.
139 Alejandro Quiroga, *Making Spaniards: Primo de Rivera and the Nationalization of the Masses* (Basingstoke: Palgrave, 2007), pp. 36–7.
140 Ibid., pp. 93–100.
141 Quiroga, *Miguel Primo de Rivera*, p. 99.
142 González Calleja, *El Máuser*, p. 308.
143 Heywood, *Marxism*, p. 85.
144 Juan Francisco Fuentes, *Largo Caballero. El Lenin español* (Madrid: Síntesis, 2005), pp. 129–30.
145 Martín Ramos, *Historia*, pp. 148–52, 160.
146 Martin, *The Agony of Modernization*, pp. 270–2.
147 Gómez-Navarro, *El régimen de Primo de Rivera*, pp. 418–31.
148 Martin, *The Agony of Modernization*, pp. 283–4.
149 González Calleja, *La España*, pp. 216, 260–1.
150 Ben-Ami, *Fascism from Above*, p. 299.
151 Gómez-Navarro, *El régimen de Primo de Rivera*, pp. 464–5.
152 Harrison, *The Spanish Economy*, p. 66.
153 Preston, *A People Betrayed*, pp. 177–85.
154 Tusell, *Radiografía*, pp. 34–5.
155 Sebastian Balfour, *Deadly Embrace: Morocco and the Road to the Spanish Civil War* (Oxford: Oxford University Press, 2002), pp. 98–100.
156 Ibid., pp. 108–14.
157 José Manuel Vera, *Primo de Rivera, 1923–1930: de la monarquía decadente a la deseada república* (Madrid: Dykinson, 2019), p. 17.
158 Quiroga, *Making Spaniards*, pp. 148–52.
159 González Calbet, *La dictadura*, pp. 128–9.
160 Quiroga, *Miguel Primo de Rivera*, p. 111.
161 Quiroga, *Making Spaniards*, pp. 58–61.
162 Ben-Ami, *Fascism from Above*, p. 206.

163 González Calleja, *La España*, p. 141.
164 Ben-Ami, *Fascism from Above*, pp. 190–1.
165 Quiroga, *Making Spaniards*, p. 173.
166 Tusell, *Antonio Maura*, pp. 260–5.
167 Gómez-Navarro, *El régimen de Primo de Rivera*, pp. 207–60.
168 Ben-Ami, *Fascism from Above*, p. 172.
169 Quiroga, *Miguel Primo de Rivera*, pp. 186–8.
170 Joseph H. Rial, *Revolution from Above: The Primo de Rivera Dictatorship in Spain* (Fairfax, VA: George Mason University Press, 1986), pp. 193–5.
171 González Calbet, *La dictadura*, pp. 171–82.
172 Vicente Marco, *Las conspiraciones contra la Dictadura* (Madrid: Giner, 1975), pp. 69–72.
173 Fernández Almagro, *Historia*, p. 358.
174 Ibid., pp. 415–17.
175 Carlos Navajas Zubeldia, *Ejército, estado y sociedad en España, 1923–1930* (Logroño: Instituto de Estudios Riojanos, 1991), pp. 58–61, 137–49.
176 González Calleja, *El Máuser,* pp. 451–66.
177 Julio Gil Pecharromán, *Conservadores subversivos. La derecha autoritaria Alfonsina, 1913–1936* (Madrid: Eudema, 1994), p. 39.
178 Marco, *Las conspiraciones*, pp. 93–114.
179 Gómez-Navarro, *El régimen de Primo de Rivera*, pp. 303–4.
180 Harrison, *The Spanish Economy*, pp. 69–70.
181 Carr, *Spain*, p. 587.
182 Ben-Ami, *Fascism from Above*, pp. 329–30.
183 Heywood, *Marxism*, pp. 103–5.
184 Ben-Ami, *Fascism from Above*, pp. 176–7.
185 Miguel Maura, *Así cayó Alfonso XIII* (Barcelona: Ariel, 1966), pp. 28–31.
186 Navajas Zubeldia, *Ejército*, pp. 70–1.
187 Maura, *Así cayó Alfonso XIII*, p. 34.
188 Quiroga, *Miguel Primo de Rivera*, pp. 298–9.
189 Romanones, *Notas de una vida*, p. 498.
190 Ben-Ami, *Fascism from Above*, pp. 390, 399.
191 Shlomo Ben-Ami, *The Origins of the Second Republic in Spain* (Oxford: Oxford University Press, 1978), p. 23.
192 Gil Pecharromán, *Conservadores subversivos*, p. 49.
193 Gómez-Navarro, *El régimen de Primo de Rivera*, pp. 388–90.
194 Shlomo Ben-Ami, 'The Republican "Take-over": Prelude to Inevitable Catastrophe?', in Paul Preston (ed.), *Revolution and War in Spain, 1931–1939* (London: Methuen, 1984), pp. 15–16.
195 Gil Pecharromán, *Conservadores subversivos*, p. 64.

196 Shlomo Ben-Ami, 'The Crisis of the Dynastic Elite in the Transition from Monarchy to Republic, 1929–1931', in Preston and Lannon (eds.), *Elites and Power in Twentieth Century Spain*, pp. 74–5, 80–1.
197 Ben-Ami, *The Origins of the Second Republic*, p. 31.
198 Ben-Ami, 'The Republican', pp. 17–18.
199 Ben-Ami, *The Origins of the Second Republic*, pp. 68–76.
200 Maura, *Así cayó Alfonso XIII*, pp. 70–1.
201 Ibid., p. 105.
202 Ben-Ami, *The Origins of the Second Republic*, pp. 103, 202–5.
203 Maura, *Así cayó Alfonso XIII*, pp. 121–3.
204 In March 1931, the *Lliga* merged with the *Mauristas* to form a new party, the *Centro Constitucional*. The objective was to establish a modern centre-right party. It came too late to save the Monarchy. See Ben-Ami, *The Origins of the Second Republic*, pp. 210–12.
205 Gabriel Maura, *Recuerdos de mi vida* (Madrid: Aguilar, 1934), pp. 198–9.
206 Moreno Luzón, *Romanones*, pp. 220–1.
207 Maura, *Así cayó Alfonso XIII*, pp. 132–8.
208 Ibid., p. 142.
209 Ben-Ami, 'The Crisis', pp. 81–3.
210 Romanones, *Notas de una vida*, p. 511.
211 Maura and Fernández Almagro, *Por qué cayó Alfonso XIII*, p. 387.
212 Maura, *Así cayó Alfonso XIII*, p. 152.
213 Romanones, *Notas de una vida*, pp. 513–14.
214 Gómez-Navarro, *El régimen de Primo de Rivera*, pp. 526–7.
215 Romanones, *Notas de una vida*, pp. 515–17; Maura, *Así cayó Alfonso XIII*, pp. 165–6.
216 Maura, *Así cayó Alfonso XIII*, p. 189.

3

Shattered Hopes: The Second Republic, 1931–1936

La Niña Bonita

It was the massive celebrations following the results of the municipal elections of April 1931 that ensured the proclamation of the Republic.[1] Jubilant crowds danced in the streets. Republican flags appeared overnight adorning balconies, lamp posts, and public buildings. Such was the euphoria that the Republic was nicknamed *la niña bonita* (the pretty girl); a young regime full of hope for the future and free from the shackles of the past.[2] Many believed that overnight all the country's maladies would magically fade away. However, the national jubilee was not able to conceal the latent social conflicts. They re-emerged in full force once the hangover of the celebrations was over. Five years later, the initial ecstasy had given way to the outbreak of a collective tragedy.

Departing from an established knowledge of events produces a certain teleologism.[3] It is spurious to suggest that the Republic's fate was a foregone conclusion, and nor can statements such as the weight of history explain the outbreak of civil war. The Republic inherited from the previous regime deeply rooted unsolved problems: socio-political radicalism, an endemic agrarian question, a militarized public order, two unreformed powerful institutions (the Church and army), and the fact that violence had become intertwined with political expression and permeated most strata of society. In a sense, the seeds of civil war were there. Still, historical accidents and contingency were crucial in their eventual germination. Ultimately, the Republic's downfall was the result of the economic framework and political decisions. As Enrique Moradiellos suggests: 'the unfolding of history does not follow one compulsory way but flows between all available paths which, in turn, offer different directions'.[4]

The new regime could not have emerged at a worse time. In 1931, Spain was going against the current elsewhere. The Republic represented the country's first genuine exercise in democracy. However, in the rest of Europe the political trend was in the opposite direction: constitutional regimes were succumbing to dictatorships and fascism. Furthermore, the entire world was plunged into the deepest economic depression ever known. Unemployment soared, incomes and exports fell, international trade plummeted, and available capital dried up. This meant that some key areas of the Spanish economy, such as the construction industry and the dynamic export sectors of metals, minerals, and citrus fruits, were gravely affected.[5]

The Republic's advent unleashed conflicting reactions. It was perceived either as a paragon of modernization or a dangerous gateway to anarchy and communism.[6] Given the context of the global economic crisis and political extremism, the new Republican administration's reformist aims had dramatic consequences. The wealthy classes feared a system that threatened their vested privileges. Simultaneously, the impossibility of borrowing foreign capital added to the huge debt inherited from the Dictatorship's years of lavish expenditure, meaning that many projects could not be implemented. When rising expectations in traditionally aggrieved groups were not met, disenchantment began to replace the previous enthusiasm.[7]

Had the monarchy been overthrown by violent means, as opposed to the rapid and bloodless transition of April 1931, the balance of power might have been radically different. The dynastic notables lost control of their strongholds. In many localities, they were unceremoniously expelled from their posts either by pro-republican crowds or newly appointed civil governors and replaced with temporary committees. However, by deserting the king out of sheer expediency, the old regime's principal pillars (the army, the Church, and the landowning oligarchy) managed to preserve their social might and were able to act as a constraint upon change.[8] Republicans soon faced the harsh reality of implementing legislation in distant corners of Spain, where real power remained largely in the hands of the traditional elites.

To complicate matters, those who defined themselves as Republicans were divided. Their alliance had been cemented only through their common opposition to the monarchy. Once in power, they were torn apart by personal rivalries and conflicting agendas. Moreover, their grassroots strength was relatively weak and concentrated amongst the urban middle classes. Real mass support was for working-class organizations (UGT-PSOE and CNT) or Catholics and, to a lesser extent, Carlists on the Right.

Initially, the Republic was able to rely on the people's enthusiasm. The parties of the San Sebastián Pact obtained a landslide victory in the general elections of June 1931. Of 470 seats, progressive republican groups returned 180 deputies. The Radicals (with 90) became the second largest group in the chamber. Alcalá's party failed to attract the moderate vote, amassing only 22 seats. With a few exceptions, dynastic politicians were swept away.[9] The new right-wing forces could only muster 41 deputies: monarchists and Catholics formed the so-called Agrarian minority and Carlists and Basque nationalists, the Basque-Navarrese coalition.[10] Although the PSOE, with

116 seats, emerged as the largest party, the birth of the Republic exacerbated its internal tensions. In 1931, the main issue was ministerial responsibility. Besteiro, the official leader, defended leaving government to Republicans, with the Socialists on the backbenches ensuring the passing of progressive legislation. He was defeated by a combined front of two other leading figures, Largo and Prieto. Both wanted to make socialism the bedrock of the new order. Thus, the Socialists retained three portfolios: Largo (Labour), Prieto (Treasury), and Fernando de los Ríos (Justice). Besteiro finally accepted the prestigious role of speaker in the Constituent *Cortes*.[11]

The Republic enshrined a powerful demand for domestic structural change.[12] The state machinery was in the hands of a new governing class committed to modernizing the country through a vast programme of reforms first introduced via emergency decrees. Modernizing Spain entailed curbing the privileges of the Church and army, drafting a progressive constitution, granting autonomy to Catalonia, social legislation, and the long-awaited agrarian reform. The new administration believed that the Republic could only survive if accompanied by a profound cultural transformation.[13] Hence, its most important mission was a pedagogical duty: to build the symbolic foundations for a secular and democratic society or, in other words, to destroy the monarchist and clerical ties that made Spaniards 'subjects' instead of 'citizens'. The essence of the transformation was public education. This was hardly surprising given the presence of so many intellectuals (university professors, writers, journalists, etc.) in the first Constituent *Cortes*.[14] Indeed, an education that stressed independent thinking, freedom from religious indoctrination, and rejection of hierarchy would perform the double function of preparing people for the new society and helping to build its foundations.[15] Schoolteachers would be the main force of this democratic revolution, transporting 'modern', civic values to the furthest corners of Spain. A laudable republican achievement was the commitment to, and financial investment in, public education, entailing the creation of new schools and teaching posts between 1931 and 1933.[16]

Simultaneously, the minister for war, Manuel Azaña, leader of a small progressive party (*Acción Republicana*), pursued the crucial task of transforming the armed forces from the monarchy's praetorian guard into a professional apolitical institution. His reforms included the abolition of the Law of Jurisdictions of 1906, the obligation of officers to take an oath of loyalty to the new regime or face discharge, and the re-opening of the question of 'responsibilities' for the disaster in Morocco. Also, measures to deal with the inflated officer corps were approved, including encouraging senior officers to take early retirement on full pay (over 10,000 accepted the offer). Promotion by war merits was frozen and some awarded during the previous years were revised downwards, infuriating colonial officers.[17]

The Socialists' foremost concern was legislation to ameliorate workers' conditions. Largo, helped by de los Ríos, devised a salient range of measures. Salaries were increased and rents were frozen so that, in a deflationary period, real wages for urban workers increased by 16 percent between 1931 and 1933, while those in the countryside virtually doubled.[18] Employees obtained seven paid days of holidays per annum and their right to strike could not lead to dismissal. There were other advances in the field of social security, such as maternity, retirement, and insurance against labour accidents. Reforms were also intended to challenge the rural oligarchy's ancestral power.[19] Primo's arbitration committees, re-named *jurados mixtos*, were extended to rural Spain. The eight-hour working day was to be applied to all professions. Two laws were introduced to improve the miserable lot of the landless peasantry: the Law of Municipal Boundaries (which forbade employers to hire outside labour in favour of local workers, so preventing strike-breaking) and that of Obligatory Cultivation (forcing owners, under penalty of confiscation, to cultivate their land).[20]

In December 1931, the approval of a new constitution marked the crowning of this period of reformist zeal. Spain was defined as a 'republic of workers of all categories' and a democratic and potentially decentralized regime. Individual rights, including the protection of private property, were recognized, but Article 44 accepted the possibility of expropriation on grounds of social utility. Two controversial issues, the concession of home rule and the awaited agrarian reform, were endorsed, but parliament was to legislate the details. Elections were to be conducted by universal secret suffrage. At that point, however, it had still to be determined whether women would be allowed to vote. There was to be a single lower chamber and a Tribunal of Constitutional Guarantees to determine the constitutionality of laws and mediate in any conflicts between the central and future autonomous governments. Parliament was to elect for a term of six years the president of the Republic, who could appoint and remove prime ministers, dissolve the chamber twice, and play an advisory role in the matter of legislation. The constitution was approved by an overwhelming majority of deputies (385 out of 470). The anti-republican forces did not vote. They simply sought to oust the Republic as soon as possible.[21]

The new regime was prepared to satisfy the claims of peripheral nationalists. This helped avoid a clash with the new hegemonic Catalan force, *Esquerra Republicana de Catalunya* (ERC), a coalition of forces whose two main components were the progressive *Partit Republicá Catalá* and the separatist *Estat Catalá*, which included a fascist-leaning paramilitary force, the Green Shirts (*Les Escamots*). Its leaders had rushed in April to proclaim the creation of the Catalan Republic within Spain's Federal Republic. Their separatist feelings were quickly tempered by the CNT's warning that the workers would not consent to separation from their brothers in the rest of Spain.[22] After a prompt visit by a governmental delegation, they agreed to recognize the capacity of the *Cortes* to grant home rule to Catalonia.

The Republic also constituted a gigantic stride in terms of women's full socio-political citizenship and legal equality. In May, the government introduced insurance to guarantee paid maternity leave and reintegration to work. For the first time, women could stand for parliament. Three were elected: Clara Campoamor (Radical), Victoria Kent (Radical-Socialist), and Margarita Nelken (PSOE). Campoamor spoke in the chamber on the right of women to vote and hold public office. Ironically, she was a lone voice within her party and was opposed by Kent.[23] Progressive Republicans were overall lukewarm since they believed that women would be easily influenced by the clergy. Only the PSOE's resolute stance secured their full political rights.[24] Women could at last vote for the first time in the general elections of November 1933.

A Short-Lived Honeymoon

The honeymoon period enjoyed by the Republic was brief. The introduction of a wide array of reforms had two rapid consequences: the breakdown of the San Sebastián Pact and the mobilization of the socio-economically dominant classes who initially had believed that the king's departure was a price worth paying in exchange for a social conservative regime.

Moderation prevailed during the first months of the Provisional Government. Ministers sought to minimize their differences until the drafting of a constitution. The Socialists excelled in the exercise of caution. Prieto was very prudent at the Treasury controlling the budget deficit and tightening spending. Largo's and de los Ríos' decrees found general endorsement, as they were perceived as necessary to mitigate the gravity of the economic crisis. It was the religious question that produced the first real fissures within the cabinet. In October, Alcalá and Maura left the government, although the election of the former in December as the first president of the Republic served to mitigate matters. The confrontation between the Radicals and Socialists was more threatening.

The Radicals had acquired a shady reputation after a long record of financial scandals. According to Miguel Maura, at the time of the San Sebastián Pact, it was agreed not to give them any portfolio related to economic matters. However, their status as the senior republican party could not be ignored. Furthermore, the Radicals returned the largest republican parliamentary contingent in June. By then, that party had definitively buried its former revolutionary stance. In 1929, its more left-wing and fiercely anti-clerical section split to form the Radical-Socialist Party (*Partido Republicano Radical-Socialista*, PRRS).[25] Lerroux presented himself in 1931 as the guarantor of a socially conservative republic. As monarchist organizations, especially in the countryside, flocked to republican parties, the Radicals benefited the most from this sudden political conversion. Thus, they managed to expand into rural areas, where they had hitherto been poorly represented, and boast that the incorporation of sectors of the old regime served to widen the Republic's social base. The drawback, however, was that the party was infiltrated by many *caciques*, hoping to safeguard their traditional power.[26] Consequently, many local authorities remained in the hands of former monarchists bent on opposing any meaningful reform approved in Madrid. This confirmed the Socialists' belief that Lerroux was an opportunist. Still, the Radicals' main constituency remained an important segment of the middle classes whose support was crucial for the new regime's political stability.[27]

During the government crisis provoked by the departure of Maura and Alcalá in October 1931, the Socialists and Radicals avoided a public clash by jointly backing Azaña's candidacy for the premiership. However, Lerroux believed this to be a temporary measure and that he, as the most senior republican leader and with the largest republican parliamentary minority, should hold the post once the constitution was approved. Hence, when in December Azaña, endorsed by the Socialists, declared his intention to remain in power and govern with the Constituent *Cortes,* the Radicals left to head the opposition.[28] The San Sebastián Pact was dead. From then on, Lerroux's objective was the removal of Socialists from office and the installation of an all-republican government. This split in republican unity was irresolvable and left the Republicans fragmented and weak.[29]

From the start, the Republic clashed head-on with the Catholic Church. For so long an unreconstructed institution, its reform was overdue and necessary to transform Spain into a modern state. Rooted aversion to democracy was embedded in the ecclesiastical hierarchy. By 1931, many Spaniards shared a strong anti-clerical identity grounded in what they regarded as the clergy's stifling ways over their everyday lives and its unflinching alliance with the more privileged sectors of society. Particularly for poor constituencies, the Church was perceived as a cog in the monarchy's architecture of repression. This was amply revealed by religious personnel helping run borstals and prisons. In these centres and other institutions (orphanages, mental hospitals, convents, etc.), the clergy validated highly authoritarian practices.[30]

Provocative outbursts like the pastorals of Spain's Cardinal Primate, Pedro Segura, in May 1931, redoubled anti-clerical feelings and persuaded the government to act. Maura, a devout Catholic, decreed the expulsion of both Cardinal Segura and the Bishop of Vitoria, Mateo Múgica, for their 'subversive activities'.[31] However, many parish priests and even leading dignitaries, such as the Papal Nuncio Monsignor Tedeschini and the Bishop of Málaga, were prepared to seek a modus vivendi. Thus, the anti-clerical discourse and measures played into the hands of the diehards of the ecclesiastical hierarchy.

The Republic allowed divorce and civil marriage, eradicated religious symbols from public buildings, and terminated the clergy's special fiscal status. State subsidies were to end within two years and the Church had to disclose its assets and revenues which, for the first time, were liable to taxation.[32] Furthermore, a radical overhaul of the education system represented a far-reaching challenge to the Church's cultural might. In May 1933, alleging that it was a question of public safety, the Law of Confessions and Religious Congregations, banning all teaching by religious orders, was introduced. That law was self-defeating and provocative. The vacuum left by ending Catholic education, especially in primary schools, could not be filled for years due to budgetary constraints: some 350,000 school places were needed.[33] This, along with unnecessarily punitive directives (such as forbidding religious burials and celebrations), offered the anti-republican forces an ideal banner – that of religious persecution – around which to rally.[34]

Azaña was prone to make spurious comments that served to rekindle hostility towards the Republic. For instance, his declaration that all the convents in Madrid were not worth the life of a Republican (after the burning of several religious buildings in May 1931) was needless. Maura obtained special powers to deal vigorously with anyone involved in disorder and arson: martial law was declared, and the army was instructed to protect ecclesiastical property. The Socialist ministers agreed that mobs should not rule the streets.[35] In October 1931, Azaña declared in parliament that Spain had ceased to be a Catholic country. That phrase was part of a speech that called for the dissolution of the Jesuits and an end to teaching by religious orders. Ironically, it sought to isolate his more anti-clerical PRRS colleagues, who pursued the disbandment of all orders.[36] Nonetheless, even though overall attendance at mass was in decline, the Church still held sway over significant sectors of the middle classes and the rural farmers of central and northern Spain.[37]

The *Asociación Católica Nacional de Propagandistas* (ACNP), staffed mostly by former Jesuit students, played a crucial role in reorganizing right-wing politics, which was in total disarray in 1931. It was behind the creation of an umbrella organization, *Acción Nacional*, to gather anti-republican deputies. Led by Ángel Herrera, the ACNP owned the largest chain of newspapers and radio stations in Spain.[38] Echoing the vitriolic attacks of the Catholic hierarchy, they portrayed the Republic as the embodiment of godless anti-Spain. That campaign was accompanied by subtle propaganda to attract the armed forces by calling the new regime unpatriotic and dominated by reds, atheists, freemasons, and separatists. The ACNP described Catalan autonomy as the beginning of the break-up of the fatherland and distorted Azaña's reforms to make them look like as an attempt to crush the army. Particularly receptive were the *Africanistas*, who were already enraged by the re-opening of the responsibilities issue and the freezing of battlefield promotions.[39]

The Republic also faced the hostility of the dominant socio-economic classes. They soon revealed their contempt for the new regime by exporting their capital.[40] In particular, the Socialist ministers were accused of plotting the destruction of the capitalist system.[41] Urban employers, however, did not present a monolithic front. They focused their anger on the arbitration committees which, presided over by the Ministry of Labour's appointees, were seen as a type of socialist dictatorship imposing conditions always favourable to the workers. Rather than seeking the immediate overthrow of the Republic, they wanted far-reaching reform of its political orientation. In July 1933, the assembly of employers demanded the prompt removal of Socialists from the government and pinned its hopes on a new Radical administration.[42]

In contrast, the rural oligarchy was united in its quest to restore the pre-1931 social order. The countryside had never seen the introduction of social reformist legislation. Hitherto, control of local power through their appointees and the compliance of the civil guard ensured the large landowners' absolute sway over the landless peasantry. The new social legislation, although far from revolutionary, if implemented could have far-reaching consequences for rural Spain. The smooth functioning of the *latifundios* depended on a vast pool of surplus labour working endless hours for miserable wages. In addition to the threat of thorough agrarian reform, labourers now worked fewer hours and had to be paid overtime whenever they worked a long day, as they inevitably did during harvest time. With Socialists dominating the arbitration committees, working contracts were bound to be favourable to the labourers. Furthermore, landowners were no longer able to keep wages down by bringing in cheap labour from outside; nor could they conduct rural lockouts by leaving vast tracks of land uncultivated.[43] In the context of a global depression, with agricultural prices and exports both falling, this meant a significant redistribution of wealth. Hence, the rural oligarchy saw its world turned upside down. The Republic represented the loss of its ancestral control of labour relations and the dismantlement of the *caciquista* system that ensured its political hegemony.[44]

Landowners' resistance to change, which added to the hopes raised amongst landless peasants, meant that the agrarian question was the central issue of the 1930s.[45] Incidents such as the lynching of four civil guards by villagers in Castilblanco (Extremadura) in December 1931, followed in January 1932 by the indiscriminate shooting and killing of 11 people in Arnedo (Logroño) by the civil guard, highlighted the vicious character of the rural conflict.[46] The Spanish countryside was the backdrop for the clash of two diametrically opposing views: clerical and traditional vis-à-vis progressive and egalitarian. It was from there that underlying social conflicts were transmitted into national politics via the country's two largest forces, the UGT-PSOE and CEDA-CNCA.[47]

The nature of the UGT was drastically altered. From being a relatively small union of Madrid's labour aristocracy and northern dockers, miners, and metalworkers, it became a mass movement of over one million members (40 percent of them were southern radicalized peasants). The introduction, for the first time, of significant rural reforms by Socialist ministers persuaded thousands of landless labourers to join the UGT's land-workers' union (FNTT). Created in June 1930 with some 28,000 affiliates, by 1933 it had

450,000 members.[48] The UGT displaced the CNT as the main representative of the rural proletariat.[49]

Simultaneously, the Agrarian Catholic Confederation (*Confederación Nacional Católica Agraria*, CNCA) became a vast force mobilizing hundreds of thousands of small landholders, sharecroppers, and farmers. It constituted the bedrock of the mass Catholic Party created in March 1933: the CEDA, *Confederación Española de Derechas Autónomas* (Spanish Confederation of Right-Wing Autonomous Groups). Despite its inter-class rhetoric and membership, the CNCA remained a confessional organization controlled by big landowners working closely with bishops and local priests.[50] By describing in apocalyptic terms the government's pursuit of land collectivization as an attempt to deprive them of their properties, it persuaded these Catholic farmers that they shared the same interests as the rural oligarchy.[51] Already aggrieved by the anti-clerical legislation, they felt economically wounded by an agrarian policy heavily biased towards the needs of landless workers. As their prosperity depended on high farm prices and low wages, the conditions imposed by the Socialist-dominated arbitration committees effectively made their farms unprofitable.[52]

Hostility towards the Republic was not limited to right-wing forces. The Communists and the anarcho-syndicalists were also declared enemies.

Since 1928, the Soviet Union had embraced a Manichaean stance in which the Socialists were considered 'social fascists', class collaborators, and enemies of the proletariat's true interests.[53] In 1931, the PCE claimed that the Republic did not differ much from the monarchy. It was just a smokescreen to divert the masses from their revolutionary path. Nevertheless, except for Sevilla and, to a lesser extent, Asturias and Vizcaya, their nationwide influence was minimal. When the Republic was proclaimed, the party only had some 3,000 members and was marked by constant squabbles and purges. The suffocating influence of the Comintern delegate in Spain, the Argentinian Victorio Codovilla, ensured the expulsion of the leadership, including its secretary, José Bullejos, in autumn 1932. Its unforgivable error was to ignore Comintern policy and support the Republic when threatened by a military coup in August 1932.[54]

Forced to endure a clandestine existence during the Dictatorship, the CNT was in a process of reconstruction in 1931. The old guard headed by the national secretary, the veteran Pestaña, welcomed the Republic as a popular regime that heralded a period of hope and liberty.[55] However, the leadership was rapidly challenged by FAI hardliners. According to Juan García Oliver, a member of *Los Solidarios* (a legendary action group of the 1920s that contained the cream of anarchist icons: Buenaventura Durruti, Francisco Ascaso, Aurelio Fernández, etc.), the FAI wanted to guide the people towards the longed-for revolution by using the CNT as its battering ram: militants needed to engage constantly in insurrectionary activities to overcome the fear of state repression and prepare for the final offensive, a practice euphemistically dubbed 'revolutionary gymnastics'.[56]

The Republic Besieged

The battle to control the CNT was fierce by the time of its national congress in June 1931. Booed and harassed, the old guard achieved a temporary victory through an agreement to establish national trade unions. However, this was never implemented due to the widespread fear that it would lead to the growth of an internal bureaucracy and destroy the CNT's federalist character.[57] The struggle began to tilt in the diehards' favour. The anarcho-syndicalist movement was inherently suspicious of top-down paternalism, let alone state intervention, which was more in tune with Socialist gradualism. Instead, it believed in direct action and condoned in certain cases criminal activities against the bourgeois enemy, such as armed robberies.[58] Azaña revealed the Republic's dichotomy: it was impossible to deal with an organization whose extremism rejected any reformist legislation, as it was perceived to diminish the militants' insurrectionary spirit.[59]

The presence in government of the historic enemy, the UGT's secretary Largo as labour minister, intensified existing apprehensions. Moreover, Socialist collaboration with the previous regime made its cadres very suspicious. They felt that they would be marginalized in a system dominated by the UGT's arbitration committees. Hence, they saw republican democracy as a particular amalgam of 'promise and threat', since its very promise of political emancipation that might now be possible through the state threatened to dislocate the libertarian movement internally.[60]

Certainly, anarchist violence contributed to the persecution of the CNT. However, the economic crisis and the application of a tough public order policy played into the hands of the hardliners. In financial matters, the government pursued moderate monetarist, budget-balancing liberal policies. Welfare benefits and public works for the jobless were noticeably absent at a time when the spread of unemployment overwhelmed local charitable initiatives and municipal projects. Additionally, the new regime proved unable to end the militarized conception of public order. Indeed, popular unrest was met with the same unreformed habits of martial law and police impunity as under the monarchy. The civil guard remained in place, unchanged. The only difference was the creation of a new corps, the assault guards, who like the civil guard were led by army officers. Trained to police the cities, they carried small guns and truncheons instead of the traditional long rifle.[61] Throughout 1931, strikes promoted by CNT or PCE militants led to huge numbers of arrests and even, in July, in Sevilla, the use of artillery and the application of the *Ley de Fugas* to four prisoners.[62]

On 1 September 1931, 30 CNT leaders, known as *Treintistas*, published a statement condemning the extremists' reckless activities. They claimed not to have abandoned the revolutionary path but were opposed to the tactics of 'audacious minorities'.[63] However, the spread of unemployment and jobless protests militated in favour of the radicals' claims that the moderate leaders sought to capitulate in the face of state power.[64] In October, the government passed the *Ley por la Defensa de la República* (Law for the Republic's Defence), based on similar legislation introduced by Germany's Weimar Republic, which endorsed exceptional measures (including the banning of spontaneous strikes as well as the arrest of suspects and their deportation).[65] Two years later, the *Ley de Vagos y Maleantes* (Law Against Vagrants and Idlers) allowed the detention of anyone who could not prove to have legal means to support themselves. For many anarcho-syndicalists, governmental legislation appeared to confirm that the Socialist-dominated Republic sought their destruction.[66] The FAI's response was to implement 'revolutionary gymnastics'.

In January 1932, there was an anarchist insurrection in Alto Llobregat (Barcelona). Failing to trigger a movement of national solidarity, it was quickly defeated and over 100 militants were deported to Equatorial Guinea (Africa).[67] It was clear that confrontation with the state was a suicidal strategy. But, accused of reformism, the old guard was hounded out of its posts. Some *Treintistas* were expelled and others broke away to form the *Sindicatos de Oposición*, with some 80,000 members, mostly in Catalonia and Valencia. Pestaña himself founded the Syndicalist Party.[68] In just over two years, the CNT had paid a heavy price, losing half of its membership after a peak of one million in 1932.[69]

The Republic was besieged by a violent pincer movement formed by the two extremes of the political spectrum. With the FAI in full control, the campaign of all-out confrontation continued unabated. It played the game of the Right whose media was eager to accuse the regime of sowing anarchy and disorder. In August 1932, it was time for the other extreme to strike. General Sanjurjo revolted in Sevilla, claiming that he intended to 'rectify' the revolutionary character that the Republic was adopting. Badly organized, the conspirators lost nine men in a rising in Madrid and only temporarily succeeded in the Andalusian city. The authorities, alerted by the lover of one of the compromised officers, were prepared.[70] Lerroux's role was ambiguous. He was in close touch with Sanjurjo before the coup. Moreover, in a vehement speech made one month earlier, he seemed to have justified an insurrection. The cabinet avoided investigating, in the belief that it could have a devastating effect on public opinion.[71] Except for the interior minister, Casares Quiroga, the government voted to commute all the death sentences to avoid staining the regime with blood.[72]

The coup's impact was the opposite of what Sanjurjo had intended. It recycled republican enthusiasm and ended the legislative paralysis: the two key pending issues, agrarian reform and the Catalan statute were passed in September. For the anti-republican forces, the former was a threat to the traditional social order in the countryside, and the latter was the first step towards the break-up of the fatherland. On 30 November, Maciá's ERC won a landslide victory in the first elections to the Catalan Parliament and became president of the Catalan government (*Generalitat*). Agrarian reform, however, was far from successful. While failing to fulfil peasants' expectations, it terrified landowners (even though compensation was to be paid at market values). After two years of several drafts, it was extraordinarily complex and contained many vague provisions. It was aimed at the south of the country in particular (where more than one-third of the total land area and about half of its cultivated land fell into one of the categories of expropriable land) but neglected measures to win over smallholders and sharecroppers. The lack of reliable statistics, technical expertise, and capital was a formidable obstacle. The agriculture minister, the Radical-Socialist Marcelino Domingo, was good-hearted but knew very little about agrarian matters.[73] Worse was that the institution established to carry through the law, the Institute of Agrarian Reform (IRA), was provided with only 50 million pesetas (1 percent of the budget) and, therefore, lacked the technical and financial resources to compensate landowners and resettle peasants with the minimum means required to make their plots productive. In the first year, of the planned 60,000 families who should have obtained land, only 10 percent had acquired it. Yet, for landowners, this was an assault on the sacred right of property. They bided their time when they would strike back.[74]

The ill-fated coup brought about the end of *Acción Nacional*.[75] Unreconstructed monarchists, unwilling to reject the conspiratorial route, founded *Renovación Española* under the leadership of the former Dictatorship minister José Calvo Sotelo. Although small in numbers, this party had enormous influence due to its members' wealth and connections with powerful interests. On the same day that the Republic was proclaimed, several aristocrats, Calvo and other leading political figures during the Dictatorship had already gathered in the house of Count Guadalhorce to start plotting against the new regime.[76] Unlike the dynastic notables of the earlier era, these monarchists rejected liberal democracy and believed in violent means to destroy the Republic. Their position was close to that of the Carlists, who were at the time organizing paramilitary militias (*Requetés*) in their Navarrese stronghold. The monarchists financed the small fascist party: Falange de las JONS (*Juntas de Ofensiva Nacional Sindicalista*, Committees of National Syndicalist Offensive). The idea was that its squads should up their violent activity to destabilize the Republic.[77] The JONS had been the result of a merger in October 1931 between two small groups: *La Conquista del Estado* (The Conquest of the State, March 1931) headed by Ramiro Ledesma and the *Juntas Castellanas de Actuación Hispánica* (Castilian Groups of Hispanic Action, August 1931) led by Onésimo Redondo. Their programme included exalted nationalism, a fierce denunciation of Marxism, harsh anti-capitalist rhetoric, and a commitment to imposing their will by violence. For their symbols, they chose the yoke and arrows of the mythical Catholic Kings, a reminder of Spain's past imperial grandeur, and to stress their revolutionary ideals their colours were the red and black of the anarchists. In February 1934, the JONS merged with Falange, founded in October 1933 by José Antonio Primo de Rivera, the Dictator's son, who became the charismatic leader of Spanish fascism.[78]

All these radical right-wing forces sought support from Fascist Italy. In March 1934, Mussolini received a delegation of monarchists and Carlists. They obtained money and training facilities and signed a secret pact that included recognition of a new Spanish regime. Also, in June 1935, José Antonio was granted a monthly contribution of 50,000 lira.[79]

Most members of *Acción Nacional* believed the ill-fated coup was a colossal error. It had destroyed overnight their successes, stalling reform through amendments and complicated technical queries about each clause of the new bills. Their stance was pragmatic. They believed that the essential issue was the regime's socio-economic content. Aware of the impossibility to destroy the Republic at the peak of its popularity, the plan was to play the democratic game, build a mass party with which to win elections and power, and then destroy the regime from within. Thus, in February 1933, they founded the CEDA, a mass Catholic party with the slogan of religion, fatherland, law, order, and property. Led by José María Gil Robles, the CNCA's secretary, it was a vast coalition of conservative groups, including the professional urban middle classes, small property owners, farmers, and big landowners. It embraced Christian Democrats and reactionary hardliners. However, its ideological dependence on the Church and financial backing from agrarian associations meant that its overall leaning was reactionary and authoritarian. Indeed, its refusal to declare its loyalty to the Republic, bellicose rhetoric, admiration for Hitler and Mussolini, and its uniformed youth wing, the *Juventudes de Acción Popular* (JAP), made its professed acceptance of the democratic process ring hollow.[80]

Spain's radical right-wing parties, like their European counterparts, underwent a process of 'fascistization' or fell under the spell of Italian fascism.[81] They rejected the basic principles of the liberal canon and, instead, were authoritarian, nationalist, and rabidly anti-democratic. They collaborated in electoral coalitions and rallies in pursuit of their main common goal: the destruction of the Republic. A crucial instrument was the journal *Acción Española*, founded in December 1931 by a group of intellectuals and collaborators of the Dictatorship. Its most visible heads were the writer Ramiro de Maeztu and the judge Eugenio Vegas Latapié. Its objective was to become an ideological school of counter-revolutionary ideas encompassing all the strands of the political right (monarchists, Alphonsines and Carlists, Catholics, and fascists). It insisted the origins of the Republic were illegitimate and justified any method for overthrowing it.[82] Despite its avowed legalism, the CEDA worked with extreme right-wing forces. Tellingly, Gil Robles confided to the monarchist leader Antonio Goicoechea that their incompatibility was not due to political differences but to reasons of tactics.[83]

As echoes of Sanjurjo's coup began to fade, the other side of the pincer closed in.[84] In January 1933, the FAI launched its second mass uprising. It was rapidly crushed everywhere. However, in Casas Viejas, a remote village of Cádiz, the rebels barricaded themselves in the house of the local anarchist leader. They were finally burned out and, together with other villagers, lined up against a wall and shot. The final death toll was 22 – three police officers and 19 peasants.[85] Rural repression was hardly new in Andalusia, but this time it had not been perpetrated by the hated civil guard but by the assault guards. As a wave of protest swept the nation, in a blatant exercise of hypocrisy, Radicals and the CEDA accused the government of persecuting innocent peasants.[86]

Much changed after Casas Viejas. The politically charged climate coincided with a worsening economic crisis. Falling productivity and growing unemployment, aggravated by the lack of a comprehensive social security system, had a devastating effect on the building and mining sectors and, above all, in the countryside, where 72 percent of the country's jobless were registered.[87] As local authorities vainly pleaded to the government for funds, the CNT continued its campaign of violent strikes, while landowners ignored legislation and attempted to starve workers into defeat. Frustration began to creep into governmental ranks, particularly the faction led by Largo. So far, the PSOE had been a bulwark of the new regime, while the UGT endeavoured to hold back the rank-and-file, often confronting Communists and anarcho-syndicalists in violent clashes. As the depression deepened, it asked its sections to avoid strikes and rely on legislation. Even in rural Spain, the FNTT's priority was to ensure the fulfilment of the conditions and contracts negotiated in the arbitration committees.[88] However, after Casas Viejas, accusations of cruelty as well as the mounting employers' offensive began to take their toll. Disillusionment grew amongst the grassroots, as they saw that reforms approved in Madrid often remained little more than lip service. There was limited machinery to enforce them in the provinces.

The section led by Largo ousted that of Besteiro to seize control of both the PSOE and the UGT in October 1932 and January 1934, respectively.[89] In 1931, Largo had welcomed the Republic. As minister of labour, he sought to use the state machinery to introduce wide-ranging social legislation and, in the process, to strengthen his organization, the UGT, vis-à-vis the CNT. Two years later, he began to question the wisdom of remaining part of the government, and thus sacrificing Socialist credibility with the masses, especially in the countryside. In addition, particularly painful to him was the CNT's significant inroads into Madrid's construction sector, the largest employer in the capital and hitherto a solid UGT stronghold.[90] The increasing radicalization of Spanish socialism was also due to the unabated rise of fascism in Europe and the belief that the CEDA was its Spanish variant.[91]

As 1933 went on, Largo, in somewhat contradictory terms, expressed disenchantment with his experience in government while rejecting altogether being dislodged from office. Feeling that the sacrifices of the previous two years would have been in vain if he lost office, he declared his identification with the Republic if the regime stood for the reforms adopted by the

Constituent *Cortes*. In the summer, he began to adopt a threatening attitude: the Socialists wanted to enjoy power, if possible, along constitutional lines; otherwise, they would do so by 'other means'.[92]

The tightening of the political noose around the government's neck throughout 1933 increased. In April, local elections in some provinces led to victory for the CEDA and the Radicals. Three months later, they won again in elections for the Tribunal of Constitutional Guarantees. Lerroux's plans gained momentum during the summer when the PRRS, one of the main groups in the government, split. Its leader, Marcelino Domingo, was opposed by a section led by Gordón Ordás who were against continuing the alliance with the PSOE.[93] The Radicals then tabled a vote of no-confidence. Although won by the government, its narrow margin provided Alcalá with the excuse to dismiss the cabinet. His manifestly bad personal relations with Azaña and unconcealed interest in taking an active part in the political process led him to appoint a Radical-dominated cabinet that he believed it would be easier to influence.[94] But, as the new cabinet lacked the requisite support in the chamber, Alcalá dissolved parliament and summoned new elections for November to be supervised by a caretaker government headed by the Radical Diego Martínez Barrio. In the two years of Azaña's administration, Spain had advanced further down the road to political modernity than in the previous two centuries. However, such change in so brief a time caused deep traumas to the traditional fabric of society.

An Illusion: A Republican's Republic

The electoral law was designed to facilitate the return of strong majorities. In an extraordinarily complex two-round ballot, the most voted party list in each provincial constituency received about 80 percent of the seats; the second the remaining 20. Consequently, it encouraged coalitions, since a small difference in votes meant huge swings in terms of seats.[95] Therefore, the PSOE made a catastrophic blunder. Although leaving room for local arrangements, it rejected a nationwide alliance. That decision was in response to the radicalization of its rural grassroots.[96] Also, regarding the end of Socialist participation in government as a betrayal due to petty political manoeuvring, Largo appeared to believe that power was within reach once the PSOE got rid of the republican ballast.[97]

The outcome was devastating for the former governing coalition. The PSOE returned 58 deputies and the progressive Republicans 37 (only the ERC with 19 fared well, but came second to its rival, the *Lliga* with 24). By contrast, the anti-republican forces presented a united front in a well-funded campaign with modern propaganda techniques. The CEDA and the Agrarian Party[98] (115 and 36 deputies, respectively) became the largest parliamentary minority. The extreme right had 53 seats. Moderate Republicans returned 140 deputies, including 102 Radicals. Lerroux's party maximized its vote through tactical alliances with different forces, depending on the region, including in some cases the CEDA in the second round.[99]

Together with a drastic political realignment, the elections produced a hung parliament. The largest force, the CEDA, even with the support of the extreme right, lacked an overall majority. The Radicals and other moderate groups also failed to have enough seats to form a government. In December, the deadlock was broken: Lerroux presided over a Radical-dominated cabinet with CEDA's backing in parliament. Some scholars have interpreted that deal as a noble attempt to widen the Republic's base by bringing into the fold the Catholic masses.[100] By contrast, others have suggested that it merely confirmed the Radicals' unprincipled opportunism: they could share the spoils of office but, in return, they had to introduce legislation put forward by the CEDA. This meant dismantling the reforms of the previous period and allowing the Republic's enemy to win back the state machinery.[101]

The middle-ground view sees the Radicals and CEDA coming together not only out of mutual self-interest but also of common hostility to the PSOE.[102] In truth, the Radicals' shady reputation could only be rigorously applied to Lerroux's inner circle and the original Barcelona section imbued by a traditional wheeler-dealer view of politics.[103] Still, morally ambiguous though they might have been, they had voted for all the major constitutional principles. In fact, a pragmatic approach marked their first weeks in office. In December, the government crushed a major new futile exercise in FAI revolutionary gymnastics (whose epicentre was this time in Aragón), but without greater violence than the previous two.[104] Ignoring some anti-clerical legislation was wise for appeasing Catholic opinion and realistic in terms of the public purse and school capacity. The state education budget was not slashed but expanded. The IRA's economic resources remained untouched and the pace of resettling peasants onto expropriated land reached in the first nine months an average of 700 per month, twice the figure achieved the previous year. Officials in the mixed juries were no longer appointed by the Ministry of Labour but belonged to the legal profession or the civil service. This rectification, although it dismayed the UGT, sought to make these bodies more independent and not necessarily a shift away from workers' interests.[105] Ongoing disputes such as the construction and waiters' strikes in Madrid in early 1934 were settled in their favour. The employers were stunned when José Estadella, the Radical labour minister, ordered the arrest of the most recalcitrant to accept a settlement.[106]

Nonetheless, the 1933 elections dispelled the illusion of a Republic governed solely by republicans. Like the previous administration, the Radicals faced the bitter truth of being dependent on the support of another mass group, in this case, the CEDA. The crucial difference was that whereas Azaña managed to build an effective working relationship with the PSOE, this was not the case with Lerroux. Gil Robles constantly outmanoeuvred the old Republican leader, who now aged 70 was well past his prime. The Republican-Socialist administration only had a major cabinet reshuffle in

June 1933, due to the PRRS's split, while the Radical-dominated legislature underwent 11 governmental crises in two years.

Once Lerroux had accomplished his dream of proclaiming the Republic and then gaining the premiership, he lacked a clear agenda beyond shifting the regime towards the centre.[107] The Radicals were willing to revise but not reject altogether the reforms of the previous administration. However, the deal with the CEDA made them highly vulnerable to the latter's well-engineered strategy. Cabinets became short-lived affairs. They were continually held to ransom as the CEDA vetoed ministers or proposals not to its liking. Such political instability resulted in the Radicals becoming a split and shrinking force. The CEDA's next step was to join the government. The final blow was to elbow out its partners from the cabinet, monopolize office, destroy the Republican constitution, and create an authoritarian corporate state.[108] This was a subtle game that entailed the right amount of pressure to undermine the Radicals but not to disrupt the political process altogether, leading to the early dissolution of parliament and new elections.

Gil Robles' first objective was to eliminate the more leftist section of the Radical Party. In February 1934, he stated he could not support an administration whose interior minister, Martínez Barrio, was unwilling to fight subversion. Following the subsequent cabinet reshuffle, the latter was replaced by Rafael Salazar Alonso, a hardliner deputy from Badajoz.[109] Alcalá wrote that this effectively initiated the process of Lerroux's capitulation before browbeating tactics.[110] Soon thereafter, the CEDA demanded the reversal of some of the anti-clerical legislation and the restoration of state contributions to the clergy and, more tellingly, a full amnesty for the August 1932 insurgents. Given the dismay expressed by Alcalá and the Radical rank-and-file, a new crisis ensued. The solution was a government headed by the Valencian Radical Ricardo Samper which signed the amnesty. Martínez Barrio and 22 other Radical deputies moved to the opposition. In September, they merged with a splinter group of the former PRRS to form *Unión Republicana* (UR).[111] By then, the Radical Party had lost over 25 percent of its strength in the chamber.

With Salazar at the Home Office, the rural oligarchy felt confident that the tide was finally turning in their favour. It could flout existing contracts, pack the mixed juries with acolytes, slash wages, and tell its workforce that if they were hungry, they should '*comed república*' ('eat Republic').[112] In May 1934, the Law of Municipal Boundaries was repealed. This meant that, during harvest time, landowners were able to bring in cheap labour from outside to local workers' detriment. One month later, the FNTT launched a general strike affecting 38 provinces. Despite its radical rhetoric, the UGT failed to support its agrarian section. Largo stressed that the entire organization could not be put at risk.[113] In contrast, Salazar took advantage to inflict a massive blow on socialist power in the countryside. He declared the harvest to be a national utility and treated the strike as a threat to public order. Amidst fierce clashes, 13 peasants were killed, hundreds of socialist militants, including councillors and even four deputies, were arrested, and their trade unions closed.[114]

Immediately, the focus of contention shifted to Catalonia. In April 1934, the *Generalitat* introduced the Law of Agricultural Contracts that gave the *rabassaires* (tenant vine-growers) the right to purchase their land after cultivating it for 18 years.[115] The irate Catalan landowners, backed by the *Lliga*, took their case to Madrid on the grounds of unconstitutionality. This brought the Catalan and central governments into conflict over legal jurisdiction. Lluis Companys, the *Generalitat*'s president and ERC's leader after Maciá's death in December 1933, agreed to withdraw it but, after some cosmetic changes in the summer, passed the same law. Although the Samper administration was willing to find a compromise, the CEDA had something else in mind: to start the next phase in its strategy.

The CEDA's Hour

On 9 September, Gil Robles presided over a huge rally in Covadonga (Asturias). The location could not have been more provocative as Covadonga is where the mythical *Reconquista* had begun. In an event reminiscent of fascist parades, the CEDA's leader, hailed by the green-uniformed JAP as *Jefe* (chief), launched a rabble-rousing speech against the Republic. Invoking parallels with the legendary past, he threatened to start a new *Reconquista* but this time against reds, separatists, and masons.[116] On 26 September, the CEDA withdrew its support for the cabinet and demanded ministerial participation in any new government. On 1 October, Samper resigned. Three days later, against the advice of moderates such as Miguel Maura, Alcalá entrusted power to a cabinet led by Lerroux containing three CEDA ministers: Rafael Aizpún (Justice), José Oriol (Labour), and Manuel Giménez Fernández (Agriculture). The Socialists responded with a revolutionary general strike.

Following electoral defeat, Largo had declared that a republic stripped of its social reforms was no longer worthy of support and that any departure from its progressive nature would force the Socialists to go down the road of civil war.[117] This radical language was aimed at squaring a circle: in the context of paralysed reform at home and ascendant fascism across Europe, to keep Spain's counter-revolutionary forces at bay, while not risking the organizational fabric of the UGT in any sudden action.[118] Largo, although increasingly dubbed 'the Spanish Lenin',[119] was ideologically miles away from the Soviet leader. His party bore no resemblance to the Bolsheviks, as Spain did not to Russia in 1917. Indeed, fierce rhetoric was not followed by deeds. In December 1933, the Socialists rapidly disassociated from the anarcho-syndicalist insurrection. Tellingly, the UGT failed to support its agrarian federation in June 1934. The Socialists appeared reluctant to abandon legality. The red line was the entry of CEDA ministers into the government. They hoped that their revolutionary threats would deter Lerroux, and ultimately Alcalá, from sharing power with declared enemies of the Republic. Thus, when a new government was formed that included CEDA ministers, the Socialists saw no option but to lead an insurrection that they neither were prepared for nor wanted.[120]

October 1934 constituted a decisive step towards the polarization of the country into two warring camps. Based on its electoral mandate, the CEDA had a fair claim to be represented in government. Without its collaboration, the legislative process could not proceed. However, that party's leaders did not conceal their admiration for fascism. Socialist misgivings were fuelled by the fear that Spain's fate might be similar to that of several other countries. In January 1933, Hitler accepted a minority of portfolios in a coalition government and then calmy destroyed the Weimar Republic. In Austria, Chancellor Engelbert Dollfuss, leader of a Catholic Party ideologically close to the CEDA, staged a coup and established a dictatorship.[121] Unlike Germany, the Austrian Socialists called for nationwide resistance, which was only suppressed after 16 days of fierce fighting in February 1934. In October 1934, the appeal to workers to strike went together with the slogan 'better Vienna than Berlin'.

The Right attempted to 'rectify' the course the new regime was taking in 1932. It was the turn of the Left in 1934. Following the precedent of August 1917, this was the second time the Socialists led a massive insurrection. However, for all the fiery talk of the previous months, they were not prepared. A revolution accomplished by squads of militants that mostly existed on paper and with few caches of weapons (most had already been seized by the police) was an utter fiasco, except for in Asturias.[122] Furthermore, the CNT claimed that this was a political struggle and remained aloof except in Asturias. Unlike the chaotic picture presented by the revolutionaries, the authorities were prepared. Martial law was declared and the army was given free rein. With the FNTT severely mauled a few months earlier, the countryside remained quiet. Thousands of leftist leaders, including Azaña and Largo, were rounded up. The latter's role was telling. In his own words, he slept the first two nights at Prieto's house, moving then to the homes of a doctor and a journalist before returning home and waiting for the police to arrest him. When interrogated, he claimed to have nothing to do with the events. He never mentioned in his memoirs any revolutionary conclusions drawn from the affair.[123] Hardly the image of Lenin on the eve of the Bolshevik Revolution. In November 1935, after nearly a year in jail, he was freed due to lack of evidence.[124]

Despite widespread shootings in some cities, including Madrid, resistance was soon overcome. In Barcelona, Lluís Companys proclaimed 'a Catalan State within the Spanish Federal Republic', but surrendered in less than 24 hours, when the army began bombarding the *Palau San Jaume*, the seat of the *Generalitat*. As in 1917, the revolution succeeded only in Asturias where an alliance of all leftist groups, including the CNT, was established and some 20,000 miners organized in columns held out for a fortnight.

Asturias foreshadowed the brutality of the civil war. With the declaration of martial law, power passed into the hands of the Radical war minister, Diego Hidalgo. However, it was General Franco, appointed as his technical adviser, who was effectively in charge. Franco ordered, for the first time, the use of colonial troops on the mainland. Paying lip service to the *Reconquista* myth, Moorish mercenaries were shipped to Asturias, the only part of Spain never conquered by the Muslims. The colonial army's decisive role in crushing the revolution encouraged their latent messianic mission to restore Spain's real identity from the barracks of Morocco, uncontaminated by metropolitan politics.[125] The revolutionaries burnt 58 churches, including the Bishop's palace in Oviedo, and took hostages amongst right-wingers and clergymen. Many of them, including 31 priests, were killed. In turn, the troops resorted to the torture and execution of prisoners to break any resistance. The miners offered to surrender, but only on the condition to give themselves up to the regular army and not to African troops. The final toll was 1,335 dead and 2,951 wounded.[126]

After October 1934, the idea of 'republicanizing' the CEDA proved to have been wishful thinking. Events seemed to vindicate the CEDA's legalist strategy. Indeed, the counter-revolution now began in earnest. Some 40,000 Republicans and Socialists languished in prisons. Many others went into hiding or abroad. A special vendetta was pursued against Azaña, who, despite his parliamentary immunity, remained imprisoned until December (when the Supreme Court released him for lack of evidence of his complicity in the October events). Catalan autonomy was suspended and the *Generalitat* was replaced by a governor general appointed by Madrid. The employers had their revenge. There were massive layoffs, wages were slashed, trade unions disbanded, and arbitration committees were suspended. The traditional order was restored in the countryside: the Socialist presence was eradicated, peasants evicted, and town councils controlled by nominees of the local *caciques*. The clock had been turned back to the monarchy's darkest days.

In 1935, the CEDA continued vetoing ministers and restructuring the government to its taste. First, Samper and Hidalgo were accused of gross negligence in allowing the insurrection to happen and were forced out. Next, the education minister, Filiberto Villalobos, was deemed too 'anti-clerical' and forced out. Simultaneously, the limits of the CEDA's social reformism became evident. The agriculture minister, Manuel Giménez Fernández, one of the three members of CEDA whose entry into the government in October had sparked the revolution, was genuinely concerned with finding a conciliatory solution in the countryside. He naively believed that landowners could be persuaded to abandon their intransigent stance at the behest of a friendly minister. When he tried to introduce some measures to forbid evictions and favour small tenants and lease holders, his party accused him of being a 'white Bolshevik'. His substitute, the Agrarian Nicasio Velayos, rapidly introduced the 'Law for Reforming the Agrarian Reform' that effectively meant its termination.[127]

In May 1935, Alcalá's insistence on commuting 21 of the 23 death sentences for the October events provoked a major crisis.[128] The solution was another cabinet reshuffle that revealed the Radicals' decline. Although still headed by Lerroux, the balance of power shifted dramatically. The CEDA emerged as the strongest partner with five portfolios. Gil Robles seized the crucial post of war minister to transform the army into a counter-revolutionary bulwark. Liberal officers were purged and replaced by *africanistas*: General Joaquín Fanjul, a rabid monarchist, became his under-secretary; Franco, for the 'outstanding' role he played in October, became chief of the general staff; anti-republican generals such as Manuel Goded and Emilio Mola were promoted to lead the air force and the army in Morocco respectively.[129]

In September 1935, the so-called *straperlo* scandal exploded – a word that has become synonymous with corruption in Spain derived from the name of a couple of international swindlers, Daniel Strauss and Joachim Perlowitz. Having found a way to rig roulette wheels, they obtained a licence to have them installed in the casinos of San Sebastián and Fomentor (Mallorca) after bribing leading Radicals, including several ministers and Lerroux's stepson.[130] When their licence was withdrawn, an infuriated Strauss dispatched a full dossier to the president of the Republic. With the initial connivance of the CEDA, the Radicals tried to hush the business up. However, Alcalá, either for reasons of moral probity or personal revenge, was unwilling to cover up the affair. He established a judicial investigation, which confirmed, in November, the Radicals' corrupt activities. By then, another scandal had surfaced involving Lerroux himself in irregular payments from colonial funds, the so-called 'Treasure of Guinea', to a bankrupt company for former services in that colony. Lerroux and his closest cronies were forced out of office. The Radicals became a spent force.[131]

The sudden turn of events convinced Gil Robles that the moment had arrived to seize power. In December, the CEDA brought down the government by torpedoing the budget drafted ironically by one of its own members. Gil Robles believed that the president of the Republic would now be compelled to entrust him with the premiership. To his chagrin, Alcalá opted for the only other available solution: the dissolution of parliament and the appointment of one of his political allies, Manuel Portela Valladares, to organize new general elections. The CEDA's leader had overplayed his hand. In this encounter, described by Gil Robles as 'extremely harsh', the president had cunningly outwitted him. Alcalá argued that the government could not be entrusted to someone who had not sworn to uphold the Constitution. The Catholic leader replied that the president had sworn his loyalty to the monarchy. Alcalá argued that his decision was due to constant political instability, knowing that Gil Robles could hardly reply that he had engineered that instability to speed up his accession to power. In vain, a despairing Gil Robles tried to lobby Franco and other officers to stage a coup. The government ordered police forces to surround the War Ministry and other strategic posts. Frustrated in the final stage of his plan, Gil Robles was forced to fight a new electoral campaign.[132]

The Slippery Path to the Abyss

Paradoxically, at such a critical stage of the Republic's life, three former ministers from the old Liberal Party – Alcalá, Portela, and Alba – occupied the vital posts of president of the Republic, prime minister, and speaker, respectively. Alcalá intended to create a new centrist force to replace the discredited Radicals, under Alba's leadership. Portela resorted to old methods of patronage and appointed trusted civil governors to secure a sizeable majority in the next parliament. However, electoral chicanery was no longer possible in the polarized Spain of 1936. Indeed, the electoral campaign was frenzied. Both sides fought the elections as a question of survival. For many on the Left, its cause represented the defence of the Republic of 1931 against the oncoming threat of fascism. In contrast, for many on the right, it was a struggle to uphold Christian traditional values against the peril of revolution. It had become clear in 1933 that electoral coalitions were crucial to maximize the vote. However, this time the Right was less successful than the Left.

The CEDA's efforts to create a grand anti-revolutionary alliance was not entirely a success. Given the tight result, it proved crucial. Conservative republican parties could not join a national front given the extremism of its members. Intransigence towards regionalist feelings also made it impossible to include the PNV. Given its xenophobic and Catholic foundations, the PNV was initially rabidly opposed to the 'heretic Republic'. It formed with the Carlists the Basque-Navarrese parliamentary minority and even abandoned temporarily the Chamber due to the Constitution's anti-clerical content. Although closer to the anti-republican right due to its confessional nature, the latter's utter rejection of any sort of home rule pushed the PNV, under the leadership of José Antonio Aguirre, to gradually embrace a Christian democratic stance. The PNV emerged as the winner in the elections of 1933 and 1936 by adopting an equidistant position in relation to the two opposing blocs. The PNV slowly began a rapprochement towards its traditional enemy, the Socialists, in exchange for autonomy.[133] Finally, infighting over names on the electoral lists led Falange to halt the negotiations, preferring political suicide: to fight the elections alone.[134]

Building a broad left-wing coalition was an arduous task, accomplished through the resilience of Azaña with the support of Prieto.[135] The defeat in 1933 and the repression after October 1934 demonstrated the need to attain some form of unity. In April 1934, Azaña headed the fusing together of several parties to form *Izquierda Republicana*.[136] In early 1935, he began a frenetic campaign that he termed 'the recovery of the original Republic'. He banked on his record as prime minister and enhanced charisma after months of humiliating imprisonment. He toured Spain holding a series of open-air rallies that culminated, in October 1935, with a vast gathering at Comillas, on the outskirts of Madrid. Before a crowd of some 400,000 people, the largest in Spanish history, Azaña outlined his programme, which encompassed immediate amnesty for the thousands of political prisoners and the return of the reformist legislation of 1931 as the basis for an electoral alliance. In November, he invited the Socialists to join him.[137]

In 1935, the Socialists were thoroughly divided. Following the defeat of Besteiro's moderate faction, the struggle was between the followers of Prieto and those of Largo. Considering it a mistake to have broken the alliance with the Republicans in 1933, the aftermath of October 1934 confirmed to Prieto that power could only be regained through a broad coalition. However, he met Largo's obstinate opposition.[138] The latter's bulwarks were the UGT and the Socialist Youth and his geographical bastions, Madrid and the south. Prieto's strength lay in the party apparatus and the northern sections (Asturias and Basque Country). The mobilization of his sections in October was an ace card that Prieto used to remind Largo's followers that their revolutionary rhetoric never went beyond mere posturing and would hand the Republic to the CEDA. Outvoted by its executive committee, Largo resigned his presidency of the PSOE in December 1935.[139]

Largo's stance was, paradoxically, difficult to sustain, following the dramatic Communist U-turn. With the fascist tide sweeping over Europe, following an attempted coup in February 1934 in Paris, the French Communist Party suggested a tactical alliance with its Socialist counterparts in June 1934 which, in October, led to the establishment of a *vaste rassamblement populaire* that included republican forces.[140] Broad alliances of progressive forces (Popular Fronts) to withstand the fascist peril were officially endorsed in the summer of 1935 during the Seventh Congress of the Comintern.[141] By then, Soviet foreign policy was attempting to build bridges with western liberal regimes, founded on their common fear of German expansionism, in the hope of checking the spread of fascism. In June 1935, a speech by José Díaz marked the PCE's shift towards an alliance with progressive forces. Still, that party's ultimate goal was the unification of Marxist forces, hoping that its small but highly disciplined ranks would give them control. Largo's radicalization offered a golden opportunity. Consequently, in 1936, the youths of the two organizations merged into the United Socialist Youth (JSU). The PCE disbanded its trade union that joined the UGT.[142]

A Republican-Socialist coalition was for Largo too reminiscent of the first years of the Republic. However, he could not maintain his stubborn opposition after being outflanked by the PCE's new stance. Furthermore,

Azaña's appeal could not be ignored after events such as Comillas. In fact, by the time that Largo met Jacques Duclos, a leading French communist sent by the Comintern to win him over to the Popular Front strategy in late 1935, he had already become enthusiastic about an alliance that included the PCE and other left-wing groups. His condition was that the PSOE would have no ministerial responsibility.[143] The Popular Front's manifesto, accepting the Republicans' moderate goals and their preponderance on the electoral lists, was sealed on 15 January 1936. The broad coalition included different republican parties, socialists, communists, Pestaña's Syndicalist Party, and the *Partido Obrero Unificado Marxista,* (POUM, a group of dissident communists[144] not affiliated with the Comintern). It could rely on many votes from CNT militants, given the support for seeing their comrades pardoned.[145]

The electoral results were tight, revealing the country's division along political lines. The National Front obtained 4,503,524 votes, consolidating its grip over Castilla, Navarra, and Galicia. The Popular Front, with 4,654,116 votes, dominated in the south, the periphery, and the main cities. Due to the electoral system, the narrow margin of victory meant a huge swing in terms of seats: the National Front returned 132 deputies (88 of the CEDA) and the Popular Front 286 (99 of them Socialists). With only 42 deputies, the centre was all but wiped out (the Radicals had only four).[146]

Gil Robles tried to prevent a fait accompli. He persuaded some generals, including Franco, to cajole the prime minister into annulling the results and declaring martial law. In turn, General Pozas, head of the civil guard, had security forces surround suspect garrisons.[147] However, 'bullying' tactics only hastened Portela to transfer power to Azaña. This meant that the constituencies that needed a second round of voting were supervised by partisan left-wing authorities, who turned a blind eye to the violence of their supporters to secure a favourable vote. However, it is misleading to argue, as some recent revisionist scholars have done, that the Popular Front's victory was fraudulent. Second round manipulation in a few places, even if it did exist, could not have reversed, but only increased, the overall majority already held by the Popular Front.[148]

The Popular Front's victory was not greeted with the same elation as in 1931. Those at the receiving end of the backlash after October 1934 moved quickly to recover lost ground. Reacting mostly to events, the new administration rapidly decreed an amnesty and promised to accelerate socio-economic reforms. A wave of industrial strikes brought cities to a standstill. The *Generalitat* was re-established and negotiations were begun regarding Basque autonomy. Arbitration committees were recreated and workers sacked for political reasons regained their jobs and were indemnified. Thousands of landless peasants occupied vast swathes of land, especially in Extremadura, encouraged by a revived FNTT. Legitimized *post hoc*, more land was redistributed now than in all the previous years of the Republic: 372,033 hectares on which 110,000 peasants were settled.[149]

Unlike 1931, the Republic did not face a hostile offensive from the Left. In March 1936, Germany's occupation and re-militarization of the Rhineland was confirmation for the Comintern of its strategy of sponsoring the Popular Front. Thus, the PCE still talked about achieving socialism but with the bourgeois Republic as a necessary step towards that goal, rather than a barrier.[150] The Communists declared their opposition to wild strikes and urged militants to avoid responding to right-wing provocations and support the government.[151] Regarding the CNT, its national congress, held in May 1936, saw the return of some of the sections which had previously left. Still, its overall membership (559,000) was only slightly above half that at its peak in 1932. After paying a heavy penalty in the past, it reaffirmed its commitment to bring about a libertarian society through revolt, but the principal concerns were high unemployment, working conditions, and the reorganization of the movement. The CNT took part in violent industrial conflicts in Madrid and Málaga. However, there was no return to revolutionary gymnastics. Tellingly, bastions such as Barcelona and Zaragoza experienced a period of social calm.[152]

Bitter internecine fighting continued to tear the Socialists apart, acquiring, at times, a level of lunacy. In May, Prieto, accompanied by the Asturian 'heroes', Ramón González Peña and Belarmino Tomás, saw their rally in Ecija (Sevilla) disrupted by the heckling of the local JSU. Amidst the ensuing havoc, they fled to safety, their cars speeding away under a hail of bullets.[153] Tensions reached a peak when Largo thwarted an initiative intended to provide a strong executive. It involved impeaching Alcalá, whose actions had antagonised every political sector, on the tenuous grounds that he had exceeded his authority by dissolving the *Cortes* twice in one term.[154] The first step of the plan, the elevation of Azaña to the presidency, was rapidly accomplished, but the second, the appointment of Prieto as prime minister, was met with Largo's total opposition and was dropped.[155] The premiership went to Casares Quiroga, an indecisive man riddled with tuberculosis, who was not a leader capable of defending the Republic.

Largo's stance was due to the frustration experienced during his time in government. He refused to be Azaña's lackey, holding back the masses, for the second time, for the sake of consolidating a bourgeois order.[156] Largo probably thought he could emulate Gil Robles in blackmailing weak cabinets without incurring ministerial responsibility. It is contested whether he had the shrewdness of the CEDA's leader to do so. Still, for all the fierce rhetoric about the fast-approaching revolution, Largo's faction never planned for it. On the contrary, in practical contexts such as the fisheries strike in Málaga or the building dispute in Madrid (both in June–July 1936), the UGT's traditional conciliatory stance led to clashes with the more radical anarcho-syndicalists that left several dead on both sides and aggravated the feeling of overall chaos. Prieto argued that a country could withstand the convulsion of a true revolution but not resist the constant drip-drop of prolonged public disorder, with the wastage of authority and economic vitality that it entailed.[157] It is debatable whether Largo was genuine in his revolutionary pronouncements. Nonetheless, his stance meant the worst of two worlds. Talking as if a revolution was imminent had the effect of terrorizing the middle classes and speeding up preparations for an insurrection. And, by vetoing Socialist participation in the cabinet, he impeded the formation of a strong government that might have averted the military sedition.[158]

Socialist deadlock coincided with the offensive to overthrow the Republic gaining momentum. The electoral defeat shattered the CEDA's legalist strategy and played into the hands of the extremists. Their plan consisted in generating a catastrophic climate of chaos and anarchy to smear the government as an accomplice of the revolutionary fervour. Simultaneously, the monarchists led by Calvo collected funds to support a military coup. They enlisted the services of the tycoon Juan March and negotiated with Italy the purchase of a significant number of planes and munitions.[159]

The Falange found its numbers swelling dramatically with the continuous inflow of JAP members. On 8 March, several leading *Africanistas* gathered at the house of the CEDA's unsuccessful candidate for Madrid, the stockbroker José Delgado, to organize a coup.[160] At the same time, a whirlpool of violence conducted by extremists on both sides rocked Spain. Right-wing gunmen unleashed a reign of terror, including bombings. Azaña, Largo, and leading jurists such as the Republican Eduardo Ortega y Gasset and the Socialist Luis Jiménez de Asúa escaped assassination attempts unscathed. A magistrate who had condemned a Falangist to 25 years in prison was killed. In turn, left-wing zealots murdered ex-minister Alfredo Martínez, churches fell prey to arson attacks, and mobs conducted assaults on right-wing centres.[161]

Between February and July 1936, a total of 384 deaths due to social violence were recorded. Such a breakdown of public order was used then, and has been defended since by certain historiography, to justify military intervention. It certainly consolidated a picture of a tragic spring of 1936 that generated an inevitable path towards civil war.[162] This climate of chaos benefited the anti-republican diehards. In 1936, its powerful media magnified every small incident to incite the army to end this 'lawless' regime. These calls were then echoed in parliament, as right-wing deputies delivered apocalyptical speeches painting a catastrophic scenario. Their denunciations were utterly cynical. They never considered the connection between social upheaval and the decades of starvation wages, endemic hunger for land, and repression. They also forgot in their vehement statements that right-wing squads caused the most casualties.[163]

The government proved incapable of curbing terrorist violence and of dismantling the military conspiracy. Their actions were either too ineffective or too timid. For instance, the idea of sending all the suspected generals to distant outposts worked in the plotters' favour, as they were able to forge a rebel network across the country. Sanjurjo, exiled in Portugal, was the visible head of the movement. The director inside Spain was General Mola, who had been sent to Navarra, a Carlist stronghold and so ideally placed to recruit a mass following. The *Unión Militar Española*, a semi-clandestine organization, founded in August 1934, which gathered together 'patriotic officers' opposed to the Republic's leftist nature, played a crucial role. In 1936, its 3,500 members were at the centre of conspiratorial cells in every province.[164] Mola's originality was to give the uprising a centripetal character: instead of seizing Madrid first, as in the past, it was to occur simultaneously in several peripheral garrisons.[165] All the anti-republican forces were aware of the coup.[166]

The government believed that the loyalty of the commanding officers of each military region would prevent any coup, or quickly thwart it as in August 1932. Casares' confidence stretched sometimes to the borders of insanity. He kept dismissing any news related to a potential coup as 'horror stories'.[167] Ángel Viñas described the stunning ineptitude of both Casares and Azaña as worthy of a Marx Brothers' comedy. Sometimes, they even disavowed those who reported military intrigues for having exceeded their duties. They seemed to be more scared of an anarchist revolution than of a Praetorian coup.[168] On 12 July, José Castillo, a lieutenant of the assault guards, was assassinated. Dismayed by the latest outrage and following the pattern of tit-for-tat retaliation, Castillo's companions decided to avenge him by killing a leading right-winger. That night, after failing to find Gil Robles, they went to Calvo's home. The monarchist leader was arrested and murdered.[169] Two days later, at a hastily assembled *Diputación Permanente* (the standing body of deputies that could be convened when parliament was not in session), right-wing politicians vented their anger. Gil Robles noted that the government, although not to blame for Calvo's murder, was responsible for creating the circumstances that made it possible.[170] Never before had a leader of the parliamentary opposition been kidnapped and assassinated by police officers. Yet, for all their justified exasperation, they concealed their level of involvement with the military preparations, none more than Calvo himself. His death, however, provided further justification for the sedition. Crucially, it persuaded dithering officers to participate in a coup that had been underway since the Right had lost the political struggle in the ballot box.

Notes

1 Santos Juliá, *Madrid, 1931–34: De la fiesta popular a la lucha de clases* (Madrid: Siglo XXI, 1984), p. 8.

2 Eduardo González Calleja et al., *La Segunda República* (Barcelona: Pasado & Presente, 2015), p. 10.

3 Eduardo González Calleja, 'Tendencias y controversias de la historiografía', in Eduardo González Calleja and Álvaro Ribagorda (eds.), *Luces y sombras del 14 de abril* (Madrid: Nueva, 2017), pp. 128–9; Francisco Pérez, '¿Una guerra

realmente inevitable? and José Luis Ledesma, 'La primavera trágica de 1936 y la pendiente hacia la guerra civil', in Ángel Viñas et al. (coords.), *Los mitos del 18 de julio* (Barcelona: Crítica, 2019), pp. 14 and 317, respectively.

4   Enrique Moradiellos, *1936. Los mitos de la Guerra Civil* (Madrid: Península, 2004), p. 70.
5   Jordi Palafox, *Atraso económico y democracia. La Segunda República y la economía española, 1892–1936* (Barcelona: Crítica, 1991), pp. 161–73.
6   Eduardo González Calleja, 'Presentación', in González Calleja and Ribagorda (eds.), *Luces*, p. 11.
7   Francisco J. Romero Salvadó, *The Spanish Civil War: Origins, Course and Outcomes* (Basingstoke: Palgrave Macmillan, 2005), pp. 27–8.
8   Nigel Townson, *The Crisis of Democracy in Spain: Centrist Politics under the Second Republic, 1931–1936* (Brighton: Sussex Academic Press, 2000), p. 19.
9   An exception was Romanones, who retained his seat as an independent deputy in the three elections of the Second Republic.
10 Manuel Tuñón de Lara, *La II República*, vol. 1 (Madrid: Siglo XXI, 1976), p. 76.
11 Heywood, *Marxism*, p. 119.
12 Helen Graham, 'Reform as Promise and Threat: Political Progressives and Blueprints for Change in Spain, 1931–1936', in Graham (ed.), *Interrogating Francoism*, p. 67.
13 Boyd, *Historia Patria*, pp. 175–6.
14 Juan Avilés Farré, *La Izquierda burguesa en la II República* (Madrid: Espasa Calpe, 1985), p. 48.
15 Radcliff, *From Mobilization to Civil War*, p. 36.
16 González Calleja et al., *La Segunda República*, pp. 323–4.
17 Santos Juliá, *Manuel Azaña: una biografía política* (Madrid: Alianza, 1991), pp. 98–110.
18 Martin, *The Agony of Modernization*, p. 305.
19 Francisco Cobo Romero, *Por la reforma agraria hacia la revolución. El sindicalismo agrario socialista durante la II República y la Guerra Civil, 1930–1939* (Granada: Universidad de Granada, 2007), p. 108.
20 Edward Malefakis, *Agrarian Reform and Peasant Revolution in Spain* (London: Yale University Press, 1970), pp. 166–71.
21 Ángel Luis López Villaverde, *La Segunda República, 1931–1936* (Madrid: Sílex, 2019), p. 55.
22 *Solidaridad Obrera* (25 April 1931).
23 López Villaverde, *La Segunda República*, pp. 145–50.
24 González Calleja et al., *La Segunda República*, pp. 94–5, 130–7.
25 Avilés Farré, *La Izquierda*, pp. 43–6.
26 Townson, *The Crisis of Democracy*, pp. 40–9.

27 Maria Thomas, *The Faith and the Fury: Popular Anticlerical Violence and Iconoclasm in Spain, 1931–1936* (Brighton: Sussex Academic Press, 2013), pp. 2, 60.
28 Juliá, *Manuel Azaña*, pp. 121, 155.
29 Luis Arranz, 'Could the Second Republic Have Become a Democracy?', in Manuel Álvarez Tardío and Fernando del Rey Reguillo (eds.), *The Spanish Second Republic Revisited: From Democratic Hopes to Civil War, 1931–1936* (Eastbourne: Sussex Academic Press, 2013), pp. 32–3.
30 Thomas, *The Faith and the Fury*, pp. 27–8.
31 Maura, *Así cayó Alfonso XIII*, pp. 293–306.
32 Lannon, *Privilege, Persecution and Prophecy*, pp. 181–2.
33 Boyd, *Historia Patria*, pp. 178–9; Stanley Payne, *Spain's First Democracy: The Second Republic, 1931–1936* (London: University of Wisconsin Press, 1993), pp. 86–7, 121–2.
34 José María Gil Robles, *No fue posible la paz* (Madrid: Planeta, 1998 [1968]), p. 53.
35 Maura, *Así cayó Alfonso XIII*, pp. 246–62.
36 Juliá, *Manuel Azaña*, pp. 131–2.
37 Lannon, *Privilege, Persecution and Prophecy*, p. 18.
38 Gil Pecharromán, *Conservadores subversivos*, pp. 92–4.
39 Balfour, *Deadly Embrace*, pp. 242–3.
40 According to Palafox (*Atraso*, p. 180), between 14 April and 30 June 1931, 917 million pesetas (13 percent of total deposits) were withdrawn.
41 Mercedes Cabrera, *La patronal ante la II República. Organizaciones y estrategia, 1931–1936* (Madrid: Siglo XXI, 1983), p. 15.
42 Ibid., pp. 215–18.
43 Malefakis, *Agrarian Reform*, pp. 166–70.
44 Francisco Espinosa, *Guerra y represión en el sur de España* (Valencia: PUV, 2012), p. 205.
45 Simpson and Carmona, *Why Democracy Failed*, p. 157; Paul Preston, 'The Agrarian War in the South', in Paul Preston (ed.), *Revolution and War in Spain, 1931–1939* (London: Methuen, 1984), p. 159.
46 Julián Casanova, *Anarchism, the Republic and Civil War in Spain: 1931–1939* (London: Routledge, 2003), pp. 24–5.
47 Paul Preston, *The Coming of the Spanish Civil War* (London: Routledge, 1994), pp. 2–3.
48 González Calleja et al., *La Segunda República*, pp. 684–5.
49 Simpson and Carmona, *Why Democracy Failed*, p. 211.
50 Cabrera, *La patronal*, pp. 63–5.
51 Preston, 'The Agrarian War in the South', pp. 160–1, 165–7.
52 Simpson and Carmona, *Why Democracy Failed*, p. 4.
53 Service, *Comrades*, p. 167.

54 Rafael Cruz, *El Partido Comunista de España en la II República* (Madrid: Alianza, 1987), pp. 30–2, 58, 115–16, 148–56; Tim Rees, 'Revolution or Republic? The Spanish Communist Party, 1931–1936', in Álvarez Tardío and del Rey Reguillo (eds.), *The Spanish Second Republic Revisited*, p. 155.
55 Casanova, *Anarchism*, pp. 3–4.
56 Juan García Oliver, *El eco de los pasos* (Paris: Ruedo Ibérico, 1978), p. 115.
57 Casanova, *Anarchism*, pp. 11–13.
58 Ealham, *Class*, pp. 125–6.
59 José M. Macarro, 'Sindicalismo y política, *Ayer,* 20 (1995), p. 152.
60 Graham, 'Reform', pp. 75, 80.
61 González Calleja et al., *La Segunda República*, p. 170.
62 Casanova, *Anarchism*, pp. 30–1.
63 *Ibid.,* pp. 53–4.
64 Ealham, *Class*, p. 122.
65 Ballbé, *Orden*, pp. 323–30.
66 Avilés Farré, *La Izquierda*, pp. 115–16.
67 Ballbé, *Orden*, p. 342.
68 Eulalia Vega, *Anarquistas y sindicalistas, 1931–1936* (Valencia: Alfons el Magnánim, 1987), pp. 56–7.
69 Casanova, *Anarchism*, pp. 50–1.
70 Manuel Azaña, *Diarios, 1932–1933* (Madrid: Crítica, 1997), p. 13.
71 Ibid., p. 38: Azaña wrote that Lerroux was *un bruto, un loco o un malvado* ('a brute, a madman, or a villain').
72 Ibid., pp. 44–8.
73 Ibid., p. 407.
74 Malefakis, *Agrarian Reform*, pp. 172–235.
75 In April 1932, *Acción Nacional* changed its name to *Acción Popular*.
76 Ángel Viñas, *¿Quién quiso la guerra civil? Historia de una conspiración* (Barcelona: Crítica, 2019), p. 23.
77 Ibid., p. 100.
78 Martin Blinkhorn, 'Conservatism, Traditionalism and Fascism in Spain', in Blinkhorn (ed.), *Fascists and Conservatives*, pp. 124–33.
79 Ismael Saz, *Mussolini contra la II República* (Valencia: Alfons el Magnánim, 1986), pp. 67–71, 138–40.
80 Preston, *The Coming of the Spanish Civil War*, pp. 40, 64–6.
81 Ismael Saz, *Fascismo y franquismo* (Valencia: PUV, 2004), p. 61.
82 Gil Pecharromán, *Conservadores subversivos*, pp. 102–4.
83 Gil Robles, *No fue*, p. 788.
84 Azaña, *Diarios*, p. 138 noted in his diary about facing the violent offensive of this pincer movement by monarchists and anarchists.

85 Ballbé, *Orden público y militarismo*, pp. 357–8.
86 The leader of the platoon of assault guards, Captain Manuel Rojas, told reporters that he had received orders to take 'neither wounded nor prisoners' and that even Azaña had used the term 'shoot them in the belly'. The subsequent investigation exonerated the government but the director general of security, Arturo Menéndez, had to resign. Rojas was brought to trial in May 1934 and sentenced to 21 years in prison, the only member of the security forces prosecuted under the Republic. Payne, *Spain's First Democracy*, pp. 131–2.
87 Palafox, *Atraso*, p. 193.
88 Cobo Romero, *Por la reforma*, p. 218.
89 Juliá, *Los socialistas*, pp. 201–3.
90 This sector was an exception for the CNT's trend of shrinking membership. As the depression worsened, the CNT's strategy of mobilization (as opposed to the UGT's reliance on negotiation) appealed to the unskilled construction workers, many of whom had quite recently arrived in Madrid, during the boom of the Dictatorship years. The general strike of September 1933 forced construction employers to recognize the CNT, thus ending a Socialist monopoly. Juliá, *Madrid, 1931–34*, pp. 143, 170–4, 240–59.
91 Heywood, *Marxism*, pp. 125–6.
92 Ibid., p. 130.
93 Avilés Farré, *La Izquierda*, pp. 191–6.
94 Juliá, *Manuel Azaña*, pp. 261–3.
95 Roberto Villa, 'The Limits of Democratization: Elections and Political Culture', in Álvarez Tardío and del Rey Reguillo (eds.), *The Spanish Second Republic Revisited*, pp. 117–18.
96 Cobo Romero, *Por la reforma*, p. 235.
97 Francisco Largo Caballero, *Escritos de La República* (Madrid: Pablo Iglesias, 1985), p. 32.
98 Founded in January 1934, the Agrarian Party was dominated by landed interests from central Spain and collaborated closely with the CEDA. However, unlike the latter, it recognized the Republic. Gil Pecharromán, *Conservadores subversivos*, p. 138.
99 Tuñón, *La II República*, vol. 2, pp. 11–15.
100 Payne, *Spain's First Democracy*, p. 185.
101 Preston, *The Coming of the Spanish Civil War*, chapter 4 (pp. 120–60).
102 Townson, *The Crisis of Democracy*, p. 191.
103 Ibid., pp. 208–10.
104 Ballbé, *Orden*, p. 364.
105 Townson, *The Crisis of Democracy*, pp. 257–61.
106 Juliá, *Madrid, 1931–34*, pp. 345–6.
107 Alejandro Lerroux, *La pequeña historia de España, 1930–1936* (Madrid: Akrón, 2009 [1937]), p. 43.

108 Preston, *The Coming of the Spanish Civil War*, p. 5.
109 Townson, *The Crisis of Democracy*, pp. 222–3.
110 Niceto Alcalá Zamora, *Memorias* (Madrid: Planeta, 1998), p. 307.
111 Avilés Farré, *La Izquierda*, pp. 238, 246–7.
112 Juliá, *Manuel Azaña*, p. 320.
113 José Manuel Macarro, 'The Socialists and the Revolution', in Álvarez Tardío and del Rey Reguillo (eds.), *The Spanish Second Republic Revisited*, p. 50.
114 Cobo Romero, *Por la reforma*, pp. 240, 252–72.
115 Townson, *The Crisis of Democracy*, pp. 249–53.
116 Preston, *The Coming of the Spanish Civil War*, p. 165.
117 Fuentes, *Largo Caballero*, pp. 209–10.
118 Graham, 'Reform', p. 84.
119 Fuentes, *Largo Caballero*, p. 19. It was the UGT's Madrid section that began to call him 'the Spanish Lenin' by the time of the 1933 elections.
120 Juliá, *Los Socialistas*, pp. 211–12.
121 Preston, *The Coming of the Spanish Civil War*, pp. 68–70.
122 Fuentes, *Largo Caballero*, pp. 140–9, portrayed the revolutionary preparations as chaotic, with arms purchases ending in losses, swindles, or police confiscations.
123 Francisco Largo Caballero, *Mis recuerdos: Cartas a un amigo* (México: Ediciones Unidas, 1976), pp. 127–8.
124 Fuentes, *Largo Caballero*, p. 262.
125 Balfour, *Deadly Embrace*, p. 256.
126 Tuñón, *La II República*, vol. 2, p. 96.
127 Cabrera, *La patronal*, pp. 169–72.
128 Gil Robles, *No fue*, pp. 138–40 called Alcalá's initiative 'an appalling episode'.
129 Preston, *The Coming of the Spanish Civil War*, pp. 189.
130 Preston, *A People Betrayed*, p. 280.
131 Townson, *The Crisis of Democracy*, pp. 315–37.
132 Gil Robles, *No fue*, pp. 352–8; Alcalá Zamora, *Memorias*, pp. 388–91.
133 Granja Sainz, *El Nacionalismo*, pp. 139–50.
134 Gil Robles, *No fue*, pp. 432–3.
135 Paul Preston, 'The Creation of the Popular Front in Spain', in Graham and Preston (eds.), *The Popular Front in Europe*, p. 84.
136 It resulted from the merging of Azaña's party with the PRRS section led by Marcelino Domingo and the Galician Republicans of Santiago Casares Quiroga. Avilés Farré, *La Izquierda*, pp. 232–4.
137 Juliá, *Manuel Azaña*, pp. 411–21.
138 Heywood, *Marxism*, p. 152.

139 Preston, *The Coming of the Spanish Civil War*, p. 234.
140 Joel Colton, 'The Formation of the French Popular Front', in Martin S. Alexander and Helen Graham (eds.), *The French and Spanish Popular Fronts: Comparative Perspectives* (Cambridge: Cambridge University Press, 1989), pp. 9–23.
141 Frank Schauff, *La victoria frustrada. La Unión Soviética, la Internacional Comunista y la Guerra Civil española* (Barcelona: Debate, 2008), pp. 74–6.
142 Antonio Elorza and Marta Bizcarrondo, *Queridos camaradas: La Internacional Comunista y España, 1919–1939* (Madrid: Planeta, 1999), pp. 245–7, 270–2.
143 Heywood, *Marxism*, p. 166.
144 The POUM was created in November 1935 by the merging of two groups led by two former anarcho-syndicalists, Joaquín Maurín's Workers and Peasants' Bloc and Andreu Nin's (Trotsky's former secretary) Communist Left.
145 García Oliver, *El eco*, p. 163.
146 Tuñón, *La II República*, vol. 2, p. 166.
147 Alcalá Zamora, *Memorias*, pp. 393–4.
148 The most recent monograph on potential electoral fraud in 1936 is Manuel Álvarez Tardío and Roberto Villa, *1936: Fraude y violencia en las elecciones del Frente Popular* (Madrid: Espasa, 2017). An effective rebuttal can be found in Francisco Sánchez Pérez, 'Las reformas de la primavera del 36 (en la Gaceta y en la calle)', in Viñas et al. (coords.), *Los mitos*, pp. 295–6.
149 Simpson and Carmona, *Why Democracy Failed*, p. 180.
150 Tim Rees, 'Revolution or Republic? The Spanish Communist Party, 1931–1936', in Álvarez Tardío and del Rey Reguillo (eds.), *The Spanish Second Republic Revisited*, p. 162.
151 Cruz, *El Partido Comunista*, pp. 269–71.
152 Casanova, *Anarchism*, pp. 94–5.
153 Gabriel Jackson, *The Spanish Republic and the Civil War, 1931–1939*, 5th edition (Princeton, NJ: Princeton University Press, 1972), p. 209.
154 Juliá, *Manuel Azaña*, p. 480.
155 Helen Graham, 'The Spanish Popular Front and the Civil War', in Graham and Preston (eds.), *The Popular Front in Europe*, p. 110.
156 Largo Caballero, *Mis Recuerdos*, p. 141.
157 Prieto's speech in Cuenca (1 May 1936) to this effect is in Indalecio Prieto, *Discursos fundamentales* (Madrid: Turner, 1975), p. 272.
158 Maura, *Así cayó Alfonso XIII*, p. 222 suggested that Largo's veto was a catastrophic blunder that sealed the Republic's fate. Preston, *The Coming of the Spanish Civil War*, pp. 241, 261–4.
159 Viñas, *¿Quién quiso la Guerra civil?*, pp. 13, 17, 139, 179–81. Preston, *A People Betrayed*, pp. 88, 163–64, 253–4, 297–8. One of the wealthiest persons in Spain and even the world, the financier and shipping magnate Juan March made his fortune through large-scale smuggling of goods and weapons during

the Great War. Charged with vast financial irregularities and imprisoned in June 1932, he escaped in November 1933 taking with him the warden and guards he had paid off. He became the main paymaster of the subversive activities against the Republic.

160 Gil Robles, *No fue*, p. 697.
161 González Calleja et al., *La Segunda República*, pp. 1144–7.
162 Ledesma, 'La primavera', p. 314.
163 According to González Calleja et al., *La Segunda República*, pp. 1132–6, right-wing terror was the cause of 30.65 percent of the killings, 29.42 were due to left-wing violence, and 29.16 to police repression.
164 Ángel Viñas, *El gran error de la República* (Barcelona: Crítica, 2021), pp. 126–8.
165 Fernando Puell, 'La trama militar de la conspiración', in Viñas et al. (cords.), *Los mitos*, pp. 55, 73.
166 Gil Robles, *No fue*, pp. 707–8, was fully informed. In early July, he donated 500,000 pesetas from the electoral funds to General Mola (p. 774).
167 Julián Zugazagoitia, *Guerra y vicisitudes de los españoles* (Madrid: Tusquets, 2001), p. 31.
168 Viñas, *El gran error*, pp. 308–10, 358. Viñas produces a list of up to 10 governmental blunders vis-à-vis prevention of the military coup (pp. 372–3).
169 Payne, *Spain's First Democracy*, pp. 354–9.
170 Gil Robles, *No fue*, pp. 797–807.

4

The Spanish Tragedy, 1936–1939

The Death of Reason

At 5 pm on 17 July 1936, colonial troops (Army of Africa) in Morocco revolted. Impervious to the unfolding tragedy, Casares joked with the press: 'If the military is rising, I am going to bed'.[1] By the morning, the rebellion had spread to the mainland. The Socialist Julián Zugazagoitia wrote that the cabinet resembled a mad house; the craziest of all was the prime minister who neither ate nor slept and kept howling.[2]

Despite the political polarization, most people were both fearful and horrified at the thought of war.[3] However, the insurrection also opened the gates to innate hatred that had been festering for generations. Spain embarked upon a dark era whose first victim was reason. Both warring camps cynically manipulated the truth. Afterwards, the triumphant insurgents enjoyed nearly 40 years in power to transform veritable myths into widely accepted certainties. One of the most egregious was the so-called Communist conspiracy. Four secret documents, miraculously discovered in the spring of 1936 and curiously labelled, by its supposedly revolutionary authors, the 'subversive movement', exposed Moscow's machinations: Comintern agents had organized, in collusion with French and Spanish left-wing partners, a coup to establish a Soviet headed by Largo Caballero. For that, they counted on well-armed assault and resistance militias, with 150,000 and 100,000 men, respectively.[4]

Published and ridiculed in May in *Claridad*, Largo's mouthpiece, the documents were a compilation of absurdities in complete contradiction with reality. Moscow was then seeking a rapprochement with the West via the Popular Front strategy and yet was plotting to overthrow this very type of government in Spain. Far-fetched, to say the least, was the supposed collaboration of so many unlikely allies: Communists, rival socialist factions, FAI members, etc. In fact, it was a mechanism of psychological warfare intended to influence the military and moderate sectors of the population to accept a counter-revolutionary coup.[5] Bombarded daily with catastrophic messages by the right-wing press, those constituencies, not well-versed in political intrigue, could believe too well that all the 'Reds' were willing partners in establishing a communist regime. Simultaneously, the insurgents sought to turn reality upside down.[6] Instead of mounting a seditious operation against the regime to which they had sworn loyalty, they were patriots prepared to sacrifice their lives to save Spain from the clutches of international communism. There only existed one conspiracy in 1936, that of reactionary elements plotting to overthrow the Republic. While cynically claiming that Moscow was behind a sinister plot, they were negotiating the purchase of weapons with Italy.[7]

The Outbreak of Apocalypse

The civil war was the unforeseen result of a partially ill-fated military sedition that tried to liquidate the Republic, on the pretext of it being in the Popular Front's dangerous hands.[8] Expecting some degree of resistance, the first of Mola's secret instructions, in April 1936, called for the use of extreme violence to crush any opposition.[9] Still, the Republic fought back and only succumbed after 33 months of brutal struggle.

By 20 July, the country was effectively divided into two zones that resembled the electoral map of February 1936. The insurgents succeeded in roughly the areas that had voted for the National Front: the centre and north-west (Galicia, Old Castilla, León, and Navarra), the colonies, and the Canary and Balearic Islands (excluding Menorca). The exceptions were Oviedo, Zaragoza, and a strip of land connecting Sevilla with other Andalusian towns (Granada, Cádiz, and Córdoba), three working-class strongholds. They were captured through the guile of the leading conspirators: General Miguel Cabanellas (Zaragoza), Colonel Antonio Aranda (Oviedo), and General Gonzalo Queipo de Llano (Sevilla) – who, given their past republican pedigree, could strike by surprise against the confident authorities. They declared martial law, and with the support of most of the local security forces, met the poorly armed government supporters with canon and machine-gun fire.

In Spain's conservative regions, the coup found little resistance. Greeted by popular jubilation, Falangist blue shirts and Carlist red berets became the dominant colours in the pretentiously called *España Nacional* and its supporters referred to as nationalists.[10] Navarra particularly experienced an atmosphere of religious exaltation. Under the slogan 'Long Live Christ the King!', crowds rushed to join the *Requetés*. Many priests carried rifles, as they held confession and gave Holy Communion.[11]

The spectacle was different in the industrial north and east, along the entire Mediterranean coast, and the south (Extremadura, Murcia, New Castilla, and eastern Andalusia). There, the insurgents were surrounded in those public buildings they initially seized (Barcelona), barricaded themselves in their garrisons hoping to receive prompt external relief (Madrid), or sat on the fence (Valencia). Successful resistance would have been impossible if a united army had revolted.[12] Most colonels and middle-ranking officers backed the uprising. However, most major generals and brigadier generals sided with the government. Cabanellas was the only major general on active command on the mainland who rebelled.[13] The balance tilted against the insurgency in most urban centres due to the stance taken by the security corps and the air force. Rebel officers' morale plummeted when they found themselves fighting not just badly armed workers but also seasoned assault and civil guards and promptly surrendered when subjected to aerial bombing.[14]

As Hugh Thomas noted, the rebellion's immediate outcome was not the emergence of two but 2,000 Spains.[15] There were no clear frontlines but disparate and fierce local clashes. A coherent Nationalist or Republican Spain hardly existed beyond the reports of foreign journalists and diplomats.

Confident in the success of the uprising, the plotters had not envisaged a protracted struggle. They expected to establish a military junta headed by Sanjurjo and, thereafter, some sort of monarchist restoration. As with Queen Isabel II, her discredited grandson, Alfonso XIII, would step aside and let his son Don Juan ascend to the throne. However, the insurrection was a partial fiasco, made worse when the insurgents soon found themselves leaderless. On 20 July, Sanjurjo died when his plane crashed and burst into flames in Cascais (Portugal) on his way to lead the insurgency.[16] Two other leading generals, Goded and Fanjul, were executed in Barcelona and Madrid, respectively. Gil Robles was discredited after the failure of his legalist strategy. Calvo Sotelo had been assassinated. José Antonio was in prison in Alicante and would be executed in November.

On 23 July, a Junta of National Defence in Burgos, under General Cabanellas, was created to offer some resemblance of unity. However, Nationalist Spain was marked by its polycentrism or the existence of a motley combination of warlords separated geographically and divided by ideological affinities. While most generals were monarchists, many young officers were attracted to the Falange. Franco remained in Morocco at the head of the Army of Africa. Queipo ruled his southern fiefdom as a despotic satrap. Mola controlled the north with Carlist support. Presiding over them, the Junta remained a toothless provisional body. Cabanellas' past links with the Radical Party undermined his authority given the existing frenzied atmosphere. Given the unreliability of the conscript soldiers, the nationalist commanders found themselves overstretched and dependent on militias to secure the rear, shore up the defensive lines, and initiate operations towards neighbouring enemy territory. As late as October 1936, some 65,000 militiamen represented a third of the total manpower.[17]

The great paradox of the insurrection was that it precipitated the very revolutionary process that it claimed to be forestalling.[18] There were three Republican cabinets in one day. Martínez Barrio replaced the hapless

Casares intending to make a last-minute effort to avert a war by negotiating with the rebels – but it was far too late. Mola told Martínez Barrio that they would be ignored by their respective radicalized followers. Azaña then appointed José Giral, one of his closest collaborators, who finally decided to arm the population.[19] But for their reluctance to act forcefully, the praetorian revolt might have been nipped in the bud. However, the Republicans were as fearful of the unknown consequences of arming the people as of the rebellion itself.[20]

Governmental authority hardly reached beyond the ministerial offices. Armed activists in the streets outgunned and outnumbered the security forces. The government decreed the demobilisation of the soldiers in regiments whose officers had revolted. Most recruits deserted their companies and either returned home or joined the various militias. The Army, as a standing corps, melted away. Loyal officers found themselves distrusted and with hardly any troops to command.[21] Militias took over military operations. They marched from Valencia and Barcelona towards Aragón and launched an ill-fated expedition to Mallorca.[22] Those from Madrid seized most bordering provinces (Guadalajara, Cuenca, Toledo, etc.) and managed to hold up the Nationalists marching southwards in the mountain passes of Somosierra and Guadarrama.[23]

All over Republican Spain, autonomous executives emerged. These newly sprung sources of power conceived military resistance in local terms, and thus worked at cross purposes with Madrid.[24] Catalan nationalists took advantage of the confusion to extend their jurisdictional powers. Basque nationalists obtained home rule in October 1936. Anarcho-syndicalist militias advancing in Aragón established a council there. There were two rival executives in Asturias, the Socialist-dominated Provincial Committee of the Popular Front in Sama de Langreo and the CNT-controlled War Council in Gijón. There were autonomous councils in Málaga, Valencia, and Murcia.

Real power lay in the streets. Everywhere there was a mushrooming of local solutions to the organization of everyday life: transport, communications, food supply, and so on.[25] Trade unions took over much of industry and public services and collectivized significant tracts of land. In Valencia, Catalonia, and Aragón, collectivisation was enforced against the resistance of many small- and middle-scale landholders. Workers' militias controlled public order. Naturally, this was far from a uniform process. Where the Socialists were strongest, the collapse of the pre-war socio-political structures was less than when the CNT was dominant. In the Basque Country, the PNV ensured minimum changes.[26]

Industrial takeovers, agrarian collectivizations, and armed militias were visible manifestations of the ongoing revolutionary process. Zugazagotia wrote: 'Madrid was in dire chaos. Public order was pulverised; it resided in the streets amongst the citizens incorporated in the struggle . . .'.[27] Workers' organizations acquired immense power in the running of the economy and upholding public order. However, they did so out of a need to fill the existing void.[28] Yet, unlike in 1917 Russia, there was no Bolshevik party seeking to overthrow liberal democracy. The legal centres of power vis-à-vis the ad hoc revolutionary committees, rather than competing, had the effect of weakening one another. The state's legitimacy, though mauled, was not in dispute. The PCE remained outspoken defenders of the inter-class alliance, the Popular Front. Within the socialist movement, the sector headed by Besteiro rapidly descended into fatalism. Prieto's followers continued their collaboration with the Republicans. Largo's wing, despite all its radical rhetoric, never considered seizing power.[29]

Even in Barcelona, revolutionary utopianism clashed with reality. On 20 July, the FAI leaders, still covered in dust from the battle, met the president of the *Generalitat*. Companys disarmed them with a combination of flattery and diplomacy. The *Generalitat* could have been swept away by the revolutionary tide but was allowed to remain in place. However, the abyss between ideological tenets and the harsh realism imposed by war eroded overnight the foundations of anarchist faith.[30] They could impose their will in Catalonia, but this would have opened an internal schism within Republican Spain, thus accelerating defeat in the war. Moreover, the CNT lacked a centralized nucleus that could articulate a revolutionary initiative across the country. Confronted with the stark military situation, the old romantic concepts of protest and struggle were redundant. The legendary Buenaventura Durruti left for the front. Most opted for collaboration and joined other Republicans in the so-called Committee of Anti-Fascist Militias. Two months later, they agreed to dissolve it and enter the *Generalitat*.[31]

Together with the crippling fragmentation of authority, terror reigned over Spain. Corpses began to appear in desolate spots and near cemeteries. Words such as *Paseo* (taken for a ride to be shot) and *Saca* (removal and execution of prison inmates) became common parlance. Social class, profession, friendships, past opinions, or just attending mass regularly or not, could carry a death sentence. Although the figures are contested, there were about 49,000 victims of Republican terror and over 130,000 were killed in Nationalist Spain during the three years of fighting.[32]

The first targets were the military. The rebel generals declared martial law and imprisoned, and often summarily executed, those officers who had been reluctant to break their oath of allegiance to the Republic.[33] No exceptions were made. The shooting of General Miguel Campíns (military governor of Granada and Franco's former deputy in the Military Academy of Zaragoza) and Franco's cousin, Major Ricardo de la Puente, showed that the Rubicon had been crossed and there was no return.[34] In Republican Spain, army plotters were arrested and, in some instances, lynched on the spot. A bloodbath occurred in *La Montaña* barracks, the main fortress in Madrid. There, false white flags of surrender were used to lure and shoot at the crowds. When, finally, the enraged masses managed to enter the fortress, they fell upon the defenders, leaving the courtyard strewn with corpses.[35]

The betrayal of supposed loyalist generals such as Queipo and Aranda fuelled the flames of suspicion and led to an all-out purge of the army corps. Mistrust and embedded left-wing anti-militarism resulted in the loss of the technical services of many military experts and the promotion of officers based only on political connections.

In Nationalist Spain, those deemed to be 'Red' were rounded up and executed without any pretence of formal justice. The same fate awaited those who had spread the Republic's pernicious principles. Teachers who had dared to challenge the prominence of Catholic education were especially targeted. Massacres acquired tragic proportions in rural areas where closer community ties facilitated the uncovering of the socio-political enemy.[36]

In Republican Spain, the targets of terror were those associated with right-wing parties or deemed social exploiters. The Church was singled out. It was a class enemy that had abandoned the gospel of poverty, amassed wealth, blessed social oppression, and demanded acceptance of the natural domination of the ruling classes.[37] Except for the Basque Country, priests were the first to be hunted down in most villages. Churches, monasteries, and convents were looted, burnt down, or transformed into shops, hospitals, canteens, even dance halls. Assaults on churches were frequently accompanied by a popular sacrophobic fiesta in which workers donned religious vestments and represented burlesque liturgical practices or other ceremonies.[38] Some 6,832 members of the clergy (including 13 bishops) were killed.[39]

The existing power vacuum facilitated the explosion of violence. Crowds ran amok, unleashing their anger against both institutions and classes associated with years of oppression. Prisons were opened and criminals allowed to walk free. By joining the growing militias, they took advantage of the ongoing chaos to rob, kill, and settle old scores.[40] Libertarian philosophy made it impossible to disavow the large sectors of the *lumpenproletariat* that now flooded the organization.[41] The CNT-FAI columns left a trail of blood throughout Catalonia in the wake of their advance into Aragón. Their militias (*patrullas de control*), which became the guarantors of the new republican order, began hunting down 'fascists'. The defence of the revolution and the enemy's physical liquidation appeared inextricably linked.[42]

However, terror in Republican Spain was neither limited to anarchists and criminals nor conducted solely by *incontrolados* (literally, 'the uncontrollable ones'), a much-abused term.[43] Nobody could claim innocence in this orgy of violence. All forces contained *exaltés* who believed that inherent to victory was revolutionary terror. Under the pretext of fighting hidden Fascists, militias took on the role of applying popular justice.[44] Large buildings were seized and transformed into improvised prisons (*checas*). They became sinister places where, after being arrested, normally at night-time, people were summarily tried and either promptly released or given their final *paseo*.[45] Republican violence was believed to offer a means of achieving *tabula rasa*. It was an instrument used consciously to ensure there could be no way back to the old socio-political order.[46]

The killings were never condoned, let alone encouraged, by the government. On the contrary, they strived to end mob justice. The *Generalitat* facilitated safe conduct and helped many of those in peril, such as Cardinal Francesc Vidal i Barraquer, the Bishops of Tortosa and Girona, to flee abroad.[47] In Madrid, the government permitted over 10,000 right-wing refugees to seek sanctuary in embassies or in private flats that, under a foreign flag, were given diplomatic status.[48] With the gradual reconstruction of the state, terror diminished. Traditional channels of order and justice were recreated, including the establishment of Popular Courts, with juries presided over by career judges, to deal with crimes of treason and sedition.[49] Nonetheless, Madrid still underwent a brutal episode that was to tarnish the Republic.

In November 1936, with the Nationalists at the gates of the city, the fate of thousands of army officers and rightists held in several prisons became a priority. The JSU (in charge of public order) and the CNT (in control of key roads on the outskirts) came up with a horrendous solution. Prisoners would be transported in large fleets of buses to a safe place to the rear. However, those deemed dangerous Fascists were to be executed. Thus, some 2,400 convicts were removed from the buses and killed by their guards in the towns of Torrejón de Ardoz and Paracuellos del Jarama, on the outskirts of the capital. Hundreds also perished as victims of *sacas*.[50] Astonishingly, it was a veteran anarchist, Melchor Rodríguez, appointed in December 1936 to manage the penitentiary system, who ended the massacres. For his extraordinary bravery, risking his own life to save thousands of others, he was nicknamed *el ángel rojo* ('the Red Angel').[51]

In contrast to the largely spontaneous terror of the other camp, the insurgents' was cold and calculated. Repression was the logical result of a deliberate plan to eradicate all that the Republic signified.[52] Terror was an intrinsic part of the nationalist ethos. The leaders, *africanistas*, conducted the war as if it was a colonial struggle with the Republicans playing the part of ungodly natives. Their cult of violence and profound disdain for human rights and liberal values forged on the cruel Moroccan battlefield was brought to the mainland.[53]

The rebel commanders implemented a surreal aberration of justice. Their declaration of martial law condemned those who defended republican legality for, incredible though it might sound, the crime of rebellion.[54] Nationalist terror had a crucial social component. It was the perfect tool to terrorize the working classes into acquiescence and to accomplish the necessary *limpieza* (cleansing). Atheists, separatists, and Reds embodied the 'anti-Spain' that had to be purified.[55] The slaughter in Andalusia reached near-genocidal levels.[56] A sick joke of the time had it that the rural labourers had finally obtained their 'land reform' – in the form of a burial plot.[57] Knowing their deficiency in numbers in southern Spain, the massacres sought to paralyse the working class through sheer panic and reassert the rightful hierarchical social order. Franco's greatest weapon in the drive on Madrid was the colonial troops' penchant for terror (pillaging of villages, mutilation of enemies, etc.). Encouraged by their commanders, it was intended to ensure that those not physically eliminated would be broken by fear and seek survival in submission. Indeed, news of advancing Moors was often enough to send the militias fleeing in panic.[58] Badajoz, the first place where the colonial army found meaningful resistance, became a turning point. Troops looted the town and some 4,000 captured prisoners were taken to the bullring and machined-gunned. Colonel Juan Yagüe, who oversaw the advance towards Madrid, explained to the US journalist Jay Allen that with his columns racing against time, he could not afford to leave Reds alive to the rear.[59]

In Nationalist Spain, there were no parallels with *el ángel rojo*. No leading voice was raised against the orgy of blood. The religious hierarchy lent its wholehearted support. Army chaplains were amongst the most ebullient voices demanding the extermination of the heretic enemy.[60] It could not be more different than the attitude of the heads of the two rival sides. Azaña broke down in tears when informed of the *saca* at Madrid prison in August 1936 that left 30 high-ranking right-wingers dead. He expressed his despair in his memoirs and in literary works such as *La Velada de Benicarló* (1939): the dreams embodied by the Republic of 1931 lay in tatters since regardless of the outcome, nothing could be the same after the civil war.[61] In contrast, for Franco peace could only come after the extermination of the enemy. In an extraordinary combination of messianic determination and cruelty, he told Jay Allen that his mission was to redeem Spain by blood regardless of the human cost.[62]

Foreign Intervention

The war was a blatant attempt to resolve, by military means, essential issues that had divided Spaniards for generations (agrarian reform, the clash between modernity and tradition, centralism versus peripheral nationalism, the role of the Catholic Church and the army in modern society). However, it can only be understood within a European context. The Spanish struggle constituted a perfect illustration of that violent period.[63] It soon transcended its borders, becoming the distorting mirror in which European countries contemplated an exaggerated image of their tensions.[64]

Based on a combination of material and human resources, it seems reasonable to speculate that the rebellion was doomed. The Republic retained control of the main cities, most of the coastline, the industrial infrastructure, and the huge gold reserves – the fourth largest in the world – the small air force and the navy, after sailors overpowered their officers. The Army of Africa, which included the Foreign Legion and the *Regulares*

(African troops commanded by Spanish officers), could not cross the Straits of Gibraltar.[65]

Lacking significant modern weaponry and an arms industry, both sides rapidly looked abroad for military supplies. The international response proved crucial to turn a seemingly ill-fated military sedition into a full-blown conflict and to dictate its course and outcome.[66]

Republican hopes of prompt international aid rested on the western democracies, particularly on the French Popular Front. Thus, after being appointed prime minister, Giral requested help from Paris.[67] The confident tone surrounding the plea seemed justified. Not only has a government, under international law, the right to acquire arms to fight an internal revolt but also a Franco-Spanish commercial agreement, signed in late 1935, provided for the purchase of weapons in France up to the value of 20 million francs.[68] Furthermore, ministers in both countries enjoyed ties of personal friendship and political identification. It was also in France's national interests that a friendly government remained on its southern border. As a consequence, the reaction of prime minister Léon Blum was favourable.[69] However, a combination of domestic and foreign pressures would drastically alter that stance.

The Republic's diplomatic staff turned out to be an obstacle in its efforts abroad. Largely recruited from the upper sectors of society, many became saboteurs of the state that they allegedly represented. Some managed to conceal their pro-rebel leanings while thwarting the instructions received from Madrid.[70] This was not the case in France where Antonio Barroso, Spain's military attaché, quickly leaked to the press Blum's plans to deliver weapons.[71] Suddenly, a seemingly straightforward operation served to exacerbate the highly polarized French socio-political milieu. Sectors of the middle classes, the Catholic Church, business elites, and the army corps loathed what the Popular Front stood for.[72] Blum himself, a Jewish Socialist, aroused a special hatred. Many officers sympathized with extreme right-wing organizations and identified with their Spanish counterparts, who were perceived to be merely defending their fatherland's ancestral values.[73]

News of the intention to aid Republican Spain gave the French right-wing media the ammunition to mount a devastating campaign against the 'treacherous Popular Front'. The uproar rocked the governing coalition. Leading elements in the Radical Party (including the president of the Republic, Albert Lebrun) and even some Socialist ministers feared that aiding the Republic militarily could spread the conflict to France. After a tumultuous cabinet meeting on 25 July, arms shipments were suspended. However, the private sector was not affected. The minister of aviation, Pierre Cot, a Radical, began to arrange the sale of weapons to Madrid via third countries. Aware that Spain had become a key battle in the forthcoming clash between the western democracies and fascism, Cot's sympathy for the Republic never wavered.[74]

Britain, seemingly, maintained strict neutrality throughout the conflict. However, that stance merely concealed a secret campaign based on disguised hostility towards the Republic.[75] Ruling economic circles feared that the triumph of a left-wing Republic could endanger their significant interests in the Spanish economy. Britain was Spain's most important trading partner (accounting for 25 percent and 10 percent of Spanish exports and imports, respectively) and controlled about 40 percent of foreign investment (13.3 percent of the total in Europe).[76] Also, for reasons of ideology, class, and upbringing, British ruling circles approved of the anti-revolutionary objectives of the Spanish insurgents.[77] For the national government, led by the Conservative Stanley Baldwin, and the diplomatic corps, an almost exclusive club of the aristocracy and upper echelons of the bourgeoisie, communism was the natural enemy. They were dismayed by the Popular Front's victories in Spain and France in 1936. Simultaneously, awareness of the empire's increasingly enfeebled economic and military position led Britain's governing classes to embrace appeasement or accommodate the fascist dictators' revisionist ambitions. The Spanish conflict's potential for creating divisions on the continent along ideological lines constituted a grave threat to that strategy.[78]

Diplomatic reports confirmed the already acute anti-revolutionary prejudice. They interpreted differently the atrocities committed on both sides: while republican brutalities were the consequence of mob rule, those in nationalist areas were necessary to restore law and order. Ambassador Henry Chilton kept stressing the similarities between Republican Spain and the Kerensky administration in 1917 Russia.[79] The British government concluded that in Spain the army was combating a virtual Soviet under the umbrella of a lifeless government.[80] Franco was viewed as a prudent leader, who had risen to fight the spectre of social revolution. A nationalist victory would be in Britain's interests. The alternative was communism tempered by anarchy.[81]

British diplomacy's problem was that the counter-revolution remained formally illegitimate.[82] Since openly supporting the rebellion was unthinkable, the government maintained for the home audience an image of scrupulous neutrality. However, its genuine position was encapsulated by Baldwin's instructions to the foreign secretary, Anthony Eden, on 26 July: 'On no account, French or other, must you bring us into the fight on the side of the Russians'[83] – a friendly democratic nation was equated with the Soviet Union. Ironically, Spain had not restored diplomatic relations with Moscow after 1917.

Britain introduced an arms embargo that put the legal government on the same footing as the insurgents. On 22 July, it accepted Franco's request to refuse fuel to the Republican navy in the ports of Gibraltar and Tangier. The Republic was inflicted a harmful blow when, on 13 August, the existing commercial payment agreement between the two countries was suspended. Also, a republican financial transaction, via Barclays Bank, to purchase arms in America was impeded, while a simultaneous nationalist operation through the Westminster Bank was permitted.[84]

While the Republic was ostracized internationally, the Nationalists received a different response. Sanjurjo had established his headquarters in Portugal, a dictatorship headed by Antonio Salazar. Once the war broke out, the Portuguese rulers perceived that a 'red' victory could have a devastating impact on the stability of their regime. Therefore, they identified with the Spanish rebellion. In October 1936, Portugal broke off relations with the Republic, giving de facto – if yet not de jure – recognition to Nationalist Spain.[85] Portuguese proximity was crucial. It became the link during the first weeks between separate nationalist areas and the perfect conduit to deliver foreign aid. In early August 1936, Franco's brother Nicolás settled in Lisbon (soon joined by Gil Robles) to procure vital supplies.[86] Salazar could only offer limited military assistance. More important contributions came from Germany and Italy.

Before July 1936, the Nazis had revealed no interest in Spain. Germany's economic interests were modest.[87] With expansionist plans focused on eastern Europe, Hitler had not even mentioned Spain in *Mein Kampf*. Consequently, its Foreign Office, fearful of international complications, promptly declined requests for aid from Mola.[88] A combination of luck and cunning led to the radical change in heart. Desperate for air transport, Franco enlisted the services of two Germans in Morocco, Johannes Bernhardt and Adolf Langenheim, members of the *Auslandorganisation*, the Nazi organization abroad. They agreed to travel to Germany to deliver a plea for military assistance. Success came after overcoming several further complications. Arriving in Berlin on the morning of 25 July, they ran into the opposition of their superiors. Eventually, one of their colleagues, Alfred Hess, found a way to bypass the bureaucratic web through his brother and deputy party leader, Rudolf. The latter contacted Hitler, then on holiday in Bayreuth (Bavaria) attending the Wagner festival, who agreed to receive them that evening. During a meeting of almost three hours, dominated by Hitler's monologues, the *Fuhrer* convinced himself to support the insurrection.[89]

Probably still under the influence of Wagner's music, Hitler set into motion 'Operation Magic Fire': the delivery of 10 *Junker* 52 transport planes that, once in Morocco, began the crucial airlift of colonial troops to mainland Spain. On 31 July, the *Usaramo* left Hamburg loaded with ten *Junker* 52s, six escort fighter *Heinkel* 51s, anti-aircraft guns, bombs, ammunition, and 85 pilots and technicians. In August, other vessels supplied more *materiel* with the complicity of the Portuguese authorities.[90]

Strategic considerations were paramount in Hitler's decision: a rapid nationalist victory was a limited risk worth taking. Nevertheless, Germany was not yet prepared for an armed confrontation in Europe. Intervention was shrouded in secrecy with the expectation of a rapid victory. However, Germany found herself dragged into a much longer campaign than initially anticipated. Consequently, other considerations became important: Spain offered raw materials that were necessary for rearmament, a testing ground for men and equipment, and an opportunity to determine the limits of the Allies' resolution.[91]

Having just signed contracts to aid the Spanish plotters with planes and other *materiel* worth £616,000, Rome was well-informed about the impending coup.[92] Still, the fiasco of the coup dampened those plans. Furthermore, Italy was militarily and economically exhausted and diplomatically isolated after the conquest of Abyssinia. Consequently, she was reluctant to get involved so soon in a new enterprise that, moreover, appeared to be failing. On 21 July, Luis Bolín, Franco's messenger, arrived in Italy. He obtained a letter of presentation from Alfonso XIII. Yet his meeting with Count Galeazzo Ciano (Mussolini's son-in-law and foreign minister) proved fruitless.[93]

On 25 July, a delegation sent by Mola arrived in Rome to advocate for the contracts arranged early that month. The *Duce* was flattered to be the recipient of pleas for help and eager to establish a potential ally in Italy's area of influence. However, his final stance was the result of a complex and anything but spontaneous decision-making process. The evaluation of diplomatic and intelligence reports led him to conclude that the covert delivery of a small amount of equipment to the insurgents was a safe risk to take. Knowledge of British hostility towards the Republic, including opposition to French involvement, was good grounds for assuming there would be no objection to discreet intervention in favour of the rebellion.[94] A further consideration were reports that the Kremlin was deeply disconcerted by the situation. Italian diplomats in Morocco – the Consul in Tangier (Pier Filippo del Rossi) and the military attaché in Tetuán (Giuseppe Luccardi) – confirmed that once colonial troops were on the mainland, the war would soon be over. On 27 July, Ciano informed Bolín that Italy was ready to help. Two days later, 12 *Savoia-Marchetti* S 81 transport planes, followed by 12 *Fiat* C.R.32 fighters and the cargo ship *Emilio Morandi* loaded with ammunition, were dispatched to Spanish Morocco.[95] On 7 August, Rome sent a further 27 fighter planes, five tanks, 40 machine guns, 12 anti-aircraft guns, and other munitions[96]

The veil of secrecy surrounding Italian intervention was soon removed. On 30 July, one *Savoia-Marchetti* plane came down in the sea and two crash-landed in French North Africa.[97] The French cabinet was bitterly divided about how to respond. The *Quai d'Orsay* (French Foreign Office) helped tilt the balance. Its principal objective after the Great War was to avoid anything that could endanger the vital alliance with Britain[98] – and London made its stance very clear. On 6 August, the French Socialist minister of finance, Vincent Auriol, told the Spanish Socialist Jiménez de Asúa that 'because of the English a delivery of arms had been suspended'. The next morning, in tears, Blum told Asúa that Baldwin had contacted President Lebrun to warn him that if France's sale of weapons to the Republic led to continental war, she would be alone. Blum was close to resigning but was convinced by the new Spanish ambassador in Paris, Álvaro de Albornoz, to stay on.[99] That day, the British ambassador, Sir George Clerk, had let the French foreign minister, Yvon Delbos, know his 'personal' view that any French commitment to the Republic would imperil the alliance between their two nations.[100] On 8 August, a rowdy cabinet meeting finally approved an initiative masterminded by Alexis Léger, the *Quai d'Orsay*'s general secretary: an appeal to all European countries to refrain from intervening in Spain.[101] Still, with Blum's connivance, Cot ensured the dispatch to Spain of 13 *Dewoitine* fighters and six *Potez* bombers that had been built for Lithuania (although they were unarmed). The novelist André Malraux, who had just returned from Madrid, oversaw the operation. While in Paris, he also raised a squadron (*Escuadra España*) of some 40 pilots and technicians.[102]

The Anglo-French concerted effort paid dividends. All 27 European nations adhered to the agreement by late August. That month, the United States also introduced a moral arms embargo on both Spanish Republicans and Nationalists, formalized later into the Embargo Act and the Neutrality Act of January and May 1937, respectively.[103] The Non-Intervention Agreement (NIA) sealed the opprobrium of denying a friendly sovereign state the means to defend itself.[104] According to the Spanish foreign minister, the Socialist Julio Álvarez del Vayo, it transformed the *Quai d'Orsay*, at least vis-à-vis Spain, into a branch of the British Foreign Office.[105] André Blumel, Blum's chef de cabinet, acknowledged French impotence: 'Non-Intervention was essentially an attempt to prevent others from doing what France was incapable of accomplishing'.[106]

Fascist aid combined with British acquiescence and French paralysis was to alter dramatically the course of the war. Nationalist desperation, embodied by Mola's confession to his secretary, on 29 July, that he was contemplating suicide, was suddenly transformed as the first successful airlift of troops in modern warfare began.[107]

Spain's tragedy brought together Germany and Italy, not long before at each other's throats over conflicting ambitions over Austria.[108] From early August, summits between the two states intensified. The dictators agreed that their activities should continue beyond the airlift, supplying weapons and allowing their air forces to engage in bombing missions. The Italians were delighted to be allowed to lead the enterprise, as the Mediterranean was their area of control, in exchange for endorsing German expansion eastwards.[109] On 1 November, Mussolini referred for the first time to the 'Rome-Berlin Axis' to describe the two countries' rapprochement.[110]

Under the protection of Axis aviation, the Army of Africa initiated the advance towards Madrid, leaving behind a staggering trail of desolation. It followed the south-western route, cutting through Andalusia and Extremadura to keep close to Portugal, its main conduit for weapons. The ill-armed militias were no match. By 10 August, the two nationalist zones were joined. In September, the dictators chose to increase their aid for what promised to be the final push. Germany launched Operation Otto: the supply of 15 additional fighter planes, 24 tanks, radio equipment, and the conversion of transport aircraft into bombers.[111] Italy dispatched thousands of hand-grenades, small arms, machine-gun cartridges, and planes that brought the total number of aircraft to 68.[112]

In September 1936, Spain was the focus of world attention. She encapsulated the microcosm of an age of political radicalism and economic depression. For conservative opinion, the Nationalists stood for the values of Christian civilization threatened by communism. For progressive circles, the Republic constituted the last-ditch stand before the advance of reaction across the continent. Aid committees sprang up in western countries to raise money and collect medicines and clothes.[113] A small number of foreigners began to cross the Pyrenees and join the diverse militias. Simultaneously, writers and artists poured into Spain. The likes of Ernest Hemingway, George Orwell, André Malraux, John Dos Passos, and many others immortalized the unfolding catastrophe with their works. This epic struggle also touched Hollywood. Scriptwriters, actors, and directors attended the numerous pro-Republican fundraising events. Errol Flynn landed in Barcelona in March 1937 to deliver a letter of support to the government, together with a cheque for 1.5 million dollars.[114]

By late September, the Republic had only received a few planes and arms smuggled from France or acquired on the black market. The first important foreign dispatch of weapons arrived in mid-October: The *Magallanes* reached Cartagena with a cargo of 20,000 rifles and 20 million cartridges from Veracruz (Mexico).[115] Mexico continued to supply weapons throughout the conflict, acted as a cover for their purchase from third countries, and represented republican interests where its diplomatic corps had defected.[116] Nevertheless, geographical distance and scarcity of resources hampered Mexico's ability to play a major role.

When the Spanish war broke out, the show trials that heralded the era of the great purges occupied Stalin's mind. Initially, the Soviet authorities were reassured by the optimistic reports from its sources in Spain.[117] The PCE was instructed to fight loyally for the governmental side.[118] The Kremlin adopted a prudent position: Platonic sympathy for the Republic, fierce denunciation of fascist aggression, and collection of food and money.[119] Axis intervention forced the Soviet Union (USSR) to act.

In late August, Georgi Dimitrov, the Comintern's general secretary, noted the possibility of organizing a force of volunteers to help the Republic.[120] Madrid and Moscow re-established full diplomatic relations that month. Marcel Rosenberg and Vladimir Antonov-Ovseenko (ambassador in Madrid and consul in Barcelona, respectively) headed large diplomatic corps, including many military advisers.[121] On 7 October, the Soviet delegation in London stated that unless violations of the NIA ceased forthwith, the USSR would consider itself freed from its obligations.[122] In fact, the Kremlin had already crossed the Rubicon: on 16 September, 'Operation X' had been launched under the utmost secrecy.[123]

Helping Republican Spain militarily constituted the USSR's first major intervention in the international arena.[124] That initiative was not intended to turn Spain into a satellite. Saving the Republic (albeit one in which revolutionary fervour was restrained) became instrumental to Russian designs to transform the strategy of domestic popular fronts into an international alliance with the Allies against Nazi aggression.[125]

On 4 October, the first delivery of small weapons arrived on board the Spanish tanker *Campeche*. From mid-October, there were intermittent but steady deliveries of *materiel*, including T-26 tanks and modern aircraft (*Polikarpov* I-15 and *Polikarpov* I-16 fighters, SB-2 *Tupolev* bombers). With them came pilots, tank crews, gunners, and military advisers.[126] Without them, the Republic would have lost the war in 1936.

On 18 September, the International Brigades were founded during a secret Comintern gathering in Moscow.[127] Communist parties were instructed to organize the enrolment and transport of individuals. André Marty, a French Communist in the Comintern Secretariat, was in charge. The objective was not to recruit Communists but instead anyone regardless of political leanings. A besieged Republic, resisting a military insurrection backed by Italy and Germany, led to a staggering number of international volunteers that was unique in modern warfare. Intellectuals were significantly represented but most came from working-class backgrounds.[128]

Everybody assumed the imminent fall of Madrid. Mola boasted that he would be taking coffee in the *Café Molinero* on the central *Gran Vía* by 12 October, the anniversary of the *Día de la Raza* (Columbus' discovery of America).[129] Mola also claimed that the four advancing columns would be aided by a fifth formed by supporters within the city. Those imprudent words unleashed a wave of frenzied liquidation of the hidden enemy.[130]

Bombed relentlessly by artillery and aviation, Madrid enjoyed a foretaste of what awaited other European cities. Faced with an apparently desperate situation, the government, then led by Largo fled, on 6 November, for the safety of Valencia, leaving behind a *Junta de Defensa* headed by General José Miaja and comprising representatives of all the political forces. Colonel Vicente Rojo, Miaja's chief of staff, oversaw the resistance. Dolores Ibarruri, the communist heroine known as *La Pasionaria*, used as a rallying cry, '¡No Pasarán!' ('They Shall Not Pass!'), the slogan from the Great War.[131]

Franco's massive frontal attack proved a strategic error. His troops' superior quality was rendered useless in street and barricade fighting.[132] On 7 November, Moorish troops pierced the defensive line through the *Casa de Campo*, the huge forest in western Madrid. The first battalions of foreign volunteers rushed to the front. Although only some 2,000 men, their presence was a formidable boost to popular morale. Madrid was no longer alone in its plight.[133] On 23 November, Franco called off the offensive.[134]

The Grand Charade

With their elite troops bogged down, short of manpower, and facing an unexpectedly well-equipped enemy, the insurgents received a deadly blow with the stalemate reached in Madrid. At this key juncture, the dictators came to the rescue. Growing foreign support for both sides transformed the Spanish affair into a veritable European civil war, where often troops from the same country found themselves fighting for the different camps.

The Nationalists sought gradually to shatter Madrid's resistance. In mid-December, they advanced towards the north-west (Coruña Road) but failed to break the stalemate.[135] On 6 February 1937, they launched an offensive towards the south-east (Jarama River) to cut off the vital road to Valencia. British and American volunteers took a bloody battering in holding onto a slope soon known as 'Suicide Hill'.[136] As both sides lost over 20,000 men, it became a costly but successful republican defensive victory.[137]

In March, Italian troops marched towards Guadalajara, to the north-east of Madrid, from where they intended to encircle the capital by linking forces with the Nationalists at Jarama. Mussolini hoped that it would lead to a spectacular conclusion of the war. In February, his troops had already been instrumental in capturing Málaga. Now, some 35,000 Italian soldiers were engaged in the so-called *Guerra Celere* (rapid war) based on a mass attack of armoured trucks and tanks covered by the air force. However, after three days of steady advances, poor weather began to disrupt the operation. The motorized columns were bogged down on icy and muddy roads, while fog grounded aircraft. To make matters worse, the Nationalists failed to renew their offensive on the other flank. Some Italian officers felt that their efforts were being sabotaged. Indeed, Franco was not entirely thrilled at the prospect of the war concluding with a stunning Italian victory. The Republican counter-attack, supported by Soviet aircraft and tanks, resulted in a rout of the Italians.[138] The Nationalists shelved the plan to capture Madrid. Yet, with his prestige now at stake, the boastful *Duce* could not withdraw troops until their reputation was rebuilt on the battlefield. From then on, Franco would direct operations, with the Italians under his command.[139]

The military deadlock did not last. The Nationalists gradually gained the upper hand courtesy of the NIA's cynical ploy.[140] Álvarez del Vayo dubbed non-intervention 'a deliberate and monstrous farce and the main cause of the collapse of the Republic'.[141] A (Non-Intervention) Committee (NIC) was created in London to oversee the agreement. Headed by the Earl of Plymouth, under-secretary to the Foreign Office, ambassadors in Britain represented their respective nations. Yet, the NIC turned out to be a body whose main task was to do little while feigning to do much.[142] It became a grandiose sham in which chicanery and hypocrisy prevailed. The Russian ambassador, Ivan Maisky, compared it to 'the ideal Japanese wife, who sees nothing, hears nothing, and says nothing'.[143] Despite vast amounts of foreign armament pouring into Spain, the NIC focused on discussing trivial matters. On other occasions, it descended into theatrical parodies, with flat denials followed by petty squabbling.[144]

The NIA's founding principles were disregarded.[145] The NIC's impotence was largely due to it being an instrument of British diplomacy whose objectives were not those portrayed by the official propaganda – that is, the prevention of foreign participation in the war. Once Madrid's resistance meant prolongation of the war, Britain's strategy became to restrain French intervention, avoid confrontation with the Axis, and maintain a semblance of impeccable neutrality for domestic opinion. The asphyxiating arms embargo imposed upon the Republic while simultaneously turning a blind eye to the flagrant Axis military assistance to the Nationalists perpetuated a structural asymmetry that determined the outcome of the conflict.[146]

In early 1937, Italy and Germany were still assessing the Allies' resolve. They intended to supply enough troops and equipment to secure a nationalist victory before the NIA's implementation but avoid a frontal clash.[147] However, they observed how the NIC, again and again, refused to act, despite their blatant breach of the agreement. Notwithstanding growing intervention, Britain was delighted to sign, with Italy, on 2 January 1937, the eloquently called 'Gentlemen's Agreement' that confirmed their mutual respect for their interests in the Mediterranean.[148] Britain, if anything, intensified its appeasement policy after Neville Chamberlain assumed the premiership in May 1937. According to Oliver Harvey, principal private secretary to the Foreign Office, Chamberlain 'believed himself with a mission to make peace with the dictators'.[149] For Ángel Viñas, he was the Republic's main nemesis.[150]

In the summer of 1937, Franco requested Mussolini's help to strangle the lifeline provided to the Republic by the convoys of Soviet supplies in the Mediterranean.[151] The press began to use the euphemism of mysterious 'pirate actions' to describe the attacks upon merchant vessels bound for republican ports. Informed by the Germans, Italy was aware that British intelligence had broken its naval codes and, therefore, knew that Italian submarines were responsible for the mayhem.[152] Ciano noted that they were confident that Britain would not risk a clash.[153]

Given the popular outcry, an international conference was held in Nyon (Switzerland) in mid-September. With the fascist powers absent, it was agreed to divide the Mediterranean between zones of patrol and intercept all pirate activity. Shockingly, the British government invited Italy to participate in the patrols. After boasting that the 'pirates had been turned into policemen', Ciano referred to such a surreal outcome as the decline of the western democracies.[154]

Blum himself, aware of the NIC's impotence, connived in the smuggling of armaments over the Pyrenean frontier, the 'Non-Intervention *Relâchée*' (relaxed non-intervention). As the Mediterranean route became too dangerous, Russian weapons had to be despatched to French Atlantic ports.

There, with the complicity of selected customs agents, they were smuggled across the border. Nevertheless, only a trickle of weapons got through.[155] France's other great service to the Republic was to allow her to establish in its territory the headquarters of international arms purchases.[156]

The stark difference between the quantity, quality, and regularity of international aid proved vital. Without its gold, the Republic would have been doomed. At the start of the conflict, the Bank of France purchased 26.5 percent of the total reserves. In October 1936, the bulk of the remaining gold (460.5 tons or US$518 million) was sent to the USSR. The currency equivalent for purposes other than the repayment for supplies was transferred to *La Banque Commerciale de l'Europe du Nord*, a Soviet Bank in Paris, to fund the acquisition of weapons.[157] Over 52 voyages, merchant ships with Russian *materiel* delivered 623 aircraft, 331 tanks, 15,008 machine guns, 379,645 rifles, and more. Some 2,100 Soviet military advisers, pilots, technicians, and secret agents served in Spain.[158] The embargo forced the Republic to operate in the black market. This meant erratic deliveries, different types of armament, shortages of supplies, and overpriced and obsolete equipment.[159] Moreover, the diplomatic corps sabotaged many of these activities. Also, the Republic's foreign volunteers were civilians who had to be armed. Their bravery in combat saw them used as shock troops in the most dangerous places, incurring an appalling number of casualties.[160]

In contrast, the Nationalists obtained their weapons on credit: from Germany (US$215 million) and Italy (US$354 million).[161] Most was to be repaid through commercial agreements in the form of raw materials. Italy's aid was extremely generous, while Germany took advantage. Two companies – HISMA at the Spanish end and ROWAK as its German counterpart, established in July and October 1936, respectively – monopolized the trading relationship. It facilitated the acquisition of crucial raw materials (pyrites, iron, copper, etc.) to aid Hitler's rearmament programme.[162]

The number of genuine volunteers joining the nationalist camp was small, some 1,500 men: 600 Irish Blue Shirts, some French monarchists, over a hundred *émigré* White Russians, a few fascist Romanians. They joined the Spanish Foreign Legion.[163] Some 78,000 African mercenaries served in Franco's colonial army.[164] They were joined by 10,000 Portuguese 'volunteers' (*Viriatos*).[165] Hitler dispatched the Condor Legion, which consisted of a permanent squadron of about 6,000 troops (over 19,000 served at different times), anti-aircraft guns, tanks, and over 700 aircraft.[166] Italy was all but in name at war with the Republic. Its *Corpo di Truppe Volontarie* included nearly 80,000 soldiers, 759 aircraft, 3,436 machine guns, and 7,400 motor vehicles.[167]

In conclusion, the Republic faced unsurmountable odds in having to maintain simultaneously a war against the Nationalists, three openly aggressive foreign powers (Portugal, Italy, and Germany), and one concealed enemy (Britain).[168]

In the City of God

The Nationalists successfully found a way of coordinating their disparate forces. As if they were 'regiments of the same army, they collaborated for the joint purpose of destroying the Republic'[169] – and readily accepted subordination to military command.

Nobody expected Franco's meteoric ascent in July 1936. A mediocre student in the military academy, Franco volunteered to serve in Morocco in February 1912. He spent the next 14 years of his life there, attaining rapid promotion for bravery in combat. He even claimed that 'without Africa he could not begin to understand himself'.[170] Franco was unhappy with the arrival of a Republic that soon introduced military reforms that hindered his career and closed the military academy of Zaragoza where he had been made director by Primo. However, he stayed clear of his fellow colonial plotters in 1932. In 1934, he supervised the crushing of the October revolt by dispatching Moorish troops to Asturias. Gil Robles rewarded him with the post of chief of the General Staff. After the victory of the Popular Front, he was banished to the Canary Islands. He was kept informed of the conspiracy but remained uncommitted. The plotters, annoyed by his vacillations, called him 'Miss Canary Islands 1936'.[171]

Franco kept his options open. He even booked holidays in Britain to learn English and play golf in July 1936. On 23 June, he sent an extraordinary letter to the prime minister, Casares. He stressed the military's profound dissatisfaction and hinted that a solution could be found if he was reassigned to Madrid. His apologists argued that this was a noble warning. A less honourable inference was that, if promoted, he was willing to turn against his comrades.[172] In early July, Luís Bolín, the London correspondent of the newspaper EL ABC chartered an aeroplane, the *Dragon Rapide*, funded by the millionaire Juan March, to allegedly take some tourists to the Canaries. Its real mission was to carry Franco to Morocco to command the Army of Africa. After the plane landed in Tenerife on 14 July, Franco needed a pretext to travel there from his base in Gran Canaria. Three days later, it was 'providentially solved'. He had to preside over the funeral of General Amado Balmes, military commander of Tenerife. Balmes' death was not a firearm accident, as then suggested, but the first assassination of the war. It facilitated Franco's trip and eliminated a loyal officer of the Republic.[173]

Franco's career was marked by a combination of caution, ambition, and good fortune. If the rebellion had succeeded, he had been promised the post of high commissioner in Morocco. Paradoxically, its partial failure together with parallel sinister disasters (death of leading generals such as Sanjurjo) transformed Franco from a hesitant rebel into an indisputable leader.

Given the urgency of achieving a unified military command, the generals gathered in Salamanca on 21 September to choose a commander-in-chief. Franco's claim was unassailable. He commanded the colonial army, the vital tool to win the war, and was the recipient of crucial Axis aid. His political ambiguity also made his candidacy palatable to all factions. Before final details were agreed upon, the generals returned to the front, after arranging to resume discussions a week later. At that crucial juncture, Franco took a polemical decision. He diverted his advance towards Madrid to relieve the besieged *Alcázar* in Toledo to the south-east of his intended route.

Toledo had remained under republican control from the start. However, some 1,000 army officers and Falangists, led by Colonel José Moscardó, barricaded themselves with their families (and some leftist hostages) in the military academy, the *Alcázar*, a fortress that overlooked the city. By choosing to relieve Moscardó, Franco gave Madrid precious time to consolidate its defences. Yet, he was aware of the spiritual propaganda at stake. On 27 September, the *Alcázar* was saved. The epic of the besieged fortress resisting against dire odds became part of the legend. Naturally, nobody mentioned the fate of the hostages or the bloodbath that followed the fall of Toledo.[174] One week later, the generals were greeted by a well-orchestrated campaign deifying the *Alcázar*'s saviour. Franco maximized the momentum to be granted the ambiguous title of head of the government of the nationalist state, but significantly only for the war's duration. However, any reference to the appointment's provisional nature mysteriously disappeared when officially published, on 1 October.[175]

The war recreated the alliance between the sword and the altar. The ecclesiastical hierarchy endorsed enthusiastically the insurrection with a zeal reminiscent of medieval times.[176] This was due not only to the bloody persecution carried out in the other zone, but also to regain its traditional privileged position.[177] The Catholic network was crucial in both mobilizing international opinion and unifying all the factions in the absence of any agreed objective other than the seizure of power.[178]

The Church brazenly falsified the facts to legitimize the sedition.[179] Various bishops used the term 'crusade' to characterize the rebel cause. On 30 September, the Bishop of Salamanca, Enrique Pla y Deniel, published the pastoral letter 'The Two Cities', which granted the conflict a confessional character. The war was a titanic struggle between two concepts of life. One was represented by a devilish city inhabited by the sons of Cain. The love of God, martyrdom, and heroism prevailed in the other. The insurgents were thus engaged in a new *Reconquista* to save Spain from the Godless hordes of Moscow.[180]

In the emerging nationalist rump state, the line between myth and reality became blurred. Franco was hailed as the *Caudillo*, the name given to medieval warrior chieftains. Victories were celebrated with *Te Deums*. The clergy endorsed the fascist salute and harangued the troops to exterminate the Reds. The Church overlooked the role played by Italy and Germany as well as that of thousands of Moors, who were at the forefront of the new *Reconquista*.[181]

Ironically, while being hailed as *Caudillo Invicto* (undefeated chieftain), Franco suffered a major defeat at the gates of Madrid. However, it again proved a blessing in disguise. Had he captured the capital and the war concluded soon thereafter, he would have lacked the time to build a messianic legend around his leadership. The Axis and many Spanish officers often despaired at what they regarded as Franco's excessive caution. Their objections were misplaced. The *Caudillo*'s baffling decisions were due to his formation: as an *africanista*, he was familiar with small-scale colonial skirmishes and not modern warfare.[182] However, there was also a hidden political agenda. The *Caudillo* pursued a long and weary war to cement his position.[183]

Throughout 1937, the Nationalists attained the military edge. In March, they turned their attention towards the relatively inactive northern front. Rich in mineral and industrial resources, it was an important prize. Cut off from the rest of Republican Spain, the three provinces of Vizcaya, Santander, and Asturias were massively outgunned and unable to receive reinforcements. To make matters worse, all of them, but Vizcaya in particular, focused their efforts on local resistance.

The PNV ensured respect for private and religious property and ignored pleas from the central authorities to apply scorched-earth policies to prevent the enemy from gaining control of Vizcaya's vast industrial resources. Terror bombing broke resistance gradually. Evacuated Basque children in foster homes in England and France expressed the horror they had endured by rushing to cellars or becoming agitated whenever an aeroplane appeared in the sky.[184] The Condor Legion trialled the mass bombardment of cities. None had more symbolic meaning than the destruction of Guernica, the ancient Basque capital, on 26 April. This small town did not present any military objectives but like Badajoz, one year earlier, it sent a clear message to those who resisted Franco's new order.[185] Pablo Picasso's painting, displayed later that year at the World Fair in Paris, immortalized the tragedy.

Mola's death in a plane crash on 3 June 1937 eliminated Franco's last serious rival. On 18 June, Bilbao's defensive perimeter was pierced through the treachery of the defences' main engineer, Alejandro Goicoechea. Basque nationalist treason escalated. Some PNV leaders used their close contacts with the Vatican to negotiate with Italy. An agreement was reached in August and several Basque regiments gathered in the small town of Santoña (Santander) to surrender to the Italians. But Franco was not prepared to honour a deal he had not sought. Basque officers were imprisoned and some were executed.[186] Two days later, Santander fell. Notwithstanding the NIA's existence, Mussolini, seeking to erase the memory of Guadalajara, boasted of the key role played by his troops.[187] Asturias' fall in October concluded the campaign. The Nationalists had broken the stalemate.

Throughout 1937, Franco consolidated his political supremacy. His brother-in-law, Ramón Serrano Suñer, was the architect of the state apparatus. An intelligent young lawyer, a close friend of José Antonio, and a

CEDA deputy for Zaragoza, Serrano was instrumental in bringing over many JAP members to the Falange in the spring of 1936. Surprised in Madrid by the outbreak of the war, he was jailed and narrowly escaped the *sacas* of August, in which many leading rightists perished, including his brothers Fernando and José. He escaped from the hospital where he had been interned due to his precarious health, managed to reach Valencia, and disguised as an Argentinean sailor boarded a vessel of that nationality, *Tucumán*.[188] In February 1937, he arrived in Salamanca. Due to his meteoric rise, he was nicknamed *el cuñadísimo* (the supreme brother-in-law) to rhyme with Franco's *Generalissimo*.

The existing administrative chaos shocked Serrano. Alongside the *Caudillo*'s headquarters in Salamanca and a secretariat, controlled by Franco's brother Nicolás, there was the so-called *Junta Técnica del Estado* (State Technical Board) in Burgos. A variety of hangers-on jockeying for influence could be found between Burgos and Salamanca.[189]

In Nationalist Spain, there were only two mass forces: the Carlists and the Falangists. Their militias had seen a massive influx of recruits. In contrast, there was no place in the new order for the 'moderate' CEDA. Gil Robles had to endure semi-exile in Portugal.[190] The monarchists possessed the best-prepared cadres and crucial links with financial centres but were few in number. They had been the most solid supporters of the idea of a unified command under Franco. However, the *Caudillo*, a master of duplicity, soon curtailed the aspirations of the royal heir, Don Juan. When in December 1936, stressing his experience in the Royal Navy, the latter requested permission to join a nationalist battleship, Franco promptly declined his offer, citing the need to keep him safe.[191]

In December 1936, Carlist ambitions were thwarted: after establishing a separate military academy for their officers without seeking Franco's approval, its political leader, Manuel Fal Conde, was presented with the stark alternative of instant exile or court-martial. The Carlist council chose to replace him with the more compromising Count Rodezno.[192]

Axis intervention appeared to offer the Falange the opportunity to impose its hegemony. However, its strength was artificial and, with most of its leaders killed in the first days of the war, it was divided. On 20 November, José Antonio was executed in Alicante, despite many Republicans believing it to be a grave error.[193] Tellingly, Franco's support for several rescue operations was lukewarm. His death was a godsend: a charismatic rival became a martyr to be worshipped as the 'absent', while the Falange remained headless.[194]

Military headquarters fuelled the flames of Falangist discord. On 18 April 1937, an armed clash between rival factions in Salamanca provided Franco with the pretext to stage a coup. The following day, he decreed the unification of all the nationalist forces under a single party: *Falange Española Tradicionalista y de las JONS* (FET), known as 'the movement'. Its symbol was the Falangist yoke and arrows. The uniform combined the Falangist blue shirt and the Carlist red beret.[195] It represented the birth of a Francoist party. Even if fascist paraphernalia and rhetoric were readily mimicked, it remained a state-controlled apparatus joined by thousands of opportunists and hitherto apolitical people. In a sense, it was a victory for the monarchists given their enormous weight in the emerging state vis-à-vis Carlists and Falangists. The former accepted it for the sake of the destruction of the atheist Republic, Catholic prominence, and the confirmation of their supremacy in Navarra.[196] Falange's social radicalism was swiftly ignored. Falangists could accept the fait accompli and enjoy access to the privileges of power or face persecution. Some revolutionary old-shirts were purged. Manuel Hedilla, José Antonio's designated successor and provisional national leader, was accused of rebellion and sentenced to death. After the intercession of Serrano and Axis diplomats, the sentence was commuted but he remained in prison until 1947. Most diehards were ready to comply.[197] After all, much of Falangist's external liturgy and jargon were adopted. They also obtained powerful positions, particularly in the security services, the labour movement, and the media.

The Church was a clear victor in the spoils of nationalist unity. In July 1937, its hierarchy published a collective letter to the bishops of the world. It represented a colossal manipulation of the truth. The rebellion was described as an 'armed plebiscite' to thwart fiendish foreign-inspired heretics.[198] Religious pomp, reminiscent of medieval times, hailed the regime. In turn, the Church experienced a golden era: a near-monopoly of education, a prominent role in social services, exemption from taxation, and much more. The Republic's secular reforms were overturned while the clergy became the guardians of people's habits. The more prudent Vatican waited until May 1938 to recognize officially Nationalist Spain.[199]

The *Caudillo* awarded himself the royal prerogative of entering and leaving religious sites *bajo palio* (under a canopy).[200] He embraced the principles of National-Catholicism: a fusion of modernizing totalitarian tendencies with medieval and religious-absolutist elements. References to the *Reconquista* and the Golden Age were merged with fascist rhetoric. The German '*Ein Volk, ein Reich, ein Führer*' was mimicked in Franco's Spain: '*Una patria, un estado, un Caudillo*'. On 2 December 1937, Franco declared himself to be responsible only to God and to history.[201]

In what would be a blueprint for future years, the first cabinet, established on 30 January 1938, represented a masterstroke in a carefully orchestrated balancing act. Serrano, at the Home Office, was to be the dominant figure overseeing administration and propaganda. The other portfolios were distributed amongst army officers, Catholics, Falangists, Carlists, and monarchists. Bound together by the so-called 'Pact of Blood' (that is, their active complicity in the ongoing brutal repression), all the nationalist factions ('families' in the Francoist jargon) shared in the spoils of office. They enjoyed enough leeway but never hegemony over the others.[202]

In the City of the Devil

A wave of widespread enthusiasm marked Republican Spain. Women acquired an unprecedented role in a male-dominated society. Some wore blue overalls and joined the militias. Others looked after the wounded or the children of the combatants, ran collective dining halls, and assumed a variety of jobs left vacant. Seized cars were painted with the graffiti of unions or parties. Prisons were emptied and court archives were destroyed. Right-wing dignitaries' houses or political headquarters were looted. Vast tracks of land and industry were collectivized. Still, the extraordinary popular resolve would be in vain unless, as Malraux noted, 'the apocalypses of fraternity' were organized.[203] This strategy, which largely coincided with that of the PCE, might have a negative impact in the medium term. It dampened the revolutionary enthusiasm of the popular revolt of the first weeks and, when it failed to produce military victory, it brough about defeatism and disaffection.

Nevertheless, focusing on the dichotomy between giving priority to the war effort or social revolution misses the core of the argument. By September 1936, the irresistible advance of Franco's troops, supplied by the Axis, had solved the question in favour of the former. The Nationalists pursued a total war and the Republic had to fight back on those terms. Resistance could no longer be based on merely local terms. Workers' courage in street fighting was crucial in crushing the insurrection, but bravery alone could not win the war. Ill-disciplined militias fared badly in open battles. Lacking experienced commanders, improvisation and rivalries often meant that while one column was fighting, others were watching, or holding a vote before an attack.[204]

With the battle for the capital looming, mobilizing all available material and human resources became imperative to stave off imminent defeat. In September, parallel to Franco's ascent, Largo Caballero, seemingly the charismatic leader best suited to rally republican forces, was catapulted to power. He attained the premiership and the War Ministry in the euphorically called 'Government of Victory', which contained six Socialists, two Republicans, one Catalan and one Basque nationalist, and two Communists. In early November, two members of the CNT – Joan Peiró (Industry) and Juan López (Commerce) – and two members of the FAI – Juan García Oliver (Justice) and Federica Montseny (Health) – joined the government.[205]

Confronted by what was a dire reality, even the CNT-FAI leaders understood that if the war were lost, there would never be a revolution. The motto was about fighting fascism above all else.[206] Emphasis was placed on restraining revolutionary chaos in the rear and creating a strong executive to run a war economy and lead a concerted military effort. Steps were taken to create a cohesive force, the Popular Army. On 29 September, a decree brought all the militias, comprising over 100,000 men, under military discipline.[207] The government established general staff and military academies, popular courts headed by professional judges, and increased the number of security forces. The minister of agriculture, the Communist Vicente Uribe, stopped the process of all-out land collectivization. In December, he founded a Peasant Federation to defend smallholders' ownership.[208]

The war accelerated the Republic's progressive programme. Women obtained equal civil rights and widow status, and the legitimacy of their offspring if they were unmarried when their partners were killed in combat. Momentum gathered for cultural enlightenment, including the conversion of abandoned estates into schools and the establishment of workers' institutes to offer two-year study plans with academic and vocational subjects for those aged between 18 and 35 years.[209] However, intrinsic problems continued to thwart the war effort. The shortage of weapons and leftist congenital aversion to military discipline were clear hindrances. Notwithstanding widespread acceptance that collaboration was imperative for victory, its genuine implementation eluded the Republicans. A Republic that was in the process of reconstructing its democratic forms could not, without destroying its raison d'être, solve this dilemma in the authoritarian fashion of the insurgents.[210]

Victory in Madrid only offered a brief respite. Largo's obstinacy in clinging to the post of war minister combined with constant displays of pettiness and refusal to accept advice, increased rivals' apprehension and friends' alienation. Málaga's fall, in February 1937, was a massive blow to his authority.[211] He often clashed with the Soviet advisers and ambassador. With resistance dependent on Russian aid, subtle diplomacy rather than a quick temper was needed. Furthermore, his relations with the PCE deteriorated. He resented communist control of the mergers he had sanctioned: the United Socialist Youth (JSU) and the Catalan United Socialist Party (PSUC). The prime minister begrudged communism's growing might. At its peak in September 1937, it had become a powerful movement with 340,000 and 250,000 members in the PCE and JSU, respectively.[212]

Indisputably, Soviet popularity, as the only major power rendering military assistance to the Republic, increased communism's prestige. However, the PCE's astonishing growth was also due to its image of competence and discipline as well as its formidable propaganda machine. Its militia (Fifth Regiment), with political commissars and professional officers, became the model for the Popular Army. The PCE emerged as the backbone of the Popular Front intra-class alliance. It maintained an important proletarian constituency, whose energies were rekindled with promises of a radical new social deal after victory. Simultaneously, its moderation (championing respect for private property and loyal collaboration between the middle and working classes) appealed to thousands of small tenants, artisans, merchants, and white-collar workers. Additionally, it made important inroads into the army and security services. They joined the PCE because it offered them a refuge in which concepts of discipline and command were respected – quite a rarity in the traumatic, post-coup times.[213]

However, the meteoric growth of the Communists mirrored that of the Falange. Their strength was largely artificial, as most of the thousands of new recruits joined not due to ideological convictions but to opportunism.

Bitter tensions persisted due not so much to the need for reconstructing the state – something even grudgingly accepted by the CNT leaders, but not by many militants – as to the struggle to control its agenda. It was in Barcelona that things would explode. The city became a fiercely contested political space. The collapse of central power provided a golden opportunity for the *Generalitat* to further its nationalist agenda. Nevertheless, the Catalan government was overwhelmed by the CNT's street power. The existence of other competing forces further exacerbated the situation.

Despite its formidable power, the CNT could no longer claim to be the only voice of Catalan labour. On 23 July 1936, the merger of four small socialist and communist groups produced a strong United Catalan Socialist Party (PSUC), which was affiliated to the Comintern. Echoing the latter's programme, the PSUC endorsed inter-class alliance, war production efficiency, and solidarity with the central government.[214] It rapidly enjoyed a large influx of members, as people sought protection against the CNT. Its trade union, the Catalan branch of the UGT, also brought together in the summer of 1936 most of the labour movement outside the CNT, including many *Treintistas*. By September, it boasted 435,000 militants.[215] Indeed, both the UGT and CNT saw a explosion in membership. However, their constituencies were radically different. Anarcho-syndicalism remained the voice of low-skilled workers and the urban poor, while its rivals attracted artisans, white-collar workers, police officers, and so on.[216] To complicate matters, a relatively small force, the POUM, had its strongest section in Catalonia. It was extremely critical of the PCE's moderate line, the Popular Front, and the USSR. Being led by Andreu Nin, who had been Trotsky's private secretary for some time in the 1920s, facilitated communist accusations of it being a Trotskyist party. Ironically, Nin had broken with Trotsky, who often lambasted the POUM in his writings.[217] There was also a history of bad blood with anarcho-syndicalists who perceived the POUM's advances as a replay of the early 1920s when Nin's faction had tried to take control of the CNT.[218]

The *Generalitat* pursued a subtle juggling act. It joined forces with the PSUC to restore state power. However, aware of the latter's centralist tendency and growing inroads into the ERC's social constituency, it needed the CNT to act as a counterweight.[219] In September 1936, a temporary solution was found: a coalition government in which all forces were represented. In a surprising surrender of ground, the CNT agreed and even dissolved the Committee of Anti-Fascist Militias.[220] Still, some militants entrenched in the patrol groups refused to disarm and abandon those vital parts of the economy seized earlier.

Tensions mounted during the first months of 1937. When in late April, the UGT leader Roldán Cortada was assassinated, an armed confrontation appeared imminent.[221] On 3 May, three truckloads of assault guards were dispatched to seize the central telephone exchange held by the CNT. It was the spark that ignited the fuse. After the police were met with a volley of shots, shops and factories began to close and barricades were erected. Barcelona experienced a four-day mini civil war which left 218 dead.[222]

Ludicrous conspiracy theories circulated. Anarchists and *Poumistas* talked of an operation orchestrated from Moscow with the complicity of the *Generalitat*. In turn, Communists spoke of an 'Anarcho-Trotskyist *putsch*' masterminded by fifth columnists directed from nationalist headquarters.[223] Comintern reports from Barcelona removed all doubts about a communist conspiracy that they had neither foreseen nor made plans to confront.[224]

Azaña, then installed in Barcelona, lived through the May Days' events. He wrote that Catalonia was in total chaos. Its population wished for a general to sweep away the ongoing madness. He described a real theatre of the absurd. He, the first symbol of the state, was not molested. The police officers at his service were sometimes shot at and others were respected.[225]

The May Days were a spontaneous outburst waiting to happen. George Orwell, another privileged witness (and despite his subjective stance as part of the POUM militia), admitted that everybody expected the fighting, but those who revolted had no precise plans.[226] The POUM's mouthpiece, *La Batalla*, printed a leaflet calling for the establishment of a revolutionary junta and the shooting of the enemies of the revolution.[227] However, the POUM was merely dragged along by events and backed down when the CNT leadership refused to sanction an armed response.[228]

The May Days produced the CNT's crisis of identity. Immersed for months in the governmental machinery, its leaders had accepted the premises of state reconstruction and could not condone insurrectionary outbursts. They knew that revolutionary success in Barcelona would mean confrontation with the rest of Republican Spain and Franco's ultimate victory. Two anarchist ministers (García Oliver and Montseny) and the national secretary (Mariano Vázquez) rushed to Barcelona. They agreed with the *Generalitat* to broadcast an appeal to their confused followers to lay down their weapons.[229]

The Republic's Dogged Resistance

The May Days strengthened those advocating for the centralization of power and discipline in the rear. The *Generalitat* lost much of its autonomy. The central government made itself responsible for public order in Catalonia and moved its headquarters to Barcelona in November 1937. The CNT, though still a huge force, emerged demoralized after what many militants regarded as the capitulation of their leaders.

The May Days compelled Largo's many enemies to act, including the PSOE. Azaña, furious by what he perceived as the prime minister's indifference to his pleas for help during the Barcelona fighting, relished his removal. On 13 May, the Communist ministers proposed a ban on the POUM and the arrest of its leaders. Largo opposed them, but after a heated dispute he discovered he only had in the cabinet the backing of his UGT comrades and the four CNT-FAI ministers. The PCE would have been content with him relinquishing his post as war minister. Moscow wanted him to remain prime minister.[230] However, everybody was shocked when Largo proposed a cabinet reshuffle reduced to only 14 ministers in which he retained the war portfolio that now incorporated the navy and air force held hitherto by Prieto.[231] He was forced to resign. Henceforth, the PSOE leadership launched a concerted assault on Largo's remaining power bases. He was removed as UGT president and a new executive seized control.[232]

The new prime minister was the Socialist Juan Negrín. Vilified afterwards as a mere communist puppet, more recent historiography has rescued his reputation and even suggested that he was a gifted war leader.[233] Negrín was a polyglot who, aged only 30, was awarded the chair of physiology at Madrid University. Siding with Prieto's faction in the PSOE, he took control of the Treasury during the Largo administration. Outspoken against the existing indiscipline, he insisted that the reconstruction of state authority was imperative to wage war successfully.[234]

Far from being a mere communist stooge, Comintern reports stressed that with Negrín in office the PCE often had to swallow a bitter pill and compromise.[235] In fact, his appointment was not due to any sort of external pressures but was Azaña's own choice. In comparison with Largo, the Republican president wrote that 'he no longer felt like he was talking to a dead man'.[236] The French military attaché, Colonel Morel, described him as a 'lucid statesman with an iron will to fight Fascism'.[237] Negrín's slogan, 'resisting is winning', encapsulated his strategy. Since victory could not be enjoyed with the existing international status quo, it was imperative to gain time to embrace different alternatives: at best, the conflict could be linked with a European war, or the Allies could be persuaded either to enforce the existing non-intervention policy or abandon it altogether and give the Republic the supplies to defend herself; at worst, an effective war effort could force Franco to negotiate a compromise peace.[238] A weakness in Negrín's emphasis on strengthening state power was the liquidation of the initial revolutionary fervour, the only asset that the Republic could truly rely upon.

The POUM became the scapegoat for the May Days. Its identification with the rebellion and its relative marginality facilitated its elimination.[239] Ludicrously accused of being 'an agent of Fascism', it was officially suppressed in June. It continued a semi-legal existence in Valencia and Madrid but hundreds of militants in Catalonia were arrested upon spurious charges of espionage. Yet Negrín's premiership did not mean the triumph of the counter-revolution but rather the reconstruction of an efficient state apparatus in command of the economy, diplomacy, and military strategy. Regaining control of public order had a price: the arrest of 3,734 militants in Catalonia alone from April 1937 to January 1939, accused of illegal possession of weapons, rebellion, or murder.[240] Such repression was the result of two parallel but not identical agendas: the internecine wars within the communist movement and the restoration of state authority with its recovery of a monopoly of legal violence and the settling of scores against the extremists.[241] Still, Comintern agents backed by the security services, which contained many Communists, murdered some foreign nationals suspected of Trotskyist leanings. A scandalous incident was Nin's kidnapping and killing by Soviet operatives led by Alexandr Orlov.[242] However, their activities should not be exaggerated. According to a recent study, at most there were 10 Soviet agents active in Spain at any one time, and they may have committed up to 20 murders.[243] Despite these flaws, legality was not altogether subverted. The POUM leaders were brought to trial in October 1938: four were sentenced to 15 years of imprisonment, another to 11 years, and two were acquitted – a verdict dubbed by Dimitrov as a 'slap in the face' to Communists.[244] They were not condemned for the grotesque charges of espionage but for endorsing a rebellion against a state at war.[245]

The pragmatic stance of the CNT leadership avoided all-out confrontation with the state.[246] After the May Days, some of its buildings were seized and militants detained. On 11 August, the government dissolved the anarchist-dominated Council of Aragón and arrested some of its members, including its president, Joaquín Ascaso, accused of jewel smuggling. The pretext was the need to reactivate a front that had remained static for months. There were few complaints; Ascaso was even expelled from the CNT.[247]

On 17 May 1937, Negrín formed a cabinet (with half the previous number of portfolios): three Socialists, two Republicans, two Communists, one Catalan, and one Basque nationalist. By June, the CNT was already soliciting representation and promising total support in the prosecution of the war.[248]

At the same time, from the original chaotic rag-tag militias, an efficient army emerged in 1937 able to mount a series of well-planned offensives: Brunete (July), Belchite (September), and Teruel (December). Still, the initial breakthroughs soon turned into battles of attrition which favoured the *Caudillo*'s plan of gradually bleeding the enemy. While both sides paid an appalling cost in terms of lives and *materiel*, the insurgents would soon make up their losses, but the Republic could not. The Nationalists' sheer material superiority would prevail over the Republicans' courage and even tactical cunning. Ultimately, as Helen Graham noted, Negrín failed to achieve victory not because his strategy was wrong but because, unlike the Axis-equipped nationalist armies, the crippling embargo not only prevented the Republic from ever engaging on an equal military footing, but also in the end undercut any attempts to sustain the physical fabric and morale of the home front, crucial to its war of resistance.[249]

In mid-March 1938, Franco abandoned his perennial caution. He launched a *Blitzkrieg* – often advocated by Axis officers – against the battered Republicans in Aragón. Under a curtain of fire produced by 1,000 Italian and German aircraft, over 100,000 troops crossed the River Ebro. On 15 April, they seized Vinaroz (Castellón) in the Mediterranean cutting the Republic in two.[250]

Franco's Victory

In the spring of 1938, the Republic appeared to be on the verge of collapse. The rear started to crumble. Subjected to constant aerial bombardments and grim news from the front, the war-weary population, whose meagre rations consisted mostly of rice and lentils, began to long for Franco's white bread and wonder when the tragedy would end.[251] By then, many Republicans, including Prieto and Azaña, had concluded that the war was lost. However, lacking any alternative apart from open capitulation, Azaña had to renew his confidence in Negrín who, on 6 April 1938, formed a new cabinet that included representatives from all the Popular Front forces. He took over the war portfolio from Prieto, Álvarez del Vayo returned to the Foreign Office, and the CNT was represented by Segundo Blanco as minister of health and education.[252] Seemingly impervious to the ongoing military debacle, Negrín continued to offer an image of optimism.[253] And indeed, two sets of events appeared to offer a glimmer of hope: Franco's baffling strategy and the international setting.

After reaching the Mediterranean, the insurgents seemed poised to seize the rest of Catalonia. Nevertheless, the *Caudillo* directed his forces south, towards Valencia. Many generals and Axis advisers were bewildered, but Franco simply sought to wage a slow war of attrition to consolidate his power and slowly bleed the enemy into total submission. This gave the Republic a breathing space. With the mountainous terrain favouring the defenders the nationalist advance was now painfully slow and very costly in terms of casualties.[254]

The Axis' increasingly undisguised ambitions revealed the hollowness of appeasement. On 12 March 1938, Germany annexed Austria (*Anschluss*). Alarm bells rang in Paris, where a second Blum cabinet was formed. The French premier believed the time had arrived to confront Nazi aggression.[255] In a hastily convened meeting of the political and military leadership (Permanent National Defence Committee), he advocated delivering an ultimatum to Franco, demanding the withdrawal of foreign troops, and dispatching arms to the Republic. Yet, most French politicians and officers felt that they could neither risk a breach with Britain nor spare any military equipment. Finally, Blum had to settle for a half-hearted formula: the opening of the border to the delivery of Soviet weapons to Spain.[256] Between March and June, over 18,219 tons of *materiel* helped re-arm the Republican army.[257]

Regardless of the *Anschluss*, the British government continued its hostility towards the Republic. In February 1938, Eden, highly critical of fascist aggression, had to resign. He was replaced by the arch-appeaser Lord Halifax.[258] The demise of 'Red Spain' was deemed to be a worthwhile sacrifice for the sake of appeasement. On 5 June, Harvey wrote: 'We seem to be drifting more and more into the position of allowing Russia to champion the Democracies while we seek to placate the Dictators . . . The government is praying for Franco's victory'.[259] Consequently, Chamberlain welcomed the fall of Blum after just one month in office and his replacement by an administration that was no longer a Popular Front but contained only Radical ministers.[260] Headed by the hesitant Edouard Daladier, it contained Georges Bonnet, a staunch supporter of appeasement, at the *Quai d'Orsay*. Halifax instructed his ambassador in France, Eric Phipps, to present Bonnet with an official communication outlining the fatal consequences of a French refusal to close the border. In the case of Bonnet, they were preaching to the converted. A doubtful Daladier finally gave way. On 13 June, Phipps happily reported that the 'hellish' border had been closed.[261]

On 1 May, an undaunted Negrín published a thirteen-point declaration destined to impress the Allies. It stipulated that post-war Spain would be a democracy, independent from foreign interference, with free elections and full civil rights.[262] In the early hours of 25 July, the Republicans launched a daring offensive, masterminded by Rojo. Predominantly led by communist commanders, the so-called Army of the Ebro had been created and trained for weeks for that operation. Profiting from the military reserves assembled before the closing of the French border, the Army of the Ebro crossed the river of that name to relieve the pressure on Valencia and ultimately gain time, as the war in Europe seemed ever closer.[263]

Catching the Nationalists by surprise, the operation was an outright success. In the first week, 800 square kilometres of ground were gained. Franco's response was to rush fresh troops and equipment, including the Condor Legion, from other fronts. The Army of the Ebro proved a formidable opponent. Entrenched on the high peaks of mountainous terrain, it withstood for weeks the hail of fire from seven major nationalist offensives. Once the Republican breakthrough was contained, the Nationalists could have resumed their operation against Valencia or pushed towards Barcelona. Instead, Franco chose a battle of annihilation, seeking to bleed the enemy regardless of the human cost.[264]

Axis leaders could not conceal their dismay. They could not understand Franco's inability to put his immensely superior firepower to decisive use. The German ambassador, Eberhard von Stohrer, expressed frustration with the existing stalemate.[265] Mussolini told Ciano: 'Today, 29th August 1938, I predict Franco's defeat. This man does not know how or does not want to make war. The Reds are fighters, he is not!'[266]

The fate of the Spanish conflict appeared inextricably linked with events on the continent. German intransigence regarding the Sudetenland

(Czechoslovakia) threatened to plunge Europe into war. On 21 September, Negrín travelled to the League of Nations in Geneva to announce the unilateral withdrawal of the International Brigades.[267] On 29 October, they staged their farewell parade in Barcelona amidst emotional scenes.[268] The loss of the remaining 12,000 foreign volunteers was a symbolic act that sought to bring about international pressure to force the Nationalists to follow suit. Franco, bereft of Axis aid, could not have pursued the war.

As Republican expectations surged, gloom dominated the other camp. After agonizing hesitations, on 27 September Franco reassured the Allies of his commitment to remain neutral in a major European conflagration. Still, his alleged neutrality had serious flaws both in terms of credibility and application. The Allies could not ignore the significant Axis *materiel* in Spain, nor could the Nationalists do without it. Francoist headquarters dreaded that, as soon as continental hostilities broke out, the Republic would declare war on Germany and link its fortune to that of the western democracies. The insurgents would find themselves geographically isolated from their friends and facing possible French intervention. In fact, the French military command had planned to send troops to Catalonia and Morocco.[269]

In the event, fate favoured Franco again. On 16 November 1938, the last Republican fighters retreated across the Ebro, putting an end to the battle.[270] Despite their massive *materiel* superiority, the Nationalists had needed almost four months to expel the Republicans from the territory captured in July. However, the campaign constituted the war of annihilation that Franco wished for. Both sides had some 60,000 casualties, including the deaths of 20,000 Republicans and 10,000 Nationalists.[271] However, it was the solution to the Czech crisis that inflicted the lethal blow on the Republic. Hopes of being rescued by the Allies were shattered.[272] On 29 September, Chamberlain and Daladier met Hitler in Munich. Bent on conserving peace *à outrance*, they chose to brow-beat the Czechs into surrendering the territory the Germans wanted.[273]

In late 1938, the two Spanish sides presented contrasting images. While Nationalist Spain enjoyed an abundance of basic goods, the Republican population had to endure shortages, a poor diet, and constant bombardment. Their war experience had been one of slow but constant defeat.[274] In military terms, both armies were exhausted after months of gruelling combat. But whereas the Republic had used up some of its best troops and *materiel*, the Nationalists managed to restore their depleted stocks rapidly. Hitler, already preparing his new coup (Poland), looked forward to ending his Spanish venture, but he would first extract massive economic gains. For months, Franco had succeeded in staving off Hermann Göring's 'Montana Project', the codename for the control of substantial Spanish mining rights. With his reserves now depleted, he granted Germany exploitation rights in over 200 mines. On 18 November, Hitler agreed to replenish the Condor Legion and deliver massive new *materiel*.[275]

In early December, Negrín sent the chief of the air force, General Ignacio Hidalgo de Cisneros, to Moscow with a personal letter for Stalin, requesting a new dispatch of weapons. In the warmest terms, he described the Soviet leader as the Republic's last chance to resist.[276] By then, Stalin had drawn crucial conclusions from Munich. In August 1939, he signed the Non-Aggression Pact with Germany. Its clauses provided a written guarantee of peace by each party towards the other, and a commitment that declared that neither government would aid or ally itself with an enemy of the other. In addition, the treaty included the Secret Protocol, which defined the borders of Soviet and German spheres of influence and control across Poland, the Baltic states, and Finland.[277] Nonetheless, in late 1938, the Nazi danger was still a reality and Stalin had not yet written off the Republic. Despite the exhaustion of Spanish gold reserves, the USSR dispatched massive military supplies (T-26 tanks, planes, cannons, machine guns, etc.).[278]

On 23 December, Franco initiated the final push into Catalonia. For that, he assembled the largest military concentration of the war: 300,000 soldiers, 300 tanks, 500 planes, and 565 pieces of artillery. Starved of supplies and heavily outgunned, the Republican defences collapsed after three weeks of dogged resistance.[279] In early January, in a desperate attempt to prevent outright defeat, the Republic launched an offensive in Extremadura. However, the attack soon fizzled out.[280] Negrín pleaded for French aid via Colonel Morel who, on 6 January, warned his superiors of the threat mounted by Axis troops on the border.[281] On 15 January, Daladier agreed to reopen the frontier to trains loaded with Soviet weapons – but it was too late.[282] Nothing short of a full-fledged French intervention could prevent the debacle; however, this was not an option. Mussolini boasted of being ready to send Italian divisions to Spain to counter any French support to the Republic.[283] After two years of shameful capitulations, for the British government it was not the advance of the Axis forces towards the Pyrenees but the potential French response that imperilled peace! By then, Bonnet was beginning to explore ways to gain the favour of the nationalist victors.[284]

Defeat in the front led to military disintegration. Many soldiers, often just recently called up, simply deserted by hiding in the haystacks of sympathetic villagers.[285] On 26 January, starved of food, packed with refugees, and under constant bombing, Barcelona fell without resistance. While many welcomed what they hoped was an end to the nightmare, for others it was just the beginning. By early February, nearly half a million beaten soldiers and civilian refugees fled along frozen roads towards the border with the few possessions that they had managed to salvage.[286] Unprepared for such a human avalanche, the French administration interned the exhausted fugitives in camps where food was scarce and shelter or proper sanitation was lacking. The appalling living conditions were a deliberate invitation for them to escape and return to Spain.[287]

A fatal diplomatic blow accompanied the military debacle. On 27 February 1939, Britain and France recognized Franco's Spain. France agreed to return whatever of Spain's assets were on its territory and prevent any operation from its soil. In return, the Nationalists promised friendly relations.[288] Tellingly, Bonnet appointed as ambassador to Madrid, the Great War hero and outspoken supporter of Nationalist Spain, Marshal Philippe Pétain.[289] Without notice, the NIC was dismantled.

On 28 February, refusing to return to Spain to continue a lost war, Azaña resigned as president of the Republic. As speaker of the chamber, Martínez Barrio agreed to temporarily occupy that post.[290] However, he also declined to travel to Spain. Party and union executives were part of the human avalanche that crossed the border in February 1939. They all chose exile save for the PCE, which followed the government back to Spain. The cabinet finally established its headquarters in the small town of Elda (Alicante).

In February 1939, it was evident that the Republic could not mount a final offensive. Nevertheless, it still controlled a roughly one-third of Spain, including the cities of Madrid and Valencia, had a population of 10 million people, and an army of half a million men, although gravely affected by lack of equipment and defeatism. At best, it could hold on until the outbreak of the expected continental war. At least its resistance might force the Nationalists to accept peace negotiations that would allow an organized retreat and the safe evacuation of those most endangered by the victor's repression.[291] Furthermore, nationalist deeds left little room for doubt about what would take place. On 13 February, with victory within his grasp, the *Caudillo* made starkly clear that there could be no reconciliation. He introduced the Law of Political Responsibilities retroactive to October 1934, which made supporters of the Republic guilty of siding with an 'illegitimate' regime. This foreshadowed the fate that the vanquished could expect.[292]

On 16 February, Negrín met with his republican army commanders at the aerodrome of Los Llanos (Albacete). Everyone except for Miaja painted a bleak picture. Shortages and war-weariness prevented further resistance. The prime minister insisted that he was willing to seek peace on honourable terms. However, the only alternative to unconditional surrender was dogged resistance to extract concessions. Channels with the enemy should remain open but secret. Otherwise, it would lead to military disintegration and catastrophic defeat.[293] However, Negrín's efforts to rekindle resistance were futile. After 30 months of combat, defeatism dominated Republican Spain.

Ultimately, the Republic's collapse came due to a lethal combination of delusion, naivety, and treachery.[294] By the time of the meeting at Los Llanos, a full-fledged plot to oust the government was being hatched. Colonel Segismundo Casado, commander of the Army of the Centre, was its leader. In October 1938, he contacted fifth columnists in Madrid. He was told that nationalist headquarters were willing to show magnanimity with those prepared to render 'good services to the cause of Spain'.[295] What better service, he might have thought, than that of both ending the war and crushing communism!

Casado gathered the support of disgruntled officers and politicians who had concluded that continued resistance was sheer lunacy. Hitherto, a rallying point due to its discipline and organization, the PCE paid the price of growing defeatism. Negrín and his government, perceived as mere puppets of the Communists, were considered an obstacle to negotiating the end of a futile war.[296] The most prominent plotter was Besteiro. Having remained in Madrid throughout the war, he refused numerous opportunities to seek safe exile and grew obsessed with the idea that Negrín was a communist stooge leading Spain to catastrophe.[297] In the naive belief that he was called for the higher purpose of stopping the bloodshed, Besteiro had been in touch with the fifth column since the spring of 1938 – meetings facilitated by the fact that some were members of the university.[298] Astonishingly, he imagined that Franco's regime would be like that of Primo, and that a reformed UGT, purged of revolutionaries, would be allowed to play a significant role in post-war Spain.[299] He met Casado at his own home for the first time on 3 February 1939. They agreed on everything, although Besteiro declined to preside over a new administration, arguing that it should be an army officer.[300]

Physical exhaustion and despair might explain the plotters' naivety and irresponsibility in ignoring the horrific scale of repression taking place in Nationalist Spain. Believing a *paz digna* (honourable peace) to be possible once Negrín was deposed, they even thought that the tragedy could end in a similar fashion to that other cruel civil war, the First Carlist War, exactly 100 years earlier: the commanders of the two armies put aside political differences and terminated the slaughter with an embrace (*Abrazo de Vergara*).[301]

On 3 March, a series of military promotions was the catalyst for the plotters to act. It was déjà vu. As in July 1936, they concealed their treason behind the delusion that their coup was a gallant effort to save Spain from a communist takeover.[302] In fact, Communists were only promoted to take command of Cartagena (Colonel Francisco Galán), Alicante (Lieutenant Colonel Etelvino Vega), Murcia (Lieutenant-Colonel Leocadio Mendiola), and Albacete (Major Inocencio Curto) – all close to the Mediterranean coast. The conclusion was clear: trustworthy officers would oversee the holding onto of key positions to safeguard a general evacuation.[303] Still, it rang alarm bells amongst those who had already decided that Negrín was a communist puppet.

On 4 March, republican officers revolted in Cartagena to prevent Colonel Galán from taking control of the vital naval base there. In a bizarre unfolding of events, fifth columnists took advantage of the situation to mount a parallel coup. After more than 24 hours of heavy fighting, reinforcements regained control for the government. Amidst the reigning confusion, the fleet departed and eventually surrendered to the French authorities in Bizerta (Tunisia). With one stroke, the Republic was deprived of the means to conduct a potential evacuation. Ironically, the affair ended with a minor nationalist disaster. Confident that their supporters were about to seize the city, they sent two warships with landing troops. They were surprised when the coastal batteries opened fire. *El Castillo de Olite* was sunk: 1,270 soldiers perished and 700 were captured. *El Castillo de Peñafiel* was hit but managed to escape with four dead and 25 wounded.[304]

On the evening of 5 March, with the battle still raging in Cartagena, Casado made his move. From the cellars of the old Treasury ministry, Besteiro, who had accepted the post of foreign minister, announced by radio that the government, lacking moral authority or political legality, was replaced by a Council of National Defence, whose objective was to negotiate with the enemy to end the slaughter.[305] During the next frenzied hours, Negrín talked in vain to Casado on the telephone while his ministers engaged with their political counterparts. Negrín understood that the jig was up. Only after a bitter struggle could the rebellion be crushed. By then, the war would be lost. The following day the government fled by plane. Communist leaders and Comintern agents followed suit.[306]

The ease with which Casado orchestrated a rebellion and conducted negotiations with the fifth column pierced the myth of the PCE's omnipresence, particularly within the army.[307] Many officers had joined that party for pragmatic reasons (career advancement, protection against revolutionary excesses, etc.). In most places, there was hardly any resistance. The exception was Madrid where the local communists' isolation combined with Casado's stringent measures against them, as a means of establishing his credentials with Franco, sparked a mini civil war. After three days of combat, the plotters were on the verge of defeat. Tellingly, they asked nationalist headquarters for help. Franco complied half-heartedly, mounting some attacks to facilitate the actions of Casado's forces. However, news of the departure of the government and the Communist leaders left the loyalist side without clear goals. Eventually, the intervention of the 4th Army Corps, led by the anarchist Cipriano Mera, tilted the balance. The battle resulted in hundreds of casualties and signalled the end of the republican army as a fighting force.[308]

Casado overlooked a crucial detail. By destroying the possibility of resistance, he removed the only reason that Franco might ever have had to concede peace with terms.[309] He effectively rendered pointless the bloodshed and sacrifices of the previous three years. Demands for time to organize the evacuation and assurances of no reprisals were dismissed. Franco reiterated what had always been his goal: unconditional surrender.[310] Bent on humiliating the enemy, he would not even let the Council mask its embarrassment with a meaningless treaty.[311] On 26 March, the Nationalists resumed the offensive virtually unopposed. Republican troops deserted en masse. Many escaped towards the coast in a final – and often futile – attempt to escape abroad.[312] When Madrid was occupied two days later, Ciano noted that fascism had won its most formidable victory to date.[313] On 1 April, the *Caudillo* announced the end of the struggle: 'Today, with the Red Army captive and disarmed, our victorious troops had achieved their final military objectives. The war is over'.[314]

Notes

1 Zugazagoitia, *Guerra*, p. 158.
2 Ibid., pp. 67–8.
3 Paul Preston, *¡Comrades! Portraits of the Spanish Civil War* (London: HarperCollins, 1999), pp. 3–4.
4 The myth is demolished in Herbert R. Southworth, *Conspiracy and the Spanish Civil War: The Brainwashing of Francisco Franco* (London: Routledge, 2002).
5 Juan Carlos Losada, 'Los momentos decisivos de la guerra. Las estrategias militares', in Juan Andrés Blanco, Jesús A. Martínez, and Ángel Viñas (eds.), *Luces sobre un pasado deformado. La Guerra Civil 80 años después* (Madrid: Marcial Pons, 2020), pp. 122–3.
6 Alberto Reig, *Violencia y terror* (Madrid: Akal, 1990), p. 22.
7 Viñas, *¿Quién quiso la Guerra civil?*, pp. 179–81.
8 Julio Aróstegui, *Por qué el 18 de julio . . . Y después* (Barcelona: Flor del Viento, 2006), p. 267.
9 Paul Preston, *The Spanish Holocaust: Inquisition and Extermination in Twentieth-Century Spain* (London: W.W. Norton, 2012), p. 132.
10 The insurgents, wanting to be identified with the nation/fatherland, called themselves *nacionales*. Rafael Abella, *La vida cotidiana durante la Guerra Civil: La España Nacional* (Barcelona: Planeta, 1976), pp. 29–30.
11 Martin Blinkhorn, *Carlism and Crisis in Spain* (Cambridge: Cambridge University Press, 1975), p. 259.
12 Moradiellos, *1936*, p. 81.
13 Cardona, *El poder*, pp. 307–9.
14 Zugazagoitia, *Guerra*, pp. 79–84.
15 Hugh Thomas, *The Spanish Civil War* (Harmondsworth: Penguin, 1986 [1961]), p. 227.
16 Viñas, *¿Quién quiso la Guerra civil?*, p. 266.
17 Reig, *Violencia*, pp. 64–5.
18 Aróstegui, *Por qué*, p. 328.
19 Thomas, *The Spanish Civil War*, p. 229.
20 Ronald Fraser, *Blood of Spain* (Harmondsworth: Penguin, 1981), p. 51.
21 Michael Alpert, *El ejército republicano en la Guerra Civil* (Madrid: Siglo XXI, 1989), p. 30.
22 Pelai Pagés, *Guerra civil espanyola a Catalunya, 1936–9* (Barcelona: A. Romero, 1997), pp. 55–8.
23 Gabriel Cardona, *Historia militar de una Guerra Civil* (Barcelona: Flor del Viento, 2006), pp. 40–2.

24 Aróstegui, *Por qué*, p. 333.
25 Helen Graham, *The Spanish Republic at War* (Cambridge: Cambridge University Press, 2002), p. 96.
26 Jackson, *The Spanish Republic*, pp. 276–83.
27 Zugazagoitia, *Guerra*, p. 76.
28 Martin, *The Agony of Modernization*, pp. 380–1.
29 Helen Graham, *Socialism and War: The Spanish Socialist Party in Power and Crisis, 1936–1939* (Cambridge: Cambridge University Press, 1991), pp. 5–6.
30 Martin, *The Agony of Modernization*, p. 383.
31 Casanova, *Anarchism*, p. 106.
32 Francisco Espinosa, 'Introducción', in Francisco Espinosa (ed.), *Violencia roja y azul. España, 1936–1950* (Barcelona: Crítica, 2010), p. 78.
33 Santos Juliá, 'De guerra contra el invasor a guerra fratricida', in Santos Juliá (ed.), *Víctimas de la guerra civil* (Madrid: Temas de Hoy, 1999), p. 17.
34 Paul Preston, *Franco* (London: HarperCollins, 1993), p. 151.
35 Javier Cervera, *Madrid en guerra* (Madrid: Alianza, 1998), p. 48.
36 Alberto Reig, *Franco: el César Superlativo* (Madrid: Tecnos, 2005), p. 233.
37 Julián Casanova, *La Iglesia de Franco* (Madrid: Temas de Hoy, 2001), pp. 38–9.
38 Ealham, *Class*, p. 187.
39 José Luis Ledesma, 'Una retaguardia al rojo. Las violencias en la zona republicana', in Espinosa (ed.), *Violencia*, pp. 180–3.
40 Rafael Abella, *La vida cotidiana durante la Guerra Civil: La España Republicana* (Barcelona: Planeta, 1975), p. 48.
41 Preston, *The Spanish Holocaust*, pp. 228–9.
42 Julián Casanova, 'Rebelión y revolución', in Juliá (ed.), *Víctimas*, p. 70.
43 Ledesma, 'Una retaguardia', pp. 195–6.
44 Preston, *The Spanish Holocaust*, p. 221.
45 Ledesma, 'Una retaguardia', pp. 190–1.
46 Helen Graham, *The War and its Shadow: Spain's Civil War in Europe's Long Twentieth Century* (Brighton: Sussex Academic Press, 2012), pp. 40–3.
47 Pagés, *Guerra civil*, pp. 72–3.
48 Cervera, *Madrid*, pp. 347–50, 369–74.
49 Reig, *Violencia*, pp. 114–15.
50 Jorge M. Reverte, *La Batalla de Madrid* (Barcelona: Crítica, 2004), pp. 577–81.
51 Alfonso Domingo, *El ángel rojo. La historia de Melchor Rodríguez* (Barcelona: Almuzara, 2010), pp. 215–45.
52 Preston, *The Spanish Holocaust*, pp. 179–80.
53 Herbert R. Southworth, *El mito de la cruzada de Franco* (Barcelona: Plaza & Janés, 1986), pp. 215–17.

54 Ramón Serrano Suñer, *Memorias* (Barcelona: Planeta, 1977), pp. 245–7.
55 Ángela Cenarro, 'Muerte y subordinación en la España franquista: El imperio de la violencia como base del nuevo estado', *Historia Social*, 30 (1998), p. 13.
56 Francisco Espinosa, 'Julio 1936', in Julián Casanova (coord.), *Morir, matar, sobrevivir* (Barcelona: Crítica, 2002), p. 117.
57 Casanova, 'Rebelión y revolución', p. 76.
58 Balfour, *Deadly Embrace*, pp. 291–6.
59 Alberto Reig, *Memoria de la Guerra Civil* (Madrid: Alianza, 1999), pp. 113–18, 133–8.
60 Thomas, *The Faith and the Fury*, pp. 6–7.
61 Preston, ¡*Comrades*!, p. 228.
62 Reig, *Memoria*, pp. 80–1.
63 Bartolomé Bennassar, 'Introduction: Portée Mondiale de la Guerre d'Espagne', in Jean Sagnes and Sylvie Caucanas (eds.), *Les Français et la Guerre d'Espagne* (Perpignan: Presses Universitaires de Perpignan, 2008), pp. 15–16.
64 *The Times* (8 September 1936), cited in Moradiellos, *1936*, pp. 148–9.
65 Francisco J. Romero Salvadó, *The Spanish Civil War: Origins, Course and Outcomes* (Basingstoke: Palgrave Macmillan, 2005), pp. 60–1.
66 Paul Preston, *The Spanish Civil War: Reaction, Revolution and Revenge* (London: Harper Perennial, 2006), p. 135.
67 Jules Moch, *Rencontres avec . . . Léon Blum* (Paris: Plon, 1970), p. 191. The text was the following: 'Surprised by dangerous military coup. Request your immediate help with arms and planes. Fraternally yours' (my translation).
68 Pierre Cot, *Triumph of Treason* (New York: Ziff-Davis, 1944), p. 338.
69 Jean Lacouture, *Léon Blum* (New York: Holmes & Meier, 1982), pp. 306–7.
70 Julio Aróstegui, 'De lealtades y defecciones. La República y la memoria de la utopía', pp. 37–8, 49 and Ángel Viñas, 'Una carrera diplomática y un Ministerio de estado desconocido', pp. 267–9, both in Ángel Viñas (ed.), *Al servicio de la República. Diplomáticos y Guerra Civil* (Madrid: Marcial Pons, 2010).
71 Gerald Howson, *Arms for Spain: The Untold Story of the Spanish Civil War* (London: John Murray, 1998), p. 23.
72 David Wingeate Pike, *The French and the Civil War in Spain* (Eastbourne: Sussex University Press, 2011), pp. 18–20.
73 Thierry Vivier, *L'Armée Française et la Guerre D'Espagne, 1936–1939* (Paris: Éditions de l'Officine, 2007), pp. 53, 60–70, 77–8.
74 Cot, *Triumph of Treason*, pp. 353–4.
75 Ángel Viñas, *La Soledad de la República. El abandono de las democracias y el viraje hacia la Unión Soviética* (Barcelona: Crítica, 2006), p. 438.
76 Enrique Moradiellos, *Neutralidad benévola: El Gobierno británico y la insurrección militar española de 1936* (Oviedo: Pentalfa, 1990), pp. 97–102.
77 Douglas Little, *Malevolent Neutrality: The United States, Great Britain, and the Origins of the Spanish Civil War* (Ithaca, NY: Cornell University Press, 1985), pp. 217–19.

78 Enrique Moradiellos, *La Perfidia de Albión: El Gobierno británico y la guerra civil española* (Madrid: Siglo XXI, 1996), p. 37.

79 Ibid., pp. 32–6.

80 Jill Edwards, *The British Government and the Spanish Civil War* (London: Macmillan, 1979), pp. 4–9.

81 Enrique Moradiellos, 'The Gentle General: The Official British Perception of General Franco during the Spanish Civil War', in Paul Preston and Ann L. Mackenzie (eds.), *The Republic Besieged* (Edinburgh: Edinburgh University Press, 1996), pp. 6–7.

82 Moradiellos, *La Perfidia de Albión*, p. 44.

83 Thomas Jones, *A Diary with Letters* (Oxford: Oxford University Press, 1954), p. 231.

84 Moradiellos, *La Perfidia de Albión*, pp. 45–8, 95.

85 Filipe Ribeiro, *Salazar* (New York: Enigma, 2009), pp. 194–6, 201.

86 Alberto Pena Rodríguez, *El gran aliado de Franco: Portugal y la guerra civil española, prensa, radio, cine y propaganda* (Coruña: Castro, 1998), pp. 174–5.

87 Britain was the main investor in Spain (687.5 million pesetas), followed by France (439.6 million pesetas); Germany had invested only 10.3 million pesetas. Ángel Viñas, *Franco, Hitler y el estallido de la guerra civil* (Madrid: Alianza, 2001), p. 236.

88 Documents on German Foreign Policy, 1918–1945, series D, vol. 3: *Germany and the Spanish Civil War* (hereafter DGFP) (London: HMSO, 1951), Doc. 10 (Memo of the Director of the Political Department, 25 July 1936), pp. 10–11.

89 Robert H. Whealey, *Hitler and Spain: The Nazi Role in the Spanish Civil War, 1936–1939* (Lexington, KY: University Press of Kentucky, 1989), pp. 5–9, 28–29.

90 Viñas, *Franco, Hitler*, pp. 422–30.

91 Whealey, *Hitler and Spain*, pp. 28–30.

92 Viñas, *¿Quién quiso la Guerra civil?*, pp. 179–81.

93 Ismael Saz, *Mussolini*, pp. 174–81.

94 Ibid., pp. 203–5.

95 Paul Preston, 'Mussolini's Spanish Adventure: From Limited Risk to War', in Preston and Mackenzie (eds.), *The Republic Besieged*, pp. 23–45.

96 John F. Coverdale, *Italian Intervention in the Spanish Civil War* (Princeton, NJ: Princeton University Press, 1975), p. 87.

97 Ibid., p. 4.

98 Jean-Baptiste Duroselle, *France and the Nazi Threat: The Collapse of French Diplomacy, 1932–1939* (New York: Enigma, 2004), pp. 215–22.

99 Pierre Renouvin and Romain Rémond (eds.), *Léon Blum* (Paris: Presses de la Fondation Nationales des Sciences Politiques, 1967), pp. 409–11.

100 Ibid., p. 360.
101 Claude Thiebaut, 'Léon Blum, Alexis Léger et la decison de Non-Intervention en Espagne', in Sagnes and Caucanas (eds), *Les Français,* pp. 24–6, 33–5.
102 Howson, *Arms for Spain,* pp. 53–6.
103 Richard P. Traina, *American Diplomacy and the Spanish Civil War* (Bloomington, IN: Indiana University Press, 1968), pp. 52–3, 100.
104 Viñas, *La Soledad,* p. 13.
105 Julio Álvarez del Vayo, *Freedom's Battle* (London: Heinemann, 1940), p. 70.
106 Lacouture, *Léon Blum,* pp. 332–3.
107 Thomas, *The Spanish Civil War,* p. 376.
108 In July 1934, an attempted coup by the Austrian Nazis, which led to the killing of the pro-Italian Chancellor Dollfuss, brought both Germany and Italy close to hostilities.
109 Galeazzo Ciano, *Diplomatic Papers* (London: Odham Press, 1948), conversation between the *Duce* and Nazi minister of justice Hans Frank (23 September 1936), pp. 43–6 and between Hitler and Ciano (24 October 1936).
110 Morten Heiberg, *Emperadores del Mediterráneo: Franco, Mussolini y la guerra civil española* (Barcelona: Crítica, 2004), p. 75.
111 Whealey, *Hitler and Spain,* p. 8.
112 Coverdale, *Italian Intervention,* pp. 127–46.
113 Tom Buchanan, *Britain and the Spanish Civil War* (Cambridge: Cambridge University Press, 1997), pp. 93–102.
114 Domènec Pastor Petit, *Hollywood responde a la guerra civil* (Barcelona: Tempestad, 1998), pp. 102–8.
115 Thomas G. Powell, *Mexico and the Spanish Civil War* (Albuquerque, NM: University of New Mexico Press, 1981), p. 71.
116 Abdón Mateos, 'Gordón Ordrás y la Guerra de España desde México', in Viñas (ed.), *Al servicio,* pp. 246–9.
117 Ronald Radosh, Mary Habeck and Grigory Sevostianov (eds.), *Spain Betrayed: The Soviet Union in the Spanish Civil War* (London: Yale University Press, 2001), Docs. 2–4, 9–11.
118 Fernando Hernández, *Guerra o revolución. El Partido Comunista de España en la Guerra Civil* (Barcelona: Crítica, 2010), pp. 88–91.
119 Denis Smyth, 'We Are with You: Solidarity and Self-Interest in Soviet Policy towards Republican Spain, 1936–1939', in Preston and Mackenzie (eds.), *The Republic Besieged,* p. 88.
120 Ivo Banac (ed.), *The Diary of Georgi Dimitrov, 1933–1949* (London: Yale University Press, 2003), p. 27.
121 Daniel Kowalsky, *La Unión Soviética y la guerra civil española* (Barcelona: Crítica, 2004), pp. 28–31.
122 Ivan Maisky, *Spanish Notebooks* (London: Hutchinson, 1966), p. 47.

123 Yuri Rybalkin, *Stalin y España* (Madrid: Marcial Pons, 2007), p. 51.
124 Schauff, *La victoria*, p. 18.
125 Smyth, 'We Are with You', pp. 96–100.
126 Howson, *Arms for Spain*, pp. 136–8.
127 Rémi Skoutelsky, *L'Espoir guidait leur pas: Les volontaires français dans les Brigades Internationales, 1936–1939* (Paris: Grasset, 1998), pp. 53–4.
128 Michael Jackson, *Fallen Sparrows: The International Brigades in the Spanish Civil War* (Philadelphia, PA: American Philosophical Society, 1994), pp. 44–5.
129 Cervera, *Madrid*, pp. 139–40.
130 Abella, *La España Republicana*, p. 134.
131 Skoutelsky, *L'Espoir*, p. 174.
132 Carlos Blanco, *La incompetencia militar de Franco* (Madrid: Alianza, 2000), pp. 294–5, 306–7.
133 Jackson, *Fallen Sparrows*, p. 16.
134 Cardona, *Historia*, pp. 95–102.
135 Ibid., pp. 113–18.
136 Bill Alexander, *British Volunteers for Liberty* (London: Lawrence & Wishart, 1983), pp. 93–107.
137 Cardona, *Historia*, pp. 125–31.
138 Coverdale, *Italian Intervention*, pp. 225–48.
139 Ismael Saz and Javier Tusell, *Fascistas en España* (Madrid: CSIC, 1981), pp. 63–4.
140 Jean-Francois Berdah, *La democracia asesinada: La República española y las grandes potencias, 1931–1939* (Barcelona: Crítica, 2002), p. 191.
141 Álvarez del Vayo, *Freedom's Battle*, pp. 2, 227.
142 Michael Alpert, *A New International History of the Spanish Civil War* (London: Macmillan, 1994), p. 60.
143 Maisky, *Spanish Notebooks*, p. 33.
144 Edwards, *The British Government*, pp. 40–7.
145 David Jorge, 'El abandono de la República por las democracias: nuevos hallazgos y enfoques', in Blanco, Martínez, and Viñas (eds.), *Luces*, p. 281.
146 Viñas, *La Soledad*, p. 447.
147 Ciano, *Diplomatic Papers*, pp. 83–6; DGFP, Doc. 202 (Telegram from Foreign Minister Constantin Neurath, 14 January 1937) p. 225, and Doc. 204 (Memo from Ulrich Hassell, German Ambassador in Italy, 15 January 1937), pp. 226–7.
148 Ciano, *Diplomatic Papers*, pp. 75–7.
149 Oliver Harvey, *Diplomatic Diaries, 1937–1940* (London: John Harvey, 1970), p. 77.
150 Ángel Viñas, *El honor de la República. Entre el acoso fascista, la hostilidad británica y la política de Stalin* (Barcelona: Crítica, 2008), pp. 47, 58–9.

151 Galeazzo Ciano, *Diary, 1937–43* (London: Phoenix, 2002 [1946]), p. 8.
152 DGFP, Doc. 418 (12 September 1937), p. 443.
153 Ciano, *Diary*, p. 5.
154 Ibid., pp. 10, 14–15.
155 Lacouture, *Léon Blum*, pp. 344–5.
156 Ricardo Miralles, 'El duro forcejeo de la diplomacia republican en París. Francia y la Guerra Civil', in Viñas (ed.), *Al servicio*, pp. 127–9.
157 Ángel Viñas, 'Gold, the Soviet Union and the Spanish Civil War', in Martin Blinkhorn (ed.), *Spain in Conflict, 1931–1939: Democracy and its Enemies* (London: Sage, 1986), pp. 224–34.
158 Enrique Moradiellos, *El reñidero de Europa: Las dimensiones internacionales de la guerra civil española* (Barcelona: Península, 2001), pp. 261–3.
159 Howson, *Arms for Spain*, pp. 250–1.
160 Some 13,000 volunteers (nearly one-third of the total) died in combat and nearly half of them were wounded. Jackson, *Fallen Sparrows*, pp. 105–6.
161 Whealey, *Hitler and Spain*, p. 56.
162 Christian Leitz, *Economic Relations between Nazi Germany and Franco's Spain, 1936–1945* (Oxford: Oxford University Press, 1996), pp. 27–31.
163 Judith Keene, *Fighting for Franco: International Volunteers in Nationalist Spain during the Spanish Civil War, 1936–39* (London: Leicester University Press, 2001).
164 Balfour, *Deadly Embrace*, p. 312.
165 Alpert, *A New International History*, pp. 54–5.
166 Whealey, *Hitler and Spain*, pp. 48-50.
167 Coverdale, *Italian Intervention*, p. 180.
168 Viñas, *El honor*, p. 551.
169 Paul Preston, *The Politics of Revenge* (London: Routledge, 1995), p. xiv.
170 Preston, *Franco*, p. 16.
171 Javier Tusell, *Franco en la Guerra Civil* (Madrid: Tusquets, 1993), pp. 31–2.
172 Blanco, *La incompetencia*, pp. 203–8; Preston, *Franco*, pp. 131–3.
173 Ángel Viñas, *La conspiración del General Franco* (Barcelona: Crítica, 2011), pp. 99–100 and *El primer asesinato de Franco* (Barcelona: Crítica, 2018), 11–12, 175–268, 542–5.
174 Southworth, *El mito*, pp. 93–116.
175 Tusell, *Franco*, pp. 52–6.
176 Hilari Raguer, *Gunpowder and Incense: The Catholic Church and the Spanish Civil War* (London: Routledge, 2007), pp. 39–40, 51.
177 Julián Casanova, 'Una dictadura de cuarenta años', in Casanova (coord.), *Morir, matar, sobrevivir*, p. 33.
178 Lannon, *Privilege, Persecution and Prophecy*, pp. 199–200.

179 Carlos Blanco, *Falacias de la Guerra Civil* (Barcelona: Planeta, 2005), p. 136.
180 Raguer, *Gunpowder and Incense*, pp. 67–9.
181 Blanco, *Falacias*, p. 144.
182 Blanco, *La incompetencia*, pp. 19–21.
183 Paul Preston, 'Francisco Franco: política y estrategia en la Guerra Civil', *Revista de Extremadura*, 21 (1996), pp. 14–17.
184 Jackson, *The Spanish Republic*, p. 385.
185 Reig, *Violencia*, pp. 135–67.
186 Coverdale, *Italian Intervention*, pp. 285–94.
187 Ciano, *Diary*, p. 2.
188 Serrano Suñer, *Memorias*, pp. 127–53.
189 Ibid., pp. 157–8.
190 Abella, *La España Nacional*, p. 100.
191 Preston, *Franco*, pp. 209–10.
192 Blinkhorn, *Carlism and Crisis in Spain*, pp. 276–7.
193 Zugazagoitia, *Guerra*, p. 270.
194 Sheelagh Ellwood, *Spanish Fascism in the Franco Era* (London: Macmillan, 1987), pp. 36–7.
195 Serrano Suñer, *Memorias*, p. 174.
196 Blinkhorn, *Carlism and Crisis in Spain*, pp. 293–5.
197 Ellwood, *Spanish Fascism*, p. 45.
198 Casanova, *La Iglesia*, pp. 78–81. Two cardinals, six archbishops, 35 bishops and five vicars-general signed the letter.
199 Ibid., p. 193.
200 Raguer, *Gunpowder and Incense*, pp. 106–16.
201 Preston, *Franco*, pp. 290–1.
202 Alberto Reig, *Franco Caudillo: Mito y Realidad* (Madrid: Tecnos, 1995), p. 187.
203 André Malraux, *L'Espoir* (Paris: Gallimard, 1937), p. 140.
204 Fraser, *Blood of Spain*, pp. 135–6.
205 Thomas, *The Spanish Civil War*, pp. 405–8.
206 Casanova, *Anarchism*, p. 116.
207 Alpert, *El ejército*, p. 140.
208 José Luis Martín Ramos, *El Frente Popular* (Barcelona: Pasado & Presente, 2015), p. 242.
209 Abella, *La España Republicana*, pp. 289–90.
210 Graham, *The Spanish Republic at War*, p. 130.
211 Zugazagoitia, *Guerra*, p. 252.
212 Hernández, *Guerra*, pp. 246–54, 303.
213 Graham, *The Spanish Republic at War*, p. 145.

214 Ferrán Gallego, *Barcelona, mayo de 1937* (Barcelona: Debate, 2007), p. 344.
215 David Ballester, *Marginalidades y hegemonías: la UGT de Cataluña, 1888–1936* (Barcelona: Bronce, 1996), pp. 200–10.
216 César Lorenzo, *Los anarquistas españoles y el poder, 1868–1969* (Paris: Ruedo Ibérico, 1969), p. 106.
217 Leon Trotsky, *The Spanish Revolution, 1931–39* (New York: Pathfinder, 1986 [1973]), pp. 245–50.
218 Lorenzo, *Los anarquistas*, p. 212.
219 Burnett Bolloten, *The Spanish Revolution* (Chapel Hill, NC: University of North Carolina Press, 1979), p. 381.
220 Casanova, *Anarchism*, pp. 119–20. The CNT controlled three departments: Economy, Supply, and Health.
221 Helen Graham, 'Against the State: A Genealogy of the Barcelona May Days', *European History Quarterly*, 29/4 (1999), p. 517.
222 Gallego, *Barcelona*, p. 486.
223 Franco and his brother boasted before the German ambassador Wilhem Faupel that 13 Nationalist agents organized the affair: DGFP, Doc. 254, p. 286. This, though, is hardly credible.
224 Radosh et al., *Spain Betrayed*, Doc. 41, pp. 178–84, Doc. 43, pp. 195–204, and Doc. 44, pp. 205–8.
225 Manuel Azaña, *Memorias políticas y de la Guerra* (Barcelona: Crítica, 1978), pp. 22–37.
226 George Orwell, *Homage to Catalonia* (Harmondsworth: Penguin, 1987 [1938]), pp. 146–7.
227 Elorza and Bizcarrondo, *Queridos*, pp. 358–9.
228 Graham, 'Against the State', p. 520.
229 Casanova, *Anarchism*, pp. 146–7.
230 Ángel Viñas, *El escudo de la República. El oro de España, la apuesta soviética y los hechos de mayo de 1937* (Barcelona: Crítica, 2007), pp. 470–3.
231 Azaña, *Memorias*, p. 53.
232 Graham, *Socialism and War*, pp. 167–81.
233 During the Cold War, Francoists, anarchists, Trotskyites, and some Socialists described Negrín as 'the Moscow man'. This thesis was advanced in academic circles by Bolloten, *The Spanish Revolution*, pp. 451–7. A vindication of Negrín can be found in Manuel Tuñón de Lara, Ricardo Miralles, and Bonifacio N. Diaz Chico, *Juan Negrín López, el hombre necesario* (Las Palmas: Gobierno de Canarias, 1996); Ricardo Miralles, *Juan Negrín* (Madrid: Temas de Hoy, 2003); and Enrique Moradiellos, *Don Juan Negrín. Una biografía de la figura más difamada de la España del Siglo XX* (Barcelona: Península, 2006). For responses to Bolloten, see Herbert. R. Southworth, 'The Grand Camouflage: Julián Gorkin, Burnett Bolloten, and the Spanish Civil War', and Helen Graham, 'War, Modernity and Reform: The Premiership of Juan Negrín', both in Preston and Mackenzie (eds.), *The Republic Besieged* (pp. 261–310 and 163–96 respectively); and Julio

Aróstegui, 'Burnett Bolloten y la Guerra Civil Española: la persistencia del Gran Engaño', in *Historia Contemporánea*, 3 (1990), pp. 151–77.

234 Zugazagoitia, *Guerra*, p. 316.
235 Radosh et al., *Spain Betrayed*, Doc. 46, p. 220 and Doc. 63, pp. 396–7.
236 Azaña, *Memorias*, pp. 55–7.
237 Anne-Aurore Inquimbert, *Un officier français dans la guerre d'Espagne* (Paris: Presses Universitaires de Rennes, 2009), p. 187.
238 Moradiellos, *1936*, pp. 182–3.
239 Gallego, *Barcelona*, p. 378.
240 François Godicheau, 'Los hechos de mayo de 1937 y los presos antifascistas: identificación de un fenómeno represivo', *Historia Social*, 44 (2002), pp. 39–63.
241 Graham, 'Against the State', p. 528.
242 Preston, *The Spanish Holocaust*, pp. 406–7; 411–13.
243 Josep Puigsech, 'La Guerra Civil Española y la política de seguridad colectiva', in Alberto Reig and José Sánchez (eds.), *La Guerra Civil española. 80 años después* (Madrid: Tecnos, 2019), p. 230.
244 Banac (ed.), *The Diary of Georgi Dimitrov*, p. 83.
245 Elorza and Bizcarrondo, *Queridos*, pp. 380–3.
246 Gallego, *Barcelona*, p. 539.
247 Casanova, *Anarchism*, pp. 134, 154–5.
248 Ibid., p. 152.
249 Graham, 'War, Modernity and Reform', p. 193.
250 Thomas, *The Spanish Civil War*, pp. 405–8.
251 Fraser, *Blood of Spain*, p. 458.
252 Tuñón et al., *Juan Negrín*, p. 81.
253 Zugazagoitia, *Guerra*, p. 441.
254 Blanco, *La incompetencia*, pp. 453–7.
255 Berdah, *La democracia*, p. 366.
256 Lacouture, *Léon Blum*, p. 349.
257 Miralles, *Juan Negrín*, p. 219.
258 Anthony Eden, *Facing the Dictators* (London: Cassell, 1962), pp. 589–92.
259 Harvey, *Diplomatic Diaries*, pp. 148–9.
260 Ibid., p. 371.
261 Moradiellos, *El reñidero*, pp. 209–10.
262 Thomas, *The Spanish Civil War*, pp. 820–1.
263 Jorge M. Reverte, *La batalla del Ebro* (Barcelona: Crítica, 2003), pp. 19–22.
264 Blanco, *La incompetencia*, pp. 471–502.
265 DGFP, Doc. 660 (19 September 1938), pp. 742–5.
266 Ciano, *Diary*, p. 119.

267 Reverte, *La batalla del Ebro*, pp. 5–6.
268 Peter N. Carroll, *The Odyssey of the Abraham Lincoln Brigade* (Stanford, CA: Stanford University Press, 1994), p. 205.
269 Reports by Ambassador Stohrer, DGFP, Doc. 658 (16 September 1938), p. 741.
270 Reverte, *La batalla del Ebro*, p. 563.
271 Cardona, *Historia*, p. 299.
272 Moradiellos, *El reñidero*, p. 231.
273 Duroselle, *France and the Nazi Threat*, pp. 271–92.
274 Cervera, *Madrid*, pp. 376–7.
275 Leitz, *Economic Relations*, pp. 85–90.
276 Santiago Álvarez, *Negrín, personalidad histórica* (Madrid: Ediciones de la Torre, 1994), pp. 45–54.
277 Geoffrey Roberts, *The Soviet Union and the Origins of the Second World War: Russo-German Relations and the Road to War, 1933–1941* (Basingstoke: Macmillan, 1995), p. 92.
278 Álvarez, Negrín, testimony of General Hidalgo, pp. 55–60.
279 Cardona, *Historia*, p. 322.
280 Ibid., pp. 325–6.
281 Inquimbert, *Un officier français*, pp. 231–2.
282 Kowalsky, *La Unión Soviética*, pp. 228–31.
283 Ciano, *Diary*, pp. 173, 179.
284 Vivier, *L'Armée Française*, pp. 34–6.
285 Abella, *La España Republicana*, p. 428.
286 Ibid., pp. 432–3.
287 Francesc Vilanova i Vila-Abadal, 'En el exilio: de los campos franceses al umbral de la deportación', in Carme Molinero, Margarida Sala, and Jordi Sobrequés (eds.), *Una inmensa prisión: los campos de concentración y las prisiones durante la guerra civil y el franquismo* (Barcelona: Crítica, 2003), pp. 81–115.
288 Moradiellos, *El reñidero*, p. 247.
289 Vivier, *L'Armée Française*, pp. 126–7.
290 Zugazagoitia, *Guerra*, p. 551.
291 Graham, *The Spanish Republic at War*, p. 399.
292 Preston, *Franco*, pp. 320.
293 Miralles, *Juan Negrín*, p. 358; Ángel Viñas and Fernando Hernández, *El desplome de la República* (Barcelona: Crítica, 2009), p. 86.
294 Paul Preston, *The Last Days of the Spanish Republic* (London: William Collins, 2016), p. 1.
295 Ángel Bahamonde and Javier Cervera, *Así terminó la guerra de España* (Madrid: Marcial Pons, 1999), pp. 259–60.
296 Ibid., pp. 350–1.

297 Preston, ¡Comrades!, p. 180.
298 Bahamonde and Cervera, Así terminó, pp. 256–7.
299 Preston, ¡Comrades!, p. 187
300 Bahamonde and Cervera, Así terminó, p. 302.
301 Ibid., pp. 245–6.
302 Viñas and Hernández, El desplome, p. 219.
303 Preston, The Last Days of the Spanish Republic, p. 175.
304 Ibid., pp. 429–38.
305 Preston, ¡Comrades!, p. 183.
306 Moradiellos, Don Juan Negrín, pp. 453–4.
307 Viñas and Hernández, El desplome, pp. 160–1.
308 Bahamonde and Cervera, Así terminó, pp. 377–404.
309 Graham, The Spanish Republic at War, p. 417.
310 Bahamonde and Cervera, Así terminó, pp. 450–3.
311 Zugazagoitia, Guerra, p. 600.
312 Thomas, The Spanish Civil War, pp. 911–12.
313 Ciano, Diary, p. 209.
314 Preston, Franco, p. 322.

5

The Long Dictatorship of General Francisco Franco, 1939–1975

The Myth of Neutrality

In September 1939, just five months after the end of the civil war in Spain, Germany invaded Poland and so began the Second World War. Spain's neutrality during that conflict was the Dictatorship's most successful myth. Official biographies depicted Franco as a far-sighted statesman who resisted the Axis's advances, allowing Spain to avert the ordeals of war. This is still widely believed by many people in Spain today. After all, the country was never at war.[1] In fact, nothing could be further from the truth. Neutrality was possible not because of but despite Franco.[2] The *Caudillo* wished for a German victory, helped the Axis as much as he could, and even tried to enter the war. Spain's eventual non-involvement was due to a combination of circumstances in which luck, as well as external factors beyond Franco's control, played a part. Spain would have entered the war if Hitler had issued an ultimatum or made enticing territorial promises, regardless of his willingness – or not – to honour them. Instead, he was contemptuous of Franco's demands and, after Mussolini's disastrous war record, was unwilling to divert German resources to rescue another impecunious ally.[3]

The *Caudillo* saw himself as a comrade in arms of Hitler and Mussolini, who had been crucial to his victory in the civil war. His regime profoundly disliked the Allies, and not just for ideological reasons. There were also territorial claims, ranging from Gibraltar to chunks of Africa, which could only be realized if the Allies were defeated.[4] In March 1939, Spain joined the Anti-Comintern pact and signed a five-year treaty of friendship with Germany. A similar agreement with Italy had existed since November 1936. In May, Spain abandoned the League of Nations. However, Germany's invasion of Poland caught Franco and Mussolini by surprise. They wanted a Nazi victory but were aware that hostilities had broken out too soon to participate in a potentially protracted and titanic struggle. Thus, they agreed to sit on the fence and wait to see how events would unfold. Yet, their feelings were clear. Mussolini even coined a new term, 'non-belligerence', to show his preference for the Third Reich without actual military participation. Spain's neutrality also concealed an implicit pro-German stance, but economic and military weakness precluded any other option at that stage.[5]

Mussolini and Franco were astonished when country after country fell to the German war juggernaut in the spring of 1940. Timing was critical. Anxious to share the spoils of victory, they felt they had to join Hitler before the conflict came to an end. However, they had to be careful not to be caught in a long war for which they were ill-prepared. The sudden fall of France in June seemed to indicate that the moment had finally arrived. The *Duce* informed Franco that he would no longer remain a spectator and, on 10 June, entered the war.[6]

Franco was more cautious than the Italian dictator. Being an army officer, he was aware of the chaotic state of his troops. Widespread food shortages and economic bankruptcy were an obstacle to any long campaign. Nonetheless, impressed by the German *Blitzkrieg*, he believed in an imminent Nazi victory and sought to clinch a good deal before entering the war.

With Britain facing defeat, the Iberian Peninsula was of strategic importance. The security of the naval base at Gibraltar was crucial for her Mediterranean commerce and communications with the empire. On 1 June 1940, Samuel Hoare, who had been an outspoken pro-Nationalist voice in the cabinet during the Spanish Civil War, was appointed ambassador to Madrid with the special mission of ensuring Spain's neutrality. His memoirs reveal explicitly how his host country was a German satellite. Under Serrano's control, who was then minister of the interior and president of the Falange's national executive, the media was awash with German propaganda. While the German ambassador, Eberhard Von Stohrer, was on intimate terms with Franco, he had to put up with constant discourtesies, pro-Axis speeches of ministers, and Falangist mobs demanding the return of Gibraltar. The *Caudillo* always met him in his office adorned with the signed photographs of Mussolini and Hitler on his desk. For fear of being kidnapped, Hoare had to be escorted everywhere: some of his servants were arrested; several British consulates were attacked. German submarines received unrestricted aid, the Gestapo collaborated with the Spanish police, and Nazi intelligence services operated at will. Hoare's strategy was to ignore all provocations, play down Germany's victories as temporary setbacks, and exacerbate internal nationalist disputes through the lavish bribery of several monarchist generals. Simultaneously, realizing the precarious situation of Spain's economy, Britain performed a balancing act, providing just enough credit and vital supplies of food and oil to show Franco how much economically he depended on them and to prevent him from joining the Axis.[7] In November 1940, Churchill appealed personally to President Franklin D. Roosevelt to join him in wielding the economic weapon against Franco.[8]

Franco sought to fulfil his imperial dreams in the slipstream of Nazi conquests. On 12 June 1940, Spain adopted the previous Italian position of non-belligerency and two days later seized the internationally administered city of Tangier in Morocco. On 17 June, he was delighted to communicate to Germany the French desire to arrange an armistice.[9] Franco wrote to Hitler expressing his warmest congratulations for his great victories and offering his constant friendship. Flattery was matched by cold calculations. The bearer of the letter, his chief-of-staff, General Juan Vigón, travelled to Berlin to negotiate the terms for joining the Axis. Franco's territorial claims included Gibraltar, French Morocco, part of Algeria, and the enlargement of Spanish Guinea. Huge economic and military aid was also requested. However, Hitler did not need Spain. He confided to Ciano, Mussolini's son-in-law, that 'it would cost more than it was worth'.[10] After all, Spain was already a friendly ally that permitted the use of its territorial waters and guaranteed the supply of its essential primary resources.[11]

In September, Serrano visited Berlin to insist on Spain's readiness to enter the war in return for Franco's colonial demands. He was shocked at being treated not as a valued ally but as the delegate of a satellite state. Moreover, the Germans were extremely vague about the Spanish claims. They regarded them as absurd, given the potential aid that Spain could offer, and even asked for the cession of one of the Canary Islands and enclaves in Morocco. In turn, Serrano's procrastination disappointed his hosts.[12]

Hitler considered Spain's demands preposterous. In the aftermath of Mussolini's intervention, he did not need further unwanted volunteers for a conflict he believed already won.[13] From his point of view, Spain should be begging to join the triumphant Axis instead of requesting a ridiculous price in exchange for a more than doubtful contribution to the war effort. A further complication was that Franco's territorial ambitions were also coveted by Mussolini and still under the control of the collaborationist French Vichy. Germany did not want to antagonize the latter for the sake of Spain's costly belligerence, a country that was hungry, defenceless, and half-destroyed.[14] The French colonial army was still capable of defending its territory against any Spanish or Italian aggression. Furthermore, any concession to Spain or Italy could see these troops get behind the emergent Free French Army of General Charles de Gaulle. Vichy's value was confirmed by its successful defence of Dakar (Senegal) in September against an Anglo-Gaullist attack.[15]

The *Caudillo* was undeterred. He blamed the German rebuff on Hitler's underlings and insisted on personally negotiating with the German leader. Thus, on 23 October, the two dictators met in the French border town of Hendaye. Franco was accompanied by Serrano who, a few days earlier, had been appointed foreign minister. For Franco's hagiographers, this was the moment, under huge pressure, he fought off the advances of the Axis and outwitted Hitler. His master plan was to ask for the impossible to keep Spain out of the war – the reality was very different. Franco's train was late, but it was not, as his propagandists later claimed, a ploy to unnerve Hitler. The delay was due to the deficient state of the Spanish railways and left Franco embarrassed.[16] Unless he was one of Hollywood's greatest actors, the *Caudillo*'s wide grin while grabbing with both hands that of the German dictator demonstrated his delight at being alongside the conqueror of Europe.

The stark truth was that Spain's fate was then, and at least until the spring of 1944, in Hitler's hands. There was nothing Franco could do if the German dictator commanded his entry into the war. Moreover, the *Caudillo* was determined to join the Axis if he could secure his precious empire. However, the Nazi leader did not accede to his territorial ambitions, neither offering empty promises nor giving him an ultimatum. The two of them simply became bogged down in obliquely opposing monologues. Hitler thought it was Franco's duty to be on his side in return for German aid during the civil war. The question of distribution of the spoils was a secondary matter which should be left until victory day. He did not even attempt to give any territorial promise since, as he had confided to his foreign minister Joachim von Ribbentrop: 'with these chattering Latins, the French will hear something about it sooner or later'.[17] When he hinted that Vichy had to be accommodated, Franco's initial bellicose rhetoric became dramatically toned down and replaced by a recital stressing Spain's appalling military and economic conditions. In the end, both were furious. Hitler concluded that Franco was an ungrateful coward who had missed his chance to join victorious Germany. He noted that 'rather than go through that again, he would prefer to have four teeth extracted', remarks which clearly showed not a threatening attitude, but frustration. The *Caudillo*, far from exuding satisfaction after heading off 'unbearable' German pressure, appeared dismayed. He told Serrano: 'these people are intolerable. They will not give us what is ours by right'. Serrano wrote that it was Franco's good fortune that Hitler was unwilling to meet his imperial ambitions. Otherwise, Spain would have entered the war.[18]

At Hendaye, Franco found himself on the receiving end of a lesson in the realities of power. His dream of territorial gains, courtesy of the Third Reich, was shattered before his eyes. It was German intransigence and not Spanish cunning that confirmed the latter's non-belligerence. Nonetheless, Franco, anxious to be at the victor's side, put his signature to a secret protocol sealing an alliance with the Axis. However, it left the precise date of Spanish entry in vague terms: until military preparations were completed.[19] For the *Caudillo*, this meant remaining sitting on the fence.

British resistance in the autumn of 1940 made it difficult for Franco to predict when to make his move. With the Battle of Britain faltering, Hitler considered initiating 'Operation Felix' (attacking Gibraltar) in February 1941. It was cancelled after Franco argued that Spain was still not prepared and German reports confirmed the appalling transport and food shortages.[20] By then, Italy's disastrous campaigns in the Balkans and North Africa had forced Germany to turn its attention to south-east Europe. Hitler concluded that it was better to have a benevolent friend in Spain than another costly and inefficient ally.

Franco's egotistical drive for greatness was revealed in the winter of 1940–41. While Europe was being devestated by war and Spain by starvation, he wrote *Raza* (Race), which was soon turned into a film. It was an embellished account of the experiences of a Galician family, identifiable with his own, from the colonial collapse of 1898 to the civil war. The romanticized protagonist (José Churruca) – in other words, himself – embodied the essence of the Spanish race: courage and heroism, even a willingness to sacrifice his life to save the fatherland from the lethal Republic.[21]

Raza showed Franco's obsession with the communist threat. Consequently, Germany's invasion of Russia in June 1941 marked the apex of his identification with the Third Reich. It fired his pro-Axis enthusiasm and offered the opportunity to secure a place at the victory table. In July, non-belligerence was replaced by 'moral belligerence'. The first contingent of a total of 47,000 volunteers (Blue Division) was sent to the Eastern Front. An agreement was signed to provide 100,000 workers for the increasingly strained German industrial force. During the annual commemoration of the outbreak of the civil war, the *Caudillo* argued before the diplomatic corps that the first battles of the war had been won in Spain. He passionately hailed Germany for 'leading the battle for which Christianity had longed for so many years, and in which the blood of Spanish youth would mingle with that of the Axis as a living expression of solidarity'. Serrano, taken aback by the reckless speech, confided to the German ambassador that Franco with his imprudence was revealing 'Spain's true stance'.[22]

Despite his impetuous statements, Franco's good luck was that the two sides of the conflict preferred the existing status quo. While the Axis considered him a loyal friend, the Allies chose to ignore his provocative rhetoric to avoid any action that might give Germany the excuse to invade Spain. Franco was also immensely fortunate that Stalin did not choose to respond to the sending of the Blue Division, the most visible Spanish contribution to the Axis, with a declaration of war.[23] Many other acts revealed where Franco's sympathies lay (submarine refuelling, deliveries of essential raw materials, aircraft facilities, the gathering of intelligence, propaganda, etc.).

The evolution of events favoured caution. Successful Russian resistance and the entry of the United States into the war in December 1941 indicated a protracted conflict. Simultaneously, internal disputes in the ruling Nationalist coalition were reaching boiling point. Initially, all the groups felt sympathy for the Axis. As the war dragged on, however, whereas Falangist enthusiasm remained undiminished, scepticism regarding an ultimate German victory grew elsewhere. Additionally, Britain's skilful strategy of bribing key monarchist generals intensified opposition to embarking on a war for which Spain was unprepared.[24] By then, many army officers had grown weary of Falangist thuggery and were wary about Serrano's power.

On 16 August 1942, tensions came to a head at the end of a religious ceremony being celebrated in Begoña (Bilbao). A group of Falangists threw a bomb at a Carlist gathering headed by General José Enrique Varela, the war minister and outspoken critic of the Falange, resulting in some 100 wounded. With the ruling coalition at breaking point, Franco proved a master manipulator. On the one hand, Varela and his ally at the Home Office, Valentín Galarza, were sacked and replaced by the pro-Axis hardliners General Carlos Asensio and Blas Pérez, respectively. On the other, one Falangist was executed, and Serrano, the main target of the army's hatred, was dismissed. The cautious General Francisco Gómez Jordana took over the Foreign Ministry.[25]

Serrano would become the perfect scapegoat.[26] His dismissal was portrayed later as proof that the *Caudillo*, aware of the forthcoming Allied victory, got rid of his ambitious brother-in-law's pernicious pro-Axis influence. In fact, Franco himself was very much in awe of Germany. Serrano's downfall was, above all, a product of domestic politics. His sacrifice was the price to appease the army. By then, Serrano's extra-marital affairs had also incurred the anger of his wife Zita and, more importantly, of his sister-in-law Carmen.[27] The *Caudillo* was happy to dismiss an intelligent politician who had been hogging the limelight and who he suspected to be building his own political position. Rather than dynamic personalities, he preferred to surround himself with sycophants and nonentities. The Falange was left in the hands of its secretary-general, José Luis Arrese, a highly reliable member of the old guard, while Admiral Luis Carrero Blanco gradually eased himself into Serrano's former position. Promoted in May 1941 to undersecretary of the presidency, Carrero was a staunch Catholic and the ideal assistant, carefully attuned to Franco's wishes, and extremely discreet in proffering his advice.[28]

Developments in the war forced Franco towards a more balanced neutrality. A turning point was 'Operation Torch', the Anglo-American landings in French North Africa in November 1942. Fearing that Spain was an Allied target, some ministers advocated letting the German army into the peninsula, but they met Jordana's obstinate opposition. Some in the American administration, including the vice president, Henry Wallace, had proposed an assault on Spanish Morocco (Operation Backbone). However, British pressure and the advice of the US ambassador in Spain, Carlton Hayes, won the day. Those plans were abandoned. Franco received personal guarantees from Roosevelt on the territorial integrity of Spain and her colonies.[29] Germany simply warned him to remain vigilant. Of course, the spectacularly swift success of the Allied offensive in North Africa abruptly brought to an end any thoughts of Spanish action.[30]

Dramatic changes on the battlefield (Germany's retreat from Russia and defeat in Africa) encouraged a distancing from the Axis orbit. Yet, it was a long and exasperating process. Mussolini's fall in July 1943 was received with alarm. Together with a news black-out there was an increasing number of arrests and executions to terrorize into submission those in Spain who sought to capitalize on the collapse of Italian Fascism.[31] Henceforth, Franco's attacks upon the decadent liberal systems were nuanced. He began to stress the differences between his regime and fascism. He even toyed with the idea of appearing as an honest peace broker. He told western diplomats that there were two separate wars. One in the east against communism in which Spain was directly involved, and one in the west in which she was neutral and could act as a mediator.[32] In October 1943, Franco, for the first time, used the term 'watchful neutrality'. That month the Blue Division was withdrawn from Russia. By early 1944, after constant complaints by the British ambassador, instructions were given to restrict German spy activities and the press adopted a less partisan tone.[33]

Even though the tide was turning clearly in favour of the Allies, tactless diplomatic incidents thwarted the prospect of establishing friendlier relations. The Republic of Saló, Mussolini's new regime in northern Italy, was not officially recognized but Spain still maintained a representative there.[34] In October 1943, an official Spanish despatch congratulating José Laurel, head of the Japanese puppet government in the Philippines, incensed the Americans. They responded by threatening an oil embargo unless Spanish deliveries of wolfram, a crucial mineral for arms production, to Germany were stopped. In February 1944, the United States stopped oil shipments. The British, more inclined to find a compromise, devised a face-saving device which brought the crisis to an end in May: the oil embargo was suspended in return for a drastic reduction of wolfram exports to Germany, the withdrawal of the existing volunteers in Russia, and the introduction of more effective measures against German spies.[35]

By then, Franco had correctly concluded that despite all provocations, the Allies preferred negotiation to force. Consequently, in a future peace settlement, they would not take direct action to remove him from power. This appeared to be confirmed when Churchill, in a speech in the Commons on 24 May 1944, praised Spain for not having joined the Axis in the grimmest period of war. The British prime minister's words were twisted in Spain into a full-scale endorsement of the ruling order.[36]

Jordana died suddenly in August 1944. He was replaced by José Félix Lequerica, the fiercely pro-Axis ambassador to Vichy, showing that the *Caudillo* still believed in German invincibility. Yet, the advance of the Red Army into central Europe and the success of the invasion of France were signs that the Allies were on the march to victory. With his main concern being survival, Franco began courting the Anglo-Americans. He reiterated that the common enemy was communism and that his regime was based on Catholic principles and averse to fascism. In the summer of 1944, Spain granted permission to evacuate Allied casualties from France through Barcelona and for flights over Spanish air space. In his farewell visit to the *Caudillo*, in October 1944, Hoare noticed that the pictures of Mussolini and Hitler had been replaced by those of the Portuguese president and the Pope.[37] That month Franco sent an astonishing personal letter to Churchill.

He stated that with the destruction of most European powers, Spain and England, the last two virile nations on the continent, should ally themselves against Russia. His startling conclusion was that the only obstacle to the deal was the sordid machinations of the British secret services. It took three months for a bewildered Churchill to reply, strongly rebuffing Franco's suggestions. Nevertheless, the *Caudillo* was relieved when the text made clear that London would do nothing to remove his regime by force.[38] Indeed, Churchill opposed Hoare and his foreign secretary Anthony Eden, who favoured heightened pressure on Franco through a forceful policy coordinated with the United States. However, with the Red Army advancing in eastern Europe, the British prime minister shared Franco's fears about the communist threat.[39]

Franco hoped until the bitter end that the Axis might avoid total defeat. Spain did not break diplomatic relations with Germany until the day of her surrender, 8 May 1945. That day the official rewriting of history began. The most extreme eulogies hailed the *Caudillo*, 'a leader chosen by the benevolence of God to bestow the gift of peace upon Spain'.[40] His blatant pro-Axis leanings were justified as a subtle game to outmanoeuvre Hitler. And so the myth of Franco's neutrality in the Second World War was born.

Francoism by the Grace of God

In Franco's long and cruel dictatorship lies the exceptional nature of Spain's modern history vis-à-vis other European nations after 1945.[41] Whether it was a fascist regime is still an ongoing debate. An evident problem when trying to define the regime was its longevity. Indeed, its long rule offered an opportunity to shape its record. The political order up to 1944, closely aligned with the Axis, was very different from that a few years later. As the Cold War unfolded, Spain sought a rapprochement with the Allies, in particular the United States, by stressing its anti-communist credentials. From the late 1950s, it embarked upon a significant chameleonic change, portraying itself as a developmental state presiding over an economic miracle.[42]

To categorize the Spanish Dictatorship is further complicated by the dichotomy between its social function and its structural foundations. Azaña noted that no genuine fascist Spain would emerge from the war, but one dominated by the habitual forces of reaction: cassocks and swords.[43] However, Franco's regime was not a traditional dictatorship, but the local variant of the violent counter-revolutionary and anti-democratic coalitions that emerged in the inter-war years. Still, equating it to fascism based solely on its social (or historical) function and regardless of the specific political format seems to be an example of *reductio ad extremum*.[44]

The Spanish Dictatorship borrowed from the fascist states a single and highly centralized party and corporatist framework. It also mimicked some of their essential features: the cult of leadership, the extensive utilization of propaganda to rewrite history, the total eradication of any signs of liberal democracy, the unprecedented levels of repression, and some of their choreography, legislation, and rhetoric. However, unlike them, the correlation of forces within the ruling coalition was detrimental to the party.[45] The original Falange had been weak and dependent on the monarchists' financial support. The civil war facilitated its rapid expansion. However, its compulsory merger with other forces, in April 1937, watered down its initial purity. Moreover, the party became a minor partner vis-à-vis traditional institutions such as the Church and the army.[46] The *Caudillo*'s rule never rested on his leadership of a mass party but on being the *Generalissimo* of the army and 'by the grace of God'.

The Spanish Dictatorship never even pretended to pursue a new revolutionary social project like the fascist states but to restore the traditional socio-economic order that had been challenged during the Republic.[47] Focusing on its historical-evolutionary dynamic, it was a reactionary military regime that suffered during its first years a remarkable but unfinished process of fascistization, eventually truncated by the outcome of the Second World War.[48] Moreover, because there was no ideology-driven campaign to remake society or forge the 'new man', regime penetration into the population and even the administration was extremely shallow.[49] Indeed, the state's main function was to control rather than to mobilize community activity.[50] Thus, the regime pursued, above all, political apathy, consent, and demobilization. Saz has concluded that the Spanish Dictatorship was more than an authoritarian regime but less than a full-fledged fascist order.[51] This facilitated its reorientation after 1945.

The new regime can be dubbed Francoism given the essential role played by a leader who claimed to be responsible only before 'God and history'. Franco did not seek to establish a 'revolutionary' fascist state but an unusually cruel and reactionary dictatorship. For the average Spaniard, this meant that obeying was prioritized over understanding or believing.[52] The *Caudillo*'s position remained unchanged. He was the supreme arbiter of a coalition of factions or families (monarchist, the army, Falange, Carlist, Catholic, etc.) competing for his favour and their own spheres of influence. His strategy was never to get too actively involved with the political minutiae but to engage in the shrewd manipulation of all of them. To achieve that, the memory of the civil war was perpetuated.[53] He would continually remind all the families that they were inextricably linked by the Pact of Blood – that is, their active complicity in the ongoing savage repression, their shared authoritarian values, and their fear of the return of the Republic. Official propaganda stressed that Franco was not just indispensable to political stability, he was consubstantial with it. While he remained in charge, they could all enjoy the spoils of victory. Their parcels of power might change according to the moment, but they would never be excluded.[54]

Francoist hegemony was based on a combination of considerable popular support, widespread demobilization, and repression. Significant segments of the population embraced the nationalist cause: the Catholic smallholders and farmers of northern Spain, the large southern landowners, the urban industrial employers, the conservative middle classes, and, in general, the many who had feared for their lives and property during the civil war. Furthermore, many Spaniards, tacitly or explicitly, supported the new regime because they had been profoundly traumatized by three years of a bloody fratricidal conflict. This apolitical 'silent' majority would be prepared to turn a blind eye to the ruthless policy of revenge conducted under the Dictatorship and opted to surrender their personal and civic freedoms for a safer, more stable social and political environment. Francoism would also acquire large swathes of support as it developed into an attractive source of promotion and *enchufismo* (cronyism and string-pulling for friends). The public sector became a bloated bureaucracy that guaranteed job security for thousands of Spaniards who, in turn, became loyal adherents to the regime. By 1942, Francoist ex-combatants had filled 50,000 state posts.[55]

Años de Hambre, Años de Silencio

Job security was one of the most precious assets in post-war Spain. In 1939, the economy was in tatters, the transport system had collapsed, and there were critical shortages of food and fuel. Until the 1950s, these were *años de hambre* (years of hunger) marked by misery, falling living standards, and the rationing of basic staples. This was largely the by-product of a decision to favour the interests of the economic elites, who now could impose conditions over the repressed workers, together with badly conceived policies regarding poor people's needs.[56]

Reconstruction was pursued through so-called 'autarky', an extreme form of economic nationalism which sought self-sufficiency by drastically cutting imports and encouraging domestic production. This fitted perfectly with the belief in the need to seal off Spain from the outside world, both politically and culturally.[57] A huge apparatus was erected to regulate wages, prices, supply, and the exchange rate. The National Wheat Service controlled all activity related to Spain's most crucial staple. The National Institute of Industry, a state-holding company created in 1941, constituted the largest national enterprise. It oversaw the country's industrial development, especially in what were considered the key areas of iron and steel, coal, electricity generation, transport, and shipbuilding.[58]

Autarky was a central part of the apparatus of repression. Its real target was to protect the interests of the social elites from foreign competition through high tariffs and administrative controls. Wages were slashed, strikes treated as sabotage and made punishable by long prison sentences, and the labour movement regimented under Falangist control through the so-called *Sindicatos Verticales* (vertical unions).[59] These official state-sponsored unions adopted Fascist Italy's corporative model of integrating workers and employers into a hierarchical structure. Their goal was to discipline the labour force because, above all, autarky gave the authorities unprecedented power over society by controlling resources, from production to distribution and consumption.[60] They imposed the politics of hunger through the rationing system, which, in the process, became another layer of repression.[61] For vital things such as a ration card or a job, it was necessary to provide evidence of loyalty to the regime through an official certificate or letter signed by an 'accredited' person (a local priest, army officer, civil guard commander, or Falange heavyweight).[62] Fear and discrimination affected every aspect of people's lives, ensured political apathy, and discouraged mobilization.

Clinging to autarky demonstrated the authorities' callousness towards the plight of ordinary people.[63] As traditional structures and technology remained unchanged, Spain failed to become self-sufficient. Foreign trade practically collapsed and production fell drastically. The decision to maintain the peseta at a ridiculously overvalued rate exacerbated the suffering. Rationing and shortages led to corruption on a spectacular scale that benefited mostly socio-political dignitaries. Abuses of power and flagrant misappropriation of funds acquired breath-taking dimensions. Indeed, the regime condoned a flourishing black market in which formidable profits were made by hoarding basic commodities and selling them at several times the official price.[64] Franco was aware of the widespread corruption and even encouraged leading members of the regime to participate. He could then use his knowledge as leverage.[65] The *Caudillo* himself and his family amassed a colossal fortune. He was the recipient of staggering gifts such as automobiles, shares, and property, including the *Pazo del Merás*, a stunning estate in his native Galicia that became his summer retreat. Simultaneously, he used his executive prerogatives to benefit from all sorts of commercial ventures. For instance, he made an extraordinary sum of over 7 million pesetas by selling Brazilian coffee.[66]

Left out of the Marshall Plan, Spain teetered on the brink of economic collapse. Its bare survival was due to the providential trade arrangements signed in April 1948 with Argentina, then headed by General Juan Domingo Perón. It advanced credit facilities amounting to 4,500 million pesetas with which to purchase essentials.[67] Meat, milk, and fish were rarely available. Since the rationed diet was scarce in proteins, only wealthy families could afford the soaring black market prices to supplement their food supply. Widespread famine meant the return of diseases and epidemics that had been eradicated before 1936, including typhus, trachoma, pellagra, and malaria. Others such as tuberculosis, influenza, and diphtheria reached unprecedented levels.[68] Some 200,000 people died between 1939 and 1945 due to malnutrition, cold, and disease.[69] Simultaneously, the housing shortage due to war damage led to huge numbers becoming homeless or living in shacks. Propaganda tried to conceal the harrowing reality. It was successful in the sense that even in today's Spain, this state of affairs is widely unknown.[70]

The enforced *silencio* of the population marked the post-war years. Official propaganda manipulated people's fear of more violence and peddled the obscene myth of Francoism being the guarantor of a golden era of social peace. Yet, while this was indeed a golden era for society's upper echelons, it meant misery for millions. The nationalist victory did not usher in a period of peace. The new order never envisaged the *abrazo de Vergara* that Casado and Besteiro had naively expected. There was never any forgiving or the mildest attempt at reconciliation but only the institutionalization of full-scale vengeance. Franco's peace was founded on the silence and submission of his opponents. Spain was to be remade in the images of the mythical crusade to save Christian civilization. Society was divided between the patriots of 'Real Spain' and the 'communist scum' who had supported 'Godless anti-Spain'. For the latter, the only possible peace was that of exile, jail, or a burial plot.[71] A battery of legislation enforced retaliation: Law of Political Responsibilities (February 1939), Law of Repression of Masonry and Communism (May 1940), Law of State Security (1941), New Penal Code (1944), New Military Code (1945), Law against Banditry and Terrorism (1947), and so on. Martial law remained in place until 1948 and most of the repressive legislation was in force until the 1960s. Tellingly, the regime never endorsed a general amnesty.[72]

Post-war reconstruction sought to build a monolithic national community by destroying republican political and cultural identities.[73] Franco's triumph was not only the fulfilment of Spain's destiny but a personal mandate from God. This mixture of providence and triumphalism produced the feeling of divine sanction for violent repression. Those who did not share the principles of the regime had to renounce their past. The collective identity of 'the defeated' was denied expression as Franco's victory was recreated day by day.[74] A life of fear, alienation, shortages, and depressed salaries did the rest. Spaniards were busy with the harsh daily task of survival and embraced what the regime wanted: socio-political demobilization.[75]

Nowhere else in twentieth-century Europe was the Church persecuted and its members massacred with such brutality as in Republican Spain during the civil war. In turn, it acquired under Franco a unique role, as the Crusade was the founding fable of the Francoist state. The narrative emphasizing martyrdom and ascetic values dominated official memory. Not only did streets, squares, and schools bear the names of nationalist leaders, but also shrines were erected to hail their sacrifices during the war.[76] One must look back to the sixteenth century – at the peak of the counter-reform and the Inquisition – for when the Church enjoyed similar power. The regime protected it, showered it with privileges, and silenced its detractors.[77] National-Catholicism, or the symbiosis between the fatherland and religion, was forged after the military rising of July 1936 as an agent to bind together the rebel groups. After the war, it was the prevailing ideology for the reactionary coalition built around Franco's authority.[78] The Church became its main source of legitimacy and its guarantor at home and abroad. In return, the clergy were left in charge of public morality, ensuring in the process the eradication of any sign of modernity and dissent. Indeed, priests became both propagandists of the state and policemen who played a leading role in the control and denunciation of those deemed to be part of the anti-Spain.[79]

The public sector was thoroughly purged. State employees had to prove their loyalty to the regime. Primary school teachers were particularly affected: over 6,000 suffered dismissal and another 6,000 were forced to work far from home.[80] At the same time, the Church acquired sweeping powers in terms of controlling instruction in the schools, which in turn became indoctrination agencies. Co-education was prohibited. Religious studies became a compulsory subject in a curriculum dominated by spiritual and patriotic values. Priests and party sycophants assumed the crucial task of rewriting history.[81] Children were not taught that Spain had undergone a devastating civil war. Instead, they learnt that a glorious movement had saved the country from the clutches of a communist-inspired conspiracy. The *Caudillo* as leader of this holy crusade was linked with the noble knights of the *Reconquista*. He had annihilated the 'Red Menace' and was a pivotal source of generosity and intelligence who had earned with his bravery the blind trust of every Spaniard. He was *Caudillo* of Spain by the grace of God, present on coins, postage stamps, in street names, and on the classroom wall to the right of the crucifix. Sunday sermons included the demand for divine protection for the Pope, the bishop of the diocese, and the head of the state, Francisco Franco.[82]

The regime highlighted the key role of women in the new state as the pillars of the family and the main regenerators of society. This meant, in practice, subordination to their fathers or husbands, something that was confirmed by the return to the 1889 Civil Code that enshrined their judicial inferiority.[83] During the Republic, the potential foundations for change had been laid (female suffrage, divorce, the right to hold office, etc.). Francoism reversed that trend. Women were relegated from the public sphere as their role as mothers and wives was reinforced. Laws were introduced against divorce, abortion, and adultery. All of them were explicitly defined as 'crimes against morality'.[84]

The Falange's female section mobilized thousands of middle- and lower-middle class women to participate in its Social Service Programme, whereby unmarried women between 17 and 35 years provided six months of state service working in schools, hospitals, orphanages, and so on. This amounted to rudimentary welfare provision on the cheap. A decree passed in 1941 forced women to fulfil social service to qualify for public jobs.[85]

Working-class women often had to supplement their household by undertaking different forms of low-paid work, including as domestic servants, seamstresses, and workers in the food-production sector.[86] The wives of Republicans were often left destitute when their husbands were tried and condemned. They had to prostitute themselves to survive. In a further cruel twist, this allowed local authorities to portray them as sinners unfit to look after their children. Some 12,000 infants, born to mothers confined to prison, were taken to be raised in state institutions or orphanages supervised by the Church. There they were often abused and told they had to expiate the 'sins of their parents'. Sometimes, their names were changed and their past erased so that they could be brought up by loyal wealthy families as their own.[87]

In fact, Franco's regime was one of the cruellest in twentieth-century Europe. He signed more death sentences than any previous Spanish head of state.[88] Compared with other right-wing dictatorships, the brutal persecution of its domestic population, even after the war, went much further than that of Nazi Germany and far surpassed that of Mussolini's Italy.[89] When visiting Sevilla in 1939, Ciano was appalled at the savage repression. It was unbelievable to him that in a city that had always been in nationalist hands, there could still be 80 executions a day. Even Heinrich Himmler was shocked by the harsh treatment of the workers when he visited Spain in October 1940.[90] With public order in the hands of *Africanistas*, there was no attempt to integrate the labouring classes. The enemy had to be vanquished, imprisoned, or terrorized into submission as the colonial natives had themselves been previously. In turn, a crusading clergy blessed the reigning terror, as it had during the *Reconquista*.

Research on Francoist repression indicates that, at the very least, over 130,000 people were assassinated.[91] These numbers are open to debate and far from complete (only 38 of the 50 provinces have been investigated). The exact figure will probably never be known. The authorities had nearly 40 years to hide all trace of their 'justice'. Thousands of Spaniards went missing during the civil war and their deaths were not registered. Many were simply executed *en masse* and buried hurriedly in unmarked mass graves. Many of these deaths were recorded as being caused by strange epidemics or bizarre accidents.[92]

In the spring of 1939, Spain resembled a militarily occupied country. Those whose political reliability was suspected were crammed into overcrowded prisons or improvised concentration camps. According to official sources, there were over 280,000 political prisoners in 1940. In total, one million people were incarcerated or suffered some sort of punishment in the post-war years.[93] This figure is astonishing given the massive exodus via Catalonia of hundreds of thousands of Republicans in February 1939.[94] Military courts worked full time delivering vindictive sentences. According to the evidence from 33 provinces, some 35,000 were condemned to death and 250,000 to long prison sentences. They all fell victim to the ingrained torture regime that marked the Francoist penal system.[95] Some 140,000 convicts were either executed or died through mistreatment and malnutrition. However, many of these deaths were recorded as caused by typhus, influenza, and other maladies.[96]

Repression was not confined to terror. The Dictatorship was also a regime of pillage. Property was confiscated on a mass scale through the judicial monstrosity of the Law of Political Responsibilities.[97] In some cases, punishment took the form of civil death. Indeed, thousands of people, because of their suspected past, were disqualified from undertaking certain jobs, banished from their place of residence, fined, and so on. Those who were freed suffered the triple burden of dire living standards, state restrictions, and employment discrimination.[98]

The regime offered those locked-up the 'opportunity' to redeem their sins through work. Labour battalions were formed to undertake public works to address the existing shortage of workers.[99] The biggest aberration of all was the construction of the *Valle de los Caídos* (Valley of the Fallen), a gigantic mausoleum to the north-east of Madrid, built between 1940 and 1959 by 20,000 political prisoners. In the process, many of them died or were gravely injured. This veritable pantheon of the Crusade was designed to commemorate those who had fallen 'for God and Spain' and, as in the times of the Pharaohs, to serve as the *Caudillo*'s final resting place.[100]

Popular collaboration was imperative for the repression to work. The authorities relied on the complicity brought about by the memories of the fear and personal losses sustained during the civil war. Denunciations of neighbours became the foundations of further accusations and judicial processes that often ended with imprisonment and execution.[101] The settlement of old scores, the willingness to prove loyalty to the new regime, and the expectation of filling the posts of those denounced were powerful motivations. It was much worse in small towns and villages where familiarity permeated the community.[102]

From International Ostracism to Respectability

Last-minute propaganda hailing Franco's impeccable neutrality was futile. The international community considered his regime the remaining anachronism of a past era of fascist hegemony.[103] At the founding conference of the United Nations (UN) in San Francisco, on 19 June 1945, the motion banning any regime installed in power by the Axis (in other words, Spain) from membership presented by the Mexican delegation was unanimously approved. Spain had become a pariah state. In 1947, she was refused membership of the European Recovery Programme (Marshall Plan) and, in 1949, the western defensive alliance, or North Atlantic Treaty Organization (NATO).[104]

To believe that international ostracism alone would herald the demise of Francoist Spain was wishful thinking. It overlooked the *Caudillo*'s resilience to cling to power. He told General Martínez Campos: 'I will not make Primo de Rivera's mistake. I do not resign. For me, it is straight from here to the cemetery'.[105] In August 1945, a report drafted by Carrero boosted Franco's determination. According to the admiral, the Anglo-Saxon countries, despite their rhetorical condemnation, would never implement sanctions that could lead to the destabilization of Spain and favour the Soviet cause.[106] His predictions proved correct. Menacing though all the measures seemed to be, they were not accompanied by an all-out economic embargo or military intervention. Furthermore, Franco benefited from the fact that of the many critical issues facing the Allies, including that of post-war European reconstruction, the Spanish question remained marginal.[107]

At the Potsdam Conference (17 July to 2 August 1945), Churchill opted not to back any measure against Franco when the Soviet delegation raised the Spanish question. He alleged that Spain's internal politics were a matter for its own citizens. Thus, the international ostracism voted by the UN the previous month was altogether toothless.[108] British foreign policy remained unaltered after the Labour victory in August 1945. The new foreign secretary, Ernest Bevin, in his first statement in the Commons, dubbed Franco and the Falange 'unfortunate anomalies' whose days were hopefully numbered. Notwithstanding his genuine longing for the end of the Spanish Dictatorship, he vetoed the kind of actions that could deliver that very objective.[109] Against a background of waning imperial power, the Labour administration shared with its predecessor the belief that ousting Franco could lead to a power vacuum or even to a new civil war that could only benefit the USSR. British misgivings were unfounded. The Kremlin acknowledged that Spain fell into the western sphere of influence. British policy was also influenced by the fear of endangering its material interests (financial investments, crucial imports of pyrites, iron ore, and potash, etc.) and the safety of Gibraltar.[110]

With the economy in tatters, Franco would have fallen if the Great Powers had backed with concrete actions their proclaimed antagonism towards his regime. The idea that he could be forced out of power peacefully by international condemnation was ludicrous. Once again, British non-intervention ensured the *Caudillo*'s survival by impeding France and the USA from taking hasty any action. Franco's close relationship with Vichy France – and the fact that 30,000 Spanish Republicans had fought with the Resistance – meant that France was the western power most inclined to act.[111] In December 1945, it appealed to London and Washington to break off all relations with Spain. It was backed by the US but vetoed by Bevin, who alleged that it might provoke a second civil war. In February 1946, France closed its southern border when Cristino García, a Republican who had reached the rank of lieutenant general in the French Resistance, was executed in Barcelona. France proposed to discuss the situation in the UN's Security Council.[112] Britain again prevailed: the three western nations finally issued a joint declaration in March 1946 condemning Francoism in the strongest terms but stopped short of taking any practical measure that could produce the regime change they otherwise appeared to advocate.[113]

On 12 December 1946, the UN's General Assembly adopted Resolution 39, which excluded the Spanish government from all its international agencies. In addition, the resolution recommended that the Security Council take the necessary measures if, within a 'reasonable time', no new government was formed whose authority was as a result of the consent of the people. The resolution also recommended the immediate withdrawal of foreign ambassadors accredited to the Spanish government. And indeed, that month, most of the ambassadors left Spain. Six countries abstained, all of them Latin American republics, and only five states kept their diplomatic corps in place: the Vatican, Portugal, Ireland, Switzerland, and Argentina. In turn, the Dictatorship launched a propaganda campaign ('Yes to Franco. No to Communism') to persuade its citizens that they were victims of a 'ruthless international siege'.[114] The regime gathered 300,000 people in Madrid to hail Franco, at which point the *Caudillo* could claim to have a popular mandate.[115] Still, the withdrawal of ambassadors was a symbolic act. It was never devised as the first instalment in a sustained campaign to unseat Franco. In the spring of 1947, the US suggested giving effective support to Franco's political opposition and issuing an ultimatum to the regime but again this was vetoed by Britain.[116] In turn, Bevin organized a meeting in October 1947 between leading rival figures of the opposition, Gil Robles and Prieto – but it was too late and nothing significant came of it.[117]

After 1945, Spain faced a dire situation economically and was dependent on the UK and the US for basic foodstuffs and oil. Thus had an economic embargo been imposed, Franco's regime would have collapsed.[118] Still, the *Caudillo* understood that the Allies would not go beyond verbal condemnation. His strategy was to hold on to the belief that sooner or later the Alliance would break up. In the meantime, official propaganda feverishly played the nationalist card portraying Spain as a state besieged by fiendish foreign powers.

It was inconceivable to believe that in a police state, physically and spiritually deprived Spaniards could overthrow the Dictatorship and that the opposition could mount an effective campaign without consistent international support.[119] Indeed, the euphoria following the defeat of the Axis gave way to frustration when it became clear that the Great Powers would not act to unseat Franco. The Republicans never presented a serious challenge. The squabbling that had marked their stance during the civil war continued in exile. Scattered and divided, they failed to form a united government that could be recognized by the Allies. The CNT split over the issue of collaboration with other groups, while the Socialists were paralysed by their opposing attitude towards the Communists and the disputes between the pro- and anti-Negrín factions. In August 1945, a government in exile headed by Giral, but which excluded the Communists, was established in Mexico. After 1939, that country opened its doors to Spanish refugees. Its consul in France, Gilberto Bosques Saldívar, saved thousands of stranded Spaniards by offering economic and diplomatic protection from the German and Vichy authorities. He also facilitated their journey to Mexico by hiring boats for that purpose.[120] Only recognized by Mexico, exiled Republicans settled there, living in their little world disconnected from reality.

As the German occupying forces began retreating in the summer of 1944, thousands of Spaniards who had fought in the French Resistance marched towards the border. In October, some 4,000 men launched a full-scale attack through the Val d'Aran in the Pyrenees. Lacking heavy weapons, they were no match for the much larger and better-armed 80,000 troops led by General Moscardó.[121] Over 7,500 guerrilla fighters kept the struggle alive over the next few years. Their failure to arouse an exhausted countryside and the civil guard's effective repressive tactics ensured their gradual liquidation. Cut off from potential sources of support, the guerrillas' quest for survival meant that their fight became entwined with robberies and kidnappings as a means of self-financing.[122] That allowed the regime to brand them mere bandits and implement a campaign of terror in those areas described as 'war zones'.[123] By 1951, most guerrillas' strongholds had been wiped out. The following year, the PCE decided to abandon the armed struggle.[124] Some anarchists continued fighting until the early 1960s.

The monarchist challenge seemed more threatening. Having fought the civil war with the hope of restoring the king, many senior officers considered Franco's rule a necessary but temporary measure. In March 1943, Don Juan, Alfonso XIII's son and heir, wrote to Franco demanding a peaceful transition of power. He felt confident that the time had arrived to replace the existing pro-Axis order with a monarchy that would be welcomed by the Allies and serve as an instrument for national reconciliation. In June, 25 leading members of Spain's socio-political elite signed a letter calling for the return of the Crown. In September, after the fall of Italian Fascism, some senior generals handed a letter to the *Caudillo* urging him 'with loyalty, respect, and affection' to consider if the time had come for restoration of the monarchy. The very respectful tone of the appeal, more a plea than an ultimatum, strengthened Franco's resilience. He knew he had the total loyalty of middle-ranking officers who did not regard him merely as 'first among equals'.[125] Thus, the dictator responded with a mixture of delaying tactics and bribery. He claimed to favour the return to a monarchy, but the time was not yet ripe. Military criticism gradually vanished when skilfully met by appeals to the *esprit de corps*, patriotism, and rewards (promotions, decorations, titles of nobility, etc.).[126]

As the Second World War dragged to an end, the monarchist cause seemed to gather momentum. On 19 March 1945, Don Juan published a manifesto in Lausanne (Switzerland) where he was living. He denounced Franco's close association with the Axis and instructed his followers in Spain to resign from their posts and form a *Junta* to oversee the expected transition. However, Don Juan's initiative received no explicit backing from the international community. Ingenuously, he was hoping that the dictator would quietly withdraw in a spirit of decency and good sense – but Franco lacked both. Resigning was never on his mind. His stubbornness left the monarchists with a choice: oust him or back him and enjoy the spoils of victory.[127] By dithering in their attempts to forcefully topple the regime and the horror at the prospect of the return of the vanquished by backing a liberal dynasty, the monarchists were indecisive and easily outmanoeuvred by the *Caudillo*.

Increasing guerrilla activity was a godsend to Franco, as it facilitated the revival of the civil war mentality and rallied the officer corps around him. Simultaneously, official propaganda portrayed diplomatic ostracism as a foreign attempt to destroy Spain. The *Caudillo* was the tireless champion of Spanish independence versus the international siege. Without him, the country would descend into the horrors of another civil war. The so-called *Noticieros y Documentales Cinematográficos* (Cinematographic Newsreels and Documentaries, NO-DO) appeared in 1943. With its screening made compulsory in all cinemas, it became the regime's voice. Before watching a movie, Spaniards had to endure the 30-minute NO-DO, wherein the *Caudillo* was portrayed almost as a superhero receiving foreign dignitaries, opening dams or factories, and ensuring the welfare of all Spaniards.[128]

The Dictatorship underwent a masterful exercise in public relations after the Second World War. The objective was to portray the appearance of popular legitimacy to counter Don Juan's activities and deflect the Allies' criticism of being close to the defeated Axis. Changes were cosmetic and did not affect the Dictatorship's authoritarian nature. The *Fuero de los Españoles* (Spaniards' Charter) was issued in July 1945 as a sort of bill of rights. Yet, there were no judicial mechanisms to guarantee them and, of course, freedom of expression was not included. It emphasized identification with Catholic principles to distinguish itself from fascism. Alberto Martín Artajo, president of Catholic Action, was appointed foreign minister. He was not only totally subservient to the *Caudillo* but could also portray Francoism as a regime founded on Catholic and anti-communist beliefs.[129] Franco reshuffled his government, increasing the number of monarchists and Catholics vis-à-vis Falangists. However, this did not mean the disappearance of the latter. On the contrary, it remained, more than ever, a docile instrument in charge of key functions such as regimenting the labour movement and organizing shows of popular support. Franco's own opinion was significant: 'It is the claque which accompanies me on my journeys through Spain'.[130] Indeed, the Falange became the most loyal family because it had no other basis for its existence after 1945.[131]

To counter Don Juan's appeal, Franco conducted a skilful campaign to appeal to monarchists. A few days after the publication of the Lausanne manifesto, the *Caudillo* alleged, with bare-faced cheek, that it was he who was responsible for putting the restoration of the monarchy on the agenda. The dictator also announced that Spain would adopt a monarchical form of government and a Council of the Realm would propose the name of the future king. In July 1947, a plebiscite took place to confirm Spain as a kingdom (Law of Succession). Manipulated by the authorities, the result was an overwhelming endorsement: 14,145,163 or 93 percent of the vote.[132]

Rather than monarchist restoration, Franco's real objective was to consolidate his rule by dividing and conquering the bulk of the monarchist camp. Indeed, although he proposed that Spain would one day be ruled by a king, no date was specified. He was to remain at the helm of the state and designate his successor. In other words, he became a regent for life. He could even claim that a popular referendum had overwhelmingly ratified his special status.[133] Most monarchists were satisfied with the outcome. Their anti-democratic values attracted them to an authoritarian monarchy based on the principles of the uprising of 1936 rather than on the liberal model preached by Don Juan. After much hesitation, Alfonso XIII's son agreed to meet Franco, in August 1948, on the dictator's yacht, the *Azor*, off the coast of San Sebastián. There the Pretender accepted the dictator's suggestion that his son Juan Carlos, then aged ten, be educated in Spain. With Don Juan's son under his control, the *Caudillo* had a hostage that enabled him to divide even further the monarchist camp.[134]

In March 1947, the Cold War became a reality when the American president, Harry S. Truman, declared his intention to defend the free world from the communist threat (Truman Doctrine). Henceforth tensions continued to grow: the USSR established communist satellites in occupied eastern European countries. In the Far East, the Chinese Civil War concluded in October 1949 with a communist victory and in June 1950 war broke out in Korea when the Communists of the north invaded the south.

As Franco expected, the deterioration of east-west relations began to alter international attitudes towards his regime. Post-war idealism was replaced by Cold War realism. In February 1948, France agreed to reopen the border. A Franco-Spanish trade agreement was signed in May.[135] One month later, Britain and Spain concluded a sterling payment agreement. With communism advancing in the world, the USA welcomed the stability provided by the dictatorships in the Iberian Peninsula. Its armed services longed for normalizing relations with Spain and installing military bases there.[136]

Spain's state resources were devoted to financing a powerful lobby in Washington headed by Lequerica. The objective was to promote a positive image of the Dictatorship and insist that Spain had the same right as communist regimes to UN membership and full diplomatic relations.[137] From the second half of 1947, the US State Department, still reluctant to establish friendly relations with a repressive regime, came under increasing pressure.[138] Ignoring his past collaboration with the Axis, US mainstream media began to praise Franco for his anti-communist zeal. The House of Representatives even voted to include Spain in the Marshall Plan in 1947 and approved the granting of loans in 1948 and 1949. Truman vetoed these measures. However, after the outbreak of the Korean War, he could no longer ignore public opinion and that of his own legislative. He finally agreed to the loan of US$62,500,000 in August 1950.[139] Truman informed Paris and London that the Department of Defence's advice had finally prevailed. He stressed his dislike of Franco's regime but could not let his personal feelings override the convictions of his military chiefs.[140]

US aid arrived providentially when the Spanish economy, beleaguered by bad harvests and lack of hard currency, was teetering on the brink of collapse. Much political capital was made from the West's diplomatic U-turn. A euphoric José Antonio Girón, the Falangist labour minister, claimed in the summer of 1950: 'the world is coming to our way of thinking'.[141] Official propaganda spared no effort to demonstrate that, finally, the international community had recognized the rightness of Franco's principles. It hailed the colossal skill of a God-guided leader who had foreseen the Cold War. The Spanish Civil War was now portrayed as the first victory against Soviet aggression and the *Caudillo was* lauded as the 'Sentinel of the West'.[142]

The winds of change brewing in the West certainly served to rehabilitate the Francoist regime. In 1949, 11 states normalized diplomatic relations with Spain.[143] On 4 November 1950, the UN General Assembly voted to rescind the resolution of December 1946 and ambassadors gradually returned to Madrid.[144] Months of arduous negotiations culminated in two diplomatic successes in 1953.

In August 1953, a concordat was signed with the Vatican. It bolstered Franco's image as the leader of a Catholic monarchy and, in turn, it officially ratified Spain as a confessional state wherein the Church played a central role and received generous financing. Henceforth, legislation was to be measured against the yardstick of Catholic orthodoxy. No other religion was allowed in public. Canon marriage became part of the civil code. All education had to conform to Catholic dogma, and religious instruction was imposed at all levels in schools.[145] The close relations with the Vatican reached a height when Pope Pius XII granted Franco, in December 1953, the highest decoration: the Supreme Order of Christ.[146]

Much more important was the agreement – covering defence, economic aid, and mutual assistance – signed with the United States, in September 1953. Despite the hostility of some senators and sectors of public opinion, the election of President Dwight D. Eisenhower, and the appointment of a new ambassador to Madrid, James C. Dunn, smoothed matters. In return for nuclear military bases, the Americans would pay a certain sum annually (between 1954 and 1961, this amounted to nearly $500 million) and provide material for the Spanish army, which up to 1963 came close to $600 million.[147] Crucially, it meant the return of Spain into the western orbit under the approval of the most powerful nation in the world. Aware of this, Franco had instructed his negotiators 'to sign anything they put in front of you'.[148] In fact, this implied that he sold a major part of Spanish sovereignty to a foreign power that was allowed to place its bases close to major urban centres.[149] Of course, the reward was US backing for his survival. Spain was admitted to the UN in 1955. By then, even the Soviet Bloc had restored diplomatic relations with Franco and broken off with the Republican government in exile. Only Mexico, Israel, and former Yugoslavia still regarded the Republic as the legitimate regime.[150]

The Economic Miracle

By the mid-1950s, the regime entered a period of stability. Franco gradually withdrew from the daily business of politics and assumed the distant air of a royal personage. The wedding of his daughter Carmen to an aristocratic playboy, Cristóbal Martínez Bordiu, the Marquis of Villaverde, broadened the family network into a powerful lobby, the *Clan del Pardo* (Pardo Clique) named after the dictator's official residence. The dictator could now relax and devote increasing amounts of time to his favourite hobbies: hunting, fishing, golf, watching westerns, etc. Of course, he remained the ultimate guarantor of favours. Indeed, enormous sums were spent to take part in hunting parties attended by Franco in the country's best private estates. They often became three- or four-day affairs in which jobs and government backing for business deals were negotiated.[151]

The *Caudillo* remained the ultimate arbiter in critical situations. For instance, in February 1956, rivalries between Catholic and Falangist students degenerated into clashes. A Falangist was severely injured, most likely due to the accidental discharge of the gun of one of his comrades. As rumours spread of a massive retaliatory attack, the captain general of Madrid, Miguel Rodrigo Martínez, threatened to call out the army.[152] Franco was forced to intervene. As in 1942, he adopted a Solomonic solution: he sacked from the cabinet both the secretary of the movement, Raimundo Fernández Cuesta, and the Catholic minister of education, Joaquín Ruiz Giménez.[153] A few months later, after France announced the concession of independence to Morocco, he showed enough realism to relinquish control of the Spanish part of the Protectorate.[154]

Political consolidation was not matched by economic recovery. Spain only began to reach pre-war levels in 1954. The failure of autarky was glaring. Import substitution to encourage self-sufficiency, state control, and heavy protectionism had worsened the economic gap with the developed West. Economic modernization was impossible, restricted to a domestic market with limited purchasing power. Protection of a backward agrarian sector had brought increasing returns to landowners, but lack of investment led to stagnation and misery for the peasantry. US loans had just averted collapse. There had been some expansion in the industrial sector and in foreign trade, which allowed for vital imports of foodstuffs, raw materials, and capital goods. However, as industrial output did not allow for sustained growth, traditional structures and technology remained unchanged. By the autumn of 1956, inflation was spiralling out of control and the deficit in the balance of payments worsened. Despite heavy state repression, rising prices and static wages sparked strikes for higher pay in the main industrial centres.[155]

Appointed minister to the presidency in 1951 and deputy prime minister in 1967, Carrero effectively oversaw daily decision-making. Aware of the poor state of the economy, he began a close association with Opus Dei, a powerful and secretive Catholic secular order founded in 1928 by the priest José María Escrivá de Balaguer, closely connected with the country's socio-economic elite.[156] The cabinet reshuffle of February 1957 – in which 12 of the 17 ministers were changed – was the turning point. For the first time, portfolios were not simply distributed amongst underlings – those relating to economic matters were now in the hands of experts belonging to Opus Dei.[157]

Although liberal in economics, the Opus ministers shared the authoritarian values of the other nationalist families. Their goal was not political reform. On the contrary, they believed that popular protest should be stifled and the regime strengthened by delivering prosperity and affluence. With Carrero's backing, the Opus team led by Laureano López Rodó, appointed in December 1956 to the post of technical general secretary to the ministry of the presidency, embraced economic liberalism and abandoned autarky. An Office of Coordination and Planning was created to change the course of economic policy. In 1958, Spain joined the Organization for European Economic Cooperation and the International Monetary Fund. Finally, the government introduced, in the summer of 1959, the so-called Stabilization Plan, whose objectives were to foster external trade, encourage foreign investment, and restore financial stability by controlling inflation. The reforms envisaged reducing public expenditure, rationalizing government controls, drastically devaluing the currency to a competitive level of 60 pesetas to the dollar, and providing incentives to liberalize trade and foreign investment. Three development plans were implemented, from 1964–67, 1968–71, and 1972–75, respectively. Their aim was to target resources to stimulate growth. Social concerns were neglected. The redistribution of wealth and income was never an objective and the age-old gap between the poorer interior provinces and the industrialized regions of the north and east widened.[158]

After many years of economic stagnation, Spain enjoyed a period of unprecedented boom. It was such that in a decade the country became part of the elite club of most developed nations. The bonanza lasted until 1973 when the West was hit with sharply rising oil prices. The upsurge in foreign trade was spectacular. Between 1961 and 1973, gross domestic product (GDP) grew at an average of 7.5 percent annually, second only to Japan. Spain ceased to be primarily an agricultural economy and became a modern industrialized society. The active labour force in the countryside fell sharply from 41.9 percent in 1959 to 25.3 percent in 1973, while industrial employment and the service sector rose from 31.8 to 36.8 percent and 26.5 to 40 percent, respectively. About 3,000,000 people left rural areas seeking jobs either abroad or in the nation's large urban conurbations: Barcelona, Madrid, Valencia, and Bilbao. In line with this, the contribution of agriculture to the economy fell dramatically to below 15 percent of GDP. Its place was taken by such industries as chemicals and metallurgy, and those related to an increasingly consumer society (washing machines, refrigerators, televisions, etc.). Spain's own automobile industry (SEAT), and the possession by so many households of its 600 model, was a sign of modern times.[159]

Spain's economic miracle was not affected by the balance of payment problems that normally bring modernization to a halt in most underdeveloped economies. This was due to three things: vast increases in overseas investment, foreign tourism, and emigrant remittances. With the dismantling of autarky, capital flowed into Spain attracted by the prospects of cheap labour, state incentives, and potential markets. Foreign investment rose from US$40 million in 1960 to US$697 million in 1970, 40 percent coming from the United States. Injections of fresh capital provided a boost to an undercapitalized industry and brought vital advanced technology. Simultaneously, the demand for manpower from western countries, particularly Germany, meant that over 1.5 million workers, mostly youngsters, left Spain in the 1960s. This facilitated the elimination of excess labour at home while amassing copious amounts of foreign currency. These were guest workers with legal contracts who only intended remaining abroad for a few years to learn crucial skills and make significant savings. This migration has been referred to as Spain's Marshall Plan: it kept the level of unemployment low, helped raise salaries in Spain, and remittances gave the economy a massive boost.[160] Finally, tourism, a poorly developed sector before 1960, became a leading industry. The number of foreigners visiting Spain rose from just below 4.2 million in 1959 to almost 34.6 million in 1973. Similarly, receipts from tourism rose over the same period from US$125.6 to US$3,091.2 million. Guaranteed sunshine, inexpensive package holiday offers, and charter flights did the rest. Earnings from tourism almost eliminated Spain's trade deficit, generated jobs in southern areas traditionally plagued by unemployment, and stimulated ambitious infrastructure developments.[161] There was an ecological price to pay as formerly small fishing towns gave way to a coastline heaving with hotels and apartment blocks.

The Falange was more than ever marginalized from central state policy-making. Veteran Falangists such as Arrese and Girón were bypassed by a new generation of more docile elements such as its new secretary, José Solís. The Law of Fundamental Principles of the Movement, approved in May 1958, confirmed the regime's vague ideological tenets. It stated that the Movement was the communion of all Spaniards who accepted the principles of the crusade. Spain was defined as a Catholic and social monarchy. This meant that instead of depending on divisive party politics, the country was an 'organic' democracy founded upon the true pillars of society: the family, the unions, and the municipality. Elections to both city councils and the *Cortes* did take place via corporatist suffrage based on these natural sectors of the community. Of course, candidates were closely scrutinized and had to abide by the regime's values.[162] In December 1966, a popular plebiscite overwhelmingly endorsed the Organic Law of the State, a semblance of a constitution that combined all the laws and principles of the regime.[163]

Although the Dictatorship had postponed material progress for almost 15 years by clinging to autarky for so long, Franco was quick to take credit for the economic miracle. He could now claim that his rule was also legitimized by Spain's flourishing economy and greatly improved living standards. However, he was now an ailing old man with Parkinson's disease. His early departure from a cabinet meeting for the first time, on 6 December 1968, gave a serious indication of his deteriorating health. Confronted by the reality of his own mortality and under Carrero's advice, the *Caudillo* finally ended years of uncertainty about the succession – on 22 July 1969, he nominated Juan Carlos as his heir, who, in turn, received the title of Prince of Spain. By breaking the royal line, Franco confirmed that he was lord and master by placing his candidate on the throne. In his speech of nomination, he noted that everything for the future was *atado y bien atado* ('tied up and well tied down'). Carrero's authority and economic prosperity would ensure the continuity of Francoism.[164]

The Twilight of the Regime

By the late 1960s, Spain was closing the economic gap with her neighbours. Consumerism was a reality, which in turn affected social values and interactions. Spanish households saw a dramatic increase in the ownership of cars, televisions, washing machines, and other signs of a modern affluent society. Yet, the rapid socio-economic modernization taking place was not matched at a political level. The Opus technocrats believed that growing prosperity would be a sufficient surrogate for ideological politics and validate the survival of Francoism. In contrast, the economic progress on which the regime prided itself engendered growing contradictions between the new society and the old state. The opening of borders and markets meant the arrival of modern ideas through foreign cinema and literature. Televisions alone were a socio-cultural phenomenon that guided people towards new lifestyle possibilities.[165] Spaniards learned from, imitated, and identified with the people of western Europe, their institutions, and their way of life.[166] By 1970, the gap between a modern society and an obsolete state still anchored on the values of the crusade had widened to the point of no return.[167] By then, sectors from without and even within the regime had concluded that the Dictatorship was an anachronism.

'Spain is different' became the slogan for an increasingly obsolete regime that was ready to project a more positive, forward-looking international image by inviting visitors to its shores to reap the economic benefits of a burgeoning tourist industry.[168] As Spain opened its doors to tourism and free market forces and the regime promoted the idea of mass consumerism, daily life became less harsh and oppressive. The liberalization of the economy brought about the so-called *apertura* (opening-up) that undermined the 'closed' and controlled society of the two decades following the civil war.

On a cultural level, it was characterized by a loosening of censorship and a more relaxed attitude towards the intrusion of foreign influences. In this sense, the arrival at the Ministry of Information and Tourism of Manuel Fraga Iribarne (1962–69) was the dawn of a new era, which saw the emergence and consolidation of a cultural universe (literature, theatre, cinema, music) whose scathing criticism contributed to undermine the Dictatorship's foundations. The heroic imperial culture hitherto spread by the Falange and the messianic image put forward by the Church sounded more and more like clichés from a distant past. Now, Spaniards were gradually able to acquire from bookshops previously banned literature, including the works of Karl Marx, Antonio Gramsci, and Albert Camus. At the same time, Spanish authors (Manuel Vázquez Montalbán, Juan Goytisolo, Carmen Martín Gaite, Montserrat Roig, Juan Marsé) and cinema directors (Carlos Saura, Victor Erice) were able to get their anti-Francoist messages to a broad audience by often couching them in allegorical terms. In some cases, the fine irony and humour in the films of Juan Antonio Bardem and Luis García Berlanga transformed the hitherto feared regime into an object of popular scorn and ridicule.[169]

Spurred by economic liberalization, internal migration from the depressed southern regions toward big cities became an exodus. These years of mass migration, the 1950s and 1960s, brought about huge demographic change. Madrid and Barcelona gained nearly 1.4 million people; Valencia 275,000. In the meantime, the population of the interior of the peninsula and the south declined in absolute numbers. In total, 34 provinces were net exporters of population.[170] The consequence was a dramatic upsurge in the industrial workforce. Neglected by the technocrats' planning, workers endured appalling living conditions. Entire families were crammed into sublet rooms in dingy neighbourhoods or emerging shanty towns on the periphery of the cities. By 1970, over 600,000 people lived in *chabolas* (self-assembled shacks).[171] More daring than their ancestors, they began to organize themselves to obtain a fairer share of the economic boom. Unrepresented by the official unions, they first found support in Catholic associations: *Hermandades Obreras de Acción Católica* (HOAC, Workers' Brotherhood of Catholic Action) and *Juventud Obrera Católica* (JOC, Catholic Workers' Youth Movement). They became a grassroots phenomenon involved in labour concerns and the only relatively safe channel for discussing social issues and airing grievances.[172] By supporting strike action and criticizing the effects of the economic measures, many young priests found themselves at odds with the Church hierarchy, who sided unequivocally with the regime. Based in poor neighbourhoods, many of them were workers themselves (plumbers, taxi drivers, builders) and so identified better with the plight of their parishioners.[173] They played a leading part in the strikes of the late 1950s and early 1960s and were the forerunners of *Comisiones Obreras* (CCOO, Workers' Commissions).[174]

Taking advantage of the legalization of collective bargaining in 1958, the CCOO first became active as ad hoc committees, negotiating grievances and wages with the employers' representatives. They appeared and dissolved once the conflict had been solved. Appointed by their fellow workers on the shopfloor to represent them in negotiations, they attracted many Catholics and even disenchanted Falangists.[175] They filled the vacuum between the clandestine and the obsolete official unions. Their success gained them the respect of the proletariat and even the tolerance of the regime overwhelmed by the fast-expanding labour movement.[176]

It was not until 1966 when the CCOO had expanded into regional networks and become an entrenched force on the shopfloor that the state realized their connection with the PCE. Unlike the UGT and CNT, whose clandestine organizations were constantly suppressed by the authorities, the Communists adopted the strategy of *entrismo* (infiltration of the official unions). The CCOO's leader, Marcelino Camacho, was himself a member of the PCE executive committee. In 1969, the government declared martial law. Ten CCOO leaders were charged with belonging to an illegal association, tried in December 1973, and sentenced to a total of 162 years imprisonment, including a sentence of 28 years for Camacho.[177] Although the sentences were later reduced, repression only served to spark labour unrest and solidarity strikes. Crucially, industrial conflicts now encompassed political objectives. Despite being punished by law, Spain in the 1970s saw the highest level of industrial action of any western country.[178]

Even sectors that previously had supported, or at least consented to, the Dictatorship began to desert it in the 1960s. Prosperity brought new values. The austere middle classes of the 1930s and 1940s became a large social section formed by engineers, doctors, teachers, white-collar workers, and so on. They increasingly rejected a regime in which they lacked a political voice and the basic freedoms that were considered natural in other western societies. Also, for the new industrial and business elites, which had replaced the landed oligarchy of the 1930s as the country's ruling economic class, Francoism was no longer the guarantor of order and prosperity. On the contrary, it was an obstacle to further economic expansion and social harmony. Its survival both impeded Spain's accession to the European Economic Community (EEC) and increased the likelihood of social unrest. Accordingly, they came to regard the Dictatorship as an irksome anachronism and so to safeguard their interests, they bet on radical change.[179]

Simultaneously, the universities became a visible focus of dissent. Campuses were no longer the refuge of an educated elite. The economic boom produced an explosion of student numbers in higher education. Despite the official discourse that defined studying as inimical to femininity, the number of women who pursued undergraduate courses doubled from 7,667 in 1950 to 15,338 in 1961.[180] They belonged to a new generation who no longer accepted that the female ideal was a submissive woman whose duty was confined to the domestic realm. Enjoying the relative liberty of academic debate and often encouraged by their tutors, students absorbed forbidden texts and embraced, like their European counterparts, pop music and the rebellious fashions of the age. Sporadic incidents such as the 1956 student clashes gave way to constant confrontation in the following two decades. Free assemblies, sit-ins, and demonstrations often ended in ritual battles with the police. The regime, having lost the loyalty of the new generation, treated their dissent as a problem of public order and resorted to repression.[181]

The 1960s also saw a resurgence of nationalism in the Catalan and Basque regions. Yet, the two models developed very differently. Despite all the attempts by the regime to eliminate symbols of national distinctiveness, the Catalan language and culture survived intact at a private level. With the liberalization of the 1960s, there was mass mobilization against the centralization of the state. Musicians, writers, clergy, and intellectuals led the campaign to defend Catalan identity. The movement spread to the Catalan-speaking areas of Valencia and the Balearic Islands. In November 1971, the so-called Assembly rallied representatives of all groups from Catholics to communists, from professional associations to delegates of working-class neighbourhoods. It demanded the re-establishment of the Catalan Statute of 1932, political freedom, and democracy.[182]

Fundamental to foster Catalan identity was the so-called Nova Cançó, which emerged in the 1960s and combined folk music with popular protest. Its most well-known members – Maria del Mar Bonet from the Balearic Islands, Raimon from Valencia, and Lluís Llach and Joan Manuel Serrat from Catalonia – exerted considerable influence, especially over the youth. Their repertoire, mainly in Catalan, was not an obstacle for them to become iconic figures all over Spain where their concerts were sold out.[183]

Basque nationalism, lacking the secure cultural roots of its Catalan counterpart, developed into a more violent phenomenon. Radical youth revolted against what they considered the passivity of their PNV elders and founded *Euzkadi Ta Askatasuna* (ETA, Basque Nation and Liberty) in 1959. Most came from Catholic circles where nationalist priests infused them with the idea of the Basque nation being occupied by a foreign army. Also influenced by the marxist understanding of imperialism, they identified their cause, the struggle for the independence of the Basque Country, with anti-colonial liberation movements then active in third world countries (Vietnam, Algeria, etc.). They initially concentrated on propaganda activities. The resort to armed struggle began with a shoot-out in June 1968 in which one *Etarra* and a civil guard were killed. In August, Melitón Manzanas, the police chief of Guipúzcoa, was slain. A wave of shootings, bombings, and robberies ensued. ETA embraced a guerrilla strategy based on action-repression-action. The idea was to provoke a brutal indiscriminate state response, which in turn would shake the population out of their apathy and rally them to the call for the independence of their homeland. The regime's brutal response played into ETA's hands. As a state of emergency was declared, the police were given a free hand, arresting and torturing hundreds of innocent people. In December 1970, 16 ETA members were tried in

Burgos by a military court. Six of them were sentenced to death. Given the international protest, Franco commuted the sentence to 30 years in prison each. The trial was a propaganda coup for ETA. The organization acquired visibility and popularity. Its members claimed to be freedom fighters. A flood of young Basques, seduced by the romantic appeal of the armed struggle, joined the terrorist group. Their activities aided by the ability to reach a safe haven in France, ETA escalated its military operations.[184]

The Church underwent the most perplexing transformation during this period. From its initial absolute identification with the Dictatorship, it moved to guarded criticism and finally to opposition. For Franco, the Church's about-turn was a betrayal and a display of ingratitude that he could never comprehend.[185]

Dissent began in the 1950s when Catholic militants from HOAC and JOC lent their support to fellow workers. Their stance clashed with the rigid position of the hierarchy. Yet, they received a spectacular boost from the Vatican with the arrival in 1958 of a progressive Pope, John XXIII. His encyclicals, *Mater et Magistra* and *Pacem in Terris*, defending social justice, civil rights, and political pluralism, meant an outright rejection of Francoist principles. The Second Vatican Council (1962–65) amounted to a political earthquake. With the Papacy extolling the advantages of dialogue and tolerance, the Spanish prelates' fundamentalism became suddenly obsolete. Spain's ecclesiastical hierarchy entered a period of trauma and self-examination.[186]

The liberal transformation continued with Paul VI, John XXIII's successor, who did not hesitate to condemn the Spanish Dictatorship's harsh repressive policies.[187] When Franco refused to relinquish his right to nominate bishops granted by the Concordat, the Pope began to name auxiliary bishops to replace the ageing old guard. He appointed Enrique Tarancón as Archbishop of Toledo and Cardinal Primate in February 1969. Churches became a place of shelter for the opposition and Catholic journals a voice of criticism of the regime. By the early 1970s, as the ecclesiastical culture of nostalgia and intolerance was in retreat, diehard prelates became a minority. In September 1971, a joint assembly of bishops and priests produced a historical statement that reflected the views of a new majority that repudiated the old underpinnings of the crusade. It preached reconciliation and asked the people's forgiveness for its partisanship in the civil war. In January 1973, bishops voted three to one in favour of formal separation from the state, the surrender of all their political prerogatives, and respect for pluralism.[188]

Losing ground in all spheres of civil society, the Dictatorship's crisis of legitimacy was a reality by the late 1960s. Claims to guarantee public order were undermined by terrorism, labour unrest, and student protest. It could not hope to deliver social peace when it was rejected by the working and middle classes. Its claim to be a Catholic state sounded ludicrous when it was not only criticized by the Church, but also was the only western nation that since 1968 had a special prison in Zamora for militant priests.[189] Still, the loyalty of the armed forces and police ensured the regime's survival while Franco lived.

The cohesion of the ruling coalition began slowly to disintegrate. The *aperturistas* believed that the regime should evolve according to the changing times. They were young pragmatists whose technical expertise and educational record, rather than ideological leanings, had gained them entry into the administration. They were recruited due to their outstanding performance in the *oposiciones*, the highly competitive exams for entry to the civil service. A good example was Manuel Fraga Iribarne, minister of information and tourism since 1962 and author of the Press Law of 1966 which, although far from allowing freedom of speech, represented a notable relaxation of censorship. Well connected with the business world, the *aperturistas* believed that clinging to an obsolete political system was simply an attempt to postpone the inevitable. Consequently, they sought to pursue reform from within to avoid a more violent revolutionary break with the past.[190]

In contrast, the *inmovilistas* were known as the 'Bunker' for their Hitlerian discourse of fighting to the end in the rubble of the Chancellery. They were old-guard Falangists and Catholics led by veterans like Girón and Blas Piñar, the head of the neo-fascist political organization and journal *Fuerza Nueva*. They rejected eveything but minimal reform. Their strength did not lay in their numbers, being a minority of diehards, but in their ability to control groups of right-wing thugs and their excellent connections with the security services, the armed forces, and Franco's inner circle, *El Clan del Pardo*.[191]

Carrero was the only person who seemed capable of maintaining the ruling coalition. In July 1969, Franco endorsed the latter's so-called *continuista* plan: the admiral would control a monarchy led by Juan Carlos so that Francoism could outlive Franco. *Continuismo* could even be presented as a middle-of-the-road position between the *inmovilismo* of the right-wing ultras and the reformism of the *aperturistas*. Carrero's firm grasp of power was not even rocked by the MATESA scandal that erupted in the summer of 1969. Juan Vilá Reyes, a member of Opus Dei and head of the textile machinery industry, *Maquinaria Textil del Norte de España SA* (MATESA), was alleged to have obtained 10 billion pesetas in export credits under false pretences, with the connivance of some ministers.[192] During the internal jockeying for influence, Fraga and Solís leaked the affair to tarnish the reputation of Opus Dei. Once again, Franco adopted a Solomonic decision: three Opus ministers connected with the scandal were dismissed, but so were Fraga and Solís. MATESA was buried. In the reshuffle of October 1969, Carrero, with the *Caudillo*'s backing, formed a cabinet that contained an even larger number of Opus technocrats.[193]

Carrero welcomed the presence of *aperturistas* in government as they could broaden the regime's base and be used as proof of tolerance of internal dissent. However, he was always closer to the *inmovilistas*, the only difference being his strong monarchism and more tempered rhetoric. In fact, as social unrest, student protest, and terrorism increased in the early 1970s, the government responded with unrestrained brutality. A state of emergency was often declared, permitting the security services to engage in an orgy of arrests and torture. Extreme right-wing groups were sponsored to act as strike-breakers and attack with absolute impunity left-wing bookshops, art galleries, and even churches where they beat up 'red' priests and their congregations. These thugs did the regime's dirty job while allowing the government to present itself as a moderate centrist administration.[194] Still, terrorist methods revealed the growing anxiety of a system whose health was deteriorating as fast as that of the *Caudillo*.

Carrero reached the peak of his career in June 1973 when Franco finally appointed him prime minister. It represented a ringing endorsement to his closest adviser to supervise the continuity of the regime after his death.[195] However, the plan suffered two devastating blows from which it would never recover.

On 20 December 1973, an ETA commando unit carried out *Operación Ogro*: Carrero's assassination. That day, shortly after leaving the Jesuit church where he attended daily mass before going to work, a huge explosive device buried under the street was detonated as his car passed over. The explosion was such that the vehicle was blown sky-high, coming to rest in the inner courtyard of a building behind the church that the prime minister had just left. The precision of the attack and the fact that for days the commando unit had been able to pursue its activities unchallenged gave rise to all sorts of conspiracy theories involving either foreign powers or Spain's secret services. It left Franco's dream of his regime outliving him via his alter ego's pair safe of hands in total disarray. A desolated *Caudillo* commented: 'they have cut my last link with the world'.[196] A few months later (April 1974), the Dictatorship suffered another lethal blow when its Portuguese counterpart was rapidly overthrown after 46 years in power following a coup staged by disgruntled young army officers.[197] This demonstrated the fragility of repressive states hitherto believed impregnable and left Spain as the last right-wing dictatorship in western Europe.

On 28 December, the choice of Carlos Arias Navarro as prime minister was considered rather astonishing. If anything, he deserved to be demoted: Carrero had been killed under his watch at the Home Office. His appointment was decided at the last minute by a senile Franco under the pressure of his inner circle, including his wife's lobbying. He was chosen due to his hard-line record: he was known as 'the butcher of Málaga' for his activities there as a public prosecutor during the civil war and years later as director of security.[198] Arias' overriding objective was to keep the governing class together and ensure the survival of Francoism's foundations after the transition of power to Juan Carlos. However, he lacked Carrero's authority. Moreover, while aware of the need to introduce some reforms to broaden the appeal of the regime, his personal feelings were closer to his Bunker's erstwhile comrades. Consequently, schizophrenia marked his government. Indeed, Arias' rule oscillated between tantalizing promises of liberalization and violent repression. He walked a tightrope between reformists and the Bunker. His irresolution succeeded in satisfying neither camp, while labour unrest and terrorism continued unabated.[199]

In a televised address to the *Cortes* on 12 February 1974, Arias seemed to side with the *aperturistas*. He announced a programme of limited reform that included the election of local officials and the right of political association. However, he was cautious to placate the *inmovilistas*, stressing soon thereafter that these associations would have to operate within the framework of the fundamental laws of the state.[200]

In February 1974, Arias ordered the arrest and exile of the Bishop of Bilbao, Antonio Añoveros, for a sermon preaching the rights of ethnic minorities. He backed down under Franco's orders when Archbishop Tarancón, supported by the Vatican, threatened to excommunicate the government.[201] The execution of two anarchists in March, followed in April by a vicious press campaign orchestrated by the Bunker, put an end to Arias' timid reformism. Indeed, on 28 April, three days after the fall of the Portuguese dictatorship, Girón backed by senior generals warned against any slide towards liberalizing the regime. Soon thereafter the moderate chief of the general staff, Manuel Díaz Alegría, was dismissed and replaced by a hard-line general, Carlos Fernández Vallespín.[202] On 9 July, Franco was taken to hospital with phlebitis and Juan Carlos reluctantly became acting head of state. By early September, Franco had miraculously recovered and resumed office. The following month, Pío Cabanillas, an outspoken reformist member of the cabinet at the helm of the Ministry of Information and Tourism, was accused of 'being too liberal' and removed. His departure was followed by a flood of *aperturistas* resigning their posts. By the end of 1974, Arias' precarious balancing act had collapsed. The diehards held the upper hand. In a televised address, he offered a pathetic image when he begged the country for confidence in the future while he presented his final Law of Associations in which the Movement's National Council held veto powers. Earlier promises of constitutional reform were effectively dashed.[203]

During 1975, the dramatic crumbling of the regime was echoed in the rapid deterioration of Franco's health. Against a background of rocketing prices in the wake of the energy crisis, industrial militancy intensified, university campuses were daily battlefields, and terrorism continued unabated. In the 20 months following Carrero's assassination, ETA killed a further 40 people (mostly policemen and civil guards) while other revolutionary left-wing groups, such as the Maoist *Frente Revolucionario Antifascista Patriótico* (FRAP, Patriotic and Revolutionary Antifascist Front), claimed victims as well.[204] In turn, diehard Francoists reverted to the nostalgic rhetoric and brutal repressive methods of the 1940s in a desperate attempt to quell dissent. Police often opened fire, killing striking workers. Protesters were rounded up in their hundreds, beaten and tortured. Right-wing squads escalated their violent campaign. In July, nine young army officers were arrested. Encouraged by the Portuguese example, they had joined a clandestine military organization, the so-called *Unión Militar Democrática*, whose objective was to turn the army into an apolitical institution alongside the nationwide drive towards democracy. The fear of many in the regime was understandable as the army was its mainstay.[205]

On 27 September, Franco made clear his determination to fight to the end. Despite worldwide pleas for clemency, including personal appeals from Pope Paul VI, three FRAP and two ETA militants were executed. The event caused consternation and massive demonstrations abroad and even attacks on Spanish embassies. Fifteen European governments recalled their ambassadors. It appeared as if Spain was returning to her isolation of the post-war years.[206]

On 1 October, four policemen were killed by a new revolutionary group, believed to be infiltrated by the security services, the *Grupos de Resistencia Antifascista Primero de Octubre* (GRAPO, Groups of Anti-Fascist Resistance First of October). That day, the *Caudillo* reacted in his usual manner. Undisturbed by mounting national and international opposition, he addressed a huge crowd of enthusiastic supporters. Revealing the extent to which he was still entrenched in a surreal universe, he claimed that Spain's problems were 'all part of a masonic leftist conspiracy of the political class in indecent concubinage with Communist-terrorist subversion in society'.[207]

This was his last public speech. Already infirm, his exposure to Madrid's freezing autumn wind proved fatal. On 15 October, he suffered a heart attack. Two days later, proving his ceaseless resistance, he still insisted on chairing a council of ministers. As his condition worsened during the following days, he was rushed to hospital. A serious risk of confrontation with Morocco over Western Sahara, the last Spanish colony in Africa, was kept secret from him. Taking advantage of the critical moment, King Hassan of Morocco, coveting a territory rich in phosphates and minerals, ordered thousands of unarmed civilians to invade ('The Green March'). The latter's cowardly opportunism was paralleled by the indecision of a panic-stricken Arias cabinet. An armed clash was avoided at the last minute when, despite earlier promises of self-determination for Western Sahara, Spain retreated ignominiously and initiated negotiations that led to the cession of that nation to its neighbours, Morocco and Mauritania.[208] In the meantime, Franco underwent three major operations. He was kept alive on life-support. When a tearful Arias confirmed Franco's demise on 20 November, most Spaniards were gripped by uncertainty and fear. Those aged below 40 had not known any other leader.

Notes

1   Paul Preston, *El gran manipulador. La mentira cotidiana de Franco* (Barcelona: Ediciones B, 2008), p. 99.

2   Reig, *Franco: El César*, p. 57.
3   Preston, *The Politics of Revenge*, p. 84.
4   Javier Tusell, *Franco, España y la II Guerra Mundial. Entre el Eje y la Neutralidad* (Madrid: Temas de Hoy, 1995), pp. 42–3.
5   Javier Tusell and Genoveva Queipo de Llano (eds.), *Franco y Mussolini* (Barcelona: Planeta, 1985), pp. 51–3.
6   Ibid., pp. 59–60.
7   Samuel Hoare, *Ambassador on Special Mission* (London: Collins, 1946), pp. 14–16, 21–5, 30–6, 45–54.
8   Richard Wigg, *Churchill and Spain: The Survival of the Franco Regime, 1940–45* (London: Routledge, 2005), p. 20.
9   Matthieu Séguéla, *Franco-Pétain. Los secretos de una alianza* (Barcelona: Prensa Ibérica, 1994), p. 51.
10 Preston, *Franco*, pp. 356–7, 377–80, 387.
11 David Wingeate Pike, *Franco and the Axis Stigma* (Basingstoke: Macmillan, 2008), p. 25.
12 Tusell, *Franco*, pp. 132–9.
13 Preston, *The Politics of Revenge*, p. 60.
14 Enrique Moradiellos, *Franco: Anatomy of a Dictator* (London: Tauris, 2018), p. 58
15 Séguéla, *Franco-Pétain*, pp. 98, 112–15.
16 Serrano Suñer, *Memorias*, pp. 289–90.
17 Séguéla, *Franco-Pétain*, p. 111.
18 Serrano Suñer, *Memorias*, pp. 285, 298–300.
19 Ibid., pp. 284–5, 313.
20 Tusell, *Franco*, pp. 158–62.
21 Preston, *Franco*, pp. 417–18. Incredibly, Churruca survives his own execution at the start of the film. He recovers in a hospital wearing 'shrewdly' dark glasses to avoid being recognized. He finally manages to flee Madrid to join the nationalist camp where he soon stands out for his courage in combat.
22 Tusell, *Franco*, pp. 262–9.
23 Preston, *Franco*, p. 442.
24 Peter Day, *Franco's Friends: How British Intelligence Helped Bring Franco to Power in Spain* (London: Biteback, 2011), pp. 169–76.
25 Preston, *Franco*, pp. 465–72.
26 Antonio Cazorla, *Franco. Biografía del mito* (Madrid: Alianza, 2014), p. 153.
27 Preston, *Franco*, p. 431.
28 Stanley G. Payne, *Fascism in Spain, 1923–1977* (Madison, WI: University of Wisconsin Press, 1999), pp. 360–4.
29 Carlton J.H. Hayes, *Wartime Mission in Spain* (New York: Macmillan, 1945), pp. 86–94.

30 Tusell, *Franco*, pp. 356–60.
31 Reig, *Franco Caudillo*, p. 201.
32 Hoare, *Ambassador on Special Mission*, pp. 184–5.
33 Pike, *Franco and the Axis Stigma*, p. 99.
34 Tusell de Llano (eds.), *Franco y Mussolini*, pp. 235–7.
35 Hayes, *Wartime Mission in Spain*, pp. 187–230; Hoare, *Ambassador on Special Mission*, pp. 259–63.
36 Ibid., p. 267.
37 Hoare, *Ambassador on Special Mission*, p. 284.
38 Ibid., pp. 300–6.
39 Wigg, *Churchill and Spain*, pp. 144, 155, 165–7.
40 Preston, *Franco*, p. 531.
41 Julián Casanova and Carlos Gil Andrés, *Twentieth-Century Spain* (Cambridge: Cambridge University Press, 2014), p. 219.
42 Laura Zenobi, *La construcción del mito de Franco* (Madrid: Cátedra, 2011), pp. 11–12.
43 Azaña, *Memorias*, pp. 312–13.
44 Moradiellos, *Franco*, p. 178.
45 Gregorio Sánchez Recio, *Sobre todos Franco. Coalición reaccionaria y grupos políticos* (Madrid: Flor del Viento, 2008), pp. 23–4.
46 Ismael Saz, 'La peculiaritat del feixisme espanyol', *Afers*, 25 (1996), pp. 629–32.
47 Julio Aróstegui, 'El régimen: derecho, doctrina y lenguaje', in Julio Aróstegui (ed.), *Franco: La represión como sistema* (Barcelona: Flor del Viento, 2012), pp. 25–9.
48 Moradiellos, *Franco*, p. 181.
49 Richard Gunther, 'The Spanish Model Revisited', in Gregorio Alonso and Diego Muro (eds.), *The Politics and Memory of Democratic Transition* (New York: Routledge, 2011), p. 20.
50 Antonio Cazorla, *Fear and Progress: Ordinary Lives in Franco's Spain, 1939–1975* (Oxford: Wiley-Blackwell, 2010), p. 41.
51 Saz, 'La peculiaritat', p. 636.
52 Cazorla, *Fear and Progress*, p. 42.
53 Reig, *Memoria*, p. 11.
54 Reig, *Franco Caudillo*, p. 187.
55 Peter Anderson, *The Francoist Military Trials: Terror and Complicity, 1939–1945* (London: Routledge, 2010), p. 79.
56 Cazorla, *Fear and Progress*, p. 61.
57 Michael Richards, *A Time of Silence* (Cambridge: Cambridge University Press, 1998), p. 92.
58 Angel Smith, *Historical Dictionary of Spain* (London: Rowman & Littlefield, 2018), p. 366.

59 Cazorla, *Fear and Progress*, p. 43.
60 Miguel Ángel del Arco, 'Hunger and the Consolidation of the Francoist Regime, 1939–1951', *European History Quarterly*, 40/3 (2010), p. 460.
61 Miguel Ángel del Arco, 'The Struggle Continues: Everyday Repression and Resistance in Post-War Francoist Repression', in Peter Anderson and Miguel Ángel del Arco (eds.), *Mass Killings and Violence in Spain, 1936–1952* (New York: Routledge, 2015), p. 163.
62 Francisco Moreno, 'La represión en la posguerra', in Juliá (ed.), *Víctimas*, p. 299.
63 Cazorla, *Fear and Progress*, p. 11.
64 Carlos Barciela, 'La España del estraperlo', in José Luis García Delgado (ed.), *El Primer Franquismo. España durante la Segunda Guerra Mundial* (Madrid: Siglo XXI, 1989), pp. 106–7.
65 Preston, *A People Betrayed*, p. 362.
66 Ángel Viñas, *La otra cara del Caudillo* (Barcelona: Crítica, 2018), pp. 292–7.
67 Qasim Ahmad, *Britain, Franco Spain and the Cold War, 1945–1950* (London: Garland, 1992), p. 184.
68 Arco, 'Hunger', pp. 468–71.
69 Cazorla, *Franco*, p. 145.
70 Cazorla, *Fear and Progress*, p. 58.
71 Richards, *A Time of Silence*, p. 7.
72 Matilde Eiroa and Ángeles Egido, 'Los confusos caminos del perdón: De la pena de muerte a la conmutación', in Aróstegui (ed.), *Franco*, p. 317.
73 Graham, *The War and its Shadow*, p. 8.
74 Richards, *A Time of Silence*, pp. 172–3.
75 Antonio Cazorla, 'Beyond They Shall Not Pass: How the Experience of Violence Reshaped Political Values in Franco's Spain', *Journal of Contemporary History*, 40/3 (2005), p. 513.
76 Michael Richards, *After the Civil War: Making Memory and Re-Making Spain since 1936* (Cambridge: Cambridge University Press, 2013), p. 85.
77 Lannon, *Privilege, Persecution and Prophecy*, p. 215.
78 Casanova and Gil Andrés, *Twentieth-Century Spain*, p. 244.
79 Casanova, *La Iglesia*, pp. 248–9.
80 Peter Anderson and Miguel Ángel del Arco, 'Introduction: Grappling with Spain's Dark Past', in Anderson and Arco (eds.), *Mass Killings*, p. 10.
81 Aurora G. Morcillo, *The Catholic Womanhood: Gender Ideology in Franco's Spain* (DeKalb, IL: Northern Illinois University Press, 2008), pp. 42–3.
82 Moradiellos, *Franco*, p. 2.
83 Helen Graham, 'Gender and the State: Women in the 1940s', in Helen Graham and Jo Labanyi (eds.), *Spanish Cultural Studies: An Introduction* (Oxford: Oxford University Press, 1995), p. 184.
84 Richards, *A Time of Silence*, p. 54.

85 Morcillo, *The Catholic Womanhood*, p. 32.
86 Graham, Graham, 'Gender and the State', pp. 187–9.
87 Anderson, *The Francoist Military Trials*, pp. 139–40.
88 Reig, *Franco Caudillo*, p. 89.
89 Of course, the Holocaust was an atrocity without comparisons. However, Nazi socio-political repression against Germans was nowhere as severe as that of Franco. The number of executions in Spain for political reasons (over 130,000) was ten times higher than that in Nazi Germany and 1,000 times higher than in Fascist Italy. In 1945, six years after the nationalists' victory, there were still over 43,000 political prisoners in Spain, ten times that in Germany in 1937. Saz, *Fascismo*, pp. 14–15, 179.
90 Ciano, *Diplomatic Papers*, p. 294; Preston, *The Politics of Revenge*, p. 9.
91 Espinosa, 'Introducción', p. 78.
92 José María García Márquez, 'El triunfo del golpe militar: el terror en la zona ocupada', in Espinosa (ed.), *Violencia*, pp. 96–7.
93 Jorge Marco, 'Debemos condenar y condenamos. Justicia militar y represión', in Aróstegui (ed.), *Franco*, p. 225.
94 Graham, *The War and its Shadow*, p. 22.
95 Richards, *After the Civil War*, p. 131.
96 Gutmaro Gómez Bravo, 'Teología penitenciaria: las cárceles del régimen', in Aróstegui (ed.), *Franco*, pp. 244–5.
97 Preston, *A People Betrayed*, p. 336.
98 Anderson, *The Francoist Military Trials*, p. 136.
99 Graham, *The War and its Shadow*, pp. 110–11.
100 Preston, *The Spanish Holocaust*, p. 509.
101 Ángela Cenarro, 'Violence, Surveillance, and Denunciation: Social Cleavage in the Spanish Civil War and Francoism, 1936–1950', in Clive Emsley, Eric Johnson, and Pieter Spierenburg (eds.), *Social Control in Europe, 1800–2000* (Columbus, OH: Ohio University Press, 2004), p. 290.
102 Conxita Mir, 'La represión franquista en la Cataluña rural', in Casanova (coord.), *Morir, matar, sobrevivir*, p. 125.
103 Florentino Portero, *Franco aislado. La cuestión española, 1945–1950* (Madrid: Aguilar, 1989), p. 33.
104 Pike, *Franco and the Axis Stigma*, pp. 139, 143.
105 Preston, *Franco*, p. 546.
106 Enrique Moradiellos, 'The Potsdam Conference and the Spanish Problem', *Contemporary European History*, 10/1 (2001), p. 89.
107 Ahmad, *Britain, Franco Spain and the Cold War*, p. 63.
108 Moradiellos, 'The Potsdam Conference', pp. 74–7, 82–6.
109 Portero, *Franco*, p. 117.
110 Ahmad, *Britain, Franco Spain and the Cold War*, pp. 33–42, 60–1.
111 Pike, *Franco and the Axis Stigma*, p. 143.

112 Boris Lietdke, *Embracing a Dictatorship: US Relations with Spain, 1945–53* (Basingstoke: Macmillan, 1997), pp. 11–14.
113 Portero, *Franco*, pp. 153–4.
114 Ibid., pp. 213–15
115 Ibid., pp. 183, 221.
116 Ahmad, *Britain, Franco Spain and the Cold War*, pp. 66–8.
117 Portero, *Franco*, pp. 253–4.
118 Ahmad, *Britain, Franco Spain and the Cold War*, p. 153.
119 Moradiellos, *Franco*, p. 66.
120 Carlos Imaz, 'España en el corazón: la ayuda y el refugio mexicano', in Reig and Sánchez (eds.), *La Guerra Civil*, pp. 262–3.
121 Francisco Moreno, 'Huidos, guerrilleros, resistente. La oposición armada a la Dictadura', in Casanova (coord.), *Morir, matar, sobrevivir*, pp. 222–3.
122 Jorge Marco, *Guerrilleros and Neighbours in Arms* (Brighton: Sussex Academic Press, 2012), pp. 140–7.
123 Richards, *After the Civil War*, p. 110.
124 Marco, *Guerrilleros and Neighbours in Arms*, p. 17.
125 Gabriel Cardona, *Franco y sus generales. La manicura del tigre* (Madrid: Temas de Hoy, 2001), p. 119.
126 Preston, *The Politics of Revenge*, pp. 101–6.
127 Portero, *Franco*, p. 62.
128 Zenobi, *La construcción*, pp. 144–5.
129 Sánchez Recio, *Sobre*, p. 177.
130 Preston, *The Politics of Revenge*, p. 11.
131 Payne, *Fascism in Spain*, p. 409.
132 Preston, *Franco*, pp. 571–2.
133 Jill Edwards, *Anglo-American Relations and the Franco Question, 1945–1955* (Oxford: Oxford University Press, 1999), p. 53.
134 Preston, *Franco*, pp. 577–80.
135 Edwards, *Anglo-American Relations*, p. 121.
136 Lietdke, *Embracing a Dictatorship*, p. 49.
137 Cazorla, *Franco*, pp. 205–6.
138 Lietdke, *Embracing a Dictatorship*, pp. 49–50.
139 Edwards, *Anglo-American Relations*, p. 171.
140 Lietdke, *Embracing a Dictatorship*, p. 106.
141 Ahmad, *Britain, Franco Spain and the Cold War*, p. 103.
142 Preston, *Franco*, p. 594.
143 Pike, *Franco and the Axis Stigma*, p. 145.
144 Ahmad, *Britain, Franco Spain and the Cold War*, pp. 212–13.
145 Shubert, *A Social History of Modern Spain*, p. 235.

146 Preston, *Franco*, p. 622.
147 Lietdke, *Embracing a Dictatorship*, pp. 175–213.
148 Preston, *Franco*, pp. 623–4.
149 Preston, *El gran manipulador*, p. 224.
150 Pike, *Franco and the Axis Stigma*, p. 146.
151 Preston, *A People Betrayed*, p. 406. This was the subject of an extremely witty satirical film, *La Escopeta Nacional* (1978).
152 Cardona, *Franco*, pp. 166–7.
153 Raymond Carr and Juan Pablo Fusi, *Spain: Dictatorship to Democracy* (London: Unwin Hyman, 1981), p. 169.
154 Preston, *Franco*, pp. 643–4.
155 Harrison, *The Spanish Economy*, p. 132.
156 Lannon, *Privilege, Persecution and Prophecy*, pp. 225–8.
157 Carr and Fusi, *Spain*, p. 53.
158 Harrison, *The Spanish Economy*, pp. 146–54.
159 Ibid., pp. 144–6.
160 Cazorla, *Fear and Progress*, p. 114.
161 Harrison, *The Spanish Economy*, pp. 154–6.
162 Pamela Beth Radcliff, *Modern Spain: 1808 to the Present* (Chichester: Wiley Blackwell, 2017), p. 220.
163 Preston, *Franco*, pp. 728–30.
164 Charles Powell, *Juan Carlos of Spain: Self-Made Monarch* (Basingstoke: Macmillan, 1996), pp. 42–3.
165 Cazorla, *Fear and Progress*, pp. 152–3, 161.
166 Víctor M. Pérez-Díaz, *The Return of Civil Society: The Emergence of Democratic Spain* (Cambridge, MA: Harvard University Press, 1993), p. 13.
167 David Gilmour, *The Transformation of Spain: From Franco to the Constitutional Monarchy* (London: Quartet, 1985), p. 33.
168 *El ABC*, 'Spain is Different! The Slogan that Changed the Image of Spain Forever' (27 March 2015).
169 Manuel Vázquez Montalbán, *La Literatura en la ciudad democrática* (Barcelona: Crítica, 2009), pp. 61–79; Carr and Fussi, *Spain*, pp. 125–31; Borja de Riquer i Permanyer, 'Social and Economic Change in a Climate of Political Immobilism' (pp. 265–6) and Peter Evans, 'Cinema, Memory, and the Unconscious' (pp. 304–7), in Graham and Labanyi (eds.), *Spanish Cultural Studies*.
170 Cazorla, *Fear and Progress*, pp. 95–6.
171 Richards, *After the Civil War*, p. 223.
172 Cazorla, *Fear and Progress*, pp. 136–7.
173 Gregorio Alonso, 'Children of a Lesser God', in Alonso and Muro (eds.), *The Politics*, pp. 116–17.

174 Lannon, *Privilege, Persecution and Prophecy*, pp. 232–6.
175 Eusebio Mujal-León, *Communism and Political Change in Spain* (Bloomington, IN: Indiana University Press, 1983), pp. 59–60.
176 Carr and Fusi, *Spain*, pp. 144–6.
177 Gilmour, *The Transformation of Spain*, pp. 92–3.
178 Mujal-León, *Communism and Political Change*, p. 66.
179 Preston, *The Politics of Revenge*, pp. 28–9.
180 Morcillo, *The Catholic Womanhood*, pp. 96–7.
181 Carr and Fusi, *Spain*, pp. 146–9.
182 Balcells, *Catalan Nationalism*, pp. 164–5.
183 Catherine Boyle, 'The Politics of Popular Music on the Dynamics of New Song', in Graham and Labanyi (eds.), *Spanish Cultural Studies*, pp. 291–4.
184 John L. Sullivan, *ETA and Basque Nationalism: The Fight for Euskadi* (London: Routledge, 1988), pp. 70–110.
185 Vicente Jesús Díaz Burillo, *Las Transiciones de la Iglesia (1962–1987). Del repliegue a la revancha* (Granada: Comares, 2019).
186 Lannon, *Privilege, Persecution and Prophecy*, pp. 46–7.
187 Gregorio Alonso, 'Children of a Lesser God', in Gregorio Alonso and Diego Muro (eds.), *The Politics and Memory of Democratic Transition* (New York: Routledge, 2011), p. 119.
188 Lannon, *Privilege, Persecution and Prophecy*, pp. 251–3.
189 Ibid., p. 109.
190 Paul Preston, *The Triumph of Democracy in Spain* (London: Methuen, 1986), p. 16.
191 Carr and Fusi, *Spain*, p. 184.
192 Preston, *A People Betrayed*, p. 435.
193 Sánchez Recio, *Sobr*, pp. 274–8.
194 Preston, *The Triumph of Democracy*, pp. 41–2.
195 Sánchez Recio, *Sobre*, pp. 250–1.
196 Preston, *Franco*, pp. 761–2.
197 Cazorla, *Franco*, pp. 306–7.
198 Preston, *Franco*, pp. 763–4.
199 Preston, *The Triumph of Democracy*, pp. 55–7.
200 Gilmour, *The Transformation of Spain*, pp. 69–70.
201 Alonso, 'Children of a Lesser God', pp. 122–3.
202 Preston, *The Politics of Revenge*, pp. 160–1.
203 Ibid., pp. 172–3.
204 The most dramatic ETA action was the blowing up, on 13 September 1974, of the *Cafetería Rolando* in Madrid, a place frequented by policemen, which left 13 dead and 70 injured.

205 Preston, *The Politics of Revenge*, pp. 183–8.
206 Cazorla, *Franco*, p. 306.
207 Preston, *Franco*, p. 776.
208 Cardona, *Franco*, pp. 255–8.

6

A Success Story: The Recovery of Democracy

Hope, Uncertainty, Fear

After Franco's death, Spaniards were gripped by a mixture of hope, uncertainty, and fear. Although most hoped that transition to a democratic regime might be managed peacefully, very few dared to predict the future. History did not augur well. Indeed, the country had no significant tradition of stable democratic governance.[1]

On 23 November 1975, the *Caudillo* was buried at the *Valle de los Caídos*. For the previous two days, Spanish television had broadcast, without interruption, images of the queues of thousands of mourners waiting to parade before his body while lying in state in Madrid's Palace of *Oriente*. Inside the building, many wept, others shouted patriotic slogans. However, to think that the regime could outlast Franco was a figment of the imagination. After Carrero's demise, there was no-one to fill the vacuum.[2] Furthermore, the now more modern and complex civil society rendered the continuity of the Dictatorship obsolete.

In late 1975, the deterioration of public order fuelled uncertainty. While strikes and mass demonstrations rocketed in number, the terrorist activities of ETA and GRAPO also escalated. Simultaneously, Francoist diehards kept their posts in the armed forces, the police, and the security apparatus. Thousands of Falangists owned guns. Ultra-right thugs continued sowing terror on university campuses and in city centres. They often stormed cafeterias and forced the attendees to hail Franco or sing the Falangist anthem, *Cara al Sol*.

Juan Carlos, duly crowned King of Spain on 22 November, remained a political enigma. Brought up under Franco's tutelage, he had been groomed to ensure continuity. Consequently, the opposition rejected his appointment outright as a desperate attempt by the regime to maintain the status quo. Santiago Carrillo, the Communist leader, even dubbed him 'Juan Carlos the Brief', predicting that his reign would not last a year.[3] In the event, the young monarch had long before concluded that his only hope for legitimacy was by becoming the king of all Spaniards in a modern democracy. The fate of his grandfather and, more recently, the defenestration of his brother-in-law Constantine II of Greece (June 1973), were stark warnings that the dynasty could only survive by endorsing thorough and rapid reform. Advised by his father and mentors, in particular his former teacher, Torcuato Fernández Miranda, he sought to build popular support for the throne through a constitutional monarchy as a guarantor of stability. However, the grip of Francoist diehards on the state's repressive apparatus meant that the king had to enact his plans slowly. Even if he wanted to be a constitutional monarch in a modern democracy, he could not repeat this openly without jeopardizing his strategy.[4]

Still, to become 'the motor of change', Juan Carlos was able to rely on certain crucial facts. The existence of a modern consumer society provided a favourable framework to build a democratic order. Moreover, traumatic memories of the civil war facilitated the establishment of a cross-class and cross-party consensus that sought to avoid the mistakes of the past.[5] The Church was a primary example of the evolving times. Having undergone a radical transformation in the 1960s, it now favoured reconciliation and political reform. By delegitimizing the regime, it was welcomed into the democratic fold. There was no question of returning to the anti-clerical policies of the 1930s.[6]

The international stage was also dramatically different. Unlike the 1930s, western Europe now provided a congenial environment for democracy. Aware of the changing times, in his many trips abroad, when still a prince, or through go-betweens, Juan Carlos obtained the support of European and American leaders for his cause. In striking contrast to the poor foreign representation at Franco's funeral where Chile's General Augusto Pinochet was the only head of state present, prominent international dignitaries, including the presidents of France and Germany, attended his coronation.[7]

Right- and left-wing politicians were also diametrically different to their predecessors during the Second Republic. Except for the Francoist diehards, most members of the governing class were *aperturistas* who recognized the need to negotiate with the opposition. The PCE, following the trend initiated by the Italian Communist Party, had embraced Eurocommunism, abandoned Soviet orthodoxy, and accepted working within the liberal democratic order. In the summer of 1974, the PCE, together with other groups, including the *Partido Socialista Popular* (PSP) led by Professor Tierno Galván, formed the *Junta Democrática*. As a sign of how times had changed, the *Junta* proposed Don Juan to lead the coalition. He travelled to Paris to meet Carrillo. However, after consulting his son, Juan Carlos, he declined.[8]

One year after the formation of the *Junta Democrática*, the remaining factions of the political opposition formed a rival alliance known as *Plataforma de Convergencia Democrática*. It was dominated by the Socialists allied with small Christian and social-democratic groups. In exile, the PSOE had become a declining force of ageing men led by Rodolfo Llopis, one of Largo's faithful lieutenants. It remained locked in the past, oblivious to the reality of Spain, and surrounded by nostalgia. By the early 1970s, the historical leaders faced a challenge from a more contemporaneous group led by much younger middle-class professionals who lived in Spain. At the Twelfth Party Congress in Toulouse in August 1972, the election of Felipe González as leader and Alfonso Guerra as his deputy represented both a dramatic generational change and a shift of power from a party dominated historically by its Madrid and northern sections to those based in the south.[9] At the Thirteenth Congress in October 1974, held in Suresnes (France), the new leadership secured the formal endorsement of the Socialist International.[10]

In March 1976, the *Plataforma* and the *Junta* joined forces in the *Coordinación Democrática*. The opposition agreed upon a *ruptura democrática* ('democratic break') from the past based on total political amnesty and free elections, supervised by a provisional government of democratic parties – a constituent parliament that would decide upon the form of the new regime.[11] However, despite its ability to mobilize public opinion, the opposition lacked the strength to defeat the state's military apparatus.

Juan Carlos, trapped between the democratic opposition demanding rupture and the still intact old order, decided to tread carefully. In his first speech to the Francoist *Cortes*, any hint of change was carefully balanced with his promise to uphold the principles he had sworn to defend. And there was a welcome surprise when, during his visit to Catalonia in February 1976, he broke with tradition and, for the first time, a head of state addressed his audience in Catalan. Crucially, he ensured the appointment of Fernández Miranda to the key positions of Speaker of the *Cortes* and president of the Council of the Realm, the body that would advise him on the appointment of a potential future premier. Despite his irreproachable Francoist past, Fernández Miranda proved to be a stealthy operator acting 'behind the scenes' to accomplish the dismantlement of the existing apparatus.[12] In this trepidatious exercise, Juan Carlos had to confirm Arias as prime minister, an unlikely leader to bring about thorough democratic reform in which he did not believe.

Arias formed a balanced cabinet of unrepentant hard-liners and *aperturistas* such as Fraga (Home Office) and the outspoken reformist José María de Areilza (Foreign Affairs). This government also included Adolfo Suárez, a young *apparatchik* who had ascended rapidly through the regime's ranks reaching the post of director of RTVE (state radio and television) in 1969. Taking advantage of that position, he established a close relationship with Juan Carlos. Thus, the king persuaded Arias in the cabinet reshuffle after Franco's death to move Solís to the Labour Ministry thereby freeing the portfolio of minister-secretary general of the Movement for Suárez.[13]

During the first half of 1976, all of the achievements made abroad by Areilza and Juan Carlos were undone by Arias in Spain. Indeed, the prime minister was ultimately loyal to the essence of Francoism and concerned about incurring the criticism of the Bunker.[14] Ambiguity and nostalgic references to the past littered his speeches. Consequently, his plans to introduce some sort of political liberalization never materialized. On 28 January 1976, he stressed in the *Cortes* that Spain was different. He contemplated the regulation of the rights of assembly and the eventual legalization of political parties, except for communists and separatists. However, he refused to grant a political amnesty, ignored crucial issues like regional autonomy and trade union freedom, never mentioned whether there would be free elections, and his language was still full of allusions to Franco's fundamental principles. His refusal to modify the strict laws of demonstrations in a time of high mobilization triggered violent repression.[15]

Arias never intended to bring about genuine change. During a televised address in April, he mentioned the *Caudillo* seven times and resorted to the old cliché of Spain being threatened by a foreign conspiracy orchestrated by international communism. Caught between his erstwhile comrades in the Bunker and the demands of the opposition, he became a victim of his ambiguities. The result was institutional stagnation, social agitation, and repression.[16]

Ironically, Fraga, with a reputation as an *aperturista*, became the main victim of Arias' dour premiership. Confronted with a formidable wave of strikes, as minister of the interior he was blamed for the brutal police response which, in Vitoria alone, resulted in the death of five workers. His authoritarian style did not help. He supervised the arrest of five leaders of *Coordinación Democrática* whom he referred to as 'his prisoners'. Asked about the people's right to demonstrate, he claimed that the streets belonged to him[17] – something that would haunt him for years to come.

In June, the *Cortes* passed the Law of Political Association, which effectively recognized political parties, except for the PCE, after an impressive speech by Suárez. Yet, in a bizarre twist, the *Cortes* simultaneously rejected the reform of the articles of the Penal Code which penalized party activities. There was widespread confusion.[18] The king declared to the US journal *Newsweek* that Arias was an 'unmitigated disaster' and forced him to resign on 1 July. The ousted prime minister compared his meeting with Juan Carlos to that in 1909 when Alfonso XIII summoned Maura only to thank him for his services and accept a resignation he had not tendered.[19] Still, for his services Arias was made a marquis.

Walking a Tightrope: The Democratic Transition

Together with the structural socio-economic conditions associated with a modern civil society, the critical decisions of key actors played a crucial role in securing democracy. Fernández Miranda compared the transition to a theatre production: the king was the impresario, Miranda the script writer, and Suárez the leading actor.[20]

Although Areilza was expected to be the next prime minister, Juan Carlos surprised everyone when, on 3 July, he appointed the charming, but relatively unknown, Suárez. Though in theory the monarch could back his candidate, the Council of the Realm presided by Fernández Miranda, on which the Bunker was well represented, had to endorse his choice. Areilza's election, an obvious reformist, might have encountered serious opposition. In contrast, the regime's diehards welcomed Suárez. Thus, initially, widespread dismay greeted the appointment of the then minister-secretary general of the Movement. However, the king had handpicked him to orchestrate the transition. Disappointment gradually gave way to astonishment, as Suárez began to prove that he was committed to leading a rapid process of democratization.

The success of the democratic transition was facilitated by the willingness of both the *aperturistas* and the opposition leaders to subscribe to the so-called *Pacto del Olvido* (Pact of Forgetfulness). This was an unwritten but explicit agreement based on the exercise of collective amnesia about past political excesses to bring closure to Spain's tumultuous past. It solved the widespread fear of reopening old wounds that Francoism had prevented from healing for 40 years. Nonetheless, given the conjuncture, there was not any sort of Truth and Reconciliation Committee.[21]

The determination and skill of Juan Carlos and Suárez were crucial to accomplishing a relatively tranquil transition. Of course, political activities did not take place in a vacuum. The dismantling of the Francoist apparatus and the building of a democratic system was not purely a piece of engineering hatched between political actors. The cultural and socio-economic transformation of the previous decade was vital. Strikes and demonstrations played a major part in convincing the ruling class of the infeasibility of *continuismo*. As civil society demanded change, the political elites were successful not because they were able to lead the people but because they were able to learn from and follow the public mood.[22]

Suárez's appointment proved an inspired choice. Despite his impeccable Falangist record, he was a pragmatic politician with few ideological principles who played a pivotal role in guiding the process through the murky waters of the Francoist apparatus. Unlike Arias, who was still anchored to the nostalgic values of the crusade, he grasped the public consensus for reform. Yet, his task was far from easy. He was walking a tightrope between the clamours of the opposition for a *ruptura democrática* and the diehards' resistance. While needing to be extremely careful to avoid a Francoist backlash, he was aware that a slow process of transition would lead to popular frustration and unrest. In the event, Suárez opted for a daring strategy. He hastened political reform to force the opposition to enter negotiations or a *ruptura negociada* ('negotiated break'). Simultaneously, he prevented a head-on clash with the Francoist establishment by adhering scrupulously to the existing legal framework. He took advantage of the Law of Succession, which stated that all fundamental laws could be reformed if they met the approval of two-thirds of the *Cortes* and were later put to a referendum. This meant the formidable task of asking the establishment to accept dismantling itself voluntarily. In this context, Miranda's Machiavellian back-door dealings, and the king's appeasement of the military (he was their commander-in-chief), were invaluable.[23]

Speed and determination were key to Suárez's success. He formed a cabinet of young *apparatchiks* like himself. Unlike Arias' ambiguity, he wasted no time. A few days after his appointment, he announced on television his total commitment to democratic reform, including the legalization of all parties followed by free elections in June the following year. Simultaneously, channels of communication were opened with opposition leaders.[24] In September, Suárez presented his programme to the army. He promised never to legalize the PCE or consent to the break-up of the fatherland. In return, he obtained its support. Crucially, at the same time, the hard-line minister of defence, General Fernando Santiago, was replaced by a liberal officer, General Manuel Gutiérrez Mellado.[25] In November, he introduced the Law for Political Reform, which guaranteed the free election of a two-chamber parliament by universal suffrage, the legalization of parties and independent unions, freedom of the press, and more. Its approval was in effect asking the Francoist establishment to commit suicide. Yet, in the heated atmosphere of 1976, only a minority of *inmovilistas* believed in the survival of an unreformed regime. The government argued that the new law was the conclusion of the *Caudillo*'s work, now fully embraced by his successor the king. Deputies were offered lucrative jobs and posts in the administration and warned that a negative vote might lead to a new civil war. Fernandez Miranda skilfully orchestrated the debate. He chose no other than José Antonio's nephew, Miguel Primo de Rivera, to defend the law. The final vote gave the government a stunning victory: 425 in favour, 13 abstentions, and only 59 against.[26]

On 15 December, the Spanish people were given the opportunity to vote in a referendum. Caught by surprise, the democratic opposition called for them to abstain. The result provided overwhelming backing for Suárez's plans: 94.2 percent for and only 2.6 percent against in a turnout of 77.4 percent.[27] The opposition could no longer speak against the reformist credentials of the government, or overlook its popular support as demonstrated by the result of the referendum. Demands for *ruptura democrática* were quietly abandoned and replaced by negotiations.[28] Henceforth Suárez could impose his agenda.

After filing for registration at the Home Office, political parties could be formally legalized. In December 1976, the PSOE celebrated its first congress in Spain for 40 years.[29] While unreformed Francoists grouped around Blas Piñar's *Fuerza Nueva*, the two more important formations emanating from the old regime were *Alianza Popular* (AP) and *Unión de Centro Democrático* (UCD). Headed by Fraga, AP was full of prominent veterans, including Arias and López Rodó. Calling themselves the civilized right, it sought to capture the vote of the so-called 'sociological Francoists' – those who remembered with a certain nostalgia the strong public order and economic prosperity of the years before the transition. While accepting democratic reform, AP's rhetoric was strongly Catholic, centralist, and anti-communist. By contrast, UCD, rather than embracing a clear ideological programme, represented a coalition of heterogeneous interests created to bask in the prestige of Suárez. It gathered 13 diverse groups including his team of *apparatchiks*, Christian-Democrats, Liberal, and Social-Democrat factions. Unlike AP, the UCD presented an image of modernity while its moderate centrist character enhanced its appeal as a buffer between the past and the future.[30]

The transition could not be completed until the PCE was legalized. Carrillo himself, feeling that he could miss the train, and aware that other opposition parties were happy to forsake communist claims for their own benefit, returned to Madrid in December 1976. By then, the PCE was pursuing openly its activities against a background of semi-legality. By organizing a conference in public, Carrillo practically forced his arrest and that of seven members of the party's central committee. His intention was to bring to the forefront the crucial issue of legalization. He was freed on bail one week later.[31]

Terrorist activities from both extremes of the political spectrum attempted to disrupt the transition. While ETA continued its murderous campaign, GRAPO intensified its provocative deeds: in December 1976, it kidnapped Antonio María de Oriol y Urquijo, a former Francoist minister and president of the Council of State. One month later, it killed three policemen and kidnapped General Emilio Villescusa, president of the Supreme Council of Military Justice.[32] In turn, an extreme right-wing squad murdered five communist lawyers at their offices in Atocha (Madrid) in January 1977. To the latter outrage, the PCE and CCOO responded with admirable restraint. In February, Suárez and Carrillo began formal negotiations. The latter proved an excellent interlocutor. In return for legalization, he recognized the monarchy, the national flag, and a social contract. In April, despite the earlier promise to the army, the PCE was legalized by royal decree. Simultaneously, the Movement was legislated out of existence.[33] The military felt especially insulted as the decree was introduced during the Easter holiday.[34]

On 15 June 1977, the first free elections since 1936 were held. People voted for closed-party lists. The outcome constituted a triumph for the government and, in general terms, for moderation. Despite dozens of parties – from the extreme right to the extreme left – it produced a two-party structure, although complicated by the *d'Hondt* electoral formula of proportional representation that favoured large and regional parties. The UCD and PSOE gathered nearly two-thirds of the vote and amassed 166 and 118 seats, respectively, out of a total of 370. The PCE with 20 and AP with 16 fared worse than expected. They paid the price for evoking memories of the past. Right-wing parties emerged as the hegemonic nationalist force in

Catalonia and the Basque Country: *Convergència i Unió* (CiU), formed by the coalition of the Conservative *Convergència Democràtica de Catalunya* (CDC) and the Christian-Democratic *Unió Democràtica de Catalunya* (UDC), and headed by Jordi Pujol, returned 11 deputies and the PNV six. Forces associated with the unreformed past, like *Fuerza Nueva*, were wiped out. Spaniards had spoken, for the first time, in over 40 years. They voted for change and laid the Franco regime to rest.[35] Indeed, one of the startling facts of the transition was the speed at which many hitherto Francoists, from politicians to journalists, became overnight lifelong democrats. This was dubbed *Chaqueteo* (changing jackets).

A Golden but Brief Honeymoon

The following two years constituted the peak of Suárez's career. He enjoyed a golden but brief two-year honeymoon. Relying on the legitimacy of his popular mandate and basking in a general mood of optimism, he succeeded in consolidating the constitutional foundations. In October 1977, he presided over the signing of a social contract: the *Pactos de la Moncloa*, named after the Spanish premier's official residence. With the economic recession worsening, inflation rising, and unemployment soaring, the government summoned the main opposition parties, the two leading trade unions (CCOO and UGT), and the employers' organization, *Confederación Española de Organizaciones Empresariales* (CEOE, Spanish Confederation of Business Organizations). The agreement was facilitated by Carrillo's eagerness to highlight his party's moderate stance. Communist flexibility made it difficult for the PSOE to reject the plans.[36] In real terms, the Left was prepared to make sacrifices to consolidate democracy. This meant that the working classes would effectively tolerate the worst of the economic crisis and accept the market economy framework. A wage ceiling of 22 percent was accepted at a time when inflation was 29 percent. Monetarist measures to restrict credit and public spending were introduced, including price controls and a 20 percent devaluation of the peseta. In return, the government made promises, which largely went unfulfilled, of major structural reforms including higher pensions and unemployment benefits, improvements in education, the health service and housing programmes, and the adoption of a more progressive income tax. Still, the *Pactos de la Moncloa* represented a significant departure from the politics of confrontation of the 1930s and offered the labour movement a role in economic decision-making and collective bargaining.[37]

The rate of unemployment and the grim financial situation concealed the existence of a vibrant underground economy that permitted many families to survive. Marked by a lack of social security contributions and controls on working hours or wages, this part of the economy boomed during the recession, relying as it did on the complicity of most Spaniards and a certain tolerance by the state.[38]

Regional autonomy was a sensitive question. Nonetheless, after years of Franco's highly centralized idea of Spain, the Left, in general, embraced the cause of a multinational state. The common struggle against the regime had solidified the bonds with peripheral nationalist forces.[39] Negotiations were remarkably smooth in Catalonia where Suárez followed an audacious strategy: direct negotiations with a legitimate interlocutor, Josep Tarradellas, a former Companys' lieutenant, and president of the Catalan government in exile. Tarradellas flew to Madrid in June 1977 and agreed to accept the monarchy in return for the restoration of Catalan autonomy, which was to be granted by the *Cortes* in Madrid. In a somewhat nostalgic atmosphere, he landed in Barcelona on 23 October and was installed as president of the *Generalitat* in charge of a provisional government. On 25 October 1979, the Statute of Autonomy, which offered the possibility of greater devolution than in 1932, was supported by 87 percent of Catalans in a referendum.[40]

In stark contrast, the Basque Country remained the black spot of the transition. Here the route to autonomy was painful. While in Catalonia all of the political parties had rallied around the Assembly of 1971, terrorism and police repression had led to a much greater radicalization in the Basque Country than anywhere else in Spain. By the time of Franco's death, ETA had acquired an aura of legitimacy among significant sectors of the population. The fact that the security forces under the same commanders continued to operate lent credence to the narrative that nothing had changed and that the new regime was just the continuation of Francoism in democratic disguise.[41] The PNV demanded a total amnesty but the government, extremely cautious not to alienate the army, was backed off making bold conciliatory steps that could be regarded as giving in to violence. Ironically, in October 1974, ETA itself had undergone a tactical and ideological split. Most members initially remained in the so-called political-military branch of that organization (ETA-PM) that was willing to collaborate with other Spanish left-wing parties. Although not yet ready to give up the armed struggle, it contemplated its gradual abandonment in exchange for genuine political concessions. The extreme nationalist hard-liners for whom the terror campaign to achieve independence had primacy, remained affiliated to the ETA military front (ETA-M). This group saw itself as a revolutionary vanguard whose mission was to continue the fight against Spain.[42]

In the Basque Country, concessions were realized only after many delays, which eroded governmental reformist credibility in the region. A comprehensive Amnesty Law was passed only in October 1977. Echoing the national reconciliation embodied in the *Pacto del Olvido*, it covered all political criminal acts up to the elections of June 1977. This benefited ETA and other terrorist groups while also guaranteeing that no members of the old regime would be prosecuted, and that no truth commission would investigate cases of human rights abuses.[43] The amnesty failed to produce the healing effect expected by the government. On the contrary, ETA concluded that its strategy was working vis-à-vis a feeble state. The wave of assassinations and bombings escalated, including that of leading army officers such as the deputy military governor of San Sebastián, Jose María Herrera and the military governor of Madrid, Constantino Ortín, both in January 1979.[44]

Unfortunately, there was no Basque Tarradellas. The PNV and the PSOE, with approximately one-third of the vote each, were the two leading parties in the region. Yet, by opting to concentrate on negotiations with the Socialists, the government managed to alienate the Basque nationalists. As a party that embraced Christian-Democratic principles, the PNV rejected violence. However, with strong xenophobic components, it competed with the more radical nationalists for the same electoral space. The result was that under the leadership of the former Jesuit Javier Arzalluz, it adopted ambiguous rhetoric criticizing the state as much, if not more, than ETA. This semi-loyal attitude, of neither opposing head-on the constitutional order nor endorsing it, exists to the present day.[45] The PNV did not take part in the constituent process in Madrid and the proportion of people abstaining in the referendum of December 1976 was ostensibly higher in that region than anywhere else (a 54 percent turnout versus 77.4 percent in Spain as a whole). Thus, the drawing of the Basque Statute of Autonomy was bitter and complex. Progress was only made after the elections of 1979 gave the PNV a bigger majority in the region. Only then did Suárez begin to deal directly with Carlos Garaikoetxea, the PNV's provisional *Lehendakari* (Basque president). In July, an agreement was reached in which the PNV obtained a crucial concession, the *concierto económico* ('economic agreement'), a historic deal that had been terminated after the Third Carlist War in 1876 by which the Basque Provinces and Navarre collected their taxes and only paid a lump sum to the state. The statute was endorsed in a referendum by a clear majority in October 1979. Among the supporters of the 'yes' vote was the Basque Left or *Euzkadiko Ezkerra* (EE), the political front for ETA-PM. However, it was too late to pacify the region. A significant sector of the population was fully behind ETA-M for whom anything short of full independence was a betrayal. An electoral coalition, *Herri Batasuna* (People's Unity, HB), was established to promote an alliance of all the radical nationalist groups. Unlike EE, which pursued collaboration with other left-wing parties, for HB the national struggle had primacy over the social, and thus the concession of autonomy was perceived as a setback – a way to delude the Basques into accepting a settlement with Madrid.[46]

Suárez's crowning success was a constitution designed to avoid the pitfalls of the past or the exclusion of key sectors of the political spectrum. It was the result of some 18 months of bargaining by a commission representing all main parties (three members from the UCD and one each from the PSOE, PCE, AP, and CiU) appointed in August 1977. Catalan nationalists and particularly the Communists proved extremely willing to find a consensus with the UCD. Disagreements between the government and the PSOE were solved in a spirit of goodwill during late-night sessions often held in restaurants or private apartments between Suárez's deputy prime minister, Fernando Abril Martorell, and Alfonso Guerra. The PSOE agreed officially to accept the monarchy. González even insisted on his party voting for the Constitution in its entirety.[47] Only a hard-line sector within AP and the PNV felt excluded in what they regarded as a UCD-PSOE private pact. When the Constitution was presented to parliament in October 1978, the overwhelming majority were prepared to endorse it. Its prime virtue lay in its ambiguity so that every significant sector of public opinion would not feel alienated.[48]

The Constitution embodied a genuine spirit of reconciliation between Right and Left, Church and secularism, capitalism and social reform, and centre and peripheral nationalisms. It defined Spain as a social and democratic state ruled by law.[49] The regime was a parliamentary monarchy with the king as head of state and commander-in-chief of the armed forces, but his authority was reduced to that of a constitutional ruler. National sovereignty resided in the people unlike the constitution of 1876, which proclaimed that it was shared with the Crown. The voting age was lowered to 18 and the death penalty was abolished. In an important departure from the past, the state had no official religion, although it recognized the historical role played by the Catholic Church. This allowed that institution to receive state funding for its cultural, social, and educational activities. The Constitution acknowledged the right to strike and universal social security, healthcare, and schooling. It emphasized gender equality before the law. An exception was article 14, which asserted male privilege in the royal line. Article 8 sanctioned the demilitarization of public order. A law passed in 1980 reinforced that military jurisdiction was restricted to its own internal matters.[50] Article 2 stressed the indissoluble unity of the nation and so denied the right of secession to any part of the country. However, it replaced rigid centralism with the recognition of what de facto could be a semi-federal state: Spain encompassed a plurality of regions and nationalities, the last concept being a concession to the areas that claimed historical identity rights (Catalonia, the Basque Country, and Galicia), with the right to self-government. This was a stunning difference compared with the Republican constitution of 1931, in which the concession of autonomy was seen as exceptional. Catalan and Basque nationalists were reluctant to accept this territorial reorganization known as *café para todos* (coffee for everyone) because it was to dilute their unique sense of identity. They argued that it was absurd to extend the autonomous framework to the entire country and, in the process, invent historical entities where none had existed before. The government argued that it responded to inter-regional solidarity and avoided discrimination.[51]

The Constitution was passed with only six votes against (either AP or EE) and 14 abstentions (all PNV or AP). Yet, Fraga and half of his parliamentary group voted for it. It was endorsed in a referendum, on 6 December 1978, by 87.9 percent of the electorate with 7.8 percent against. The only setback was the high abstention rate registered in the Basque Country: 55 percent versus 32 percent in the rest of Spain.[52] Parliament was then dissolved. The elections of 1 March 1979 confirmed the trend of 1977: the UCD and PSOE remained the two leading parties with 168 and 121 seats, respectively. The PCE experienced a slight improvement (23 seats) and AP saw its representation reduced (just nine). The extreme right obtained a single seat, that of its leader Blas Piñar. Yet, ETA obtained significant support: EE obtained one seat and HB three.[53]

Francoism's Last Stand

The electoral triumph of March 1979 marked the zenith of Suárez's career – henceforth, everything was to go wrong. His popularity began to be eroded by the underlying issues of army subversion, terrorism, mass unemployment, and economic stagnation. Simultaneously, his boldness and inspiration deserted him.[54]

As in 1931, many people believed that democracy would solve every single problem overnight. With expectations unfulfilled, the press alluded to the *desencanto* ('disenchantment') that contrasted with the enthusiasm of the transition's early years. Utopia and exaltation gave way to the less exciting life of democratic normality. This phenomenon was most conspicuous amongst the youth. Faced with an uncertain future and the thrilling era of mobilization against Francoism over, many abandoned their earlier political activism and retreated into a subculture of drugs, abstentionism, and alienation known as *pasotismo* ('caring about nothing'), a nihilistic approach to life that entailed complete apathy.[55]

Confronted by recession and worsening public order, Suárez seemed to be overwhelmed. Constant references were made to the UCD's *desgobierno* ('lack of government').[56] The economy, neglected for the sake of political expediency, failed to recover. The future appeared even more bleak after the steep oil-price increase in June 1979, which raised Spain's energy costs by 70 percent in six months. The result was a hard recession that led to a severe drop in domestic demand, a spate of company bankruptcies, and factory closures. From a low of 2.94 percent in 1974, unemployment soared to 12.60 percent in 1980, 15.37 percent in 1981, and 17.06 percent in 1982.[57]

The government's inability to halt the escalation of terrorist activities exacerbated the widespread climate of gloom. In a sense, both ETA and the Bunker seemed, for different purposes, to be combining forces to destroy the new regime. Extreme right-wing squads continued their terror campaign often undeterred by a police force still headed by Francoist elements. Infamous Italian and Latin American Fascists who had found refuge in Franco's Spain took an active role in this strategy of tension. So-called 'national' zones or areas where these thugs operated existed in every major city. Cinemas, journals, and bookshops suffered bomb attacks. They also carried out assassinations: the Socialist Yolanda González and the trade unionist Vicente Cuervo (February 1980), the CNT militant Jorge Caballero (March 1980), the president of a neighbours' association Arturo Pajuelo (May 1980), and so on. In the Basque Country, right-wing squads murdered leaders of the separatist cause, including Argala, the historical leader of ETA-M.[58]

In turn, ETA increased its lethal attacks. While 74 people were killed by ETA between 1968 and 1977, it was responsible for 176 killings between 1979 and 1980.[59] Crucially, the targets were often senior army officers in an attempt to provoke major repression. And indeed, it played straight into the hands of the Bunker. The funerals of policemen and army officers became the rallying point of demonstrations urging the army to take power.[60]

Since Suárez broke his promise and legalized the PCE, army *golpismo* ('plotting') intensified. The rightist press made simplistic comparisons with the prosperity of the previous regime to conclude that 'we lived better under Franco'. Simultaneously, continuous diatribes against Suárez and Gutiérrez Mellado went unpunished. That leniency towards military sedition was regarded as proof of democratic weakness and served to embolden the hard-liners. A flagrant example was the handling of the so-called 'Galaxia Operation', named after the cafeteria in Madrid where some army officers, in November 1978, planned to kidnap the entire cabinet while in session at the Moncloa. Uncovered by the intelligence services, the main conspirator, a lieutenant colonel of the civil guard, Antonio Tejero, was sentenced to a meagre seven-month jail sentence and then returned to his post where he continued plotting. By late 1980, the rumours of an imminent coup became deafening.[61]

Once the Constitution was approved, the politics of consensus were over. To further aggravate matters for Suárez, the UCD began to disintegrate. It had always been a broad church of disparate interests bound together by the common goal of presiding over a peaceful transition and sharing the spoils of office. Once the foundations of the new regime had been laid, the basic purpose for its existence was lost. Suárez could not govern with both his cabinet and parliamentary group divided into antagonistic factions who held opposing views about most legislation and bickered among one another for key posts. The local elections of April 1979 returned a massive victory for the Left. The first autonomic elections in March 1980 in Catalonia and the Basque Country delivered a victory for the CiU and the PNV, respectively. While the PSOE did well, the UCD suffered a humiliating result.[62] This steep decline in electoral fortunes exacerbated the latter's internal tensions. By the spring of 1980, the press kept referring to the 'revolt of the barons' or the different faction leaders who were increasingly unhappy with Suárez's presidential style of government. Sensing the growing crisis, González began to talk about the need for a new majority formed by the PSOE and the UCD's left-wing faction, while Fraga referred to the creation of a 'natural majority' formed by AP and the UCD's more conservative groups.[63]

By 1980, Suárez was no longer the exuberant leader of the transition. Living basically on coffee, cigarettes, and pills, he withdrew to his office in the Moncloa surrounded by his small loyal team of *apparatchiks* and advisers known as *fontaneros* ('plumbers').[64] As his status began to wane, that of González was growing. From the almost skeletal party he inherited in 1974, the PSOE under his leadership had emerged in 1977 as the main opposition force. Massive aid from the Socialist International, especially the German Social-Democrats, and the youthful image of his party helped relegate the PCE to second place. The PSOE's hegemony of the Left was increased by the absorption of rival groups such as Galván's PSP in 1978. González's next step was to shift to the centre to expand the party's constituency and win the next elections. Consequently, at the PSOE's 28th Congress in May 1979, he proposed to abandon its old class-based Marxist rhetoric and embrace Social-Democracy. When a majority voted against it, the entire executive resigned. The gamble paid off. Aware that one of the party's main electoral assets was González's personal charisma, none of his rivals were ready to take over. In the subsequent interregnum, Guerra, in charge of the party apparatus, masterminded internal changes that led to a reduction in the number of delegates and gave greater control to the largest section, Andalusia. In an extraordinary congress held in September, González was returned in triumph as secretary and his thesis was approved by a party more dominated by the leadership than ever before.[65]

In May 1980, the PSOE passed a vote of no-confidence against the government. Suárez narrowly avoided defeat even though he performed poorly in the televised debates and offered an image of an ageing politician, while González emerged with his prestige enhanced and reinforced as a real alternative to power.[66] In September, Suárez played his last roll of the dice, a cabinet that incorporated all the main barons, but soon they renewed their bickering.[67] On 29 January 1981, the prime minister stunned the nation when he announced his resignation. Tired and embittered by his party's infighting, savaged by the press, and vilified by the army, he had had enough. He was replaced by Leopoldo Calvo Sotelo, the dull minister of the economy. Unlike the flamboyant Suárez, he was a lugubrious figure. It was his lack of ambition that made him the ideal compromise candidate for all the UCD's factions.[68]

According to Javier Cercas, the 'placenta of a coup d'état' was by then effectively borne.[69] Suárez, the statesman who had surprised everyone by successfully piloting the democratic transition, had become the target of several different but converging forces. For Francoist diehards, he was a traitor. Ruling economic circles, who had lauded his early achievements, now openly considered him an upstart. For them, he was a 'bellboy' who, while given the role of foreman to dismantle the Francoist apparatus due to his experience after years of climbing through its ranks, had now outstayed his welcome. The Church had gone from openly supportive to critical of his duplicity as he had approved a Law of Divorce that went beyond earlier promises. For Fraga, he was simply a usurper who had stolen the limelight. The Socialists, relative neophytes to power machinations but sensing their opportunity to grasp power, even explored with some army officers the establishment of a government of national unity. The king also, realizing the growing decline of Suárez's popularity, was increasingly looking forward to his departure. Even the Reagan administration longed for the demise of someone who had legalized the PCE and was averse to joining NATO. Its intelligence services were aware of a military conspiracy. Finally, the UCD had become a cauldron of intrigues.[70]

On 23 February, parliament was in full session for the investiture of Calvo Sotelo. At 6.20 pm, the long-feared military conspiracy was revealed.[71] Lieutenant Colonel Tejero, pistol in hand, followed by some 200 civil guards, stormed the chamber interrupting the vote. Simultaneously, units of the crack *Brunete* armoured division took control of key points in Madrid and Captain General Jaime Miláns del Bosch declared martial law in Valencia, the third largest city, and ordered tanks onto the streets. Tellingly, the US secretary of state, Alexander Haig, did not condemn the coup. He merely claimed that it was Spain's internal problem. With the entire political class sequestrated, the young democracy appeared to be finished. History seemed to be repeating itself, as it recalled the storming of the *Cortes* by General Pavía in January 1874, which brought to an end the short-lived democratic experiment of the First Republic. However, Karl Marx proved correct in his assessment of great historical events occurring twice: the first time is a tragedy and the second a farce.

Spaniards watched the coup play out live on their televisions. The image of a civil guard with an enormous moustache brandishing his gun and shouting abuse at politicians was a pathetic reminder of a past they wanted to forget. Faced with the stunning bravery of Gutiérrez Mellado in confronting them, the *golpistas* responded with a burst of gunfire into the air. All the deputies except Suárez and Carrillo, who remained unperturbed in their seats, dived for cover. In the next scene, Tejero was seen trying to knock Gutiérrez Mellado down, who, despite his advanced age, managed to stay on his feet. Suddenly, the live broadcast was cut.

The plotters, still anchored in the mentality of the 1930s, were unaware of how much both the international and domestic context had evolved. Unlike 1936, there was no sign of civilian support for the insurrection. Furthermore, the coup was a hurried combination of three separate conspiracies. First, some colonels pursued the imposition of military rule followed by a draconian policy of repression. Second, Miláns, one of the most awarded generals and a veteran of the Blue Division, led a group of senior officers who sought to end the perceived growing political chaos. Finally, there was a sophisticated plot headed by General Alfonso Armada, the former head of Juan Carlos' Military Household and now deputy head of the General Staff. It did not seek the destruction but instead the rectification of democracy by the formation of an executive of national salvation headed by himself. In the process, he became the link between the other two. Suárez's sudden resignation precipitated the events.

Miláns, a staunch monarchist, proceeded with the belief, reinforced by Armada, that he had royal backing, an assumption that was to be proved wrong. When Armada called the palace during the night to offer his services, he was turned down. Juan Carlos never intended to play Alfonso XIII to a new Primo de Rivera. In fact, on 23 February, he pursued a similar strategy to that of his grandfather: he contacted the senior commanders of every region. As in 1923, most were sympathetic to the coup but also confirmed their loyalty to the throne. A reassured Juan Carlos then did the opposite of Alfonso XIII. He paralysed any backing for the coup in Madrid by mobilizing two key senior military figures: José Gabeiras, the head of the General Staff, and Guillermo Quintana Lacacci, captain general of Madrid. He also established a provisional government formed by the undersecretaries of every department headed by Francisco Laína at the Home Office. Finally, dressed as commander-in-chief, he appeared on television at 1.15 am sternly declaring his total opposition to any movement against the constitutional order. The coup unravelled fast. Miláns himself, after talking to the king, called his soldiers back to the barracks. Amidst the confusion, Armada appeared in parliament to implement his plan. Seeing himself as a patriotic saviour, Tejero could not believe that he was offered a flight into exile so that Armada could preside over a government of national unity with some of the politicians he held hostage. He threw Armada out. By noon it was all over. A frustrated Tejero surrendered himself.

The ill-fated coup of 23 February represented the final nail in the coffin of the old regime. Anchored in discipline, the Francoist generals obeyed the king. They acted through their sense of loyalty to their commander-in-chief who had been placed in that post by the *Caudillo*, rather than genuine respect for democracy. Despite having kidnapped the whole political class leadership, the rebellion ended in disarray and ridicule.[72] The trial of 32 army officers and one civilian took place between February and June 1982. Tejero and Miláns were sentenced to 30 years imprisonment, Armada to six, and most others to between one and five years. Judged to be too lenient, the Military Supreme Court revised the original verdict, doubling most of the sentences and raising that of Armada to 30 years to match that of the other two ringleaders.[73]

In the aftermath of the coup, there was a re-awakening of mass enthusiasm for democracy. Spaniards marched in support of the new order. The demonstration in Madrid alone saw one million people on the streets.[74] The king won adulation and respect for his decisive role. Even the most recalcitrant Republicans declared themselves to be *Juancarlistas*.[75] Absurd rumours circulated years later about his possible knowledge of, and sympathy for, the coup given his past close links with Armada. He may indeed have had his suspicions, as most Spaniards had, that some army officers were plotting. Yet, if he had wished it, a successful coup would have been guaranteed. Instead, his decisiveness at the key moment was crucial in its failure.[76]

The UCD could not bask for long in the national euphoria. Calvo Sotelo successfully negotiated the slowing down of the autonomic process for the non-historical regions with the opposition but infuriated everyone when, without much debate, he negotiated the entry of Spain into NATO. Both measures were designed to curry military favour. The spectacle of the UCD's disintegration dominated his hapless premiership. Throughout 1982, its diverse constituents broke apart. The Social-Democrats went over to the PSOE and the Christian-Democrats joined AP. Even Suárez formed his own group, the *Centro Democrático y Social* (CDS).[77]

The UCD's implosion shared headlines with the internecine struggles raging in the PCE. Carrillo still controlled the party with a tight fist, but poor electoral results intensified dissent. His leadership was under attack from different tendencies. The orthodox wing regretted the adoption of Eurocommunism. The Catalan PSUC demanded more autonomy from the centre. Its Basque section, against the instructions of the PCE's executive, initiated a dialogue to merge with EE. Finally, the 'liberal' wing began to demand the revision of the party statutes to permit greater internal democracy. Carrillo still managed to defeat all the opposing tendencies at the PCE's Tenth Congress of July 1981. During the following year, he tightened his control in the best Stalinist manner. Those dissidents who did not leave were purged or expelled, such as the Basque central committee, which was replaced by one imposed by Madrid. The PSUC split into Leninist and Eurocommunist factions.[78]

The End of the Transition: The PSOE in Power

Observing the disintegration of the UCD, Calvo Sotelo decided to call a general election. The disarray was such that he even refused to be the UCD's candidate. Landelino Lavilla, the Speaker of the *Cortes*, took upon himself that thankless task.

The elections of October 1982 marked the end of the transition and initiated an era of socialist hegemony that was to last 14 years. Even though the PSOE's electoral victory was a foregone conclusion, the scope of it surpassed all predictions: an overall majority – over 10 million votes (48.43 percent of the total) – and a record 202 seats. Fraga's coalition emerged as the main opposition, with 106 seats. Regional nationalists increased their representation slightly, with the CiU on 11 seats and the PNV on six. The centre all but collapsed: the UCD managed 12 seats and the CDS just two. The PCE returned only four deputies.[79] Faced with his party's stunning decline, Carrillo resigned.[80]

The PSOE's electoral slogan was ¡Por el Cambio! ('For Change!'). The emphasis was on moderation: consolidating the climate of national reconciliation, sealing the estado de las autonomías ('state of self-governing communities'), and accepting the market economy. The Socialists intended to adopt social-democratic measures to build a fairer and more progressive society through the improvement of public services and the consolidation of universal health and education systems. In international terms, the objective was to fulfil the longed objective of joining the European Economic Community.[81]

The Socialists proved not only to be willing to respect the institutional framework but also to be their staunchest defender.[82] Embracing this moderate reformist strategy, they enjoyed two further landslide victories (June 1986 and October 1989). There are several reasons for such political dominance.

The rebranding of the official ideology and discourse was a timely manoeuvre. Indeed, scrapping Marxism and former reductionist positions and instead adhering openly to social-democratic principles, facilitated the appeal of the Socialists to a much wider multi-class constituency than ever before. Furthermore, unlike the UCD, the PSOE functioned, at least until the early 1990s, as a highly disciplined machine under Guerra's tight control.[83]

The PSOE benefited from financial and international connections with other western socialist parties. Influential personalities such as Germany's Willy Brandt, France's François Mitterrand, and Sweden's Olof Palme, lent their prestige to the 1982 campaign. Consequently, the Spanish Socialists could claim to be the best vehicle for European integration.[84]

The Socialists offered a youthful image (the ministers had an average age of 40 years). Nobody could match the appeal of its leader, usually referred to only as Felipe. In contrast, AP was perceived as a party headed by old leaders with close links to the past. Indeed, unlike the UCD, it had been reluctant to embrace democracy wholeheartedly, thus putting off prospective moderate centrist voters. Thus, it did not fare much better in the next two general elections: 105 and 107 seats in 1986 and 1989, respectively. In fact, the gradual erosion of the socialist vote did not benefit AP but regional forces. Consequently, the Basque and particularly Catalan nationalist minorities acquired a decisive influence in the Cortes while consolidating their hegemony in their local parliaments. The PNV, however, after an internal split, was forced to form a coalition with the PSOE in 1987 to retain control of the Basque government.[85] It was not until 1989, when Fraga finally retired to serve as president in his native homeland, Galicia, that a proper bipartisan system began to take shape. AP underwent a relaunch with a new image and name, Partido Popular (PP). A young team led by José María Aznar, a former tax inspector and president of the autonomous region of Castilla-León (1987–1989). Aznar's aloof nature could not be more distant from González's image. Yet, his efforts to modernize his party, shedding its neo-Francoist reputation, and identifying with the European Christian-Democrats, paid off. By then, it had dropped its opposition to critical social issues such as the right to abortion and accepted the quasi-federal structure of the state. The PP also encouraged the participation of women in the party and their promotion to senior posts.[86] In an attempt to portray himself as the right leader for political change, Aznar tellingly did not invoke past right-wing statesmen but compared himself with a modernizer like Azaña.[87] His popularity increased after surviving an ETA car bomb in April 1995.

The UCD broke up in 1983. Suárez's project, the CDS, survived a little longer but after failing to make clear headway, collapsed in 1991. Simultaneously, the PCE after numerous schisms only began to recover part of its lost ground in the late 1980s by becoming the core of an alliance of leftist groups, the United Left (*Izquierda Unida*, IU) headed by the charismatic former mayor of Córdoba, Julio Anguita.[88]

As for the terrorist challenge, following the PSOE victory, ETA's politico-military faction officially declared its abandonment of the armed struggle on 30 September 1982.[89] However, the military wing continued its operations. The killing in November 1982 of General Lagos Román, head of the *Brunete* armoured division, was a declaration of war to the new administration. In March 1983, it kidnapped the financier Diego Prado, a friend of the king. He was kept in captivity for 72 days until his family paid an undisclosed ransom. In February 1984, the PSOE senator Enrique Casas was assassinated. Murders, kidnappings, and robberies continued unabated. Especially lethal were two car bombs in 1987: the first, on 19 June, at the *Hipercor* shopping centre in Barcelona killed 21 people and injured 45; the second, on 11 December, at the civil guard barracks in Zaragoza resulted in 11 dead, five of them children, and 88 injured. Secret meetings took place in Algiers from November 1986 to April 1989 with ETA to end the terrorist campaign. However, there was to be no satisfactory outcome.[90] In parallel, two cross-party pacts were signed first in the *Cortes* (November 1987) and later in the Basque Parliament (January 1988), in which only HB was excluded, condemning ETA's violence, and stressing the commitment to pursue democratic solutions to solve political conflicts.[91]

By the late 1980s, ETA's power was in decline. It had hitherto enjoyed a degree of sympathy in France where its activists could move at liberty. This was due to the erroneous comparison with the Resistance during the German occupation. However, the arrival in office of President Mitterrand saw closer collaboration between the security services of the two countries. The arrest by French police, in March 1992, of the ETA leadership, together with the seizure of vital documents proved a watershed.[92] Nevertheless, despite dwindling operational capability, ETA was still able to carry out lethal attacks and raise funds through the so-called revolutionary tax, a euphemism for the gross extortion of Basque businessmen. Its list of potential targets included journalists, civil servants, intellectuals, businessmen, academics, and others. This meant a growing number of people requiring police protection in the Basque Country or fleeing that region. Politicians became one of the most common terrorist targets. Some 23 members of the PSOE and PP were killed between 1995 and 2003. Simultaneously, ETA's shrinking number of attacks due to police efficacy and French collaboration led to a new tactic, the so-called *Kale Borroka* or constant urban violence (riots, the burning of buses and cars, breaking of shop windows, etc.) carried out by bands of hooded young radical nationalists in the streets of the Basque Country.[93] By then, however, the simplifying narrative of the Basques living in an occupied country was becoming untenable. It was now the local police constabulary (*Ertzainza*) that assumed most of the tasks formerly assigned to the national police, including, of course, the suppression of street violence.[94]

In the 1980s, Spain became one of the most decentralized countries in the world. Following the fast-tracking concession of the statutes of autonomy to the Basque Country and Catalonia (both in 1979) and Galicia (1981), by 1983 fifteen other regions had acquired their respective home rule with executives, presidents, and legislative chambers. The two North African enclaves of Ceuta and Melilla became autonomous cities in 1995. This shaped the territorial compromise known as *el estado de las autonomías*, or a hybrid system that involved federalist features based on self-governing regions that gradually acquired control of key areas such as health, education, public infrastructure, and transport. The Spanish state retained the overall structure of a unitary body politic.[95] Henceforth, all the autonomous communities devoted a good deal of energy to fostering, when not blatantly inventing, their distinctive identities: flags, national days, anthems, cultural symbols, nostalgic remembrance of past events, and so on. Simultaneously, they established a vast bureaucracy to support their administrations. Devolution in education meant that universities and schools were filled with nationalist-leaning teachers. Local languages were promoted to the detriment of the common Castilian. In March 1981, 2,300 Barcelona intellectuals published a manifesto accusing the *Generalitat* of implementing policies that discriminated against Castilian speakers, more than half of the population. They defended the right to be taught in Spanish. One of its leaders, Federico Giménez Losantos, was kidnapped by a radical nationalist group, *Terra Lliure*, tied to a tree and shot in the leg. Then a leftist journalist, Losantos, fled to Madrid where he soon embraced a hard right line and became one of the best-known voices in the daily *tertulias* (chat shows). Most of the other co-signatories of the manifesto and some 14,000 primary or secondary teachers left Catalonia.[96] In 1983, the Catalan parliament passed the so-called *inmersión lingüística* ('language immersion') or Law of Linguistic Normalization, which imposed Catalan as the language of public education by alleging its weakness vis-à-vis the dominant Castilian Spanish. Similar versions were introduced in the following decades in other communities.[97]

Regional governments subsidized numerous cultural projects and entities to shore up the claims of existential uniqueness. Madrid's reluctance to intervene facilitated the local nationalists' goals, including their defiance of the constitutional order. A telling moment occurred in 1984 when Pujol was investigated due to possible irregularities committed for years in the bank (*Banca Catalana*) founded by his father, which had even led to suspension of payments. The Catalan president's response was to summon his supporters. In front of a mass audience of 300,000 people, he compared the attack on his person to that of Spain against the Catalan nation. Madrid blinked. The investigation was gradually dropped. The affair was finally dismissed in 1990.[98] Thus, Pujol was able to continue unchallenged his nationalist agenda.[99]

The 1980s were marked by optimism. The PSOE's overall strategy was in line with the previous administration: a conciliatory tone towards the military, no official unburdening of the past, and no question of returning to a republic.[100] However, the fact that the Left was finally in power seemed to offer hope and, in a sense, rectify the past. González presided over the radical transformation of the country. By the 1990s, Spain was a modern European society in which democratic values were firmly rooted. *Golpismo* was successfully eradicated. There were two more serious conspiracies, the first on the eve of the elections of October 1982 and the second in June 1985, but they involved only a minority of hard-liners and were swiftly dismantled.[101]

As a matter of fact, the PSOE dealt swiftly with the military question. Its strategy combined appeasement with a determination to stamp out revolt. Gradually but firmly it imposed a sense of subordination to constitutional legality through the modernization of the corps. Those officers who espoused anti-democratic views were progressively replaced by others known to be loyal. In 1984, the National Defence Law extended the power of the prime minister and the minister of defence. At the same time, the budget of the armed forces remained high to bring the pay of the military in line with that of the public sector. Troops received more sophisticated training and new and improved equipment. A welcome renovation was the official incorporation of women into the corps in 1988. In the 1990s, after the retirement of the remaining officers who had participated in the civil war, the army no longer represented a threat to the constitutional order.[102] By then, it was a professional force integrated into the western defence system. Significantly, it even took an active role in UN peacekeeping missions and helped train its counterparts in Latin American countries in democratic values.

Foreign policy proved an area of remarkable success. In a decade, Spain abandoned its peripheral role to play a central part in Europe. Diplomacy followed a path radically different from that of the Francoist period. Until 1975, Spain had adopted a pro-American and pro-Arab stance while remaining semi-ostracized in Europe. The Socialists instead pursued a Eurocentric strategy. In January 1986, Spain established full diplomatic relations with Israel and achieved its long-sought goal of joining the EEC after overcoming previous French reticence under President Valéry Giscard d'Estaing (1974–1981) owing to the potential competition of the Spanish agrarian sector. The good rapport between González and Mitterrand, elected president of France in 1981, which was consolidated after a meeting in Paris in December 1983, represented a dramatic improvement in Franco-Spanish relations.[103]

In March 1986, a referendum confirmed Spain's membership of NATO. Ironically, the PSOE's manifesto of 1982 had stressed the intention of leaving that alliance following Calvo Sotelo's unilateral decision to join. This was in tune with the wishes of most Spaniards, who blamed the USA for propping up the Dictatorship and were wary about becoming part of an international military pact.[104] However, once in office, the Socialists followed the path of pragmatism over idealism. A key reason was their belief that NATO membership was a formula for democratizing the armed forces. Also, adherence to NATO appeared to facilitate entry into the EEC. To help persuade the unconvinced among their ranks, they introduced certain provisos, including not joining the integrated military structure, a ban on nuclear weapons being stored on Spanish territory, and the gradual reduction of the US military presence. The propaganda campaign pursued through RTVE paid off: 56.9 percent voted in favour (in a turnout of 59.4 percent).[105]

By backing entry to NATO, the Socialists emphasized their intention of being part of the western bloc while maintaining a certain distance from the line taken by the United States. Spanish diplomacy was often different from that pursued by the USA in Latin America. For instance, excellent relations were maintained with Castro's Cuba and Spain condemned the US-sponsored *Contras* in Nicaragua, instead endorsing the so-called Contadora Plan to find a negotiated solution in that country. In the 1990s, Spanish forces participated in two important world missions, the Gulf War and Bosnia. In 1991, Madrid held the crucial Arab-Israeli Peace Conference. The year 1992 was a veritable *annus mirabilis* for Spain, reflecting its new standing in the world. Apart from the celebrations for the 500th anniversary of the discovery of America, Madrid was designated Europe's cultural capital, Barcelona staged the Olympic Games, and Sevilla hosted the World Trade Exhibition. The *Observer* noted that Spain's arrival on the international scene could no longer be ignored.[106] In 1995, the Socialist Javier Solana was appointed NATO's secretary general. By then, Spain was a key mediator between Europe and Latin America and had a strong friendship with the Arab countries.[107]

With the PSOE in office, the establishment of a solid welfare state became a reality. In 1986, the General Health Law planted the seeds for the creation of a highly sophisticated medical system available to everyone. Since 1985, children aged 6–16 years had a right to compulsory free education. Public spending reached European levels, increasing from 40 to 48 percent of GDP between 1985 and 1993. The Socialists also established a generous new pension scheme and a progressive tax system. However, investment in research remained at low levels, the government instead choosing to fund social security, unemployment benefits, and an expanded public sector.[108]

Socialist handling of the economy produced more ambiguous results. When the PSOE assumed office, structural weaknesses had not been resolved. The public deficit had reached 5.4 percent of GDP, inflation remained at 15 percent, and the rate of unemployment had risen to 17 percent. At the time, the social-democratic principles of Keynesian demand management techniques, state interventionism, and nationalization of key sectors, were being abandoned in favour of strict monetary regulations throughout the western world. Following that trend, the ministers of the economy – Miguel Boyer (1982–1985) and Carlos Solchaga (1985–1993) – abandoned traditional principles of state control and high taxation to redistribute wealth. They instead placed an emphasis on sound finance, fighting inflation, modernizing crucial infrastructure, and improving competitiveness. Boyer immediately announced an 8 percent devaluation of the peseta to arrest the outflow of foreign currency reserves. Monetary policy was tightened, and a ceiling on wage demands was established.[109] In February 1983, he decided to appropriate the enormous but tottering Rumasa holding company to safeguard some 60,000 jobs in 400 separate enterprises, including 17 banks. To the disappointment of many Socialists, he soon declared his intention to re-privatize most of it.[110]

Straight after assuming office, Boyer also introduced a Plan of Industrial Reconversion, the objective of which was to establish a modern industrial base capable of competing internationally. This meant that the public sector was pruned of inefficient plants. The old steel, iron, and shipbuilding industries were closed or sold off.[111] Also, within in a few years, dozens of hitherto symbolic enterprises were sold, the most significant being SEAT to Germany's Volkswagen. This restructuring programme was relatively successful if judged in terms of conventional macroeconomic indicators: the rate of inflation was halved, productivity improved, and there was an economic boom in the second half of the 1980s. After joining the EEC, Spain benefited from large inflows of foreign capital attracted by high interest rates, relatively low labour costs, and a massive popular thirst for consumer goods. It also profited from having access to the so-called cohesion funds to support less developed regions. This boosted investment in modern infrastructure, which included motorways, the dramatic modernization of *Red Nacional de Ferrocarriles Españoles* (the state-owned railway company), which included a cutting-edge high-velocity system (*Alta Velocidad Española*, AVE), and world-class airports. However, to join the EEC Spain had to sacrifice some of its competitive advantages, especially in the agricultural and fishing sectors. Still, the annual rate of economic growth, at almost 5 percent, was the highest amongst the western economies. Yet, like the rest of the world, by 1993 the boom had given way to a recession and the economy showed no sign of picking up again until 1995. By then, the peseta had been devalued four times and interest rates cut from 14.3 to 7.5 percent.[112]

The government's economic policy was lauded by the financial world but criticized by the organized labour movement because of it having to endure most of the harsh adjustment measures. Modernization meant unpopular job-cutting policies that a right-wing party could never have got away with. An electoral promise of 1982, the creation of 800,000 new jobs within the following four years, was not only dropped but reconversion meant a notable increase in the number of unemployed. By 1992, the unemployment rate hovered around 20 percent of the working population, the largest in western Europe. It reached 24 percent by 1993. Bureaucratic red tape around getting rid of the excess labour force made employers reluctant to hire new staff on permanent contracts The government tried to soften this by turning a blind eye to the buoyant underground economy, estimated at around 25 percent of GDP, increasing pensions and social security, protecting those on fixed-term contracts, and presiding over a bloated public sector.[113]

The PSOE's economic approach put it on a collision course with the unions. In 1988, Nicolás Redondo Urbieta, the UGT leader, gave up his parliamentary seat. His organization joined the CCOO in a general strike on 14 December. It led to a historic divorce, made official in 1990, between the PSOE and the UGT.[114] The former was now seen as openly pro-business and anti-worker, a remarkable turnaround for a party which, in the 1970s, had defended Marxist principles.[115] In the 1990s, tensions with the labour movement increased. After signing the Maastricht Treaty in February 1992, which transformed the EEC into a closer, more integrated association (the European Union, EU), the government found itself further constrained by the need to meet the convergence criteria for economic and monetary union. As one of the first wave of nations to join the single currency (Euro), these measures included a tightening of fiscal policy and cuts to public services. There were further general strikes on 24 May 1992 and 27 January 1994.[116]

Under the leadership of González and Guerra, the PSOE was transformed beyond recognition. It became a successful electoral machine but, simultaneously, the frugality which had hitherto characterized it was jettisoned. Once in power and lacking any serious challenge, the government began to identify itself with the state. González gradually adopted a presidential stand, failed to attend a parliament that simply rubber-stamped government decisions, and created a 'royal court' around his residence at the Moncloa.[117] The PSOE grew gradually contemptuous of public opinion, considered the public sector its possession, and fostered clientelism. By 1994, at its 23rd Congress, 72 percent of delegates held official posts.[118]

In turn, the socialist constituency changed. After being catapulted to power by the young and urban middle and working classes in particular in 1982, the PSOE became a catch-all party that attracted support from all sectors of society. Many whose first choice would have been Communist ended up giving their 'useful' vote to the PSOE. However, an increasing part of its electoral support came from those quarters who benefited from governmental action: pensioners, public employees, and the rural vote in Andalusia and Extremadura. In these southern strongholds, a clear example of clientelist politics could be seen to operate. Being designated poor regions, funds – in the shape of the *Plan de Empleo Rural* (Rural Employment Plan) – were set aside for development projects to offer employment and improve village life. Anyone who could document working for 60 days qualified for community benefits for the entire year. In practice, with the complicity of local socialist authorities, the scheme became a colossal fraud. In some cases, relatives took it in turns to work the minimum 60 days so that they all received benefits. In others, villagers were credited with working on projects that never existed. A vulnerable sector of the population might have been able to get through hard times, but it was also a 'captive' vote for the Socialists.[119]

In the 1990s, González's statesmanship was hailed in Europe where he was rumoured to be a strong candidate for the post of EU president. Yet, his reputation – along with that of his party – was being tarnished by the natural erosion that occurs after being in power for over a decade. Moreover, following the euphoria of the Olympic Games and Expo '92, Spain awakened to an economic recession marked by a dramatic fall in production and an upsurge in unemployment.[120] At the same time, there was such an avalanche of corruption scandals that the economist Ramón Tamames called Spain a 'kleptocratic state'.[121] On 24 May 1993, *El Mundo* printed a devastating editorial entitled 'Corruption: A Cancer for the Democracy'. Unlike Restoration times when scandals were mostly connected with the activities of political bigwigs, they were now also related to party financing.[122] Clearly, a lack of executive accountability, corruption, nepotism, and other crimes are not uniquely Spanish phenomena. Countries like France, Greece, and above all Italy have also experienced comparable crises.

The first monumental scandal emerged in Andalusia, the socialist heartland. In December 1989, Juan Guerra, brother of the deputy prime minister, seized the headlines. Previously unemployed, after the electoral victory of 1982 he acquired an office in the PSOE's headquarters in Sevilla. He rapidly amassed a huge fortune, which included the possession of a big estate with fine horses, several luxury cars, and shareholdings in numerous enterprises. Leaks to the press by his ex-wife led him to be accused of *tráfico de influencias* ('influence-peddling') and he was sentenced to two years in prison.[123] Under fierce criticism in parliament, Alfonso denied knowledge of his brother's misdoings. He resigned from the government in 1991 but retained his key position in the party. Henceforth, despite the executive's attempts to obstruct judicial investigations, magistrates and journalists launched themselves into a relentless campaign that exposed a myriad of scandals involving the RTVE, RENFE, Red Cross, banks, Expo '92, and more. The biggest uproar was at the discovery in May 1991 of a series of artificial consulting companies (FILESA) which acted as fronts for the PSOE. They obtained millions of pesetas from banks and industries in return for unknown services. Guillermo Galeote, responsible for the PSOE's finances, was forced to resign and was tried along with 50 others. Twelve of them received prison sentences in 1997.[124]

The opinion polls suggested that most Spaniards believed that Felipe must have been aware of the ongoing scandals. Crucially, although revelations of widespread governmental misconduct fuelled public scepticism about the political class, they also – in a roundabout way – confirmed the foundations of democratic politics in Spain. Had the scandals emerged in the transition years, the new regime might have collapsed. However, not a single voice in the 1990s called for a return to the past. Of course, political corruption was no worse than during past regimes; the essential difference was that, then, it might never have come to light.

In March 1993, González visited Madrid's Central University. Believing to be on friendly ground among students, he was shocked at being dubbed a 'thief'. Soon thereafter, he called for an early election in May. During the subsequent campaign, he proved again to be a formidable performer. He stressed both his commitment to building a fairer society and fighting corruption. As proof of that promise, he placed Baltasar Garzón, a prominent anti-corruption judge, as number two, behind him, on the Madrid party list. The PSOE won a fourth consecutive victory but lost its overall majority, falling to 38.8 percent of the vote (159 seats). The PP, for the first time, broke through its previous electoral ceiling of 25 percent to reach 34.8 percent (141 seats). IU also saw its vote increase (18 seats). Given the hostility between the PSOE and IU, the government had to rely on the CiU, which, with its 18 seats, became 'kingmaker'. The Catalan nationalists refused two portfolios but obtained a bigger share of the tax receipts.[125]

The PSOE's fourth term in office soon turned into a nightmare. The exposure of another string of scandals further tarnished the PSOE's reputation and facilitated the fierce offensive undertaken by the PP and IU, who continued to portray the government as a sleazy machine.[126] In less than a year, five members of the cabinet were forced to resign and dozens of top officials in the civil service, local government, and the police force faced criminal charges or were under investigation. Particularly toxic for González was the imprisonment of both the former governor of the Bank of Spain and the president of Madrid's stock exchange, Mariano Rubio and Manuel de la Concha, respectively. They were charged with widespread fraud and insider trading. That led to the resignation of the minister of the economy, Carlos Solchaga who had appointed Rubio. Equally astonishing was the fall of Luis Roldán, a taxi driver's son and the first civilian head of the civil guard who had been favourite to be the next minister of the interior. In April 1994, he fled abroad after being accused of embezzling public funds, taking kickbacks on building contracts, and laundering money. The government tried to portray his arrest by Spanish policemen, in February 1995, at Bangkok airport as proof of its determination to stamp out corruption. Yet, it turned into a disaster when it was discovered that Roldán, who allegedly was hiding in Laos, had agreed to his extradition on the condition of being tried on limited charges only. He was sentenced to 31 years of jail.[127]

Judge Garzón uncovered another damaging affair for the government. Between 1983 and 1987, a mysterious organization, the *Grupos Antiterroristas de Liberación* (GAL), had murdered 27 members or sympathizers of ETA in their safe haven in south-west France. The GAL's accurate intelligence aroused the suspicion that they were death squads composed of foreign mercenaries hired as part of a dirty war orchestrated by Spain's security services and financed by the *fondos reservados* ('slush funds'). It ended its activities after pressure brought by the French authorities.[128] In 1988, two police inspectors, José Amedo and Michel Domínguez, were charged with having created GAL and sentenced to 100 years in jail. The affair had almost been forgotten when, feeling himself conned by González after being given the role of drug tsar instead of the Justice portfolio, Garzón resumed the investigation into GAL activities. His findings revealed that millions of pesetas from slush funds of the Interior Ministry had been used to finance the death squads. Amedo and Domínguez were scapegoats in an operation engineered by top officials. To buy their silence, both were receiving a 'salary' of half a million pesetas a month into secret Swiss accounts and had been promised a pardon.[129] Under pressure, however, they implicated in their confessions the former civil governor of Vizcaya, Julián Sancristobal; the former chief of the anti-terrorist brigade, Francisco Álvarez; the chief of police in Bilbao, Miguel Planchuelo; the former secretary of the Basque socialists, Ricardo García Damborenea; and a former director of state security, Rafael Vera. Under interrogation, all but the latter incriminated José Barrionuevo, the former minister of the interior, and an even more high-profile figure described only as Mr X, who could be none other than González. Barrionuevo and Vera were sentenced to 10 years in prison in 1998 and pardoned in 2001.[130] A new scandal, in the summer of 1995, revealed that the secret services had been illegally tapping the conversations of opposition politicians and even the king. This led the CiU to withdraw its support of the PSOE in the chamber. The government dissolved parliament and called early elections for March 1996.[131]

Towards a New *Turno*: The Return of the Right

The electoral campaign of 1996 was the most acrimonious in the democratic era. Fighting for his credibility, Felipe proved he was still a formidable candidate. He claimed to be the victim of a smear campaign. Still, a combination of the Socialists' tarnished image, economic recession, and a willingness to change helped the PP to electoral success. However, it was a bitter victory. Far from the massive swing that the opinion polls predicted, their 156 seats left them 20 short of an overall majority and dependent on the CiU and PNV who, with 16 and 5 deputies respectively, became the arbiters of politics. In general, the better-educated, young, and urban middle classes went over to the PP. The 'coalition' that had kept the PSOE in power for 14 years – pensioners, subsidized urban and rural workers, and public sector employees – remained largely loyal. Far from being routed, the Socialists returned 141 deputies. Those who had hoped that a crushing defeat would usher in a period of self-examination and renewal within Spanish Socialism were disappointed. The IU, with only 21 seats, also saw its hopes of displacing the PSOE as the new hegemonic leftist force – by focusing on the government's immoral activities – shattered.[132]

Although Aznar's idol was Margaret Thatcher because of her strong right-wing stance,[133] pragmatism dominated policy-making during the PP's first term in office. A clear example was the government's approach to regional nationalists. Past centralist outbursts suddenly changed into wide-ranging concessions, greater than those made by the Socialists. Everything that the PP had previously described as the PSOE giving up national sovereignty was now branded as a model of political logic.[134] Indeed, paradoxically, Aznar was responsible for the largest ever devolution in economic, cultural, and administrative prerogatives. Initially, when polls closed, his supporters, believing in an overwhelming victory, chanted 'Pujol, you dwarf, now you will have to speak Castilian'. However, the tune changed dramatically as it became evident that CiU was the key to breaking the deadlock. After two months of negotiations, the Majestic Pact, named after the hotel in Barcelona where they took place, was reached. In return for its support in parliament, the *Generalitat* would keep up to 30 percent of tax revenue,[135] and gain greater control of policing as most duties conducted by national forces were transferred to the local constabulary (*Mossos d'Esquadra*). Crucially, it also allowed for the replacement of the hitherto powerful figures of civil governors, the government's representatives in the provinces. Henceforth, government delegates would simply become figureheads. Aznar also agreed to abolish military service and to remove Alejo Vidal-Quadras, a bitter foe of Pujol, from the presidency of the Catalan PP. Finally, when the CiU lost its overall majority in the Catalan parliament in 1999, the PP shored up the minority administration.[136] Simultaneously, the PP obtained the support of the PNV in exchange for an extension of the *concierto económico*: the collection of more taxes (petrol, alcohol, etc.), jurisdiction on labour matters, and a commitment to developing the local statute of autonomy. Arzalluz boasted to have snatched more from Aznar in 14 days than from González in 14 years.[137] This ground-breaking shift from the Spanish Right seemed to pave the way for greater national harmony. However, hopes were soon dashed.

With Aznar in office, ETA's operational capacity continued to fall away. A record 250 activists were jailed. The government took the controversial decision of ordering the detention of the 23 members of HB's national committee, later condemned to 7 years imprisonment, due to their links with the terrorist apparatus. On 1 July 1997, the police liberated José Antonio Ortega Lara, a prison officer who had been kidnapped and held in captivity in inhumane conditions in a tiny dudgeon for 532 days. Aznar had refused ETA's demands to have its jailed activists moved to Basque prisons nearer their homes. A week later, Miguel Ángel Blanco, a young PP councillor from Ermua, a small Basque town, was abducted. The government was given an ultimatum: facilitate the transfer of prisoners within 24 hours or he would be shot. When this did not happen, ETA carried out its threat. This brutal assassination not only revealed the terrorists' desperation but also their increasing isolation. It sparked the largest spontaneous mass mobilization in Spanish history. Millions of people across the country, including a record half a million in Bilbao, came out to condemn ETA.[138] Many Basque intellectuals and NGOs were no longer prepared to remain quiet. In a snowball effect, Blanco's death became the symbolic end of what hitherto had been a 'spiral of silence'. ETA had once and for all lost its appeal and resonance.[139]

In September 1998, the Basque question experienced a new twist with the announcement of the *Pacto de Estella*. In a moment, when the entire nationalist universe seemed to be in the doldrums, the PNV embraced a legitimate initiative – although it was not exempt from controversy.[140] It broke its pact with mainstream Spanish forces for the sake of a Basque nationalist front which endorsed a good deal of ETA's programme. This included the demand to negotiate with the state based on the right of Basque self-determination and to establish a greater nation that incorporated Navarra and the Basque regions in Spain and France. This offered ETA the alternative of pursuing its strategic goals through the existing institutional structures. In exchange, the terrorist organization declared a truce, although not the end of the *Kale Borroka*.[141] The PNV metamorphosed from an ambiguous acceptance of the status quo to embracing openly the right to sovereignty; even if this potentially meant the end of the armed struggle, it was not welcomed in Madrid. The expulsion of the PNV from the Christian-Democratic international at the behest of the PP was one of the consequences of the growing hostility between the two parties.[142] In May 1999, negotiations took place in Switzerland between ETA and representatives of the government but again ended in deadlock. The truce was broken in January 2000 when a car bomb killed an army officer (Lieutenant Colonel Pedro García Blanco) in Madrid.[143]

Following the economic recovery that had begun in the last years of González, the PP presided over an economic boom. Spain, together with Ireland, experienced the highest growth of the EU nations: 3 percent annually against a European average of just 1.2 percent. This meant macroeconomic stability, interest rate cuts, a significant diminution of the national debt and public deficit, and a reduction in the unemployment rate from 23 percent in 1996 to 14 percent in 2000. This provided the climate for social cooperation with the trade unions. The government also followed the trend initiated during the previous administration, raising over 4 billion pesetas by liberalizing and privatizing formerly nationalized sectors, including some of its most valued assets, including telecommunications (Telefonica), aviation (Iberia), electricity (Endesa), and oil (Repsol).[144]

Given the widespread feeling of socio-economic well-being, the PP was not just re-elected in March 2000 but gained an overall majority, taking 44.5 percent of the votes cast and 183 seats. The PSOE was still tarnished by recent scandals. Its new leader, Joaquín Almunia, had a reputation as an honest technocrat; however, unlike Felipe's abundant charisma, he was a dull communicator. Moreover, the strategy of local electoral coalitions with the IU, facilitated by the replacement of Anguita by Francisco Frutos, smacked of despair and both parties were penalized in the polls. The PSOE fell to 34 percent of the vote (125 seats), while the IU only took 5.45 percent (eight seats). The regional nationalists cemented their previous results: the CiU and PNV won 15 and seven seats, respectively.[145] A new *turno pacífico* appeared to have been consolidated.

Notes

1. Omar G. Encarnación, *Spanish Politics* (Cambridge: Polity, 2008), p. 30.
2. Antonio Rivera, *20 de diciembre de 1973. El día en que ETA puso en jaque al régimen franquista* (Barcelona: Taurus, 2021).
3. Powell, *Juan Carlos of Spain*, p. 46.
4. Gilmour, *The Transformation of Spain*, p. 138.
5. Paloma Aguilar, *Memory and Amnesia: The Role of the Spanish Civil War in the Transition to Democracy* (Oxford: Berghan, 2002), p. 151.
6. Lannon, *Privilege, Persecution and Prophecy*, p. 5.
7. Powell, *Juan Carlos of Spain*, pp. 82–4.
8. Ibid., pp. 64–5.
9. Juliá, *Los Socialistas*, pp. 419–29.
10. https://www.cambridge.org/core/journals/contemporary-european-history/article/like-father-like-son-willy-brandt-and-felipe-gonzalez-democracy-social-democracy-and-internationalism-in-motion-in-the-late-cold-war/424C24F11D9BADB5DEBBF4E6A955157E
11. Carr and Fusi, *Spain*, p. 209.
12. Powell, *Juan Carlos of Spain*, p. 86.
13. Ibid., p. 89.
14. Gilmour, *The Transformation of Spain*, p. 141.
15. Santos Juliá, *Transición* (Barcelona: Galaxia Gutenberg, 2017), p. 352.
16. Encarnación, *Spanish Politics*, p. 33.
17. Ramón Tamames, *La economía española. De la transición a la unión monetaria* (Madrid: Temas de hoy, 1996), p. 103.
18. Gilmour, *The Transformation of Spain*, p. 144.
19. Powell, *Juan Carlos of Spain*, pp. 104, 110.

20 Ibid., p. 133.
21 Encarnación, *Spanish Politics*, p. 2.
22 Pérez-Díaz, *The Return of Civil Society*, p. 34.
23 Preston, *The Triumph of Democracy*, pp. 94–6.
24 Juliá, *Transición*, p. 367.
25 Preston, *The Triumph of Democracy*, pp. 97–8.
26 Powell, *Juan Carlos of Spain*, pp. 118–22.
27 Gilmour, *The Transformation of Spain*, pp. 156–8.
28 Gunther, 'The Spanish Model Revisited', p. 30.
29 Juliá, *Los Socialistas,* p. 406.
30 Aguilar, *Memory and Amnesia*, pp. 234–6.
31 Mujal-León, *Communism and Political Change*, p. 151.
32 On 11 February 1977, both were rescued when the police stormed the hideout where they were kept captive. This seemed to confirm the rumours about the GRAPO being infiltrated by the intelligence services.
33 Mujal-León, *Communism and Political Change*, pp. 152–3.
34 Encarnación, *Spanish Politics*, p. 37.
35 Preston, *The Triumph of Democracy*, p. 119.
36 Mujal-León, *Communism and Political Change*, pp. 167–8.
37 Tamames, *La economía española*, pp. 139–62.
38 Víctor M. Pérez-Díaz, *España puesta a prueba* (Madrid: Alianza, 1996), p. 152.
39 Alejandro Quiroga, 'Salvation and Betrayal, The Left and the Spanish Nation', in Alonso and Muro (eds.), *The Politics,* pp. 138–9.
40 Andrew Dowling, *Catalonia since the Spanish Civil War* (Brighton: Sussex University Press, 2013), pp. 113–15.
41 Nicholas Manganas, *Las dos Españas: Terror and Crisis in Contemporary Spain* (Brighton: Sussex University Press, 2016), pp. 52–3, 56.
42 Diego Muro, *Ethnicity and Violence: The Case of Radical Basque Nationalism* (London: Routledge, 2008), p. 113.
43 Carsten Humlebæc, 'The Pacto del Olvido', in Alonso and Muro (eds.), *The Politics*, p. 188.
44 Juliá, *Transición*, p. 442.
45 Gunther, 'The Spanish Model Revisited', p. 29.
46 Sullivan, *ETA and Basque Nationalism*, pp. 200–1.
47 Juliá, *Los Socialistas*, p. 503.
48 Paul Heywood, *The Government and Politics of Spain* (London: Macmillan, 1995), p. 51.
49 https://www.constituteproject.org/constitution/Spain_2011.pdf?lang=en.
50 Ballbé, *Orden*, pp. 460–1, 468, 474.
51 Aguilar, *Memory and Amnesia*, pp. 184–5.

52 Muro, *Ethnicity and Violence*, p. 120.
53 Gilmour, *The Transformation of Spain*, pp. 207–10.
54 Preston, *The Triumph of Democracy*, p. 122.
55 Pablo Sánchez León, 'Radicalism without Representation', in Alonso and Diego Muro (eds.), *The Politics,* p. 108; Carr and Fusi, *Spain*, pp. 257–8.
56 Preston, *The Triumph of Democracy*, p. 171.
57 Harrison, *The Spanish Economy*, pp. 177, 181.
58 Mariano Sánchez Soler, *Los hijos del 20-N. Historia Violenta del Fascismo Español* (Madrid: Temas de Hoy, 1993), pp. 210–59.
59 Muro, *Ethnicity and Violence*, p. 122.
60 José Luis Rodríguez Jiménez, *Reaccionarios y golpistas. La extrema derecha en España: del tardofranquismo a la consolidación de la democracia, 1967–1982* (Madrid: CSIC, 1994), pp. 278–9.
61 Preston, *The Triumph of Democracy*, pp. 148–9.
62 Ibid., p. 251.
63 Carr and Fusi, *Spain*, p. 253.
64 Gilmour, *The Transformation of Spain*, p. 249.
65 Juliá, *Los Socialistas,* pp. 528–45.
66 Preston, *The Triumph of Democracy*, p. 174.
67 Ibid., p. 179.
68 Gilmour, *The Transformation of Spain*, p. 253.
69 Javier Cercas, *Anatomía de un instante* (Barcelona: Mondadori, 2009), p. 77.
70 Ibid., pp. 55–76.
71 I have used the excellent analysis of Cercas for the narrative of the events and outcome of the coup.
72 Cardona, *Franco*, p. 323.
73 Cercas, *Anatomía*, pp. 415–19.
74 Juliá, *Transición*, p. 540.
75 Powell, *Juan Carlos of Spain*, p. 173.
76 Cercas, *Anatomía*, pp. 160–1.
77 Gilmour, *The Transformation of Spain*, p. 264.
78 Mujal-León, *Communism and Political Change*, pp. 207–19.
79 Gilmour, *The Transformation of Spain*, p. 267.
80 Mujal-León, *Communism and Political Change*, pp. 221–2.
81 Juliá, *Transición*, p. 539.
82 Juliá, *Los Socialistas*, p. 581.
83 Heywood, *The Government and Politics of Spain*, p. 93.
84 Encarnación, *Spanish Politics*, p. 53.
85 The PNV split in 1986 when the *Lehendakari* Garaikoetxea broke away to lead his own party, *Eusko Alkartasuna*.

86 Encarnación, *Spanish Politics*, p. 61.
87 Juliá, *Transición*, p. 550.
88 Heywood, *The Government and Politics of Spain*, p. 203.
89 *El País*, 'ETA's Politico-military Faction Announces during its 7th Assembly the End of the Armed Struggle' (1 October 1982).
90 Sullivan, *ETA and Basque Nationalism*, pp. 249–50.
91 Muro, *Ethnicity and Violence*, pp. 145–7.
92 *El País*, 'ETA Leadership Arrested Near Biarritz' (30 March 1992).
93 Muro, *Ethnicity and Violence*, pp. 155–7.
94 Manganas, *Las dos Españas*, p. 60.
95 Encarnación, *Spanish Politics*, p. 3.
96 Quiroga, 'Salvation and Betrayal', p. 136.
97 Encarnación, *Spanish Politics*, p. 108.
98 Julia Navarro, *1982–1996. Entre Felipe y Aznar* (Madrid: Temas de Hoy, 1996), pp. 55–9.
99 Dowling, *Catalonia since the Spanish Civil War*, p. 133.
100 Richards, *After the Civil War*, pp. 314–15.
101 In the second, the conspirators apparently planned to assassinate the king and leading politicians by blowing up the official stand at the Armed Forces Day parade in La Coruña on 1 June 1985. Cardona, *Franco*, p. 323. These coups were exposed in a special edition of *El País*, 'Objective: to Kill the King' (17 February 1991).
102 Heywood, *The Government and Politics of Spain*, pp. 64–5.
103 José M. Magone, 'The Role of the EEC in the Spanish, Portuguese, and Greek Transitions', in Alonso and Muro (eds.), *The Politics*, pp. 229–30.
104 Benny Pollack, *The Paradox of Spanish Foreign Policy* (London: Pinter, 1987), p. 153.
105 Heywood, *The Government and Politics of Spain*, pp. 98–9, 267.
106 *The Observer*, 'The Spanish Resurrection' (23 February 1992).
107 Heywood, *The Government and Politics of Spain*, p. 262.
108 Pérez-Díaz, *España*, pp. 55–6.
109 Tamames, *La economía española*, p. 207.
110 Harrison, *The Spanish Economy*, p. 184.
111 Tamames, *La economía española*, p. 212.
112 José Luis García Delgado and Juan Carlos Jiménez, *Un siglo de España. La economía* (Madrid: Marcial Pons, 2001), p. 178.
113 Ibid., pp. 140–1.
114 Navarro, *1982–1996*, p. 227.
115 Heywood, *The Government and Politics of Spain*, p. 248.
116 Navarro, *1982–1996*, p. 278.

117 Cándido, *La sangre de la rosa. El poder y la época, 1982–1996* (Madrid: Planeta, 1996), p. 14.
118 Pérez-Díaz, *España*, p. 40.
119 Preston, *A People Betrayed*, p. 512.
120 García Delgado and Jiménez, *Un siglo*, p. 180.
121 Tamames, *La economía española*, p. 291.
122 Jaume Muñoz, *La España corrupta* (Granada: Comares, 2016), p. 89.
123 Ibid., p. 94.
124 Full coverage of these scandals can be found in *El Mundo*, 'González against the Ropes' (29 December 1994). Tamames, *La economía española*, pp. 291–332; Pérez-Díaz, *España*, pp. 107–12.
125 Heywood, *The Government and Politics of Spain*, p. 181.
126 Plans to execute the pincer operation between Aznar and Anguita were made at the house of Pedro J. Ramírez, editor of *El Mundo*. Javier Tusell, *El Aznarato. El gobierno del Partido Popular, 1996–2003* (Madrid: Aguilar, 2004), pp. 24–5.
127 Preston, *A People Betrayed*, pp. 520–1.
128 Sullivan, *ETA and Basque Nationalism*, pp. 254–7.
129 *El Mundo*, 'The Government Paid 200 Million Pesetas from the Slush Funds in Secret Swiss Accounts to Remain Silent' (9 January 1995).
130 Navarro, *1982–1996*, p. 79.
131 Ibid., p. 469.
132 Pérez-Díaz, *España*, pp. 168–9.
133 Tusell, *El Aznarato*, pp. 57–8, 39.
134 Fernando García de Ortazar and J. Manuel González Vega, *Breve historia de España* (Madrid: Alianza, 2017), p. 625.
135 Even though all the autonomous communities raised some taxes, others, including income tax, were collected by the state who later redistributed the revenue based on a complex formula based on population, per-capita income, etc.
136 Tusell, *El Aznarato*, pp. 68–9.
137 *Voz Pópuli*, 'The PNV's Yes to González, Aznar, and Sánchez Came at a Price' (1 January 2020).
138 *El País*, All the Country against ETA' (13 July 1997).
139 Manganas, *Las dos Españas*, p. 58.
140 *El País*, 'From Ajuria Enea to Estella' (17 September 1998).
141 Muro, *Ethnicity and Violence*, p. 165.
142 Tusell, *El Aznarato*, p. 157.
143 *The Guardian*, 'Madrid Car Bomb Kills Soldier' (22 January 2000).
144 Encarnación, *Spanish Politics*, pp. 116–17.
145 Tusell, *El Aznarato*, pp. 190–2.

7

Quo Vadis Spain? The Challenges of a New Century

From Euphoria to Disillusion

At the beginning of the twenty-first century, Spain constituted a success story. In comparative terms, she was a positive model to emulate rather than one which elicited pity or encouraged avoidance.[1] Abroad, departments of political sciences taught its rapid and relatively peaceful democratic transition and socio-economic modernization as the ideal blueprint for the states emerging then in eastern Europe and Latin America after decades of dictatorships. Indeed, given its history of political turmoil and fratricidal conflict, as well as 40 years of authoritarian rule, Spain's was an extraordinary achievement. Today, Franco represents a spectre from the past, uncomfortable but very real. The most common attitude towards him is one of subtle indifference that conceals the more negative feelings aroused by his character and reactionary politics.[2]

Over a single generation, Spain joined the club of advanced western societies. The speed of transformation was startling. Between 2000 and 2007, it became the biggest recipient of foreign labour in the EU: some five million immigrants arrived mostly from three areas (Latin America, North Africa, and eastern Europe, especially Romania). They were concentrated mostly in the low-wage sector: construction, hospitality, agriculture, domestic service, and so on. Consequently, the percentage of residents born abroad went from minimal to 12 percent of the population. This was in stark contrast to a country that used to be a net exporter of people.[3] It helped enormously to make up for the rapid fall in the birth rate, which at 1.1 is one of the lowest in the world, and an ageing population with its negative impact on the pension and social security system. Simultaneously, there was a profound renovation of its institutions. Spain is now one of the most decentralized systems in Europe and provides universal education and healthcare, a generous pension scheme, and unemployment benefits. It can also boast of being the second most preferred destination for tourists and a favourite place for retirees. It has an outstanding transport infrastructure, including the largest motorway system in Europe, which spans 15,000 kilometres, and one of the best national health systems in the world. Its population enjoys one of the highest life expectancies, second only to Japan. A recent study confirmed that Spain is one of the most tolerant countries in terms of feminist policies and sexual inclination.[4] It was one of the first nations to legalize same-sex marriages and gender parity. Women have achieved significant visibility on citizens' platforms and lead men in terms of professional qualifications. In the last two decades, only the post of prime minister has eluded them. They have occupied over 40 percent of the seats in the *Cortes*, presided over the two chambers, and held the key position of deputy prime minister in the last three administrations, in which they also filled nearly 50 percent of cabinet posts, including those of the interior, foreign affairs, defence, and economy ministers. Madrid, Barcelona, and Valencia have all had lady mayors and twice women have served as state attorney general. Women have also enjoyed prominent jobs in the financial world: Ana Botín (Santander Bank), Marta Ortega (Multinational Inditex), and Dolores Dancausa (Bankinter) are just three examples. There is still, however, much work to be done in terms of wage discrimination and the horrific rates of spousal abuse. In 2016 alone, 134,000 women reported episodes of domestic violence.[5]

Following the hosting of the Olympic Games in Barcelona in 1992, Spain experienced a an astonishing period of success in many sports, including football, basketball, tennis, Formula 1, and motorbike racing. Crucially, it also appeared to have averted the distressing trend of powerful extreme right-wing or anti-immigrant populist forces. Also, political violence, a protagonist in the spiral of revolution and reaction which had marked its modern history, disappeared. ETA, the last terrorist group, declared a unilateral ceasefire in October 2011.[6]

This idyllic image began to fade during the second decade of the twenty-first century, however. A feeling of confidence gave way to pessimism owing to the negative consequences of the global world recession: rising unemployment and economic precariousness. In turn, national and regional populist movements challenged the ruling order. Even the democratic transition, once a prominent symbol of pride, is now being questioned. Tellingly, a famous political reporter titled his book on Spain's contemporary history: 'From Illusion to Disappointment'.[7]

Spain's current maladies are shared across the world. While globalization has brought about technological advances and facilitated international integration, it has made countries more vulnerable to major socio-economic and political upheavals. Europe has been rocked by the consequences of recent disasters: a seismic financial crisis in 2008, the outbreak of a pandemic ten years later, and the war in Ukraine since February 2021. Yet, many of Spain's deficiencies were structural problems that had only been anaesthetized during the first decades of democracy.

The Fragile Foundations of the Economic Miracle

By the late 1990s, Spain was hailed as one of the most dynamic economies within the EU. It could boast an annual growth much higher than that of its partners. Thus, it was able to meet the stringent conditions of the Growth and Stability Pact and was among the first group of nations to adopt the euro as the new single currency. The bonanza continued under the Socialist José Luis Rodríguez Zapatero, Aznar's successor in office. The fact that there were only three pragmatic ministers in charge of the economy between 1985 and 2009 ensured stability: Carlos Solchaga (1985–1993), Pedro Solbes (1993–1995 and 2004–2009), and Rodrigo Rato (1996–2004).[8] During 2006 and 2007, the economy grew at a significant rate, 3.9 and 3.8 percent, respectively. Unemployment fell to 7.95 percent in the first half of 2007 (the lowest level since 1978), and Spain became the second eurozone country – only behind Germany, with a much larger economy – to create the most jobs (an average of 600,000 per year over one decade). Spain's GDP per capita reached 107 percent of the EU level, ahead of Italy (101 percent) and just behind France (111 percent). In 2008, Spain enjoyed its fourteenth year of uninterrupted growth, the longest cycle of expansion in its history. And the success was repeated in the private sector. In 2006, Spanish companies spent over €140 billion on domestic and overseas acquisitions, just behind their British and French counterparts. For instance, *Iberdrola*, an electricity company, purchased *Scottish Power*; *Banco Santander* bought the British *Abbey National Bank*; and *Ferrovial*, a construction enterprise, acquired *BAA*, which operates the UK's three main airports.[9]

The introduction of the euro heralded a long period of low interest rates and cheap money, which drove the cost of borrowing down. In the process, Spain underwent a mind-boggling housing bubble fuelled by easy access to loans. Its importance in creating employment led both the PSOE and the PP to encourage the spending spree by relaxing supervision of the financial sector.[10] Borrowers could acquire massive mortgages without any real scrutiny. After all, property kept being revalued upwards – house prices rose 200 percent from 1996 to 2007 – building companies saw their profits soar, and the housing stock grew by 5.7 million units. More houses were built than in the USA, which had a population eight times that of Spain. Between 2000 and 2007, the debts amassed by households and non-financial companies rose from 94 to 191 percent of GDP.[11] The seemingly never-ending economic boom served to conceal crucial underlying shortcomings. It was based on high levels of private consumption, tourism, and the construction industry. Spain also lagged far behind the EU average in research spending and productivity growth.[12]

The global financial crisis that began in 2008 brought to an abrupt end this era of speculative fever. The sudden credit crunch squeezed borrowers and burst the property bubble. As prices began to plummet, panic ensued. Hundreds of thousands of newly built properties remained unsold. By 2009, the construction sector had ground to a halt, leaving over 600,000 workers jobless.[13] Many cities presented a ghostly image of abandoned construction sites and half-built deserted apartment blocks. Houseowners found themselves facing fast-rising negative equity as their properties became gradually worth less than the mortgage they had taken out. Some three million middle-class families faced poverty.[14]

The 2008 crash became a fiscal tsunami. Locked in an international currency (the euro), the country could not resort to traditional devaluation to foster production and exports. The worst consequence was soaring unemployment, peaking in 2013 at 27 percent of the population, reaching 56 percent for those aged below 25. Faced with such daunting reality, many managed to survive thanks to the underground economy and the persistence of a deeply rooted family-centred culture. It was indeed a common occurrence to see three generations of the same family living together on the pension of the grandparents. The crisis reversed decades of belief in a better future. The Spanish youth was now worse off than their forebears.[15]

Zapatero worsened the lethal impact of the crisis either by sheer ignorance or, even worse, by fearing the potentially negative consequences of taking drastic but unpopular measures on the eve of a general election. His high public spending budgets for 2008 and 2009 only contributed to increasing the national debt. Moreover, the dramatic fall in revenue blew a hole in government accounts resulting in a large deficit.[16] It was only after pressure from Brussels and Washington that Zapatero acknowledged officially, after two years of delay, what everyone knew: the entire world was undergoing an unprecedented recession.[17] On a fateful 12 May 2010, he announced in a two-minute speech the freezing of pensions, severe cuts in public investment and civil servants' salaries, an increase in VAT, a rise in the retirement age from 65 to 67, and the abandonment of all his social schemes.[18] Moreover, to satisfy Brussel's demands, the PSOE joined forces with the PP to make a substantial constitutional amendment: the introduction of a cap on the state's structural deficit allowance, obliging all tiers of government, including local and regional, to adhere to the budget stability principle.[19] This was only the second time that the 1978 constitution had been amended, the first being in 1986 owing to Spain's accession to the EEC. The boom was over. The subsequent hangover presented a bleak image: *desahucios* ('evictions'), growing unemployment, and rising dependence on charitable handouts and soup kitchens. The crisis also resulted in an unprecedented brain drain as a highly educated generation began to emigrate abroad.[20]

In November 2011, months ahead of schedule, an overwhelmed Zapatero called a snap election. Tellingly, he did not seek a third term in office. One of his lieutenants, Alfredo Pérez Rubalcaba, was the one to suffer the wrath of the electorate. Indeed, the PSOE recorded its worst results since 1977: just 110 seats after a loss of 4.3 million votes. The PP, catapulted to power by their promise to repair the economic disaster and led by the man handpicked by Aznar to replace him, Mariano Rajoy, enjoyed a landslide victory, with an overall majority of 186.[21]

The new government further increased austerity. It introduced a Law of Budget Stability that entailed supplementary cuts to public spending, including imposing a ceiling on those of the autonomies, freezing civil servants' salaries, raising taxes, reducing unemployment benefits after six months, and introducing labour reforms to facilitate low-paid contracts.[22] Unable to refinance their debt or obtain further funding, as the international markets had downgraded their bonds to junk status, the regional governments had to obtain loans from the state but, in return, had to adhere to strict deficit reduction targets.[23] Madrid avoided a comprehensive bailout but needed, in June 2012, financial support from Brussels to help its over-indebted banking sector. The introduction of a market reform that year helped lower the rate of unemployment but to the detriment of workers, since it significantly reduced severance payments and gave employers greater powers to dismiss redundant staff and impose badly paid temporary contracts.[24] It was only in 2013 that Spain slowly began to come out of a long recession in which it had shredded over 9 percent of its GDP in five years. Yet, the economy only picked up momentum in 2017: the rate of unemployment, although still high (nearly double the EU average), fell to 17.22 percent and GDP registered 3 percent growth for the third year in a row. This was largely due to a substantial recovery of the export sector, a boom in the tourist industry – facilitated by the political instability of its cheaper rival destinations in North Africa – and the plunge in energy prices.[25]

As the impact of the economic crisis appeared largely overcome, two major unexpected catastrophes struck: Covid-19 and war in Ukraine. Spain was one of the worst affected eurozone countries, with some 3.2 million infections and 75,000 deaths, after Covid-19 began to spread in February 2020.[26] Most non-essential activity came to a halt between March 2020 and May 2021 due to partial or total lockdowns. GDP shrank by 10.8 percent in 2020, the deepest recession in 80 years and the harshest in Europe owing to the impact on two crucial sectors: tourism and hospitality.[27] Yet, unemployment only rose to 16.2 percent in late 2020, far less than predicted because of the success of the furlough scheme, ERTE (*Expedientes de Regulación Temporal de Empleos*).[28]

With Europe seeming to have recovered after the mass vaccination of its population, the outbreak of war in Ukraine, in February 2022, again rattled the world economy. Despite not being as exposed as other EU nations in terms of dependence on Russia for energy and agrarian imports from Ukraine, shortages of key foodstuffs and the climbing price of oil and gas produced galloping inflation that had been unknown for decades. The subsequent hike in interest rates in the USA and the eurozone curbed the economic recovery and generated a wave of protest.[29] In March 2022, while some 400,000 farmers and cattle breeders flocked to Madrid to vent their anger, the country was paralysed by a general strike of lorry drivers which lasted nearly three weeks (from 14 March to 2 April).[30]

The Three Fateful Cs: *Caínismo*, *Crispación*, Corruption

Democracy brought about the modernization of political habits and institutions. Yet, the governing classes failed to mirror the strengths of the Restoration dynastic notables, while indulging in some of their worst deficiencies, including glaring cronyism and corruption. The dynastic elites were almost without exception gifted orators, many of them authors of excellent historical, literary, and economic works. They also showed the ability to rally together in the face of a major crisis, particularly after 1917. After Franco, the transition leaders demonstrated, despite their ideological differences, remarkable foresightedness to negotiate and establish a new democratic order. However, that quality deteriorated dramatically over time. The compromise that marked the transition was replaced by *crispación* ('acrimony') and political *caínismo* ('fratricide'). Naturally, the power struggle began in earnest once democracy was consolidated. Yet, the new generation that took control of the PSOE and the PP seemed to be concerned only with remaining in power at any cost, and transformed party competition into undisguised hostility.

The PSOE opened Pandora's Box during the elections of 1996. For the first time, as the Right appeared to be poised to gain office, the Socialists resorted to a murky propaganda campaign. The PP was depicted in a video as a barking Dobermann and the electorate were warned that a PP victory represented a return to Francoism.[31]

The *crispación* escalated during Aznar's second term in office. With an absolute majority, he displayed growing arrogance by pushing his policies through the *Cortes* without much dialogue. A dangerous chasm opened up vis-à-vis the regional nationalists, especially in the Basque Country, where tensions increased after the arrival of a new PNV *lehendakari*, Juan José Ibarretxe, who in September 2001, three months after winning an extremely virulent regional election, introduced a highly contentious plan, named after himself, that took the *Pacto de Estella* to a new level. It proposed to reform the Statute of Autonomy to enable the Basque people to have the right to decide their future. Ibarretxe endorsed the idea of a free-associated state with its own penal system, judiciary, social security, and the right to sign international bilateral agreements. This initiative, which amounted to open conflict with the constitutional order, was narrowly approved by the Basque parliament two years later.[32] In August 2002, the Supreme Court backed a government proposal to ban *Herri Batasuna* (HB), accused of being part of ETA's terrorist network.[33]

Aznar's most polemic decision was taken in the realm of foreign policy. Despite the lack of a valid UN mandate, he supported the US intervention in Iraq, which began on 19 March 2003, based on the spurious claim of that country possessing weapons of mass destruction. Three days earlier, he stood in Terceira (the Azores) shoulder to shoulder with the American president George W. Bush, the British premier Tony Blair, and their host, the Portuguese prime minister, José Manuel Durão Barroso. Aznar's hawkish pro-Atlanticism represented a radical departure from Spain's long-standing Europeanism and clashed with the anti-war stance of the two leading EU nations, France and Germany. His decision was not debated in parliament and defied the overwhelming will of the country. Opinion polls showed 92 percent of Spaniards opposed. Three million people took to the streets to express their anger. Aznar's choice was based on his belief that it would put Spain at the centre of a post-Cold War new international order that Bush seemed bent on establishing.[34] Yet, it came to haunt him just a year later.

A general election was scheduled for Sunday, 14 March 2004. Having taken the laudable decision not to seek a third mandate, Aznar appointed his successor, Mariano Rajoy, a property registrar from Galicia. Given the buoyant state of the economy, most opinion polls indicated that the PP was poised to claim victory, the only doubt being whether it could renew its absolute majority. The PSOE was then led by a practically unknown, José Luis Rodríguez Zapatero, who had won the leadership of his party by beating the apparatus candidate and former minister of defence, José Bono.[35] Yet, the Socialists won 164 seats to the PP's 148.[36] The deadliest terrorist attack in Spanish history proved crucial to the election outcome.

Three days before the elections, there were ten near-simultaneous explosions on four commuter trains about to enter Atocha Station in Madrid during the morning rush hour. The blasts killed 193 people and wounded 2,000.[37] The PP's defeat was not determined by the attack but by the government's response to it. Shocked by the scale of the slaughter, Aznar feared a popular backlash given its staunch pro-US stance during the Iraq War. Thus, it continued to blame ETA even when it became evident that it was the work of Islamic fundamentalists. Having access to worldwide news that confirmed that Al-Qaeda was behind the terrorist havoc, Spaniards felt cheated by a government blatantly concealing evidence for electoral reasons. Popular anger led to thousands protesting outside PP headquarters in several cities during the day of reflection, in the 24 hours before the polls, when political activities are suspended.[38] The right-wing media later fostered the idea of a constitutional coup that achieved the objective sought by the terrorists: to oust the PP from office. The latter never accepted the results and, consequently, denied Zapatero's government legitimacy.[39] It hardly changed matters when the PSOE won the next election, in March 2008, winning five more seats.[40]

Such a wide-ranging number of reforms took place during Zapatero's period in office that some authors have called it a second transition.[41] For his supporters he was a reformist crusader, while for his enemies he was a reckless or naïve politician.[42] The politics of *crispación* reached a new peak.

Zapatero's first initiative was to restore the traditional collaboration with the Franco-German partnership and fulfil his pledge of immediate withdrawal of Spanish troops from Iraq. This was somehow mollified by deploying a military mission to Afghanistan.[43] There were no major fissures between the two mainstream parties regarding the economy or ameliorating the welfare state due to the country's rising prosperity. The policies included a significant increase in the minimum wage; subsidized rents for young adults ('emancipation money'); a Law of Dependency, which enabled universal aid for those who for reasons of age, illness, or disability were permanently dependent on nursing care to carry out day-to-day tasks; mothers were to receive €2,500 for the birth of a child ('the baby cheque'); free nursery places for toddlers; and paternity and maternity leave to be increased to 3 and 13 weeks respectively.[44] However, four essential issues led the PP, backed by conservative sectors of society, to adopt an intransigent stance: the social agenda, the historical memory, ETA, and the territorial question.

Having embraced liberal pro-market policies, European social-democracies' emphasis shifted from workers' demands and economic redistribution to socio-cultural themes (gay rights, environmental protection, multiculturalism, etc.). Zapatero himself claimed to pursue a feminist agenda. In 2007, the *Cortes* passed the Law of Gender Equality for all walks of life, including the requirement for parties to fill at least 40 percent of their electoral lists with women.[45] He established more than parity in his first cabinet: nine of his 17 ministers were women, including the vice president, María Teresa Fernández; Bibiana Aído, Spain's youngest ever minister (31 years old) at the newly created portfolio of Equality; and the seven-month pregnant Carmé Chacón as the country's first-ever woman minister of defence.[46] Rajoy decreased the number of female ministers (four out of 13) but retained the tendency to promote them to powerful posts: the party's two most powerful figures, after him, were the otherwise bitter rivals, Soraya Sáenz de Santamaria (vice president and cabinet spokesperson) and María Dolores de Cospedal (general secretary and minister of defence).

Within the social agenda, the major causes of friction were the legalization of same-sex marriages, the right of gay couples to adopt children, easier accessibility to abortion, the replacement of Religious Studies in schools with Citizenship Education, and the end of the practice of displaying religious symbols in public buildings. The Church responded by abandoning its previously politically neutral stance. By then, the Holy See had taken a radical turn under conservative popes: the Polish Karol Wojtyla (John Paul II, 1978–2005) and the German Joseph Ratzinger (Benedict XVI, 2005–2013). Acting in tandem with the PP, the Church organized mass demonstrations to denounce the depravity of legislation that imperilled the foundations of the traditional family.[47]

Zapatero's intention of making the recovery of the historical memory official state policy constituted a clear departure from González's great care to avoid the backlash that unearthing the troubled past could provoke. Indeed, the PP and the right-wing media quickly dubbed it an instrument of division and a betrayal of the spirit of the transition that relegated historical memory to the academic world.[48] In fact, the recovery of historical memory responded to the growing demands of the younger generations. They were the grandchildren and the great-grandchildren of the war, who wanted to know the truth about their missing ancestors. By the turn of the century, a groundswell of social memory, formed from direct recollection of the painful past, passed on generation to generation, had gathered momentum.[49]

Apart from the generational change, an external factor played a big part. In October 1998, while seeking medical treatment in England, Chile's former dictator, General Pinochet, was detained on an international warrant requested by the Spanish judge Garzón, based on the universal jurisdiction for crimes of genocide and crimes against humanity. Pinochet would spend 503 days under house arrest after the House of Lords ruled that he did not enjoy immunity. Finally, he was allowed to return to Chile when the British home secretary, Jack Straw, decided against his extradition to Spain.[50] Pinochet's arrest proved a catalyst in the struggle for the recovery of historical memory in Spain. It was, after all, ironic to force another democracy to face its dark past while refusing to face its own.[51]

A civil society movement, the *Asociación para la Recuperación de la Memoria Histórica* (Association for the Recovery of Historical Memory), emerged in 2000. Branches opened across Spain to pursue several objectives: to recover and identify the 'unidentified', estimated to be at least 30,000, who were in mass graves; to establish an archive that would preserve the historical memory; to disseminate knowledge about the victims of the civil war; and to fight for justice for those repressed by Francoism.[52] On a symbolic date, 20 November 2002, the anniversary of Franco's death, all the parties in the *Cortes* agreed to a declaration condemning the coup of 1936 and recognizing the sacrifices of its victims.[53]

That agreed parliamentary declaration represented for the PP the end of any discussion on the subject. In fact, party allegiances have shaped the politics of memory. Aznar tried to hinder any investigation and even to turn the clock back. In 2003, he unveiled a new educational programme that followed traditional lines and made religion a compulsory subject. Also, grants were given to private foundations and think-tanks with conservative leanings, including, controversially, the Francisco Franco Foundation, which is dedicated to the memory of the *Caudillo* and is administered by his daughter Carmen.[54] Aznar appeared to have forgotten his initial identification with Azaña when he provocatively told the assembled press in 2003 that amongst the books he was taking for his summer holidays was the *Myths of the Civil War* by Pío Moa, a former member of the GRAPO transformed into a leading figure of the badly termed revisionist authors. Emerging in the

1990s, they were an eclectic group of professional writers who boasted of being the spearhead of a rebellion against what they claimed was a left-dominated academia. Rather than revision, their work merely attempts to justify the military uprising of July 1936 by repeating some glaring Francoist clichés. Hailed by the right-wing media, they were often invited to participate in *tertulias* that reached large audiences. Their works, available everywhere, from department stores to airport lounges, became bestsellers.[55]

Once the PSOE was back in office, the *Cortes* voted that 2006 would be the Year of Historical Memory and approved, after much-heated debate, in October 2007, the Law of Historical Memory.[56] It dashed hopes for a deep reconciliation with the past since its focus was on the identification of the repressed but not the repressors, shifting responsibility to the local and regional authorities, which in practice meant that conservative town halls or autonomies could thwart any efforts to unmask the guilty. It was, nonetheless, a symbolic achievement.[57] It formally condemned, for the first time, the Francoist regime, sanctioned the removal of the remaining symbols of the Dictatorship from public buildings and spaces, and provided aid to help trace and exhume the thousands of unaccounted victims of Francoist repression. There were 740 exhumations between 2000 and 2018, with over 9,000 bodies retrieved.[58]

The historical memory was put on the back-burner during Rajoy's mandate, as the PP resisted opening the Francoist past to scrutiny. It returned to the forefront when the Socialist Pedro Sánchez became prime minister in June 2018. Franco's exhumation and removal from his resting place in the *Valle de los Caídos*, in October 2019, after a prolonged legal battle, was a landmark victory and a long overdue step.[59] The last initiative on the subject was the approval by the *Cortes*, in June 2022, of a Law of Democratic Memory, which included the creation of a census of victims of Francoism; the investigation of Francoist crimes; the right to compensation for seized assets and economic sanctions; and the abolition of noble titles granted to 33 dignitaries of the Dictatorship. Its passing was mired in controversy, as it needed the votes of *Bildu* (HB's most recent reincarnation), which imposed a clause investigating the victims of police torture in the context of the fight against ETA until 1983, eight years after Franco's death.[60]

There is the danger of using historical memory for political purposes and thus to generate further *caínismo*. While the response of some sections on the Right has been histrionic, some on the Left appear to be bent on either trying to fight the war all over again or pursuing a revisionist process in which the transition is simplified and misleadingly described as surrender, betrayal, trickery, and so on.[61] As Javier Cercas noted, the truth is exactly the opposite. The transition was a success and responded to the social demand of the times. There was no sell-out. On the contrary, the Left made important concessions, but the Francoist elites were forced to accept genuine democratic reform and give up the absolute power they had held for decades. Total justice was not done, republican legitimacy was not restored, those responsible for the Dictatorship were not judged, nor were its victims compensated. Yet, democracy might not have succeeded if the primary objective had been to amend the past and not to build the future.[62] It is the spirit of that era that, unfortunately, is missing right now. The sensitive issue of the historical memory needs to be backed by a negotiated pact between the country's mainstream forces and not used as a political football. Certainly, its insertion in the political debate has not been motivated by popular pressure.[63] Yet, the recovery of the historical memory should be about honouring and acknowledging victims' suffering and about inquiring self-critically about the consequences of society's past decisions.[64] Furthermore, it is the best way to reveal the strength of Spain's democracy and to put to rest the ghosts of a previously dark era.[65]

Zapatero took on the complex task of ending ETA terrorism. The Northern Ireland Good Friday agreement of 1998, which ended decades of violence in that province, had been a recent successful precedent. ETA's announcement of a permanent ceasefire, in March 2006, facilitated the opening of negotiations. Puzzling and even cynical was the fierce opposition of the PP supported by the associations of victims of terrorism. They claimed that it amounted to 'a betrayal of the dead'.[66] That vitriolic stance not only broke the traditional bipartisan unity on the subject but also was false. Both the PP and the PSOE had entered negotiations with ETA in the past. Moreover, the government refused to make any concessions until disarmament had been completed. A fairer criticism would have been to argue that it was futile to pay any price to a terrorist organization that had, by then, been seriously weakened through the concerted action of the French and Spanish security services. The dialogue lasted just nine months when ETA broke the ceasefire by detonating a bomb in the car park of Madrid airport in December 2006, killing two Ecuadorian immigrants who were sleeping there.[67] ETA could never regain its past strong position. During the next four years, it murdered six people, but most of its operations involved small explosive devices and car bombs. In the process, it committed the fatal error of killing two French police officers in shootouts with activists, in March and April 2011, respectively. Fearing an all-out French clampdown, in October 2011 ETA announced the end of its armed struggle. In May 2018, it proclaimed the complete dissolution of all its structures. By then, ETA had undertaken 2,472 terrorist acts and killed 856 people.[68]

Zapatero also entered the murky waters of the territorial question. He first had to contend with Basque defiance. After seeing his plan rejected in the *Cortes*, on 1 February 2005, by an overwhelming 313 to 29 votes, Ibarretxe brought forward regional elections. Crucially, the PNV suffered a shock defeat, for the first time, losing out in government. The Basque socialist leader, Patxi López, with the votes of the PP, was elected *Lehendakari*.[69] After dealing with the Basque challenge, the government tried to finalize the issue of the relationship between the state and the autonomies. Six regions had new statutes of autonomy approved. The process went smoothly in Valencia, the Balearic Islands, Andalusia, Aragón, and Castile-León, but not in Catalonia.

Zapatero had promised, during the electoral campaign, possibly thinking that he would never be prime minister, given the latest opinion polls, that he would support any new statute of autonomy approved by regional parliaments. Thus, his unforeseen victory bolstered regional demands for enhanced powers. Once in office, he also felt forced to act due to unprecedented circumstances. In Barcelona in 2003, for the first time, the Catalan socialists (*Partit dels Socialistes de Catalunya*, PSC) led by Pasqual Maragall gained control of the *Generalitat* by forming a three-party coalition with the left-wing ecologists of *Iniciativa per Catalunya-Verds* and the old republican party ERC, which had had independence as part of its manifesto since 1989. In Madrid, Zapatero needed the support of other minorities, including the ERC, to govern.[70]

The debate in the Catalan parliament turned into a competition between CiU and ERC to assert themselves as the most nationalist party.[71] In September 2005, the final draft included some controversial clauses, including the demand for an economic pact based on the Basque model, the definition of Catalonia as a nation, the contention that Catalonia's powers of self-government emanated from the Catalan people and not the Spanish Constitution, and a demand for greater control over taxation, immigration, and judicial affairs. This maximalist plan sounded alarm bells in Madrid. Once before the *Cortes*, it was attacked not only by the PP but also by many Socialists. A committee led by Alfonso Guerra finally agreed to a watered-down version that included a preamble that avoided calling Catalonia a nation, but recognized its desire to be called so, and offered a greater share of the taxes raised in the region but rejected the existence of an independent tax agency. The impasse was finally overcome when an agreement was reached between Zapatero and the new CiU leader, Artur Mas, behind the back of the Catalan government.[72] This was considered a slap in the face by Maragall and the ERC refused to back it. In November 2006, Maragall was replaced by José Montilla. Born in Extremadura, he was the first non-ethnic Catalan president of the *Generalitat*.[73] Marta Ferrusola, Pujol's wife, commented that Montilla was 'an Andalusian who could not speak Catalan properly'.[74]

In June 2006, in a referendum in Catalonia, 74 percent voted in favour of the Statute and 21 percent against – the proportion abstaining, however, was high at 50.6 percent, suggesting many were indifferent or tired of a process that had monopolized political debate for two years. Yet, the saga was not over. The PP conducted a vociferous campaign across Spain with apocalyptic slogans such as *España se rompe* ('Spain is breaking up'), calling for a boycott of Catalan products, collecting signatures against the Statute, and asking the Constitutional Court to intervene. However, it did not protest the Andalusian Statute, which largely mirrored the Catalonian one.[75] On 28 June 2010, after more than four years of deliberations, the Constitutional Court rewrote 14 articles that mostly related to the primacy of Catalan as the vehicular language of that region and the extension of autonomous judicial and economic powers. It also stressed that the term 'nation' had no legal standing.[76]

It was not the judicial changes (only a small number of the 227 articles were amended) but the PP's old-fashioned centralist campaign and the long delay in the Constitutional Court's decision that dismayed many Catalans. Indeed, it contributed to the false but largely felt perception that it was a diminution of their self-government. Nationalists claimed it was an attack on Catalan identity and a judicial assault on a political agreement backed by a referendum.[77] Over 400,000 people (one million according to the organizers) gathered on the streets of Barcelona to demonstrate, including most current and former political dignitaries. And for the first time, flags of independence (*Estelada*) created in 1917 after the Cuban model were on view.[78] As a sign of the polarization, Montilla was accused of *botifler*[79] and forced to abandon the march.[80]

Corruption is the last of the fateful Cs. Nepotism, cronyism, and widespread immorality were inherent to Restoration and Francoist politics. They did not disappear with the arrival of democracy. The vital difference is that today neither the rule of law nor public opinion can be ignored. Politicians' illegal activities were exposed before, as freedom of the press existed in Restoration times. Yet, it is only now that they are indicted and sometimes jailed. Furthermore, in a democracy, political parties depend on genuine popular support, and thus any misdeeds are likely to be punished at the polls.

The historical tolerance in southern Europe towards corrupt practices ceased when the economic bubble burst.[81] In turn, increasing cynicism towards the political class increased exponentially. A good deal of the population believes that politicians are parasites who abuse their power to enjoy the spoils of office. Once exposed, they rarely resign or are forced to do so. Their colleagues normally close ranks and engage in a blame game with the opposition. It is staggering how many of them stand for election with charges still pending. Of course, they do not represent a constituency. Parties present lists for each electoral district containing as many names as seats are available. The candidates depend on being chosen by local or national officials. Therefore, dissent is almost unheard of, since deputies vote as directed. All must toe the line or risk being deselected at the next election. Conformism tends to be the norm. This, in turn, devalues parliament as a debating chamber.[82]

When a wave of breathtaking scandals exploded during the financial crisis, they acquired a particular political dimension. Most were related to regional governments and the construction boom.[83] Entrepreneurs paid vast sums to local authorities in return for licences to build. By 2010, more than 150 town halls were under investigation for fiscal fraud, money laundering, and acceptance of bribes. According to opinion polls, corruption became the second biggest concern after unemployment.[84]

The so-called *Gürtel* affair was the most devastating scandal associated with the PP. It was named after one of its main suspects, the construction mogul, Francisco Correa (Correa means belt in English and *Gürtel* in German). It came to public attention in 2009 when two whistleblowers confirmed that in the PP's regional strongholds of Madrid and Valencia, there existed a vast network of influence peddling, tax fraud, money laundering, and embezzlement of public funds, involving both entrepreneurs and politicians.[85]

In the following years, PP dignitaries from these two regions were indicted for different financial crimes. A by-product of the investigation was the discovery, in 2013, that one of those implicated, Luis Bárcenas, a former PP treasurer, possessed a secret Swiss bank account containing millions of euros. Extracts of Bárcenas' handwritten notes, released by *El País*, revealed that he oversaw a parallel bookkeeping system, lasting from 1999 to 2009 at least, to funnel undeclared cash donations into a slush fund to finance party activities and boost the salaries of senior PP members, including allegedly Rajoy. The latter's reputation was further stained when *El Mundo* published text messages that he had sent to Bárcenas. One of them said, 'Luis, be strong'.[86] In May 2018, 29 PP politicians and businessmen were convicted. Correa and Bárcenas received 51 and 33 years, respectively. The court also ruled that the PP had benefited from the racket and the party was fined €245,000. This led to the PSOE tabling a vote of no-confidence the following month.[87] Known for his bone-dry sense of humour, Rajoy also revealed an unparalleled level of apathy. A great believer in the maxim that with time all problems can be solved, he was naturally inclined to avoid mistakes by doing nothing.[88] The end of his premiership was underwhelming, to say the least. On 31 May 2018, confronted with a vote of no-confidence that he appeared poised to lose, the socialist leader Pedro Sánchez offered him the alternative of resigning and announcing new elections. Rajoy declined. Yet, instead of fighting for his record, he simply took advantage of the lunch recess to flee with his lackeys to a nearby restaurant where he drowned his sorrows until late in the evening. He never returned to the *Cortes*.[89]

The most harmful affair for the PSOE was that of the ERES, or *expedientes de regulación de empleo* ('employment contract severance'), in Andalusia, a socialist stronghold. It surfaced in 2011 when an investigation revealed that leading regional officials had set up a fraudulent scheme to syphon off vast amounts of money allegedly destined to help jobless workers. The final sum was about €1 billion.[90] This led to 26 senior PSOE officials being indicted and sentenced to prison. In 2019, two former presidents, Manuel Chaves and José Antonio Griñán, were tried and sentenced to 9 years of political disqualification and 6 years of jail and 15 years of disqualification, respectively.[91]

In Catalonia, scandals embroiled the CiU. The most important was the so-called 3 percent affair, which first surfaced in 2005 when President

Maragall mentioned it in the Catalan parliament. This was allegedly the amount that CiU officials charged to companies in exchange for the allocation of public work contracts. In 2018, twelve people were convicted, including two former CiU treasurers, Fèlix Millet and Daniel Osàcar.[92] María Victoria Álvarez, the ex-lover of Pujol's eldest son, confessed that the family held secret accounts in Andorra. To pre-empt an inquiry, Pujol confessed in July 2014 that for over 30 years, including 23 of them as president of the *Generalitat*, he had maintained foreign bank accounts to avoid paying tax on the inheritance from his father. The investigation concluded that the family had cashed in on his power to amass a vast fortune that had been hidden in Andorra and offshore accounts. In April 2021, the judicial authorities charged Pujol, his wife, Marta Ferrusola, and their seven children, with being a criminal organization at the centre of influence peddling, tax evasion, and money laundering.[93]

Corruption also tarnished the credibility of the highest institution of the state, the monarchy. Before the economic crisis, King Juan Carlos was very popular. Even his well-known extra-marital affairs could not tarnish him. However, several shady incidents were to rock the royal family. The first was the so-called Nóos, named after the non-profit foundation created by the king's son-in-law, Iñaki Urdangarín, a former handball star married to the *Infanta* Cristina. In 2011, he and his partner Diego Torres were accused of raising vast amounts of money from diverse public administrations to allegedly organize charity and sporting events. Instead, the proceedings had been syphoned off to shadow companies to fund their lavish lifestyles. In 2016, nine people were tried, accused of fraud and tax evasion, including Urdangarín and his wife. The prosecution argued that the *Infanta* could not have been ignorant of her husband's activities. Cristina was acquitted but Urdangarín was sentenced to six years and three months of jail and fined €512,000.[94]

In April 2012, while the Nóos affair was still ongoing, Juan Carlos' reputation suffered a serious setback. It was revealed that he had been injured and needed an urgent hip operation during a safari in Botswana. Pictures of Juan Carlos posing next to a dead elephant caused a storm of anger from pro-animal activists and fuelled anti-monarchist feelings. Many Spaniards were dumbfounded that the monarch could be enjoying a luxury holiday while people were faced with austerity and soaring unemployment. Further revelations suggested that his lover, the German-Danish entrepreneur Corinna zu Sayn-Wittgenstein-Sayn, had arranged and accompanied him on the hunting trip.[95] She was also rumoured to have been the king's go-between for business deals between Spanish and Saudi companies for which lucrative commissions were forthcoming. In June 2014, Juan Carlos chose to abdicate in favour of his son Felipe (VI) to save the monarchy. Besieged by revelations of secret accounts and tax evasion from kickbacks, he fled the country and settled in Abu Dhabi. In March 2022, prosecutors dropped the investigation, alleging the improbability of proving the charges.

The Democratic Transition under Attack

The combination of a devastating economic crisis and corruption scandals proved the perfect storm. There was a certain feeling of déjà vu with 1898. Nearly 120 years later, new forces from different sides of the political spectrum pursued substantial reform or even destruction of the transition settlement. However, once again, the current *turno pacífico* and the monarchy seem to have managed to weather the challenge.

On Sunday, 15 May 2011, following the pattern adopted by movements such as Occupy Wall Street, a civil association called *Democracia Real Ya* (Real Democracy Now) organized a demonstration to highlight the democratic deficit that allowed austerity policies to shatter people's lives. Nobody could have imagined that this was the beginning of a social movement that would adopt the name 15-M, due to the date of its birth, and mobilize some 3.5 million people in 2011 alone. Those who heeded the call to demonstrate their anger were *Los Indignados* (the Outraged). They were mostly Spanish youth with no prospects of finding a decent job or home, in spite of their excellent educational background, owing to a society ravaged by savage public spending cuts and evictions. Feeling cheated by a political class that appeared anchored in endemic corruption, they wanted a real democracy to represent them and rejected the austerity policies hatched between politicians and bankers. They had not only failed to protect citizens against the worst effects of the crisis but also forced them to assume the losses by capitalist speculation. When the demonstration ended in Madrid's central square, *Puerta del Sol*, many decided to turn it into a campsite. The attempt by the police to evict them had the opposite effect, as thousands turned up to defend the camp. By 18 May, the occupation had spread to 52 cities. This leaderless movement was kept alive due to social media. It was apolitical and inclusive, and thus rejected all flags and partisan banners.[96] In June, the demonstrators voted to dismantle the camps. The next phase was the creation of popular assemblies that would meet regularly in the squares while continuing to spread their message across city neighbourhoods.[97]

A significant by-product of this movement was the collective *15MpaRato*, created in 2012, on the anniversary of 15-M. It was named after Rodrigo Rato, Aznar's minister of economy and later chairman of the International Monetary Fund (2004–2007) and president of *Bankia* (2010–2012). That collective brought a lawsuit against the executives of *Caja Madrid*, Spain's oldest building society, and *Bankia*, the new bank that had resulted from the merger of *Caja Madrid* with six other building societies. Consequently, 64 politicians and bankers were charged with having defrauded over €2 billion from thousands of investors through forgery, misleading information, and embezzlement. Rato was sentenced to four and a half years' imprisonment. Related to this affair was the 2014 Black Card Scandal, concerning the issue of credit cards to *Bankia*'s directors and used for scandalous personal expenses and tax evasion.[98]

In late May, the *indignados* were dislodged from Barcelona's central square (*Plaça de Catalunya*) by the *Mossos* (local constabulary) after a veritable pitched battle that left 121 injured. As a response, on 15 June, they laid siege to the Catalan parliament. There were unprecedented scenes when some deputies trying to enter the chamber on foot were booed and pushed. To avoid the angry crowds, Artur Mas and other politicians arrived by helicopter.[99]

The Catalan Challenge: *El Procés*

Nobody expected that Mas would accomplish such a radical transformation of his persona in less than a year following the rowdy scenes outside the Catalan parliament. Indeed, from being the target of popular anger, he managed to transform himself into the quasi-messianic leader of the *Procés* (Independence Process) that was to rock Spain, dominate its media, and shape its politics.

On 27 October 2017, the Catalan parliament proclaimed independence. It is widely believed to have been the third time in 100 years; in fact, this is not exactly true. Declaring the independence of Catalonia constituted extraordinary news.[100] When the monarchy imploded in April 1931, Maciá rushed to announce the Catalan Republic but also called upon the rest of Spain to form a confederate state. He backtracked when a delegation from Madrid promised that the *Cortes* would approve legislation to grant Catalan home rule. In October 1934, Companys proclaimed 'the establishment of a Catalan State within the Spanish Federal Republic'. Yet, this was part of a wider revolutionary movement that was rapidly crushed.

Non-nationalist Catalan authors, baffled by the sudden upsurge of separatism in the region, felt like they were living in a madhouse and described el *Procés* as living in a madhouse or a Kafkaesque tale.[101] It was puzzling to them that the secessionist movement in Catalonia, which had never been an independent nation or a colony, acquired mass support in 2017 when Spain was recognized as a leading democracy above countries such as France and the United States[102] and one of the most decentralized nations in the world.[103] Catalonia enjoys a far greater degree of autonomy than during the Second Republic or that of federal systems, such as those of the German *Länders* or the US states. Moreover, Catalan wealth comes largely from exporting products to the rest of Spain: it sells more to Aragón than France, more to Valencia than the UK, and more to Madrid than the USA.[104]

It also seems baffling that secessionism erupted in Catalonia when, ironically, the Basque Country was becoming an oasis of peace. The PNV and CiU seemed to have reversed roles: the *Lehendakari*, Íñigo Urkullu, in power since 2012, abandoned Ibarretxe's adventurism.[105] Before the dangers of global financial and geopolitical instability, the PNV put its territorial demands on the backburner and pragmatically backed central administrations in exchange for concessions. In contrast, Catalan nationalists seemed bent on a strategy of confrontation with the state.

The roots of the *desencuentro* ('falling out') or failed *encaje* ('fit') between regional nationalists and the centre lay, of course, in the nature of the former: for nationalists, their ultimate objective is, logically, to have their own nation-state. With the *estado de las autonomías*, the government sought to solve the sensitive issue of the relationship between the centre and the regions. However, Catalan and Basque nationalists regarded it as a façade to avoid acknowledging the existence of different nations within the state and sharing sovereignty with them. To make matters worse, the fathers of the Constitution planted the seeds of a problem for the future: the open-ended nature of the decentralization process meant there was no demarcation of powers. Consequently, regional forces, well represented in the *Cortes* due to *d'Hondt* Law, have been pivotal for the governability of the country. In turn, this has enabled them to keep demanding further powers, which has helped them build parallel state structures.[106]

The *estado de las autonomías* meant that the local governments filled the role left by the withdrawal of the centre. Yet, the main national parties have revealed a staggering level of naivety vis-à-vis the obvious disloyalty of their alleged partners. A wake-up call should have been the declaration of Barcelona, in July 1998, when Catalan, Basque, and Galician nationalists referred to the lack of legal-political recognition of their identity, including being sovereign nations.[107] For them, democracy and self-government were not the end of the voyage, but instead a step towards independence.[108]

The mass enthusiasm and ongoing support for Catalan secessionism is undeniable, and seems to indicate the existence of a bottom-up movement that has forced the political class to act. Although presented as a purely grassroots movement that caught Mas by surprise, the reality is much more nuanced. Indeed, nobody has forced hundreds of thousands of Catalans to attend the annual *Diada* (Catalonia's national day) or other demonstrations to demand independence with a faith of almost millenarian proportions.[109] Still, nation-building and identity formation in Catalonia over the decades suggests that top-down, elite-led activity has preceded and influenced an apparently popular movement.[110]

Indeed, the far-reaching exercise in social engineering behind *el Procés* should be a fascinating subject of future study. Politicians have shaped the agenda and controlled every phase of the pro-independence roadmap. Clara Ponsatí, a member of the *Generalitat* that proclaimed independence, compared *el Procés* to a poker game: 'it was a bluff and we lost'.[111] Having become victims of their own self-deception, when the central government acted, the secessionist leaders offered no resistance.

In fact, many Catalans did not embrace secessionism out of the blue. To cross the Rubicon, Julius Caesar had first to lead his legions across Gaul.[112] *El Procés* could not have happened without its path being paved during Pujol's long term in office (1980–2003).[113] By excelling at obtaining concessions through bargaining, the so-called *Peix al cove* ('bird in hand'), Pujol, who never embraced a clear-cut secessionist stance, secured crucial jurisdiction over policing, transport, health, public works, and education. However, these step-by-step concessions were only instalments in the objective of *Fer Patria*, or laying the foundations of a nation-state.[114] A crucial initiative in that direction was the 1983 Law of Linguistic Normalization. Indeed, what had first been advocated as the defence of the weaker Catalan language gradually became the imposition of linguistic uniformity and the practical disappearance of Castilian Spanish in public life, despite being the co-official language according to the Constitution and the Catalan Statute. In 1997, new legislation enshrined Catalan as the only language for public education.[115]

In 1990, *El País* and other newspapers revealed the existence of 'Programme 2000': a roadmap to awaken Catalan national consciousness through the appointment of nationalist-minded people in all the key sectors of civil society, including the media – in particular, the public-owned radio (*Radio Catalunya*) and television (TV3) stations – the education system, the commercial world, sporting and cultural organizations.[116] The historian Álvarez Junco noted how the invented narrative that has driven the secessionist movement is mainly facilitated by public television and schools, where the existence of a Catalan nation is explained in terms of good and evil or the struggle of a millenary nation against an oppressive Spain.[117] This emphasis on the unique nature of Catalan culture has led to mindboggling outcomes such as the financing of the *Institut de Nova Historia* (Institute of New History), which has claimed that Christopher Columbus, Miguel de Cervantes, Leonardo da Vinci, and even William Shakespeare were all Catalans.[118]

Some believe that the turning point for the upsurge of Catalan separatism occurred in July 2010, when the Constitutional Court's ruling on the statute frustrated Catalan hopes that Spain could become a genuine multinational state. Yet, bridges seemed to have been mended after the return to power of two conservative administrations, the CiU headed by Mas (December 2010) and the PP under Rajoy (November 2011). Mas had his budget approved thanks to the votes of the Catalan PP. In fact, much more important was the advent of the global crisis. The cocktail of corruption scandals and financial distress persuaded many Catalans to revolt against an inefficient state that, furthermore, had revealed disdain for their feelings of identity.[119] Still, there would have been no *Procés* without Mas' abrupt about-turn. Proving to be a versatile politician, he adjusted his position to maximize the gains but ultimately failed. Being a neo-liberal in economics, he had no qualms in decreeing harsh austerity measures to confront the economic crisis. With the recession worsening, Catalonia became the highest indebted region and faced bankruptcy. His administration increasingly depended on loans from Madrid that came with stringent budgetary measures imposed by the deficit targets set by the EU. This intensified long-standing resentment over the vexing issue of Catalonia's contribution to a fiscal system that redistributed tax revenues to poorer regions.[120]

On 11 September 2012, over 600,000 people marched in the annual *Diada* under the overtly pro-independence slogan, 'Catalonia: A New State in Europe!' They carried the separatist *Estelada* instead of *la Senyera*, the traditional Catalan flag.[121] Two weeks later, Mas called elections for 25 November, two years ahead of schedule. For the first time, the CiU based its electoral manifesto around the question of sovereignty. Between the *Diada* and the summoning of elections, Mas had travelled to Madrid to demand a new fiscal pact but encountered Rajoy's flat rejection. Given Spain's dire situation, the only thing that the Spanish prime minister could redistribute was misery.[122]

Facing a situation of social revolt, as the siege of the parliament revealed, and anticipating the emergence of a myriad of scandals related to the CiU, Mas sought to square the circle by riding the separatist bandwagon. In the event, he managed to reinvent himself as the Messiah of a crusade for national liberation. Indeed, he sought to deflect responsibility for his unpopular economic measures by resorting to the well-known formula of an external foe, Spain.[123] In the process, Mas undertook a 180-degree political transformation, going from being an austerity-prone conservative politician to a street protester.[124] He was the first to mention and describe, in March 2012, the word *Procés* as a journey towards a new Ithaca.[125] One of his ministers, Santiago Vila, confessed that without the secessionist narrative, the *Generalitat* would have faced major social upheaval given the scope of the austerity measures.[126] However, after opening Pandora's Box, Mas found that it was impossible to backtrack and gradually became hostage to more radical forces. Ultimately, *el Procés* was to destroy his political career and the CiU's political hegemony as well as produce a badly fractured society.[127]

Little was left to chance. The two organizations behind the popular mobilization, *Òmnium Cultural* and *L'Assemblea Nacional Catalana* (ANC),[128] received a steady flow of public money.[129] Their leadership emanates from the nationalist political class. Local television and radio stations provided ample coverage and advertised with fanfare, months in advance, the *Diada* and other secessionist displays.[130] Experts in communication designed every detail (symbols, choreography, etc.) to produce a gigantic demonstration of willpower – civic, festive, and aesthetically sensational.[131] Such a grandiose spectacle was to give it popular legitimacy. In turn, Madrid's silence would lead to its discredit and entice Brussels to intervene and force a referendum.[132]

Catalan secessionism won by a landslide in the propaganda war. Whereas Madrid appeared to respond badly and much too late to the challenge, the *Generalitat* promoted an effective narrative based on a mixture of victimization and hope.[133] The Catalan media, especially TV3 and Radio Catalunya, offered an image of a united Catalonia in its pursuit of freedom. They presented the bid for independence as the story of a prosperous

European-looking Catalonia that aspired to obtain, through impeccable democratic procedures, the people's right to choose their future. In contrast, the state was cast as still anchored in Franco's times, refusing to settle the issue in a civilized way, by authorizing a referendum, unlike Britain allowing Scotland to vote.[134]

El Procés represented the local version of a series of unprecedented events marked by anti-establishment sentiment combined with a xenophobic form of nationalism: the Scottish referendum, Brexit, Donald Trump's victory in the US presidential elections, the upsurge of populist and Europhobe parties across Europe.[135] It echoed those grievances used by the Brexit campaign, Flemish nationalists, and the Italian *Lega Nord*:[136] Spain's fiscal plundering of Catalonia ('Spain robs us') – an annual figure of €16 billion was cited (effectively debunked by Josep Borrell, the Catalan socialist who in 2019 became the EU's High Commissioner for Foreign Affairs);[137] and 'taking back control' or the right to decide democratically (a euphemism for self-determination) the future.[138]

Some have dubbed *el Procés* a postmodern coup, or an assault on the state, ambiguous and not overtly violent, so that, when necessary, it could be denied by its protagonists by claiming the symbolic nature of their actions. Yet, that ambiguity also served to portray symbolism as facts.[139] Others have described the Catalan separatist movement as a revolution of the rich dressed up as a progressive cause. It was a major challenge to a recognized liberal democracy from a wealthy region whose per capita income was over €25,000. A Catalan humourist highlighted the paradox that the rich in Catalonia claimed to be oppressed.[140] Indeed, most of its adherents live in the wealthiest quarters. They follow the news through public regional media and Catalan is their dominant language.[141] They are the socially conservative constituency who used to vote for CiU: the rural hinterland, the urban managerial classes, and the bureaucracy linked to the *Generalitat*.

Sandrine Morel, *Le Monde*'s correspondent in Spain, noted that while the *Generalitat* assiduously courted foreign journalists and even offered to buy advertising space in exchange for favourable editorials, Madrid ignored them in the belief that the less information on the subject the better.[142] Consequently, it was easy to project a sole perspective on the matter, as these journalists were often unfamiliar with Spanish politics. The Catalan government spent some €417 million in its international campaign to promote independence, including the establishment of *DiploCat* (Catalan Diplomacy) and the opening of embassies in several countries.[143] Despite being faced with a movement that could mobilize over a million people, Rajoy's response was dumbfounding. He dismissed *el Procés* as a *souflée* that would eventually vanish once the economy improved. It never crossed his mind to make the case for better together. Thus, he fell back on his favourite solution: to do nothing except recite the law and threaten judicial action if the constitution was transgressed.[144]

Expecting an overwhelming majority, Mas – who had inundated Catalonia with posters of himself opening widely his arms as a new Messiah – suffered a serious setback in the elections of November 2012, losing 12 seats (down from 62 to 50 out of a total of 130). He chose to double down on the challenge. To stay in power, he required the support of the ERC, a party that had genuinely embraced independence long before, and had obtained 21 deputies, 11 more than in the previous contest.[145] After gaining backing in the Catalan parliament for the ambiguous formula of 'the right to decide', he called for a referendum on self-determination. When in April 2014, as expected, the *Cortes* voted against it and the Constitutional Court declared it illegal, Mas simply ignored them. To avoid penal prosecution for disobedience, he tried to present it as a non-binding popular consultation organized by volunteers. In November, residents in Catalonia over 16 years of age, including foreigners, were invited to answer a double question: Should Catalonia be a state? And if yes, should that state be independent?[146]

The referendum was conducted in a festive atmosphere. There were instances, some of which were filmed, of people voting several times in places that only had ballots favourable to secession. According to the *Generalitat*'s data, 80.76 percent answered 'yes' to both questions. Yet, their own intelligence recognized that less than 35 percent of the electorate voted.[147] In March 2017, Mas' defiance led to his being tried with two of his ministers and sentenced to two years of political disqualification and a fine of €36,500.[148]

Undeterred by the lack of a clear secessionist majority, Mas chose again to raise the stakes: a snap election in September 2015 with the character of a plebiscite.[149] He managed to concoct a temporary coalition of all the pro-independence forces on a single platform called *Junts Pel Si* ('*Junts*, Together for Yes'), except for the *Candidatura d'Unitat Popular* (CUP, Popular Unity Candidacy), an assembly-based organization, founded in 1991, whose programme combines fierce anti-capitalism and the struggle for the independence of the so-called Catalan countries (Catalonia, Valencia, and the Balearic Islands). *Junts*' manifesto listed just one item, the right to self-determination. In the process, the CiU imploded when, in June 2015, its junior partner UDC broke away after voting by a narrow minority to reject the secessionist roadmap.[150] In July 2016, tarnished by corruption scandals, Mas presided over the re-foundation of his party now to be called *Partit Demòcrata Europeu Català* (PDeCAT, Catalan European Democratic Party).[151]

The plebiscitary elections fell short of expectations. The secessionist forces did not reach 48 percent of the vote: *Junts* won 39.5 percent (62 deputies, the same that the CiU alone had in 2010) and the CUP 8.2 percent (10 deputies). Still, they had a majority in the chamber given that the Catalan electoral system rewards the rural over the metropolitan vote.[152] To remain in office, *Junts* needed to rely on the CUP, which, in turn, was able to influence the agenda. Its first price was Mas' head, a leader tainted by his party's scandals and record of spending cuts. He was replaced by a new figure of consensus, Carles Puigdemont, the relatively unknown CiU mayor of Girona.[153]

Puigdemont declared that his period in office would constitute a post-autonomist or pre-secessionist phase. The final rupture with Spain would occur after a second and definitive referendum. In the summer of 2017, Puigdemont reshuffled his cabinet. All the ministers had to sign a pact committing themselves to hold the referendum regardless.[154] On 6 September, the Catalan government finally crossed the Rubicon: it introduced, amidst acrimonious scenes and the symbolic departure of almost half of the deputies, the so-called 'laws of disconnection', even though they were not on the day's agenda and against the advice of the chamber's own legal advisers. They affirmed Catalan sovereignty and thus its prevalence over any legislation emanating from Spain. Catalan lawmakers conferred upon themselves the prerogative to organize a referendum on 1 October. The Constitutional Court suspended it automatically.[155] It was not even legal according to Catalonia's Statute of Autonomy, which requires a two-thirds majority for its modification. Eva Granados, the socialist spokesperson in the Catalan parliament, noted that the secessionists had not just exacerbated social tensions but also broken the constitutional contract.[156]

A collision with Madrid was nigh. *El Procés*' previous atmosphere of carnival gave way to the much darker xenophobic side of nationalism: the destruction of the windows of non-secessionist parties, violent graffiti, threats, *escraches* (surrounding the homes of enemies while proffering insults and blowing horns and whistles), and so on.[157] Anyone who opposed the *Procés* was called a *botifler*. This included left-wing Catalan figures such as the songwriter Joan Manuel Serrat, the film director Isabel Coixet, and the novelist Javier Cercas.[158] Awakening to the scope of the defiance, Rajoy reinforced the national police presence in Catalonia and promised that the referendum would not take place.[159] Amidst a fast-deteriorating situation, the deployment of police agents to search the Catalan Department of Economy on 20 September led to one of the most precarious moments. In a matter of minutes, some 40,000 people, alerted by social media, laid siege to the building. Atop the roofs of vandalized police cars, the leaders of ANC and Òmnium, Jordi Sànchez and Jordi Cuixart, harangued the angry crowd with megaphones. The *Mossos* managed to extricate the police officers in the early hours of the morning. Others, including a court clerk, made their escape across the roof of the building.[160] On 16 October, Sànchez and Cuixart were charged with rebellion and jailed.[161]

Sunday 1 October constituted a massive propaganda coup for the secessionist movement. The referendum went ahead despite Rajoy's promise. The organizers had seized the voting centres by having groups of supporters, in some cases three generations of the same family, camp inside the entire weekend.[162] Because of the passivity of most *Mossos*, neighbours were able to transport the hidden ballot boxes in the early hours of the morning. An overwhelmed Rajoy declared on television that the referendum had been successfully halted while calling out the national police to stop it. The outcome was not at all good for Spain's image. The entire world witnessed how policemen attempted to confiscate the ballot boxes by raiding polling stations and beating protesters.[163] Images of the heavy-handed repression of voters by the Spanish police dented the country's democratic credentials. The illegal nature of the referendum did not matter anymore; nor did its lack of impartial scrutiny (some images revealed ballot boxes already packed with votes) or the gross distortion of reality (claims that 900 people had been hospitalized and photos of alleged police violence that were later found to be from such distant places as Chile).

The *Generalitat* had declared that it was enough to win the referendum by a single vote. In the event, it claimed to have received 90 percent of the vote – although only 43 percent of the electorate turned out to vote. This relatively low turnout, even according to the secessionists' scrutiny, suggested that the majority stayed at home.[164] Notwithstanding the euphoria of the moment, *el Procés* began to unravel during the following days.

On 10 October, in a televised address from the Catalan parliament, Puigdemont affirmed that despite police violence, holding the referendum had earned Catalonia the right to be a sovereign republic. Yet, a few seconds later he proposed to suspend the declaration of independence and called on Madrid to enter negotiations. The pro-independence deputies then signed a symbolic declaration of independence with no legal effect.[165] During the following two weeks, Madrid and the *Generalitat* engaged in a dialogue of the deaf: Rajoy kept asking if independence had been declared while Puigdemont called for international mediation in negotiations.

Several key events revealed to the secessionist leaders that they were entering a cul-de-sac. Madrid showed that it was prepared to use repression to quell the secession. At the same time, the profusion of national flags and symbols in windows and balconies across the country indicated the emergence of Spanish nationalism with unpredictable consequences.[166] Furthermore, on 3 October, Felipe VI delivered an unusually strongly worded televised address. He sought to reassure the non-secessionist part of the population in Catalonia while reminding the pro-independence leaders that their illegal actions were threatening social coexistence and breaking the most elementary democratic rules enshrined in the Constitution.[167] While many Catalans showed their fury at a monarch who failed to mention the violence of 1 October, others felt emboldened. On 8 October, one million people took to the streets of Barcelona, under the slogan 'let's recover our common sense' to demonstrate their opposition to independence. They were addressed, among others, by Borrell, the Barcelona-based Peruvian Nobel Prize for Literature winner Mario Vargas Llosa, and the former secretary of the PCE (1998–2009) Francisco Frutos, who declared himself proud to be a *botifler*.[168] This was a major setback to the narrative of a united people in their quest for sovereignty, since it revealed that at least half of the population was prepared to fight back.[169]

Finally, *el Procés* also suffered two major blows. In the diplomatic realm, practically the entire world turned down Catalan approaches for mediation and declared its support for Spain's unity.[170] Economically, instead of the fantastic boom promised by the secessionists, there was a mass exodus of both capital and hundreds of businesses, including the two Catalan Banks (*Caixa* and *Sabadell*). The official data from the College of Registrars revealed that in the week following the referendum, the flight of companies reached the extraordinary figure of 544, and in one year, 2,344. They mostly moved their headquarters to Madrid, Valencia, and Aragón.[171]

Having gone as far as it had, the *Generalitat* could not back down for fear of a backlash from its hundreds of thousands of followers. Puigdemont appeared to have accepted the last-minute mediation of Urkullu, who advised him to call new elections. Yet, he failed to do so after being lambasted as a traitor.[172] On 27 October, in a half-empty Catalan parliament, 70 deputies (a further two abstained) proclaimed independence. This was a civilian *pronunciamiento*.[173] However, in contrast to the jubilant CUP deputies, those from *Junts* looked as if they were staring into the abyss.[174] Almost immediately, with the support of the PP, the PSOE, and *Ciudadanos*, the Senate voted to activate Article 155 of the Constitution that authorized Madrid to suspend any region's autonomy when the Constitution was violated. Rajoy dissolved the Catalan government and chamber and imposed direct rule. He also accused the *Generalitat* ministers of rebellion and embezzlement of public funds. On 30 October, Puigdemont and five of his ministers appeared in Belgium, where they still reside, to avoid extradition. The others were prosecuted and sentenced to different prison terms for sedition.[175] Mas' journey to Ithaca lay in ruins. However, although the hopes for independence were quelled when its leaders were jailed or fled abroad, *el Procés* was far from over. It had just entered a new phase whose outcome remains difficult to predict.

Rajoy's application of Article 155 surprised everyone. Instead of a long spell of central control, he called for a snap election three months later to counter the expected secessionist victimization rhetoric.[176] Their parties were not outlawed but encouraged to participate. Catalan public media was allowed to broadcast without hindrance. In parts of Catalonia, graffiti and yellow ribbons began to occupy public and neutral spaces to express solidarity with the jailed or exiled leaders. They symbolized territory markers and defiance of the state. This led to confrontation when groups of people proceeded to remove them.[177]

The elections to the Catalan parliament of December 2017 saw the highest popular vote ever (79 percent). Once again, the secessionist parties obtained 47.5 percent of the vote, which ensured them a majority in parliament, even though the most voted for party had been the anti-nationalist *Ciudadanos*.[178] This exposed a society divided both in geographic and economic terms. Catalan humourists joked that the so-called *Tabarnia* should have the right to decide and separate from *Tractoria*. *Tabarnia* refers to that small but most densely populated urban and coastal strip of Barcelona, including its metropolitan belt, to the city of Tarragona. This is a cosmopolitan area that contains a high percentage of mostly Spanish speakers who vote non-nationalist.[179] Albert Boadella, a well-known theatre director persecuted by the Franco regime and later self-exiled to Madrid after the backlash produced by one of his plays criticizing Pujol, was declared its virtual president.[180] They called *Tractoria* (given the abundance of tractors in the countryside) the pro-independence territory that comprises the hinterland towns and villages, including the entire provinces of Lleida and Girona. They coincide remarkably well with the old Carlist strongholds.[181]

In May 2018, after months of wrangling between the CUP, ERC, and *Junts Per Catalunya* (the coalition that included PDeCAT, headed by Puigdemont), Quim Torra, a lieutenant of the exiled leader in Brussels, was elected president of the *Generalitat*, with Pere Aragonès, from ERC, as his deputy. Torra elicited strong criticism due to him being the author of several xenophobic essays in which he described Castilian Spanish speakers in Catalonia as scavengers, hyenas, and vipers.[182] Without crossing the line that could trigger the reimposition of Article 155, he adopted a stance of permanent defiance, including sympathy for street demonstrations that occasionally turned into riots and occupations of the airport and train stations. The most violent displays coincided with the sentencing of the secessionist leaders in October 2019.[183] Between October 2017 and July 2018, 12 people had been tried by Spain's Supreme Court, including the previous Catalan vice president, Oriol Junqueras, most cabinet ministers, as well as the activists Jordi Sánchez and Jordi Turull, leaders of the *Òmnium Cultural* and ANC respectively, and the former Speaker of the Catalan parliament, Carme Forcadell. They were charged with organizing the celebration in 2017 of an independence referendum after being declared illegal by Spain's Constitutional Court, the passing of laws to override the Spanish Constitution, and declaring independence (on 27 October 2017). The trial proceedings officially ended on 12 June 2019 and the verdict made public four months later. Nine of the accused received prison sentences for the crimes of sedition, four of whom were also found guilty of misuse of public funds. Their sentences ranged from 9 to 13 years. The remaining three accused were found guilty of disobedience and were sentenced to pay a fine but received no prison term. The court dismissed the charges of rebellion.[184]

In September 2020, Torra was ousted after the Supreme Court confirmed his charges of disobedience due to his refusal to obey the Central Electoral Board to remove partisan symbols from public buildings during the national elections of the previous year.[185] Torra was replaced by Aragonés, who retained his post after the regional elections of February 2021 that were won by the PSC. The secessionists reversed roles, as the ERC beat *Junts* to third place, but together they formed a government. The fact that this election had the lowest turnout ever (51.2 percent), unlike the two highly charged previous contests – 77.4 percent in 2015 and 79.09 percent in 2017 – might indicate that the exultation generated by *el Procés* might be fading.[186]

Challenge in Madrid: The Emergence of New Parties

At the same time as the pro-independence upsurge in Catalonia, the global economic crisis led to the emergence of national parties, from across the political spectrum, to challenge the bipartisan grip of power held by the PSOE and the PP. Initially, the two strongest challengers were *Podemos* ('We Can') and *Ciudadanos* ('Citizens'), both of which appeared to offer hope and political regeneration. They expressed the popular malaise resulting from the financial upheaval and corruption scandals and were the local version of a phenomenon that spread throughout Europe. Yet, unlike France or Italy, they failed to dislodge Spain's two dominant forces from power. Nevertheless, they put an end to the smooth functioning of Spain's modern *turno pacífico*.

Born out of the 15-M movement, *Podemos* was an assembly-type organization founded in January 2014 by political scientists from Madrid University. It sought to channel the popular discontent against what they dubbed the *casta* or the socio-politically dominant class that was responsible for the crisis.[187] Borrowed from Barack Obama's electoral slogan – 'We Can' – *Podemos* was intended to offer a message of hope. Its programme was anti-monarchist, anti-capitalist, feminist, and federalist to the extent of accepting the right to regional self-determination.[188] *Podemos* burst onto the political scene in the European elections of May 2014, returning five deputies, having obtained over 5 million votes. Consolidation was achieved in the municipal elections of October of that year. Forming alliances with diverse local alternatives, *Podemos* and its partners shocked the establishment. They seized control of the town halls of several cities, including Madrid (Manuela Carmena, an independent judge heading a left-wing coalition called *Ahora Madrid*), Barcelona (Ada Colau, an anti-eviction activist who headed the platform *Barcelona en Comú*), and Valencia (Joan Ribó, the leader of *Compromís*, a left-wing ecologist coalition).[189] In November, some opinion polls put *Podemos* in first place.[190]

Ciudadanos also stood to fight corruption and promote political transparency. Its birth dated back to July 2006 following the publication of a manifesto, in June 2005, by some Catalan intellectuals who, hitherto close to the PSC, had grown frustrated by the latter's inability or unwillingness to combat the socio-cultural hegemony built by Catalan nationalism and its discrimination of Catalan Castilian Spanish-speakers.[191] Its programme was based on social-democratic principles. In 2013, it decided to branch out into national politics with the double objective of imposing moral regeneration and ending the extortion by regional parties in Madrid based on their crucial role in securing parliamentary majorities.[192]

Both new parties seemed to bring a breath of fresh air to the stale political climate. Their leaders, the former swimming champion Albert Rivera (*Ciudadanos*) and the pony-tailed lecturer Pablo Iglesias Turrión (*Podemos*), were photogenic and excelled at media relations. They became familiar faces, often appearing jointly in *tertulias*. However, from together lambasting the vices of the ruling system, their initial good rapport grew into outright hostility. Their desire for prominence, authoritarianism, and hyperactive leadership resulted in their early demise. In the process, their parties went from touching distance of power to a waning force.

The general elections of December 2015 represented a political sea change. Pundits described the emerging situation as surrealist because, regardless of the challenge presented by *el Procés*, political intrigues were to dominate.[193] Although the two main parties still topped the polls, their joint support plummeted to barely 50 percent of the popular vote. This, in turn, meant more deadlock and instability due to the difficulty of cobbling together an effective working government. The PP returned 123 deputies (down 63) and the PSOE 90 (down 20). Together, they were nowhere near the 176 seats required to achieve a majority and were forced to work with a myriad of regional forces and the new national parties. *Podemos* had 69 seats and *Ciudadanos* 40, representing 24.5 and 13.9 percent of the vote, respectively.[194]

Despite having the largest minority, Rajoy declined to stand for the premiership. Instead, he did what he always did: do nothing and let others try but fail. Consequently, *Ciudadanos* and the PSOE, led by Pedro Sánchez, the party's general-secretary since July 2014, agreed to form a centre-left administration that needed *Podemos* to abstain if it was to take power. Yet, Iglesias not only torpedoed the deal but stunned the chamber when he recalled the PSOE's past links with *Grupos Antiterroristas de Liberación* (GAL). Behind his tough stance was his ambition to emulate the achievement of *Syriza* in Greece, which overtook the Socialists (PASOK) in 2012.[195] Similar outcomes were to occur later in Italy with the 5 Star Movement and France with *La France Insoumise*.

The elections of June 2016 cemented the existing gridlock.[196] The PP increased its representation (137 seats) slightly. Although the PSOE saw its worst result in democratic circumstances (85 seats), there was overall relief because *Podemos*' aim of becoming Spain's dominant left-wing force failed to materialize. To achieve that, *Podemos* headed a strong left-wing coalition, *Unidas Podemos* (UPOD, 'United We Can'), which included various regional forces as well as a declining IU. However, it only gained two deputies (71).[197] In turn, *Ciudadanos* suffered a small setback, losing eight seats (32).

Once again, Spain experienced months of intrigue and confusion. Rivera supported Rajoy's investiture despite his past promise of never backing a government with ministers mired in corruption. Yet, they were still short of a majority. The PSOE old guard and regional barons put pressure on Sánchez to abstain; they believed that otherwise, new elections would bring greater chaos to a country rocked by socio-economic dislocation, discredit in Europe, and offer *Podemos* the chance to overtake them. However, Sánchez stuck to his motto, 'No is No!' Rumours began to circulate that he was contemplating leading a 'Frankenstein government', a term first used by his predecessor Rubalcaba to define the monstrosity of a coalition dependent on the votes of practically all the regional forces, including *Bildu* and the Catalan secessionists.[198] Increased squabbling finally led to an extraordinary meeting of the PSOE's national committee in October 2016. Amidst histrionic scenes, Sánchez was ousted and resigned his seat in the *Cortes*. The acting leadership duly abstained and allowed Rajoy to be invested.[199]

Sánchez might have been out but he was not down. Over the following months, he travelled across Spain appealing to the grassroots. Against the odds, in May 2017, he was re-elected secretary general by beating the apparatus candidate, Susana Díaz, the leader of the most powerful section (Andalusia). Sánchez immediately began to alter the party's constitution, transforming it into a more hierarchical organization whereby the power of the barons was weakened vis-à-vis what was an omnipotent leader only responsible to the party membership.[200]

The PSOE resembled a dwindling force in 2017. With Sánchez absent from parliament, Iglesias increasingly assumed the role of leader of the opposition. The successful application of Article 155 seemed to consolidate Rajoy's position. Yet, in May 2018, the *Gürtel* affair offered Sánchez the opportunity to make a comeback by introducing a vote of no-confidence. Ironically, Rivera had used the court ruling to launch a scathing attack on the government. *Ciudadanos* was then top of the opinion polls, having been catapulted to a historic victory: it was the most voted for party in the Catalan elections of December 2017, although the united secessionist forces retained the *Generalitat*. Despite *Ciudadanos*' original centre-left credentials, Rivera believed that power could be attained by moving to the right. This became increasingly possible when many frustrated centre-right voters appeared to desert a discredited PP headed by an ineffective Rajoy. Accordingly, Rivera introduced radical change, dropping *Ciudadanos*' social-democratic principles and instead emphasizing a liberal ideology, espousing a hard-line Spanish nationalist discourse, and competing with the PP as the party of low taxes. The vote of no-confidence rattled Rivera. Reluctant to let the PSOE reap the benefits of the PP's disrepute, *Ciudadanos* was the only party to vote against the motion in the *Cortes*. As Rivera moved further from the centre, the intellectual founders of the party began to depart.[201]

The new socialist administration was short-lived but offered nearly one year of respite with a cabinet of fresh faces untainted by past scandals. It included well-regarded personalities such as Borrell at the Foreign Office, Nadia Calviño – a veteran EU economist – at the Treasury, and two independent judges, Fernando Grande-Marlaska and Margarita Robles, at the Home Office and Defence, respectively. In April 2019, Spain went to the polls. The result confirmed the trend of the previous two elections but this time with the PSOE and the PP reversing roles. The former obtained 123 seats and the latter slumped to a record low of 66; the third force was *Ciudadanos* (57) followed by UPOD (42).[202]

Ciudadanos and the Socialists could now muster a majority to form a centre-left administration, which was the only viable option for a stable legislature. But the two leaders' relationship had deteriorated dramatically. Despite colleagues' pleas and even high-profile resignations, such as that of the party's economic spokesperson Toni Roldán, Rivera continued to accuse Sánchez of having 'a plan to destroy Spain by leading a gang formed by all the country's enemies'.[203] Ironically, the socialist leader even claimed on TV that, like most Spaniards, he would suffer sleepless nights if Iglesias was ever in office. He also used tougher rhetoric than the PP in his references to Basque or Catalan separatists.[204]

Blinded by his aversion to Sánchez and ambition to lead the centre-right, Rivera forgot that the PP had shrugged off *Ciudadanos*' challenge and remained the second most popular party. Moreover, its new leader since July 2018, Pablo Casado, presented a much more belligerent leadership than Rajoy. Crucially, there was also a new right-wing challenger, *Vox*. Previously, Spain had been the exception in Europe, lacking a successful populist far-right party since Franco's death. *Vox* now entered parliament with 24 deputies. Launched in January 2014 by disgruntled PP members, including its leader, the Basque Santiago Abascal, *Vox*'s programme promoted an ultra-centralist agenda, including rewriting the Constitution to abolish regional autonomy, anti-immigrant and Eurosceptic policies, and fierce opposition to progressive issues such as feminism, same sex-marriage, and abortion.[205]

The deadlock continued after the election of November 2019, the fourth in four years. The Right increased its representation but failed to achieve a majority. Fighting for the same political space, the tactical vote favoured the PP, which obtained 89 seats and *Vox*, with 52 deputies, became the third force in parliament. Rivera paid a heavy price for his stubbornness. *Ciudadanos* returned only 10 deputies, upon which he promptly resigned. Both the PSOE and *Podemos*, with 129 and 35 seats, respectively, saw their representation diminished. This time Sánchez did not waste time. In January 2020, he became prime minister, having mustered 176 votes, including those of the ERC and *Bildu*. His cabinet contained five ministers from *Podemos*. Iglesias was one of its vice presidents. The Frankenstein administration reviled by Rubalcaba was beginning to take shape.

Quo Vadis, Spain?

Analysing current Spanish affairs, from around the 1970s' transition, belongs more to the realm of the political journalist than to the historian whose research relies on the semantic principle of working critically and objectively with an exhaustive catalogue of verifiable primary sources and academic literature. It is, therefore, an even harder task to assess today's political scenario, let alone predict the near future. Thus, it is too early to tell whether by accepting to lead an unprecedented left-wing coalition Sánchez made a grave blunder or embraced a courageous and novel initiative.

Spain is today more fractured than at any point in its democracy. The politics of consensus have given way to fratricidal polarization. Sánchez's reputation has been shredded under the attacks of both friends and foes. Derided as Pedro I 'the insomniac', given his comments about allying with Iglesias, he has been the target of vitriolic hostility from right-wing parties and the media. Yet, bitter criticism has also emanated from his camp, particularly from the old guard who were in office with González. Joaquín Leguina, the former president of Madrid's regional government (1982–1995) and Nicolás Redondo Terreros, the former secretary general of the Basque Socialists (1989–1997) and son of the historic head of the UGT, have warned that the Socialists are committing a brutal error by clinging onto power with the support of enemies of the democracy.[206] Juan Carlos Rodríguez Ibarra, the former socialist president of Extremadura (1983–2007), noted that the height of infamy was to pass the new democratic memory law with the support of *Bildu*. Accepting the latter's amendment to extend the period until 1983 will turn the past upside down: the terrorists will be freedom fighters and their victims and the governments headed by Suárez and González accomplices of Francoism.[207]

Given the scope of Sánchez's victory over the socialist barons in 2017, their opposition has been more nuanced but has grown steadily. It is a survival exercise for them. Recent regional elections have been devastating for the PSOE. Andalusia, the natural breadbasket of socialist votes, saw the most shocking setback. They held its government until 2018 when, despite still having the most votes, control was lost to a coalition of the PP and *Ciudadanos*. In June 2022, the PP obtained an absolute majority, something that would have been unbelievable a decade earlier.[208]

Political juggling and baffling U-turns have acquired a whole new dimension with Sánchez. One of the last episodes in a saga of astonishing decisions concerns the sensitive issue of the Western Sahara, the last Spanish colony in Africa. Since its occupation by Morocco during the so-called Green March, coinciding with Franco's death in November 1975, this territory has witnessed a bitter dispute between that country and the *Polisario* Front, the Sahrawi liberation movement backed by Algeria. All Spanish administrations have adopted a pragmatic stance: support for the UN resolution calling for a referendum when circumstances allow. Sánchez reneged on that position and managed to alienate everyone. He caused a major diplomatic clash with Morocco by secretly allowing Brahim Ghali, the *Polisario* secretary general, to receive hospital treatment in Spain. Following the subsequent diplomatic scandal, Ghali was forced to leave.[209] Barely a year later, a published letter from the king of Morocco made clear that Sánchez now endorsed wholeheartedly his country's claims over the

Western Sahara. To add insult to injury, Morocco did not even, in return, renounce its demands over the North African Spanish enclaves of Ceuta and Melilla. Such a puzzling about-turn has given rise to all sorts of rumours, including that secret information held by the Moroccan intelligence services was used to blackmail the Spanish prime minister.[210] Still, Sánchez seems to have taken a unilateral decision that not only broke with decades of bipartisan consensus but also was extraordinarily self-defeating. Coinciding with the war in Ukraine and the reality of soaring energy prices, he managed to offend Algeria, Spain's main supplier of natural gas, which duly suspended the two countries' treaty of friendship.[211]

Constant squabbling in the ruling coalition, from economic policy to foreign affairs, dominated the headlines. *Podemos* ministers used the media to express their dissent as if they were the opposition rather than part of the government. Yet, despite the infighting, nobody was contemplating a break-up knowing that this could result in a resounding electoral defeat. For the PSOE, having UPOD members in the cabinet avoided civil unrest due to the worsening socio-economic hardship. In turn, *Podemos'* strength has been progressively weakened. Its hybrid structure presents the glaring contradiction of an anti-system force anchored in a grassroots assembly movement becoming a traditional left-wing party. Iglesias solved this by establishing a hierarchical structure dominated in the classical Leninist style by himself, the charismatic leader, and his inner circle. In the process, practically all the founding members gradually departed. Iglesias' most publicized clash took place with his lieutenant, Íñigo Errejón, who ended up leaving, in early 2019, to form his own political grouping, *Más Madrid*, which that year gained three seats in the general elections as part of a coalition called *Más País*.[212] Iglesias' popularity plummeted due to his hyperactive character and nepotism. Just after his resounding victory at the party congress of 2016, he installed his wife, Irene Montero, as the parliamentary spokesperson in place of Errejón. Montero was promoted to minister of equality in Sánchez's ruling coalition in 2020. Also highly controversial was Iglesias' decision to move from his modest flat in Vallecas, a working-class quarter of Madrid, to a magnificent mansion in Galapagar, on the outskirts of the city.[213]

In May 2021, such was the popular hostility against him that Iglesias made a surprising decision. He announced his resignation as vice president to stand in the Madrid regional elections to combat the 'fascist threat' embodied by the local autonomy's president, Isabel Díaz Ayuso, a rising star in the PP. The results had far-reaching consequences. Ayuso secured an amazing victory after nearly doubling the PP vote.[214] *Ciudadanos* lost all its seats in confirmation of its growing irrelevance. It soon might have to face the choice between its dissolution or a return to its original progressive stance.[215] *Podemos* came last, even beaten handsomely by *Más Madrid*. Iglesias resigned from active politics to pursue a career in *tertulias*. He left behind a dual leadership that could generate further infighting: Yolanda

Díaz, the minister of labour, an IU militant, who succeeded him in the government and Ione Belarra, minister of social affairs, *Podemos*' new secretary general.[216] In November 2021, Díaz announced her intention to initiate a 'listening process' leading to the establishment of a political platform called *Sumar* ('To Add') to contest the next general election. It is a tall order for Iglesias, who still controls *Podemos* behind the scenes, and his inner circle to accept being a minor partner in that project. Ayuso's victory also activated a rebellion against Casado who had sought to undermine her popularity by leaking allegations that her brother had profited from kickbacks to procure healthcare products during the pandemic. In April 2022, he was forced to resign and was replaced by Alberto Núñez Feijóo, known for his moderate disposition and winning reputation: president of Galicia (2009–2022) with four consecutive election victories.[217]

Sanchez's relationship with and dependence on a myriad of small regional forces to remain in office, including *Bildu* and the ERC, fuelled intense hostility. Their votes were vital in the passing of laws and annual budgets. In turn, they extracted concessions triggering diatribes against Sánchez as an unprincipled prime minister who had mortgaged the nation to its enemies. In June 2021, the government took the decision to pardon the jailed secessionist leaders despite their threats to act again.[218] Sánchez countenanced the establishment of a round table with the ERC that permitted the latter to brand it as bilateral talks between two countries, Spain and Catalonia.[219] The government also refused to implement a court order mandating that a minimum of 25 percent of subjects be taught in Spanish in Catalan public schools.[220] According to the historian Jordi Canal, relying on the secessionists' loyalty is naive and a gross mistake. It has permitted *el Procés* to advance under new formulas. The secessionists retain control of the *Generalitat* and continue to use public money to maintain their patronage networks and control over education and the media.[221]

However, others viewed Sánchez's initiatives as brave and necessary to break the political deadlock and crucial to demonstrate Spain's democratic foundations. The jailed secessionist leaders were not granted an amnesty but benefited from pardons, a generous but valid procedure that does not eradicate their crimes and counters their victimization rhetoric.[222] Sánchez's change of tack on the territorial question is proof for many of his opportunism and thirst for power. However, his shift is arguably based more on rhetoric than real substance. The PSOE insisted that nothing can be done outside the constitutional framework, including the right to self-determination. In the process, the secessionist camp split, with *Junts* and the ERC exchanging roles. The former, led by Puigdemont in Brussels, is stuck in an uncompromising position, while the latter has gradually embraced the pragmatism formerly practised by Pujol. Furthermore, support for independence has fallen to about 38 percent. Significantly, the youth has abandoned *el Procés*.[223] Even the CUP has experienced a breakaway faction, *Horitzó Socialista* (Socialist Horizon), which has given up independence to focus on the socialist revolution.²²⁴ The secessionist cause also suffered crucial setbacks in the European Parliament, including the defeat by 437 to 170 votes, in November 2020, of the proposal by Diana Riba, an ERC Eurodeputy, for the right of self-determination.²²⁵

After a massive defeat on 28 March 2023, both in the municipalities as well as in twelve of the autonomous communities and the two enclaves in North Africa, Sánchez decided to call a general election on 23 July, six months early. Tellingly, the two forces that had emerged in recent times to embody political renovation have practically disappeared. *Ciudadanos* finally decided not to stand in the election and *Podemos* was forced to be just one of the many groups under the platform of *Sumar* led by Díaz.

Until the eve of the general election, which were held on 23 July 2023, most opinion polls had prophesized a clear victory for the PP. On being elected and with the support of *Vox*, the PP could have formed a new administration. This would have meant a radical right-wing U-turn in politics and exemplified the politics of revenge that have plagued recent times. Instead, against all odds and despite the definitive surge in the number of PP deputies (from 89 to 137), the PSOE managed to increase, if only by just one seat, its representation in parliament (121). A campaign based largely on stoking the widespread fear of *Vox* was successful. And indeed, *Vox* lost a significant number of deputies (from 52 to 33) while *Sumar* retained most of *Podemos*' vote (from 33 to 31).²²⁶ However, negotiations to form a new government were lengthy and problematic. The governing coalition, ubiquitously derided as 'Frankenstein-like', needed now to include the indispensable eight votes of *Junts*. Eventually, Sánchez was inaugurated prime minister in November but in the process he was forced to make concessions, such as a new transfer of powers to the *Generalitat* that included control over emigration and RENFE, and the promise of an amnesty law, which is not consistent with the letter of the Constitution.²²⁷ The stability of the new administration is somewhat precarious. Its narrow parliamentary majority (179 seats) was weakened by the desertion of the five elected members of *Podemos* who defected *Sumar* and have become a sort of left-wing opposition.²²⁸ And, above all, the continuity of the government is in the hands of Puigdemont. This became blatant when *Junts* voted against the amnesty decree that the PSOE had brought to parliament.²²⁹ Tellingly, despite their claims not to change a word from the original text, the Socialists finely capitulated and passed in March 2024 a new law of amnesty which fulfilled all the demands of Catalan Separatists.²³⁰

The world is beset by unprecedented economic, geopolitical, and health crises. Yet, Spain finds itself in a dangerous quagmire, the most evident symptoms of which are gridlock, the persistence of the territorial question, and the growing discredit and distrust of politicians. It is, therefore, vital to rediscover the spirit of the transition. However, this is only possible if there are statesmen capable of setting aside their partisan agendas, with a long-term state view, and willing to reach a compromise. It is disquieting that when confronted with a dire situation, the two main parties are more willing to cosy up to the extremes on either side of the political spectrum than collaborate in a grand coalition such as in Germany and other western nations.

Constitutional reform to underpin the democratic foundations of the nation is imperative. It must be consensual and generous in an appeal to national and regional forces. In exchange, constitutional loyalty should be expected, including regional administrations not using public funds or the media attacking the state from which, after all, their powers emanate and their salaries are paid. Once approved in the *Cortes*, any suggested reform must be put to the nation. Amongst its many essential goals, three stand out.

First, the territorial question must finally be settled. As Koldo Casla argues, we find ourselves in a world of increasing xenophobia and nationalist hubris. Nationalists (centralist or peripheral), in Spain and elsewhere, manipulate the symbols of the nation for their own political agenda and exclude a supposedly underserving *other* from society's protection.[231] The Constitution should enshrine national unity, as is the case in practically the entire world. No modern state, including the western democracies, accepts its evident self-destruction by recognizing the right of regional self-determination. As Álvarez Junco contends, this is a recipe for Balkanization.[232] It can be argued that it is legitimate to break up a country if its government behaves in an oppressive and discriminatory manner. But Spain is today a genuine democracy and the regional communities enjoy levels of political self-rule uncommon elsewhere in the world. The autonomies are here to stay but the demarcation of powers must be fixed. No country, including those that have a federal structure, allows their regions to constantly demand new jurisdictions dependent on the balance of power. In turn, the Constitution must recognize that Spain is a multinational state whose diverse identities are an asset that must be defended. There is room for further decentralization, particularly in terms of taxation and financial devolution. However, other areas such as education need to become more centralized so that all Spaniards learn from similar curriculums and have the same opportunities in terms of employment and mobility, for example.

Secondly, the Constitution should adopt stringent measures to uproot political corruption. To achieve that, a new electoral system is required, one that forges a link between each constituency and the candidates, who, above all, are supposed to be public servants representing their electorate. Closed party lists for provincial districts, where the candidates are handpicked by regional or national barons, should be abandoned, as they only encourage nepotism and hierarchical subordination.

Finally, the Constitution must guarantee a real division of powers. An existing dysfunctional feature is the politicization of the judicial system. Many judicial bodies – including, crucially, the Constitutional Court – are politically appointed depending on the parliamentary balance of power. The judges and prosecutors should instead be elected by their peers.

Despite the existing adversities and uncertainties, hope should not be lost. As Fernando Ónega, a leading political journalist, recalls, the German Iron Chancellor Otto Von Bismarck affirmed: 'Spain is the strongest country in Europe. Its inhabitants have been trying to destroy it for 500 years and have not yet succeeded'.[233]

Notes

1. Radcliff, *Modern Spain*, p. 251.
2. Moradiellos, *Franco*, p. 14.
3. Sebastián Arroyo, *Why Banks Fail: The Political Roots of Banking Crises in Spain* (New York: Palgrave, 2020), p. 124.
4. *La Vanguardia*, 'Eighty-One Percent of Spaniards would Support a Gay Prime Minister' (27 September 2019).
5. Fernando Ónega, *Qué nos ha pasado, España. De la ilusión al desencanto* (Barcelona: Plaza Janés, 2017), p. 318.
6. *El País*, 'Eta Ends 43 Years of Terror' (20 October 2021).
7. Ónega, *Qué nos ha pasado*.
8. Sebastián Royo, 'Reforms Betrayed? Zapatero and Continuities in Economic Policy', in Bonnie N. Field (ed.), *Spain's Second Transition? The Socialist Government of José Luis Rodríguez Zapatero* (London: Routledge, 2011), p. 64.
9. Arroyo, *Why Banks Fail*, pp. 121–3.
10. Luis Buendía and Ricardo Molero-Simarro, 'Introduction: The Political Economy of the Spanish Growth Model and its Structural Adjustment Process', in Luis Buendía and Ricardo Molero-Simarro (eds.), *The Political Economy of Contemporary Spain: From Miracle to Mirage* (London: Routledge, 2020), p. 4.
11. Tobias Buck, *After the Fall: Crisis, Recovery, and the Making of a New Spain* (London: Weidenfeld & Nicolson, 2020), pp. 74–5.
12. Arroyo, *Why Banks Fail*, pp. 127–8.
13. *The Guardian*, 'Building Boom Reduced to Ruins by Collapse of Spain's Economic Miracle' (19 January 2009).
14. Ónega, *Qué nos ha pasado*, p. 237.
15. Ibid., pp. 240–1.
16. Arroyo, *Why Banks Fail*, pp. 130–2.
17. 'Zapatero Forced to Impose Reforms', https://www.expansion.com/2010/06/02/economia-politica/1275515700.html
18. *El País*, 'Two Minutes that Changed Spain' (18 May 2010).
19. Caroline Gray, *Territorial Politics and the Party System in Spain* (New York: Routledge, 2020), p. 30.
20. https://www.bloomberg.com/view/articles/2015-09-28/spain-s-brain-drain-poses-a-threat-to-the-euro#xj4y7vzkg
21. Ónega, *Qué nos ha pasado*, p. 142.

22 Alfonso Botti, 'From Opposition to Government: The Popular Party of Mariano Rajoy', in Bonnie N. Field and Alfonso Botti (eds.), *Politics and Society in Contemporary Spain: From Zapatero to Rajoy* (Basingstoke: Palgrave, 2013), pp. 54–6.
23 Gray, *Territorial Politics*, p. 31.
24 Buendía and Molero-Simarro, 'Introduction', p. 11.
25 *The Guardian*, 'Ten Years on. How Countries that Crashed are Faring' (16 June 2018).
26 https://www.worldometers.info/coronavirus/#countries (29 March 2021).
27 *Real Instituto Elcano*, 'Challenges and Opportunities for Spain in Times of COVID-19' (April 2021).
28 *El País*, 'Spain's ERTE Furlough Scheme is Extended to September' (28 May 2021).
29 *Real Instituto Elcano*, 'The Effects of the Invasion of Ukraine on the Spanish Economy' (11 March 2022).
30 *El Español*, 'Massive Countryside Protest against the Government in the Streets of Madrid' (20 March 2022); *El País*, 'Lorry Drivers Halt Temporarily their Strike after 20 Days of Mobilizations' (2 April 2022).
31 Tusell, *El Aznarato*, p. 30.
32 Ibid., pp. 178–81.
33 Muro, *Ethnicity and Violence*, p. 172.
34 Tusell, *El Aznarato*, pp. 335–41.
35 Fernando Jáuregui and Federico Quevedo, *El desengaño* (Madrid: Almuzara, 2017), p. 80.
36 https://www.historiaelectoral.com/e2008.html
37 *The Guardian*, 'Bombers Wreak Havoc in Madrid' (11 March 2004).
38 *El País*, 'Thousands Gather in front of the PP Headquarters throughout Spain' (13 March 2004).
39 Ónega, *Qué nos ha pasado*, p. 90
40 https://www.electionguide.org/elections/id/423/
41 Bonnie N. Field, 'A Second Transition in Spain? Policy, Institutions and Interparty Politics under Zapatero (2004–8)', in Field and Botti (eds.), *Politics and Society in Contemporary Spain*, pp. 1–2.
42 Omar G. Encarnación, 'Spain's New Left Turn: Society Driven or Party Instigated', in Field and Botti (eds.), *Politics and Society in Contemporary Spain*, p. 21.
43 Thomas G. Powell, 'A Second Transition, or More of the Same? Spanish Foreign Policy under Zapatero', in Field and Botti (eds.), *Politics and Society in Contemporary Spain*, p. 148.
44 Eloísa del Pino, 'The Spanish Welfare State from Zapatero to Rajoy: Recalibration to Retrenchment', in Field and Botti (eds.), *Politics and Society in Contemporary Spain*, pp. 211–12.
45 *The Guardian*, 'Zapatero's Feminist Agenda' (1 April 2011).

46 https://www.lamoncloa.gob.es/gobierno/gobiernosporlegislaturas/paginas/IXLegislatura.aspx
47 *El País*, 'The March against Gay Weddings Brings together Families, Bishops, and PP Leaders in Madrid (18 June 2005).
48 *El País*, 'The Enduring Myths around Spain's Historical Memory Law' (26 June 2009).
49 Richards, *After the Civil War*, p. 334.
50 *The Guardian*, 'Pinochet Leaves Britain' (2 March 2000).
51 Manganas, *Las dos Españas*, p. 29.
52 https://memoriahistorica.org.es/
53 *El País*, 'The PP Condemns Franco's Coup and Promises to Honour all the Victims of the Civil War' (21 November 2002).
54 Encarnación, *Spanish Politics*, p. 63.
55 Alberto Reig, *Anti-Moa, la subversión neofranquista de la historia de España* (Madrid: Ediciones B, 2006), pp. 15–16; Matilde Eiroa, 'Del estudio del pasado a la trasmisión en el presente: ¿Qué papel desempeñan los historiadores a los 80 años de la Guerra Civil?', in Blanco, Martínez, and Viñas (eds.), *Luces*, p. 31.
56 Koldo Casla, *Spain and Its Achilles' Heels* (London: Rowman & Littlefield, 2022), p. 88.
57 Graham, *The War and its Shadow*, p. 147.
58 Francisco Etxeberria, 'Fosas comunes de la Guerra Civil en el Siglo XXI: antecedentes, interdisciplinariedad y legislación', *Historia Contemporánea*, 60 (2019), pp. 404–5.
59 *El Confidencial*, 'The Government Removes Franco from the Valley of the Fallen' (24 October 2019).
60 *Público*, 'The Government Manages to Save the Democratic Memory Law Thanks to the Support of Bildu' (28 June 2022).
61 Ónega, *Qué nos ha pasado*, pp. 15–16.
62 Cercas, *Anatomía*, pp. 433–4.
63 Aguilar, *Memory and Amnesia*, p. 123.
64 Casla, *Spain and Its Achilles' Heels*, p. 170.
65 Saz, *Fascismo*, pp. 284–9.
66 Manganas, *Las dos Españas*, p. 155.
67 *The Guardian*, '10 Years on from the End of Basque Terror Group ETA' (20 October 2021).
68 Ónega, *Qué nos ha pasado*, p. 71.
69 Ibid., pp. 178–81.
70 Dowling, *Catalonia since the Spanish Civil War*, p. 140.
71 Gray, *Territorial Politics*, p. 9.
72 Ónega, *Qué nos ha pasado*, p. 164.
73 Diego Muro, 'Territorial Accommodation, Party Politics, and Statute Reform in Spain', *South European Society and Politics*, 4 (2009), p. 461.

74 *La Vanguardia*, 'Ferrusola Attacks Montilla' (19 March 2008).
75 Muro, 'Territorial Accommodation', pp. 459–61, 464.
76 https://www.catalannews.com/politics/item/the-spanish-constitutional-court-shortens-the-current-catalan-statute-of-autonomy
77 Casla, *Spain and Its Achilles' Heels*, p. 46.
78 Enric Ucelay-da Cal, *Breve historia del separatismo catalán* (Barcelona: Penguin, 2018), p. 43.
79 This term was originally given to the supporters of the Bourbon Philip V during the War of the Spanish Succession (1701–1714). Catalan nationalists used it to insult those people they considered traitors to the fatherland.
80 *El País*, 'Tens of Thousands of Catalans Take to the Streets against the Statute Cuts' (10 July 2010).
81 Gray, *Territorial Politics*, p. 25.
82 Heywood, *The Government and Politics of Spain*, pp. 169–70.
83 Bonnie N. Field and Alfonso Botti, 'Introduction', in Field and Botti (eds.), *Politics and Society in Contemporary Spain*, p. 7.
84 Preston, *A People Betrayed*, p. 530.
85 Muñoz, *La España corrupta*, p. 99.
86 Ónega, *Qué nos ha pasado*, pp. 210–14.
87 *The Guardian*, 'Court Finds Spain's Ruling Party Benefited from Bribery Scheme' (24 May 2018).
88 Jáuregui and Quevedo, *El desengaño*, p. 267.
89 *El País*, 'The President Disappeared at Lunchtime and Left the Restaurant at Ten at Night' (1 June 2018).
90 Preston, *A People Betrayed*, p. 513.
91 *The Guardian*, 'Socialist ex-Presidents of Andalusia Guilty in €680m Fraud Case' (19 November 2019).
92 Preston, *A People Betrayed*, p. 535.
93 *La Vanguardia*, 'The Pujol Ferrusola Family Facing Years of Jail' (7 May 2021).
94 *The Guardian*, 'Spain's Princess Cristina Acquitted in Tax Fraud Trial' (17 February 2017).
95 Muñoz, *La España corrupta*, pp. 107–8.
96 Cristina Flesher Fominaya, *Democracy Reloaded: Inside Spain's Political Laboratory from 15-M to Podemos* (Oxford: Oxford University Press, 2020), pp. 2–3, 61, 72–3.
97 Manganas, *Las dos Españas*, pp. 203–4.
98 Fominaya, *Democracy Reloaded*, pp. 166–76.
99 *La Vanguardia*, 'Artur Mas and Núria de Gispert Access Parliament by Helicopter' (15 June 2011).
100 Ucelay-da Cal, *Breve historia*, p. 15.
101 Ramón de España, *El manicomio catalán* (Barcelona: La esfera de los libros, 2013); Jordi Canal, *Con permiso de Kafka. El proceso independentista en Cataluña* (Barcelona: Península, 2018).

102 https://www.democracymatrix.com/ranking. In this complete index for 2020, Spain is ranked number 11, Britain 17, France 19, and the United States 36.
103 https://www.oecd.org/regional/regional-policy/Decentralisation-trends-in-OECD-countries.pdf
104 Ferran Brunet, *Economía del separatismo catalán* (Barcelona: Planeta, 2022), pp. 66–7, 118, 304–9.
105 Jáuregui and Quevedo, *El desengaño*, p. 86.
106 Encarnación, *Spanish Politics*, p. 107.
107 Juliá, *Transición*, pp. 589–91.
108 *El País*, 'Catalan Nationalism Explained by José Álvarez Junco' (29 September 2018).
109 Ucelay-da Cal, *Breve historia*, p. 253.
110 Gray, *Territorial Politics*, pp. 45–6.
111 Ucelay-da Cal, *Breve historia*, p. 280.
112 David Jiménez Torres, *2017. La crisis que cambió España* (Barcelona: Deusto, 2021), p. 68.
113 Canal, *Con permiso*, p. 103.
114 Tamames, *La economía española*, p. 387.
115 Encarnación, *Spanish Politics*, p. 108.
116 *El País*, 'The Catalan Government Debates a Document that Advocates Nationalist Infiltration in All Social Spheres' (28 October 1990); *Voz Pópuli*, '30 Years of the Programme 2000: The Plan with which Pujol Designed the Procés' (17 July 2020).
117 Interview with José Álvarez Junco, in *El Confidencial* (5 February 2018).
118 *The Guardian*, 'Catalonia Pays €3m to Firms Linked to Theory that Shakespeare was Catalan' (9 March 2020).
119 Germà Bel, *Disdain, Distrust and Dissolution: The Surge of Support for Independence in Catalonia* (Eastbourne: Sussex University Press, 2015), pp. 1, 143–4.
120 Raphael Minder, *The Struggle for Catalonia* (London: Hurst, 2017), p. 204.
121 *El Periódico*, 'Catalonia Cries Out for Independence' (11 September 2012).
122 Sandrine Morel, *En el huracán catalán* (Barcelona: Planeta, 2018), p. 36.
123 Canal, *Con permiso*, p. 174.
124 Casla, *Spain and Its Achilles' Heels*, p. 48.
125 Joaquim Coll, 'El *Procés*', in Joaquim Coll, Ignacio Molina, and Manuel Arias Maldonado (eds.), *Anatomía del Procés* (Barcelona: Debate, 2018), p. 21.
126 Ibid., p. 26.
127 Adolf Tobeña, *Fragmented Catalonia: Divisive Legacies of a Push for Secession* (London: Rowman & Littlefield, 2021), pp. 4, 19–20.
128 *Òmnium Cultural* was created in 1961 as a cultural organization to promote the Catalan language and culture. *L'Assemblea Nacional Catalana* (ANC)

was formed in 2011 as a social movement whose objective is the independence of Catalonia.
129 Minder, *The Struggle for Catalonia*, p. 13.
130 Lola García, *El naufragio* (Madrid: Península, 2018), p. 35.
131 Tobeña, *Fragmented Catalonia*, p. 33.
132 Morel, *En el huracán*, pp. 13–14, 43–6.
133 Canal, *Con permiso*, p. 218.
134 Tobeña, *Fragmented Catalonia*, pp. viii–ix.
135 Ignacio Molina, 'La dimensión internacional y europea del *Procés*', in Coll, Molina, and Arias Maldonado (eds.), *Anatomía del Procés*, p. 203.
136 Dowling, *Catalonia since the Spanish Civil War*, p. 154.
137 Josep Borrell and Joan Llorach, *Las cuentas y los cuentos de la independencia* (Madrid: Catarata, 2017), pp. 20–2.
138 Rafael Arenas, 'El *Procés*, un intento de secesión de hecho', in Coll, Molina, and Arias Maldonado (eds.), *Anatomía del Procés*, p. 68.
139 Daniel Gascón, *El golpe posmoderno* (Barcelona: Penguin, 2018).
140 Editorial written by Albert Soler in *Voz Pópuli* (27 February 2020). He is also the author of a sarcastic book on the subject, *Estàvem cansats de viure bé* (Barcelona: Sagasse, 2019).
141 Borrell and Llorach, *Las cuentas*, pp. 11–12; *Voz Pópuli*, 'The Youth and the Families with Less Income are the least Secessionist in Catalonia' (14 July 2021).
142 Morel, *En el huracán catalán*, pp. 111–14.
143 Juan Pablo Cardenal, *La telaraña. La trama exterior del Procés* (Barcelona: Ariel, 2020), p. 20.
144 Jáuregui and Quevedo, *El desengaño*, p. 271.
145 García, *El naufragio*, p. 73.
146 Coll, 'El *Procés*', pp. 32–4.
147 *El País*, '1.8 Million People Vote for Catalan Independence on 9-N' (10 November 2014).
148 *El País*, 'Mas Sentenced to Political Disqualification for the 9N' (13 March 2017).
149 García, *El naufragio*, pp. 97–8.
150 *La Vanguardia*, 'CDC and Unió Consider their Alliance Broken after 37 Years' (17 June 2015).
151 *El País*, 'The New Party Created by Mas Embraces Independence' (10 July 2016).
152 A deputy needs 49,500 votes to be returned to parliament in the province of Barcelona while it is 21,019 in Lleida. https://www.rtve.es/noticias/20210205/sistema-electoral-catalan-reparto-votos-provincias/2073047.shtml.
153 Coll, 'El *procés*', pp. 38–9.
154 García, *El naufragio*, p. 157.
155 *El Mundo*, 'The Catalan Parliament Completes its Plan of Insubordination' (8 September 2017).

156 *Crónica Global*, 'Interview with Eva Granados' (21 September 2019).
157 Pau Marí-Klose, 'Cataluña deshilachada', in Coll, Molina, and Arias Maldonado (eds.), *Anatomía del Procés*, p. 237.
158 Gascón, *El golpe posmoderno*, p. 145.
159 García, *El naufragio*, p. 168.
160 https://www.rtve.es/noticias/20170921/mossos-desalojan-guardia-civil-conselleria-economia/1621007.shtml
161 *The Guardian*, 'Spain High Court Jails Catalan Separatist Leaders Pending Investigation' (17 October 2017).
162 García, *El naufragio*, pp. 177–80.
163 Gascón, *El golpe posmoderno*, pp. 167–9.
164 Gray, *Territorial Politics*, p. 41.
165 *The Guardian*, 'Catalan Government Suspends Declaration of Independence' (10 October 2012).
166 Morel, *En el huracán catalán*, pp. 173–4.
167 Tobeña, *Fragmented Catalonia*, p. 20.
168 *The Guardian*, 'Catalonia: Hundreds of Thousands Join Anti-Independence Rally in Barcelona' (8 October 2021).
169 Coll, 'El *procés*', p. 45.
170 Gascón, *El golpe posmoderno*, p. 177.
171 *El País*, '540 Companies Have Left Catalonia since the Referendum on October 1' (13 October 2017); Brunet, *Economía*, p. 354.
172 Morel, *En el huracán*, pp. 199–200.
173 Interview with Santos Juliá in *El País* (16 April 2018).
174 García, *El naufragio*, p. 226.
175 *El País*, 'Sentences of 9 to 13 years for the Leaders of the *Procés* for Sedition and Embezzlement' (14 October 2019).
176 Jáuregui and Quevedo, *El desengaño*, p. 301.
177 Marí-Klose, 'Cataluña deshilachada', p. 232.
178 https://resultados.elpais.com/elecciones/2017/autonomicas/09/index.html
179 Tobeña, *Fragmented Catalonia*, pp. 7–10.
180 Jiménez Torres, *2017*, p. 148.
181 Canal, *Con permiso*, p. 249.
182 *El País*, 'A Nightmare in Barcelona' (15 May 2018).
183 *The Guardian*, 'Chaos at Barcelona Airport as Protesters React to Sentencing over 2017 Bid for Independence' (14 October 2019).
184 *Político*, 'Spain's Supreme Court Jails Catalan Leaders for up to 13 Years' (24 October 2019).
185 https://www.rtve.es/noticias/20200928/supremo-inhabilita-torra-unanimidad-como-presidente-generalitat/2043005.shtml
186 Tobeña, *Fragmented Catalonia*, p. 9.

187 Manganas, *Las dos Españas*, p. 207.
188 Gray, *Territorial Politics*, pp. 95–6.
189 Ónega, *Qué nos ha pasado*, p. 183.
190 Richard R. Weiner and Iván López, *Los Indignados: Tides of Social Insertion in Spain* (Alresford: Zero Books, 2016), p. 18.
191 *Crónica Global*, 'The Legacy of Ciudadanos' (1 July 2022).
192 Gray, *Territorial Politics*, p. 33.
193 Jáuregui and Quevedo, *El desengaño*, p. 121.
194 *The Guardian*, 'Spanish Election: National Newcomers End Era of Two-Party Dominance' (21 December 2015).
195 Weiner and López, *Los Indignados*, p. 27.
196 *The Guardian*, 'Spanish Elections: Renewed Deadlock Beckons as No Party Wins Majority' (27 June 2016).
197 Weiner and López, *Los Indignados*, p. 173.
198 Joaquín Leguina, *Pedro Sánchez. Historia de una ambición* (Barcelona: Planeta, 2021), p. 66.
199 Ónega, *Qué nos ha pasado*, p. 168.
200 Jáuregui and Quevedo, *El desengaño*, pp. 134–5.
201 *Crónica Global*, 'Rivera's Labyrinth' (5 July 2019).
202 https://resultados.elpais.com/elecciones/2019-28A/generales/congreso/
203 Gray, *Territorial Politics*, pp. 143–4.
204 *Crónica Global*, 'A Marriage of Convenience' (24 July 2019).
205 Gray, *Territorial Politics*, pp. 124–6.
206 Leguina, *Pedro Sánchez*, p. 111.
207 *Voz Pópuli*, 'Against Disloyalty' (2 March 2021) and 'They Are Not Socialists. What Are They?' (12 July 2022).
208 *El País*, 'The PP Sweeps Andalusia with a Historic Victory' (19 June 2022).
209 *El Español*, 'The Leader of the Polisario Front admitted to a Spanish Hospital for Humanitarian Reasons' (23 April 2021).
210 *Voz Populi*, 'Algeria Confirms: Sánchez Was Blackmailed' (12 June 2022).
211 *El País*, 'Algeria Suspends the Friendship Treaty and Freezes Trade with Spain after the Turn of the Government on the Sahara' (21 June 2022).
212 Fominaya, *Democracy Reloaded*, pp. 254–5, 274–5.
213 *La Vanguardia*, 'Iglesias: From Sherwood to Galapagar' (17 April 2019).
214 *El País*, 'Ayuso Sweeps Madrid' (4 May 2021).
215 *Voz Pópuli*, 'Ciudadanos: Refoundation or Dissolution' (28 June 2022).
216 *El Periódico*, 'Iglesias Leaves Politics after Crashing in Madrid' (5 May 2022)
217 *El País*, 'Feijóo is Elected to Lead the PP' (4 April 2022).
218 *El País*, 'The Government Approves the Pardons for the Prisoners of the Procés' (22 June 2021).
219 *Crónica Global*, 'Sánchez's Blindness' (1 January 2021).

220 *El Diario*, 'The Government Rules Out Requesting the Execution of 25 Percent of Classes in Spanish in Catalonia' (29 March 2022).
221 Interview with Professor Jordi Canal in *El Confidencial* (11 July 2021).
222 *Analytiks*, 'A Courageous Initiative' (29 May 2021).
223 *Voz Pópuli*, 'The Youth and the Families with Less Income are the Least Secessionist in Catalonia' (14 July 2021); *El País*, 'Support for the Independence of Catalonia Plummets to 38 Percent' (17 March 2022).
224 *The Objective*, 'The CUP Splits: A New Communist Faction Gives Up the Independence Goal' (22 July 2022).
225 Leguina, *Pedro Sánchez*, p. 238.
226 *El País*, 'General Election Results' (24 July 2023).
227 *El Periódico*, 'Junts Will Make Sánchez Prime Minister' (16 November 2023).
228 *El País*, 'Podemos Quits Sumar' (5 December 2023).
229 *La Razón*, 'Junts Humiliates Sánchez by Voting Down the Amnesty Law' (30 January 2024).
230 *El Mundo*, 'the Cortes Approves the Amnesty Law wished by Puigdemont (14 March 2024).
231 Casla, *Spain and Its Achilles' Heels*, pp. 176–7.
232 Interview with José Álvarez Junco, in *El Confidencial* (5 February 2018).
233 Ónega, *Qué nos ha pasado*, p. 268.

BIBLIOGRAPHY

Abella, Rafael, *La vida cotidiana durante la Guerra Civil: La España Republicana* (Barcelona: Planeta, 1975).
Abella, Rafael, *La vida cotidiana durante la Guerra Civil: La España Nacional* (Barcelona: Planeta, 1976).
Aguilar, Paloma, *Memory and Amnesia: The Role of the Spanish Civil War in the Transition to Democracy* (Oxford: Berghan, 2002).
Ahmad, Qasim, *Britain, Franco Spain and the Cold War, 1945–1950* (London: Garland, 1992).
Alcalá Zamora, Niceto, *Memorias* (Madrid: Planeta, 1998).
Alexander, Bill, *British Volunteers for Liberty* (London: Lawrence & Wishart, 1983).
Alonso, Gregorio, 'Children of a Lesser God', in Gregorio Alonso and Diego Muro (eds.), *The Politics and Memory of Democratic Transition* (New York: Routledge, 2011).
Alonso Ibáñez, Ana I., 'Las Juntas de Defensa de las clases de tropa, 1917–18', *Cuadernos de Historia Contemporánea*, 21 (1999).
Alpert, Michael, *El ejército republicano en la Guerra Civil* (Madrid: Siglo XXI, 1989).
Alpert, Michael, *A New International History of the Spanish Civil War* (London: Macmillan, 1994).
Álvarez, Santiago, *Negrín, personalidad histórica* (Madrid: Ediciones de la Torre, 1994).
Álvarez Junco, José, *El Emperador del Paralelo. Lerroux y la demagogia populista* (Madrid: Alianza, 1990).
Álvarez Junco, José, 'La nación en duda', in Juan Pan-Montojo (ed.), *Más se perdió en Cuba. España, 1898 y la crisis de fin de siglo* (Madrid: Alianza, 1998).
Álvarez Junco, José, *Spanish Identity in the Age of Nations* (Manchester: Manchester University Press, 2011).
Álvarez Tardío, Manuel and Roberto Villa, *1936: Fraude y violencia en las elecciones del Frente Popular* (Madrid: Espasa, 2017).
Álvarez del Vayo, Julio, *Freedom's Battle* (London: Heinemann, 1940).
Anderson, Peter, *The Francoist Military Trials: Terror and Complicity, 1939–1945* (London: Routledge, 2010).
Anderson, Peter and Miguel Ángel del Arco, 'Introduction: Grappling with Spain's Dark Past', in Peter Anderson and Miguel Ángel del Arco (eds.), *Mass Killings and Violence in Spain, 1936–1952* (New York: Routledge, 2015).
Arco, Miguel Ángel del, 'Hunger and the Consolidation of the Francoist Regime, 1939–1951', *European History Quarterly*, 40/3 (2010).
Arco, Miguel Ángel del, 'The Struggle Continues: Everyday Repression and Resistance in Post-War Francoist Repression', in Peter Anderson and Miguel

Ángel del Arco (eds.), *Mass Killings and Violence in Spain, 1936–1952* (New York: Routledge, 2015).
Arenas, Rafael, 'El *Procés,* un intento de secesión de hecho', in Joaquim Coll, Ignacio Molina, and Manuel Arias Maldonado (eds.), *Anatomía del procés* (Barcelona: Debate, 2018).
Aróstegui, Julio, 'Burnett Bolloten y la Guerra Civil Española: la persistencia del Gran Engaño', in *Historia Contemporánea*, 3 (1990).
Aróstegui, Julio, *Por qué el 18 de julio . . . Y después* (Barcelona: Flor del Viento, 2006).
Aróstegui, Julio, 'De lealtades y defecciones. La República y la memoria de la utopía', in Ángel Viñas (ed.), *Al servicio de la República. Diplomáticos y Guerra Civil* (Madrid: Marcial Pons, 2010).
Aróstegui, Julio, 'El régimen: derecho, doctrina y lenguaje', in Julio Aróstegui (ed.), *Franco: La represión como sistema* (Barcelona: Flor del Viento, 2012).
Arranz, Luis, 'Could the Second Republic Have Become a Democracy?', in Manuel Álvarez Tardío and Fernando del Rey Reguillo (eds.), *The Spanish Second Republic Revisited: From Democratic Hopes to Civil War, 1931–1936* (Eastbourne: Sussex Academic Press, 2013).
Arroyo, Sebastián, *Why Banks Fail: The Political Roots of Banking Crises in Spain* (New York: Palgrave, 2020).
Avilés Farré, Juan, *La Izquierda burguesa en la II República* (Madrid: Espasa Calpe, 1985).
Avilés Farré, Juan, *La fe que vino de Rusia: la revolución bolchevique y los españoles, 1917–1931* (Madrid: Biblioteca Nueva, 1999).
Avilés Farré, Juan, *Francisco Ferrer Guardia. Pedagogo, anarquista y mártir* (Madrid: Marcial Pons, 2006).
Avilés Farré, Juan, 'Contra Alfonso XIII: atentados frustrados y conspiración revolucionaria', in Juan Avilés and Ángel Herrerín (eds.), *El nacimiento del terrorismo en Occidente. Anarquía, nihilismo y violencia revolucionaria* (Madrid: Siglo XXI, 2008).
Avilés Farré, Juan, *La daga y la dinamita. Los anarquistas y el nacimiento del terrorismo* (Barcelona: Tusquets, 2013).
Avilés, Juan and Ángel Herrerín, 'Propaganda por el hecho y propaganda por la represión: anarquismo y violencia en la España de fines del Siglo XIX', *Ayer*, 84 (2010).
Azaña, Manuel, *Memorias políticas y de la Guerra* (Barcelona: Crítica, 1978).
Azaña, Manuel, *Diarios, 1932–1933* (Madrid: Crítica, 1997).
Bachoud, Andrée, *Los españoles ante las campañas de Marruecos* (Madrid: Espasa, 1988).
Bahamonde, Ángel and Javier Cervera, *Así terminó la guerra de España* (Madrid: Marcial Pons, 1999).
Balcells, Albert, *Catalan Nationalism* (London: Macmillan, 1996).
Balcells, Albert, *El pistolerisme. Barcelona, 1917–1923* (Barcelona, Pòrtic, 2009).
Balfour, Sebastian, 'Riot, Regeneration and Reaction in Spain in the Aftermath of the 1898 Disaster', *Historical Journal*, 38 (1995).
Balfour, Sebastian, 'The Lion and the Pig: Nationalism and National Identity in *Fin-de-Siècle* Spain', in Clare Mar-Molinero and Angel Smith (eds.), *Nationalism and the Nation in the Iberian Peninsula: Competing and Conflicting Identities* (Oxford: Berg, 1996).

Balfour, Sebastian, *The End of the Spanish Empire, 1898–1923* (Oxford: Oxford University Press, 1997).
Balfour, Sebastian, *Deadly Embrace: Morocco and the Road to the Spanish Civil War* (Oxford: Oxford University Press, 2002).
Ballbé, Manuel, *Orden público y militarismo en la España constitucional, 1812–1983* (Madrid: Alianza, 1985).
Ballester, David, *Marginalidades y hegemonías: la UGT de Cataluña, 1888–1936* (Barcelona: Bronce, 1996).
Banac, Ivo (ed.), *The Diary of Georgi Dimitrov, 1933–1949* (London: Yale University Press, 2003).
Bar, Antonio, *La CNT en los años rojos: Del sindicalismo revolucionario al anarcosindicalismo, 1910–1926* (Madrid: Akal, 1981).
Bar, Antonio, 'The CNT: The Glory and Tragedy of Spanish Anarchosyndicalism', in Marcel Van der Linden and Wayne Thorpe (eds.), *Revolutionary Syndicalism: An International Perspective* (Brookfield, VT: Scholar Press, 1990).
Barciela, Carlos, 'La España del estraperlo', in José Luis García Delgado (ed.), *El Primer Franquismo. España durante la Segunda Guerra Mundial* (Madrid: Siglo XXI, 1989).
Barrio Alonso, Ángeles, *La modernización de España, 1917–1939. Política y sociedad* (Madrid: Síntesis, 2004).
Bel, Germà, *Disdain, Distrust and Dissolution: The Surge of Support for Independence in Catalonia* (Eastbourne: Sussex University Press, 2015).
Ben-Ami, Shlomo, *The Origins of the Second Republic in Spain* (Oxford: Oxford University Press, 1978).
Ben-Ami, Shlomo, *Fascism from Above: The Dictatorship of Primo de Rivera in Spain, 1923–1930* (Oxford: Oxford University Press, 1983).
Ben-Ami, Shlomo, 'The Republican "Take-over": Prelude to Inevitable Catastrophe?', in Paul Preston (ed.), *Revolution and War in Spain, 1931–1939* (London: Methuen, 1984).
Ben-Ami, Shlomo, 'The Crisis of the Dynastic Elite in the Transition from Monarchy to Republic, 1929–1931', in Paul Preston and Frances Lannon (eds.), *Elites and Power in Twentieth Century Spain: Essays in Honour of Sir Raymond Carr* (Oxford: Oxford University Press, 1990).
Bengoechea, Soledad, *Organització Patronal i conflictivitat social a Catalunya* (Barcelona: L'Abadia de Montserrat, 1994).
Bengoechea, Soledad, *El Locaut de Barcelona* (Barcelona: Curial, 1998).
Bennassar, Bartolomé, 'Introduction: Portée Mondiale de la Guerre d'Espagne', in Jean Sagnes and Sylvie Caucanas (eds.), *Les Français et la Guerre d'Espagne* (Perpignan: Presses Universitaires de Perpignan, 2008).
Berdah, Jean-Francois, *La democracia asesinada: La República española y las grandes potencias, 1931–1939* (Barcelona: Crítica, 2002).
Bergasa, Francisco, *¿Quién mató a Ferrer i Guardia?* (Madrid: Aguilar, 2009).
Blackbourn, David and Geoff Eley, *The Peculiarities of German History: Bourgeois Society and Politics in Nineteenth-Century Germany* (Oxford: Oxford University Press, 1991).
Blanco, Carlos, *La incompetencia militar de Franco* (Madrid: Alianza, 2000).
Blanco, Carlos, *Falacias de la Guerra Civil* (Barcelona: Planeta, 2005).
Blinkhorn, Martin, *Carlism and Crisis in Spain* (Cambridge: Cambridge University Press, 1975).

Blinkhorn, Martin, 'Introduction: Allies, Rivals or Antagonists? Fascists and Conservatives in Modern Europe', in Martin Blinkhorn (ed.), *Fascists and Conservatives* (London: Unwin Hyman, 1990).
Blinkhorn, Martin, 'Conservatism, Traditionalism and Fascism in Spain', in Martin Blinkhorn (ed.), *Fascists and Conservatives* (London: Unwin Hyman, 1990).
Bolloten, Burnett, *The Spanish Revolution* (Chapel Hill, NC: University of North Carolina Press, 1979).
Bookchin, Murray, *The Spanish Anarchists: The Heroic Years, 1868–1939* (New York: Free Life, 1977).
Borrell, Josep and Joan Llorach, *Las cuentas y los cuentos de la independencia* (Madrid: Catarata, 2017).
Botti, Alfonso, 'From Opposition to Government: The Popular Party of Mariano Rajoy', in Bonnie N. Field and Alfonso Botti (eds.), *Politics and Society in Contemporary Spain: From Zapatero to Rajoy* (Basingstoke: Palgrave, 2013).
Boyd, Carolyn P., *Praetorian Politics in Liberal Spain* (Chapel Hill, NC: University of North Carolina Press, 1979).
Boyd, Carolyn P., *Historia Patria. Política, historia e identidad nacional en España: 1875–1975* (Barcelona: Pomares, 2000).
Boyd, Carolyn P., 'El Rey-Soldado', in Javier Moreno Luzón (ed.), *Alfonso XIII* (Madrid: Marcial Pons, 2003).
Boyle, Catherine, 'The Politics of Popular Music on the Dynamics of New Song', in Helen Graham and Jo Labanyi (eds.), *Spanish Cultural Studies: An Introduction* (Oxford: Oxford University Press, 1995).
Brennan, Gerald, *The Spanish Labyrinth: An Account of the Social and Political Background of the Civil War* (Cambridge: Cambridge University Press, 1943).
Bru Sánchez-Fortún, Alberto, 'Para repensar la Juntas Militares de 1917', *Hispania*, LXXVI/252 (2016).
Brunet, Ferran, *Economía del separatismo catalán* (Barcelona: Planeta, 2022).
Buchanan, Tom, *Britain and the Spanish Civil War* (Cambridge: Cambridge University Press, 1997).
Buck, Tobias, *After the Fall: Crisis, Recovery, and the Making of a New Spain* (London: Weidenfeld & Nicolson, 2020).
Buendía, Luis and Ricardo Molero-Simarro, 'Introduction: The Political Economy of the Spanish Growth Model and its Structural Adjustment Process', in Luis Buendía and Ricardo Molero-Simarro (eds.), *The Political Economy of Contemporary Spain: From Miracle to Mirage* (London: Routledge, 2020).
Bueno Madurga, Jesús I., *Zaragoza, 1917–1936. De la movilización popular y obrera a la reacción conservadora* (Zaragoza: Fernando el Católico, 2000).
Burgos y Mazo, Manuel, *El verano de 1919 en Gobernación* (Cuenca: Tipos, 1921).
Buxadé, José, *España en crisis. La bullanga misteriosa de 1917* (Barcelona: Bauzá, 1917).
Cabrera, Mercedes, *La patronal ante la II República. Organizaciones y estrategia, 1931–1936* (Madrid: Siglo XXI, 1983).
Cabrera, Mercedes, Francisco Comín, and José Luis García Delgado, *Santiago Alba. Un programa de reforma económica en la España del primer tercio del Siglo XX* (Madrid: Instituto de Estudios Fiscales, 1989).
Cabrera, Mercedes and Fernando del Rey Reguillo, 'De la oligarquía y el caciquismo a la política de intereses. Por una relectura de la Restauración',

in Manuel Suárez Cortina (ed.), *Las máscaras de la libertad. El liberalismo español, 1808–1950* (Madrid: Marcial Pons, 2003).
Cacho Viu, Vicente, *Repensar el noventa y ocho* (Madrid: Biblioteca Nueva, 1997).
Callahan, William J., *The Catholic Church in Spain, 1875–1998* (Washington, DC: Catholic University of America Press, 2000).
Cambó, Francesc, *Memorias* (Madrid: Alianza, 1987).
Canal, Jordi, *El Carlismo* (Madrid: Alianza, 2000).
Canal, Jordi, *Con permiso de Kafka. El proceso independentista en Cataluña* (Barcelona: Península, 2018).
Cándido, *La sangre de la rosa. El poder y la época, 1982–1996* (Madrid: Planeta, 1996).
Capel, Ana María, 'Life and Work in the Tobacco Factories: Female Industrial Workers in the Early Twentieth Century', in Victoria Lorée Enders and Pamela Beth Radcliff (eds.), *Constructing Spanish Womanhood* (New York: State University of New York Press, 1999).
Carden, Ron M., *German Policy Toward Neutral Spain, 1914–18* (New York: Garland, 1987).
Cardenal, Juan Pablo, *La telaraña. La trama exterior del Procés* (Barcelona: Ariel, 2020).
Cardona, Gabriel, *El poder militar en la España contemporánea hasta la guerra civil* (Madrid: Siglo XXI, 1983).
Cardona, Gabriel, *Franco y sus generales. La manicura del tigre* (Madrid: Temas de Hoy, 2001).
Cardona, Gabriel, *Historia militar de una Guerra Civil* (Barcelona: Flor del Viento, 2006).
Cardona, Gabriel, *Alfonso XIII, el rey de espadas* (Barcelona: Planeta, 2010).
Carr, Raymond, *Spain, 1808–1975* (Oxford: Oxford University Press, 1982).
Carr, Raymond and Juan Pablo Fusi, *Spain: Dictatorship to Democracy* (London: Unwin Hyman, 1981).
Carroll, Peter N., *The Odyssey of the Abraham Lincoln Brigade* (Stanford, CA: Stanford University Press, 1994).
Casanova, Julián, 'Rebelión y revolución', in Santos Juliá (ed.), *Víctimas de la guerra civil* (Madrid: Temas de Hoy, 1999).
Casanova, Julián, 'La cara oscura del anarquismo', in Santos Juliá (ed.), *Violencia política en la España del Siglo XX* (Madrid: Taurus, 2000).
Casanova, Julián, *La Iglesia de Franco* (Madrid: Temas de Hoy, 2001).
Casanova, Julián, 'Una dictadura de cuarenta años', in Julián Casanova (coord.), *Morir, matar, sobrevivir* (Barcelona: Crítica, 2002).
Casanova, Julián, *Anarchism, the Republic and Civil War in Spain: 1931–1939* (London: Routledge, 2003).
Casanova, Julián and Carlos Gil Andrés, *Twentieth Century Spain* (Cambridge: Cambridge University Press, 2014).
Casla, Koldo, *Spain and Its Achilles' Heels* (London: Rowman & Littlefield, 2022).
Castillo, Santiago (ed.), *Historia de la Unión General de Trabajadores*, 2 vols. (Madrid: Unión, 1998).
Castillo, Santiago, (ed.), *Historia de la UGT, vol. 1: Un sindicalismo consciente, 1873–1914* (Madrid: Siglo XXI, 2008).
Castro Alfín, Daniel, 'Agitación y orden en la Restauración', *Historia Social*, 5 (1989).

Cazorla, Antonio, 'Beyond They Shall Not Pass: How the Experience of Violence Reshaped Political Values in Franco's Spain', *Journal of Contemporary History*, 40/3 (2005).
Cazorla, Antonio, *Fear and Progress: Ordinary Lives in Franco's Spain, 1939–1975* (Oxford: Wiley-Blackwell, 2010).
Cazorla, Antonio, *Franco. Biografía del mito* (Madrid: Alianza, 2014).
Cenarro, Ángela, 'Muerte y subordinación en la España franquista: El imperio de la violencia como base del nuevo estado', *Historia Social*, 30 (1998).
Cenarro, Ángela, 'Violence, Surveillance, and Denunciation: Social Cleavage in the Spanish Civil War and Francoism, 1936–1950', in Clive Emsley, Eric Johnson, and Pieter Spierenburg (eds.), *Social Control in Europe, 1800–2000* (Columbus, OH: Ohio University Press, 2004).
Cepeda Gómez, José, 'La invención de dos mitos: norteamericanos y españoles ante sus guerras de Independencia', in Antonio Rodríguez and Rosario Ruiz (eds.), *1808. Controversias historiográficas* (Madrid: Actas, 2010).
Cercas, Javier, *Anatomía de un instante* (Barcelona: Mondadori, 2009).
Cervera, Javier, *Madrid en guerra* (Madrid: Alianza, 1998).
Ciano, Galeazzo, *Diplomatic Papers* (London: Odham Press, 1948).
Ciano, Galeazzo, *Diary, 1937–43* (London: Phoenix, 2002 [1946]).
Cierva, Juan de la, *Notas de mi vida* (Madrid: Reus, 1955).
Cobo Romero, Francisco, *Por la reforma agraria hacia la revolución. El sindicalismo agrario socialista durante la II República y la Guerra Civil, 1930–1939* (Granada: Universidad de Granada, 2007).
Cobo Romero, Francisco, 'The Red Dawn of the Andalusian Countryside: Peasant Protest during the Bolshevik Triennium, 1918–1920', in Francisco J. Romero Salvadó and Angel Smith (eds.), *The Agony of Spanish Liberalism: From Revolution to Dictatorship, 1913–1923* (Basingstoke: Palgrave, 2010).
Coll, Joaquim, 'El *procés*', in Joaquim Coll, Ignacio Molina, and Manuel Arias Maldonado (eds.), *Anatomía del procés* (Barcelona: Debate, 2018).
Colton, Joel, 'The Formation of the French Popular Front', in Martin S. Alexander and Helen Graham (eds.), *The French and Spanish Popular Fronts: Comparative Perspectives* (Cambridge: Cambridge University Press, 1989).
Confederación Nacional del Trabajo, *Memoria del Congreso celebrado en el Teatro de la Comedia de Madrid, los días 10 al 18 de diciembre de 1919* (Barcelona: Cosmos, 1932).
Confederación Regional del Trabajo, *Memoria del Congreso celebrado en Barcelona, los días 28, 29, 30 de junio y el 1 de julio de 1918* (Barcelona: CRT, 1918).
Costa, Joaquín, *Oligarquía y caciquismo como la forma actual de gobierno en España: urgencia y modo de cambiarla* (Madrid: Biblioteca Nueva, 2001 [1898]).
Cot, Pierre, *Triumph of Treason* (New York: Ziff-Davis, 1944).
Coverdale, John F., *Italian Intervention in the Spanish Civil War* (Princeton, NJ: Princeton University Press, 1975).
Cowans, Joe, *Modern Spain: A Documentary History* (Philadelphia, PA: University of Pennsylvania Press, 2003).
Cruz, Rafael, *El Partido Comunista de España en la II República* (Madrid: Alianza, 1987).
Cruz Artacho, Salvador, Francisco Acosta Ramírez, Francisco Cobo Romero et al., 'El socialismo español y la cuestión agraria, 1879–1923. Luces y sombras en el debate teórico y en la práctica sindical y política', *Ayer*, 54 (2002).

Cuadrat, Xavier, *Socialismo y Anarquismo en Cataluña, 1890–1911* (Madrid: Revista de Trabajo, 1976).
Culla i Clara, Joan B., *El Republicanisme Lerrouxista a Catalunya, 1901–1923* (Barcelona: Curial, 1986).
Dalmau i Ribalta, Antoni, *El Cas Rull. Viure del terror a la ciutat de las bombas, 1901–1908* (Barcelona: Columna, 2008).
Dalmau i Ribalta, Antoni, *Set dies de fúria. Barcelona i la Setmana Trágica* (Barcelona: Columna, 2009).
Dalmau i Ribalta, Antoni, *El procés de Montjuïc. Barcelona al final del Segle XIX* (Barcelona: Base, 2010).
Dalmau i Ribalta, Antoni, 'La oleada de violencia en la Barcelona de 1904–1908', *Ayer*, 85 (2012).
Dardé, Carlos, 'Sagasta o cómo sobrevivir en política', in Javier Moreno Luzón (ed.), *Progresistas* (Madrid: Taurus, 2006).
Day, Peter, *Franco's Friends: How British Intelligence Helped Bring Franco to Power in Spain* (London: Biteback, 2011).
Díaz Burillo, Vicente Jesús, *Las Transiciones de la Iglesia. (1962–1987). Del repliegue a la revancha* (Granada: Comares, 2019).
Díaz del Moral, Juan, *Historia de las agitaciones campesinas andaluzas* (Madrid: Alianza, 1995 [1929]).
Documents on German Foreign Policy, 1918–1945, series D, vol. 3: *Germany and the Spanish Civil War* (London: HMSO, 1951).
Domingo, Alfonso, *El ángel rojo. La historia de Melchor Rodríguez* (Barcelona: Almuzara, 2010).
Dowling, Andrew, *Catalonia since the Spanish Civil War* (Brighton: Sussex University Press, 2013).
Duroselle, Jean-Baptiste, *France and the Nazi Threat: The Collapse of French Diplomacy, 1932–1939* (New York: Enigma, 2004).
Ealham, Chris, *Class, Culture and Conflict in Barcelona, 1898–1937* (London: Routledge, 2005).
Ealham, Chris, An Impossible Unity: Revolution, Reform and Counter-Revolution and the Spanish Left, 1917–23', in Francisco J. Romero Salvadó and Angel Smith (eds.), *The Agony of Spanish Liberalism: From Revolution to Dictatorship, 1913–1923* (Basingstoke: Palgrave, 2010).
Eden, Anthony, *Facing the Dictators* (London: Cassell, 1962).
Edwards, Jill, *The British Government and the Spanish Civil War* (London: Macmillan, 1979).
Edwards, Jill, *Anglo-American Relations and the Franco Question, 1945–1955* (Oxford: Oxford University Press, 1999).
Ehrlich, Charles E., '*Per Catalunya i l'Espanya Gran*: Catalan Regionalism on the Offensive, 1911–1919', *European History Quarterly*, 28/2 (1998).
Eiroa, Matilde, 'Del estudio del pasado a la trasmisión en el presente: ¿Qué papel desempeñan los historiadores a los 80 años de la Guerra Civil?', in Juan Andrés Blanco, Jesús A. Martínez, and Ángel Viñas (eds.), *Luces sobre un pasado deformado. La Guerra Civil 80 años después* (Madrid: Marcial Pons, 2020).
Eiroa, Matilde and Ángeles Egido, 'Los confusos caminos del perdón: De la pena de muerte a la conmutación', in Julio Aróstegui (ed.), *Franco: La represión como sistema* (Barcelona: Flor del Viento, 2012).
Ellwood, Sheelagh, *Spanish Fascism in the Franco Era* (London: Macmillan, 1987).

Elorza, Antonio and Marta Bizcarrondo, *Queridos Camaradas: La Internacional Comunista y España, 1919–1939* (Madrid: Planeta, 1999).
Elorza, Antonio and Elena Hernández Sandoica, *La Guerra de Cuba, 1895–98* (Madrid: Alianza, 1998).
Encarnación, Omar G., *Spanish Politics* (Cambridge: Polity, 2008).
Encarnación, Omar G., 'Spain's New Left Turn: Society Driven or Party Instigated', in Bonnie N. Field and Alfonso Botti (eds.), *Politics and Society in Contemporary Spain: From Zapatero to Rajoy* (Basingstoke: Palgrave, 2013).
Esenwein, George R., *Anarchist Ideology and the Working-Class Movement in Spain, 1868–1898* (Berkeley, CA: University of California Press, 1989).
España, Ramón de, *El manicomio catalán* (Barcelona: La esfera de los libros, 2013).
Espinosa, Francisco, 'Julio 1936', in Julián Casanova (coord.), *Morir, matar, sobrevivir* (Barcelona: Crítica, 2002).
Espinosa, Francisco, 'Introducción', in Francisco Espinosa (ed.), *Violencia roja y azul. España, 1936–1950* (Barcelona: Crítica, 2010).
Espinosa, Francisco, *Guerra y represión en el sur de España* (Valencia: PUV, 2012).
Espuny Tomás, María José, 'Eduardo Dato y la legislación obrera', *Historia Social*, 43 (2002).
Etxeberria, Francisco, 'Fosas comunes de la Guerra Civil en el Siglo XXI: antecedentes, interdisciplinariedad y legislación', *Historia Contemporánea*, 60 (2019).
Evans, Peter, 'Cinema, Memory, and the Unconscious', in Helen Graham and Jo Labanyi (eds.), *Spanish Cultural Studies: An Introduction* (Oxford: Oxford University Press, 1995).
Fernández Almagro, Melchor, *Historia del reinado de Alfonso XIII* (Barcelona: Montaner y Simón, 1977 [1933]).
Fernández Vargas, Valentina, *Sangre o dinero. El mito del ejército nacional* (Madrid: Alianza, 2004).
Ferrer, Sol, *Vida y obra de Francisco Ferrer* (Barcelona: Luis de Caralt, 1980).
Field, Bonnie N., 'A Second Transition in Spain? Policy, Institutions and Interparty Politics under Zapatero (2004–8)', in Bonnie N. Field and Alfonso Botti (eds.), *Politics and Society in Contemporary Spain: From Zapatero to Rajoy* (Basingstoke: Palgrave, 2013).
Field, Bonnie N. and Alfonso Botti, 'Introduction', in Bonnie N. Field and Alfonso Botti (eds.), *Politics and Society in Contemporary Spain: From Zapatero to Rajoy* (Basingstoke: Palgrave, 2013).
Finer, Samuel E., *The Man on Horseback: The Role of the Military in Politics* (London: Pall Mall Press, 1967).
Fomento del Trabajo Nacional, *Memoria de la Junta Directiva del Fomento del Trabajo Nacional correspondiente a 1919–1920* (Barcelona: Hijos de Domingo Casanova, 1920).
Fomento del Trabajo Nacional, *Memoria de la Junta Directiva del Fomento del Trabajo Nacional correspondiente a 1923–1924* (Barcelona: Hijos de Domingo Casanova, 1924).
Fominaya, Cristina Flesher, *Democracy Reloaded: Inside Spain's Political Laboratory from 15-M to Podemos* (Oxford: Oxford University Press, 2020).
Forner, Salvador, *Canalejas y el partido liberal democrático* (Madrid: Cátedra, 1993).

Fraser, Ronald, *Blood of Spain* (Harmondsworth: Penguin, 1981).
Fuente Monge, Gregorio de la, *Los revolucionarios de 1868, elites y poder en la España liberal* (Madrid: Marcial Pons, 2000).
Fuentes, Juan Francisco, *Largo Caballero. El Lenin español* (Madrid: Síntesis, 2005).
Fuentes Codera, Maximiliano, *España en la Primera Guerra Mundial: una movilización cultural* (Madrid: Akal, 2014).
Fundació Ferrer i Guàrdia, *Causa por Regicidio frustrado (31 mayo 1906)*, 5 vols. (Madrid: Sucesores de J.A. García, 1911).
Fundació Ferrer i Guàrdia, *Ferrer, páginas para la historia. Consejo de Guerra: acusación, defensa y sentencia* (Barcelona, 1912).
Fusi, Juan Pablo, *Política obrera en el País Vasco, 1880–1923* (Madrid: Turner, 1975).
Gabriel, Pere, 'Red Barcelona in the Europe of War and Revolution, 1914–30', in Angel Smith (ed.), *Red Barcelona: Social Protest and Labour Mobilization in the Twentieth Century* (London: Routledge, 2002).
Gabriel, Pere, 'El ugetismo socialista catalán, 1888–1923', *Ayer*, 54 (2004).
Gallego, Ferrán, *Barcelona, mayo de 1937* (Barcelona: Debate, 2007).
García, Lola, *El naufragio* (Madrid: Península, 2018).
García Delgado, José Luis (ed.), *Las ciudades en la modernización de España. Los decenios interseculares* (Madrid: Siglo XXI, 1992).
García Delgado, José Luis (ed.), *La modernización económica en la España de Alfonso XIII* (Madrid: Espasa, 2002).
García Delgado, José Luis, and Juan Carlos Jiménez, *Un siglo de España. La Economía* (Madrid: Marcial Pons, 2001).
García Márquez, José María, 'El triunfo del golpe militar: el terror en la zona ocupada', in Francisco Espinosa (ed.), *Violencia roja y azul. España, 1936–1950* (Barcelona: Crítica, 2010).
García Oliver, Juan, *El eco de los pasos* (Paris: Ruedo Ibérico, 1978).
García de Ortazar, Fernando and J. Manuel González Vega, *Breve historia de España* (Madrid: Alianza, 2017).
García Sanz, Fernando, *España en la Gran Guerra. Espías, diplomáticos y traficantes* (Madrid: Galaxia Gutenberg, 2014).
Garriga, Joan, *Memòries d'un liberal catalanista, 1871–1939* (Barcelona: Edicions 62, 1987).
Geary, Dick, *European Labour Protest, 1848–1939* (London: Methuen, 1984).
Gerwarth, Robert, *The Vanquished: Why the First World War Failed to End, 1917–1923* (London: Penguin, 2016).
Gil Andrés, Carlos, *Echarse a la calle. Amotinados, huelguistas y revolucionarios, La Rioja, 1890–1936* (Zaragoza: Prensas Universitarias de Zaragoza, 2000).
Gil Pecharromán, Julio, *Conservadores subversivos. La derecha autoritaria Alfonsina, 1913–1936* (Madrid: Eudema, 1994).
Gil Robles, José María, *No fue posible la paz* (Madrid: Planeta, 1998 [1968]).
Gilmour, David, *The Transformation of Spain: From Franco to the Constitutional Monarchy* (London: Quartet, 1985).
Godicheau, François, 'Los hechos de mayo de 1937 y los presos antifascistas: identificación de un fenómeno represivo', *Historia Social*, 44 (2002).
Golay, Michael, *The Spanish-American War* (New York: Facts on File, 1995).
Golden, Lester, 'The Women in Command: The Barcelona Women's Consumer War of 1918', *UCLA Historical Journal*, 6 (1985).

Gómez Bravo, Gutmaro, 'Teología penitenciaria: las cárceles del régimen', in Julio Aróstegui (ed.), *Franco: La represión como sistema* (Barcelona: Flor del Viento, 2012).

Gómez-Navarro, José Luis, *El régimen de Primo de Rivera* (Madrid: Cátedra, 1991).

Gómez Ochoa, Fidel, 'El conservadurismo canovista y los orígenes de la Restauración: la formación de un conservadurismo moderno', in Manuel Suárez Cortina (ed.), *La Restauración, entre el liberalismo y la democracia* (Madrid: Alianza, 1997).

González Calbet, María Teresa, *La dictadura de Primo de Rivera. El Directorio Militar* (Madrid: El Arquero, 1987).

González Calleja, Eduardo, 'Una perspectiva de la violencia política en la España de la Restauración', *Ayer*, 13 (1994).

González Calleja, Eduardo, *La razón de la fuerza. Orden público, subversión y violencia política en la España de la Restauración, 1875–1917* (Madrid: CSIC, 1998).

González Calleja, Eduardo, *El Máuser y el sufragio. Orden público, subversión y violencia política en la crisis de la Restauración, 1917–1931* (Madrid: CSIC, 1999).

González Calleja, Eduardo, *La España de Primo de Rivera. La modernización autoritaria 1923–1930* (Madrid: Alianza, 2005).

González Calleja, Eduardo, 'Tendencias y controversias de la historiografía', in Eduardo González Calleja and Álvaro Ribagorda (eds.), *Luces y sombras del 14 de abril* (Madrid: Nueva, 2017).

González Calleja, Eduardo, 'Presentación', in Eduardo González Calleja and Álvaro Ribagorda (eds.), *Luces y sombras del 14 de abril* (Madrid: Nueva, 2017).

González Calleja, Eduardo and Paul Aubert, *Nidos de espías. España, Francia y la Primera Guerra Mundial* (Madrid: Alianza, 2014).

González Calleja, Eduardo and Fernando del Rey Reguillo, *La defensa armada contra la revolución* (Madrid: CSIC, 1995).

González Calleja, Eduardo, Francisco Cobo Romero, Ana Martínez Rus, and Francisco Sánchez Pérez, *La Segunda República* (Barcelona: Pasado & Presente, 2015).

González Casanova, José Antonio, *Federalismo y autonomía. Cataluña y el estado español, 1868–1938* (Barcelona: Crítica, 1979).

González Cuevas, Pedro Carlos, 'El pensamiento político de Antonio Cánovas', in Javier Tusell and Florentino Portero (eds.), *Antonio Cánovas y el Sistema político de la Restauración* (Madrid: Biblioteca Nueva, 1998).

González Hernández, María Jesús, *Ciudadanía y acción. El conservadurismo maurista, 1907–1923* (Madrid: Siglo XXI, 1990).

González Hernández, María Jesús, *El universo conservador de Antonio Maura* (Madrid: Biblioteca Nueva, 1997).

González de Molina, Manuel, 'Los mitos de la modernidad y la protesta campesina. A propósito de rebeldes primitivos de Eric J. Hobsbawm', *Historia Social*, 25 (1996).

Graham, Helen, 'The Spanish Popular Front and the Civil War', in Helen Graham and Paul Preston (eds.), *The Popular Front in Europe* (London: Macmillan, 1987).

Graham, Helen, *Socialism and War: The Spanish Socialist Party in Power and Crisis, 1936–1939* (Cambridge: Cambridge University Press, 1991).

Graham, Helen, 'Gender and the State: Women in the 1940s', in Helen Graham and Jo Labanyi (eds.), *Spanish Cultural Studies: An Introduction* (Oxford: Oxford University Press, 1995).
Graham, Helen, 'War, Modernity and Reform: The Premiership of Juan Negrín', in Paul Preston and Ann L. Mackenzie (eds.), *The Republic Besieged* (Edinburgh: Edinburgh University Press, 1996).
Graham, Helen, 'Against the State: A Genealogy of the Barcelona May Days', *European History Quarterly*, 29/4 (1999).
Graham, Helen, *The Spanish Republic at War* (Cambridge: Cambridge University Press, 2002).
Graham, Helen, *The War and its Shadow: Spain's Civil War in Europe's Long Twentieth Century* (Brighton: Sussex Academic Press, 2012).
Graham, Helen, 'Reform as Promise and Threat: Political Progressives and Blueprints for Change in Spain, 1931–1936', in Helen Graham (ed.), *Interrogating Francoism* (London: Bloomsbury, 2016).
Graham, Helen and Paul Preston, 'The Popular Front and the Struggle against Fascism', in Helen Graham and Paul Preston (eds.), *The Popular Front in Europe* (London: Macmillan, 1987).
Granja Sainz, José Luis de la, *El Nacionalismo Vasco: Un siglo de historia* (Madrid: Tecnos, 2002).
Gray, Caroline, *Territorial Politics and the Party System in Spain* (New York: Routledge, 2020).
Grupo de Afinidad Quico Rivas, *La Barcelona de la dinamita, el plomo y el petróleo, 1884–1909* (Barcelona: El ojo portátil, 2009).
Gual Villalbi, Pedro, *Memorias de un industrial de nuestro tiempo* (Barcelona: Sociedad General de Publicaciones, 1923).
Gunther, Richard, 'The Spanish Model Revisited', in Gregorio Alonso and Diego Muro (eds.), *The Politics and Memory of Democratic Transition* (New York: Routledge, 2011).
Gutiérrez Molina, José Luis, *El estado frente a la anarquía. Los grandes procesos contra el anarquismo español, 1883–1982* (Madrid: Síntesis, 2008).
Hall, Morgan C., *Alfonso XIII y el ocaso de la monarquía liberal, 1902–1923* (Madrid: Alianza, 2005).
Harrison, Joseph, *The Spanish Economy in the Twentieth Century* (London: Croom Helm, 1985).
Harrison, Joseph, 'The Catalan Industrial Elite, 1898–1923', in Paul Preston and Frances Lannon (eds.), *Elites and Power in Twentieth Century Spain: Essays in Honour of Sir Raymond Carr* (Oxford: Oxford University Press, 1990).
Harvey, Oliver, *Diplomatic Diaries, 1937–1940* (London: John Harvey, 1970).
Hayes, Carlton J.H., *Wartime Mission in Spain* (New York: Macmillan, 1945).
Heiberg, Morten, *Emperadores del Mediterráneo: Franco, Mussolini y la guerra civil española* (Barcelona: Crítica, 2004).
Hernández, Fernando, *Guerra o revolución. El Partido Comunista de España en la Guerra Civil* (Barcelona: Crítica, 2010).
Herrerín López, Ángel, *Anarquía, dinamita y revolución social. Violencia y repression en la España de entre siglos, 1868–1900* (Madrid: Catarata, 2011).
Heywood, Paul, *Marxism and the Failure of Organized Socialism in Spain, 1879–1936* (Cambridge: Cambridge University Press, 1990).

Heywood, Paul, *The Government and Politics of Spain* (London: Macmillan, 1995).
Hoare, Samuel, *Ambassador on Special Mission* (London: Collins, 1946).
Hobsbawm, Eric J., *Primitive Rebels* (Manchester: Manchester University Press, 1959).
Hobsbawm, Eric J., *The Age of Revolution, 1789–1848* (London: Weidenfeld & Nicolson, 1962).
Hobsbawm, Eric J., *Age of Extremes: The Short Twentieth Century, 1914–91* (London: Penguin, 1994).
Howson, Gerald, *Arms for Spain: The Untold Story of the Spanish Civil War* (London: John Murray, 1998).
Huertas, Josep Maria, *Obrers a Catalunya* (Barcelona: Avenç, 1982).
Humlebæc, Carsten, 'The Pacto del Olvido', in Gregorio Alonso and Diego Muro (eds.), *The Politics and Memory of Democratic Transition* (New York: Routledge, 2011).
Hurtado, Amadeu, *Quaranta anys de advocat. Història del meu temps, 1894–1936* (Barcelona: Edicions 62, 2011 [1956]).
Ignacio, León, *Los años del pistolerismo. Ensayo de una guerra civil* (Madrid: Planeta, 1981).
Imaz, Carlos, 'España en el corazón: la ayuda y el refugio mexicano', in Alberto Reig and José Sánchez (eds.), *La Guerra Civil española. 80 años después* (Madrid: Tecnos, 2019).
Inquimbert, Anne-Aurore, *Un officier français dans la guerre d'Espagne* (Paris: Presses Universitaires de Rennes, 2009).
Instituto de Reformas Sociales, *Movimiento de los precios al por menor durante la guerra y la posguerra, 1914–1922* (Madrid: Sobrinos de la Sociedad de M. Minuesa, 1923).
Jackson, Gabriel, *The Spanish Republic and the Civil War, 1931–1939*, 5th edition (Princeton, NJ: Princeton University Press, 1972).
Jackson, Michael, *Fallen Sparrows: The International Brigades in the Spanish Civil War* (Philadelphia, PA: American Philosophical Society, 1994).
Jáuregui, Fernando and Federico Quevedo, *El desengaño* (Madrid: Almuzara, 2017).
Jiménez Torres, David, *2017. La crisis que cambió España* (Barcelona: Deusto, 2021).
Joll, James, *The Anarchists* (London: Eyre & Spottiswoode, 1964).
Jones, Thomas, *A Diary with Letters* (Oxford: Oxford University Press, 1954).
Jorge, David, 'El abandono de la República por las democracias: nuevos hallazgos y enfoques', in Juan Andrés Blanco, Jesús A. Martínez, and Ángel Viñas (eds.), *Luces sobre un pasado deformado. La Guerra Civil 80 años después* (Madrid: Marcial Pons, 2020).
Jover Zamora, José María, *España en la política internacional. Siglos XVIII–XX* (Madrid: Marcial Pons, 1999).
Juliá, Santos, *Madrid, 1931–34: De la fiesta popular a la lucha de clases* (Madrid: Siglo XXI, 1984).
Juliá, Santos, *Manuel Azaña: una biografía política* (Madrid: Alianza, 1991).
Juliá, Santos, *Los Socialistas en la política española, 1879–1982* (Madrid: Taurus, 1997).
Juliá, Santos, 'De guerra contra el invasor a guerra fratricida', in Santos Juliá (ed.), *Víctimas de la guerra civil* (Madrid: Temas de Hoy, 1999).

Juliá, Santos, *Transición* (Barcelona: Galaxia Gutenberg, 2017).
Keene, Judith, *Fighting for Franco: International Volunteers in Nationalist Spain during the Spanish Civil War, 1936–39* (London: Leicester University Press, 2001).
Kowalsky, Daniel, *La Unión Soviética y la guerra civil española* (Barcelona: Crítica, 2004).
Lacomba, Juan Antonio, *La crisis española de 1917* (Málaga: Ciencia Nueva, 1970).
Lacouture, Jean, *Léon Blum* (New York: Holmes & Meier, 1982).
Lannon, Frances, *Privilege, Persecution and Prophecy: The Catholic Church in Spain, 1875–1975* (Oxford: Oxford University Press, 1987).
Laporte, Pablo, 'The Moroccan Quagmire and the Crisis of Spain's Liberal System', in Francisco J. Romero Salvadó and Angel Smith (eds.), *The Agony of Spanish Liberalism: From Revolution to Dictatorship, 1913–1923* (Basingstoke: Palgrave, 2010).
Largo Caballero, Francisco, *Mis recuerdos: Carta a un amigo* (México: Ediciones Unidas, 1976).
Largo Caballero, Francisco, *Escritos de La República* (Madrid: Pablo Iglesias, 1985).
Ledesma, José Luis, 'Una retaguardia al rojo. Las violencias en la zona republicana', in Francisco Espinosa (ed.), *Violencia roja y azul. España, 1936–1950* (Barcelona: Crítica, 2010).
Ledesma, José Luis, 'La primavera trágica de 1936 y la pendiente hacia la guerra civil', in Ángel Viñas, Fernando Puell de la Villa, Julio Aróstegui et al. (coords.), *Los mitos del 18 de julio* (Barcelona: Crítica, 2019).
Leguina, Joaquín, *Pedro Sánchez. Historia de una ambición* (Barcelona: Planeta, 2021).
Leitz, Christian, *Economic Relations between Nazi Germany and Franco's Spain, 1936–1945* (Oxford: Oxford University Press, 1996).
Lerroux, Alejandro, *La pequeña historia de España, 1930–1936* (Madrid: Akrón, 2009 [1937]).
Lida, Clara, 'Para repensar la mano negra. El anarquismo español durante la clandestinidad', *Historia Social*, 74 (2012).
Liedtke, Boris, *Embracing a Dictatorship: US Relations with Spain, 1945–53* (Basingstoke: Macmillan, 1997).
Little, Douglas, *Malevolent Neutrality: The United States, Great Britain, and the Origins of the Spanish Civil War* (Ithaca, NY: Cornell University Press, 1985).
López Villaverde, Ángel Luis, *La Segunda República, 1931–1936* (Madrid: Silex, 2019).
Lorée Enders, Victoria and Pamela Beth Radcliff, 'Introduction', in Victoria Lorée Enders and Pamela Beth Radcliff (eds.), *Constructing Spanish Womanhood* (New York: State University of New York Press, 1999).
Lorée Enders, Victoria and Pamela Beth Radcliff, 'Part II: Work Identities', in Victoria Lorée Enders and Pamela Beth Radcliff (eds.), *Constructing Spanish Womanhood* (New York: State University of New York Press, 1999).
Lorenzo, Anselmo, *El proletariado militante. Memorias de un internacional* (Madrid: Solidaridad Obrera, 2013 [1901–1923]).
Lorenzo, César, *Los anarquistas españoles y el poder, 1868–1969* (Paris: Ruedo Ibérico, 1969).

Losada, Juan Carlos, 'Los momentos decisivos de la guerra. Las estrategias militares', in Juan Andrés Blanco, Jesús A. Martínez, and Ángel Viñas (eds.), *Luces sobre un pasado deformado. La Guerra Civil 80 años después* (Madrid: Marcial Pons, 2020).

Macarro, José M., 'Sindicalismo y política', *Ayer*, 20 (1995).

Macarro, José M., 'The Socialists and the Revolution', in Manuel Álvarez Tardío and Fernando del Rey (eds.), *The Spanish Second Republic Revisited: From Democratic Hopes to Civil War, 1931–1936* (Eastbourne: Sussex Academic Press, 2013).

Magone, José M., 'The Role of the EEC in the Spanish, Portuguese, and Greek Transitions', in Gregorio Alonso and Diego Muro (eds.), *The Politics and Memory of Democratic Transition* (New York: Routledge, 2011).

Maisky, Ivan, *Spanish Notebooks* (London: Hutchinson, 1966).

Malefakis, Edward, *Agrarian Reform and Peasant Revolution in Spain* (London: Yale University Press, 1970).

Malefakis, Edward, *Reforma agraria y revolución campesina en la España del Siglo XX* (Barcelona: Ariel, 1971).

Malraux, André, *L'Espoir* (Paris: Gallimard, 1937).

Manganas, Nicholas, *Las dos Españas: Terror and Crisis in Contemporary Spain* (Brighton: Sussex University Press, 2016).

Marco, Jorge, 'Debemos condenar y condenamos. Justicia militar y represión', in Julio Aróstegui (ed.), *Franco: La represión como sistema* (Barcelona: Flor del Viento, 2012).

Marco, Jorge, *Guerrilleros and Neighbours in Arms* (Brighton: Sussex Academic Press, 2012).

Marco, Vicente, *Las conspiraciones contra la Dictadura* (Madrid: Giner, 1975).

Marcuello, Juan Ignacio, 'Las Cortes de Cádiz, Monarquía y gobierno de Asamblea. Valoraciones historiográficas sobre la formación de gobierno en el Sistema constitucional de 1812', in Antonio Rodríguez and Rosario Ruiz (eds.), *1808. Controversias historiográficas* (Madrid: Actas, 2010).

Marí-Klose, Pau, 'Cataluña deshilachada', in Joaquim Coll, Ignacio Molina, and Manuel Arias Maldonado (eds.), *Anatomía del procés* (Barcelona: Debate, 2018).

Márquez, Benito and José María Capó, *Las Juntas Militares de Defensa* (La Habana: Porvenir, 1923).

Martin, Benjamin, *The Agony of Modernization: Labor and Industrialization in Spain* (New York: Cornell University Press, 1990).

Martín Corrales, Eloy, 'Movilizaciones en España contra la guerra de Marruecos, julio-agosto de 1909', in Eloy Martín Corrales (ed.), *Semana Trágica. Entre las barricadas de Barcelona y el Barranco del Lobo* (Barcelona: Bellaterra, 2011).

Martín Ramos, José Luis (ed.), *Historia de la UGT, vol. 2: Entre la revolución y el reformismo, 1914–1931* (Madrid: Siglo XXI, 2008).

Martín Ramos, José Luis, *El Frente Popular* (Barcelona: Pasado & Presente, 2015).

Martínez Fiol, David, *La Setmana Trágica* (Barcelona: Pòrtic, 2009).

Martorell Linares, Miguel, *El santo temor al déficit* (Madrid: Alianza, 2000).

Martorell Linares, Miguel, *José Sánchez Guerra. Un hombre de honor, 1859–1956* (Madrid: Marcial Pons, 2011).

Mateos, Abdón, 'Gordón Ordrás y la Guerra de España desde México', in Ángel Viñas (ed.), *Al servicio de la República. Diplomáticos y Guerra Civil* (Madrid: Marcial Pons, 2010).

Maura, Gabriel, *Bosquejo histórico de la dictadura* (Madrid: Tipografía de archivos, 1930).
Maura, Gabriel, *Recuerdos de mi vida* (Madrid: Aguilar, 1934).
Maura, Gabriel and Melchor Fernández Almagro, *Por qué cayó Alfonso XIII: Evolución y disolución de los partidos históricos durante su reinado* (Madrid: Ambos Mundos, 1948).
Maura, Miguel, *Así cayó Alfonso XIII* (Barcelona: Ariel, 1966).
Maurice, Jacques, 'A propósito del Trienio Bolchevique', in José Luis García Delgado (ed.), *La crisis de la Restauración: España entre la Primera Guerra Mundial y la II República* (Madrid: Siglo XXI, 1986).
Mayer, Arno, *The Persistence of the Old Regime: Europe to the Great War* (London: Croom Helm, 1981).
McDermott, Kevin and Jeremy Agnew, *The Comintern: A History of International Communism from Lenin to Stalin* (London: Macmillan, 1996).
McHarg, Farquhar, ¡*Pistoleros! 1: 1918* (Hastings: Christie Books, 2009).
Meaker, Gerald, *The Revolutionary Left in Spain 1914–23* (Stanford, CA: Stanford University Press, 1974).
Meaker, Gerald, 'A Civil War of Words', in Hans A. Schmitt (ed.), *Neutral Europe between War and Revolution, 1917–1923* (Charlottesville, VA: University of Virginia Press, 1988).
Mendoza, Eduardo, *The Truth About the Savolta Case* (London: HarperCollins, 1993).
Milán García, José Ramón, 'La revolución entra en Palacio. El liberalismo dinástico de Sagasta, 1875–1903', *Berceo*, 139 (2000).
Minder, Raphael, *The Struggle for Catalonia* (London: Hurst, 2017).
Mir, Conxita, 'La represión franquista en la Cataluña rural', in Julián Casanova (coord.), *Morir, matar, sobrevivir* (Barcelona: Crítica, 2002).
Miralles, Ricardo, *Juan Negrín* (Madrid: Temas de Hoy, 2003).
Miralles, Ricardo, 'El duro forcejeo de la diplomacia republican en París. Francia y la Guerra Civil', in Ángel Viñas (ed.), *Al servicio de la República. Diplomáticos y Guerra Civil* (Madrid: Marcial Pons, 2010).
Moch, Jules, *Rencontres avec . . . Léon Blum* (Paris: Plon, 1970).
Molina, Ignacio, 'La dimensión internacional y europea del *procés*', in Joaquim Coll, Ignacio Molina, and Manuel Arias Maldonado (eds.), *Anatomía del procés* (Barcelona: Debate, 2018).
Moradiellos, Enrique, *Neutralidad benévola: El Gobierno británico y la insurrección militar española de 1936* (Oviedo: Pentalfa, 1990).
Moradiellos, Enrique, *La Perfidia de Albión: El Gobierno británico y la guerra civil española* (Madrid: Siglo XXI, 1996).
Moradiellos, Enrique, 'The Gentle General: The Official British Perception of General Franco during the Spanish Civil War', in Paul Preston and Ann L. Mackenzie (eds.), *The Republic Besieged* (Edinburgh: Edinburgh University Press, 1996).
Moradiellos, Enrique, *El reñidero de Europa: Las dimensiones internacionales de la Guerra civil Española* (Barcelona: Península, 2001).
Moradiellos, Enrique, 'The Potsdam Conference and the Spanish Problem', *Contemporary European History*, 10/1 (2001).
Moradiellos, Enrique, *1936. Los mitos de la Guerra Civil* (Madrid: Península, 2004).

Moradiellos, Enrique, *Don Juan Negrín. Una biografía de la figura más difamada de la España del Siglo XX* (Barcelona: Península, 2006).
Moradiellos, Enrique, *Franco: Anatomy of a Dictator* (London: Tauris, 2018).
Morato, Juan José, *Pablo Iglesias* (Barcelona: Ariel, 2000 [1931]).
Morcillo, Aurora G., *The Catholic Womanhood: Gender Ideology in Franco's Spain* (DeKalb, IL: Northern Illinois University Press, 2008).
Morel, Sandrine, *En el huracán catalán* (Barcelona: Planeta, 2018).
Moreno, Francisco, 'La represión en la posguerra', in Santos Juliá (ed.), *Víctimas de la guerra civil* (Madrid: Temas de Hoy, 1999).
Moreno, Francisco, 'Huidos, guerrilleros, resistente. La oposición armada a la Dictadura', in Julián Casanova (coord.), *Morir, matar, sobrevivir* (Barcelona: Crítica, 2002).
Moreno Luzón, Javier, 'El poder público hecho cisco. Clientelismo e instituciones políticas', in Antonio Robles (ed.), *Política, Política en penumbra* (Madrid: Siglo XXI, 1996).
Moreno Luzón, Javier, *Romanones: Caciquismo y política liberal* (Madrid: Alianza, 1998).
Moreno Luzón, Javier, 'El rey de papel', in Javier Moreno Luzón (ed.), *Alfonso XIII* (Madrid: Marcial Pons, 2003).
Moreno Luzón, Javier (ed.), *Progresistas* (Madrid: Taurus, 2006).
Moreno Luzón, Javier, 'José Canalejas. La democracia, el estado y la nación', in Javier Moreno Luzón (ed.), *Progresistas* (Madrid: Taurus, 2006).
Moreno Luzón, Javier, 'Alfonso XIII, 1902–1931', in Ramón Villares and Javier Moreno Luzón, *Historia de España, vol. 7: Restauración y Dictadura* (Madrid: Marcial Pons, 2009).
Moreno Luzón, Javier, 'The Government, Parties and King, 1913–1923', in Francisco J. Romero Salvadó and Angel Smith (eds.), *The Agony of Spanish Liberalism: From Revolution to Dictatorship, 1913–1923* (Basingstoke: Palgrave Macmillan, 2010).
Moreno Luzón, Javier, *Modernizing the Nation: Spain During the Reign of Alfonso XIII, 1902–1931* (Brighton: Sussex Academic Press, 2012).
Mosher, John R., *The Birth of Mass Politics in Spain: Lerrouxismo in Barcelona, 1901–1909* (New York: Garland, 1991).
Mujal-León, Eusebio, *Communism and Political Change in Spain* (Bloomington, IN: Indiana University Press, 1983).
Muñoz, Jaume, *La España corrupta* (Granada: Comares, 2016).
Muro, Diego, *Ethnicity and Violence: The Case of Radical Basque Nationalism* (London: Routledge, 2008).
Muro, Diego, 'Territorial Accommodation, Party Politics, and Statute Reform in Spain', *South European Society and Politics*, 4 (2009).
Nadal, Jordi, 'The Failure of the Industrial Revolution in Spain, 1830–1914', in Carlo M. Cipolla (ed.), *The Fontana Economic History of Europe, vol. VI, Part Two: The Emergence of Industrial Nations* (Hassocks: Harvester Press, 1976).
Nadal, Jordi, 'A Century of Industrialization in Spain, 1833–1930', in Nicolás Sánchez-Albornoz (ed.), *The Economic Modernization of Spain, 1830–1930* (New York: New York University Press, 1987).
Nadal, Jordi, *El fracaso de la revolución industrial en España, 1814–1913* (Barcelona: Ariel, 1991).

Nash, Mary, 'Un/Contested Identities: Motherhood, Sex Reform and the Modernization of Gender Identity in Early Twentieth Century Spain', in Victoria Lorée Enders and Pamela Beth Radcliff (eds.), *Constructing Spanish Womanhood* (New York: State University of New York Press, 1999).

Navajas Zubeldia, Carlos, *Ejército, estado y sociedad en España, 1923–1930* (Logroño: Instituto de Estudios Riojanos, 1991).

Navarro, Julia, *1982–1996. Entre Felipe y Aznar* (Madrid: Temas de Hoy, 1996).

Núñez de Prado, Guillermo, *Los dramas del anarquismo* (Barcelona: Maucci, 1904).

Núñez Florencio, Rafael, *El terrorismo anarquista, 1888–1909* (Madrid: Siglo XXI, 1983).

Núñez Florencio, Rafael, 'El terrorismo', in Julián Casanova (ed.), *Tierra y Libertad. Cien años de anarquismo en España* (Barcelona: Crítica, 2010).

Ónega, Fernando, *Qué nos ha pasado, España. De la ilusión al desencanto* (Barcelona: Plaza Janés, 2017).

Ortega y Gasset, José, *La España invertebrada* (Madrid: Espasa Calpe, 1964 [1921]).

Orwell, George, *Homage to Catalonia* (Harmondsworth: Penguin, 1987 [1938]).

Ossorio, Ángel, *Barcelona. Julio de 1909* (Madrid: Imprenta de Ricardo Rojas, 1910).

Pabón, Jesús, *Cambó, 1876–1947* (Barcelona: Alpha, 1999 [1952–1968]).

Padilla, Fernando, *Volunteers of the Spanish Empire, 1855–1898* (PhD thesis: University of Bristol, 2018).

Pagés, Pelai, *Guerra civil espanyola a Catalunya, 1936–9* (Barcelona: A. Romero, 1997).

Palacios, Joaquín J., *Las cartas de Clonard* (Madrid: Visión, 2013).

Palafox, Jordi, *Atraso económico y democracia. La Segunda República y la economía española, 1892–1936* (Barcelona: Crítica, 1991).

Pan-Montojo, Juan, 'Introducción. ¿98 o fin de siglo?', in Juan Pan-Montojo (ed.), *Más se perdió en Cuba. España, 1898 y la crisis de fin de siglo* (Madrid: Alianza, 1998).

Pantoja Antúnez, José Luis and Manuel Ramírez López, *La Mano Negra. Memoria de una represión* (Cádiz: Quorum, 2010).

Pastor Petit, Domènec, *Hollywood responde a la guerra civil* (Barcelona: Tempestad, 1998).

Payne, Stanley, *Spain's First Democracy: The Second Republic, 1931–1936* (London: University of Wisconsin Press, 1993).

Payne, Stanley, *Fascism in Spain, 1923–1977* (Madison, WI: University of Wisconsin Press, 1999).

Pena Rodríguez, Alberto, *El gran aliado de Franco: Portugal y la guerra civil española, prensa, radio, cine y propaganda* (Coruña: Castro, 1998).

Perea Ruiz, Jesús, 'Guerra submarina en España', *Espacio, Tiempo y Forma*, 16 (2004).

Pérez, Francisco, '¿Una guerra realmente inevitable?', in Ángel Viñas, Fernando Puell de la Villa, Julio Aróstegui et al. (coords.), *Los mitos del 18 de julio* (Barcelona: Crítica, 2019).

Pérez Blasco, Santiago, *Cullera, 1911. La protesta d'un poble* (Valencia: 7 i Mig, 1999).

Pérez-Díaz, Víctor M., *The Return of Civil Society: The Emergence of Democratic Spain* (Cambridge, MA: Harvard University Press, 1993).

Pérez-Díaz, Víctor M., *España puesta a prueba* (Madrid: Alianza, 1996).
Pérez Ledesma, Manuel, *El obrero consciente* (Madrid: Alianza, 1987).
Pérez Ledesma, Manuel, 'La sociedad española, la guerra y la derrota', in Juan Pan-Montojo (ed.), *Más se perdió en Cuba. España, 1898 y la crisis de fin de siglo* (Madrid: Alianza, 1998).
Pestaña, Ángel, *Lo que aprendí en la vida*, 2 vols. (Murcia: Zero, 1971 [1933]).
Pich Mitjana, Josep, *La Setmana Tràgica (1909): Sagnant, Roja, Negra o Gloriosa* (Barcelona: UPF, 2009).
Pike, David Wingeate, *Franco and the Axis Stigma* (Basingstoke: Macmillan, 2008).
Pike, David Wingeate, *The French and the Civil War in Spain* (Eastbourne: Sussex University Press, 2011).
Pino, Eloísa del, 'The Spanish Welfare State from Zapatero to Rajoy: Recalibration to Retrenchment', in Bonnie N. Field and Alfonso Botti (eds.), *Politics and Society in Contemporary Spain: From Zapatero to Rajoy* (Basingstoke: Palgrave, 2013).
Pollack, Benny, *The Paradox of Spanish Foreign Policy* (London: Pinter, 1987).
Ponce, Javier, 'Propaganda and Politics: Germany and Spanish Public Opinion', in Troy R.E. Paddock (ed.), *World War I and Propaganda* (Leiden: Brill, 2014).
Portero, Florentino, *Franco aislado. La cuestión española, 1945–1950* (Madrid: Aguilar, 1989).
Powell, Charles, *Juan Carlos of Spain: Self-Made Monarch* (Basingstoke: Macmillan, 1996).
Powell, Thomas G., *Mexico and the Spanish Civil War* (Albuquerque, NM: University of New Mexico Press, 1981).
Powell, Thomas G., 'A Second Transition, or More of the Same? Spanish Foreign Policy under Zapatero', in Bonnie N. Field and Alfonso Botti (eds.), *Politics and Society in Contemporary Spain: From Zapatero to Rajoy* (Basingstoke: Palgrave, 2013).
Prados, León, *De imperio a nación, 1780–1930* (Madrid: Alianza, 1988).
Preston, Paul, 'The Agrarian War in the South', in Paul Preston (ed.), *Revolution and War in Spain, 1931–1939* (London: Methuen, 1984).
Preston, Paul, *The Triumph of Democracy in Spain* (London: Methuen, 1986).
Preston, Paul, 'The Creation of the Popular Front in Spain', in Helen Graham and Paul Preston (eds.), *The Popular Front in Europe* (London: Macmillan, 1987).
Preston, Paul, *Franco* (London: HarperCollins, 1993).
Preston, Paul, *The Coming of the Spanish Civil War* (London: Routledge, 1994)
Preston, Paul, *The Politics of Revenge* (London: Routledge, 1995).
Preston, Paul, 'Mussolini's Spanish Adventure: From Limited Risk to War', in Paul Preston and Ann L. Mackenzie (eds.), *The Republic Besieged* (Edinburgh: Edinburgh University Press, 1996).
Preston, Paul, 'Francisco Franco: política y estrategia en la Guerra Civil', *Revista de Extremadura*, 21 (1996).
Preston, Paul, *¡Comrades! Portraits of the Spanish Civil War* (London: HarperCollins, 1999).
Preston, Paul, *The Spanish Civil War: Reaction, Revolution and Revenge* (London: Harper Perennial, 2006).
Preston, Paul, *El gran manipulador. La mentira cotidiana de Franco* (Barcelona: Ediciones B, 2008).

Preston, Paul, *The Spanish Holocaust: Inquisition and Extermination in Twentieth-Century Spain* (London: W.W. Norton, 2012).
Preston, Paul, *The Last Days of the Spanish Republic* (London: William Collins, 2016).
Preston, Paul, *A People Betrayed: A History of Corruption, Political Incompetence and Social Division in Modern Spain, 1874–2018* (London: HarperCollins, 2020).
Prieto, Indalecio, *Discursos fundamentales* (Madrid: Turner, 1975).
Pro Ruíz, Juan, 'La política en tiempos del Desastre', in Juan Pan-Montojo (ed.), *Más se perdió en Cuba: España, 1898 y la crisis de fin de siglo* (Madrid: Alianza, 1998).
Puell, Fernando, 'La trama militar de la conspiración', in Ángel Viñas, Fernando Puell de la Villa, Julio Aróstegui et al. (coords.), *Los Mitos del 18 de julio* (Barcelona: Crítica, 2019).
Puigsech, Josep, 'La Guerra Civil Española y la política de seguridad colectiva', in Alberto Reig and José Sánchez (eds.), *La Guerra Civil española. 80 años después* (Madrid: Tecnos, 2019).
Quiroga, Alejandro, *Making Spaniards: Primo de Rivera and the Nationalization of the Masses* (Basingstoke: Palgrave, 2007).
Quiroga, Alejandro, 'Nation and Reaction: Spanish Conservative Nationalism and the Restoration Crisis', in Francisco J. Romero Salvadó and Angel Smith (eds.), *The Agony of Spanish Liberalism: From Revolution to Dictatorship, 1913–1923* (Basingstoke: Palgrave, 2010).
Quiroga, Alejandro, 'Salvation and Betrayal, The Left and the Spanish Nation', in Gregorio Alonso and Diego Muro (eds.), *The Politics and Memory of Democratic Transition* (New York: Routledge, 2011).
Quiroga, Alejandro, 'La nacionalización en España. Una propuesta teórica', *Ayer*, 90 (2013).
Quiroga, Alejandro, *Miguel Primo de Rivera. Dictadura, Populismo y Nación* (Barcelona: Crítica, 2022).
Radcliff, Pamela B., *From Mobilization to Civil War* (Cambridge: Cambridge University Press, 1996).
Radcliff, Pamela B., 'Women's Politics: Consumer Riots in Twentieth Century Spain', in Victoria Lorée Enders and Pamela Beth Radcliff (eds.), *Constructing Spanish Womanhood* (New York: State University of New York Press, 1999).
Radcliff, Pamela B., *Modern Spain: 1808 to the Present* (Chichester: Wiley Blackwell, 2017).
Radosh, Ronald, Mary Habeck and Grigory Sevostianov (eds.), *Spain Betrayed: The Soviet Union in the Spanish Civil War* (London: Yale University Press, 2001).
Raguer, Hilari, *Gunpowder and Incense: The Catholic Church and the Spanish Civil War* (London: Routledge, 2007).
Rees, Tim, 'Revolution or Republic? The Spanish Communist Party, 1931–1936', in Manuel Álvarez Tardío and Fernando del Rey (eds.), *The Spanish Second Republic Revisited: From Democratic Hopes to Civil War, 1931–1936* (Eastbourne: Sussex Academic Press, 2013).
Reig, Alberto, *Violencia y terror* (Madrid: Akal, 1990).
Reig, Alberto, *Franco Caudillo: Mito y Realidad* (Madrid: Tecnos, 1995).
Reig, Alberto, *Memoria de la Guerra Civil* (Madrid: Alianza, 1999).

Reig, Alberto, *Franco: el César Superlativo* (Madrid: Tecnos, 2005).
Reig, Alberto, *Anti-Moa, la subversión neofranquista de la historia de España* (Madrid: Ediciones B, 2006).
Renouvin, Pierre and Romain Rémond (eds.), *Léon Blum* (Paris: Presses de la Fondation Nationales des Sciences Politiques, 1967).
Reverte, Jorge M., *La Batalla del Ebro* (Barcelona: Crítica, 2003).
Reverte, Jorge M., *La Batalla de Madrid* (Barcelona: Crítica, 2004).
Rey Reguillo, Fernando del, 'El Capitalismo Catalán y Primo de Rivera: En torno a un golpe de estado', *Hispania*, XLVIII/168 (1988).
Rey Reguillo, Fernando del, 'El empresario, el sindicalista y el miedo', in Rafael Cruz and Manuel Pérez Ledesma (eds.), *Cultura y movilización en la España contemporánea* (Madrid: Alianza, 1997).
Rial, Joseph H., *Revolution from Above: The Primo de Rivera Dictatorship in Spain* (Fairfax, VA: George Mason University Press, 1986).
Ribeiro, Filipe, *Salazar* (New York: Enigma, 2009).
Richards, Michael, *A Time of Silence* (Cambridge: Cambridge University Press, 1998).
Richards, Michael, *After the Civil War: Making Memory and Re-Making Spain since 1936* (Cambridge: Cambridge University Press, 2013).
Riquer i Permanyer, Borja de, *Regionalistes i Nacionalistes, 1898–1931* (Barcelona: Dopesa, 1979).
Riquer i Permanyer, Borja de, 'La débil nacionalización española del Siglo XIX', *Historia Social*, 20 (1994).
Riquer i Permanyer, Borja de, 'Social and Economic Change in a Climate of Political Immobilism', in Helen Graham and Jo Labanyi (eds.), *Spanish Cultural Studies: An Introduction* (Oxford: Oxford University Press, 1995).
Riquer i Permanyer, Borja de, 'El surgimiento de las nuevas identidades contemporáneas: propuestas para una discusión', *Ayer*, 35 (1999).
Riquer i Permanyer, Borja de, *Alfonso XIII y Cambó. La monarquía y el catalanismo político* (Barcelona: RBA, 2013).
Riquer i Permanyer, Borja de, *Francesc Cambó, L'últim retrat* (Barcelona: Edicions 62, 2022).
Rivera, Antonio, *20 de diciembre de 1973. El día en que ETA puso en jaque al regimen franquista* (Barcelona: Taurus, 2021).
Robert, Vincent, 'La protesta universal contra la ejecución de Ferrer: las manifestaciones de octubre de 1909', *Historia Social*, 14 (1992).
Roberts, Geoffrey, *The Soviet Union and the Origins of the Second World War: Russo-German Relations and the Road to War, 1933–1941* (Basingstoke: Macmillan, 1995).
Robles, Antonio (ed.), *Política en penumbra* (Madrid: Siglo XXI, 1996).
Rocker, Rudolf, *En la borrasca, Años de destierro* (Puebla: Cajica, 1967).
Rodríguez, Antonio and Rosario Ruiz (eds.), *1808. Controversias historiográficas* (Madrid: Actas, 2010).
Rodríguez Jiménez, José Luis, *Reaccionarios y golpistas. La extrema derecha en España: del tardofranquismo a la consolidación de la democracia, 1967–1982* (Madrid: CSIC, 1994).
Romanones, Conde de, *Las responsabilidades del antiguo régimen, 1875–1923* (Madrid: Renacimiento, 1923).
Romanones, Conde de, *Notas de una vida, 1912–1931* (Madrid: Marcial Pons, 1999 [1934]).

Romero Maura, Joaquín, *La Rosa de Fuego. El obrerismo barcelonés de 1899 a 1909* (Madrid: Alianza, 1989 [1975]).
Romero Maura, Joaquín, *La Romana del diablo* (Madrid: Marcial Pons, 2000).
Romero Salvadó, Francisco J., 'The Views of an Anarcho-Syndicalist on the Soviet Union: The Defeat of the Third International in Spain', *Revolutionary Russia*, 8/1 (1995).
Romero Salvadó, Francisco J., 'The Failure of the Liberal Project of the Spanish Nation-State, 1909–1923', in Clare Mar-Molinero and Angel Smith (eds.), *Nationalism and the Nation in the Iberian Peninsula* (Oxford: Berg, 1996).
Romero Salvadó, Francisco J., *Spain, 1914–1918: Between War and Revolution* (London: Routledge, 1999).
Romero Salvadó, Francisco J., 'The Great War and the Crisis of Liberalism in Spain, 1916–17', *Historical Journal*, 46/4 (2003).
Romero Salvadó, Francisco J., 'Fatal Neutrality: Pragmatism or Capitulation? Spain's Foreign Policy during the Great War', *European History Quarterly*, 33 (2003).
Romero Salvadó, Francisco J., *The Spanish Civil War: Origins, Course and Outcomes* (Basingstoke: Palgrave Macmillan, 2005).
Romero Salvadó, Francisco J., *The Foundations of Civil War: Revolution, Social Conflict and Reaction in Liberal Spain, 1916–1923* (London: Routledge, 2008).
Romero Salvadó, Francisco J., 'The Comintern Fiasco in Spain: The Borodin Mission and the Birth of the Spanish Communist Party', *Revolutionary Russia*, 21/2 (2008).
Romero Salvadó, Francisco J., 'Spain's Revolutionary Crisis of 1917: A Reckless Gamble', in Francisco J. Romero Salvadó and Angel Smith (eds.), *The Agony of Spanish Liberalism: From Revolution to Dictatorship, 1913–1923* (Basingstoke: Palgrave, 2010).
Romero Salvadó, Francisco J., '*Si Vis Pacem Para Bellum*: The Catalan Employers' Dirty War, 1919–1923', in Francisco J. Romero Salvadó and Angel Smith (eds.), *The Agony of Spanish Liberalism: From Revolution to Dictatorship, 1913–1923* (Basingstoke: Palgrave, 2010).
Romero Salvadó, Francisco J., 'Antonio Maura: From Messiah to Fireman', in Alejandro Quiroga and Miguel Ángel del Arco Blanco (eds.), *Right-Wing Spain in the Civil War Era: Soldiers of God and Apostles of the Fatherland* (London: Continuum, 2012).
Romero Salvadó, Francisco J., 'Building Alliances against the New? Monarchy and the Military in Industrializing Spain', in Helen Graham (ed.), *Interrogating Francoism* (London: Bloomsbury, 2016).
Romero Salvadó, Francisco J., '¡España no era Rusia! La revolución española de 1917: anatomía de un fracaso', *Hispania Nova*, 15 (2017).
Romero Salvadó, Francisco J., 'Between the Catalan Quagmire and the Red Spectre, Spain 1918–19', *Historical Journal*, 60/3 (2017).
Romero Salvadó, Francisco J., 'Spain and the First World War: The Logic of Neutrality', *War in History*, 26/1 (2019).
Romero Salvadó, Francisco J., *Political Comedy and Social Tragedy: Spain, a Laboratory of Social Conflict, 1892–1921* (Brighton: Sussex University Press, 2020).
Romero Salvadó, Francisco J. and Angel Smith, 'The Agony of Spanish Liberalism and the Origins of Dictatorship', in Francisco J. Romero Salvadó and Angel Smith

(eds.), *The Agony of Spanish Liberalism: From Revolution to Dictatorship, 1913–1923* (Basingstoke: Palgrave, 2010).
Rosenbusch, Anne, 'Total War in Neutral Territory: German Activity in Spain during the First World War', *Hispania Nova*, 15 (2017).
Rowold, Katharina, *The Educated Woman: Minds, Bodies, and Women's Higher Education in Britain, Germany, and Spain, 1865–1914* (London: Routledge, 2010).
Roy, Manabendra Nath, *Memoirs* (London: George Allen & Unwin, 1964).
Royo, Sebastián, 'Reforms Betrayed? Zapatero and Continuities in Economic Policy', in Bonnie N. Field (ed.), *Spain's Second Transition? The Socialist Government of José Luis Rodríguez Zapatero* (London: Routledge, 2011).
Rubí, Gemma, 'Protesta, desobediencia y violencia subversiva; La Semana Trágica de julio de 1909 en Cataluña', *Revista de Historia Contemporánea*, 10 (2011).
Rybalkin, Yuri, *Stalin y España* (Madrid: Marcial Pons, 2007).
Saborit, Andrés, *Julián Besteiro* (México: Pablo Iglesias, 1961).
Saborit, Andrés, *Asturias y sus hombres* (Toulouse: UGT, 1963).
Saborit, Andrés, *La huelga de agosto de 1917* (México: Pablo Iglesias, 1967).
Sánchez Alonso, Blanca, 'Those Who Left and Those Who Stayed Behind: Explaining Emigration from the Regions of Spain, 1880–1914', *Journal of Economic History*, 60 (2000).
Sánchez León, Pablo, 'Radicalism without Representation', in Gregorio Alonso and Diego Muro (eds.), *The Politics and Memory of Democratic Transition* (New York: Routledge, 2011).
Sánchez Pérez, Francisco, 'La crisis social: Las tres huelgas de agosto', in Eduardo González Calleja (ed.), *Anatomía de una crisis. 1917 y los españoles* (Madrid: Alianza, 2017).
Sánchez Pérez, Francisco, 'Las reformas de la primavera del 36 (en la Gaceta y en la calle)', in Ángel Viñas, Fernando Puell de la Villa, Julio Aróstegui et al. (coords.), *Los mitos del 18 de julio* (Barcelona: Crítica, 2019).
Sánchez Recio, Gregorio, *Sobre todos Franco. Coalición reaccionaria y grupos políticos* (Madrid: Flor del Viento, 2008).
Sánchez Soler, Mariano, *Los hijos del 20-N. Historia Violenta del Fascismo Español* (Madrid: Temas de Hoy, 1993).
Saz, Ismael, *Mussolini contra la II República* (Valencia: Alfons el Magnánim, 1986).
Saz, Ismael, 'La peculiaritat del feixisme espanyol', *Afers*, 25 (1996).
Saz, Ismael, *Fascismo y franquismo* (Valencia: PUV, 2004).
Saz, Ismael and Javier Tusell, *Fascistas en España* (Madrid: CSIC, 1981).
Schauff, Frank, *La victoria frustrada. La Unión Soviética, la Internacional Comunista y la Guerra Civil española* (Barcelona: Debate, 2008).
Seco Serrano, Carlos, *Militarismo y civilismo en la España contemporánea* (Madrid: IEC, 1984).
Séguéla, Matthieu, *Franco-Pétain. Los secretos de una alianza* (Barcelona: Prensa Ibérica, 1994).
Serrano, Carlos, *Final del Imperio. España, 1895–1898* (Madrid: Siglo XXI, 1984).
Serrano, Carlos, *Le Tour Du Peuple. Crise nationale, mouvements populaires et populisme en Espagne, 1890–1910* (Madrid: Bibliotheque de la Casa de Velázquez, 1987).
Serrano Suñer, Ramón, *Memorias* (Barcelona: Planeta, 1977).

Service, Robert, *Comrades – Communism: A World History* (Basingstoke: Macmillan, 2007).
Shipman, Charles, *It Had to be Revolution: Memoirs of an American Radical* (Ithaca, NY: Cornell University Press, 1993).
Shubert, Adrian, *The Road to Revolution in Asturias* (Chicago, IL: University of Illinois Press, 1987).
Shubert, Adrian, *A Social History of Modern Spain* (London: Unwin Hyman, 1990).
Simarro, Luis, *Los sucesos de agosto en el parlamento* (Madrid: LIF, 1918).
Simpson, James and Juan Carmona, *Why Democracy Failed: The Agrarian Origins of the Spanish Civil War* (Cambridge: Cambridge University Press, 2020).
Skoutelsky, Rémi, *L'Espoir guidait leur pas: Les volontaires français dans les Brigades Internationales, 1936–1939* (Paris: Grasset, 1998).
Smith, Angel, *Anarchism, Revolution and Reaction: Catalan Labour and the Crisis of the Spanish State, 1898–1923* (Oxford: Berghahn, 2007).
Smith, Angel, 'The Catalan Counter-revolutionary Coalition and the Primo de Rivera Coup, 1917–1923', *European History Quarterly*, 37/1 (2007).
Smith, Angel, 'The Lliga Regionalista, the Catalan Right and the Making of the Primo de Rivera Dictatorship', in Francisco J. Romero Salvadó and Angel Smith (eds.), *The Agony of Spanish Liberalism: From Revolution to Dictatorship, 1913–1923* (Basingstoke: Palgrave, 2010).
Smith, Angel, *Historical Dictionary of Spain* (London: Rowman & Littlefield, 2018).
Smith, Joseph, *The Spanish-American War: Conflict in the Caribbean and the Pacific, 1895–1902* (London: Longman, 1994).
Smyth, Denis, 'We Are with You: Solidarity and Self-Interest in Soviet Policy towards Republican Spain, 1936–1939', in Paul Preston and Ann L. Mackenzie (eds.), *The Republic Besieged* (Edinburgh: Edinburgh University Press, 1996).
Soler, Albert, *Estàvem cansats de viure bé* (Barcelona: Sagasse, 2019).
Southworth, Herbert, R., *El mito de la cruzada de Franco* (Barcelona: Plaza & Janés, 1986).
Southworth, Herbert, R., 'The Grand Camouflage: Julián Gorkin, Burnett Bolloten, and the Spanish Civil War', in Paul Preston and Ann L. Mackenzie (eds.), *The Republic Besieged* (Edinburgh: Edinburgh University Press, 1996).
Southworth, Herbert, R., *Conspiracy and the Spanish Civil War: The Brainwashing of Francisco Franco* (London: Routledge, 2002).
Stevenson, David, *Cataclysm: The First World War as Political Tragedy* (New York: Basic Books, 2005).
Suárez Cortina, Manuel, *El reformismo en España* (Madrid: Siglo XXI, 1986).
Suárez Cortina, Manuel, 'Introducción', in Manuel Suárez Cortina (ed.), *La Restauración, entre el liberalismo y la democracia* (Madrid: Alianza, 1997).
Sueiro, Susana, 'El asesinato de Canalejas y los anarquistas españoles en Estados Unidos', in Juan Avilés and Ángel Herrerín (eds.), *El Nacimiento del terrorismo en Occidente. Anarquía, nihilismo y violencia revolucionaria* (Madrid: Siglo XXI, 2008).
Sullivan, John L., *ETA and Basque Nationalism: The Fight for Euskadi* (London: Routledge, 1988).
Taibo II, Paco Ignacio, *Que sean fuego las estrellas. Barcelona, 1917–1923* (Barcelona: Crítica, 2016).

Tamames, Ramón, *La economía española. De la transición a la unión monetaria* (Madrid: Temas de Hoy, 1996).
Tamburini, Francesco, 'Michelle Angiolillo e l'assassinio di Cánovas del Castillo', *Spagna Contemporanea*, 9 (1996).
Tavera, Susanna, 'La historia del anarquismo español: una encrucijada interpretativa nueva', *Ayer*, 45 (2002).
Termes, Josep, *Anarquismo y sindicalismo en España, 1864–1881* (Barcelona: Crítica, 2000 [1961]).
Thiebaut, Claude, 'Léon Blum, Alexis Léger et la decison de Non-Intervention en Espagne', in Jean Sagnes and Sylvie Caucanas (eds.), *Les Français et la Guerre d'Espagne* (Perpignan: Presses Universitaires de Perpignan, 2008).
Thomas, Hugh, *The Spanish Civil War* (Harmondsworth: Penguin, 1986 [1961]).
Thomas, Maria, *The Faith and the Fury: Popular Anticlerical Violence and Iconoclasm in Spain, 1931–1936* (Brighton: Sussex Academic Press, 2013).
Tobeña, Adolf, *Fragmented Catalonia: Divisive Legacies of a Push for Secession* (London: Rowman & Littlefield, 2021).
Towson, Nigel, *The Crisis of Democracy in Spain: Centrist Politics under the Second Republic, 1931–1936* (Brighton: Sussex Academic Press, 2000).
Traina, Richard P., *American Diplomacy and the Spanish Civil War* (Bloomington, IN: Indiana University Press, 1968).
Trebilcock, Clive, *The Industrialization of the Continental Powers, 1780–1914* (London: Longman, 1981).
Trice, Thomas G., *Spanish Liberalism in Crisis: A Study of the Liberal Party during Spain's Parliamentary Collapse, 1913–1923* (New York: Garland, 1991).
Trotsky, Leon, *The Spanish Revolution, 1931–39* (New York: Pathfinder, 1986 [1973]).
Tuñón de Lara, Manuel, *La II República*, 2 vols. (Madrid: Siglo XXI, 1976).
Tuñón de Lara, Manuel, *Poder y sociedad en España, 1900–1931* (Madrid: Espasa-Calpe, 1992).
Tuñón de Lara, Manuel, Ricardo Miralles, and Bonifaco N. Diaz Chico, *Juan Negrín López, el hombre necesario* (Las Palmas: Gobierno de Canarias, 1996).
Tusell, Javier, *La política y los políticos en los tiempos de Alfonso XIII* (Barcelona: Planeta, 1976).
Tusell, Javier, *Radiografía de un golpe de estado: El ascenso al poder del General Primo de Rivera* (Madrid: Alianza, 1987).
Tusell, Javier, 'El sufragio universal en España (1891–1936): un balance historiográfico', *Ayer*, 3 (1991).
Tusell, Javier, *Franco en la Guerra Civil* (Madrid: Tusquets, 1993).
Tusell, Javier, *Antonio Maura. Una biografía política* (Madrid: Alianza, 1994).
Tusell, Javier, *Franco, España y la II Guerra Mundial. Entre el Eje y la Neutralidad* (Madrid: Temas de Hoy, 1995).
Tusell, Javier, *El Aznarato. El gobierno del Partido Popular, 1996–2003* (Madrid: Aguilar, 2004).
Tusell, Javier and Juan Avilés, *La derecha española contemporánea: sus orígenes, el Maurismo* (Madrid: Espasa Calpe, 1986).
Tusell, Javier and Genoveva Queipo de Llano (eds.), *Franco y Mussolini* (Barcelona: Planeta, 1985).
Tusell, Javier and Genoveva Queipo de Llano, *Alfonso XIII* (Madrid: Taurus, 2001).

Ucelay-da Cal, Enric, *Breve historia del separatismo catalán* (Barcelona: Penguin, 2018).
Ullman, Joan Connelly, *The Tragic Week: A Study of Anticlericalism in Spain, 1875–1912* (Cambridge, MA: Harvard University Press, 1968).
Valle Inclán, Ramón del, *La corte de los Milagros* (Madrid: Espasa Calpe, 1968 [1927]).
Varela Ortega, José, *Los amigos Políticos. Partidos, elecciones y caciquismo en la Restauración, 1875–1900* (Madrid: Alianza, 1977).
Varela Ortega, José, 'Aftermath of the Splendid Disaster: Spanish Politics Before and After the Spanish American War of 1898', *Journal of Contemporary History*, 15 (1980).
Varela Ortega, José, 'De los orígenes de la democracia en España, 1845–1923', in Salvador Forner (ed.), *Democracia, elecciones y modernización en Europa, Siglos XIX–XX* (Madrid: Cátedra, 1997).
Varela Ortega, José (ed.), *El poder de la influencia. Geografía del caciquismo en España, 1875–1923* (Madrid: Marcial Pons, 2001).
Vázquez Montalbán, Manuel, *La Literatura en la ciudad democrática* (Barcelona: Crítica, 2009).
Vega, Eulalia, *Anarquistas y sindicalistas, 1931–1936* (Valencia: Alfons el Magnánim, 1987).
Vera, José Manuel, *Primo de Rivera, 1923–1930: de la monarquía decadente a la deseada república* (Madrid: Dykinson, 2019).
Vilanova i Vila-Abadal, Francesc, 'En el exilio: de los campos franceses al umbral de la deportación', in Carme Molinero, Margarida Sala, and Jordi Sobrequés (eds.), *Una inmensa prisión: los campos de concentración y las prisiones durante la guerra civil y el franquismo* (Barcelona: Crítica, 2003).
Villa, Roberto, 'The Limits of Democratization: Elections and Political Culture', in Manuel Álvarez Tardío and Fernando del Rey (eds.), *The Spanish Second Republic Revisited: From Democratic Hopes to Civil War, 1931–1936* (Eastbourne: Sussex Academic Press, 2013).
Villacorta Baños, Francisco, *Profesionales y burócratas. Estado y poder corporativo en la España del Siglo XX, 1890–1923* (Madrid: Siglo XXI, 1989).
Villares, Ramón, 'Alfonso XII y Regencia, 1875–1902', in Ramón Villares and Javier Moreno Luzón, *Historia de España, vol. 7: Restauración y Dictadura* (Madrid: Marcial Pons, 2009).
Villares, Ramón and Javier Moreno, 'Prólogo', in Ramón Villares and Javier Moreno Luzón, *Historia de España, vol. 7: Restauración y Dictadura* (Madrid: Marcial Pons, 2009).
Viñas, Ángel, 'Gold, the Soviet Union and the Spanish Civil War', in Martin Blinkhorn (ed.), *Spain in Conflict, 1931–1939: Democracy and its Enemies* (London: Sage, 1986).
Viñas, Ángel, *Franco, Hitler y el estallido de la guerra civil* (Madrid: Alianza, 2001).
Viñas, Ángel, *La Soledad de la República. El abandono de las democracias y el viraje hacia la Unión Soviética* (Barcelona: Crítica, 2006).
Viñas, Ángel, *El escudo de la República. El oro de España, la apuesta soviética y los hechos de mayo de 1937* (Barcelona: Crítica, 2007).
Viñas, Ángel, *El honor de la República. Entre el acoso fascista, la hostilidad británica y la política de Stalin* (Barcelona: Crítica, 2008).

Viñas, Ángel, 'Una carrera diplomática y un Ministerio de estado desconocido', in Ángel Viñas (ed.), *Al servicio de la República. Diplomáticos y Guerra Civil* (Madrid: Marcial Pons, 2010).
Viñas, Ángel, *La conspiración del General Franco* (Barcelona: Crítica, 2011).
Viñas, Ángel, *El primer asesinato de Franco* (Barcelona: Crítica, 2018).
Viñas, Ángel, *La otra cara del Caudillo* (Barcelona: Crítica, 2018).
Viñas, Ángel, *¿Quién quiso la guerra civil? Historia de una conspiración* (Barcelona: Crítica, 2019).
Viñas, Ángel, *El gran error de la República* (Barcelona: Crítica, 2021).
Viñas, Ángel and Fernando Hernández, *El desplome de la República* (Barcelona: Crítica, 2009).
Vivier, Thierry, *L'Armée Française et la Guerre D'Espagne, 1936–1939* (Paris: Éditions de l'Officine, 2007).
Weiner, Richard R. and Iván López, *Los Indignados: Tides of Social Insertion in Spain* (Alresford: Zero Books, 2016).
Whealey, Robert H., *Hitler and Spain: The Nazi Role in the Spanish Civil War, 1936–1939* (Lexington, KY: University Press of Kentucky, 1989).
Wigg, Richard, *Churchill and Spain: The Survival of the Franco Regime, 1940–45* (London: Routledge, 2005).
Zenobi, Laura, *La construcción del mito de Franco* (Madrid: Cátedra, 2011).
Zoffmann, Arturo, 'An Uncanny Honeymoon: Spanish Anarchism and the Bolshevik Dictatorship of the Proletariat, 1917–22', *International Labour and Working Class History*, 94 (2018).
Zugazagoitia, Julián, *Guerra y vicisitudes de los españoles* (Madrid: Tusquets, 2001).

INDEX

Abascal, Santiago, 282
Abd el-Krim, Muhammad ibn, 73
Abrazo de Vergara (1839), 163, 188
Abril Martorell, Fernando, 229
Acción Española, 107
Acción Nacional, 101, 106–7, 124n.75
Acción Republicana, 97
ACNP (Asociación Católica Nacional de Propagandistas), 101
Afghanistan, 260
Africanistas, *see* Army of Africa
Agrarian Party, 109, 129n.98
Agrarian Reform, 97–8, 102, 105–6, 136
  Institute of, 106, 110
Aguilera, Gen. Francisco, 77
Aguirre, José Antonio, 116
Aído, Bibiana, 260
Aizpún, Rafael, 112
Al-Qaeda, 259
Alba, Santiago, 51, 59, 80, 88n.99, 116
Albornoz, Álvaro de, 141
Alcalá Zamora, Niceto
  becomes the first president of the Republic, 100
  and the corruption scandals of 1935, 115
  dismisses Azaña, 109
  and the elections of April 1931, 84
  and the elections of February 1936, 116
  is impeached, 119
  leaves the Provisional Government, 99
  and October 1934, 112–13
  and the Radicals in power, 111
  refuses to give power to Gil Robles, 115
  and the San Sebastián Pact, 81

Alcázar de Toledo, 148
Alfonso XII, King of Spain, 1, 6–7
Alfonso XIII, King of Spain
  and Canalejas, 33
  and the Civil War, 140
  and the crisis of 1917, 55
  is crowned, 26
  and the *Dictablanda*, 80–2
  different to King Juan Carlos, 234
  dismisses Maura, 29
  electoral defeat and exile, 84–5
  and the Great War, 54
  and Morocco, 27
  object of terrorism, 26–7
  and Primo de Rivera, 78
Algeria, 179, 204, 283–4
Alhucemas (landing, 1925), 74
Alhucemas, Marquis of (Manuel García Prieto), 54–5, 58–9, 67, 70, 81, 83, 88n.59
Alianza Republicana, 81
Almunia, Joaquín, 248
Álvarez, Francisco, 245
Álvarez, María Victoria, 267
Álvarez, Melquiades, 25
Álvarez Junco, José, 271, 287
Álvarez Mendizábal, Juan, 3
Álvarez del Vayo, Julio, 141, 144, 158
Allen, Jay, 136
Amadeo of Savoy, King of Spain, 5, 36n.19, 43n.138
Amedo, José, 245
anarchism, *see also* CNT, FAI
  anti-Francoist guerrillas, 194
  arrival in Spain, 13–14, 16–17
  and *Casas Viejas* (1933), 107–8
  and the Civil War, 133–4, 155
  and the FAI, 103
  and the Great War, 63–4

myth, 13–14
  success in Spain, 13–14
  terrorism and martyrdom, 18–19, 29–30, 33
  violence after the Great War, 66
Anarchist Federation, see FAI
Anarcho-Syndicalism and Anarcho-Syndicalist trade union, see CNT
ANC (L'Assemblea Nacional Catalana), 272, 275, 278, 292–3n.128
Anschluss (1938), 158–9
Andalusia
  and the Civil War, 130, 135, 141
  Latifundios, 14
  new statute, 264
  Reconquista, 3
  rural insurrections and repression, 18, 108
  scandals, 243, 266
  Socialist electoral defeat (2022), 283
  Socialist stronghold in democracy, 232, 242
  and the *Trienio Bolchevique*, 60, 65
Andorra, 267
Angiolillo, Michelle, 19
Anguiano, Daniel, 58
Anguita, Jesús, 237, 248, 252n.126
Annual (Battle of, 1921), 68, 73, 80
Antonov-Ovseenko, Vladimir, 142
Añoveros, Bishop Antonio, 208
AP (Alianza Popular), 224–5, 228–31, 235–6
Aperturistas, 206, 208, 220–1, 223
Aragón, 14, 110, 132, 134, 157–8, 264, 277
Aragonès, Pere, 278
Arana, Sabino de, 24
Aranda, Gen. Antonio, 130, 134
Areilza, Jose María de, 221, 223
Arias Navarro, Carlos, 207–9, 221–4
Armada, Gen. Alfonso, 233–4
Army of Africa, 52, 73, 77, 101, 115, 120, 129, 131, 135–6, 140, 147, 190
Arnedo events (1932), 102
Arrese, José Luis de, 182, 200

Arzalluz, Javier, 228, 246
Asamblea Nacional Consultiva, 74–5
Ascaso, Francisco, 103
Ascaso, Joaquín, 157
Asensio, Gen. Carlos, 182
Asociación para la Recuperación de la Memoria Histórica, 261
Assembly of Parliamentarians, 55–7, 59, 67
Asturias, 10, 16, 57, 103, 113–14, 117, 132, 147, 149
Auriol, Vicent, 140
Autarky, 186–7, 198–201
Azaña, Manuel
  and anarchism, 101
  anticlericalism, 101
  appoints Giral as Prime Minister, 132
  and Aznar, 237, 261
  backs Juan Negrín for the premiership, 156
  becomes president of the Republic, 119
  becomes prime minister, 100
  believes the Franco regime is not Fascist, 184
  and *Casas Viejas*, 125n.86
  demoralized by the course of the war, 158
  escapes being assassinated, 120
  ineptitude towards coup, 121
  loses office in 1933, 109
  and the May Days of 1937, 155
  and October 1934, 113–14
  overwhelmed by the outbreak of the war, 136
  and the Popular Front, 116–17
  President of the *Ateneo* in the 1920s, 81
  and the Reformist Party, 25
  resigns his post of president, 162
  returns to power in February 1936, 118
  War Minister, 97
Atocha (massacre of lawyers, 1977), 225
Atocha Station (terror attack, 2004), 259

Aznar, José María, 236–7, 246–7, 257–9, 261
Aznar, Adm. Juan Bautista, 83–4

Badajoz (massacre, 1936), 136, 149
Bakunin, Mikhail, 14
Baldwin, Stanley, 138, 140
Balmes, Gen. Amado, 147
Bankia scandal, 268
Barcelona
    anarchist stronghold, 14
    and the Assembly of 1917, 55
    capital of the Republic, 155
    and the coup of 1923, 67–70
    and ¡Cu-Cut! (1905), 25
    demographic growth, 10, 80, 199, 202
    emergence of nationalism, 24
    and *El Procés*, 276–8
    and ETA's terror attack (1987), 237
    falls in 1939, 161
    farewell to International Brigades, 160
    food riots, 60–1
    insurrection in 1932, 105
    and Lerroux, 25
    and the May Days (1937), 154–6
    microcosm of the social struggle, 27
    and the military uprising in 1936, 130–3
    and October 1934, 113
    and relief of casualties in the Second World War, 183
    site of Olympic Games (1992), 240
    and social warfare after the Great War, 62–3, 66
    Socialist failure, 14–15
    terrorism in the 1890s, 18–19
    and the Tragic Week, 31
Barcelona en Comú, 279
Bárcenas, Luis, 267
Bardem, Juan Antonio, 202
Baroja, Pío, 22
Barret, Josep Albert, 64
Barrionuevo, José, 245
Barroso, Antonio, 137
Bas, Carlos, 66
Basque Country
    and Carlism, 2
    and the Civil War, 118, 132, 134, 149
    and the creation of the PNV, 24
    home rule and PNV's hegemony after transition, 226, 228–9, 231, 236, 270
    and the Ibarretxe's Plan, 263–4
    and industry, 10
    oasis of peace, 269
    and the resurgence of nationalism in the 1960s, 204
    Socialist stronghold, 15–16, 117
    and terrorism, 204–5, 227, 231, 237–8, 247, 258
Basque Nationalism, *see* PNV, HB, Bildu, ETA
Basque Nationalist Party, *see* PNV
Bayonne (abdication, 1808), 1
Belarra, Ilone, 285
Belchite (Battle of, 1937), 157
Benedict XIII, Pope, 260
Berenguer, Gen. Dámaso, 79–84
Bernhardt, Johannes, 139
Besteiro, Julián
    attitude towards the Second Republic, 97
    joins Casado's plot, 163–4, 188
    loses power in the Socialist movement, 108, 117
    and the revolutionary strike of 1917, 54, 58
    spiritual agony during the war, 133
    succeeds Pablo Iglesias as Socialist leader, 72
Bevin, Ernest, 192
Bilbao, 10, 38n.48), 57, 68, 149, 199, 247
(Euskal Herria) Bildu, 262, 281–3, 285
Black Card scandal, 268
Blair, Tony, 259
Blanco, Miguel Ángel, 247
Blanco, Segundo, 158
Blasco Ibáñez, Vicente, 25, 76
Blue Division, 181, 183, 233
Blum, Léon, 137, 141, 145, 158–9
Blumel, André, 141
Boadella, Albert, 278
Bolín, Luis, 140
Bonet, María del Mar, 204

Bonnet, Georges, 159, 161–2
Bono, José, 259
Borodin, Mikhail, 61
Borrell, Josep, 273, 276, 281
Bosnia, 240
Bosques Saldivar, Gilberto, 193
Botín, Ana, 254
Boyer, Miguel, 241
Brabo Portillo, Manuel, 64, 90n.101
Brandt, Willy, 236
Bresci, Gaetano, 19
Brunete (Battle of, 1937), 157
Bulgaria, 70, 91 (126
Bullejos, José, 103
Burgos, 131, 150
   military trial (1970), 204–5
Burgos y Mazo, Manuel, 66
Burguete, Gen. Ricardo, 83
Bush, George W., 259

Caballero, Jorge, 230
Cabanellas, Gen. Miguel, 130–1
Cabanillas, Pío, 208
Caciquismo, 7–8, 11–12, 22–3, 25, 29, 34, 55, 67, 71, 84, 100, 102, 114
Cádiz, 1, 35n.4, 107, 130
Calviño, Nadia, 281
Calvo Sotelo, José, 74, 106, 120–1, 131
Calvo Sotelo, Leopoldo, 232–3, 235, 240
Camacho, Marcelino, 203
Cambó, Francesc, 24, 28, 59, 70
Campíns, Gen. Miguel, 133
Campoamor, Clara, 99
Camus, Albert, 202
Canal, Jordi, 285
Canalejas, José, 28, 32–4
Cánovas del Castillo, Antonio, 5–6, 8–9, 19, 22, 41n.100
Carlism
   and the *Abrazo de Vergara*, 163
   a declining force in 1890s, 23
   and Franco's enforced political unification, 151
   and General Varela, 182
   and nineteenth-century wars, 2–3, 5
   part of Franco's governing coalition, 185
   and Restoration Spain, 11
   and the Second Republic, 96, 106–7
   and *Solidaridad Catalana*, 28
   strongholds in Catalonia and Basque Country, 24
Carlos, Don (Carlos María Isidro de Borbón), 2–3
Carmena, Manuela, 279
Carr, Raymond, 67
Carrero Blanco, Adm. Luis, 182, 191, 198–9, 201, 206–8, 219
Carrillo, Santiago, 219–20, 225–6, 233, 235
Cartagena (uprising, 1939), 163–4
Casado, Pablo, 282, 285
Casado, Col. Segismundo, 5, 162–4, 188
Casas, Enrique, 237
Casas Viejas (rebellion, 1933), 107–8
Casares Quiroga, Santiago, 82, 105, 119, 121, 129, 132, 147
Caserio, Sante Geronimo, 19
Castilblanco events (1931), 102
Castilla, 118, 130–1, 236
Castillo, Lt Jesús, 121
Castro, Américo, 25
Castro, Fidel, 240
Catalan Nationalism, *see* Lliga Regionalista, CiU, ERC, Junts pel Si, Junts per Catalunya
Catalonia
   and 1898, 20
   in the 1960s, 204
   anarchist stronghold, 51
   Catalanism, 43n.126
   and the Civil War, 132–4
   and corruption scandals, 266
   and *El Procés*, 269–78
   falls to Nationalists, 161
   hegemony of Nationalist parties in democracy, 225–6, 231
   industry and protectionism, 10
   and the May Days of 1937, 154–7
   origins of nationalist movement, 24
   and Pedro Sánchez, 285
   and the revolution of October 1934, 113–14
   and the Second Republic (Home Rule), 81, 97–8, 105, 112

social conflict in the 1890s, 18–19
and social violence after the Great
   War, 66–8
and Socialist failure, 15
Statute and home rule, 227–9, 238
and the Tragic Week, 31–2
Catholic Church, *see also* CEDA and
   Opus Dei
and the 1876 constitution, 8–9
against the Second Republic, 97,
   100–1
and Antonio Maura, 28–9
and Basque and Catalan
   nationalism, 24
becomes backbone of the
   Nationalist regime, 151, 188–9,
   195
and Carlism, 2
and the CEDA, 103, 107, 113
clashes with Falange, 198
and the Concordat (1953), 197
and the democratic transition, 229,
   260
and education in the 19th century, 6
and Miguel Primo de Rivera, 74–6
moves against Franco, 202, 205
and the rise of Opus Dei, 199
running orphanages, 190
supports coup in 1923, 70
supports the Nationalists, 148
victim of Republican atrocities, 134
CCOO (Comisiones Obreras), 202–3,
   225–6, 242
Cercas, Javier, 232, 261, 275
Chacón, Carme, 260
Chamberlain, Neville, 145, 159–60
Charles IV, King of Spain, 1
Chaves, Manuel, 266
Chilton, Henry, 138
Churchill, Winston, 178, 183–4, 192
CDC (Convergència Democratica de
   Catalunya), 226, 274
CDS (Centro Democrático y Social),
   235, 237
CEDA (Confederación Española de
   Derechas Autónomas
blackmails Radical Party, 111–12
and *Casas Viejas*, 108
and the CNCA, 102

in Covadonga (1934), 112
creation and ideology, 103, 107
declining force in the Civil War,
   150
and the elections of February 1936,
   116, 118, 120
electoral success (1933), 109–10
fails to seize power, 115
hegemonic role in 1935, 114–15
and October 1934, 112–14
pact with Radical Party, 110–11
perceived as fascist, 108
CEOE (Confederación Española de
   Organizaciones Empresariales),
   226
Ciano, Count Galeazzo, 140, 145, 159,
   164, 179, 190
Cierva, Juan de la, 29, 31, 34, 58–9,
   83–4, 88n.59
Ciudad Real, 77
CIU (Convergència i Unió), 226, 228,
   231, 235, 244–6, 248, 264,
   266–7, 269, 271–5
Ciudadanos, 277, 279–84, 286
Civil Guard
and the Civil War, 131
and the coup of February 1981,
   231, 233
creation, 4
and the elections of April 1931, 84
and ETA, 204, 208, 237
and Franco's regime, 187
and Luis Roldán, 244
paramilitary force in countryside, 9
repression of guerrillas, 194
repressive force, 13
and the Second Republic, 102, 104
Claridad, 129
Clerk, Sir George, 141
CNCA (Confederación Nacional
   Católica Agraria), 102–3
CNT (Confederación Nacional del
   Trabajo
in 1930, 82
banned by Primo de Rivera, 72
after the Civil War, 193, 203
and the Civil War, 132–5, 152,
   154–8
and the Comintern, 61–2

expansion and class struggle after the Great War, 62–5
foundation, 32
illegalized in 1911, 33
and the Labour Pact (July 1916), 51
and October 1934, 113–14
and the Popular Front, 118
and the Second Republic, 103–5, 108, 125n.90
Codovilla, Victorio, 103
Coixet, Isabel, 275
Colau, Ada, 279
Collective *15MpaRato*, 268
Combes, Émile, 37n.36
Comillas (Azaña's speech, 1935), 117–18
Comintern, 60–2, 65, 103, 117–19, 129, 143, 154–7, 164
Communism and Communist Party, see PCE
Communist International, see Comintern
Communist trade union, see CCOO
Companys y Jover, Lluis, 112–13, 133, 227, 269
Compromís, 279
Concordat with Vatican (1953), 197, 205
Concha, Manuel de la, 244
Concierto Económico, 228, 246
Condor Legion, 146, 149, 159–60
Confederación Patronal Española, 65–6
(La) Conquista del Estado, 106
Conservative Party
  and the *Dictablanda*, 81–2
  founded by Cánovas, 6
  led by Sánchez Guerra, 67, 77
  and the *turno pacífico*, 7
  under Maura and splits in October 1913, 28–9, 34, 88n.59
  under Silvela, 22
  vetoed by Catalan employers in 1919, 66
Constitution
  1812, 2, 35n.5
  1876, 6, 8–9, 13, 71, 77, 81
  1931, 97–100, 116
  1978, 228–9, 231, 256, 264, 270–1, 273, 276–8, 282, 286–7
Constantine I, King of Greece, 56
Constantine II, King of Greece, 220
Coordinación Democrática, 221–2
Córdoba, 130, 237
Corruption, 11, 16, 24, 52, 69, 73, 115, 187, 243–4, 258, 265–8, 271, 274, 279–80, 287
  see also Bankia, Black Card, ERES, FILESA, MATESA, Gürtel, Nóos, Straperlo, Three per cent
Cortada, Roldán, 154
Correa, Francisco, 267
Cospedal, María Dolores, 260
Costa, Joaquín, 22–3, 69
Cot, Pierre, 137
Council of Aragón, 132, 157
Council of National Defence, 164
Council of the Realm, 195, 221, 223
Covid-19, 257
Cristina, Infanta of Spain, 267
CTV (Corpo di Truppe Volontarie), 146
Cuba, 5, 19–22, 28, 240
Cuervo, Vicente, 230
¡Cu-Cut! incident (1905), 27
Cuixart, Jordi, 275
Curto, Major Inocencio, 163
CUP (Candidatura d'Unitat Popular), 274, 277–8, 285
Czechoslovakia, 160

Daladier, Edouard, 159–61
Dancausa, Dolores, 254
Dato, Eduardo, 23, 34, 49, 55–9, 66, 88n.59
Delbos, Yvon, 141
Delgado, José, 120
Desamortización, 2–3
Desencanto, 230
Díaz, José, 117
Díaz, Susana, 281
Díaz, Yolanda, 284–6
Díaz Alegría, Gen. Manuel, 208
Díaz Ayuso, Isabel, 284–5
Dimitrov, Georgi, 142, 157
DiploCat, 273
Dos Passos, John, 142

Dollfuss, Engelbert, 113, 169n.108
Domingo, Marcelino, 106, 109, 126n.136
Domínguez, Michel, 245
Doval, Gerardo, 63, 66
Duclos, Jacques, 118
Dunn, James C., 197
Durão Barroso, José Manuel, 259
Durruti, Buenaventura, 103, 133

Ebro (Battle of, 1938), 158–60
Eden, Anthony, 138, 159, 184
EE (Euzkadiko Ezkerra), 228–30, 235
EEC (European Economic Community), 203, 239–42, 256
Eisenhower, Dwight D., 197
El ABC, 70
El Correo Catalán, 70
El Diario Universal, 52
El Mundo, 243, 266
El País, 266, 271
El Progreso, 25
El Socialista, 15, 20
elections (national)
   April 1901, 43n.127
   April 1907, 28–30
   April 1916, 51
   February 1918, 59
   December 1922, 67
   June 1931, 96–7
   November 1933, 99, 109–10
   February 1936, 116, 118
   June 1977, 225–6
   March 1979, 230
   October 1982, 235–6
   June 1986, 236
   October 1989, 236
   June 1993, 244
   March 1996, 245, 258
   March 2000, 248
   March 2004, 259
   March 2008, 259
   November 2011, 256–7
   December 2015, 280
   June 2016, 280
   April 2019, 281–2
   November 2019, 282
   July 2023, 286
elections (local)
   April 1931, 83–4, 95
   April 1933, 109
   April 1979, 231
elections (Catalan)
   November 1932, 105
   March 1980, 231
   November 2012, 274
   September 2015, 274–5
   December 2017, 277–8, 281
   February 2021, 278–9
elections (Madrid Community)
   May 2021, 284
emigration, 10, 24, 64, 200, 202, 253–4, 264, 282
Equatorial Guinea, 53, 105, 115, 179
ERC (Esquerra Republicana de Catalunya), 98, 105, 109, 264, 274, 278, 282, 285–6
Erice, Victor, 202
Errejón, Íñigo, 284
ERTE (Expedientes de Regulación de Empleo), 257
Ertzainza, 238
Escrivá de Balaguer, José María, 199
Estat Catalá, 76, 98
ETA (Euskadi Ta Askatasuna
   and Atocha massacre (2004), 259
   bombing at *Cafetería Rolando*, 216n.204
   at the Burgos Trial (1970), 205
   declares unilateral ceasefire (2011), 258
   and the democratic transition, 230–1
   ends armed struggle (2011), 263
   ETA's PM abandons armed struggle (1982), 237
   founded, 204
   and the GAL, 245
   growing isolation and vulnerability, 246–7
   killing of Miguel Ángel Blanco (1997), 247
   militants executed, 209
   negotiations fail in Algiers, 237
   and Operation Ogro (Killing Adm. Carrero Blanco), 207
   and the *Pacto de Estella*, 247

peace negotiations (2006), 263
popular in Basque Country, 227
splits, 227–8
terror campaign after Carrero's killing, 208, 219, 225
terrorist operations in the 1980s, 237–8
EU (European Union), 242–3, 247, 253, 255, 257, 259, 271
Extremadura, 1, 102, 118, 130, 141, 161, 242, 283

FAI (Federación Anarquista Ibérica), 72, 103, 105, 107–8, 110, 133–4, 152, 156
Fal Conde, Manuel, 150
Falange (de las JONS), 106, 116, 120, 130–1, 151
Falange Española Tradicionalista (FET) y de las JONS
  creation, 150–1
  growth during the Civil War, 154, 185
  marginal force, 200, 206
  part of the Francoist state, 185–7, 195, 198
  and the Second World War, 178, 181–2
Fanelli, Giuseppe, 14
Fanjul, Gen. Joaquín, 115, 131
Faupel, Wilhem, 173n.223
Felipe VI, King of Spain, 267, 276
Ferdinand VII, King of Spain, 1–2, 35nn.3 and 5
Fernández, Aurelio, 103
Fernández, María Teresa, 260
Fernández Cuesta, Raimundo, 198
Fernández Miranda, Torcuato, 220–4
Fernández Vallespín, Gen. Carlos, 208
Fernández Villaverde, Raimundo, 23–4
Ferrer, Eduardo, 64
Ferrer Guardia, Francisco, 26–7, 31–2
Ferrusola, Marta, 264, 267
Five Star Movement, 280
Flynn, Errol, 142
FNTT (Federación Nacional de Trabajadores de la Tierra), 15, 102, 111, 113, 118

Forcadell, Carme, 278
Foreign Legion, 136, 146
  see also Army of Africa
Fraga Iribarne, Manuel, 202, 206, 221–2, 224, 229, 231, 233, 235–6
France
  and the 1938 crisis, 158
  alliance against Abd-el Krim, 73–4
  and anarchism, 14–15
  anti-clericalism in Third Republic, 37n.36
  and the Carlist Wars, 3
  demonstrations in favour of Ferrer Guardia, 32
  education under the Third Republic, 12
  and ETA, 205, 237–8, 245, 247, 263
  exile of Queen Isabel II, 6
  and Franco during Cold War, 192
  helps the Republic, 142, 146
  and the Great War, 50, 53
  intervention in 1823 to back Ferdinand VII, 35n.5
  investments in Spain (1930s), 168n.87
  and the Iraq War (2003), 259
  and military service, 7
  and non-intervention, 140–2
  and the outbreak of the Spanish Civil War, 137–8
  and the partition of Morocco, 27
  Popular Front, 117
  Protectorate in Morocco, 33
  recognizes Franco, 161–2
  reopens border in 1948, 198
  scandals, 243
  and the Second World War, 178, 183
  under British pressure (border), 159
  and the War of Independence, 1–2, 35n.2
  war with Prussia (1870–71), 5, 22
(La) France Insoumise, 280
Francisco de Asís, Consort of Queen Isabel II, 5
Franco Polo, Carmen, 198, 261
Franco, Nicolás, 139, 150

Franco y Bahamonde, Gen. Francisco
  in the 1950s, 158
  and the *Alcázar* of Toledo, 148
  appoints Juan Carlos as his
    successor (1969), 201
  and the Battle of Guadalajara, 144
  and Carrero Blanco, 206–7
  and the Casado's coup, 163–4
  and the Church's U-turn, 205
  Concordat with the Vatican (1953),
    157
  the conquest of Catalonia, 161
  corruption, 187
  deteriorating health and death,
    207–9
  director of the Military Academy
    (1928), 77
  dismisses Serrano Suñer, 181–2
  and Don Juan, 194–6, 198
  early days in Morocco, 73–4
  and the economic miracle, 201
  enforces Political Unification,
    149–51
  fails to capture Madrid, 143
  favours war of attrition, 149,
    158–60
  funeral, 219–20
  and Gil Robles, 115–17
  heads the Army of Africa, 131,
    136
  hesitant plotter, 147
  his new order, 185–9
  and the international community
    after 1945, 191–3, 196
  and José Antonio, 150
  and the May Days of 1937,
    173n.229
  meteoric rise to Power, 147–8
  and Mussolini, 140, 145
  nostalgia, 231
  in October 1934, 114
  removed from *El Valle de los
    Caídos* (2018), 261
  and repression, 136, 184, 188, 190,
    213n.89
  and the Second World War, 177–84
  sends emissaries to Hitler, 139
  today's memory, 253
  Treaty with USA (1953), 157
  viewed by British diplomacy in
    1936, 138
FRAP (Frente Revolucionario
  Antifascista y Patriótico), 208–9
FRE (Federacion Regional Espanola de
  la Primera Internacional), 14
FRTE (Federacion Regional de
  Trabajadores Españoles), 14
Frutos, Francisco, 248
Fuero de los Españoles, 195
Fuerza Nueva, 206, 224, 226

Gabeiras, Gen. José, 234
GAL (Grupos Armados de Liberación),
  245, 280
Galán, Capt. Fermín, 82
Galán, Col. Francisco, 163
Galarza, Valentín, 182
Galaxia, Operation (1978), 231
Galeote, Guillermo, 243
Galicia, 61, 118, 130, 181, 187, 229,
  236, 238, 259, 270, 285
Gana, Francisco, 19
Garaikoetxea, Carlos, 228, 250n.85
García, Lt Gen. Cristino, 192
García Berlanga, Luis, 202
García Blanco, Lt Col. Pedro, 247
García Damborenea, Ricardo, 245
García Oliver, Juan, 103, 152, 155
Garzón, Baltasar, 244–5, 261
Gasset, Rafael, 88n.59
Gaulle, Gen. Charles de, 179
generation of 1898, 22, 42n.112
Germany
  activities in Spain during the First
    World War, 53–4, 56, 63–4
  and domestic repression, 190,
    213n.89
  and the EU, 255
  German Socialists support PSOE,
    232, 236
  against Iraq invasion (2003),
    259–60
  occupation of the Rhineland
    (March 1936), 119
  purchase of Spain's Pacific islands,
    21
  rising great power, 22
  and the Second World War, 177–84

and the Spanish Civil War, 139,
    141–3, 145–6, 158–61, 168n.87
  Spanish migrants in the 1960s,
    200
  and universal conscription, 12
Ghali, Brahim, 283
Gibraltar, 73, 138, 177–80, 192
Gil Robles, Jose María
  Accidentalismo, 107
  aware of coup in 1936, 128n.66
  at Covadonga (1934), 112
  electoral defeat in February 1936,
    118
  escapes assassination, 121
  fails to become prime minister,
    115–16
  leads CEDA, 107
  meets Indalecio Prieto (1947), 193
  outmanoeuvres Lerroux, 110–11
  shunned by the Nationalists, 131,
    139, 150
  strategy vis-à-vis the Radical Party,
    111, 119
  War Minister (1935), 115
Giménez Losantos, Federico, 238
Giménez Fernández, Manuel, 112,
  114–15
Giral, José, 132, 137, 193
Girault, François, 18
Girón de Velasco, José Antonio, 197,
  200, 206, 208
Giscard d'Estaing, Valéry, 239
Goded, Gen. Manuel, 79, 115, 131
Goicoechea, Alejandro, 149
Goicoechea, Antonio, 34, 107
(Gómez) Jordana, Gen. Francisco,
  182–3
González, Felipe
  backs constitution (1978), 221
  charisma, 236
  consolidates power in the PSOE,
    232
  criticized by students (1993), 244
  elected leader of the PSOE (1972),
    221
  loses power (1996), 245
  and Mitterrand, 240
  modernization of Spain, 239
  and NATO, 240
  presides over smooth electoral
    machine, 242
  rising electoral strength vis-à-vis the
    UCD, 231–2
  scandals, 243–5
González, Yolanda, 230
González Peña, Ramón, 119
Golpismo, 231, 233, 239
Göring, Hermann, 160
Goytisolo, Juan, 202
Gramsci, Antonio, 202
Granados, Eva, 275
GRAPO (Grupos Revolucionarios
    Antifascistas Primero de
    Octubre), 209, 219, 225,
    249n.32, 261
Great Britain
  appeasement, 145
  and the Carlist Wars, 3
  and Franco during Cold War,
    192–3, 196
  investments in Spain (1930s),
    168n.87
  and non-intervention, 144–5
  and the outbreak of the Spanish
    Civil War, 138, 140
  Pinochet is detained (1998), 261
  recognizes Franco, 161
  and the Second World War, 178,
    180, 182–4
  stops French intervention, 141,
    158–9
  and the War of Independence,
    35n.2
Greece, 56, 87n.51, 220, 243, 280
Griñán, José Antonio, 266
Guadalajara, 84, 132
  (Battle of, 1937), 144, 149
Guadalorce, Conde de (Rafael
    Benjumea y Burín), 106
Guam, 21
Guernica, 149
Guerra, Alfonso, 221, 229, 232, 242–3,
  264
Guerra, Juan, 243
Guerrilla, 3, 20, 194–5, 204
Gulf War, 240
Gutiérrez Mellado, Gen. Manuel, 224,
  231–3

Haig, Alexander, 233
Halifax, Lord (Edward Woods), 159
Harvey, Oliver, 145
Hassan, King of Morocco, 209
Hayes, Carlton J. H., 182
HB (Herri Batasuna), 228, 230, 237, 258
Hearst, William Randolph, 21
Hedilla, Manuel, 151
Hemingway, Ernest, 142
Hendaye (France) meeting (1940), 179–80
Herrera, Major José María, 228
Herrera y Oria, Ángel, 101
Hess, Alfred, 139
Hess, Rudolf, 139
Hidalgo, Diego, 114
Hidalgo de Cisneros, Gen. Ignacio, 161
Himmler, Heinrich, 190
Historical Memory, 260–3, 283
Hitler, Adolf, 107, 113, 139, 146, 160, 177–80, 183–4
HOAC (Hermandades Obreras de Acción Católica), 202, 205
Hoare, Samuel, 178, 183–4
Horitzó Socialista, 285
Horthy, Adm. Miklós, 70
Hoyos, Marquis of (José María de Hoyos y Vinent), 83
Hungary, 70, 91n.126

Ibarretxe, Juan José, 258, 263, 269
Ibarruri, Dolores (La Pasionaria), 143
Iglesias Posse, Pablo, 14–15, 31–3, 57, 72
Iglesias Turrión, Pablo, 280–5
IMF (International Monetary Fund), 199, 268
Iniciativa per Catalunya-Verds, 264
(Los) Indignados, 268
inflation
  in 2022, 257
  in the democratic transition, 226
  and the Great War, 50, 60
  under Franco, 198–9
  under PSOE government, 241
Inmovilistas, 206, 208, 224
Institut de Nova Historia, 272
International Brigades, 143, 160

Iraq, 259–60
IRS (Instituto de Reformas Sociales), 23, 42n.122), 52, 72
Isabel II, Queen of Spain, 2–5, 131
Israel, 197, 239
Italy
  against the Second Republic, 107, 120, 130
  defeated in Adowa (1896), 22
  domestic repression, 190, 213n.89
  Fascist take-over, 70
  friendship Treaty with Franco, 177
  and the Great War, 50
  intervention in the Spanish Civil War, 139–40, 142–6, 148–9, 158
  large public sector, 73
  and the libertarian movement, 14
  new parties in the 21st century, 279–80
  political scandals, 243
  and Primo de Rivera, 75
  and the Second World War, 178–9, 183, 194
  Socialism, 15
  Trasformismo, 37n.32
  unification (*Risorgimento*), 5, 37n.36
IU (Izquierda Unida), 237, 244, 246, 248, 280, 285
Izquierda Republicana, 117, 126n.136

Jaca (rebellion, 1930), 82
JAP (Juventudes de Acción Popular), 107, 112, 120, 150
Japan, 22, 199, 254
Jarama (Battle of, 1937), 144
Jerez, 17–18
Jesuits, 101, 128
Jiménez de Asua, Luis, 120, 140
JOC (Juventud Obrera Católica), 202, 205
John XXIII, Pope, 205
John Paul II, Pope, 260
JONS (Juntas de Ofensiva Nacional Sindicalista), 106
Joseph I Bonaparte, King of Spain, 1, 35n.2
JSU (Juventudes Socialistas Unificadas), 117, 119, 135, 153

Juan, Don (Juan de Borbón y Battenberg), 131, 150, 194–6, 220
Juan Carlos I, King of Spain
  acting head of state (1974), 208
  appointed Franco's successor, 201, 206
  and Arias Navarro, 221–2
  and the coup of February 1981, 233–4
  and the democratic transition, 220–1, 223
  returns to Spain to be educated by Franco, 196
  scandal and abdication, 267
  settles in Abu Dhabi, 267
  and Suárez, 221, 223, 233
  target of *golpistas*, 251n.106
Junqueras, Oriol, 278
Junta Democrática, 220–1
Junta de Defensa (Madrid), 143
Junta Nacional de Defensa, 131
Junta Técnica del Estado, 150
Juntas Castellanas de Actuación Hispánica, 106
Juntas Militares de Defensa, 52, 55–6, 58–9, 73, 77
Junts Pel Si, 274, 277
Junts Per Catalunya, 278, 285–6

Kale Borroka, 238, 247
Kent, Victoria, 99

La Acción, 70
La Batalla, 155
La Canadiense (Ebro Power and Irrigation) strike (1919), 63, 65, 68
La Correspondencia Militar, 55
La Veu de Catalunya, 27
Lafargue, Paul, 14
Laína, Francisco, 234
La Montaña (military fortress, 1936), 133
Langenheim, Adolf, 139
Largo Caballero, Francisco
  and the agrarian revolution of June 1933, 111
  and the alleged Communist conspiracy of 1936, 129
  becomes minister of Labour, 97, 99, 104
  becomes prime minister, 143, 152–3
  the May Days of 1937 and ousted from office, 155–6
  and the military rebellion, 133
  and October 1934, 114
  and the Popular Front, 117–20, 127n.158
  and the revolutionary strike of 1917, 58
  radicalized by course of events, 108–9, 112, 126 (119
Latifundismo, 3–4, 102
Latin America, 10, 54, 87n.37), 193, 230, 239–40
Lavilla, Landelino, 235
Law
  against Banditry and Terrorism (Franco), 188
  of Amnesty (Democracy), 227
  of Amnesty under Pedro Sánchez (Democracy), 286
  of Associations (Restoration), 6
  of Budget Stability (Democracy), 257
  of Confessions and Religious Congregations (Republic), 101
  of Democratic Memory (Democracy), 262
  of Dependency (Democracy), 260
  of Disconnection (Catalan parliament), 275
  of Disentailment (Restoration), 3
  of Divorce (Democracy), 232–3
  of Fundamental Principles of the National Movement (Franco), 200
  of Gender Equality (Democracy), 260
  of General Health (Democracy), 240
  of Historical Memory (Democracy), 262
  of Jurisdictions (Restoration), 28, 30, 97

of Linguistic Normalization
    (Catalan parliament), 238, 271
of Local Administration
    (Restoration), 29
of Municipal Boundaries
    (Republic), 98, 111
of National Defence (Democracy),
    239
of Obligatory Cultivation
    (Republic), 98
Organic of the State (Franco), 200
of Political Association (Franco),
    208, 22
of Political Reform (Democracy),
    224
of Political Responsibilities
    (Franco), 162, 188, 190–1
of Press (Franco), 206
of Reform of the Agrarian Reform
    (Republic), 115
of Repression of Masonry and
    Communism (Franco), 188
Salic (Absolute Monarchy), 2
of State Security (Franco), 188
of Succession (Franco), 195, 224
see also Ley
Le Monde, 273
Lebrun, Albert, 137, 140
Ledesma, Ramiro, 106
Léger, Alexis, 141
Leguina, Joaquín, 283
Leo XIII, Pope, 9
León, 236, 264
Lequerica, José Félix, 183, 196
Ley, *see also* Law
    Ley del Candado (Restoration), 32
    Ley de Fugas, 66, 90 (107), 104
    Ley por la Defensa de la República
        (Republic), 105
    Ley de Vagos y Maleantes
        (Republic), 105
Llach, Lluis, 204
Laussane (Manifesto of, 1945), 194
Lenin (Vladmir I. Ulianov), 53, 113
Lerroux, Alejandro
    clashes with the PSOE, 100
    controversial role, 25
    and the coup of August 1932, 105,
        124n.71

electoral defeat in 1907, 28
Emperor of the *Paralelo*, 25–6
and Ferrer Guardia, 26–7
forced to resign after *Straperlo*
    scandal (1935), 115
greets the Republic, 99
ideological shift after the Tragic
    Week, 32
and Maura, 28
in office with CEDA's backing,
    109–11
and October 1934, 112–13
and street violence, 30
and the Tragic Week, 30–1
Liberal Party
    and Canalejas, 32–3
    and *¡Cu-Cut!* incident, 27
    and *Dictablanda*, 81–2
    and February 1918 elections, 59
    and the Great War, 34, 51, 54,
        88n.59
    last cabinet in 1923, 67–8
    and Lerroux, 25
    and Maura, 28–30
    splits, 88n.59
    and the Tragic Week, 32
    and *turno pacífico*, 7
Liceu Theatre (bomb, 1893), 18
Lliga Regionalista de Catalunya, 24–5,
    43n.127), 51, 55, 58, 83,
    94n.204), 109, 112
Llopis, Rodolfo, 220
López, Juan, 152
López, Patxi, 263
López Rodó, Laureano, 199, 224
Loubet, Émile François, 26
Louis XVIII, King of France, 35n.5
Luccardi, Giuseppe, 140

Maastricht (Treaty, 1992), 242
Maciá, Francesc, 76, 105, 112, 269
Madoz, Pascual, 3
Madrid
    and the advance of the Army of
        Africa, 141–4, 148
    Atocha Station terror attack (2004),
        281
    Azaña's speech in 1935, 117
    burning of convents in 1931, 101

and Carlist War, 3
and the Casado's conspiracy, 162–4
corruption scandals, 266, 268
and the coup of 1981, 233–4
and the coup of August 1932, 105
and the CNT's inroads in the construction sector, 125n.90
demographic growth, 10, 80, 199, 202
and *El Procés,* 277–8
and the elections of April 1931, 84
Europe's cultural capital (1992), 240
experiences labour clashes in 1936, 119
food riots in 1919, 63
and the military rebellion and outbreak of Civil War, 131–3, 135–6
murder attack on Alfonso XIII (1905), 26–7
and *Podemos,* 279, 284
and the revolution of 1934, 113
and the revolutionary strike of 1917, 57
site of Arab-Israeli Peace Conference (1991), 240
Socialist stronghold, 15, 117
strikes in 1920, 61
stronghold of the PP, 284–5
terrorist attack (1977), 225
visited by Eisenhower in 1959, 197
Maeztu, Ramiro, 107
Maine USS (1898), 21, 41n.107
Majestic (Pact, 1996), 246
Maisky, Ivan, 144
Málaga, 10, 100, 119, 132, 144, 207
Malraux, André, 141–2, 152
Mancomunidad, 33, 70, 76
(La) Mano Negra (1882), 17
Manzanas, Melitón, 204
Maragall, Pasqual, 264, 267
March, Juan, 120, 127n.159), 147
Maria Christina of Austria, Queen of Spain, 4
Maria Christina of the Two Sicilies, Queen of Spain, 2, 4–5
Márquez, Col. Benito, 52
Marsé, Juan, 202

Marshall Plan (European Recovery Programme, 1949), 187, 191, 196, 200
Martín Artajo, Alberto, 195
Martín Gaite, Carmen, 202
Martínez, Alfredo, 120
Martínez Anido, Gen. Severiano, 66, 68, 71
Martínez Barrio, Diego, 109, 111, 131–2, 162
Martínez Bordiu, Cristobal (Marquis of Villaverde), 198
Martínez Campos, Gen. Arsenio, 1, 5
Marty, André, 143
Marx, Karl 202, 233
Mas, Artur, 264, 269–72, 274–5, 277
Más Madrid, 284
Más País, 284
MATESA (Maquinaria Textil del Norte de España SA, 1970), 266
Matos, Leopoldo, 56
Maura, Antonio
  advises Alfonso XIII in 1923, 69
  aftermath of the Tragic Week, 30–3
  and the Assembly of 1917, 55–6
  and Barcelona, 30
  criticizes Dictatorship, 75
  as 'fireman', 88n.66
  heads a national government in 1918, 59, 83
  Morocco and the Tragic Week, 30
  and national regeneration, 28–9
  ousted from leadership and splits the Conservative Party, 34, 88n.59
Maura, Gabriel, 55, 69, 83–4
Maura, Miguel, 56, 79, 81, 84–5, 99–101
Maurismo, 34, 55, 58, 83
Maurín, Joaquín, 61, 127n.44
Mauritania, 209
May Days (1937), 154–7
McKinley, William, 21
Mendiola, Lt Col. Leocadio, 163
Menéndez, Arturo, 125n.86
Menorca, 130
Mera, Cipriano, 164
Mexico, 61, 142, 191, 193, 197
Miaja, Gen. José, 143, 162

Miláns del Bosch, Gen. Jaime, 233–4
Miláns del Bosch, Gen. Joaquín, 63, 66, 69
Millet, Félix, 267
Mitterrand, François, 236–7, 240
Moa, Pío, 261
Mola, Gen. Emilio, 115, 120–1, 128n.166), 130–2, 139–41, 143
Moncloa (Pacts of, 1977), 226
Montana Project (1938), 160
Montañés, Carlos, 63, 66
Montero, Irene, 284
Montero Ríos, Eugenio, 27
Montilla, José, 264–5
Montjuïc (Castle of/tortures, 1896), 18–19, 25
Montseny, Federica, 152, 155
Morel, Col. Henri, 156, 161
Morel, Sandrine, 273
Moret, Segismundo, 27, 30, 32
Morocco
  and Alfonso XIII, 33
  and the Civil War, 139–40
  colonial occupation, 27
  and Franco, 131, 147
  gains independence, 198
  and Maura's fall, 30
  and occupation of the Western Sahara, 209
  and Pedro Sánchez, 283–4
  and Primo de Rivera, 73, 79
  and the Second Republic, 97
  and the Second World War, 179, 182
  Spain's defeat at Annual (1921), 68–9
Morral, Mateo, 26–7
Moscardó, Gen. José, 148, 194
Mossos d'Esquadra, 246, 269, 275
Múgica, Bishop Mateo, 100
Munich (Agreement, 1938), 160–1
Murcia, 84, 130, 132, 163
Mussolini, Benito, 69, 75, 107, 140–1, 144–5, 149, 159, 161, 177–9, 182–3, 190

Napoleon, Emperor of France, 1
Napoleon III, Emperor of France, 5
National Assembly, 74–8

National Council of the Economy, 73
National Institute of Industry, 186
National Movement, *see* Falange
National Wheat Service, 186
NATO (North Atlantic Treaty Organization), 191, 233, 235, 240
Nath, Manabendra, 61
Navarra, 2, 118, 121, 130, 151, 228, 247
Negrín, Juan
  becomes prime minister, 156–7
  and the Comintern, 156
  faces revolt and flees Spain, 163–4
  fall of Catalonia and failure to rekindle resistance, 162
  launches diplomatic offensive in 1938, 159–60
  pleas to Daladier, 161
  reasons for defeat, 157
  requests military aid from Stalin, 161
  reshuffles the cabinet in April 1938, 158
  scholarly debate on his role, 156
  war strategy, 156
Nelken, Margarita, 99
NIA (Non-Intervention Agreement), 141–2, 144–5, 149, 156
NIC (Non-Intervention Committee), 144–5, 162
Nicholas II Romanov, Tsar of Russia, 53–4, 60
Nin, Andreu, 61, 127n.144), 154
NO-DO (Noticieros y Documentales Cinematográficos), 195
Nóos scandal, 267
Non-Intervention Agreement, *see* NIA
Non-Intervention Committee, *see* NIC
Northern Ireland Good Friday Agreement (1998), 263
Numancia (mutiny, 1911), 33
Núñez Feijóo, Alberto, 285
Nyon Conference (1937), 145

Obama, Barack, 279
October Revolution (1934), *see* Revolution

Òmnium Cultural, 272, 275, 278, 292n.128
Ónega, Fernando, 287
Operation Backbone (1942), 182
Operation Felix (1941), 180–1
Operation Galaxia (1978), 231
Operation Magic Fire (1936), 139
Operation Ogro (1973), 207
Operation Otto (1936), 142
Operation Torch (1942), 182
Opus Dei, 198–9, 201, 206
Ordás, Gordón, 109
Oriol, José, 112
Oriol y Urquijo, Antonio María, 225
Orlov, Alexandr, 157
Ortega, Marta, 254
Ortega y Gasset, Eduardo, 120
Ortega y Gasset, José, 12, 22, 25, 27, 42n.112
Ortega Lara, José Antonio, 246–7
Ortín, Gen. Constantino, 228
Orwell, George, 142, 155
Osàcar, Daniel, 267
Ossorio, Ángel, 29, 34, 56, 81
Ottoman Empire, 22
Oviedo, 114, 130

Pact of Blood, 151, 185
Pacto de Estella (1998), 247, 258
Pacto del Olvido, 223, 227
Pactos de la Moncloa (1977), 226
Pajuelo, Arturo, 230
Palme, Olof, 236
Paracuellos del Jarama, 135
Pardo (Pact of, 1885), 7
Pardo (Clan del), 206
Pardiñas, Manuel, 33–4
Paris (Treaty of, 1898), 21
Partido Radical Republicano
    and the *Alianza Republicana*, 81
    and *Casas Viejas*, 108
    electoral oblivion in 1936, 118
    electoral strength in 1931, 96
    foundation (1908), 28
    led by Alba, 116
    and October 1934, 113–14
    opposes Azaña, 100
    in power, 109–10
    scandals and crisis, 115
    shady reputation, 99
    splits in 1929, 99
    and the Tragic Week and its aftermath, 31–2
    vis-à-vis the CEDA, 110–11
PASOK, 280
Pasotismo, 230
Paul VI, Pope, 205, 209
Pavía, Gen. Manuel, 5, 233
PCE (Partido Comunista de España
    abandons guerrilla strategy against Franco, 194
    accused of international conspiracy, 129–30
    against the Second Republic, 103–4, 108
    Atocha massacre of lawyers (1977), 253
    and the battle of the Ebro, 159
    beaten by PSOE, 232
    and the Casado's coup, 162–4
    clashes with Largo, 153–4
    and the constitution of 1978, 228
    and the coup of 1923, 68
    the defence of Madrid, 143
    and the elections of 1977, 225
    and the elections of 1979, 230
    embraces Eurocommunism, 220
    embraces the Popular Front, 117–19
    excluded from the Republican government in exile, 193
    experiences massive growth, 153–4
    fails to make inroads in the labour movement, 62
    and the fall of Largo Caballero, 156
    foundation, 61
    infiltrates the labour movement, 203
    internal divisions and electoral decline (1982), 235
    and IU, 237
    is legalized, 222, 224–5
    and the May Days of 1937, 155
    and the *Pactos de la Moncloa*, 226
    and reaction to war, 133, 142
    supports Negrín, 157
PDeCAT (Partit Democrata Europeu Català), 274, 278

Peiró, Joan, 152
Pérez, Blas, 182
Pérez Rubalcaba, Alfredo, 256, 281–2
Perón, Gen. Juan Domingo, 187
Pestaña, Ángel, 62, 64, 72, 77, 103, 105, 118
Pétain, Marshall Philippe, 162
Philippines, 19–21, 23, 183
Phipps, Eric, 159
Picasso, Pablo, 149
Pinochet, Gen. Augusto, 220, 261
Piñar, Blas, 206, 224, 230
Pius IX, Pope, 37n.36
Pius XII, Pope, 197
Pla y Deniel, Bishop Enrique, 148
Plan de Empleo Rural, 243
Plan of Industrial Reconversion, 241
Planchuelo, Miguel, 245
Plataforma de Convergencia Democrática, 220–1
Plymouth, Earl of (Ivor Miles Windsor-Clive), 144
PNV (Partido Nacionalista Vasco
  and the 1977 electoral results, 226
  arbiter of state politics, 245–6
  becomes the hegemonic force in the Basque Country, 231, 235, 248
  and the Civil War, 132, 149
  and the democratic transition, 227–9
  electoral defeat in Basque elections (2005), 263
  and the emergence of ETA, 204
  foundation, 24
  Ibarretxe and the *Pacto de Estella* (1998), 247, 258
  regional coalition with the PSOE (1987), 236
  and the Second Republic, 116
  splits in 1986, 250n.85
  under Urkullu, 269
Polavieja, Gen. Camilo, 23
Poland, 70, 91n.126), 160–1, 177
Polisario Front, 283
Polo de Franco, Carmen, 182
Polo, Zita, 182
Ponsati, Clara, 270
Portela Valladares, Manuel, 115–16, 118

Portugal, 22, 50, 70, 91n.126), 120, 131, 139, 141, 146, 150, 193, 207–8
Potsdam (Conference, 1945), 192
POUM (Partido Obrero de Unificación Marxista), 118, 127n.144), 154–7
Pozas, Gen. Sebastián, 118
PP (Partido Popular),
  against negotiations with ETA, 263
  Atocha's terrorist massacre and electoral defeat in 2004, 259
  backs constitutional demands imposed by Brussels, 256
  campaigns against new Catalan Statute, 265
  described as a 'barking Doberman', 258
  dislodged from office after losing non-confidence vote (2018), 281
  and the economic boom, 247
  electoral victory in 2011, 256–7
  and the elections of 2015, 280
  and the elections of 2023, 286
  and the emergence of VOX, 282
  and Gürtel Affair, 266
  and the Historical Memory, 261–2
  introduces Law of Budget Stability, 257
  led by Aznar, 235–6
  led by Casado and defeated in the elections of 2019, 281–2
  mobilizes against Zapatero, 260
  new electoral victory in 2000, 248
  in office after the electoral victory of 1996, 245–6
  regional hegemony of Díaz Ayuso, 284
Prado, Diego, 237
Prat de la Riba, Enric, 24
Prieto, Indalecio
  and the Civil War, 133, 156, 158
  clashes with Largo Caballero, 119
  meets Gil Robles (1947), 193
  and the Pact of San Sebastián (1930), 81
  and the Popular Front, 116–17
  and Primo de Rivera, 72, 78
  Treasury Minister, 97, 99

Primo de Rivera, Gen. Miguel
   attempts to consolidate his rule, 74
   backed by Alfonso XIII, 68–70
   captain general of Barcelona, 68
   and its critics, 76–7
   and the economic crisis and fall, 78–80
   and the economy, 72–3
   endorsed by Catalan bourgeoisie, 70
   European context, 70
   and the labour movement, 72
   leads coup in 1923, 68–9
   and Morocco, 73–4
   opposed by sections of the army, 77
   power vacuum afterwards, 80
   and regeneration, 71
   unlike Franco, 191
Primo de Rivera, José Antonio, 106–7, 131, 149–50
(El) Procés, 269–80, 285
PRRS (Partido Republicano Radical Socialista), 99, 101, 109, 111, 126n.136
PSC (Partit dels Socialistes de Catalunya), 264, 278–9
PSOE (Partido Socialista Obrero Español
   back to power with Zapatero (2004), 251
   backs joining NATO in 1986 referendum, 240
   backs the constitutional demands imposed by Brussels, 256
   backs women's vote, 99
   challenged by new parties, 280
   clashes with the Radicals, 100
   and Communism, 61–2
   and corruption scandals, 243
   declining force in exile, 220
   defeat at the polls in 1996, 245–6
   in democratic transition, 224
   and drafting of the constitution (1978), 228–9
   and the economy, 241–2
   and the elections of June 1931, 96
   electoral defeat in 1933, 109
   electoral defeat in 2011, 256
   electoral machine, 242
   electoral strength and social reforms, 102–4
   electoral success and in power in 1982, 235–6
   ERES scandal, 266
   and ETA, 237–8
   fails to achieve significant support in Barcelona, 15
   the fall of Largo Caballero, 155–6
   first (municipal) electoral success, 15
   and the First World War, 50, 56
   foundation and slow growth, 14–16
   González consolidates his leadership (1980), 232
   in government, 96–9
   historical break with the UGT (1990), 242
   and the Historical Memory, 262
   and the housing bubble, 255
   Iglesias elected deputy, 32
   internal polarization and the Popular Front, 117–20
   and the Labour Pact with the CNT (1916), 51–2
   Largo Caballero seizes the Premiership, 152
   leading opposition force, 225, 228, 230
   led by Felipe González (1972), 221
   loses electoral majority, 244–5
   and the municipal elections of April 1931, 83–4
   negotiates with ETA (1998), 263
   and Negrín, 157
   and the new Catalan Statute (2005), 266
   new defeat in elections of 2000, 248
   and October 1934, 112–14
   optimism of 1980s, 239
   and polarization, 258
   and Primo de Rivera, 72–8
   and the radicalization of Largo, 108–9
   and the revolutionary events of 1917, 54–8
   and the San Sebastián Pact (1930), 81–2

seals alliance with Republicans in 1909, 32
signs *Pactos de la Moncloa* (1977), 226
social reforms, 240
tables and wins vote of no-confidence against Rajoy (2018), 266
tables non-confidence vote (1980), 232
and the Tragic Week (1909), 31
and the transfer of power from Besteiro to Largo, 108
under the controversial leadership of Sánchez, 280–6
PSP (Partido Socialista Popular), 220, 232
PSUC (Partido Socialista Unificado de Cataluña), 153–4, 235
Puente, Major Ricardo de la, 133
Puerto Rico, 19, 21
Puigdemont, Carles, 275–7, 285–6
Puig i Cadafalch, Josep, 76
Pujol, Jordi, 226, 239, 246, 264, 267, 270–1, 278, 285
Pulitzer, Joseph, 21

Queipo de Llano, Gen. Gonzalo, 130–1, 134
Quintana Lacacci, Gen. Guillermo, 234

Rabassaires, 112
Radical Party, *see* Partido Republicano Radical
Radio Catalunya, 271–2
Raimon, 204
Ramírez, Jesús, 61
Ramírez, Pedro J., 252n.126).
Rajoy, Mariano
    and *Ciudadanos*, 281
    and the corruption scandals, 266
    and *El Procés*, 271–3, 275–6
    and the feminist question, 260
    and the Historical Memory, 262
    loses elections in 2004, 259
    loses office in non-confidence vote (2018), 266
    narrow victories in the elections of 2015 and 2016, 280–1
    replaced by Casado, 282
    succeeds Aznar and electoral victory in 2011, 256–7
Rato, Rodrigo, 255, 268
Reagan Ronald, 233
Reconquista, 3, 8, 112, 114, 148, 151, 189–90
Redondo, Onésimo, 106
Redondo Terreros, Nicolás, 283
Redondo Urbieta, Nicolás, 242
Reformist Party, 25, 58
Regeneration, 22–4, 27–8, 33–4, 69, 71, 74
RENFE (Red Nacional de los Ferrocarriles Españoles), 241, 243, 286
Renovación Española, 106
Requetés, 2, 106, 130
Revolution
    August 1917, 56–7
    'Glorious' of September 1868, p 5
    October 1934, 113–14
    Russian (March 1917), 53–4
    Russian (November 1917), 53–4
Riba, Diana, 286
Ribó, Joan, 279
Ribbentrop, Joachim von, 180
Ríos, Fernando de los, 81, 97, 99
Rivas, Natalio, 67, 91n.112
Rivera, Albert, 280–2
Robles, Margarita, 281
Rodezno, Count (Tomás Domínguez Arévalo), 150
Rodrigo Martínez, Gen. Miguel, 198
Rodríguez, Melchor, 135–6
Rodríguez Ibarra, Juan Carlos, 283
(Rodríguez) Zapatero, José Luis
    becomes leader of the PSOE, 259
    economic bonanza, 255
    effects of the economic crisis, 256
    electoral victory in 2004 and 2008, 259
    feminist agenda, 260
    foreign policy, 260
    Historical Memory, 261
    negotiations with ETA, 263
    quits office and calls early elections, 256

reformist administration, 259–60
and the territorial question, 263–4
Roig, Montserrat, 202
Rojo, Gen. Vicente, 143, 159
Roldán, Luis, 244
Roldán, Tony, 282
Rojas, Capt. Manuel, 125n.86
Román, Gen. Lagos, 237
Romania, 146, 253
Romanones, Count (Alvaro de Figueroa y Torres),
   and the *Dictablanda*, 81
   and the Great War, 50–4, 88n.65
   La Canadiense strike and ousted (1919), 66–7
   in the last monarchist cabinet in 1931, 83–4
   maverick leader of the Liberal Party, 34
   in the national government of 1918, 59
   and Primo de Rivera, 77, 79
   returns to power in late 1918, 63
   splits in the Liberal Party, 88n.59
   and the Second Republic, 122n.9
Roosevelt, Franklin D., 178, 182
Roosevelt, Theodore, 21
Rosenberg, Marcel, 142
Rossi, Pier Filippo del, 140
RTVE (Radio y Television Española), 221, 240, 243
Rubio, Mariano, 244
Ruiz Giménez, Joaquín, 198
Ruiz Zorrilla, Manuel, 25–6, 43n.138
Rull, Joan, 30
Rumasa, 241
Russia
   according to Oliver Harvey (1938), 159
   and Andalusia (*Trienio Bolchevique*), 65
   and the Blue Division, 181, 183
   compared with Second Republic by Ambassador Chilton, 138
   defeated in the war against Japan (1904–5), 22
   differences vis-à-vis Spain, 77, 112, 133
   epicentre of revolution, 53

exporting grain, 10
and the Holy Alliance, 35n.5
impact of Bolshevism, 60–2
revolutionary events in 1917, 54–5
and the Second World War, 181–2
and the Spanish Civil War, 143, 145–6, 153
strength of the libertarian movement, 14
see also Soviet Union

Saborit, Andrés, 58
Sadi Carnot, Marie François, 19
Sáenz, Soraya de, 260
Sagasta, Mateo Práxedes, 6, 21–2, 36n.19), 41n.100
Sala, Alfonso, 76
Salamanca, 147–8, 150
Salazar, Antonio, 139
Salazar Alonso, Rafael, 111–12, 114
Salmerón, Nicolás, 24, 28
Samper, Ricardo, 111, 114
Sànchez, Jordi, 275, 278
Sánchez, Pedro, 262, 266, 280–6
Sánchez Guerra, José, 67, 77, 80, 82–3
Sánchez Moya, Antonio, 33
San Fulgencio (Sinking of, 1917), 54
Sancristobal, Julián, 245
Sandhurst (Manifesto of, 1874), 6
Sanjurjo, Gen. José, 73, 84, 105, 107, 120, 131, 139, 147
San Sebastián, 69, 115, 196
   (Pact of, 1930), 81–2, 96, 99–100
Santander, 149
Santiago, Gen. Luis, 224
Santiago, Salvador, 18
Santoña, 149
Saura, Carlos, 202
Sayn-Wittgenstein-Sayn, Corinna zu, 267
SEAT, 200, 241
Second International, 15
Seguí, Salvador, 62, 64, 66
Segura, Cardinal Pedro, 100
Serrano, Gen. Francisco, 5, 36n.19
Serrano Suñer, Ramón, 149–51, 179–82
Serrat, Joan Manuel, 204, 275

Sevilla, 10, 103–5, 119, 130, 190, 240, 243
Shipman, Charles, *see* Ramírez, Jesús
Silvela, Francisco, 22, 28
Silvestre, Gen. Manuel Fernández, 69
Sindicatos de Oposición, 105
Sindicatos Verticales, 186–7
Socialism and Socialist Party, *see* PSOE
Socialist trade union, *see* UGT
Socialist Youth, *see* JSU
Solana, Javier, 240
Solbes, Pedro, 255
Solchaga, Carlos, 241, 244–5
Solidaridad Catalana, 28, 30–1
Solidaridad Obrera, 26, 31–2
Solís Ruiz, José, 200, 206, 221
Somatén, 66, 74–5
Soviet Union
  behind alleged Communist coup in 1936 Spain, 129–30
  compared to Spanish Republic by Prime Minister Baldwin, 138
  endorses Popular Fronts, 117
  large public sector, 73
  at Potsdam Conference (1945), 192
  restores diplomatic relations with Franco, 197
  and the Spanish Civil war, 142–6, 153, 156–8, 161
  strategy against the Socialist movement, 73
  see also Russia
Stabilization Plan (1959), 199
Stalin, Joseph, 142, 161, 181
Stohrer, Eberhard von, 159, 178
Straw, Jack, 261
Suárez, Adolfo
  is appointed prime minister, 221
  and the army, 225
  attacked in the historical memory law, 283
  and the Basque Country, 228
  and Catalonia, 227
  and the coup of 1981, 232–3
  electoral victory in 1977, 226
  growing opposition and crisis, 230–2
  leads CDS, 235, 237
  leads UCD, 225

  obtains backing from the Francoist *Cortes*, 222
  and the PCE, 225
  presides over the democratic transition, 223–4
  the zenith of his career, 228–30
Sumar, 285–6
Switzerland, 13, 145, 193–4, 247
Syndicalist Party, 105, 118
Syriza, 280

Tamames, Ramón, 243
Tancament de caixes (1899), 24
Tangier, 33, 138, 140, 179
Tarancón, Cardinal Enrique, 205, 208
Tarradellas, Josep, 227–8
Tedeschini, Nuncio Monsignor Federico, 100
Tejero, Lt Col. Antonio, 231, 233–4
Terra Lliure, 238
Terrorism, *see* Anarchism, ETA, FRAP, GAL, GRAPO
Teruel (Battle of, 1937–38), 157
Thatcher, Margaret, 246
Three per cent scandal, 266–7, 272
Tierno Galván, Enrique, 220, 232
Tomás, Belarmino, 119
Torra, Quim, 278
Torrejón de Ardoz, 135
Torres, Diego, 267
Tourism, 200–1, 255, 257
Tragic Week, 31–2
Trump, Donald, 273
Truman, Harry S., 196
Turull, Jordi, 278
TV3, 271–2

UCD (Unión de Centro Democrático
  and the constitution, 228–9
  creation, 224–5
  in crisis, 230–1
  defeat in 1982 and implosion, 235–6
  electoral victory in 1977, 225
  electoral victory in 1979, 230
  led by Calvo Sotelo, 232
UDC (Unió Democratica de Catalunya), 226, 274
UGT (Unión General de Trabajadores
  after *Casas Viejas,* 108

backs *Pactos de la Moncloa* (1977), 226
creation, 14
in exile, 203
expands in Catalonia from 1936, 154
historical break with the PSOE (1990), 242
Largo Caballero's fiefdom, 117
Largo as Labour minister, 108
leader assassinated in Barcelona in 1937, 154
loses ground in Madrid (1933), 108, 125n.90
Madrid strikes in 1920, 61
massive expansion and change in 1930s, 102
membership in 1920, 89n.84
moves headquarters to Madrid (1899), 15
and Primo de Rivera, 72, 78
rattled by the repression of 1917, 62
and the revolutionary strike of 1917, 56–7
and the rural strike of June 1934, 111–12
seals Labour Pact with CNT (July 1916), 51–2
threatens nationwide strike (1919), 63
Ukraine, 254, 257, 284
Umberto I, King of Italy, 19
UMD (Unión Militar Democrática), 209
UME (Unión Militar Española), 121
UP (Unión Patriótica), 74–5, 78
UN (United Nations), 191–3, 196–7, 239, 259, 283
Unamuno, Miguel de, 22, 76
Unión Republicana, 111
United Kingdom, *see* Great Britain
United States
  and the Cold War, 184, 192
  and the Cuban War (1898), 20–1
  and the Great War, 54, 87n.37
  and the invasion of Iraq (2003), 259
  investments in Spain, 200
  rising great power, 22
  and the Second World War, 181–4
  and Spain joining NATO, 240
  and the Spanish Civil War, 141
  Treaty with Franco (1953), 196–7
UPOD (Unidas Podemos), 280, 282, 284
Urdangarín, Iñaki, 267
Uribe, Vicente, 153
Urkullu, Íñigo, 269, 277

Valencia
  and Blasco Ibáñez, 25
  and Carlism, 2
  and the Civil War, 131–2, 143, 158–9, 162
  and the coup of February 1981, 233
  and *El Procés*, 277
  and the end of Francoism, 204
  and the foundation of FAI, 72
  and the *Ley de Fugas*, 90n.107
  population growth, 10, 38n.48), 80, 199, 202
  and the *pronunciamiento* of 1874, 1
  and the *pronunciamiento* of 1929, 77
  and the *Sindicatos de Oposición*, 105
  and social violence after the Great War, 66
  and the strike of 1911, 33
  and the transport conflict in 1917, 56–7
Valle de los Caídos, 191, 215, 262
Valle Inclán, Ramón del, 5
Varela, Gen. José Enrique, 182
Vargas Llosa, Mario, 276
Vatican, 149, 151, 197, 205, 208
Vázquez, Mariano, 155
Vázquez Montalbán, Manuel, 202
Vega, Col. Etelino, 163
Vegas Latapié, Eugenio, 107
Velayos, Nicasio, 115
Venizelos, Eleftherios, 87n.51
Ventosa, Joan, 24, 59

Vera, Rafael, 245
Vichy, 179–80, 183, 192–3
Victoria Eugenie of Battenberg, Queen of Spain, 26
Vidal i Barraquel, Cardinal Francesc, 135
Vidal-Quadras, Alejo, 246
Vigón, Gen. Juan, 179
Vila, Santiago, 272
Villalobos, Filiberto, 114
Villescusa, Gen. Emilio, 225
Viñas, Ángel, 121, 146
Viriatos, 149
Vittorio Emanuele II, King of Italy, 5
Vittorio Emanuele III, King of Italy, 70, 78
Vizcaya, 24, 103, 149, 245

Wallace, Henry, 182
Western Sahara, 209, 283–4
Weyler, Gen. Valeriano, 77
Wolfram, 183
Women, 2, 6–7, 13, 23, 36n.24, 60–1, 75–6, 98–9, 152–3, 189, 203, 239, 254, 260

Yagüe, Col. Juan, 136
Yugoslavia, 70, 197

Zanjón (Pact of, 1878), 4
Zapatero, *see* Rodríguez Zapatero, José Luis
Zaragoza, 10, 66, 77, 82, 119, 130, 147, 150, 237
Zugazagoitia, Julián, 129